MORE THAN A WOMAN

MORE THAN A WOMAN

AN INTIMATE BIOGRAPHY OF

BETTE DAVIS

JAMES SPADA

BANTAM BOOKS

New York Toronto London Sydney Auckland

MORE THAN A WOMAN
A Bantam Book / September 1993

All rights reserved.
Copyright © 1993 by James Spada

Book design by Michael Mendelsohn of MM Design 2000, Inc.

No part of this book may be reproduced or transmitted
in any form or by any means, electronic or mechanical,
including photocopying, recording, or by any information
storage and retrieval system, without permission in
writing from the publisher.
For information address: Bantam Books.

Library of Congress Cataloging-in-Publication Data
Spada, James.
    More than a woman : an intimate biography of Bette
Davis / James Spada.
        p.   cm.
    Includes bibliographical references (p.   ) and index.
    ISBN 0-553-09512-9
    1. Davis, Bette, 1908–1989.   2. Motion picture actors
and actresses—United States—Biography.   I. Title.
PN2287.D32S62   1993
791.43′028′092—dc20
[B]   93-7366
                                                        CIP

Published simultaneously in the United States and Canada

Bantam Books are published by Bantam Books, a division of Bantam Doubleday Dell Publishing Group, Inc. Its trademark, consisting of the words "Bantam Books" and the portrayal of a rooster, is Registered in U.S. Patent and Trademark Office and in other countries. Marca Registrada. Bantam Books, 1540 Broadway, New York, New York 10036.

PRINTED IN THE UNITED STATES OF AMERICA
RRH   0 9 8 7 6 5 4 3 2 1

For Kathy Robbins—
agent, mentor, friend.

CONTENTS

An actor is something less than a man;
an actress is more than a woman

           —Inscription on Bette Davis's
              cigarette case

PART ONE

"A High-Strung Young Filly"

ONE

T he little girl sat next to her father on the back porch of their clapboard Victorian house as a warm summer breeze stirred the crystal-clear night air. Here and there a strand of her wispy blond hair strayed from under the wide satin ribbon at the back of her head and fell across her forehead, above the huge eyes that grew ever larger with the wonderment she felt at the sight above her.

The New England sky was aglow with thousands of tiny sparkling stars, more than she had ever seen. "The sky was silver with them," she recalled. "I was bewitched."

As he too gazed above him, her father's face remained wintry and expressionless, framed by the high starched collar and necktie he wore even while at leisure. The man rarely spoke to his daughter, barely heard the child's incessant, excited chatter about this discovery or that. But this evening it was he who broke the silence of the girl's reverie as he turned to see her staring with such awe at the unfathomable enormity above her.

"Do you see all those stars up there?" he asked her.

She followed his gaze back up toward the sky and her heart jumped with excitement—her father was going to explain the mysteries of the heavens to her.

He turned to her again. "There are millions and millions of them. Remember that always and you'll know how unimportant you are."

Bette Davis spent the rest of her life trying to prove her father wrong.

On both sides of the family, her heritage courses back through long lines of bedrock New Englanders. There was the Pilgrim, James Davis, who sailed from Wales to the New World in the early 1600s and helped found the city of Haverhill, Massachusetts. There was Colonel Jabez Mathews, a Revolutionary War hero, and a line of Hinckleys with resonantly Puri-

3

tan Christian names like Reliance, Thankful, Experience, Mercy, and Admire.

James Davis became a selectman of his community, and during the simmering seventeenth-century religious persecutions that flamed into the hysteria of the Salem witch trials, he accused a man named John Godfrey of "familiarity with the Devil." At the trials, twenty people—mostly women—were executed, some of them hanged in a public square while the good townspeople watched, mouths agape.

The Sturm und Drang of Bette Davis's personality, the elements that warred within her, may well have stemmed from the fact that another one of her ancestors, on her mother's side, was one of those women killed. Clearly, she was the product of diverse family traits—the rock-solid industry and stoicism of Reliance and Experience and Thankful on her father's side, and the emotional, artistic bent of her mother's ancestors, the French Huguenot LeFievres, who numbered among themselves inventors, musicians, and actors, including an early vaudeville star named Eddie LeFavour. *Fièvre* means "fever" in French, and sangfroid seems not to have been one of their strong points. As Bette put it, they were "perhaps more than titularly feverish."

The LeFièvres anglicized their name to Favour over the years, then Americanized it to Favor. Bette's uncle, the Reverend Paul Favor, ascribes some of the fabled Bette Davis drive as well to the Keyeses, the progenitors of Bette's grandmother Eugenia Thompson. "This elemental driving force of the Keyeses through the generations," Favor wrote in a family memoir, "was a double power, the power of vision to see what they wanted to accomplish, and the power to release an uncommon degree of energy which recognized no obstacle strong enough to deter them from achieving their ends."

Eugenia Thompson married William A. Favor, a civil engineer, in 1878, and had four children. Paul, their first child, recalls his mother being "as persistent as a flowing river and as irresistible." Her granddaughter, Elizabeth Carmichael, recalls Eugenia as "a little bitty thing with a strong will. I guess you could say that she was a little hyper." Her first daughter, Ruth, born on September 16, 1885, inherited all her mother's "elemental force" and then some—and handed it down to her own daughter, Bette Davis.

Eugenia Favor's mission, in her son Paul's words, was to teach him, Ruth, and their younger siblings Mildred and Richard "lessons of order, industry, obedience and enterprise." She dominated her household in the big, maple-shaded yellow clapboard house at 22 Chester Street in

Lowell like a whirlwind, assuming the role of father as much as mother. Her husband rarely related to his children, preferring to spend most of his spare time at a private club; Paul Favor writes nothing of him in his family history. Eugenia, her cheekbones high, her manner imperious, and her carriage ramrod straight, ran her home with an iron hand. She gave her children piano lessons at precisely the same time each day, and for exactly an hour; if the children were late for a meal, she removed their plates from the table; she set aside time each evening to read aloud to the children from Emerson, Tennyson, Longfellow, Wordsworth, and the Bible. On Sundays she brought them to services at the First Baptist Church of Lowell in their best starched clothes. Church attendance was mandatory, even as they became young adults.

While Paul Favor admitted that such strict homes can be difficult for children to live in, he grew up to believe that "they are certainly the most satisfactory to look back upon." His decision to pursue a life in the ministry suggests a personality well suited to such regimentation, whereas his sister Ruth wasn't nearly as influenced by their upbringing. Along with her drive, Ruth Favor's predominant traits proved to be independence, rebellion—and complexity.

Although Ruth was a pretty girl, she hated being one. She insisted on being called "Fred," wore her brother's shirts and trousers, and roughhoused with the neighborhood boys on Lowell's rolling, grassy hills. At the same time she enjoyed putting on little skits in the attic of her house with other girls, and took elocution and dance lessons from Miss Sadie Porter during her family's summer vacations in Ocean Park, Maine.

In the summer of 1897, before Ruth's twelfth birthday, she took part in a local talent recital at The Temple, Ocean Park's assembly hall. She read a dramatic portion of Lew Wallace's *The Prince of India* in which the hero, Tamerlane, dies. Although the reader was just a young girl, Paul Favor professed that "through her the great audience was transported to distant Persia . . . and brought face to face with one of history's most thrilling moments." The applause, Paul recalled, was deafening, and forty years later members of the audience still talked about the power of the performance.

Although Sadie Porter influenced a number of her students toward theatrical careers, utilizing the free expressionist theories of the French dramatic coach François Delsarte, neither she nor the Delsarte school had any such profound effect on Ruth Favor. As she grew into a bright, industrious, and efficient teenager, Ruth's creative energies focused instead on writing: she wrote dozens of short stories and achieved the literary editorship of the Lowell High School monthly magazine through sheer determination.

Ruth rebelled against academic regimentation and proved a mediocre student, but she had inherited her mother's drive, and was "in her element," Paul Favor tells us, when she became the senior commanding officer of the Girls' Battalion at the school, where she could amply exercise her "dominating" nature.

At nineteen, graduated from high school, Ruth Favor was expected, as were all girls her age, to marry and begin a family. It didn't matter that she possessed talent and drive and qualities of leadership; women around the turn of the century weren't allowed any ambition higher than landing a husband. It didn't take long for Ruth to find one, for she had flowered into a lovely young woman, "a painting by Mr. Sargent," as Bette put it, "gay, graceful and full of the joy of life." A tomboy no longer, she now called herself Ruthie, fluttered with femininity, giggled freely, projected a Gibson Girl delicacy with her upswept hairdos. She grew excited about marriage, the only real future allowed her, and played shy and demure with the many young men who were attracted by her coquettishness and intrigued by her one blue and one gray eye.

Among the suitors who presented themselves at her door, however, she allowed only one to make a serious bid for her hand. He was a young man she had known since the age of seven named Harlow Morrell Davis.

He might have sprung from the imagination of Charles Dickens. Harlow Davis was an only child and every inch a stolid, staid New Englander, a brilliant legal scholar with little sense of humor and less tolerance for emotionalism. His pale, thin face, topped by a bulbous forehead, was framed by protruding ears, small round wire-rimmed glasses, and the starched high collar and tie he had worn every day since grade school. His face seemed frozen in a perpetual scowl, even when photographed with his family on holiday outings.

Little is known about his childhood except that he was born in Augusta, Maine, on March 9, 1885, the son of Edward E. Davis, a men's clothier and a deacon of the local Baptist church, and the former Eliza Jane Morrell. The family lived a comfortable life between a sprawling Victorian mansion in Augusta and a seaside cottage at Old Orchard Beach. Harlow's maternal grandfather, the Reverend A. H. Morrell, had been a founder of Storer College in Harpers Ferry, West Virginia, one of the South's first Negro colleges after the Civil War.

Harlow Davis's own scholastic achievements were of a high order. He was chosen valedictorian of his high school class, and at Bates College in Lewiston, Maine, he served as president of his class four times, captained the debating team, and headed up the athletic association. A Bates classmate of Harlow's recalled, "His legal papers were flawless, and he was an indefatigable worker who could concentrate longer upon a problem in patent law than anyone I ever knew. His memory was prodigious, retaining endless figures and facts."

Davis decided not to attend Oxford University in England when he learned that the school didn't allow students to smoke; instead, he moved to Boston and enrolled at Harvard Law School. It was during his last year at Bates College that he had begun his courtship of Ruth Favor, whom he had first met in 1892 during a summer vacation in Ocean Park with his family when she was seven and he eight. They spent time together every summer thereafter.

Ruthie was flattered by such ardent romantic attentions from a long-time friend, which aroused interest in her if not passion. Harlow's mother, Eliza, had warned her early on that her son was "brilliant but disagreeable" and that if she ever were to marry him he would "destroy your life." Despite these severe admonitions, Eugenia Favor decided that the match would be a good one for Ruthie because Harlow seemed to have such a solid future. He had inherited his father's business and both family houses after his father's death in 1903 and his mother's in 1906, and he fairly shone with the promise of a brilliant law career. Unsure, Ruthie vacillated. But Eugenia praised the pairing to her daughter, Harlow wrote Ruthie effusive love poems, and she finally acquiesced. The date was set. The bride was twenty-one, the groom twenty-two.

The couple were wed on July 1, 1907, in the Favor home on Chester Street, Ruthie a vision in a simple, button-necked white gown with a heavy, decorous veil, attended by her sister Mildred as maid of honor. According to Ruthie, the marriage began on a number of sour notes that reminded her immediately of her mother-in-law's dire warnings. After the ceremony, as the bride and groom left for their honeymoon, a group of friends and relatives threw handfuls of rice at them. Harlow turned angrily and yelled, "Goddamn you, I'll get you for this!"

On July 4, as the new Mr. and Mrs. Davis honeymooned on Squirrel Island in Maine, their hotel was forced to shut off the water supply for several hours. The couple had just had sex, and there was no water for

Ruthie to use as a contraceptive douche. Harlow soared into a rage, harangued the hotel staff, and lashed out at his bride. When Ruthie missed her period a month later, Harlow found himself suffused with dread and fear. He felt financially and emotionally incapable of fatherhood. He had no job; he had let the family business founder. He would be entering law school in a matter of weeks, and he knew it would take all his concentration to do as well as everyone expected him to do. He and Ruthie were living in her mother's house, surrounded by her family, and they already enjoyed little of the privacy he coveted so much. The *last* thing he wanted at this juncture in his life was a child. According to Ruthie, she burst into tears when he suggested that she give the baby up for adoption.

With her fervid sense of the dramatic, Bette Davis always maintained that she was born on Sunday, April 5, 1908, amid great tumult, between a crack of thunder and a bolt of lightning that almost hit the Favor house and split a nearby tree in two. The day's weather reports, however, show that Ruthie's later description of the elements—a "lovely" spring shower —was far closer to the truth. As was customary in the New England of the time, the little girl was delivered by a midwife in her parents' bedroom. She weighed a healthy enough five and three quarter pounds, but she looked frail and her color was poor. When Ruthie's sister Mildred peered down at the infant in her bassinet for the first time, she muttered, "Too bad. Too *bad*."

The baby, christened Ruth Elizabeth Davis and nicknamed Betty, further crowded the house on Chester Street, three-storied and spacious though it was. There were Grandmother and Grandfather Favor (as everyone called them after Betty's birth), their children Paul, Mildred, and Richard, Ruth and Harlow Davis, baby Betty, and her nurse, Mrs. Hall.

The birth of his child didn't soften Harlow Davis's attitude toward fatherhood, but the baby seemed to be trying her best to accommodate his habitual bad temper. She seldom cried, rarely fussed, slept soundly through most nights. "She was quiet and easy to care for the first few years," Ruthie later said. Then she added, "Perhaps in compensation for the years to come."

Harlow paid the child little mind. Hunched over his law books, uneasy around infants, he left Betty's nurturing entirely to Ruthie. As young as she was, the little girl noticed, and as her personality developed, most of her energies were directed toward her father. Her first word, uttered when she was ten months old, was "Poppa"; her first sentence, "Poppa forgot his rompers—he catch cold." After Betty learned to crawl, Ruthie always knew where to find her whenever she disappeared—in her father's study, often clambering onto his leather couch.

The baby's efforts to win her father's attention usually failed. Grandpa Favor was an occasional substitute, and Bette's earliest memory was of her grandfather standing on the second-floor landing of their house, encouraging her as she tentatively crawled up the long flight of stairs to him. When she reached the top step she grabbed his legs for support and felt a surge of "triumph."

Harlow remained so indifferent to his daughter that he forbade his wife to discuss the child in his presence outside the home. Whenever they vacationed, their acquaintances thought they were honeymooning. After the couple moved into a house of their own in nearby Winchester, and Ruthie gave birth to a second daughter, Barbara, on October 25, 1909, neither child was allowed downstairs while their father was home.

Sensitive to Betty's lack of paternal attention, Ruthie overcompensated for her husband's rigidity by giving her daughter free rein most of the time. "I am afraid I was more lenient than I should have been in an endeavor to offset his harshness," she said. By the time Betty was nineteen months old, she had developed a strongly defined personality. After her sister Barbara's birth, she stayed with her grandmother back in Lowell for nearly a month. When she returned, she looked at her little sister and chirped, "My big doll!"

A few days later, Barbara's nurse, Mrs. Worthington, left Betty in the nursery for a few moments while Barbara lay in the crib that had earlier been Betty's. When she returned, the woman found the infant lying facedown on a small couch across the room. She watched as Betty stood next to her sister, stamped her foot, and yelled, "Stay there, stay there!"

When she reached the age of three, Betty grew eager to emulate her father. A stickler for organization, Harlow demanded that Ruthie keep a spotless home, and he saw to it that he was able to walk through his pitch-dark bedroom and locate any item of clothing he wanted from any closet or drawer, from memory. When Ruthie once dressed Betty in a gingham smock that had a small spot and some wrinkles in it, the child screamed and cried until her mother brought out a fresh dress and changed her. "She became all smiles," Ruthie recalled. Then she added ruefully, "Perhaps I should have curbed her." Bette later agreed: "I should have gotten a good swat on the behind."

She almost never did, even when she cut off all her baby sister's hair and announced, "Now she won't be pretty anymore!" The only time she could remember being physically disciplined was after she and Barbara ate some forbidden unripe grapes from the family's arbor, and her father spanked her. Even as her buttocks burned with pain she smiled with a secret pleasure that she had finally won some attention from Harlow, because otherwise "I never felt I had a father." After that she repeatedly made childish attempts to rouse something, anything, in him that might let her know he cared a whit about her; once she carried a dead field mouse into the dining room while her parents were entertaining. Her behavior only solidified Harlow's determination to keep as much distance between him and his daughters as possible. Betty soon learned that her best course was to keep out of his way. Her sister, nicknamed Bobby, never grasped the lesson. "Bobby spent every waking moment trying to please Daddy," Bette recalled. But Bobby's efforts were no more successful than Betty's had been.

Harlow Davis wouldn't allow his daughters to dine with their parents except on Saturday evenings and holidays. Even then, Harlow had no patience with childish meanderings or lapses of etiquette. "I can remember sitting at their table during a holiday celebration," Bette's cousin Elizabeth Carmichael said, "and we children weren't allowed to speak. He was a cross man, and he wasn't nice to children." Ruthie recalled that after nearly every meal the family shared, the sisters left the table in tears.

As Betty's personality began to express itself more and more forcibly, Harlow actually grew to dislike her. Her penchant for screeching appalled him, and even he was annoyed by the extremes to which she would now take her fastidiousness. One afternoon he took Betty and Bobby to the circus, and Betty sat thrilled by the clowns and elephants and acrobats until she noticed that the carpeted runway for the animals had a crooked seam down the middle. It drove her to distraction; it ruined her day. She brooded while all those around her hooted at the three-ring antics. "Daddy simply decided I was an ungrateful brat," Bette said. "He only knew that he had sacrificed an afternoon for nothing." Even her laughter grated on Harlow. "He once promised me a dollar if, after a year, I learned to laugh like a lady. I never collected."

Photographs of the Davis family taken around this time show Ruthie flanked by her daughters, playing with them on the beach or on the lawn of their home. In almost all of the pictures Harlow appears off to one side, sitting or standing alone, not interacting with his children at all.

One Bette Davis biographer has described Harlow Davis as a "monster," but as Bette herself put it, "It is so difficult to label people." She recalled his frequent gifts to Ruthie, and his generosity when he paid for his brother-in-law Richard's tuition at Harvard Law School after Grandfather Favor died and Eugenia found herself in "reduced circumstances." Bette's fondest memories of her father centered around Christmas time, "Daddy's favorite holiday." On Christmas Eve, he would cheerfully decorate the family tree, stringing twinkly lights and carefully hanging colorful glass balls. Then he would dress up in a red costume, wear a white cotton beard, clang a bell, and shout "Ho! Ho! Ho!" as his children tumbled excitedly down the stairs to find the living room filled with so many gifts they "spilled into the hallway."

But Christmas was the only time Betty got anything that even approached love or attention from her father. "He was barely conscious of us," she said, and Harlow's demanding work made the situation all the worse. He had graduated from Harvard Law School in 1910 with a specialty in patent law and was hired as an in-house attorney for the United Shoe Machinery Corporation of Boston. He worked long hours of overtime, rose quickly through the ranks, and took charge of United's patent department within a few years. He spent his entire working life with the firm.

Harlow Davis made a good salary; the family soon moved to a large, two-story house, and they vacationed every summer in Maine. His daughters were well dressed, the family car was a Cadillac. Financially, he proved to be the ideal provider Eugenia Favor had wanted for her daughter. Emotionally, he left Ruthie and her children impoverished.

Her childhood memories, except for the cold vacuum left by her father, were happy ones for Bette Davis. Her mother provided sunlight, she said, to balance her father's "dark cloud." Ruthie encouraged her daughter's boundless fascination with the world around her, answered her questions without condescension, never attempted to quash her enthusiasms. If her father wanted her to remember how "unimportant" she was, her mother taught her that she was the center of the universe.

Almost from the beginning, Ruthie behaved as much like a friend to Betty as a mother, and it was all a part of Ruthie's rebellion against her own rigid upbringing. "Even though the family thought my ideas about children's individuality a little eccentric," she said, "I still had my own ideas and kept to them. I do believe obedience is not as important as good companionship and I never insisted on a schedule of discipline merely for discipline's sake."

Bette's fondest early memories remained inextricably entwined with the New England seasons and Yankee customs: the first tulips and warm breezes of springtime; picking berries with Bobby in the dense and enveloping woods behind their house; the profuse vegetable garden that provided a groaning board of green and yellow produce for the dinner table; the salty spray that whipped off the ocean during summer clambakes in Maine; the nip of autumn as Ruthie sewed their Halloween costumes; the windows fogged up on a cold Thanksgiving morning while the turkey crackled in the oven and its wonderful aroma filled the house; the frigid winter days when she and Bobby would slide down the nearby hills, snow stinging their faces, using only their behinds as sleds.

The idyll might have been total but for Harlow, and as the years passed the marriage of Ruthie and Harlow deteriorated. Even at seven, Betty sensed that her father had become as indifferent to Ruthie as he was to her and Bobby. Marriage to the surly Harlow had never been easy for Ruthie, and now it was almost unbearable; his simmering hostility toward the children, his long absences and silences, all took their toll. Ruthie had inherited the high-strung Favor personality, the characteristics Elizabeth Carmichael had called "hyper" in her grandmother. There was as well an emotionally fragile strain in the family, and it led Ruthie to take her husband's small cruelties very hard. Just three years into the marriage, photos of her show a downcast, weary woman, dark circles under her eyes, a nearly haunted look on her face.

Nervous and fidgety, Ruthie now burst into tears at the slightest provocation. In 1911, on the edge emotionally, Ruthie checked herself into a sanatorium for a rest. It was a juncture in her life that she never again mentioned, not even to Bette; the shame of it in this unenlightened period was too painful a memory.

A few months later, Ruthie returned home in a better frame of mind, but over the next several years her marriage continued to crumble. When Betty was eight, she sensed that "a shadow" had fallen over the Davis home. She would sit rigidly on the living room sofa and listen to her parents argue in the kitchen, then watch, afraid to speak, as her father walked stone-faced up the stairs and her mother cried. Soon the arguments were replaced by hushed conferences, and the normally talkative Ruthie would sit in long cold silences at the dinner table, silences that seemed strange and ominous to the eight-year-old. She felt tortured by the realization that "my mother was unhappy, that something was wrong." While Betty tried to intellectualize the problems in her childlike way, Bobby withdrew into herself and suffered her own bout with mental instability. During the 1916–1917 school term, Bobby's condition got so bad that Ruthie was forced to remove her from her second-grade classes.

Finally, in February 1918, just as the tension threatened to become unbearable, Ruthie told the children that she was taking them on a vacation to St. Petersburg, Florida—without their father. On the evening they were scheduled to board the train south, Harlow took the family to dinner at the Copley Plaza Hotel in Boston. The sounds of a gay string orchestra filled the restaurant, but the meal was a typically strained affair; Ruthie picked at her food and said nothing. Harlow, Bette recalled, acted oddly "attentive and kind" to her and Bobby.

She retained a vivid memory of the next scene for the rest of her life. At the railway station, Harlow kissed them all good-bye. As the train pulled out of the depot, Betty peered through the window and watched her father standing on the platform, tall and thin, waving sadly back at them. Then he receded into a cloud of smoke as the train chugged off down the track.

When they returned to Massachusetts in early April, Ruthie told her daughters that their father would no longer live with them. Bobby ran to her room in tears, but Betty just piped up happily, "Well, anyway, now we can go on picnics and have a baby sister!" Ruthie later wondered how Betty knew her father hadn't wanted any more children. "She must have overheard something and grasped the idea."

On April 5—Betty's tenth birthday—Ruthie filed a "libel for divorce" action against Harlow. She accused him of years of "cruel and abusive treatment" that ended only when they separated on February 24, and asked for a dissolution of the marriage, custody of Betty and Bobby, and alimony. Harlow contested none of it. Perhaps because he was an attorney, the case proceeded with unusual speed: two and a half months later, the divorce was final. No provision was made for Harlow's visitation rights to his daughters; he hadn't asked for any. He was ordered to pay Ruthie $200 a month in alimony, and Bette always maintained that because he was a lawyer he had pulled strings to "pay as little as possible." The amount was certainly not enough for the Davis girls to enjoy anything near the lifestyle they had been used to with Harlow.

Bette later said she was "glad" that her parents divorced. "I hated the way he treated my mother," she said. "I hated him, really." For years afterward, she insisted that her father's absence from her life had none but the positive effect of allowing her to become an actress, something Harlow opposed even from afar and surely would have forbidden had he remained head of the family. But she admitted much later that after that farewell meal at the Copley Plaza, she couldn't hear the strains of a string orchestra without crying. Forty years later, working on her memoirs, she denied to her ghostwriter that Harlow's absence meant much to her. After he probed and prodded, Bette finally had to admit that she was kidding herself. "Father's departure *was* and *is* to be reckoned with," she said. "[It's] something I'll never get over."

Unquestionably, her parents' parting affected Bette more than anything else in her childhood. It strengthened her independence, fueled her rebellion, and left her with both a deep-seated need for men and an equally strong distrust of them. Harlow's legacy to Bette was her sometimes punishing combination of driving ambition and crippling insecurity. All he had to do, on the rare occasions over the years when they saw each other or corresponded, was to mock one of her ideas, and the notion would stiffen into stony resolve.

When she wrote to him that she was thinking of changing the spelling of her name to Bette after Honoré de Balzac's novel *La Cousine Bette,* he called it a "silly" idea. She made the change at school the next day. When he suggested that she become a secretary instead of an actress, her theatrical ambitions crystallized in her mind. "He certainly inspired me no end to prove he was wrong. He made me prove a lot." What she left unsaid was that his lack of faith in her also left her with deep doubts about her own abilities.

Bette's most lasting impressions of her father were filtered through the perceptions of Ruthie, who carried bitterness toward Harlow Davis for the rest of her life. Years after the divorce, Ruthie told friends that Harlow had left her to marry Minnie Stewart, a woman she described as his "mistress." She probably hoped this piece of information would win her sympathy as a woman wronged, but it wasn't true. Harlow didn't marry Minnie Stewart until September 21, 1926, more than eight years after his divorce.

Again and again throughout her life, Ruthie painted a picture of Harlow as an unremittingly cold, heartless man, indeed a "monster," with no redeeming characteristics. But Virginia Conroy, Bette's later dramatic school roommate and longtime friend, thinks Harlow Davis deserves a more evenhanded assessment. According to Virginia, "Bette had been meticulously brainwashed about her father. He had 'deserted' the family. The word suggests a feckless, irresponsible man, a ne'er-do-well who took it on the lam. Nothing could be further from the truth— which was that Ruthie deliberately schemed to drive him away and pose as the injured party."

Virginia had heard so many terrible things about "Harlow the Heinous" that she decided to "collect evidence" from other family friends about his life with Ruthie and the children. "First I established in my mind what he did not do. He did not drink, gamble, womanize, resort to physical abuse. One of his crimes was to request that he and Ruthie dine separately, with the children being fed first. In view of Bette's penchant for screaming—she told me her father used to put his hands over his ears to block out the noise—it does not seem unreasonable for a man at the end of a hard day to want to dine in peace."

Of the story that Harlow suggested Ruthie give Bette up for adoption, Conroy feels "the idea is so fantastic that it hardly bears repeating. The social implications of such an act would be unimaginable in a small community where the Davis and Favor families were well known. It was incredible to me that Bette would take this statement seriously. The only explanation for it that I can imagine is that during one of Bette's screaming spells, Harlow might have said, 'For God's sake shut her up or give her away!' And Ruthie put the remark down in her little black book for future use."

A friend of Harlow's once asked him why his marriage failed. His reply was terse and enigmatic: "If a man gets a cup of coffee thrown in his face every morning, he can't keep his self-respect." A thought crossed Conroy's mind when the remark was repeated to her: *If this is what happened at the breakfast table, what went on in the bedroom?*

The truth about Harlow Davis clearly lies somewhere between Ruthie's colorings and Virginia Conroy's. Apparently, Harlow felt equally wronged by Ruthie. So much so that after his second marriage he took out his anger on both his daughters by expressly excluding them from his will.

One thing is certain: In his absence, Harlow was as important a force in Bette's future success as her mother, who hovered over her and pushed, pushed, pushed her toward stardom. "The very thought that he valued her genius (as yet unproved) so little as to want her to become a *secretary* made her mind boggle," Virginia Conroy recalls. "But secretarial experience has often proved a bulwark against the casting couch in many a talented girl's struggle, and that's what Harlow Davis was concerned about.

"Yet the memory of her father's secretarial plans for her served as a goad through all her theatrical setbacks. It spurred her in a negative way as much as her mother's positive praise. Bette would rant and rave and weep at fate, and through her tears she would gasp aloud to the invisible Harlow Davis, *'I'll show you!'*"

TWO

Ruthie Davis and her daughters, once part of a securely upper-middle-class nuclear family, were now cast adrift. Divorce was rare in this era; the girls were so ashamed that Bette never mentioned her father, and Bobby told friends he had a job outside the country. "The children of divorced parents feel a little strange, a little different," Bette said. "I never once told anyone that my parents were divorced. I remember thinking, 'There *is* something funny about us.'"

Just as bad as the psychological impact was the financial. With a little scrimping, the $200 a month from Harlow would have been enough to rent a small apartment and send the girls to public school. But by now Ruthie was determined that her daughters should have the very finest education, and that could come only from private schools, which were expensive. Ruthie vowed to give her girls the best no matter what, and for the next fourteen years she struggled to keep "the three musketeers" (as they came to think of themselves) a step ahead of the bill collector. Ruthie later estimated that between 1918 and 1932 they lived in *eighty* different residences, many of them boardinghouses. Sometimes they made their moves in the middle of the night to avoid paying the rent.

Most other women of her era would have set about at once to find a new husband. Ruthie did not, partly because of her experience with Harlow and partly because as a mature woman of thirty-three she found she liked her independence and wanted to follow her own dreams. She was much ahead of her time in that respect, and when she set out to find a job she was hit by the fact that this was not an easy task for an untrained woman of her social position and financial needs in 1918. Most working women of this era who did not teach, nurse, or become secretaries were either impoverished factory workers or servants in wealthy homes. When she first went looking for work she wore her shoes "down to holes" before finding a well-paid position as a governess in New York for three small boys who had become "animals" after the death of their wealthy father—a tough job, Ruthie recalled, but one that allowed her to

16

send her daughters to one of the finest boarding schools in Massachusetts.

There was the crux of it—Ruthie's determination to give Bette and Bobby the same lifestyle and education they could have had with a successful patent attorney for a father. Sadly, Ruthie realized that this would require that she be separated from the girls—her job was in New York, the school she had chosen—Crestalban—was in the Berkshire Hills. Bette and Bobby, barely used to the absence of their father, now were faced with their mother's removal from their daily lives as well. But Ruthie saw Crestalban as "one big happy family" and a place where the lives of her girls could be "molded into a fine pattern." It was, she felt, the perfect situation for children whose parents could not keep "a normal home."

She first inspected the school on a snowy afternoon. Crestalban's director, Marjorie Whiting, ran the school with her brother and two sisters, and she met Ruthie's train in a small sleigh. They rode a mile or so with blankets wrapped around their knees, the sleigh's silver bells tinkling gaily, and when they arrived Ruthie was met with a Currier & Ives tableau: a white farmhouse at the crest of a low hill, surrounded by several huge red barns and a brown-shingled building. That, Miss Whiting pointed out, was the schoolhouse.

Ruthie loved what she saw and heard of Crestalban. Indeed more like a family than an institution, it had just thirteen students, all girls, and all expected to tend to the farm's pigs, cows, horses and chickens, and the upkeep of the house. The students learned to care for their own clothes and bedding, to sew, and to cook. In short, to rely on themselves.

The buildings had no electricity, no central heating or plumbing; the food was prepared on a wood-burning stove. The students spent sixteen hours of their day outdoors, including their lessons. Overnight they slept on a porch that sometimes left them covered with a thin blanket of snow in the morning. The outdoorsy aspects of Crestalban appealed to Ruthie because her daughters "had never been robust children." Bette in particular was pale and skinny at eleven; her brilliantly blue eyes, huge and protruding and heavily lidded, only added to her waiflike aura.

Ruthie brought the girls to Crestalban after a shopping spree to buy them sleeping bags, woollen "sitting bags" for lessons on the porches, warm underwear and leggings and mittens, woollen bloomers, middie blouses, and sweaters. When they arrived, each put on a brave face for the others; neither Bette nor Bobby shed a tear. Ruthie felt it wise to remain only a few hours, to hasten the girls' adjustment to their new environment. "Then, too, I was pretty sad, and didn't want them to know how I felt. So they waved good-bye—a little wistfully. I can see their faces as if it were yesterday."

The first night, Bette and the painfully shy, wraithlike Bobby shared a sleeping bag in the corner of the porch, trembling with fear and cold and clinging to each other "like orphans in a storm." But within days they had fallen in love with their new home, joyously taking naked snowbaths in the mornings, milking cows, and birthing livestock. Soon their constitutions improved markedly.

Their education was top-notch. Nothing but French was spoken during lunch, and every evening the students gathered around the great roaring fireplace in the main room to sew and listen to Miss Whiting read to them from the classics. It was at Crestalban that Bette, who had inherited her father's keen, analytical mind, developed a passion for books. Most playtimes she could be found sitting alone under a spreading tree, engrossed in some novel or other, oblivious of all the other children romping nearby. Whenever she did join the horseplay, she made sure she became either the leader of the activity or the center of attention. It was a pattern that would continue for the rest of her life.

Even in a moment of near tragedy when she was eleven, Bette's main concern was to capture as much attention and sympathy as she could. It was an early morning a few days before her second Christmas at Crestalban, and as she had the previous year, she was playing Santa Claus in preparation for the exchange of gifts among the students and faculty. Her suit was red wool, with white cotton batting at the cuffs and collar, and a cotton beard. Playing Santa reminded Bette of Harlow, and she imitated his rousing "Ho! Ho! Ho!" that had filled their home with rare happiness once a year.

The school's tree—huge, freshly cut, aromatic, and gaily decorated with cranberry garlands the children had strung together—stood in the center of the great room, aglow with dozens of burning wax candles. Bette had been warned to stay away from it until one of the adults could gather the presents from underneath for her to hand out. But alone in her Santa suit, poking around to see which boxes were for her, Bette's curiosity got the best of her, and she reached down to grab one shiny gift with her name on it. In a flash her cuff caught on fire. She shook her arm to put out the flames, but that only fanned them as they spread to her beard.

Bette heard her own screams, then panicky voices as she felt herself pushed down on the floor and rolled up in a rug. Bobby, who couldn't bear to look, turned away. Once the flames were snuffed out, everyone stared in horror as Bette lay still on the floor, the sides and top of her face red and bubbly, her eyebrows singed, her eyes seemingly seared shut. She heard one of the teachers cry, "She is blind! Oh God, she is blind!"

She remained frozen and lapped it up. "I didn't know if I was blind or not. But I do remember feeling, with thrills and chills of morbid pleasure, that this was my moment, my big dramatic moment. And I deliberately kept my eyes tight closed, groped helplessly around with my hands, until the full savor of that moment was extracted."

Miss Whiting couldn't reach a doctor, and the school nurse decided that applications of cold cream to Bette's face would be enough treatment until the following day, when she, Bobby, and some of the other children were to return to their parents in New York in the company of several teachers. After an eight-hour journey, Bette and Bobby rushed off the train to greet Ruthie. She recognized only Bobby; by now Bette's face was a mass of blisters that had become encrusted with cinders from the train. Ruthie let out a yelp and one of the teachers ran forward to explain what had happened and that Miss Whiting suggested she take Bette to a doctor. Ruthie recalled saying "unprintable" things. "Like a mother lioness with a sick cub, I literally snarled as I hurried [Bette and Bobby] away in a taxi."

The cabbie rushed them a few blocks to St. Bartholomew's Hospital, where only one doctor, a Japanese intern, was on Christmas Eve duty. For more than an hour, the man carefully peeled off the blisters that covered Bette's forehead and the sides of her face, and gingerly removed the cinders with a pair of tweezers. When he was through, little of the outer layer of Bette's skin remained. He wrapped her head with bandages, leaving just the bottom half of her eyes, her nose, and her mouth visible, and told Ruthie that in order to prevent lifelong scarring, the burns would have to be swabbed with boric acid and moistened with grease every two hours around the clock for two weeks. "If you can do this," the doctor said, "the burns will not heal and form scar tissue. They will just slough off and new skin will form." Then he added, "Unless you hire a nurse, I don't think you can do it."

Ruthie did it. For fourteen days she changed the dressings around the clock; at night she rose to the jangle of her alarm clock every two hours to daub Bette's burns and try to ease the pain that made it impossible for her to sleep more than a few minutes at a time. She tied Bette's hands down every night to keep her from scratching, and Bobby held them during the day as Ruthie read stories to distract her. It took years for Bette's skin to return to normal, and even then the burns left her with a thin, almost translucent epidermis that left her vulnerable to severe sunburns.

By now Ruthie was employed as a housemother at Miss Bennett's, a girls' finishing school in Millbrook, New York, where she was provided room and board as part of her compensation, and where she took Bette to recover. Ruthie had agreed to give up her own Christmas vacation to look after the students who couldn't go home for the holidays, provided that her own daughters could stay with her. This was necessary because Ruthie didn't have the money to send them anywhere else.

After Bette and Bobby completed their third year at Crestalban in 1920, Ruthie lost her job at Miss Bennett's and could no longer afford to pay their tuition. Her unemployment forced her to make a decision that she had agonized over for some time: She screwed up her courage and enrolled in the Clarence White School of Photography on West 128th Street in Manhattan. Ruthie had become intrigued by the possibilities of the camera after her divorce, and she had taken many family photos and experimental portraits, usually with Bette as her model. All of her creative yearnings seemed to be satisfied by photography, and she hoped that formal training might allow her to set up a studio. Then she would have a career, be her own boss, not have to worry about finding or losing jobs. And she was sure she could make enough money to keep Bette and Bobby well dressed, well housed, and well educated.

In the meantime, however, they would have to endure some hardship. Ruthie sat the girls down and explained that they would be living with her in Manhattan, and they would have to go to a public school. She hoped that they would understand the need for sacrifice now in order that they might have a brighter future. She told them she had rented a nice apartment, and although the girls were heartbroken not to be returning to Crestalban, they thought this new adventure might be fun. Best of all they would be reunited with Ruthie full time. "For the first time since Winchester," Bette recalled, "the three musketeers were together again."

But the reality of the change traumatized the sisters. When they entered the cramped one-bedroom walk-up at 144th Street and Broadway, the only apartment Ruthie could afford, they found it "so dismal and so foreign to everything we had known" that they retreated to the bedroom moments later and burst into tears. "Do you really believe that she thinks this is a nice place?" Bobby asked.

"I'm afraid she does," Bette replied. "But we must be brave and not hurt her feelings."

Ruthie knew her girls were "horrified" by the place, but there was nothing she could do; Harlow's $200 a month covered fewer and fewer expenses these days, and the tuition at the White School wasn't cheap. Bobby slept in the same bed as Ruthie, with Bette on a cot next to them. After the fresh air and hillsides of Crestalban, this claustrophobic apartment was a very hard adjustment indeed.

P.S. 186 was even harder for Bette to take. The school looked to her like a "big, brown fortress. Forbidding, impersonal." At Crestalban there were thirteen students on two hundred acres; here there were fifty pupils to a class, three thousand students in all. When she was first herded into a general assembly hall with all of them, she sat there "terrified," sure that she would be trampled, beaten up, or killed. There had been so much fresh air and nature at Crestalban; what Bette most remembered about P.S. 186 was "the smell of steam heat mingled with chalk and children." To make matters worse, Bette had been put back half a year to the second half of the seventh grade, because the school principal didn't consider private school education on a par with the New York City curriculum.

But just as she had come to love country life, Bette soon found herself enchanted by the charms of 1921 New York. Children named Esperanzo and Seymour and Nuncio, at first frighteningly alien to her, proved "warm and friendly," and they became her pals. In summer they roller-skated down the hill between Broadway and Riverside Drive, bought colorful shaved-ice cones from an Italian man under an umbrella pushcart, played hopscotch on the asphalt, opened fire hydrants to keep cool during heat waves. In winter, snow transformed the hill into an icy speedway for sledding, and the glittery beauty of the Christmas window displays in the fancy Fifth Avenue shops that Ruthie took her to see left Bette's huge eyes wide with wonder. After two seasons in New York, Bette recalled, "we were having a glorious time."

Even their tawdry apartment, it turned out, could offer entertainment. At night, Ruthie would turn out the lights and raise the window shades, and the three of them, as though in a scene from Alfred Hitchcock's *Rear Window*, would watch their neighbors as they went through their often quirky routines of daily life across the courtyard. "We rocked with laughter," Bette recalled. "Ruthie had made our dreary place into the first box at the Palace."

That spring in New York, Bette saw her first movie, *Four Horsemen of the Apocalypse* with Rudolph Valentino, and the lights and shadows she saw up on that huge silvery screen left her "tremendously impressed." She loved *Little Lord Fauntleroy* with Mary Pickford, and when she saw *Black Beauty* a while later, she came home and cried herself to sleep on her cot next to Ruthie and Bobby. It was in a movie theater that Bette Davis felt her first nameless stirrings of desire for something more exciting than the future that seemed to be in store for her.

Bette joined the Girl Scouts in New York and became so dedicated to the organization's credo and goals that "I would have tripped an old lady in order to pick her up." She won dozens of merit badges and became a patrol leader, gaining the reputation of a tough-as-nails drill sergeant. She didn't care whether she was popular; she had a mission—to march her patrol before Mrs. Herbert Hoover, the wife of the U.S. Secretary of Commerce, in a competition at Madison Square Garden. When she won the contest, she was in her glory. "I had to be the best. Nothing less ever satisfied me."

The summer of 1922, Ruthie used money she had painstakingly saved over the previous nine months and sent Bette and Bobby to Camp Mudjekeewis in Maine, where they swam, made jewelry, rode horses, and canoed down the fast-moving river that linked Upper Kezar Lake to Lower Kezar. The expense of that "glorious summer" left Ruthie no longer able to afford her classes at the White School, nor even the modest apartment in Manhattan. But she felt she now had enough knowledge to set up her photography business, and when a piano teacher of Bobby's at Mudjekeewis suggested they move to East Orange, New Jersey, so that Bobby could continue her lessons, Ruthie packed the musketeers up once again.

This time Ruthie could afford only boardinghouse rooms for herself and the girls, and the situation proved unbearable for Bette. She despised their tiny attic space, hated the shabby decor, dreaded having to share her meals with strangers at the long dining room table. She grew miserably unhappy, and frustrated that the nebulous dreams she had started to nurse of someday being "somebody important" seemed more and more remote by the day. "My imagination took me around the world," she recalled, "and I was stuck in a boardinghouse in East Orange, New Jersey."

Ruthie placed a small notice in the local paper and started to pick up some photography business, trundling her camera and reflectors and tripods over to the neighbors' houses to take family portraits. It wasn't much, but it was a start, and Ruthie loved it. Finally, she was able to express her creativity and make money at it too.

Bette entered East Orange High School as a freshman after she insisted on taking a special examination that made up for the half-year she had been put back at P.S. 186. But her alienation was so great that she made no friends at the school, and she offered no remembrances of her studies there in her autobiography. Her life during this period, she felt, was little more than "a monotone. If I had any distinguishing emotion at all it was that I was waiting for something. I didn't know at all what . . . I can't remember that I ever thought, much less said, that I would become an actress. . . . I just sort of lived in a static mist . . . punctuated with occasional rages when something I wanted penetrated the coma."

Ruthie later admitted that she had been "petrified" by those rages, and she tried to placate Bette at every turn, but without success. Bette enjoyed her power over her mother but Ruthie's permissiveness also "irritated" her. It was at this point in her life that Bette's feelings about her mother turned ambivalent. Bette with her mercurial temperament and willfulness was always first and foremost in Ruthie's heart and mind, far ahead of the withdrawn, undemanding Bobby. Anything Bette wanted, Ruthie would try to get. Anything Bette disliked, Ruthie would try to change. She did whatever was necessary to keep Bette's moods on an even keel, keep Bette happy, keep Bette from tearing off into a terrible tantrum.

The closeness between mother and daughter grew so strong that it sometimes took on an almost unnatural cast. After Bette's face was burned, Ruthie had begun bathing her daughter every night, carefully sponging her sensitive skin and helping it to heal. Long after Bette recovered, Ruthie continued to give her tub baths; she didn't stop the practice, in fact, until Bette was well into her teens.

But for all of Ruthie's ministrations to Bette, for all her attempts to keep her happy, Bette in her adolescent angst lost respect for Ruthie. She felt disdain at how easily she could manipulate her, embarrassment at how silly she sometimes seemed. When Ruthie would chatter in an attempt to lighten the atmosphere around her sullen daughter, Bette would smirk and call her a "flibbertigibbet."

Bette's behavior in East Orange so alarmed Ruthie that she consulted a doctor, but to little avail. The man simply advised her that Bette was "a high-strung young filly" and that the best thing to do would be to leave her alone because "she needs a free rein." As Bette recalled it, Ruthie had little choice anyway: "The filly became a bucking bronco."

One evening, as they prepared for dinner, Ruthie suggested a game: She and Bette would exchange clothes and assume the other's personality throughout the meal. Bobby and another girl would wear each other's jumpers and do the same. After they joined the other boarders at the sprawling dining room table, Bette began to chatter incessantly, ending every other sentence with a giggle. Ruthie sat, uncharacteristically silent, staring sullenly at her plate. Finally Ruthie looked up and started to laugh, recognizing herself in Bette's impression. But Bette, "as if a bomb had exploded under both of us," started screaming at her mother. "I'm *not* like that!" she cried and stood up so violently that her chair toppled over. She barreled out of the room as the laughter of the other boarders rang in her ears.

Later, calmed, Bette realized what her mother had tried to do, but the attempt was futile. "I couldn't help the way I was acting. I felt like a misfit." She longed for something more, something that would "penetrate the coma."

After two months in East Orange, Ruthie fell ill. She felt feverish, her jaw ached. A dentist told her that she had osteomyelitis of the jawbone, a serious bacterial infection. The doctor cleaned out the infection, closed Ruthie's jaw with twenty stitches, and sent her home. When she stepped off the trolley car in front of the boardinghouse, she collapsed on the sidewalk. Frightened by the experience, she felt she needed to be near her sister Mildred in Newton. A few days later, Mildred and her husband came to New Jersey to help the musketeers come home.

They moved into another boardinghouse, this one even worse than the first, and Bette was so miserable that Ruthie swallowed her pride and approached Harlow for financial help. To her great humiliation, he refused her, and she had no other recourse but to try to regain her strength in the noisy, unpleasant environment of the lodging house. Still, she recovered quickly, and before long she rustled up enough photography business among family and old friends in Newton to afford the rent on the second floor of a two-family house, a living situation closer to what she and the girls had been used to in Massachusetts. Not much later, Ruthie bought a used Model T Ford. Now they were more like a traditional family than they had been for years.

By Newton standards, however, they were the height of eccentricity. Ruthie turned part of the apartment into a studio and advertised her photography in the local newspaper—"Portraits with a Personality—At

Your Home or Mine." Most days when Bette and Bobby came home from school, they would find their living room overrun with people eager to have their pictures taken and Ruthie bustling around directing the lamps, adjusting the backdrops, posing her subjects. Then she would get behind her "Big Bertha" black box camera standing on its tripod, poke her head under its heavy black fabric, and set off a burst of gunpowder to produce a flash—and an eight-by-ten-inch glass negative she could print and retouch into a lovely portrait or family tableau.

Bette didn't mind all this chaos because she was now in a much better humor. Ruthie seemed so much happier "in her element," and Bette's "coma" had been penetrated by "something I wanted": to be accepted by her Newton High School classmates. After a rocky start she did indeed blossom into one of the most popular girls in the school. The transformation occurred between her first and second school dances. She was reluctant to attend the first, held early in the school year, because she had no friends and no beau. Since she'd spent most of her school years at girls' academies, she recalled, she was "petrified of boys."

Ruthie convinced her to go, and dressed her, as usual, in her schoolgirl outfit of corduroy jumper and flat shoes, her long hair combed straight down her back. Bette spent the first hour standing alone along a wall of the school gymnasium, "praying for someone to ask me to dance." Finally one "sympathetic soul" did, but he soon regretted it—because no one offered to cut in. When Bette glanced into a mirror and saw him gesture frantically to the boys on the sidelines for rescue, she made an excuse and fled. Back home, she sobbed inconsolably to Ruthie that she would always be a wallflower. "Bette," her mother replied, "I think it's about time you put your hair up and started to dress like a young lady."

She appeared at the second dance looking like a vision in a long white chiffon dress, with a sweeping skirt trimmed in turquoise and a neckline so daring—just below the collarbone—that the visiting Grandmother Favor exclaimed, "Bette, you're not going to wear that where gentlemen can see you, are you?" *That's exactly what I'm going to do,* she thought, and with her hair in a glamorous upsweep and her cheeks pink with excitement, she looked into a mirror and thought to herself for the very first time, *You're pretty.*

The boys at the party agreed. Bette's dance card filled quickly, and the cutting-in was constant. At the end of the evening, she recalled, she had acquired two boyfriends—John Holt and George Dunham, whom everyone called "Gige." When Ruthie picked Bette up in the Model T, she drove the boys home as well. Beginning the next day, the rivals walked Bette home the two miles from school every afternoon. From this point on, John Holt recalls, Bette's personality flowered. "She was bright and intelligent and vivacious and everybody liked her. We sort of prized our association with her because we liked her very much. After we'd walk her home we'd play around in her yard, play with her dog, things like that. One afternoon the dog was chasing Gige around and he ran afoul of some barbed wire on a fence and tore his pants. Bette's mother spent the afternoon stitching them up, which amused us all no end."

Master Dunham won this initial competition for Bette's affections. "Gige was a fun-loving person," John Holt says, "full of beans and energy. More so than I was. I was more the serious type—much duller." When Gige asked Bette if he could be her beau she was "dizzy" with joy —and so drunk with this new power she exerted over boys that John Holt's mother cautioned him against her: "She thought Bette was always 'making eyes,' " Holt recalls, "and she didn't approve of girls making eyes."

Bette admitted that she careered "from crush to crush" now, but her series of boyfriends was important to her mainly because they brought with them invitations to football games, hayrides, dances, marshmallow roasts, sleigh rides—in short, they made Bette a part of the Newton social life that she coveted and came to love.

As flirtatious as she was, Bette "zealously guarded" her chastity. While Ruthie may have been ahead of her time as a single working mother, when it came to sexual frankness with her daughters, her Puritan ancestry came to the fore in a rush of silence. What little Bette knew about the birds and the bees she had picked up in tittery whispers from classmates. This information was scarce and inaccurate; the first time a boy kissed Bette, she was so certain she'd have a baby that her stomach expanded into a hysterical pregnancy. "My terror," she recalled, "the possible disgrace to Ruthie, was indescribable."

When she had her first period, a similar panic gripped Bette: no one had warned her about menstruation, and she was sure she was dying. Ruthie told her this was part of a girl's growing up, and the "burden women must bear" to have children. Wistfully, Bette wrote in her auto-biography that the younger Bobby was spared this "jump into the un-known."

As Bette developed into young womanhood, her mother took on a strange new role in her life: rival. Ruthie was just thirty-six when Bette was fifteen, and still a lovely, vibrant woman. Bette remembered feeling a deep twinge of jealousy when one of her older boyfriends complained that she didn't have her mother's maturity.

Ruthie had several suitors herself at this point, and for the first time since her divorce she allowed herself thoughts of marrying again. But whenever she would introduce a gentleman to Bette and Bobby, and afterward gently inquire whether they might accept him as a stepfather, her daughters invariably, adamantly said no. And that would be that. According to Bette, "She let us wreck her personal life. She never thought of herself, only of us."

And still she struggled to pay the bills. Even though the girls hadn't been in a private school for several years, inflation had been so high during that period that Harlow's $200 alimony payment, worth the contemporary equivalent of $1,800 four years earlier, was worth a quarter of that in 1922. The income from Ruthie's photography business wasn't enough any longer, and the summer after Bette's first year at Newton High, Ruthie took a two-month job as a live-in cook/housekeeper for a young minister in Provincetown. The position included free room and board and gave Bette and Bobby a fun July and August by the sea. Bette remembered it as "wonderful," particularly a summer romance with a young man about to enter Harvard.

To have a "college man" as a beau at fourteen kept Bette in a perpetual state of euphoria. She never admitted to it, but she may have let him believe she was older; it wouldn't have been hard to do. Bette had posed for Ruthie just about daily ever since her mother had purchased studio equipment and began to experiment with lighting and focus and how to pose her models. The experience gave Bette the carriage and self-possession of a young adult, and her strong intelligence and quick wit belied her age. Only her naïveté might have given her away, although it wasn't unusual in this era for women much older to be equally unworldly, and Bette's beau may have left for the ivy-covered campus in Cambridge with no idea just how young his girlfriend had been.

At the end of the summer, the Davis gypsies returned to Newton, where Bette completed her sophomore year of high school in 1923 without distinguishing incident. By then, inflation had subsided and the cost of living was 20 percent lower than it had been for the previous two years. Necessities cost Ruthie less, and the increased buying power enjoyed by everyone else perked up her photography business to the point that she felt she could afford to send Bette and Bobby back to boarding school.

She chose the all-girl Northfield Seminary primarily for its reasonable tuition, but both her daughters were miserable there. They felt overworked, and found the instruction too religious and the food "hopeless." Although they tried to keep their letters to Ruthie upbeat, she sensed their unhappiness and took them out of the school over the Christmas holidays of 1924. In January she enrolled them in an alma mater of her own, Cushing Academy in Ashburnham, Massachusetts, a small, well-regarded prep school, considered by many a stepping-stone to Dartmouth College. Cushing was coeducational and had a strong dramatics department, and while its $1,000-a-year tuition for each of her girls put Ruthie on the cusp of poverty once again, she thought that Bette, especially, would love the place.

She did. Although the classrooms were part of a huge stone building with a two-hundred-fifty-foot bell tower at its center, Cushing's several acres of country setting reminded Bette of Crestalban. She enjoyed the curriculum, much more liberal than Northfield's, and she gravitated toward the school's revered dramatics coach, Lois Cann; she had begun to have a vague inkling now that she might want to act in school plays.

It was during her two years at Cushing that the diverse facets of Bette Davis's personality coalesced into the irresistible force they would remain for the rest of her life. She entered the school in the middle of her junior year and not only became a top-grade student but won such popularity that she was voted president of her sorority.

Her fellow students remember her with a tinge of wonder. "She was a very forceful, assertive person," Bob Hendricks, a year behind her, recalls. "Alert, aggressive, pop-eyed. We were all somewhat in awe of Bette. She was poised, assured—and ambitious. In both the best and worst senses of the word."

With her new social status came jealousy from her fellow students. Although Hendricks remembered that "there was nothing high-hat about her at all," Bette would recall that some at the school found her "stuck up." She denied it. "I was just sure of myself. This is and always has been an unforgivable quality to the unsure."

Still, one of Bette's own recollections suggests that she had lost little of the snobbery that had made her hate the small apartments and boardinghouses that Ruthie's financial woes had forced her to live in. Ruthie had notified Cushing's headmaster, Dr. Cowell, that she would have difficulty meeting the next semester's tuition, and Cowell called Bette into his office. Nervous and unsure about why she had been summoned, Bette trembled as she knocked on Cowell's massive oak door. When she sat down in front of the white-haired man's desk, she was pleased, if a little puzzled, by his initial comment. "You have a wonderful and brave mother, Bette," he said in his cultured and even voice. "You are truly fortunate in having someone to make great sacrifices to give you an education." But as Cowell continued, Bette felt as if she had been slapped in the face.

The headmaster suggested that Bette help Ruthie meet her tuition by waiting on tables in the girls' dining room. "I was afraid that I might cry," Bette recalled. "How could anyone suggest such a thing to me? I was much too fine a person to demean myself by carrying trays in and out of a kitchen." Although she was "burning with indignation," she told Cowell "hypocritically" that she thought it was a wonderful idea and she would write to her mother and ask her permission. "I was absolutely positive Mother would refuse. She would *never* let her daughter be a waitress!"

She "pulled out all the stops" in the letter, Bette recalled. "I made the whole thing appear not only disagreeable but revolting. For the next few days I was highly pleased with myself." Came her mother's reply and "my world seemed to fall apart." Ruthie wrote that Cowell's notion was "very sweet" and that Bette should "go right ahead." For three days, she remained in her room and sulked. She was convinced that the minute her friends saw her waiting on them they would never speak to her again. "I wanted to leave the school. I made desperate plans for running away." She lay in her bed the night before her first day as a waitress and thought, *I wish I were dead.*

The next morning she picked up a tray laden with bowls of oatmeal from the kitchen counter, took a deep breath, pushed through the swinging doors into the dining room, and began to place the bowls in front of her fellow students. To her astonishment, there were no whispers, no titters, no finger-pointing. In fact, she noticed that her classmates were friendlier than usual. One girl who Bette knew didn't like her much said "Good morning" to her for the first time since her arrival at the school. Soon, to her delight and amazement, her humbling dining room duties had won her more friends than ever.

Bette waited on tables three meals a day for the rest of her two years at Cushing—"My snobbishness was a thing of the past." One of her classmates, Eleanor Coffin, did feel a little uncomfortable having a friend serve her. "I used to feel so guilty that Bette was waiting on tables and I would sit there. I didn't like that. But we knew she didn't have too much and her mother was struggling along as a photographer to make ends meet. Bette was helping her mother out, and we admired her for that."

THREE

ette sat in English class and stared out the window, the sounds of a
classmate's recitation of "Beowulf" droning in her ears. Suddenly
she perked up: passing outside the window was a tall, gangly, lik-
able-looking young man she found very attractive. Later, after class, she
saw him again, and asked around to discover that he was Harmon O.
Nelson, Jr., a senior and a musician whom everyone called "Ham."
Bette later described him as "lean, dark curly-haired, with a funny
nose and beautiful brown eyes." She was smitten. "I think I liked him
at first," she said, "because he had such cold, curious eyes, promising warmth. Then I liked him because he was such an indifferent
louse. He didn't pay the slightest attention to me. I went home and
told Ruthie about him. I said, 'I'm going to get him if it's the last thing I
do!'"

At the next school dance, Bette had her usual fill of male attention, but Ham Nelson, playing the piano to help pay his tuition, never
approached her during any of his breaks, and Bette went home
frustrated.

They got to know each other when Ham invited her to join a musi-
cale he was putting on at the school. She as yet had no burning desire to
perform; she had enrolled in Lois Cann's Expression class, but she had
never had any problem expressing herself and the exercises brought her
no creative epiphany. But she immediately said "Yes!" to Ham's request,
because she knew it would bring them closer together. For weeks Ham
coached her with her song, and during the show he provided the accom-
paniment for her rendition of "Gee, I'm Mighty Blue for You," one of
the hit songs of the day. "I had a lot of fun," Bette recalled, "skipping
octaves on him and doing all kinds of little tricks."

Ham sang "Paddlin' Madeline Home," and Bette noticed that he
had a beautiful voice and was "a gifted musician." Bette mustered up the
courage to ask him why he had ignored her for so long. Shyly Nelson
replied that he had liked her the moment he first saw her, months earlier,

31

but he was certain that if he had let his interest be known, she would have rebuffed him. She let out one of her raucous laughs, and from that moment on she and Ham Nelson were "an item." When Ham began trumpet lessons, he interrupted her studies every night by playing taps for her from his dormitory room, directly across a courtyard from hers— "A definite agony for all concerned," Bette recalled. She scarcely minded. "I was wading in those velvety brown eyes. I was truly in love. So was he."

But he had competition. Art Walsh, a fellow senior who didn't much like Ham Nelson anyway, decided that *he* should be Bette Davis's beau. As Bob Hendricks recalls it, "Art and Ham had a big fight on the gymnasium floor, to see who would win the hand of the fair damsel." Bette was taking dance classes directly above the gym while this was going on, and word got to her in a flash. While she waved her arms and kicked her legs and smiled prettily, she could hear "these awful *sloshing* noises and tremendous thumps and bangs." Ham seems to have gotten the worst of it: "Art just about killed me," he admitted.

Ham may have lost the battle, but he won Bette. Soon everyone took it for granted that they were "the class couple." At his senior prom in June 1925, they danced every dance together; no one dared cut in. The night before, she had played Lola Pratt in the senior class play, Booth Tarkington's *Seventeen,* but the acting bug hadn't yet bitten her as deeply as the love variety: she did the show only because Ham played Uncle Georgikins. At a party on the last day of school, it was less a comment on her acting than her love life when Bette, blushing deeply, was presented with a large baked ham.

That summer, Ruthie took Bette and Bobby to Peterboro, New Hampshire, a small artistic community whose local photographer had recently passed away. Mariarden, a noted theater school, was nearby, and Ruthie was sure they'd need a photographer to record their recitals. She found a small, two-hundred-year-old clapboard building with space for a photography studio and darkroom below and living quarters above. She hung a shingle from the small portico above the front door announcing "The Silhouette Shop," took out an ad in the local paper, and drummed up business among the residents of the picturesque town. Peterboro, Bette recalled, offered Ruthie "a feast of cultural and creative opportunity."

It did Bette as well, for it was in Peterboro that she experienced the first thrill of real stage accomplishment and felt her nascent notion that she might want to be an actress blossom into the implacable ambition that would propel her through the rest of her life. And all because she liked dancing and thought it would be fun to study it with Mariarden's exotic instructress, the British *danseuse* and designer Jane Cradduck, who had been raised in India and went by the *nom d'artiste* of Roshanara.

But Mariarden's tuition was too high for Ruthie, and Bette enrolled instead with the Outdoor Players of Marie Ware Laughton, who waived tuition in exchange for Ruthie's photographs of the students' activities. From Miss Laughton's staff, Bette said, she learned "nature dances à la Isadora Duncan." Classes were held on an acre of green lawn with a background of tall pines. On a Monday afternoon about a week into the session, as Ruthie took pictures of Bette and her classmates practicing, a wave of excitement rolled through the students: Roshanara was on her way to visit the class. Ruthie watched in awe as the Great Lady, her long black robe trailing behind her, moved across the grass with such grace she seemed like a swan. Bette was spellbound by the spectacle as well, and barely able to concentrate on her own movements from then on. When the class was over, Roshanara thanked the students and just as grandly took her leave.

The next morning, she sent a note asking to see Bette at four o'clock that afternoon. Ruthie's face lit up, but Bette assured her that the woman probably just wanted to give her private lessons because she'd been so bad, and they wouldn't be able to afford them anyway. When they arrived for the meeting, Roshanara told them that Bette had great potential and that she wanted her as a student. "I do not mean to embarrass you, Mrs. Davis," she said, "but I know you are short of funds; I have heard." She suggested that Bobby—who had shown a talent for the piano—play at rehearsals three hours a day, in exchange for which Roshanara would pay her five dollars a week and waive Bette's tuition.

Thrilled by the prospect of studying with Roshanara more than she had been by anything before, Bette worked "harder than I had ever thought possible." She rehearsed eight hours a day in punishing heat to prepare for her role as a dancing fairy in a public performance of *A Midsummer Night's Dream*. Ruthie later learned that Bette had had a painful plantar wart on her foot during all this time that had "caused her agony even to step," and that later took three months of treatment to cure. But Bette had said nothing because she was afraid that if she did, she wouldn't be allowed to dance—and by now she was completely under the spell of Roshanara, who "made my head reel" with the way she combined movement and emotion. When she, Ruthie, and Bobby saw the woman dance her own "Prayer," Bette felt more reverence than she ever had in a church.

A Midsummer Night's Dream, Bette Davis's first performance before a paying audience, was presented on July 23, 1925, and as she danced in ensemble and heard the crowd's applause she felt a thrill wash over her. But it was nothing compared to her next performance, as The Moth. For this highly theatrical dance, a solo turn on an outdoor stage, she wore a flowing white silk gown with enormous sleeves extended over long bamboo sticks to simulate wings. Bette's body fluttered as smoothly as the silk did in the warm evening breeze, as she enacted the birth, flight, and death of the moth on the glass stage, shimmering in silhouette above colored lights that slowly changed from white to blue to amber. The moonlight from above, Ruthie recalled, "seemed to cast its kindly light down upon this graceful child who herself was coming out of her cocoon."

Bette's performance caught the audience in its spell, and when she drooped to the floor and the moth died, they burst into a sustained ovation that almost overwhelmed her. Ruthie and Bobby had huddled close together as they watched Bette, astonished by the power and the beauty she had projected on that colorful stage. Afterward, Bette recalled, they looked at her "as if they'd never seen me before."

Frank Conroy, an instructor and director at Mariarden, walked up to Ruthie moments later. "Mrs. Davis," he said, "throughout my life I have religiously abstained from advising a mother to put her daughter on the stage. But Bette has something you can't buy and you can't imitate. Even if she doesn't open her mouth, she has that quality that draws an audience to her. I think that someday, if she works hard, she will be a fine actress." Ruthie and Bette stared at Conroy for a few seconds, then glanced at each other. Both looked as though a light had been turned on behind their eyes.

When Bette returned to Cushing for her senior year in the fall of 1925, her triumphant summer at Mariarden carried over into an "obsession" with the theater. She had so loved the acclaim, the matchless sense of accomplishment she had felt, that she became fiercely determined to experience it again and again. She also knew that if she could achieve some measure of theatrical success, she would be able to help Ruthie avoid the financial struggles she had grappled with for so many years.

With Ham no longer at Cushing to divert her attention, Bette plunged herself into dramatics. Florence Melanson Rogers, who had returned to the school as an instructor soon after her graduation and was only four years older than Bette, recalls that "she was in rehearsal every single afternoon. She always wanted to be in the plays, and she loved it when they would go public and take them to neighboring towns for a night or two."

Bette discovered that she often felt more natural on the stage than she did away from it. "I loved rehearsing. I learned the lines easily. I never suffered from stage fright. I felt no self-consciousness." Bob Hendricks recalled that Bette soon became Lois Cann's "great white hope." She also represented hope to Ruthie, who knew better than her daughter how much success on the stage could mean to the Davis family. Ruthie had always encouraged Bette in whatever enthusiasm she embraced, but she now became something akin to a stage mother. According to Bob Hendricks, "She was a martinet. She pushed Bette hard. I think she thought, *Well, which of my daughters is gonna make it?* And then she just pushed the hell out of Bette."

With Bette more than ever in the forefront, her sister found herself shuffled even further into the background. Although Bobby was intelligent, musically talented, and, some thought, prettier than Bette, her painful shyness and secondary position in the family left her "completely overshadowed by Bette," Bob Hendricks recalls. "A punishing overshadowment. It was extremely bad." Florence Rogers remembered helping Bobby with her posture. "She was a dear, sweet, shy, overshadowed little sister. It was pathetic. She was just *shoved* into the background. She was so mousy that I don't even know if most people knew Bette *had* a sister at Cushing."

Bette's main goal that year was to play the lead in her own senior play—and of course she did, on June 12, 1926. The piece was *The Charm School* by Alice Miller and Robert Milton, in which art imitated life: Bette played Elise Benedotti, the student leader at a girls' boarding school. She did so "vivaciously," according to her yearbook.

When she was graduated from Cushing, Bette's classmates voted her the "prettiest," the "busiest," and the "best actress" in the class. Her yearbook photo is accompanied by this legend:

> One of the fairest girls we know is Bette Davis—Ham says so! Bette may be the busiest girl in the senior class, but she is never too busy to help out when she is asked. Her giggle is a delight far more pleasing than the "Laughing" record on the "vic." Bette's talents are numerous, for she has a lovely singing voice, is the best actress, and the class beauty—what more could anyone wish?

To pay for Bette and Bobby's tuition that semester, Ruthie had photographed the entire graduating class and single-handedly developed the proofs and retouched each finished portrait. She stayed up night after night until the early-morning hours to finish the work, and when it was completed she felt tired unto death.

As Bette proudly walked across the stage to accept her diploma on June 13, she scanned the audience for her father. He wasn't there. Then she spotted Ruthie, and the sight of her mother that day, more than anything before it, galvanized her determination to succeed. Ruthie weighed about ninety pounds, looked drawn and tired, and had signs of developer poisoning on her face. "A braver, more exhausted mother was not there that day," Bette recalled. "I wanted to cry."

The next three months, according to Ruthie, were Bette's "last carefree summer." Ruthie rented a small fishing shack in Ogunquit, Maine, for one hundred dollars the season; it had one large room with a fireplace and a small alcove as a bedroom. Because there was so little room, Bobby went to live with Ruthie's best friends, a husband and wife and their family, where she was expected to "earn her keep" by doing chores. She was made to wash dishes every day for thirteen or fourteen people, and the wife accused her of chipping several dishes through carelessness. Finally, as Ruthie later put it, "she just went to pieces," and she was brought home by the husband, who told his wife she had been taking advantage of Bobby. She had never complained.

Bette, by contrast, hadn't a care in the world. She became the only female lifeguard in Ogunquit and acquired a new boyfriend, a handsome Yale man named Fritz Hall who rode a motorcycle and reminded Bette of the dashing aviator Charles Lindbergh. Smitten for the first time since she met Ham Nelson (who was out of sight at Amherst College and soon out of mind), Bette wrote Ham a Dear John letter, returned his fraternity pin, and declared her love for Fritz.

When the summer ended, Fritz returned to Yale and the Davis family went back to Newton. There, the melancholia Bette had suffered five years earlier in New Jersey returned. For the next two years, she made no progress whatsoever toward her dream of a stage career, and felt herself totally adrift and alienated. She helped Ruthie around the house, typed manuscripts for a local author to earn extra money for the family, and pined over Fritz. Her loneliness was worsened by the fact that most of her old Newton High friends had gone on to college or careers, and few of them were left in town.

Ruthie's photography business had sagged, and she was badly pinched for money again. Unsure that she could meet the next month's rent, she suggested to Bette, now eighteen, that she pose for an acquaintance, an elderly sculptor who lived on Beacon Hill in Boston. The woman, Ruthie explained hesitantly, was willing to pay very well for a model for a life-sized embodiment of Spring in the form of a young . . . lovely . . . *naked* girl.

Bette stared at her mother, her eyes larger than ever, and gulped. "It will be okay, darling," Ruthie soothed. "She's a lovely woman, very high in Boston society. There's nothing to be embarrassed about. It's for the sake of art."

Two days later, the artist's long black limousine pulled up in front of their house, a uniformed driver at the wheel, and whisked Bette to Boston. As she sat in the back seat, she looked eagerly out the window to see whether any of the neighbors had noticed her. To her intense disappointment, no one had.

Horror rippled through her when she walked into the studio and saw the sculptor's handsome young male assistant. Ignoring the look on Bette's face, the woman told her that the dressing room was at the top of the stairs. "Please remove your clothes," she said matter-of-factly, "and we'll begin." Bette's face burned with embarrassment as she scurried up the stairs. Fifteen minutes later, she still hadn't mustered the courage to come down. "Miss Davis," the woman called up the stairs, "we're *ready* for you."

"I was absolutely panicked," Bette recalled. "I was so modest." But, finally, she descended the steps. "I tell you, I was *mortified*. It took me years to get over it, as a matter of fact." She stuck to the commitment she'd made, however, and felt better when she realized the young man was "impersonal about the whole thing." Within a few days, she felt less self-conscious, more comfortable with her body—attributes that served her very well as a budding actress.

When the sculpture was completed, Bette adored it. "It was lovely, beautiful. I had the perfect figure for it." Still, she reflected years later that the entire episode "does present a picture of a sad little girl, earning money for the family."

At this point in her life, Bette *was* sad—and confused. She couldn't fathom what the future held for her. Ruthie didn't have the money to send her to the kind of acting school she now felt ready for, one in New York that would prepare her for a career on Broadway. She knew she didn't want to be a housewife and spend the rest of her life in Newton. When Ham came home from Amherst that Christmas and visited her, she forgot Fritz and fell back in love with the doe-eyed musician she had met at Cushing: "A beau—on hand—is worth two in the bush." She sat with him, staring at the Davis Christmas tree, and dreamed of the future —dreams she felt were "hopeless" at this point in her life.

When Ham returned to school, Bette thought she would "lose my mind with ennui." Sensitive as always to her daughter's moods, Ruthie surprised her with a trip to Boston to see a production of Henrik Ibsen's *The Wild Duck,* starring Blanche Yurka, with Peg Entwhistle as the Norwegian Ekdal family's sensitive, ill-fated fourteen-year-old daughter Hedvig. It was Bette's first exposure to legitimate theater, and it affected her more deeply than anything since her summer at Mariarden.

She had watched the first act of the play with interest, but when the second-act curtain went up and revealed for the first time Hedvig and the Ekdal home, she gasped. Peg Entwhistle looked just like her! And scattered around the living room was all manner of photographic equipment; Hedvig's father earned a meager living as a photographer and retoucher. She felt more and more empathy for Hedvig as more and more similarities to her own family came to light: Hedvig's father thinks of his wife as intellectually inferior to him, and when he learns that Hedvig is not his daughter he deserts the family. When he leaves, Hedvig flies into a frenzy of pain and bewilderment. As Peg Entwhistle wept and pleaded hysterically for her father not to go, Bette held her breath for fear that she would jump up and cry out, too.

At that moment she was no longer just a member of the audience. She felt she had *become* Hedvig. "I was watching myself," she recalled.

"There wasn't an emotion I didn't anticipate and share. . . . It seemed as though everything in my life fell into place. . . . There had been a glimmer here and there; but this time was the vision. . . . I knew now that more than anything—despite anything—I was going to become an actress."

Ruthie turned to Bette at the end of the play and saw that she was sitting stock-still, dry-eyed, her face "a graven image. It went beyond tears with her."

"Mother," Bette said, "if I can live to play Hedvig I shall die happy. And someday I *will* play her!"

Back in Newton, that day seemed a million years away. Still without a regular job, Ruthie had swallowed her pride and pleaded with Harlow yet again to help her finance Bette's acting ambitions. "Let her become a secretary!" he bellowed in reply. "She'll earn money quicker. Bette could never be a successful actress. Or better yet, find her a husband!" Bette wasn't surprised when Ruthie came home empty-handed. "This was my second reason for succeeding," Bette said. "To prove Daddy wrong. He truly challenged me."

In September 1927, Ruthie read about a new repertory company on Fourteenth Street in Manhattan, run by the acclaimed young actress Eva Le Gallienne. When she saw that the students earned their tuition by appearing in the company's plays, she swept Bette into the Model T and drove off for New York. At the audition the next day, Ruthie remained in the waiting room while Bette was interviewed by Le Gallienne's assistant in her outer office. She was taken aback by the woman's questions, among them whether she knew why actors should study the movements of animals. "That's what I've come here to find out!" she blurted. She had never received that kind of training, and the whole exercise "made me feel stupid and I wasn't used to that. I have never functioned well when anyone is doubting my ability to do something."

The assistant looked at Bette reprovingly and handed her a play from which she was to read for Miss Le Gallienne. When she realized that her part was an elderly Dutch woman, Bette was dumbfounded. *Why should a girl of eighteen portray a woman of seventy?* she thought. She took a deep breath and entered the sanctum sanctorum of Le Gallienne's office. The woman asked "cold and impersonal" questions about Bette's background, her ambitions, whether she could sustain herself while attending school. The last question rankled her; she replied curtly that "I would not become a public charge, inasmuch as I would live with my mother in New York."

Le Gallienne sat in silence and looked at Bette expectantly. She dug in her heels and read as well as she could, but knew instinctively she was doing a poor job. Still, Le Gallienne's look of disinterest while she read angered her, and she stopped. "What I said is beyond recall, but Miss Le Gallienne interpreted it, and rightly, as an outburst of defiance. Fixing me with a frigid eye, she said, 'I can see that your attitude toward the theater is not sincere enough to warrant taking you as a pupil. You are a frivolous little girl.' "

Hot with anger, Bette stalked out of the school while Ruthie padded along behind her, pleading, "What happened, what *happened?*" The anger she felt, Bette said, "was a lifesaver. Humiliation and defeat were outweighed by my indignation. All I had asked for was an opportunity to try, and I felt this had been denied me. I was mad." But by the time she and Ruthie were on the highway headed back to New Rochelle, New York (where they were staying with Ruthie's brother Paul), Bette was in tears. She had lost an extraordinary opportunity, and she knew it.

As Ruthie lay in bed and listened to Bette's bitter sobs most of the night, she resolved that her daughter would try again. The next day, she drove Bette back into Manhattan to the Robert Milton/John Murray Anderson School of the Theatre. Not long into their preliminary interview with John Anderson's brother, Hugh, Ruthie asked about the tuition. She reacted with shock when the man replied, "$500 a term."

Ruthie's head began to fill, as usual, with alternatives, possible solutions, deals. But Bette stood up, said firmly, "Mother, let's go, we can't do it," and that was that. As ambitious as Bette was, she easily accepted rejection at this point in her life. She allowed herself to be deterred much more readily than Ruthie did, as though each rejection and each obstacle were a personal affront. "Funny thing," Ruthie wrote after Bette became a star, "this very famous woman has always had this negative approach." Perhaps somewhere in her subconscious Bette believed that Harlow was right, that she "could never be a successful actress." As much as his lack of faith could egg her on, it could also hold her back.

At home again in Newton, Bette received an official rejection from Le Gallienne, who wrote that she lacked the seriousness to become an actress. "If I ever could have become a mental case," Bette said, "it was at this time." She sagged into a depression, terrified that she would never become the "something" she had dreamed about since childhood, that she would be doomed, like Flaubert's Emma Bovary, to a deathly life in the provinces. Miserably the fear gripped her that her father might be right about her lack of potential, and her mood further soured, leaving her by turns irritable and melancholy. One day she would argue and snap at Ruthie, the next day she would do her household chores like an automaton, silent and pale, overwhelmed by hopelessness.

Ruthie's heart broke for her daughter, but the only thing she could do for her now was find work and make the money Bette needed to attend the Milton/Anderson School. She heard about a photo retouching job in Norwalk, Connecticut, and she and Bette moved yet again. (Bobby was now a senior at Newton High and wanted to complete her term there. She remained behind with her Aunt Mildred and Uncle Myron.) They took another dreary room in a boardinghouse, and Ruthie began long hours of delicate retouching. For the first time in her life, Bette looked for work herself, and when she couldn't find any her depression deepened. She slept most of the day. "Lying there I would think—*There's no reason for my getting up. If I can stay in bed long enough the day will be shorter . . . and maybe I can forget that Ruthie's eyes are red-rimmed from strain and that she must sit cramped in a chair all day long.*"

But as though to worsen her suffering, as though to punish herself, Bette was drawn every day to a coffee shop across the street from Ruthie's studio. She would sit on a stool at the lunch counter, silently drinking one cup of black coffee after another, and watch her mother work in front of a picture window, hunched over the drafting table, squinting at negatives. "I don't know why that photographer's window drew me like a horrible magnet," Bette said. "I don't know why I wanted to inflict pain on myself. I only knew that I couldn't keep myself away from it—that I must watch Ruthie even though it was unbelievable agony to do so."

Even the weather mirrored Bette's melancholy, and most of the time she watched her mother through wind-blown sheets of rain or sleet. "Sometimes I would rush away from that lunch counter, dash down the street, walking until I had passed the last house and was on the state highway, hoping that perhaps I would stop seeing Ruthie, stop remembering within my heart that for me there was nothing to do but wait. But always that tableau of Ruthie was just ahead of me, no matter how many miles I walked, no matter how wet and cold and dreary I was, how completely exhausted I became. And so I would go back to the lunch counter.

"As I sat there I thought to myself—*I'm going mad. This can't go on. Isn't there ever going to be an end to this?*"

FOUR

uthie shook Bette awake. "Come on, get up. Put on your navy dress. I think it's your best. And that blue hat. We're going to New York. You're going on the stage." Ruthie had been aware that Bette watched her work day after day, and it broke her heart. She couldn't stand her daughter's suffering any longer. "Hurry!" she ordered. "We haven't much time." Bette had no idea what was going on, but she obeyed without a word. "I wondered if some miracle had happened, but I feared to break the enchantment by asking questions." It was Wednesday, October 29, 1927.

The Model T had broken down, so they took the train from Norwalk to Grand Central Terminal, and during the ride Ruthie wouldn't answer Bette's incessant queries about what was going on. It wasn't until their taxi pulled up in front of the Milton/Anderson School that Bette realized what Ruthie was doing. "But Mother," she protested, recalling their previous visit and the $500 tuition, "how can we—?" She had barely finished the sentence before they were inside Anderson's office. "Mother was quite wild-eyed," she recalled. "Mr. Anderson never knew what hit him." While Bette sat mute beside her, Ruthie began. "My daughter is going to be an actress," she stated flatly. "I haven't any money to pay her tuition in full. But you are going to take her as a student, and you will get your money eventually." Ruthie caught her breath and looked at Mr. Anderson.

"Has she any talent?" he asked.

In a rush, Ruthie told Anderson about Roshanara and Frank Conroy and how spellbinding Bette had been as The Moth and, after a deep breath, concluded, "You *must* take her!"

Anderson chuckled and cast a perplexed glance at Bette, who turned her eyes downward in embarrassment. "Years later," Bette said, "he told me he didn't know what to think that day. He was too bewildered." But when Bette read for him, his brother John, and Robert Milton—far better than she had for Le Gallienne—he and Milton were impressed.

42

John was less so. Years later he told associates that he didn't think Bette had much talent, but the opinions of his partners carried the day, and Bette was accepted as a student. Ruthie arranged to pay the tuition in three monthly installments. Bette later said that Hugh Anderson was amenable to all this less because of her talent than Ruthie's *chutzpah*.

Bette was to begin her studies the following Monday. By Saturday, Ruthie had quit her job in Norwalk, piled all their earthly belongings into the repaired Model T, and found a position as a housemother at St. Mary's School in Burlington, New Jersey, in order to be closer to Bette. On Sunday, Ruthie helped Bette settle into her "dormitory," a huge boardinghouse next door to the converted mansion that housed the Milton/Anderson school. The building—two brownstones converted into one—offered tepid water, drafty hallways, a chaperon on each floor, and a restaurant in the basement where students ate all three of their daily meals, along with paying members of the public.

When Bette and Ruthie arrived, Bette's roommate wasn't there, but the girl seemed unconcerned with housekeeping: the room, a small bed-sitter with two cots, was in chaos. Once Ruthie left, Bette found herself alone in a strange new environment, with neither her mother nor her sister for emotional support, and on the threshold of an exciting—and frightening—new chapter in her life.

When Bette's roommate, Virginia Conroy, returned, she was struck by her first sight of Bette Davis. "She was sitting on the floor in the middle of a small Navajo rug wearing short homemade pajamas, her golden hair cascading down her back. Over and over she kept playing the same song on her hand-wound phonograph, 'Someone to Watch Over Me,' about a little lamb lost in the woods."

Ginny introduced herself and asked Bette what was wrong. Bette quickly rose off the floor and muttered, "Nothing. Nothing at all." But Ginny recognized the signs of loneliness and homesickness and tried to make light conversation. Bette's replies were monosyllabic until Ginny mentioned she was from a small town in Massachusetts. Suddenly, they were soulmates in Bette's mind, and a fast friendship began.

Still, Bette and Ginny should never have gotten along. There was the matter of the housekeeping, very important to Bette, whose childhood obsession with neatness had only grown over the years. Ginny, at sixteen, was three years younger than Bette. And their personalities clashed. "She was a Clara Bow type," Bette recalled, "a true flapper, who entertained few serious thoughts. . . . She was the first girl I'd ever known who used lipstick and much too much of it."

Ginny recalled that whenever she danced the Charleston, sang, and played her ukulele while Bette was trying to study, Bette would "bug out her eyes, switch her tail, stretch her neck like a hostile greylag goose and say in an icy tone, '*Do* you mind?'" Intimidated at first by Bette's intensity, Ginny would quiet down, but later she told her, "You know, Bette, you could be the bee's knees if you wouldn't take life so *seriously.*"

One afternoon, Ginny took a cigarette out of her purse, fumbled to light it, and took a puff. Bette was shocked. "*Ginny!* How can you do that?" she cried.

"Oh, you should try it, Bette," Ginny replied nonchalantly. "All the smart people do it." Bette refused and afterward pointedly opened the windows or left the room whenever Ginny lit up.

Despite their differences, Bette soon considered Ginny "delicious" and "a dear," and they developed a strong, lifelong friendship. Although Bette was better educated, she found that Ginny was "Phi Beta Kappa in most of the subjects worth knowing about." Ginny was surprised to discover that Bette was "even more naïve and innocent than I was. Of course we both knew, as did all damsels of our generation, that if we ever spoke to a stranger or even let him catch our eye, we would be in imminent danger of landing up in the South American white slave market." Bette felt compelled to warn Ginny further about men: "They will tell you," she began, and then paused to find the words, "that *certain things* are . . . all right. But Ginny, they are *not!*"

Ginny was fascinated and perplexed by the inconsistencies in Bette's character. "She could be brash and battling, frightened and lonely, violent and vulnerable." She seemed a "bundle of nerves and talent" who hovered between bravado and terror: "She carried a bottle of spirits of ammonia and a spoon in her pocketbook—in case she should faint on the subway."

The one steady trait in Bette at this point was her dedication to her studies. She loved the school and its grand stage, was thrilled by the immersion into drama, speech, and dance that her classes offered her. She learned to soften her broad Boston A's, and was told by the revered actor George Arliss, a guest lecturer, not to "adopt that exaggerated speech we hear so much of today on the stage. Be clear and simple!" She studied movement, stage technique, the projection of one's voice. She wasn't taught how to act—"There are things that cannot be learned"— but rather she acquired the tools an actor must possess: poise, grace, confidence, technique.

As Roshanara had before her, the instructor who most influenced Bette was her exotic, extravagant dance teacher: Martha Graham. "To *act* is to *dance!*" Graham would proclaim as Bette sat in her class, riveted. "She had just finished her Oriental period," Ginny recalled, "and usually wore a henna-colored tunic with long full skirt split up one side. Her jet-black hair was pulled back in a knob and she affected the continental makeup popular at the time—white face, red lips, no rouge."

Graham conducted her classes once a week, and she was a "hard taskmaster," according to Ginny. "The confrontation one had to go through to be excused from a class of hers was hideous. If we had a cold, she would remind us that 'Ruth St. Denis *dahnced* with a temperature of one hundred and *four!*' " Several students who didn't dip properly at the ballet barre were abruptly pulled up by their hair, and others—including Ginny and Bette—took more than one whack from Graham on a recalcitrant thigh.

Graham had her students wear bathing suits to make them "uninhibited" about their bodies. Ginny found "hair-raising" Graham's theory that every citizen should be forced by law to stand naked in a public place once a year and be either punished or rewarded for what they had done to their bodies.

Graham taught her students everything from the ethereal theories of interpretive dancing ("Positive emotions lift your body up toward the heavens") to the practicalities of how to fall down a staircase without getting hurt. One's walk, Graham told her students, should be from the hip and not the knee, with head up and shoulders back: "Carry your body *proudly!*"

One afternoon Ginny and Bette decided to follow Graham as she walked to the subway station after class "to see if she really walked that way all the time." She did, and Ginny recalled that she "seemed like some kind of immortal goddess thrusting her way through the tired, bedraggled, round-shouldered denizens of the sidewalks of New York."

Bette soon seized upon Graham's walk, Conroy recalled, and "exaggerated it into a swivel and made it her own, a characteristic later beloved by her imitators." Years hence Bette observed that whenever she climbed a flight of stairs in a film ("I spent half my life on them"), she was being Martha Graham every step of the way.

Although Bette could be as serious as a tragic muse in her studies, Ginny saw another side of her. "I believed she was the world's greatest comedienne. At night she would often trail around in an oversized lavender rayon nightgown of her mother's, tottering on the rickety heels of mules cut down from old shoes. She would emote, wave her arms about, roll her eyes wildly. One time she recited some lines we used in school: 'She left the web / She left the loom / She made three paces through the room / She saw the water lilies bloom.' When she got to the three paces she took three big hops toward me. I laughed so hard I fell out of my cot and the mattress tumbled over on top of me."

A different kind of hysteria sometimes overtook Bette when Ruthie paid her a visit. "It was a real show," Ginny recalled, "and I loved drama. There were several big rows." Ginny had noticed that Ruthie doted on Bette, seemed to sacrifice everything for her. "When I first met Ruthie she had only one pair of stockings that she had to wash out every night and pray she wouldn't get a run. She gave Bette her fur coat so that she could make an impression at school, even though she only had to go two doors down the block to classes—leaving Ruthie with a cheap cloth coat for the cold trips back and forth from New Jersey."

Ginny noticed that Bette would grow fidgety whenever her mother visited, as though she were "unconsciously resentful" of her. "There would be wild screams and slammed doors," Ginny recalled, "but these dustups always ended in kissing, cooing, and tears. I came to think the tears were therapeutic in nature—the object of the exercise. After they'd make up, Ruthie would go into her little-girl act—she'd duck her head, blink her eyes, purse her mouth, and murmur baby talk."

Because these confrontations were usually about "practically nothing," Ginny suspected that Ruthie "deliberately offered herself as a sacrificial lightning rod, a safety ground for the charge of Bette's built-up voltage. It was as if Bette generated a kind of poison that had to be got rid of and put onto someone else."

The storm currents of Bette's personality disturbed Ginny. She was puzzled by the warring elements of her psyche, her obvious loathing of her father, her love/hate relationship with her mother—so much so that she suggested to Bette that she seek some psychiatric counseling. Bette rejected the idea out of hand. "She regarded anything like psychoanalysis as a cop-out," Ginny said. "She thought of it as people placing the blame on others for their failures."

Once when Bobby came along with Ruthie to see Bette, Ginny became aware of the younger sister's distant third-place position among the three musketeers. It was shortly after Valentine's Day, 1928, and Bobby noticed two greeting cards taped onto the mirror over a dresser—one for Bette, one for Ginny. Both were from Ruthie; Bette's featured a globe with a ribbon around it that proclaimed, "You are all the world to me."

Bobby, who was still living with her aunt and uncle in Newton, turned to Ruthie and said in a small voice, "You didn't send me a valentine."

"But I couldn't send one to Bette without sending one to Ginny," Ruthie explained, "and I only had the money for two valentines."

Even the sixteen-year-old Ginny was amazed by Ruthie's tortured reasoning. "Somehow, even then, I knew Bobby would have few valentines in her life. She was like a flower deliberately pinched in the bud, so that all the life force of the maternal plant could go to that perfect bloom—Bette."

Her studies at Milton/Anderson occupied Bette so thoroughly that her head rarely turned for her attractive male classmates. She was still much interested in boys, however, and she continued to correspond with both Fritz at Yale and Ham at Amherst. One of her few dates during this period came about through a new beau of Bobby's, Hunter Scott, who introduced her to an aspiring twenty-three-year-old actor during a break in classes. His name was Henry Fonda. Bette found him "very beautiful," and she was thrilled when Bobby's beau suggested the four of them go on a double date.

The day before, Hunter had goaded Henry into a contest: every time one of them kissed a girl, he would get a point, and whoever had the most points after a certain amount of time would win some prize or other. Fonda despaired of keeping up. "Hunter had a girl pinned in every state in the country, it seemed. I had been dating a girl for two years and never kissed her."

The foursome drove into New Jersey to the Princeton University athletic stadium, and while Hunter and Bobby strolled under the moonlight on the empty playing field, Henry and Bette remained in the back seat of Scott's car in awkward silence. "I had just met this girl and she didn't really attract me," Fonda recalled. "I didn't think she was very pretty." He knew he'd never win the contest, but "I didn't want to disgrace myself by not having one point. I knew Hunter would be scoring. Some way or other, I just leaned over and gave her a peck, so that I was at least even with Hunter."

That was all Bette needed—she fell head over heels. A few days later, Henry got a letter from her accepting his proposal of marriage. "I've told Mother about our lovely experience in the moonlight," she wrote. "She will announce our engagement when we get home."

"She scared the shit out of me!" Fonda exclaimed. "I thought, *One kiss and I'm engaged! Is that how it happens?*" He ignored the letter, and when he didn't hear anything more about it from Bette, he sighed with relief.

If Henry Fonda didn't want to marry Bette, Fritz Hall did. He invited her to his senior prom, and Ruthie made her a lovely white net dress and cape in which Ginny thought she "looked as beautiful as an angel." At the end of the evening, Fritz proposed, and when Bette accepted him, he gave her a ring.

The engagement lasted three days. Fritz planned to follow his father into business, and he wanted a helpmate and hostess as his wife, not an actress out on the road most of the time. On prom night, Bette had been blithely noncommittal when Fritz asked her to give up acting. But when he pressed her by phone the next day, she told him she had serious reservations. By Tuesday he was in New York to demand a definitive response.

Ruthie was there too, and Ginny wondered why she was away from her job on a weekday. In retrospect she realized "how agitated Ruthie must have been. Fritz was a definite danger to her grand plans for Bette to become a star." Ruthie and Ginny left Fritz and Bette alone in the room and "huddled around a corner of the hallway, shivering with cold, straining to pick up what we could of what was going on behind that closed door. At last Fritz emerged and stormed off with an awful slam of the door, as dramatic as in an Ibsen play. Ruth let out a sigh of relief." When the eavesdroppers went back into the room, they found Bette "a shaking, pink-eyed wreck." She had given Fritz back his ring. According to Ginny, "Ruthie had done her work well. Bette had avoided her first temptation to bask in romantic domesticity. Now she was well and truly set upon her career."

Bette acted in a play a week at Milton/Anderson, and soon she, Ginny, and their fellow student Ted Scharf made a two-reeler screen test. The few remaining frame blowups of the footage show the trio in casual dress and attitude, enacting a variety of facial expressions. Bette seems relaxed, but her tight, prim hairdo, simple shirt, and lack of makeup give her a drab appearance that belies the loveliness she possessed in person. Nothing came of the test for any of the participants.

Bette won the lead role of Sylvia Fair in the school's end-of-term examination play, *The Famous Mrs. Fair,* to be directed by James Light. The production was to be presented publicly, and if Bette's performance was judged favorably, she would win a scholarship for the next semester's tuition. Two days before the show, Bette awakened, to her horror, with laryngitis. She tried every old wives' remedy and over-the-counter medication she could find until her voice improved serviceably the night of the play. By the third act, she could barely croak out her lines. But since Sylvia Fair at this point in the play has grown dissolute, Bette's "whiskey baritone" added much to her characterization and made her far more believable playing a much older woman. So did her nervousness, which heightened the fidgety mannerisms she had begun to develop and which lent her a neurotic air that belied her youth.

The audience cheered her performance, and immediately after the show the scholarship winners were announced. "Ruthie's look of gratitude when my name was read as the winner was worth a lot to me," Bette recalled.

Bette's instructors and directors were clearly impressed with her, and her eyes widened when she read a Hugh Anderson press release in the local paper that called her "the perfect modern Venus." Had Anderson not thus presented Bette to the public at this time, she might have been forever known as Bette Favor. Ruthie had decided that her maiden name would be a more unusual, mellifluous stage name for her daughter than Davis, and both Bette and Ginny agreed. (Unmentioned, but understood, was the underlying break from any remnant of Harlow. One family friend observed acidly, "Ruthie probably figured that this way she could pretend that Bette had been immaculately conceived.") Robert Milton argued against the change; since Bette had already received public attention as a student of the school under the name Davis, he said, it would be unwise to change her name now. Ruthie dropped the idea.

Not long after Bette's triumph as Sylvia Fair, James Light asked her to appear in *The Earth Between,* a play he planned to direct at the Provincetown Playhouse in Manhattan's Greenwich Village. It was Bette's first offer of paid work, and she was thrilled. But in order to accept, she would have to leave school and forgo the scholarship. Hugh Anderson advised her that the opportunity was too good to pass up, and she accepted Light's offer.

But problems arose. The play had to be postponed until the following fall, and Bette found herself with neither a scholarship nor a job. She asked her Mariarden instructor Frank Conroy—who was now directing a play on Broadway—if he could recommend her to anyone in need of an ingenue. Conroy put her in touch with George Cukor, who had a stock company along with George Kondolf at the Lyceum Theatre in Rochester, New York. Cukor had not yet cast a small part as a chorus girl in his current production, *Broadway,* a backstage melodrama that had been a hit in New York. Cukor was unsure when he met Bette in his Manhattan office that anyone as mousy as she seemed to him could carry off the role of a brassy chorine. But rehearsals for the show were already in progress, and he told her, "Okay, we can use you." She later commented, "I can't think of a more eloquent speech to be delivered to a girl who wants a job on the stage."

Ruthie came in from New Jersey to help Bette pack, and saw her off with an elaborate letter of instructions in which she addressed her daughter, now twenty, as though she were a child. "Read this first!" she scrawled across the top page of the first of six numbered sections of the letter. She then told her how she should deport herself on the train ("Let the porters take care of the luggage"), how to settle into her room in Rochester, and the fine points of the conduct she expected of Bette during rehearsals. She admonished her to telephone her Uncle Paul, and to use the name "Bette Favor Davis" on business correspondence and checks. Ruthie concluded her manifesto, "God watch over my little girl, as I can't—but you help him!"

As Ruthie put Bette on the train, she insisted that she be sure to learn the part of Pearl, the lead female role, because "the actress playing it is going to have an accident!"

"Oh, Mother," Bette laughed, "you and your hunches." But she had had enough experience with Ruthie's often uncannily accurate sixth sense over the years that she spent the entire trip studying the other actress's lines and ignoring the beautiful countryside as it rushed past her compartment window. She wasn't surprised when Ruthie's prediction proved dead on the mark. During the third performance, Rose Lerner, the actress cast as Pearl, twisted her ankle in a fall down a staircase. The next day, Cukor asked to see "the dame who has the smallest part." When Bette appeared, he asked if she could learn the larger part—a brassy, hard-bitten show gal who shoots her lover—by that evening. When Bette replied that she already knew it, Cukor was skeptical. He then asked her if she knew how to fall down a staircase safely. Thanks to Martha Graham, she did. She proved in rehearsals that she indeed had the part committed to memory, and she took the stage as Pearl that evening.

Bette was shocked by the way she looked in the skimpy costume she had to wear, and she decided she needed to chew gum during the performance to help her affect the necessary toughness. Early in the second act, she was supposed to shoot her lover twice, and he was to stagger offstage to die. Bette was so nervous, and had such a fear of guns, that when the moment came she fired at her costar so many times there was no way for him to do anything but drop on the spot. "He was in agony holding his breath for the rest of the act," Bette recalled.

The play ran, as scheduled, for just one week, but Bette had acquitted herself so well that Cukor and Kondolf asked her to join the company as its lead ingenue the following fall. She was ecstatic, but her euphoria evaporated when she got back to Manhattan and began to make the rounds of casting offices in New York's crushing summer heat. It was her first taste of that ego-battering experience, and she hated it. She felt like a piece of meat, and was so tired of being told she looked too young that she thought she'd scream if she heard it one more time. Again and again she was told to "come back tomorrow," but she was smart enough to know a brush-off when she heard it. She felt "shattered" by the disregard she was shown "as a human being," and after a week of this she took to her bed and refused to get up. Ruthie pleaded for days with Bette to get out of bed until finally her persistence paid off —her daughter was back in the fight. Bette loved her mother for it: "I never would have made it without Ruthie."

Spurred on more by her mother's determination that she succeed than her own, Bette "badgered" the New York agency representing the Cape Playhouse, a theater company formed the year before in Dennis, Massachusetts, that had already drawn actors of the repute of Basil Rathbone, Peggy Wood (who later starred in *I Remember Mama* on television), and Laura Hope Crews, best known to today's audiences as Aunt Pitty-Pat in *Gone With the Wind*. Finally she got an appointment with a man described to her as the director of the Playhouse—in his hotel room. When she arrived the man was in his underwear, shaving. Fearful and skeptical at first, Bette left in ecstasy after he proved harmless and told her she was hired as the company's ingenue for the 1928 summer season and should report in a few weeks.

Ruthie was just as thrilled, and she made arrangements to rent a house on Cape Cod. Then she and Bette attended Bobby's graduation from Newton High, after which all three piled up their new car, a used Chevrolet, with everything from camera equipment to a wire-haired terrier Bette had adopted and named Boojum, and off they went.

Bette stared ahead wide-eyed as they drove up to the Playhouse, part of a colorful arts colony comprising a remodeled church as the theater, a paint shop where the scenery was made, a moving-picture house, and a restaurant. She bounded into the theater as if to say, "Well, you lucky people, here I am," and announced herself to Raymond Moore, the owner of the Playhouse. Moore seemed perplexed. "Who did you say hired you?"

Bette repeated the partially clad man's name. "Why, he has no authority to engage players!" Moore sputtered. "Our company is already full. The season has begun. I'm terribly sorry, but there is no place for you here." Bette thought of the lease Ruthie had signed, of the anticipation and excitement she'd felt, and wanted to cry. She looked so shocked and crestfallen that Moore took pity on her and asked if she would be willing to usher for the season. Of course, he added, she would be paid. "Yes!" Bette fairly shouted.

Despite what she saw as "the tragedy of my fall," Bette ushered with gusto, all the while learning every line the company's ingenue spoke. She reminded Mr. Moore at every opportunity that should he ever need an actress—"even a deaf-dumb maid to remove the tea things in the second act"—she was available. Ruthie had no premonitions of broken legs this time, but Bette kept a watchful eye on the ingenue's health.

The young lady remained intact, and as Bette guided people to their seats one evening she saw Henry Fonda take the stage. She nearly gasped —she still thought he was "the most beautiful boy I had ever seen." After the show, she said hello to him but mentioned nothing about her unheeded letter of a year before. Neither did he. She invited him to the cottage for dinner with her and Ruthie, and he accepted. They served steamed clams, a New England delicacy reserved for special occasions. Fonda, a Nebraskan, loathed them. Once again nothing came of Bette's crush, and she was philosophical about it: "He just never took to me."

Although the company ingenue continued in good health, she was not suited for the role of Dinah in the company's last play, *Mr. Pim Passes By.* In July, Bette had taken a brief break from her ushering chores to reprise her Cushing senior play role of Elise Benedotti in *The Charm School* with the Cape Playhouse Junior Players in East Dennis, so Moore knew she could act. When Laura Hope Crews, who was to star in and direct *Mr. Pim,* asked Moore to find another actress to play Dinah, an English girl, he suggested Bette. Crews told her that if she could learn to sing the English ballad "I Passed by Your Window" by the following morning, the part would be hers.

Bette had never heard it, but she assured Miss Crews she'd be ready. No one else in the company knew the song either. While Bette stayed behind to usher that evening, Ruthie motored to every music store in Dennis and Hyannis, on the other side of Cape Cod, but none had the sheet music. Frantic, she began to knock on doors where pianos were visible through the front windows. Again no luck. Then she stopped at a local church and asked the organist; he not only had the music but offered the use of his piano so that Bette could practice the piece. Ruthie called Bette, who borrowed a car after the night's performance ended, drove to Hyannis, and stayed up until three in the morning learning the song by heart: "There is no stopping a girl when she really decides to be an actress."

On the first day of rehearsals, Laura Hope Crews, who was renowned for her elegant hand gestures, watched Bette gesticulate nervously on almost every line. A few scenes into the play, she told everyone to stop and turned to Bette. "No good ingenue *ever* moves her hands," she told her. Bette was mortified. She had not been trying to imitate or upstage Crews; she had used her hands to communicate all her life. She resisted the temptation to remind Crews that she wasn't playing a cripple, and that her hand gestures had helped her characterize Sylvia Fair. Instead, she made such a strong attempt to resist her natural mannerisms when she resumed the scene that "I looked like a Rembrandt figure."

She slipped during an emotional moment in the last act of the rehearsal and let her arm move up "about twelve inches." Immediately she felt a sharp slap from behind her that pushed her hand down to its prior limp position. She turned to see Miss Crews, who went on with her line readings as though nothing had happened. "My face burned and I must have counted to ninety-five before I regained control of myself," Bette recalled. "It was just as well that I did. I was an unknown; she was famous. Any display would have meant my ruin."

Bette thought that Crews's restriction on her made her performance stiff, but she was a crowd pleaser as Dinah—partially, she thought, because the subscription audience knew her as their usher and were rooting for her. In any case, Raymond Moore was impressed enough to invite her back the following summer as the company ingenue.

Overjoyed, Bette returned with Ruthie to New York, while Bobby, eager to continue the independence that had allowed her to become more her own person while she completed high school at Newton, went back to stay with Aunt Mildred and Uncle Myron while she waited to see whether she had been accepted as a student at Denison University in Granville, Ohio. "She was showing signs of wanting to go *far* away," Bette recalled. "I think she had a desire to establish her own identity."

Bette and Ruthie took an apartment on Fifty-third Street along with a childhood girlfriend of Bette's from Maine, also an aspiring actress. The quarters were so cramped Ruthie had to sleep on a suitcase held up by two chairs. The first night, the girls were awakened by a crash and found Ruthie on the floor, inextricably entwined in the bedclothes. "Although we protested, she tried it again and finally learned to keep her balance," Bette recalled. "She insisted that we get our rest; she said she could sleep days while we were looking for work."

Bette had no success "making the rounds," and September 1928 turned into "the darkest period of my life." She suffered a solid month of unrelieved rejection—audition after audition, turndown after turndown. "Eating was a problem. I felt sorry for any man who asked me to dinner, for it meant that I could conserve my resources during the day and order everything on the menu at the poor fellow's expense."

Bette felt she couldn't possibly fall any lower after she entered a Vilma Banky look-alike contest in the hope of winning a fifty-dollar prize. She rented appropriate vamp clothes from a costumer; Ruthie did her hair and makeup. She looked so much like Banky, she and Ruthie both agreed, that "I left for the theater with the fifty dollars as good as in my pocket."

There were nearly one hundred girls lined up inside the theater when Bette arrived, and as she looked them over she felt more confident than ever that she would win. Then she and the others saw a girl being escorted to the center of the stage and assumed she was the first contestant. Instead, the girl was announced as the winner. "It was such a palpable fake that I wanted to shout my resentment," Bette recalled. "There was nothing to be done, but I learned a lesson. Never again did I get on that side of a Hollywood publicity stunt."

With Ruthie prodding her as usual, Bette kept knocking on doors, but matters remained bleak until she returned to Rochester in October to join the Cukor/Kondolf stock company for a full season as its ingenue. With this job and her promise of another season on Cape Cod, Bette now had professional acting commitments for the next twelve months. Ecstatic, she and Ruthie piled back into the Chevy and drove to Newton, where they were joined by Bobby, who was equally overjoyed about her acceptance at Denison.

The three musketeers then drove Bobby to school in Granville, Ohio, before Ruthie and Bette headed for Rochester. There was barely room to breathe in the car, what with clothes and Boojum and Ruthie's camera equipment and all the things the university required Bobby to have in her dorm room. But all three women were happier than they had been for a long time, each with visions of a better future ahead of her.

None more so than Bette. After she and Ruthie kissed Bobby good-bye in Granville, they turned around and headed back East for Rochester and Bette's first full season as an employee of a theater company. Bette sat next to Ruthie, with Boojum in her lap, and chirped happily about this subject and that. For the first time in her life, she truly felt like an actress.

FIVE

It was nearly midnight when Ruthie and Bette arrived at their new apartment building in Rochester. Bette clambered up the steps, laden down with luggage, exhausted from the long drive, dripping wet from the rain. When she opened the door to the apartment and flipped on the light, she let out a shriek: the walls were papered with bold red-and-white stripes that seemed to vibrate as she looked at them. More jittery than ever about starting a full season with Cukor, Bette turned to Ruthie as she came up behind her and proclaimed, "I *cannot* stay here. These stripes will make me *mad!*"

Ruthie thought of the three-month lease she had signed and the month's rent she had paid in advance and murmured soothingly, "If you put out the lights, darling, you won't see them." But Bette would not be placated. "I'll see them in my *sleep,*" she screamed. "Throughout *eternity!*"

Ruthie knew better than to upset her "high-strung filly" on the eve of so important a professional breakthrough. She may have thought wistfully once again that if only she had swatted Bette's behind on that long-ago day when she howled her lungs out about a crease in her dress . . . But now it was too late: she had helped create a daughter who was willful, self-centered, and used to getting her way. Yes, Ruthie thought, Bette could be a spoiled brat, but it was so clear to her that she was headed for a brilliant stage career that at this point Ruthie's only concern was to keep her on an even keel emotionally so that she could do her best work on the stage. More than ever, anything Bette wanted, Ruthie would do for her. Anything Bette hated, Ruthie would remove from her life.

While Bette sat on the edge of the sofa, theatrically covering her eyes with her hands, Ruthie's mind raced. Within a few minutes she put on a pair of heavy boots, went out into the rainy night, and stealthily left a trail of footprints leading up to the apartment window. She came back, changed into a nightdress, then let out a piercing scream just before she tore over to the landlady's apartment, babbling that she'd seen a prowler peering in her window and couldn't possibly remain in so dangerous a place—she had a young daughter with her! They would leave first thing in the morning and have that month's rent back!

When the landlady sputtered that Ruthie must have had a nightmare, that such a thing was not possible, Ruthie indignantly told her to go outside and see for herself. When she returned, muttering under her breath, the woman gave Ruthie her money back. While Bette was at the theater the next day, Ruthie found another place. It was in the city's red-light district, which gave her some pause, but it was even less expensive than the first apartment and closer to the Cukor company's new home, the Temple Theatre. Besides, Bette liked the wallpaper.

Calmed, Bette began a week of intense rehearsals, and was delighted to find that she liked most of her fellow actors. They included Frank Mc-Hugh, an amiable Irishman, and Wallace Ford, a mug with a gleam in his eye. Bette found them both "loads of fun," and was fascinated by a mysterious young man named Sam Blythe who eventually was found out as Ethel Barrymore's son. The publicity helped bring audiences into the theater at prices that started at twenty-five cents and "soared to $1.50 for the choice seats," Bette recalled. (Bette's salary was twenty-five dollars a week.)

Her first play was *Excess Baggage,* with Wallace Ford and Miriam Hopkins, and the Rochester *Times* singled Bette out for praise as "a pretty blonde slip of a miss." She, however, was enchanted by Hopkins, the twenty-six-year-old leading lady. "She was the prettiest golden-haired blonde I had ever seen," she recalled. "I will never forget her before a performance—emerging from a shower and simply tossing her curly hair dry. She was the envy of us all."

Bette's fondness for Miriam soon stopped cold. With all her beauty and talent, Hopkins was immensely insecure, mean-spirited, paranoid, and given to the most outrageous scene stealing, even from the lowliest extra. Whenever a fellow actor commanded what Miriam deemed an excess of audience attention, she would wave her handkerchief, rearrange flowers, wind a clock, leaf through a book—anything to divert the audience's eyes back to herself. It was not a propensity likely to endear her to her costars.

At first Bette was only disconcerted by Miriam's habit of patting her on the backside and telling her what a beautiful neck she had. Naïve as

Bette was, she didn't know about the rumors that Hopkins's sexual preferences included women as well as men. Although she'd been married twice, Miriam raised eyebrows in the company when she introduced a lovely young girl as her "protégée" and shared a bungalow with her every night. Ruthie's antennae were more attuned than her daughter's, and when Bette told her that Hopkins had invited her to join her and her friend one evening in the bungalow, Ruthie told her urgently, "Stay away from her—she's *trouble!*" Bette took her mother's advice.

Hopkins was angered by this rejection, and she turned viciously on Bette a few days later. In the middle of a rehearsal, she spun away from her and screamed at Cukor, "She's stepping on my lines! The bitch doesn't know her place! *I'm* the star of this show—not that little nobody!" Then Hopkins stalked off, leaving a mortified Bette alone on the stage.

Bette appeared in half a dozen productions with the Cukor company, and while the repertoire that season didn't thrill her, she recalled that she "settled down and regarded my work without emotion. Acting was what I wanted to do and I was determined to learn all I could. . . . Rochester was providing me with solid schooling."

And a new beau. Shortly after her arrival, she met Charles Ainsley, a young man about her age, and "fell in love" once again. Charlie came to every one of her performances and sent yellow roses to her dressing room each night. He was from a good family, Bette recalled, and "risked his reputation" nightly by dating an actress and being seen at her apartment in "the bad part of town." But he loved the fact that Bette was an actress; he glowed with pride whenever her picture popped up in the local paper. Within a few weeks, Bette and Charlie were engaged to be married.

Early in November, as rehearsals for *The Squall* neared an end, the company manager approached Bette. "We won't need you after this show," he said.

Shocked, Bette could only whisper, "Why?"

"Cukor says you won't be needed anymore." And that was that. For years Bette maintained that she was mystified by the firing, and that all she could imagine was that she had been considered standoffish because she went directly home to Ruthie or out with Charlie immediately after each performance. But in a 1981 *Playboy* interview, she admitted that there was more to it than that: "I didn't live up to what was expected in those days of a stock company ingenue, who had *other* duties . . . you know what I'm talking about. Socializing. Socializing very seriously, let us say, with people in the company. That was just not my cup of tea." What she left unsaid was how much she suspected that Miriam Hopkins's angry hand had helped to stir the vat of ill-feeling against her.

Louis Calhern, a guest star with the company, was more blunt. Bette was let go, he said, because she wouldn't "put out."

Devastated, Bette went home to Ruthie and fell into her arms. She must be an incompetent actress, she sobbed; she had blown this golden opportunity; she had no future on the stage. Ever plucky, Ruthie suggested that she and Bette go down that minute to the telegraph office and send a wire to Jimmy Light: maybe he was finally ready to put on his Greenwich Village production of *The Earth Between*.

Bette said she'd rather go to bed, but Ruthie pushed her out the door and they sent the wire. The next night, as Bette walked offstage after her last performance in Rochester, Ruthie showed her Light's reply: "If you can come to New York, I think I can do the show." Ruthie had their packed bags with her, and they went directly from the theater to board the overnight train to New York. The next morning they sat in a small, chilly coffee shop in Grand Central Terminal and had breakfast with Light, who told them that he had raised the money for the show, and could put it on within a few months. Bette signed a run-of-the-play contract with Light for thirty-five dollars a week, and he advised Ruthie to find them an apartment in Greenwich Village near the Provincetown Theatre. She did, on Eighth Street near MacDougal.

The wait for rehearsals to begin gave Bette time to grow nervous about her Off Broadway debut. The Provincetown was already famous for the quality of its productions, playwrights, and stars—including Helen Hayes, Eugene O'Neill, Edna St. Vincent Millay, and Katharine Cornell. It had been called the American equivalent of England's revered Old Vic, and Bette fretted over whether she'd be up to its demands. "One could forgive a shiny new ingenue in a stock company almost anything," she said, "but this was the real thing. I had to be good. This was New York. Not Broadway, but still New York!"

The play, too, was first-rate. Written by Virgil Geddes, *The Earth Between* was an evocative drama of a widowed Nebraskan farmer and his sixteen-year-old daughter, its style redolent of Eugene O'Neill. Bette thought as she read the script that the farmer's demands on his daughter as a replacement for his wife were a bit excessive, but she read no more into it than that. In fact, the play dealt subtly with the man's incestuous desire for his daughter, and its final scene strongly suggested her acquiescence.

According to Bette, the subtext of the play never did dawn on her, and Light never clued her in: he sensed that her lack of insight would add to the innocence he wanted her characterization to exude.

As opening night of *The Earth Between* loomed, Bette felt more pressure than she ever had before. There was so much for her to prove—to Ruthie and the rest of her family, to her friends and boyfriends (present and past), to John Murray Anderson, to Eva Le Gallienne, to George Cukor. More than anything else, she wanted to show her father that he had been wrong about her. The hurt she felt at his refusals to help her pay for her studies was still fresh, and his words—"Bette could never be a successful actress"—rang in her ears at the most inopportune times, sapped her self-confidence, made her think of quitting. Then, at Ruthie's urging, she would take those same words and use them to renew her determination to prove her father wrong.

Harlow Davis, in his bitter absence, helped Bette find a key to her characterization of Floy, the naïve farm girl with a close, loving relationship with her father. Bette used her fantasies of what life might have been like had Harlow been a different man, had their family stayed together, had her father loved her. It wouldn't be the last time that Harlow's departure from the Davis family circle would inspire Bette to a brilliant performance.

James Light, as good a showman as he was a director, scheduled the play's opening for an evening on which he knew no other plays were set to premiere—in order to assure a larger turnout by the New York theater critics than was usual for an Off Broadway show. Bette knew that good reviews for her performance would help her career immeasurably. She also knew that the reverse was just as true. The pressure rendered her nearly catatonic. Whenever Ruthie couldn't penetrate one of these moods of Bette's, she'd chirp, "I wonder when Bette's coming back from Canada?" She asked the question a lot in the days before *The Earth Between* opened.

Years later, Bette could recall little of that first performance on March 5, 1929, except that the night was stormy with mixed snow and rain and that after the final scene, in which her character yields to her father in a wheat field, she felt a huge rumble build and vibrate throughout the theater. She thought at first the roof was about to cave in. Then she realized it was applause—ecstatic, sustained applause, the loudest, most fervent she had ever heard on a stage—and most of it directed at her. She couldn't believe it: she had thought her performance was "awful."

She felt as though she floated to her dressing room, which was full of flowers and telegrams, family and friends. There was a wire from Bobby and yellow roses with a note from Charlie Ainsley: "I love you." She felt more loved that night than she ever had before; her head swirled with visions of stage stardom, and of marriage to Charlie. But there was one big aching void: her father wasn't there. Amid all the bouquets she was drawn to one small basket of flowers by its scent, which reminded her somehow of her childhood in Winchester. She opened the envelope attached and found an engraved card that read only, "Harlow Morrell Davis."

The reviews for the play were mixed, but to a man the critics praised the newcomer. Brooks Atkinson of *The New York Times* wrote, "Miss Bette Davis, who is making her first appearance, is an enchanting creature who plays in a soft, unassertive style." The *Daily News* critic called Bette "a wraith of a child with true emotional insight."

"That was the greatest night of my life," Bette recalled. "I have played in finer theaters; I have experienced the thrill of thousands of people jamming the streets for a premiere of a film in which I appeared." But nothing would ever equal the emotion Bette felt that night.

Three weeks later, Cecil Clovelly, the road manager for Blanche Yurka, came backstage to Bette's dressing room after a performance and asked her, "How would you like to go on the road with Miss Yurka in Ibsen?" Bette was struck dumb. She knew that Yurka was still touring in the production of *The Wild Duck* that had so affected her three years earlier in Boston, and there was only one role Yurka could have wanted her to play: Hedvig. Clovelly confirmed it. Linda Watkins, the actress playing the part, was about to leave, and Clovelly had suggested Bette to replace her. He had been impressed with her in *The Earth Between* and knew the show was set to close, as scheduled, in a week.

Bette met with Yurka the next day at the Bijou Theatre, intensely nervous but captivated by the forty-one-year-old stage legend's extraordinary intensity, her magnetism, her swanlike neck. Bette read just a few lines before Yurka's rich, mellow voice interrupted her. "That's fine, my dear," she said. "We'll have one week of rehearsal after you close in *The Earth Between*." The Yurka company was in repertory with three Ibsen plays, and Bette was to replace Linda Watkins in a small part as a maid in *The Lady from the Sea* for one week, then settle into *The Wild Duck*.

The rest of that day stood out in Bette's memory for the remainder of her life. She felt aglow, giddy, incredulous that she would get to play Hedvig just as she had told Ruthie she would. Minutes before her evening's performance as Floy, she began to feel queasy and feverish, and by the time the final curtain fell, she felt dreadful. Weak and nauseated, she slumped into her dressing-room chair after the performance and the room began to whirl. Just then she looked up at the doorway and sat bolt upright: standing there was the imposing figure of her father, wearing a topcoat, homburg hat, and leather gloves. She hadn't seen him in years, and she was amazed at how little he had changed. Now forty-four, he had grayed a bit, and had a few lines around his eyes and mouth. Otherwise, he looked just as she remembered him.

He seemed ill at ease. Bette jumped up and asked him to come in. There was no kiss, no hug, no handshake. Harlow stood stiffly and told her that he had enjoyed the play. He then enumerated, point by point, all the positive qualities of each of the actors in the cast—except for Bette. "He never mentioned my performance," she recalled. "I . . . was hurt."

Tentatively, inarticulately, Harlow suggested that Bette join him for dinner that evening. She told him that she didn't feel up to it; she thought she was coming down with something. "I'm sorry, Daddy," she croaked, "but I feel wretched—really."

"I see," Harlow replied.

Bette knew her father didn't believe her and protested, "I have a chill and I'm soaking wet. . . ." But by this point she felt too sick to care. She also knew that even had she not been ill, there could never be a reconciliation between her and Harlow. He had hurt her too deeply; there was too much mutual distrust, too much misunderstanding, too much awkwardness between them. They were, simply, too unalike. Looking sad, Harlow said good-bye and left.

She went home and collapsed into bed; the next morning she awoke covered with spots and a frantic Ruthie sent for a doctor. The diagnosis: one of the worst cases of measles the man had seen, and he ordered her not to get out of bed until she recovered. Ruthie and Bette both panicked. Not only would Bette miss out on the last week of *The Earth Between*, but there was no way she could attend rehearsals of *The Lady from the Sea* and *The Wild Duck* in time to learn her parts. Bette was shattered, sure that her chance to play Hedvig was gone. "The suffering from my malady was not nearly so intense as the pain from my broken heart," she recalled.

Yet again, Ruthie saved the day. She assured Cecil Clovelly that if Linda Watkins could remain with the company for just one more week, Bette would know both parts by heart, without rehearsals, in two weeks. Bette told her mother she was being ridiculous; surely Blanche Yurka wouldn't change everyone's plans for *her*. But that's exactly what happened. Yurka wanted her, and whatever had to be done would be.

Ruthie didn't allow Bette's astonishment to last very long; she started to coach her for the parts that day. Bette remembered the next two weeks of illness as a "nightmare." She lay in bed, feverish, achy, her eyes so sensitive to the light that Ruthie had to read the scripts to her with a flashlight in the pitch-dark apartment. Wearing a flannel nightshirt, her hair in bedtime braids, Ruthie sat on a chair next to Bette's bed and read to her late into the night, cueing her responses when she forgot them, tugging the proper emotions out of her when she felt too weak to call them up. Bette threw temper tantrums, grabbed the script out of Ruthie's hand and flung it across the room, howled that she couldn't concentrate, her eyes hurt, she wanted to be left *alone*! But Ruthie never let up.

By the night before she was due at the Bijou for her one rehearsal for *The Lady from the Sea*, Bette knew both her parts by instinct. The next morning she and Ruthie awoke at 9:30—exactly the hour Bette was supposed to begin the rehearsal. After all that work, Ruthie had forgotten to set the alarm. Bette became hysterical, screaming with rage as her mother pushed and pulled her into her clothes and got her down to Eighth Street and Sixth Avenue. There wasn't a taxi in sight. Mad with frustration, Bette grabbed Ruthie and bit her on the shoulder, her teeth cutting into her mother's flesh through a woollen dress.

They ran into the theater an hour late, and Ruthie started breathlessly to explain what had happened to an angry Cecil Clovelly. Bette turned on her furiously. "Get *out*, Mother!" she screamed. "And *stay* out!" Ruthie, carrying a thermos of milk and a bottle of wine she had brought to give Bette fortitude, did as she was told and sat quietly by the stage door as Bette began her rehearsal.

It went off without a hitch, and Bette felt confident she would at least know her lines at her first performance—that same day at a 2:30 matinee. But when she was handed her costume, she lost her composure once again. It was soiled and torn, and had not been altered to fit her.

"It was unbelievable," Bette recalled. "I announced my displeasure, which was even more incredible, and crawled off to a lunch that I prayed I could keep down."

When she returned, she found that the costume had been washed, ironed, starched, sewn, and laid out in her dressing room along with freshly shined shoes and a crisp white cap—all by Ruthie. With her mother plying her with milk and wine every time she came offstage, Bette got through the performance—even though she hadn't even seen the play's set before she took the stage. As a Broadway debut, it was inauspicious (and unreviewed), but Bette felt grateful that she wouldn't have to play Hedvig under such adverse conditions. By the time the company traveled to Jackson Heights, Queens, for Bette's first performance in *The Wild Duck,* she was recovered, in a better frame of mind, and totally ready for the challenge.

Blanche Yurka, who staged as well as starred in *The Wild Duck,* had seen Bette in *The Earth Between* and thought she had the makings of a "great" Hedvig. Although Bette was now twenty-one, she could pass easily for fourteen with her sylphlike body and the big-eyed innocence she exuded. More important, Yurka felt instinctively that Bette would "attack the part, not with technique, but with her nerves and her heart." Yurka decided not to rehearse Bette fully in the big emotional scene, where Hedvig weeps hysterically as her father leaves her. "It was a risky thing to do with such an inexperienced youngster," Yurka recalled, "but I followed my hunch and merely told her to let herself go when she came to the spot. But on opening night, even I was not prepared for the torrent of emotional intensity which rocked that frail body as she lay downward on the sofa, crying her heart out."

Yurka had no way of knowing, of course, that at this pivotal moment in Ibsen's play she was not watching Hedvig Ekdal plead with her father not to leave her, but rather Bette Davis crying out to Harlow.

When *The Wild Duck* left New York to continue its tour, Ruthie insisted that she accompany Bette. Blanche Yurka was not pleased. She considered Bette's mother a silly woman whose apron strings were far too tightly tied to her daughter, and "the archetype of the classic stage mother—only worse!" Yurka had found Bette to be "overeager and full of tears and tantrums," and she realized that Ruthie's worried hovering merely worsened matters.

Nevertheless, Yurka allowed Ruthie to travel with the company, and she was generous to Bette professionally as well. She would sometimes hand entire scenes to her; she told the press at the time, "I've had my day—let's see this eager, talented young girl commence to have hers!" Bette recalled that "the critics were exceptionally nice" about her performance, and they were. "She acts with all her heart and being," a New York reviewer felt. "On view here is a sincerity that is as compelling as it is electric."

In Philadelphia, one critic singled Bette out for special praise: "The strikingly effective portrayal in the production is that of Bette Davis. . . . Miss Davis—wan, sickly, yet cheerful as a child should be—thrills us with the poignant grief that comes with the revelations of the child's great tragedy." This time, Bette felt she deserved the praise heaped upon her in city after city. "For the first time I felt that I was really accomplishing something in my career."

One of the Washington, D.C., critics, however, sounded a discordant note amid the litany of praise with stinging observations that telegraphed some of the criticisms Bette would later face as a screen actress. "She had about the same amount of the much-maligned sex appeal as a kippered herring," Mabelle Jennings wrote in the *Washington Post*. "There were occasions when I knew perfectly well that she had forgotten there was anyone else on stage but herself. . . . In twelve months' time she will be doing harder and heavier roles than she is today. But this enlargement of experience will also see the passing of the naturalness of her Hedvig characterization."

Her success in *The Wild Duck* brought Bette her first request for an interview. She and Ruthie were agog with excitement at the prospect, and when the reporter entered her dressing room, Bette sat at her vanity mirror, her legs crossed demurely, her attitude suffused with as much sophistication as she could muster. "I've read sufficient interviews given by prominent personages of the stage," Bette announced to the bemused journalist, "to have a comprehensive idea of the information you desire."

For Bette, the "grand triumph" of the *Wild Duck* tour was her opening in Boston. It was nearly spoiled when she read a letter from Charlie Ainsley just before the performance: he was breaking off their engagement because his parents disapproved of actresses. Bette was furious: why hadn't Charlie fought harder for their relationship? Why hadn't he talked to her about it? He never could have *really* loved her!

But she forgot it all out on that stage, where her only problems were Hedvig's. She had found first nights "a nightmare," and this one more than any because "word had gone out among my schoolmates that a hometown girl was coming back." Friends came from Winchester, New-ton High, Mariarden, and Cushing, and every relative within a three-hundred-mile radius sat in the front rows—including her father. She peered out from behind the curtain, mesmerized, petrified, and thrilled by the enormous theaterful of people eagerly waiting to see *her*.

Aware that Bette had "come home," Blanche Yurka broke one of her strictest rules during the curtain call. None of the supporting cast members ever took bows alone, but as she and Bette acknowledged the cheers in Boston, Yurka slipped away and let Bette bathe in the hosannas all by herself. The audience erupted. People stood on their chairs and cheered for the hometown girl who'd made it. Bette said she felt "wave after wave of love" wash over her until she simply stood there and cried. "The weight that was Charlie lifted like a miracle. . . . I was alone—onstage and everywhere; and that's the way it was obviously meant to be. . . . My heart almost burst. This was the true beginning of the one, great, durable romance of my life."

The "waves of love" followed Bette backstage, where her dressing room was jammed with well-wishers. Harlow Davis saw the mob and slipped away; but several months later he caught the show again in New York, where its tour ended at the Shubert Riviera on Ninety-sixth Street. Again he went backstage to see Bette. Again he asked her to join him for supper and again she declined, pleading weariness.

The similarities between Hedvig and her father and Bette and him-self could not have been lost on Harlow. Prompted perhaps by a twinge of guilt, he wrote her a long letter after seeing *The Wild Duck* for the second time. It was a "big kick" for him to see her in the play, he said, and he was "very proud" of the "fine debut" his daughter had made in New York. After expressing his regret that once again Bette had been unable to dine with him, he admonished her to take good care of herself ("You need lots and lots of cream, milk, eggs, fruit, green vegetables") and closed by saying, "[I] was glad to see my so accomplished daughter do so very well."

This note doesn't suggest an ogre of the sort Ruthie had painted over the years. Perhaps Harlow Davis had mellowed. Perhaps Ibsen had made him realize the pain he had caused his daughter. Perhaps he was more comfortable complimenting her in writing than in person. But it was all too little, and too late. And Ruthie, still bitter, had little desire to close the chasm between her ex-husband and her daughter. "A loving mother might have tried to mediate," Ginny Conroy felt, "but Ruthie did no such thing. Rather, she continually bad-mouthed Harlow, used every possible occasion to drive the wedge further between father and daughter. That way, she could be assured that Bette—the center of her universe—would forever be exclusively hers."

Bette returned to the Cape Playhouse in the summer of 1929, after she and Ruthie drove to Ohio to pick up Bobby. During the ride back, Bobby bubbled with excitement about her studies as an English major at Denison and about all the friends she had made in the Kappa Kappa Gamma sorority. Secretly, Ruthie was pleased that Bobby finally had a life of her own to talk about, and the topic of conversation didn't always have to be Bette. Still, they were headed to Cape Cod purely for Bette's sake, and by the time they got there, the discussion rarely strayed away from what the summer held for her.

Her first assignment—as an older sophisticate in *The Constant Wife* —made her so nervous on opening night that she passed out on stage. According to Bette, the play's star, Crystal Herne, "turned playwright" and hastily invented a new ending on the spot to explain what had happened. "The audience never knew the difference." Next she did *The Patsy,* her first comedy, and during rehearsals she woke up every night in a cold sweat, terrified that she wouldn't get a single laugh. When her first line was met with guffaws, she relaxed. "I proved to be a laugh riot."

Her third show, Bernard Shaw's *You Never Can Tell,* featured a guest actor, the handsome leading man Dodd Meehan, and Bette fell for him. Meehan took advantage of her moon-eyed adoration and had her cue him for all his lines during rehearsals, which left her with little time to learn her own part. At the morning dress rehearsal, she "blew up" in her lines so often that Raymond Moore told her, "If you don't learn your part we will have to cancel the opening tomorrow night."

Ruthie had been at the rehearsal, and when she and Bette got home she spent the next fifteen straight hours coaching her; they didn't finish until four in the morning. The next night, Bette was letter perfect, but Ruthie still fantasized about running Dodd Meehan over with her car.

By now, Bette had a theatrical agent, Jane Broder, and when she returned from Cape Cod, Broder had an offer for her: to play Donald Meek's daughter in a new domestic comedy by Martin Flavin, *Broken Dishes.* At first Flavin and the show's director, Marion Gering, found Bette's acting merely serviceable, and considered firing her. But after eight days of rehearsals she warmed to the role, and "they changed their minds about that." She was to be paid a salary of seventy-five dollars a week—nearly a fortune to her and Ruthie.

Broken Dishes opened at the Ritz Theatre on November 5, 1929; Bette and the play won mostly positive reviews. One critic called her "delightful in her girlishness, her little feminine tricks, her tenderness and sympathetic feelings for her father, her diffident happiness with her lover." Another called her "something of an artiste . . . pretty and believable as Elaine."

Bette glowed with amazement and joy as she read the words. Finally, she had originated a role in a major Broadway show, she had been reviewed favorably by the top critics, and the play looked as if it was going to be a hit. She could scarcely believe it; now she was in the company of Gertrude Lawrence, Leslie Howard, Laurence Olivier, Alfred Lunt and Lynn Fontanne, George M. Cohan, Helen Morgan—all of whom were also on Broadway that season of 1929. She daren't let herself dream that someday she might be among their peers.

Broken Dishes played 178 performances in New York, and had a successful road tour later in the year. After the first three months, Bette's salary was doubled to $150 a week, the equivalent of $1,200 in 1993 dollars, and she and Ruthie went on an ecstatic shopping spree. The stock market had crashed several months earlier, and many investors (including Donald Meek) had lost large amounts of money. But the Great Depression hadn't yet taken its stranglehold on the country, Bette was in a hit, and the Davis women felt blithely wealthy.

About a month into the New York run, Bette had received an "imperious" summons from the Hollywood mogul Samuel Goldwyn, who wanted to test her for a movie role opposite the popular British romantic actor Ronald Colman. Although the prospect intrigued her, she couldn't summon up much enthusiasm about going to Hollywood. She loved Broadway and disliked cameras—"I had been Mother's model so often I had a phobia about them." But Ruthie, who was well aware of the fame, money, and power available to an actress in the burgeoning film industry, insisted that she do it.

The test, made at the Paramount studios in Astoria, was "ghastly," Bette recalled. She shook with nerves and fainted briefly just as the cameras began to roll. She was given no direction, was poorly lit, badly dressed and made up, and had a crooked tooth that stood out on film "like a locomotive." After Goldwyn saw the film he thundered, "Who wasted my time with *that* one?!" Bette agreed with the assessment, and put thoughts of Hollywood out of her head. But she did go directly to a dentist to have her tooth straightened.

In the summer of 1930, Bette returned to Cape Cod for her third season with the Playhouse. One Sunday evening in August, she, Ruthie, and Bobby sat in the Hyannis Port cinema, riveted on Joan Crawford in *Our Blushing Brides.* As the film ended and the lights went up, Bette let out "a blood-curdling yell": four rows in front of her she saw the back of a curly-headed young man who couldn't have been anyone but Ham Nelson. She ran up to him and he picked her up in his arms and twirled her. They hadn't seen each other for four years, "and yet we were both acutely aware of the existence of the other. Ham had always been important to me."

Ham was on the Cape to lead the Amherst College orchestra during their summer gig at the Old Mill Tavern. He and Bette talked into the early morning hours that first night, and resumed their romance with long days at the beach, drives in Ruthie's Chevy, walks around the Cape. "It was as though we had never been apart," Bette recalled. "We just talked and talked and talked, and grew to know, even though no words were said, that this was somehow very right, that we belonged together." But marriage, at the time, was out of the question. Bette had to return to New York, Ham to Amherst, and once again circumstances kept them apart.

A week into the road tour of *Broken Dishes* later that year, Bette got an offer to star again on Broadway, this time as Alabama ("Bam") Follonsby in a new comedy by Lawton Campbell, *Solid South,* starring Richard Bennett, father of the movie stars Constance and Joan. Bette liked the idea of originating another role, but she was reluctant to leave *Broken Dishes.* She had heard that Mr. Bennett could be difficult, and she would have to be ready to open in ten days. With "misgivings," she took the night train from Washington to New York and went directly to Bennett's office for an interview.

"I suppose that you are another of those young ham actresses," Bennett sniped in greeting. Tired, cranky, and ambivalent, Bette snapped back, "I've been on the train all night, Mr. Bennett. Unless you show me more consideration than this, I'll go home and we'll forget the matter."

Bennett smiled, told her, "You'll do," and added that she would be paid $125 a week, more than she was getting for the *Broken Dishes* tour. (Salaries were lower on the road because of the expenses involved in moving a show from town to town, and the lower ticket prices in smaller cities.) Bette thought a few minutes, realized that to create a new character was more important than any of the drawbacks, and accepted Bennett's offer.

She later recalled *Solid South* as "a good play," and it did receive favorable reviews when it opened on October 14, but Bette was rarely singled out for praise. She blamed the fact that the show lasted just three weeks on Bennett's temperament, unprofessionalism, and heavy drinking even while he worked. The second night, he stepped out of character in the middle of a scene and bellowed, "Stagehand, where's my cigar?" A few nights later he became irritated when the audience didn't respond to a comic speech he was delivering. He left Bette and another actress alone in the middle of the stage and walked down to the footlights to berate them: "I suppose I'll have to tell you a dirty story to get you to laugh." He then walked off the stage and left his leading ladies to their own devices.

On the Monday of the fourth week of the run, Bette walked into the theater and saw a notice posted on the bulletin board. *Solid South* had been closed, it said, "by act of God." The god, Bette thought bitterly, must have been Bacchus.

The show-business gods, however, had smiled on Bette the previous Friday. She had taken another screen test, this one for Carl Laemmle at Universal, for a role in their movie version of Preston Sturges's hit play *Strictly Dishonorable*. Once again Bette had felt ambivalent. "I was not fooled for a moment into thinking that the screen was the same thing as the stage," she recalled, "nor did I suspect that it might someday overthrow the theater. [But] it was new and it was big and it was impressive, and it certainly was worth investigating."

This time, Bette did her own makeup, wore her own clothes, and had straight teeth. She came off much better than she had in the Goldwyn test, and after a long series of transcontinental phone calls, Universal offered her a contract at the staggering pay of $300 a week, with renewal options with pay raises every three months. Ruthie couldn't believe it when Bette vacillated. "Don't you realize what an *opportunity* this is?" she pleaded. "Movies are seen around the world, by millions more people than ever see plays. And Hollywood could make us rich, Bette! You haven't done a thing for them yet and they're willing to pay you twice as much a week as any Broadway producer ever has. I read that Constance Bennett makes *$30,000 a week,* what with her acting and her cosmetics business! Imagine that, Bette! You must accept this offer. You *must!*" Bette sat mutely, overwhelmed by her mother's tirade. Finally, Ruthie took a deep breath and quietly concluded the lecture. "If you don't, you're a perfect fool."

Bette signed the contract in the office of David Werner, Universal's New York talent scout. She sat in front of his desk, in awe of the opulence around her; the huge room was resplendent with wood paneling and thick red carpeting and shiny brass furnishings. She had brought Boojum with her, convinced that she would seem more "Hollywood" carrying a dog to a meeting. The contract was the longest document she had ever seen, and just as she put pen to paper to sign it, Boojum jumped off her lap and proceeded to relieve herself on that thick wool carpet.

"I don't know why I've done this," Werner muttered to her as she handed him the signed pages. "You're the greatest gamble I've ever sent to Hollywood. You don't look like any actress I've ever seen on the screen. And yet, for some reason I can't analyze, I think that I'm right. I think you'll go a long way."

Bette's theater friends disagreed. Unanimously, they were appalled that she had "sold out" to Hollywood, and they warned her of dire consequences: "If you're serious about being an actress you'll never get a chance out there," they told her. "You can't lick them." She was certain they were right after her first meeting in New York with Universal's publicity department. Several gentlemen sat behind a great oak desk with their feet up, soles of their shoes toward Bette, and peered at her critically. They asked her for facts about her life they could use in press releases, then announced that of course her name would have to be changed. "We feel that 'Bette Davis' lacks glamour," one of them told her. "It doesn't have the fan appeal that it should."

Bette bristled. "It's done all right on the stage."

The man was all patience. "You don't understand," he replied. "Picture names must excite the fans. They must possess that intangible allure that makes customers think that actresses are different from ordinary people."

And what name, Bette inquired, did they have in mind?

"Bettina Dawes!" they replied in unison. "It's a natural!"

Bette almost gagged. *"Bettina Dawes!"* she cried. "I may not know anything about Hollywood, and Davis may not sound as romantic as Bernhardt, but I *like* it and I'm going to *keep* it!"

Several of the men began to object when Bette added, "Besides, I refuse to be called 'Between the Drawers' all my life."

The men laughed, then Bette laughed, and finally one of them said, "Okay, we'll discuss this again later." To her immense relief, nothing more was ever said about changing her name.

Bette and Ruthie drove to Madison, where Bobby had transferred to the University of Wisconsin, to pick her up for the start of her Thanksgiving break. (Bobby's reasons for the switch have been lost to posterity.) After a Thanksgiving sojourn with Aunt Mildred and Uncle Myron in Newton, Bobby took a train back to Madison, and Ruthie and Bette returned to Manhattan to make the arrangements for their journey to Hollywood. Ruthie sold the Chevy, arranged to sublet their apartment, and on the snowy morning of December 8, Davis *mère et fille* boarded the train to California, Bette with Boojum in her arms. Both women's emotions were a jumble of anticipation, uncertainty, excitement, and fear. With fifty-seven dollars left to her name after she had made all the arrangements to leave, Ruthie thought of Constance Bennett's $30,000-a-week income and sighed.

It saddened Bette to think that she might never again see the New England she so loved, and she knew she would miss her friends and family. But she was thrilled by the promises that Universal had made to her: *Strictly Dishonorable* would be a prestigious picture, and it was sure to make her a star overnight: "Clearly, my future was dazzling."

As she sat with her mother on the observation deck, Ruthie chattering incessantly about all the adventures that awaited them, Bette fell silent. Her mind wandered back over all the sacrifices that Ruthie had made for her, all the times she had pushed and prodded and browbeat her to gather up that one last ounce of gumption when Bette was sure she had none left.

The train sped along toward Bette's future, and all she could think about was the tableau that had haunted her three years earlier: Ruthie framed by the window of that photography studio as she retouched negatives, her head bowed, her eyes strained. "I have never paraded sentiment," Bette said. "I have always thought that my mother sacrificed far too much to be paid with empty lip service. But there is a shrine in my heart to her, and that shrine is the memory of a woman hunched in a window, to make it possible for her daughter to have the chance which only her mother's mind could conceive."

PART TWO

—————— ❧ ——————

"The Little Brown Wren"

SIX

ette and Ruthie stood on the dusty platform of the railway station in Pasadena, stranded. They had traveled for more than five days in the coach section of a chilly train that had been stopped by snowdrifts several times. Unable to afford berths, they had slept fitfully in the uncomfortable seats, and when they arrived on the Saturday morning of December 13, they were tired, downcast, and irritable. A publicity man from Universal was supposed to have met them, but no one was there.

They stood for what seemed an eternity amid their baggage, shielding their eyes from the hot, harsh California sun as they peered up and down the long, now-deserted platform for a sign of their escort. Bette held Boojum and struggled to keep calm. They felt, Ruthie recalled, like "strangers in a strange land."

Finally they had no choice but to take a taxi to the Hollywood Plaza Hotel, an expensive twenty-mile journey. Bette hung out the window as the cab drove into Hollywood, amazed and entranced by the warm, dry air two weeks before Christmas and the rows of exotic palm trees. She was sure that she'd see stars like Douglas Fairbanks, Norma Talmadge, and Vilma Banky every other block. To her disappointment, the fabled intersection of Hollywood and Vine seemed little more than a main street corner like any other.

After Ruthie paid the cabbie, she had seven dollars left in her purse. They went to their room and Bette called John Johnston, Universal's publicity director. Johnston was relieved to hear from her; he had sent one of his men to meet her, but he had returned alone because he hadn't seen anyone who looked remotely like an actress. "I may not have had a mink coat," Bette retorted, "but I *was* carrying a dog. That should have made him think I was an actress."

The studio sent a representative to the hotel (who made arrangements for the Davises to remain there until they could find a house to rent) and a photographer, who took the first pictures of Bette Davis in Hollywood. She held Boojum and posed next to Ruthie in the hotel lobby, and in the one surviving photo, mother looks more the budding movie star than daughter. While Bette cast her eyes down toward the dog, Ruthie looked directly into the camera and smiled prettily. But neither looked the least bit glamorous in their drab cloth coats and cloche hats.

Bette was told that a studio car would pick her up on Monday morning. On Sunday, as soon as she and Ruthie finished lunch (which they charged to the room and thus the studio), they began their house hunt. They stopped at a "smart" realty office near the hotel and told the broker, Mrs. Carr, that they had a very limited budget but hoped for a small house. Mrs. Carr replied that she thought she had something in their price range, but first she wanted them to see a "simply adorable" house that was far too expensive but that she liked to show to newcomers to Hollywood.

The house was at 4435 Alta Loma Terrace in the Hollywood hills, and the minute Ruthie and Bette saw it they fell in love. It was a two-story California bungalow-style cottage, completely furnished, with a thatched roof, a heavy redwood door, a ladder that led to a little balcony above the step-down living room, a built-in sofa, rows of bookcases filled with richly bound volumes, and a goldfish bowl built into a window. There was a rooftop sun deck, a patio out back, and—wonder of wonders—a flower garden in full bloom in December. To Ruthie, it was a "Hollywood house such as you dream about when you are far away."

As Mrs. Carr had suspected they might, Bette and Ruthie wanted to live there. But the rent was $150 a month, and Bette wouldn't receive her first paycheck from Universal for at least two weeks. Ruthie begged her to ask the studio for an advance, but she refused. Undeterred, Ruthie told Mrs. Carr that they were interested and would let her know their decision by Monday. Bette suspected that her mother had lost her mind, and she was sure of it later when Ruthie told the same thing to a car salesman about a green Ford phaeton because she thought Bette looked "just right" behind the wheel.

"You must have a car in this city, Bette," Ruthie cajoled. "Everything's so far away, and you can't hail a taxi like you can in New York. Besides, you must give the appearance of being a promising young actress. Just ask the studio for the money, Bette. Surely they'll—"

"*No,* Mother!" Bette exploded, and Ruthie realized that further pleas would be useless. They returned to their hotel, where Bette cried herself to sleep over their inability to afford that charming house, and Ruthie lay awake wondering how she could make things right. She considered wiring Harlow and asking for the $400 she needed, but decided the expense of the wire would be wasted. The next morning at 6 she awoke with an idea. She skulked out of the Plaza and hurried to the nearby Hollywood Roosevelt Hotel, where she knew that a long-time family friend, the wealthy former governor of Maine, Carl Milliken, was staying. She inquired about Milliken, and was told he would be down in a few minutes to play his daily game of tennis. When Milliken, tall and dapper in his tennis whites, stepped out of the elevator and saw Ruthie, he was both surprised by her presence and alarmed by the frantic expression on her face. "What in the world is the matter, Ruthie?"

"I must have four hundred dollars," she blurted.

Milliken pulled out his wallet and peeled off four hundred-dollar bills. "What are you going to do with the money?"

Ruthie told him and promised to repay the loan within a few weeks. Milliken went off to his tennis match and Ruthie walked back to the Plaza, wondering what she would tell Bette: she knew her daughter would be furious that she had borrowed the money. As she passed a Western Union office, a plan struck her. She walked in and asked the young man on duty to print a message on their yellow paper, and give it back to her rather than send it. He eyed her skeptically but did as he was asked. Ruthie took the telegram and envelope, put the four hundred dollars inside, and slipped it under their hotel room door. Within a few seconds she heard a shout from Bette. She had read the message: "Am sending money your mother asked to borrow. Dad."

Late that afternoon, Bette and Ruthie drove the phaeton up Alta Loma Terrace and moved their luggage into their new home.

The next day, Bette's first at Universal, was not nearly as propitious, perhaps because Ruthie wasn't there to smooth everything out. Bette knew that word had spread about "the Davis girl's arrival," and she noticed that a number of people made excuses to be in Universal founder Carl Laemmle's outer office while she was there, just to get a gander at her. She sensed she was in trouble when Laemmle's twenty-two-year-old son, Junior, a handsome man renowned for his appreciation of beautiful women, stuck his head out of his office door, took a look at her, and retreated back inside without so much as a word.

Bette knew she was a far cry from the beautiful, glamorous, often exotic girls who populated Hollywood movies. Junior Laemmle saw, she said, "a girl without makeup, one who had never been to a beauty parlor and whose eyebrows were thick and unplucked, whose long hair was wound up in back and broken only by two curls at her face." Bette had thought she was fairly good-looking (many of the New York theater critics had made a point of how "pretty" she was), but she sensed by the reactions of Junior Laemmle and the other men who came and went through the office that—by Hollywood standards, at least—she wasn't.

Her insecurities peaked when she met the elder Laemmle, whose face remained stony while he sized her up in his office. After a few perfunctory exchanges, the sixty-three-year-old film pioneer told her that she would be notified when she was to report to work on a production. Bette didn't know it, but Laemmle had decided immediately that she was wrong for the provocative role he had planned to give her in *Strictly Dishonorable*.

In the meantime, she toured the studio, met with publicity men, wardrobe mistresses, and makeup artists, and was introduced to some of the other actors and actresses on the lot. To her, Universal Pictures seemed the apex of Hollywood studios. In November, Carl Laemmle's personal fiefdom had won the third Best Picture Academy Award for *All Quiet on the Western Front,* and Bette was convinced the studio would offer her films just as prestigious. She couldn't know, of course, that Universal wouldn't win another top Oscar for forty-three years. *All Quiet on the Western Front* had been an aberration, a fleeting break in the studio's long line of Western, crime, and (starting in 1931) horror programmers. Laemmle Senior believed in saving money above all else, and had such a propensity for hiring his relatives that the humorist Ogden Nash was inspired to write a couplet: "Uncle Carl Laemmle / Has a very large faemmle."

Universal's production values were minimal, and the studio expended little effort grooming stars. (They had none, except for Boris Karloff and Bela Lugosi in their monster makeup, until Deanna Durbin in the late '30s.) Universal was probably the worst studio Bette could have signed with, but as 1931 opened, she was blissfully ignorant of the fact.

During the next few weeks, she posed for a seemingly endless series of still photographic tests, during which the photographer struggled to find the perfect lighting and angles to make Bette look as much as possible like America's idea of a movie star. In between photo sessions, she waited around the house for a summons from the studio. Finally it came. They wanted to do another screen test—this time of her "gams," the cinematographer told her. She had never heard the word. "Your *legs*," he explained. "The studio wants to see if you've got good legs."

"What have legs got to do with acting?"

The man sighed. "You don't know Hollywood, do you?"

Bette was mortified the next day as the cameraman continually prodded her to hike up her skirt "just a little higher." Finally he stopped when he saw her discomfort, and asked her to do some emoting. She mimed happiness, sadness, fright. In between, unaware that the camera was running at all times, she mugged outrageously, made faces, stuck her tongue out. When she saw the finished film, complete with her childish antics, she ran out of the screening room in tears. She hated everything about what she'd just seen on the screen. "I can't bear it," she cried to Ruthie when she got home. "We'll pack up tonight. I'll never be seen on the screen again."

Ruthie calmed her down. "The test they made in New York was good, wasn't it?" Bette had to admit she had liked that one. "You'll get used to it," Ruthie murmured consolingly. "They'll learn how to photograph you and you'll be all right." Bette felt a little better but her mood remained melancholy. She heard from the studio again a few days later, when she was told to be on the soundstage the next morning to test for a new movie. Thrilled, she arrived early and stared, mouth agape, as she roamed around the enormous hangar that housed the sets, the huge scaffolding that held the lights, the disassembled bits of scenery and backdrop that littered every inch of the building's periphery.

She was puzzled when she wasn't given any script sides to read. Instead, she was told to lie down on a divan. James Hall, a young actor popular as one of the stars of *Hell's Angels,* approached the divan, knelt by it, made an impassioned speech of undying love for Bette, then kissed her lustily. Hall slipped away, and a breathless Bette heard the director call out, "That's fine. Okay, who's next?"

Who's next?! Before Bette could react, the first of a succession of fifteen varyingly well-known actors knelt beside her, each repeating the lines and the passionate kiss. It didn't take Bette long to realize that she wasn't the actor being tested. "I might as well have been a dummy for all the good it did me. My face was hidden every time." Of the fifteen men, only the matinee idol Gilbert Roland sensed her dismay. "Don't be upset," he told her. "This is the picture business. We've all gone through it. Just relax!"

At the end of the morning, Bette went home to Ruthie and sobbed with abject misery. She felt abused and degraded by what she'd just been through. The studio obviously hated her. She was sorry she'd come to Hollywood. She missed her friends and the theater and New York. She hated the "obscenely" warm weather; she wanted it to "feel like Christmas." And on and on. Ruthie, as usual, tried to buck her up with assurances that everything would turn out for the best, but Bette remained in a blue mood for weeks.

Finally, Universal decided on a picture for her: Booth Tarkington's *The Flirt*. Bette loved the idea of playing a spoiled rich girl who runs off with a smooth con man. But then she heard that Sidney Fox had been cast as the girl, and that she would play her virtuous sister, a role she thought far less interesting than the colorful title character. Bette already resented Fox, who had played the role she'd been promised in *Strictly Dishonorable*, and this didn't help matters. Bette later claimed that Junior Laemmle and the twenty-one-year-old actress were romantically involved, and that Fox's minimal talent didn't warrant her casting in such important roles. She may have been right: Fox made just eleven movies in Hollywood, the last in 1934. She died at thirty-two of an accidental overdose of sleeping pills.

The title of *The Flirt* was changed to *Bad Sister,* and while Bette enjoyed working with Conrad Nagel and Humphrey Bogart, she loathed playing virtue. "I think it was that picture that gave me a horror of nobility. Ever since then I have fought against portraying saccharine characters. Give me the part of a vixen and I'm happy."

Still, she had finally appeared in her first motion picture, and on the day of a preview screening, she was "all adither." She and Ruthie drove sixty miles east of L.A. to San Bernardino, a sleepy community of citrus farms, and took rear balcony seats in the town's only theater to avoid being recognized. As the film progressed, Bette sank lower and lower in her seat. She and Ruthie left before the film ended, and Bette cried all the way home.

"Everything about me was wrong," she recalled. "I regarded myself as a hopeless mess. . . . My face was proportioned wrong. My mouth was too small. To overcome this they had smeared on make-up so that it looked like a tunnel. When I am embarrassed I smile crookedly, and for 7000 feet of film my mouth was distorted. . . . My clothes were bad and my hair was abominable."

Bette expected Universal to tear up her contract, which was about to expire, and she was amazed when Laemmle not only renewed it but raised her salary to $450. She later learned that they had indeed decided to drop her before Karl Freund, the cinematographer on *Bad Sister,* urged them to keep her on. His reason? "Davis has nice eyes."

"While his words saved my career," Bette recalled, "they were as cruel as can be uttered about a girl who thinks that she is fairly easy to look at and who has the hope that somebody will regard her as a capable actress.''

Matters did not improve for Bette during the second half of 1931. She made two more pictures, *Seed,* a bad film in which her part was so negligible that no critic commented upon it, and *Waterloo Bridge,* a better movie in which she again had little to do: her name appeared in the cast list just before "Old Woman."

After he screened *Waterloo Bridge,* Carl Laemmle turned to his son and said, "What audience could ever imagine the hero going through hell and high water just to kiss her at the fadeout?" Junior had made his own assessment of Bette after *Bad Sister:* "She has about as much sex appeal as Slim Summerville."* Bette already knew that around the lot she had been unkindly dubbed "the little brown wren," and when she heard about the younger Laemmle's remark, she was crushed. "I didn't recover for a long time."

Universal was ready to drop Bette when the RKO producer Pandro Berman asked to borrow her services for *Way Back Home,* a cornspun film based on the popular "down-home Yankee" radio character Seth Parker. Laemmle was pleased to comply; the studio always made a profit whenever they lent out one of their contract players. While *Way Back Home* turned out to be a rather silly film that drew lambasts from most critics, it was the first picture in which Bette felt she looked good. The cinematographer, J. Roy Hunt, took care with her and offered her "the first encouragement I had had, as to my face on the screen. I was truly overjoyed."

Bette's hair was bleached a light blond for the role, and she felt the look became her. Still, she wrote a friend that it made her "a little sick" that she had to do it. The lighting was flattering, and she did look pretty in the film. She also gave a charming performance, which was generally overlooked in the mass of bad reviews.

The picture was shot on location in Santa Cruz, California, and its production was resonant for Bette. Not only was she playing a small-town New Englander in a film replete with Yankee customs like taffy pulls, barn dances, and singing bees, but Santa Cruz provided her with her first look at pine trees in almost a year. "I've missed those so much

---

* Summerville was a lanky forty-year-old character comedian with a hangdog expression.

ever since I left home," she told Ginny Conroy. "They don't have any in Hollywood."

Way Back Home also proved to Bette that while she might not seem sexy to her bosses, she possessed animal magnetism enough for a number of men. Her love interest in the picture, Frank Albertson, a handsome twenty-two-year-old leading man, was "obviously in love with her," according to the film's director, William Seiter. "She handled him very gently, onscreen and off."

Albertson acknowledged that he had had "a crush" on Davis. "She was very warm and sweet. I know people think of her as a fussy, man-hating dynamo, but she wasn't like that then, not at all. I really *felt* the love scenes."

Now that she was a budding movie star, Bette felt she needed to become a part of the Hollywood social scene. The studio arranged for her to be invited to her first Beverly Hills soiree, and she and Ruthie shopped at Magnin's to find her a slinky, sophisticated, low-cut evening gown that would show those movie people just how sexy Bette Davis could be.

Bette had also decided that if she were truly to become a sophisticate, she would have to smoke and drink. "I thought if I learned to swear and smoke cigarettes, they would think I was an actress." She did both at this party, trying to project a worldliness she didn't possess, but if she had hoped her newly adult persona would attract virile and handsome men to her side, she was very disappointed. Standing self-consciously alone in the middle of the room for nearly an hour, she finally retreated to a window along a far wall, painfully reminded of her wallflower days at Newton High. Suddenly, a beautiful young man introduced himself. He was Douglas Fairbanks, Jr., the estranged husband of Joan Crawford.

Bette chatted with him a few moments, and before she knew what had happened, Fairbanks had slid his hand into her dress, fondled one of her breasts, and then told her, "You should use ice on your nipples the way Joan Crawford does." Flustered, Bette pulled away from him and ran to a telephone to call Ruthie.

Bette's next two films, *The Menace* and *Hell's House,* were again made on loan-out, for two other studios. Both took less than two weeks to film.

Bette called the former "a monstrosity; my part consisted of a great many falls out of closets. The picture was made in less than eight days. I knew that I had reached bottom."

Hell's House kept her there, with its hokey story of a naïve teenager (Junior Durkin) who unwittingly fronts for a petty bootlegger (Pat O'Brien) and is sent to reform school. Bette played O'Brien's moll as well as could be expected (complete with platinum hair, moxie, and a heart of gold), but the picture, which one critic rather daintily suggested "projects of having been put together in a slipshod manner," did her in. Pat O'Brien said he and Bette both knew the results would be dismal and formed a "mutual consolation society" during filming. "It took two weeks to shoot," O'Brien recalled, "and looked like it had taken a day and a half."

Like Frank Albertson, Junior Durkin was soon smitten with Bette. The good-looking, sensitive sixteen-year-old, who received top billing in *Hell's House,* had gained popularity early in 1931 playing the title role in *Tom Sawyer,* which he repeated six months later in *Huckleberry Finn.* Bette went out of her way to be nice to Durkin, whom she looked on as the brother she never had. It was a shock to Bette, Pat O'Brien recalled, "when I tipped her off that the poor kid, all of sixteen, no less, had fallen hook, line, and sinker for her!"

Durkin's infatuation caused him some embarrassment. During a scene in which Bette's character comforts Durkin, he sprouted an erection that was so noticeable the scene had to be cut from the picture. A few of Durkin's friends pirated the excised footage and screened it at stag parties—much to their merriment and Durkin's mortification. He got into a few fistfights over it, and cried to Pat O'Brien, "What do I do?" O'Brien told him not to worry. "So you got a hard-on with Bette Davis in a movie. Great! Proves you're a man!"*

Bette "couldn't imagine" what Durkin saw in her. After her first six films, her insecurities were deeper than ever—about her appearance, her talent, her future. She rightly felt unappreciated and poorly used by Universal, and she knew she was on tenuous footing every time her contract neared renewal. "Failure to me is death," she said, and she was sure she had failed. Her depression grew so deep that she contemplated suicide.

In September 1931, Universal dropped her contract. Again, Bette immediately accepted the defeat; in spite of Ruthie's pleas, she decided she would prefer to return home and admit she'd flopped in movies than

---

* Durkin's career foundered after *Hell's House,* and he made just five more films before he was killed in an automobile accident at twenty. A fellow child star, Jackie Coogan, survived.

to hang on like the thousands before her who had refused to face reality and eventually failed, as Bette put it, "with their money and their friends vanished."

This time she wouldn't be swayed by Ruthie's importunings. She was in the shower, her bags packed and ready to go, when the telephone rang. The caller told Ruthie that George Arliss would like to speak to Bette about a role in his new film. Ruthie raced into the bathroom and screamed the news at Bette. She was maddeningly unimpressed. This had to be one of her friends pulling her leg—George Arliss was one of the most respected actors in the country; to Bette he "loomed as the greatest figure in the theater." That he would want her for a movie, with her track record, was absurd. "Oh, Mother," she answered as she shampooed her hair, "it's just someone playing a practical joke. I'm never going to make another film."

Ruthie pulled Bette out of the shower, frantically wrapped a towel around her, and dragged her to the phone. Dripping wet, she decided to play along with the prank. The voice on the other end of the line said, "Miss Davis, this is George Arliss. Would it be possible for you to come to Warner Brothers immediately for an interview with me for my next film, *The Man Who Played God*?"

Bette replied in a ridiculous English accent. "Of *course*, Mr. Arliss! How *jolly* decent of you!" She did this again in response to the man's next three statements, until finally he realized what was happening. "Miss Davis!" he boomed. "This *is* George Arliss!" Bette gasped—she remembered that intimidating tone from her classes with Arliss at Milton/Anderson. "Oh, I'm so sorry, Mr. Arliss," she stammered. "I really thought . . ."

"Never mind that. Can you come now?"

"Of course—I'll be right there!"

For a few moments, Bette and Ruthie sat there speechless. Then Bette roiled into action and was dressed and ready within fifteen minutes. Driving over the hills of Laurel Canyon to the Warner Brothers lot in Burbank, Bette marveled at her good luck. An Arliss film was a prestige production, peopled with actors with stage backgrounds, and always an event picture. This could be her big break! She drove onto the twenty-three-acre complex and felt overwhelmed. She had never seen a studio so large, with its seven huge soundstages and its rambling back lot. *This place could be a factory,* she thought.

As she walked into Arliss's office, Bette was scared, her nerves on the brink of snapping. But a few minutes later, as she sat across from Arliss, she felt oddly unafraid. "I was meeting my own kind," she explained. "A citizen of the theater." Arliss told Bette that Murray Kinnell, who had appeared in *The Menace* with her at Columbia, had recommended her after Arliss had unsuccessfully tested twenty other young actresses to play the major role of his fiancée in *The Man Who Played God*. Bette wasn't sure what to say until candor got the better of her. "I don't know how he could tell from my work in that terrible picture," she said.

Arliss laughed. "Discernment," he replied. "A sixth sense."

When Bette told him that she had been on the stage for three years, Arliss allowed as how that was long enough to "wear off the rough edges." He then sat silently, appraising this young girl. Staring back at him, she was struck anew by his bemonocled, skeletal face, the skin so taut she suspected that there was a great knot of it at the nape of his neck. His eyes seemed to bore into her. "Universal had asked to see my legs," Bette remembered thinking. "Mr. Arliss was examining my soul."

She passed the inspection. "The part is yours," Arliss announced. "Go to the casting office right away. They will take you to the wardrobe department." Bette felt faint with joy and thanked Arliss profusely. She tried to retain her dignity, but by the time she got to the casting office, she was hugging strangers and shouting, "I don't believe it! I don't believe it!"

Warner Brothers offered her a one-picture contract at a salary of $300 a week, with an option for further employment if the studio wished. Ruthie thought she should have been paid more—after all, Universal had paid her $450 a week—but Bette was less interested in her salary than the opportunity. She signed the contract on November 18, 1931. Its only unusual clause stipulated that she was required, for some unfathomable reason, to provide her own shoes and stockings for the film—"Black, white, silver or gold will suffice."

Bette was so overjoyed to be working with George Arliss that she never paused to think that she, at twenty-three, had been chosen to play the fiancée of a sixty-three-year-old man.

The Man Who Played God is the story of a brilliant concert pianist, Montgomery Royale (Arliss), who loses his hearing when a bomb goes off near him in Paris. He returns to New York, at first bitter and suicidal, but then he begins to study the people in Central Park below his window, reading their lips through binoculars. Royale learns of their problems and sends them anonymous gifts, "playing God" by helping them. He soon also sees his fiancée, Grace, talking with a young man in the park, and he learns that she loves the young man yet feels that she must remain with Royale because of his disability. Unselfishly, he asks her to break off the engagement, and she agrees. Royale then turns to a woman closer to his age who has loved him for many years.

Arliss had played Royale nine years earlier in a silent film version, and even then the age difference between him and Grace was a potential problem. In 1922 there had been a twenty-year difference between Arliss and his leading lady; now the gap was forty years. Arliss felt it important that Grace be seen as a character who was infatuated with Royale's artistry, who loved him as a person but also worshiped him as a musical hero. There would be no intimation of a physical affair; Grace would have to be played as naïve, loyal, and sacrificing. Arliss's problem had been to find an actress who could play these characteristics without seeming dumb, silly, or opportunistic. Bette, he thought, could do it.

He wasn't disappointed. After he saw the final cut of the film, Arliss turned to Bette, released his monocle, and said, "My dear, not even *I* saw all the dimensions you gave to Grace. Thank you!" In his autobiography Arliss wrote, "I felt rather humbled that this young girl had been able to discover and portray something that my imagination had failed to conceive. She startled me because quite unexpectedly I got from her a flash that illuminated mere words and inspired them with passion and emotion."

Bette loved working with Arliss; his habit of completely rehearsing a film before the cameras rolled reminded her pleasurably of the theater and resulted in an on-time, one-month shooting schedule. Later she said that Arliss "was like a father to me." Not only had he filled for a while the void that Harlow had left in Bette's life, but he did it, she said, as "the first major fosterer of my creative life." Bette's complex feelings about Harlow, and her use of them in her characterization of Grace, once again added texture to one of her performances.

Warner executives were as impressed by Bette's acting as Arliss had been. Hal Wallis, one of the studio's top producers, recalled that "anyone who could hold her own with George Arliss in a scene and not look like a prop was outstanding in my book. Indeed, there were moments when you weren't looking at Arliss, you were looking at her instead. . . . She didn't just act with her eyes. She acted with her whole body. . . . She was *alive;* she jumped out of the screen."

Bette considered *The Man Who Played God* the most important picture of her career, and it may well have been. Not only did it keep her in Hollywood; it elevated her standing as an actress overnight. The picture's popularity (it grossed nearly $1 million) brought her to the attention of far more film fans than had ever seen her before. And most importantly, it marked the beginning of her relationship with Warner Brothers. As soon as filming wrapped, the studio offered Bette a five-year contract, with renewal options twice a year. Her salary would start at $400 a week and rise to $1,250 a week if all the options were exercised. Thus began one of the longest, most mutually rewarding, and most tempestuous professional associations in Hollywood history. "The greatest eighteen years of my life," Bette called it.

Warner Brothers Pictures, Inc. was less than nine years old in 1932, but it had already carved out a major niche for itself in Hollywood with pioneering forays into sound production. In 1926, the studio had released *Don Juan,* the first film to include synchronized music and sound effects, and a year later had an enormous success with *The Jazz Singer,* which thrilled audiences with bits of dialogue and songs—and made it clear that talkies were the cinematic wave of the future.

Formed in 1923 by four brothers, Harry, Albert, Jack, and Sam, the company gained profitability with its sound breakthroughs and a combination of meager budgets and major showmanship. As Bette signed her contract on Christmas Eve, 1931, she felt that she had at last found a hospitable home in Hollywood. Jack L. Warner, thirty-nine, soon became the studio's head of production,* and in him Bette found another surrogate father. As a paternal figure, "J.L." Warner was more Harlow Davis than George Arliss. He ran his studio with a whip hand, insisted that productions be lean, mean, and snappy, and excelled at keeping recalcitrant children in line. His son, Jack Junior, describing Warner, could have been talking about Harlow Davis: "He existed behind a self-made wall. Besides, a lot of him wasn't that nice to know. At times he gloried in being a no-good son of a bitch."

Bette's relationship with Warner, like that with her father, wavered between love and hate. At the outset, however, Bette was convinced that the Warner studio's no-nonsense approach to production would be compatible with her no-nonsense style of acting, and that their appreciation of her would translate into better films than she had been offered at Universal. Occasionally this was so. But for the most part, at first, the studio provided Bette with scripts that were not much better than the

---

* Harry Warner was the president of the studio, Albert its treasurer. Sam, whose idea it had been to pursue sound production, died the day before *The Jazz Singer* opened.

ones she had hated in the past. Her first picture as a Warner contract player, *So Big,* starring Barbara Stanwyck, offered her little to do and brought mixed reviews; one critic was moved to call Bette's acting "unusually competent." Bette later said that her part as Dallas O'Mara, an idealistic young artist, was one of her favorites because Dallas had "a naturalness similar to my own personality . . . even though my career was dedicated to character parts from the beginning, every now and then I selfishly wanted an audience to know what kind of a person I really was. Anyway, the kind of person I *felt* I was."

Bette's afterthought is revealing, because Dallas was in fact quite *unlike* Bette Davis. In fact, Bette was so terrified of Stanwyck that she was a bundle of nerves on the film, and her unnaturally kinetic behavior irked the star badly. When Bette forgot her lines in the middle of a scene, lit a cigarette, and complained, "It all makes me so jittery, the pace of this scene," Stanwyck shot back, "You make *yourself* jittery! Try to fit into things!" Stanwyck later told William Wellman, the film's director, that Bette was "an egotistical little bitch. Why doesn't she relax, for Christ's sake! She'll get her turn. There's plenty of room at the top for talent in Hollywood."

It wouldn't be the last time that sheer, gut-wrenching terror in Bette would be misunderstood as ego and temperament.

So Big proved memorable for Bette, mainly because it introduced her to George Brent, a handsome twenty-eight-year-old who had fled Ireland in 1921 to escape British retribution for his revolutionary activities. After a Broadway stage career, he won great popularity in Hollywood as a suave, if less than charismatic, leading man. Bette had first noticed Brent back in New York a year earlier, and she had immediately developed an "all-time crush" on him.

Her heart ached on the set of her next picture, *The Rich Are Always With Us,* which also featured Brent, because she could only watch helplessly as he fell in love with the film's star, Ruth Chatterton. A legend of the theater, Chatterton scored a success in movies at thirty-nine with her rich voice and her sophisticated manner. Bette was so terrified by her the first day of filming that she was unable to speak her first line. Chatterton simply stared at her "in a superior sort of way" and waited for her to say something. Finally Bette blurted out, "I'm so damned scared of you I'm speechless!"

According to Bette, this "broke the ice," and she found Chatterton surprisingly willing to help her after that. But the burgeoning romance between Brent and Chatterton left her with "a saddened heart," and she wept bitterly when she heard that the couple had been married.

∾

Bette was heartsick as well over something else in 1932: Jack Warner was putting her into more and more B films, quickies made on minuscule budgets and cut to run just over an hour. In most of them Bette provided mere window dressing for the studio's patented "male-oriented" stories about politics (*Dark Horse*), mobsters in prison (*20,000 Years in Sing Sing*), and pilots (*Parachute Jumper*).

B picture directors took scant care to make a leading lady look her best; flattering close-ups of the actresses were rare. Still, Bette had one opportunity to shine, in a B+ picture, *The Cabin in the Cotton*, which paired her with Richard Barthelmess. She played Madge Norwood, the flighty daughter of a wealthy planter for whom Barthelmess goes to work. Amid chicanery by her father to cheat his sharecroppers, their threats of rebellion, and Barthelmess's efforts to force his boss into fairness toward his tenants, Bette's character, at once seductive and coy, flirts and vamps outrageously toward Barthelmess. The script gave Bette one of her all-time favorite lines: "Ah'd like t' kiss ya, but ah just washed mah ha-ir."

Bette adored this vixenish Southern belle, and she used her Martha Graham training to give her movements a sensual, serpentine quality that worked well for the character. But the film's director, Michael Curtiz, didn't seem to appreciate what she was doing. He hadn't wanted her for the role in the first place; the studio's production chief, Darryl Zanuck, had forced her on him. Curtiz "made my life hell" during the shoot, Bette recalled. While she thought she was doing a great job conveying Madge's simmering sexuality Curtiz would crouch behind his camera and grumble about her under his breath. Once she overheard him sputter, "Goddamned-nothing-no-good-sexless-son-of-a-bitch!"

"What with Barthelmess's wife sitting beside the director appraising our love scenes and Curtiz's heckling," Bette recalled, "it's a wonder I made it." She went home every night, she said, "irritated, exhausted and hungry . . . ready to explode . . . eager to be soothed by a well-run household and a soft-spoken wife."

Despite all of this, Madge Norwood emerged as Bette Davis's first memorable screen characterization, and film critics sat up and took real notice of her for the first time. Regina Crewe in the New York *Journal American* called Bette "that flashy, luminous newcomer," and added that she "romps off with first honors, for hers is the most dashing and colorful role. . . . The girl is superb."

But Warners immediately lumbered her with another dud, *Three on a Match,* a sixty-three-minute marvel with a great deal of cigarette smoking and heavy-handed melodrama in which she played a stenographer. She costarred with Joan Blondell and Ann Dvorak; the director, Mervyn LeRoy, made constant mention of the stellar future that awaited Blondell while pointedly ignoring Bette. This, Bette said, "hardly encouraged me in my daily work." She had come to realize that "something in me created resistance in these men." She was certain that what she called her "background and assurance" caused resentment among her male colleagues. "They were used to empty, passive slates they could scribble on," she felt—and they didn't like the fact that this young starlet had her own very definite ideas about acting.

With her professional life so full of ups and downs, so emotionally draining, and so fraught with ego destruction, Bette longed more than ever to be "soothed by a well-run household and a soft-spoken wife." Ruthie tried her best. When Bette came home from a day at the studio, exhausted and overwrought, her mother would hand her a martini to calm her down, draw her bath, lay out her robe. Ruthie tried to make Bette's life easier, but more often than not their personalities would clash as they always did and she would infuriate her daughter in the process.

So that Bette wouldn't have to suffer through the heat of another stifling Los Angeles summer, Ruthie convinced her to rent a cottage at the seashore in Zuma Beach, near Malibu, and to trade in the phaeton for a secondhand Auburn for the ride to and from Hollywood every day. Before long the three musketeers were together again when Bobby left the University of Wisconsin on the advice of a doctor and moved back in with her mother and sister. She had not been able to handle the pressures of advanced college work, and when she came to Hollywood she was once again nervous, melancholy, and withdrawn. A local physician confirmed that Bobby needed prolonged rest and should not return to school.

Part of Bette was pleased by this family reunion, but another part of her longed for freedom after so many years of daily life with her mother and sister. Even more, she pined after the intimate company of an attentive man. In a matter of weeks, her wish came true: in the late spring of 1932, Ham Nelson re-entered her life.

SEVEN

vening fog rolled in off the Pacific Ocean and enveloped Bette's Zuma Beach house. Inside, she sat at the dinner table with Ruthie, Bobby, and her Aunt Mildred and cousin Donald, who were visiting from Newton. All evening long, she had felt ganged up on. First one, then another of her relatives pleaded with her to listen to her mother. Ruthie had rallied everyone to her latest crusade: to convince Bette that the sensible thing for her to do was marry Ham Nelson. The only person at the table with misgivings was Bette.

Nelson had come out to California late in June 1932, after he was graduated from college, and Bette had been "thrilled" to see him again. She had found him more attractive than ever, especially since he had lost little of the boyish charm and New England provincialism she had fallen in love with. As they had on Cape Cod four years ago, they fell back easily into a pleasant, comfortable relationship. Now, the inevitability of their ultimate marriage, which they had "sensed" in Cape Cod, stared them in the face.

Ham was all for it. Whenever he and Bette were alone—during long drives up the California coast, or as they sipped wine in a fancy restaurant or a milk shake with two straws in a soda shop on Hollywood Boulevard —Ham would say to her, "I think we ought to be married while I'm here." Bette would invariably reply, "Oh, I think that would be sort of silly. . . ."

They volleyed back and forth like this for most of the summer. When Ruthie became aware of the debate she immediately urged Bette to accept Ham. She felt that marriage—and a regular sex life—might calm her daughter's chronic jitters. Finally, the matter came to a head.

Ham was staying with the Davises at the beach cottage (sleeping, of course, in a separate bedroom), and on August 16, he sat in the living room with Bette and Ruthie and their visiting relatives and listened as Ruthie listed yet again all the reasons Bette should marry him. It was time she got married, Ruthie said. She had always loved Ham, and if she didn't accept him now he might return East and never ask again. And then wouldn't she be sorry? Bette listened silently, thoughtfully. A little embarrassed that Ruthie was saying all these things in front of Ham, she still sensed that her mother was right. "I knew *how* sorry I'd be if I didn't marry Ham," she recalled.

Still, she felt deeply ambivalent about becoming Ham's wife. Yes, she loved him; yes, she thought they had a good chance to be happy together. But she was worried. "I was afraid for Ham, afraid of what Hollywood would do to his career, afraid of putting him in a position of being a star's husband." All evening she vacillated from a firm "No" to a conditional "Maybe" ("If you get a job here I'll think about it") to a possible "Yes" ("Weelll . . .").

One of the main factors pulling Bette toward "Yes" was her frustration at being a twenty-four-year-old virgin living in the same house with a man she found sexually exciting. "I was hopelessly puritan, helplessly passionate," she recalled, and the combination was driving her crazy. Still bound by Ruthie's moralistic values, she was afraid that unless she got married soon, she wouldn't be able to avoid the temptation to sin. Her ambivalence that night knew no bounds. Whenever she would say "Weelll," Nelson would start to dress for their wedding trip; then she would have second thoughts and say "No" and he'd undress and go back upstairs to bed. Then he'd come down and ask again.

Finally, at midnight, Bette agreed to marry him, and Ham wasn't going to give her time to change her mind. He corralled the entire household—six people and Boojum—into two cars and set off for Yuma, Arizona, in the smallest hours of the morning. By daybreak, they were still a hundred miles short of their destination, the desert temperature was already in the nineties, and Bette had been silent the whole time. "It was on the tip of my tongue to say, 'This is horrible. I won't go on.' "

Ruthie, who could read Bette's mind by now and knew exactly how to handle her, spoke up first. "Let's not go on," she said. Bette reacted as Ruthie had expected. "The mule in me immediately gave a back-kick of the heels and told Ham to step on the gas."

When the wedding party arrived in Yuma, their clothing was soaked through with perspiration. ("It was 107 in the shade!" Bette marveled.) The six of them booked two motel rooms for the four women and a third for the two men, and took turns taking showers, then wrapped themselves in the bedspreads while their clothes dried. Ham went out to buy a new shirt and searched all day to find a wedding ring in the small town. Bette kept muttering, "This is so awful it's funny."

The next morning, August 18, Harmon O. Nelson, Jr., and Ruth

Elizabeth Davis were married in the cramped home of a Methodist minister. Boojum loudly slurped herself with her tongue throughout the ceremony, and Ham dropped the ring twice, once losing it between two loose floorboards. Bette couldn't get the thought out of her mind that this wasn't the kind of wedding she had imagined she'd have. She was once again drenched in perspiration, which turned patches of her drab tan dress a deep brown. "This is love's greatest test," she said to herself. "If Ham doesn't look at me and scream, 'Good God, is *that* what's going to be Mrs. Harmon Nelson?,' then I know that nothing matters to him."

The fantasy wedding Bette had always pictured for herself flashed through her mind: she'd be "dewy and divine," dressed in white satin and orange blossoms. To the lovely strains of Mendelssohn, she would walk up a church aisle bedecked with white ribbons. She was jerked back to reality by the sound of locomotives chugging in a nearby railway yard. Perhaps it was all these lost fantasies that led Bette into a little mischief when the minister asked her if this was her first marriage. "No, sir," she replied, "it's my third."

Mr. and Mrs. Nelson returned to the Zuma Beach house and shared a bedroom for the first time. In her autobiography, Bette rhapsodized that "This was Ruth Elizabeth's golden moment. The proper bliss of a wedding night was here. The union under God and everything between a man and an honest-to-goodness maid was hers; and her joy was boundless. . . . Passion formalized, love ritualized, sex smiled upon by Society."

In fact, Bette's wedding night wasn't nearly so blissful. As she told her friend, the writer Jerry Asher, Ham's provincial naïveté extended to matters sexual. He had never been with a woman before, and was used to masturbating. He behaved awkwardly in bed, and remained passive with his bride, not quite sure what he should do.

Bette was, more than anything else, surprised. Nelson had played in bands for years; surely he must have had his pick of available women. Later she would wonder about the depth of Ham's interest in the opposite sex, but for now she became the aggressor. No sexual sophisticate herself, she masturbated him to climax, and he never satisfied her that first night. It was, she told friends, months before she had "trained" him to please her, but still he seemed to prefer masturbation or fellatio to coital intercourse.

Sexual problems were not the only ones the couple faced. Ham soon got a job as an orchestra leader at the Colony Club, a popular night spot on the Sunset Strip, and returned home each night only a few hours before Bette left for work. By the time she got home after a day at the studio, Ham was getting ready to leave again. They barely saw each other except on Sundays.

Still, Bette gave her all to make her marriage to Ham Nelson work. When he took a gig at the Villa Mateo in Daly City, a suburb of San Francisco, late in 1933, she drove north every weekend to see him, accompanied by a new friend, Liz Fisher, and turned Ham's tacky lodgings, cottage number 10 in the Mission Auto Court, into as close an approximation of a home as possible. She and Liz "cooked up a storm" and decorated an evergreen for Christmas with gay cutouts from the Sunday comics. There wasn't a place in the world, Bette recalled, that she couldn't "make seem like home. Ruthie had given me this ability . . . money is not the biggest ingredient. Imagination and being adaptable help the most."

It took a few visits before others staying at the Mission Auto Court recognized Bette. "How does it feel to be the husband of a famous movie star?" Ham was asked. "She's just Bette to me," he replied. People "made fun" of her, Bette said at the time, when they found out that she "cooked, swept, cleaned, and kept house for my husband just as women do all over the world. I needed that experience, and because of the demands of my work, I had never been able to have it in Hollywood. I wanted it, not only for my own good but also to prove to Ham that I could be a real wife in every sense of the word, not just a part-time wife whose job is pretty important to her, too."

This "admission" of Bette's was more disingenuous than it was candid. While she did assume, happily, the role of "the little woman" when she wasn't working, when she was on a set her career took precedence over her marriage. Emoting for the camera, exhausted at the end of a day's shooting, Bette longed for the "wife" she had talked about earlier, and Ham seemed more than happy to accommodate her. When she suggested that he do some housework, he agreed, but Bette found herself less pleased by Ham's contributions than dismayed that he hadn't refused to do "woman's work" as a "real man" would have.

Publicly, they played out the charade of a happily modern "percentage" marriage; Ham's $100 a week, they claimed, would pay for 10 percent of what Bette's $1,000 a week (by 1934) could buy. Bette bought furs, gowns, a black Packard "to keep up her business position," and Ham bought suits off the rack and a Ford roadster that cost him

$19.50. So far, Bette said, the arrangement had "worked beautifully and enabled each to keep our self-respect and the respect of the other."

The reality was less comfortable, and Ham Nelson would learn that he couldn't win with Bette one way or the other. When he refused to allow her to pay for a more extravagant lifestyle than his $100-per-week income could keep up with (as her "real man" would have), she flew into a fury. They had moved into a white, ivy-covered English Tudor house on Horn Avenue in Hollywood; Ruthie and Bobby lived in a guest house in the back. When Bette wanted to move to a larger, more fashionable home, Nelson said firmly, "We can't move, not yet."

"We can afford to move," Bette insisted. "I've got the money."

"We can't buy a house with your money," Nelson shot back.

"What *difference* does it make, Ham?" she shouted. But Nelson had already turned and walked away.

Early in 1933, Bette discovered she was pregnant. Initially ecstatic, she was stopped cold by her husband's reaction to the news. "You're much too busy to have a baby," he told her. "It would be stupid to jeopardize your career." Then he added something that to Bette was the real point: "You don't think I'm going to have *you* pay the hospital bills for the baby, do you?"

It was *their* baby and *their* money, Bette replied. But Ham had grown more and more adamant about living largely on his income. Ruthie sided with Ham and told Bette that to have a baby now could derail her career. Bette saw the point, but the only way out of her pregnancy was to undergo an operation, and the thought of it made her feel "wretched." Still, she said, "I did as I was told."

Unlike other young women of this era, Bette didn't have to undergo the ordeal of a back-alley operation performed by a quack. A studio doctor performed the procedure, quickly and safely, in a medical setting. After a silent drive home with Ham, Bette took to her bed and cried for hours, shaking with misery and guilt.

Even so, she would undergo another abortion while married to Ham Nelson.

By now, the fan magazines had taken notice of Bette: She was featured in fashion layouts arranged by the studio; she did more than her share of silly publicity poses with huge Valentine hearts and oversized beach balls; and she appeared on her first cover in 1933. As her career began to burgeon, more and more articles about her private life and her marriage appeared with each new film. She earned a reputation for candor; just about every interviewer pointed out that the "outspoken" Bette Davis rarely shied away from subjects about which most actresses remained mute. She owned up to the fact that she had been "fired" from Universal; and admitted to the reporter Laura Benham that her "arrangement" with Ham Nelson wasn't as successful as she had earlier claimed it was: "In Hollywood there are so many households in which the wife earns either the entire income or the greater portion of it. Mine is one of those households. And therein exists the problem."

Benham commented, "I was surprised by her frankness. All too many times have I broken bread with beautiful young ladies of the screen who were bearing the economic responsibility of their families. This was the first time one of them had admitted it." The title of the Benham article could not have pleased Ham Nelson: "Marriage Costs Bette Plenty."

Bette's openness about some subjects gave her leeway to be less than honest about others. Her questioners were so sure she was being straightforward with them that they tended to believe everything she said. In fact Bette was less than truthful about a number of elements in her life.

She sometimes led reporters to believe that her parents were still married, and she invariably painted Ruthie as a tower of virtue who sacrificed everything for her daughter's career. While there were elements of truth in that, Bette never revealed her growing resentment against her mother because of Ruthie's dominating personality, her continual meddling in Bette's affairs, and especially her lavish spending. At one point Bette wrote a note listing all the things that most vexed her; foremost was "Ruthie's growing extravagance." Bette often did without something she wanted in order to buy Ruthie a new fur, put her behind the wheel of a shiny new car, or send her on vacation. But what irked her even more was Ruthie's apparent belief that *she* deserved the kudos for Bette's career as much as Bette did. Ruthie always walked ahead of Bette at premieres, prompting Bobby to observe, "You'd think she was the movie star and Bette just the also-ran relative."

Bette's profound ambivalence toward Ruthie tore at her heart. On the one hand, she felt that her mother had sacrificed so much for so long that she deserved creature comforts and a share of the spotlight. And yet she grew more and more upset with Ruthie's profligacy, and increasingly hurt by her suspicion that her mother's sacrifices had been made more with an eye toward her own future happiness than Bette's. These mixed feelings left her very uncomfortable, racked with anger one minute, awash with guilt the next.

The situation with Bobby didn't help. In December 1934, Los Angeles newspapers ran the story that Bette Davis's sister was a "new Warner Brothers actress" who wanted to follow in Bette's footsteps. Without Bette's knowledge, Ruthie had taken Bobby to Warner Brothers for a screen test, and the Warner executives were interested. When the press items appeared, Bette told reporters that "I mean to help Barbara as much as possible." Instead, she stepped in and killed the prospect cold. The reason, Ruthie told Ginny Conroy, was that "Hollywood isn't big enough for two Davis girls."

That was only part of it. Bette was less concerned about any competition Bobby might be to her than she was about keeping her sister's increasingly delicate emotional state out of the limelight. Bobby, even more high-strung than Bette, had lived in her sister's shadow for so many years, and that shadow was now so long and so dark, that the young woman had teetered over the edge into mental illness a year earlier.

Always timid, quiet, and nervous, Bobby's behavior had grown increasingly bizarre. Now her withdrawals verged on the catatonic, but often they were bracketed by violent outbursts of laughter or screaming. Several times, she hit Ruthie and had to be restrained from doing herself physical harm. Finally, there was no choice but to hospitalize her. Ruthie took her to a sanatorium in New York, where she remained for over a year. She didn't utter a word the entire time.

Bobby's mental problems deeply disturbed Bette, and for reasons much more complex than worry about her sister's welfare. Bobby's symptoms of untrammeled energy followed by crippling depressions hit much too close to home for Bette; she often exhibited the same pattern. Ginny Conroy said of Bette: "Certainly there were times when she seemed as though she were manic/depressive." In her most private moments Bette wondered, *Could I go nuts like Bobby?*

It was a genuine concern; mental illness remained a thread throughout Bette Davis's life. It is impossible to know whether similar problems afflicted Bette's ancestors, because in those eras such illness was hidden at all costs within families; even had Ruthie or Bette heard rumors about mental instability in the family, they wouldn't have spoken of it publicly. But it is perhaps significant that one of Bette's forebears had been labeled a witch; many of those so accused suffered from mental illnesses that made them behave so strangely that they seemed, in this period before scientific enlightenment, to be "possessed by the devil."

Bette tried to put it out of her mind. In her memoirs, she attributes Bobby's emotional turmoil to the fact that after Bette's marriage her sister "felt she had lost me and her anxieties took on the proportions of a nervous breakdown." There was far more to it than that, but Bette was never able to accept the fact that whatever was in the genes, Bobby's instability was badly exacerbated by the "punishing overshadowment" to which Bette and Ruthie had subjected her since her childhood. When Bobby returned to Los Angeles after her confinement back East, in good spirits and hoping for a film career, only to have her exciting new aspirations shot down by Bette, it was crystal clear that nothing had changed.

Around this time Bette's beloved Boojum died, and she was profoundly saddened by the loss. She had never liked being alone, and with Ham working nights and Bobby away, the adorable little terrier had provided warmth and company for her whenever she most needed it. Ruthie quickly found a replacement, a Scottie Bette named Tam-O-Shanta, and within a few years the Davis home had become a dog sanctuary with the addition of a Sealyham, a Doberman, and two poodles. But Bette always kept a special place in her heart for Boojum, who had been with her when all of this started. Her pet's death and her sister's illness were melancholy reminders to Bette that she was no longer the New England girl she had been when Boojum first came into her life.

Bette's career ups and downs continued, as if on a parallel graph with her personal highs and lows. She was earning $1,000 a week by mid-1934, and at the height of the Great Depression, when the cost of living bottomed out, this salary was equivalent to nearly $10,000 in 1993 dollars. She was touted as Hollywood's "hottest new star" in Sunday supplements, she dressed in designer gowns and expensive furs, she appeared on the covers of more and more movie magazines, was mobbed by adoring fans at premieres. She made seven films between January 1933 and April 1934; with *Ex-Lady,* released in May 1933, she was billed over the title for the first time. She was starting to feel like a "star."

But the undertow of mediocre films Warners so often gave her threatened to wash this promising career out to sea. Only one of those seven films, *The Working Man,* which reteamed her with George Arliss, proved creatively satisfying for Bette. Most of the others, while successful at the box office, were either artistic clunkers or failed to utilize Bette's talents properly. *Bureau of Missing Persons,* she said, had an "appropriate enough title, I guess." *Fashions of 1934,* although a box-office success that many critics considered "clever and lively," left Bette unhappy because Warners had tried to make her over into a blond Greta Garbo, with a platinum wig styled to resemble Garbo's coiffure—"to say nothing of the false lashes and huge mouth and the slinky clothes." She felt, she said, "glamorized beyond recognition."

That was where Bette Davis differed from most screen actresses of the early thirties. She had little interest in glamour; she wanted to be praised for her talent, not her legs or her eyes or her hair. And that was why, when she learned that the director John Cromwell wanted to borrow her from Warners to play Mildred in the RKO movie version of W. Somerset Maugham's bestseller *Of Human Bondage,* a beacon of light seemed to shine out at her from the edges of her ever-deepening doubt about the direction of her career. *Mildred!* she thought. *What a marvelous part for an actress!*

No other star in Hollywood would touch it. Mildred Rogers in Maugham's semiautobiographical novel is one of the most unsympathetic characters ever transferred to film. A sullen, slatternly, barely literate Cockney waitress, she coldly manipulates Philip Carey, the shy, sensitive, club-footed artist-turned-medical-student who obsessively loves her. She leaves him twice for other men, one of whom makes her pregnant and both of whom desert her. She returns to Philip each time; he is still so possessed by her that he takes her in. But he rebuffs her physical overtures when he realizes they are rooted not in love or even sexual attraction, but rather pity and a sense of indebtedness. Infuriated by the rejection, Mildred rails viciously against him, destroys his paintings, and burns the bonds he has inherited and needs to continue medical school.

With Mildred out of his life, Philip begins a fulfilling relationship with Sally, a gentle, caring, decent young woman. Then he learns that Mildred is dying of tuberculosis. Still in bondage to his obsession, he goes to see her. He gives her some money, but she succumbs to the ravages of the disease and dies in the hospital where Philip is an intern. He is finally free to love and be loved by Sally.

Bette didn't care that dozens of actresses had turned the role down before it was offered to her; she was thrilled to be offered such a strong dramatic opportunity. Her joy was short-lived: Jack Warner refused to lend her out. "It's a terrible role for anybody who wants a career in

Hollywood," Warner told her. "You'll destroy any film following you ever had. You'll never live it down."

What Bette feared she would never live down was the succession of second-rate movies and cardboard characters she'd been forced to play, and she was willing to take a risk with Mildred. She couldn't see how such a vivid role could hurt her career, no matter how unsympathetic the character. She suspected Warner was being petty. How could he lend her out to play Mildred, she asked sarcastically in her memoirs, when he "needed me desperately for such historic milestones as *The Big Shake-down* and *The Man with the Black Hat*"?

She wouldn't take no for an answer. One morning Warner walked into his office at sunrise and found Bette sitting in the waiting room.

"What can I do for you, Miss Davis?" he asked.

"Let me play Mildred," Bette replied.

Warner again refused, and Bette appeared at J.L.'s door just about every morning for months. Finally, he relented—mainly, Bette felt, to get rid of her. In fact it was a classic Hollywood quid pro quo that turned the trick: RKO would lend Warner Irene Dunne only if they could have Bette. "The role may hurt you," he told her, mentioning neither the trade-off nor the fact that RKO was paying Warners $2,250 a week for her services. "The public may recoil from Mildred, associate her with you, and back off from you—but go ahead and hang yourself if you must."

Jack Warner wasn't alone in his concern about Bette's playing Mildred; Ham and Ruthie both counseled her against it. But she would not be dissuaded, and she plunged herself into preparation for the role. To master Mildred's Cockney accent she hired an Englishwoman as an assistant, and soon began to speak like a born East Ender. "I drove my family wild," Bette laughed. Ham put up with it at first, but grew more and more irritated. When Bette fell into the accent in bed one night, he packed an overnight bag and left the house.

Of Human Bondage began production on February 12, 1934, on a soundstage on the RKO lot in Hollywood, and Bette quickly became aware that she was not a popular girl among her fellow actors. The cast was largely English, and to a man and woman they resented an American actress playing Mildred—unmindful of the fact that RKO was unable to find any English actress willing to play the role.

Leslie Howard, the handsome, aristocratic Britisher cast as Philip, was already a major star, although his most indelible screen performance wouldn't come until five years later when he played Ashley Wilkes in *Gone With the Wind*. Bette found him "as cold as ice" on the set, resentful of her casting, dismissive of her ability to pull off the role, and unattracted to her physically. Bette was hurt by all of it. "I had admired him for years. I wanted him not only to like me as a person but to approve of me as an actress." Bette realized that neither was the case when she saw Howard sitting on the edge of the set, reading a book, and looking up disinterestedly whenever he had to feed her a cue line.

Howard's attitude changed the moment he saw the first daily rushes. Not only was he amazed at Bette's complete disappearance into her character, but he saw that her performance could easily steal the picture from him if he remained so nonchalant. He didn't.

Bette's total metamorphosis into Mildred Rogers, more evident with each day of filming, astounded everyone—including Bette. Her upbringing, she said, "was what you'd call protected," and she was appalled when she realized that she was able to understand Mildred's "vileness" and "machinations." That she not only felt compassion for the character but could actually empathize with her left her "ashamed."

Mildred's vilest moment comes when Philip refuses her sexual advances and she turns on him ferociously:

> "Yew cad, yew dirty swine! I never cared for yew—not once! I was always makin' a *fool* of yuh! Yuh *bored me stiff*! I *hated* yuh! It made me *sick* when I had to let yuh *kiss me*! I only did it because yuh *begged* me. Yuh *hounded* me, yuh *drove me crazy,* and after yuh kissed me, I always used to wipe my mouth! *Wipe my mouth!* . . . You know what you are, you gimpy-legged monster?! You're a cripple, a cripple, a *cripple*!"

The viciousness and abandon Bette brought to this monologue left the cast and crew gasping, and shocked audiences into horrified silence. No actress before her had allowed herself to be so raw, so bilious, so hateful on screen. What had Bette called upon from within herself to deliver these lines with such indelible bitterness? In her memoirs, she admitted that "I was always Bette Davis," no matter what role she was playing, and she clearly drew upon her own emotions in that scene. It reveals a woman with deep-seated fury at the world around her.

If Bette in *Of Human Bondage* was the first actress to allow herself to be so emotionally naked on screen, she was also the first to insist that she *look* exactly as she should. For her death scene, Bette asked John Cromwell if she could do her own makeup. He agreed. "I let Bette have her head," he said. "I trusted her instincts."

Even so, Cromwell was shocked when he saw Bette walk onto the set. Her skin was sallow, her hair dry and strawlike, her eyes sunken and hollow and underscored by dark pouches. In short, exactly as a dying woman would look. Everyone told Bette that she had overdone it, but she wouldn't budge. "I made it very clear," Bette recalled, "that Mildred was not going to die of a dread disease looking as if a deb had missed her noon nap. The last stages of consumption, poverty and neglect are not pretty and I intended to be convincing-looking." It was unheard-of in 1934 for a star to look bad on film willingly (afterward most actors were still loath to do it), but Bette got her way.

When Leslie Howard first saw her makeup, Bette recalled, he smiled slowly at her and said, *"Damn!"*

In April, Ham went to a public preview of the film in Santa Barbara. Bette stayed home, too nervous to join him. "I was afraid to go because the reaction to that picture meant so much to me," she said soon afterward. "I didn't sleep, naturally. I lay awake, every nerve tense. I worked myself into a lather." When she heard Ham's car in the driveway around midnight, she bolted out of bed and rushed down the stairs. When he came through the front door, Bette tried to read his face. She couldn't. His expression was blank, and he said nothing to her for several long seconds.

Bette thought she'd burst. "*Well?!* Can't you say *something?!*" she shrieked.

Ham finally told her that her performance had been painful for him to watch, and he feared it would be so for others too. "I doubt that it will do your career much good," he told her. "It might even do you harm." Bette knew Ham was being brutally honest, and she went to the next preview to see if he was right. "I was stunned. I was so much nastier than I had expected. So unforgivably mean. And I looked so ghastly." The two-month wait until the picture opened and she would find out whether she had destroyed her career was almost too much for her to bear.

When the film debuted in New York on June 28, Ham was proven right. Audiences were dumbstruck by Mildred's tirades against Philip, shivered and averted their eyes from her horribly dissipated appearance at the end, and actively despised her. Mordaunt Hall, the film critic for *The New York Times,* wrote that "at the first showing yesterday of the picture, the audience was so wrought up over the conduct of this vixen that when Carey finally expressed his contempt for Mildred's behavior, applause was heard from all sides."

It took a while—an agonizingly long while for Bette—but at last it became clear that the critics *were* able to separate their loathing for Mildred from their admiration for Bette's achievement. *Life* magazine called it "probably the best performance ever recorded on the screen by a U.S. actress," and to this day it remains one of the best.

The strongest indication of Bette's accomplishment in *Of Human Bondage* is the impact her performance retains even now. While the film itself, stagy and contrived, dates badly, Bette's acting is just as impressive today as it was in 1934. She brought everything she was, and everything she had learned, to bear for Mildred. She uses her body sinuously early in the film, utilizing her Martha Graham training to the fullest; later she harnesses all the nervousness and kineticism of her own personality to imbue Mildred with an electricity that rivets the viewer's eyes to her. Her vicious tirade against Philip, although it has become familiar because it is shown so often at Davis tributes and in various documentaries, can still shock with its power. Even Bette's reaction in a much quieter moment— when Philip tells her she has tuberculosis and her body crumples as she emits three soft sobs—sends chills down the spine.

As Bette put it without a trace of modesty, "*Bondage* made movie history"—and not only because of her groundbreaking histrionics. When the Academy Award nominations for 1934 were announced on February 5, 1935, both the film and Bette's performance were ignored. Only three actresses—Claudette Colbert, Norma Shearer, and Grace Moore— were nominated, in accordance with Academy rules at the time. Bette's omission created such an uproar among the many who admired her performance that when the ballots were mailed to the seven hundred voters the Academy announced that they would, for the first time, be allowed to write in a name other than one of the three nominees. Even so, Bette came in fourth; Claudette Colbert won the award for *It Happened One Night*—in a role Bette had turned down to play Mildred.

Bette always maintained that Jack Warner actively campaigned against her selection, had even sent letters to his employees ordering them not to vote for her, because he was peeved at having been proven wrong, and because he didn't want another studio to make too much money with one of his players. That makes little sense; J. L. Warner was too shrewd a businessman not to realize that an Oscar for Bette would only increase her future value to *him,* no matter what film won her the award.

What more probably worked against Bette was the Academy's rules at the time. Nominees in each category were chosen not by all the members of a particular branch (acting, directing, writing, etc.) as they are today, but rather by committees made up of selected members of each branch. The Academy, then and for years afterward, was a very conservative organization, and committee members chosen by its president were likely to be just as conservative. Like some others, they may have been uncomfortable with the way Bette as Mildred had etched out the raw underbelly of a certain segment of humanity, and felt it "unbecoming" of the Academy to nominate her performance. *It Happened One Night,* by contrast, was a lighthearted, likable story that was far more popular with mainstream audiences. It received five nominations and won them all.

Still, the uproar over what many pundits called Bette's "unconscionable" snub—and the suspicion by some that the vote could not have been completely honest—helped prompt changes in the rules the following year. Starting with the ninth annual awards in 1936, all members of each branch were allowed to vote on nominations, and five nominees were allowed for each award (ten for Best Picture). The Academy also enlisted the accounting firm of Price, Waterhouse to tabulate the ballots beginning in 1937.

Although she was "heartbroken" not to win an award many people had assured her she couldn't lose, Bette knew that the tremendous play the press gave her snub generated as much favorable publicity as a victory might have. In some respects, she actually felt relieved. "It was just as well," she mused shortly afterward. "It would have looked like fast work —too fast. Not good for me."

With or without what was then called "the Academy statuette," Bette felt she had finally convinced Jack Warner of her abilities, and she was certain he would rush to put her into first-rate motion pictures with topflight production values and juicy, full-dimensional roles. She was wrong, and it didn't take long before she began to think of her employment at Warners as a nightmarish bondage of her own.

EIGHT

H am and Bette lay in bed on a chilly evening in the spring of 1934. Their second-floor bedroom was illuminated only by the flames in the fireplace and Bette's small bedside lamp, under which she was reading the latest script that Warner Brothers had ordered her to do. As Ham drifted off to sleep beside her, a frown hardened on Bette's face. She read a few more pages of the script, then started to leaf through it quickly. Finally she threw it across the room.

"Christ!" she bellowed, startling Ham out of his slumber. "I can't *believe* they still want me to do *crap* like this!"

Ham turned to her groggily. "What's wrong with it?"

"It's *shit,* that's what's wrong with it!" Bette fumbled for a cigarette and lit it, then crossed her arms and stared hard into the fire. "This character they want me to play has *nothing* to do! She's *unnecessary.* It's just another Warner Brothers gangster epic. All they want me for is *window* dressing. Well, I'm not going to do it!"

"If you don't do it," Ham replied, turning his back to her, "they'll suspend you. Now go to sleep."

The scene was not an isolated one, and it illustrates a number of Bette Davis's problems at this time. Professionally, she was often so frustrated she felt like screaming. Bette had expected that after Jack Warner had seen her work in the soon-to-be-released *Of Human Bondage,* he would take her much more seriously as an actress. Instead, he stuck her in a melodrama called *Housewife,* of which she later said, "Dear God, what a horror!" When J.L. told her in June 1934 that her next role would be as Della Street in a Perry Mason mystery, *The Case of the Howling Dog,* she refused to report. As Ham had warned her, she was immediately placed on suspension.

Bette's professional troubles spilled over into her personal life and affected her marriage. She resented Ham's increasing lack of interest in her career. "He had no idea how time-consuming and enervating it was," she said. "There were times when he was as distantly related to my present crises as a fur trader on the Yukon."

Ham shared her resentment, to a degree she never imagined. His wife was no longer the woman he had married three years earlier; Hollywood had changed her. He had never heard Bette swear until her battles with Jack Warner began. She had never smoked until she came to Hollywood; now she "smoked like a chimney" as Ham put it, lifetimes removed from the nineteen-year-old girl who was shocked by Ginny Conroy's first puff. Worst of all for Ham, Bette was so wrapped up in her career that she often neglected him. Even when he wasn't working—and his employment was sporadic—he rarely got to interact with Bette in any meaningful way. She left for the studio at six in the morning and often worked until eight or nine at night. Then she would lie in bed and study her script for the next day's shooting, and put out the lights by 11 in order to get a full night's sleep. Ham wondered whether Bette cared more about her career than she did him; that she pooh-poohed the idea did little to calm his anxiety.

He would never have admitted it to Bette, but Ham had ambivalent feelings about her ambition. He wanted her to succeed to whatever degree she desired, but he worried that every advance in her professional standing would put a further wedge between them, take up more of her time, increase the discrepancy between their incomes. What Bette interpreted as Ham's indifference to her career was just as much cold fear that he would lose the woman with whom he had expected to spend the rest of his life.

One has to feel compassion for Ham Nelson's classically show-business predicament, even if elements of it have become cliché. None was more so than the romantic and sexual jealousy that now tugged at him whenever Bette was in close proximity to one of the many handsome, often sexually profligate leading men with whom she interacted. He had known nothing of Bette's infatuation with George Brent, but when the Nelsons attended a screening of *Front Page Woman,* which paired the two once again, he seethed at the doe-eyed way she stared at Brent through most of the picture. The film's director, Michael Curtiz, was sitting behind them and recalled this exchange: "You must be in love with that guy the way you ogle him constantly," Ham hissed in a too-loud whisper.

Bette took a deep breath. "But Ham, I'm paid to be an actress, and you have to look interested in your leading man."

"Horseshit!" Ham shot back, and walked out of the room.

Bette's suspension over her refusal to do *The Case of the Howling Dog* lasted just two weeks; after her astonishing reviews for *Of Human Bondage,* Warner at last gave her a meaty role as a mentally unbalanced housewife in a Paul Muni picture, *Bordertown,* which she began to film in August 1934. Her performance—especially in a scene where her character goes mad on the witness stand—won critical praise. "The most interesting phase of the picture," *The New York Times* critic noted, "is Bette Davis's performance as a cheap and confused wife who murders her husband and then degenerates under the strain. . . . Miss Davis plays the part with the ugly, sadistic and utterly convincing sense of reality which distinguished her fine performance in *Of Human Bondage.*"

Bette had, in fact, underplayed her "mad scene"; Jack Warner and the film's director, Archie Mayo, wanted her to chew the scenery and act as they felt audiences expected a "nut" would. Bette argued that the crack-up would be far more effective if it was subtle, and she told them, "Believe me, I know something of psychopathic women. I've seen it." Her performance, based more on nervous mannerisms and sudden unexpected movements, was clearly inspired by her experiences with Bobby's breakdowns.

The dramatic reprieve of *Bordertown* didn't last long, however, and Bette once again was maddened by the pictures Warner told her to do. Whether she was playing challenging roles in trashy pictures (*The Girl from 10th Avenue*) or dull, secondary parts in above-average productions (*Special Agent*), it galled her that she was still so often merely a feminine cog in the machinery of Warner's men's pictures. She was well aware that she wasn't being showcased by Warner the way she would be at another studio—MGM, for instance. She knew she had the potential to become one of the screen's premiere stars, and that with that would come the finest roles from Broadway and literature. But she felt so misused that she suspected Jack Warner and his executives of deliberately sabotaging her career: "It seemed that they *wanted* me to fail."

Finally, a year after her triumph in *Of Human Bondage* and after incessant pleading by Bette, her studio finally gave her another challenging role. The film was *Dangerous,* and this time the character, Joyce Heath, was an alcoholic, self-destructive former Broadway star who believes she is a jinx to all who meet her. Dan Bellows, a handsome young architect (played by Franchot Tone, on loan from MGM), falls in love with her, helps her to dry out, and finances her stage comeback. He proposes to her, but she has a husband she's never mentioned, and he won't give Joyce a divorce. In a scene of high melodrama, she deliberately drives herself and her husband into a tree, crying, "It's going to be your life or mine! If you're killed, I'll be free. . . . If I'm killed, it won't matter any longer . . . and if we both die—good riddance!"

Joyce escapes injury, but her husband is paralyzed. Racked with guilt, she pushes Bellows away from her with despicable behavior and vows to take care of her husband. From the hospital, she can see Bellows leave a church after marrying another woman.

The script for *Dangerous* (loosely based on the tragic life of the stage and silent film star Jeanne Eagels, who died of a drug overdose in 1929 at the age of thirty-five) was a dramatic hodgepodge replete with much soap-opera silliness. But it gave Bette a meaty, rangy role to play. Joyce is seen wandering the streets in a drunken haze as the picture opens, then becomes desperate for alcohol at Bellows's country home. The character goes through anger, girlishness, vindictiveness, psychosis, remorse, and rehabilitation. The character, if not the plot, was complex and finely layered.

Dangerous brought Bette together with Franchot Tone; and with her marriage so unsatisfying, she was ripe for infatuation. The thirty-year-old leading man, aristocratically handsome, with his mellifluous voice and a sophisticated demeanor more British than American, was catnip for the ladies, and he dutifully romanced as many of them as he could fit into his schedule. Bette admitted that she "fell in love" with Tone during the filming, and her passion was returned. For the first time, Bette became enmeshed in an extramarital affair—with the man who was now engaged to marry Joan Crawford.

The career of the strikingly handsome MGM actress had long tweaked Bette. She considered her rival less talented than herself, and envied the quality scripts, strong directors, and high production values that MGM routinely gave her. As jealous as she was of Crawford's image as a beautiful and glamorous star, Bette's decision to become sexually involved with Crawford's fiancé might well have carried a dollop of malice. Crawford was alerted to the liaison, but she was working long hours at MGM to finish *I Live My Life,* and there was little she could do.

Clearly, the much-celebrated later feud between Davis and Crawford had its genesis in Franchot Tone's dalliance with Bette.

One afternoon during *Dangerous* production, the film's producer, Harry Joe Brown, walked through the open door of Bette's dressing room and stopped dead in his tracks. There were Bette and Franchot in what he delicately described as "a very tight position." When they saw Brown, neither seemed perturbed. Tone just laughed, and Bette asked him to close the door when he left. Later, Brown recalled, "they were all over each other on the set."

Tone returned Bette's passion, but not her love. For him, she was just another in a long line of conquests that had begun in college, when he was called Jack the Ripper—for all the panties he'd torn off young women in the back seat of his car. When the filming ended, so did the affair, and soon thereafter Tone married Joan Crawford—who never forgave Bette for diddling with her fiancé.

Although the production values on *Dangerous* were typically Warner cheapjack, Bette's acting knocked the film up a few rungs, and the critics raved. Grace Kingsley said in the *Los Angeles Times* that Davis "seems actual flesh and blood in *Dangerous.* That's how penetratingly alive she is and how electric, varied as to mood and real her performance in the picture." André Sennwald in *The New York Times* thought that "This Davis girl is rapidly becoming one of the most interesting of our screen actresses."

More and more, audiences and critics had begun to notice and comment on Bette's oddly nervous mannerisms, especially in moments of high drama. She seemed sometimes like a puppet on a string, or a toy wound too tightly. Some viewers loved this kinetic quality about Bette, others found her jerky movements off-putting. E. Arnot Robertson, in *Picture Post,* gave Bette an interesting and perceptive notice for *Dangerous,* one that harkened back unknowingly to her Salem ancestry: "I think Bette Davis would have been burned as a witch if she had lived two or three hundred years ago. She gives the curious feeling of being charged with power that can find no ordinary outlet."

This time, between the quality of the performance and the Academy's chagrin over her *Bondage* snub, there was no denying Bette the Best Actress prize. On February 7, 1936, she became the first Warner Brothers actress nominated for the award, and on March 5 she won it. Bette later recalled that as she stood behind the podium, clutching the fifteen-inch-tall gold-plated man, she peered down at her mother, sitting between Bobby and Ham. Ruthie looked proud and regal, beaming as the applause rose around her. Bette thought to herself, *If I don't quiet the audience down and accept the award, Mother will!* To hear Bette tell it, she might not have minded: "In a sense, it was Ruthie's triumph and I knew it."

When Bette returned to her table, she inspected the statuette and noticed something intriguing about it: the well-built man holding the scepter had a backside that reminded her of Ham's. Harmon O. Nelson's middle name was Oscar, and although he hated it (and hadn't told Bette until after their marriage what the "O" stood for), she decided to call her award "Oscar." The press picked up on it, and a nickname was born.

Bette was brought back to earth in her moment of triumph by a confrontation in the ladies' room with an irate Ruth Waterbury, the editor of *Photoplay*. Waterbury harangued Bette about her attire, a loose-fitting, simple dress with a small print and wide white lapels: "How *could* you? A print! You could be dressed for a family dinner. Your photograph is going around the *world*. Don't you realize? Aren't you aware? You don't look like a Hollywood star!" *Oh, that again!* Bette thought. By the end of the tirade Waterbury had backed Bette up against the pink-tiled walls like the object of a firing squad.

Waterbury later said she suspected that Bette had purposely dressed down to show her disdain for the award, but Bette denied that. The dress "was very simple," she recalled, "and very expensive." But with the evening's attire formal—Ham wore white tie and tails, Ruthie an evening dress and fur—Bette *did* look a bit like the hired help. She didn't care. She was determined to carve out an individualistic niche for herself in Hollywood, despite all the dire predictions of professional disaster hurled her way. The determination sprang largely from her conviction that she needed to be different to succeed, but there was also about it a soupçon of in-your-face contrariness. What Ruth Waterbury had really told her in that powder room, Bette suspected, was that she was no longer free to do exactly as she wished. Her reaction? "Never say this to a Yankee."

Harlow Davis sat across from Bette and Ham and sipped the soup that Bette's maid, Dell Pfeiffer, had served them. Harlow had come to Los Angeles on company business, and he telephoned Bette to ask if he could take her to dinner and meet her husband. Flustered, Bette asked him if he would like to come to her home for supper, and he agreed. During the meal, her hands shook so badly she couldn't hold the spoon without splashing the soup; finally she pushed the bowl away.

Ham carried the day, engaging Harlow in conversation as Bette sat silently, conflicted emotions churning inside her, angry that Ruthie and Bobby had refused to join them but understanding their reluctance, especially as the evening progressed. As so often before, her father seemed incapable of giving her a compliment. When the subject turned to Bette's career, Harlow said he thought her acting in *Of Human Bondage* had been "hysterical." While Bette looked away, Ham said, "But surely you enjoyed *Dangerous*? Of course you know Bette won the Academy Award for her performance."

"Yes," Harlow conceded, "that was a good job. But I did think the movie was trashy and tasteless."

It went on like that for the rest of the evening, and by the time Harlow left Bette's stomach was in knots. "Christ, he'll *never* change!" Bette railed at Ham, who tried to soothe her by saying that her father was obviously a cold and supercilious man and she shouldn't let him get to her. It was scant comfort.

When Harlow returned to Boston, he wrote Bette a note. He thanked her for dinner and added, "Your husband is a nice young boy." *How contemptuous he can be!* Bette thought. *How superior!*

As 1936 approached, Bette's career was building in an ever-increasing crescendo, and she should have been the happiest girl in the world. She wasn't. Her problems with Ham had mounted in direct proportion to her successes; the financial disparity between them increased every time she got a raise, and she was now making $1,350 a week. Ham had given in a little; he and Bette now lived in Greta Garbo's former house in Brentwood. There were more of the creature comforts that Bette felt she simply *had* to have in order to project the "proper image" of a movie star—servants, fancy clothes, grand transportation. (Forgotten in these instances, it seems, was her often vociferous determination to resist the trappings of stardom.) Clearly, Bette could be as complex and contradictory as her better characters. And the more his wife needed, the less Ham was able to supply her with it.

They both had begun to fear that theirs was, as Bette put it, a "misalliance," but neither would admit it. Each hoped that their problems would somehow go away, but instead the chasm between them widened.

In her memoirs, Bette called the marriage at this point "antiseptic"—surely a death knell for any romantic union.

Still, the thought of his wife with another man enraged Ham. He had heard whispers about Bette and Franchot Tone, but refused to believe them. Now, in retrospect, he wasn't so sure, and his jealousies exploded early in 1936 when a young Warner contract player, Ross Alexander, developed an obsession for Bette, undeterred by her marital status. A handsome, well-built, bisexual twenty-eight-year-old, Alexander was tortured by his homosexual yearnings and compensated for them with indiscreet and desperate pursuits of strong-willed women, despite his marriage to the actress Anne Nagel. While Bette was vulnerable to romantic overtures, she sensed Alexander's sexual confusions and shied away from him. She turned down his advances with a flip riposte ("I'm a married woman!"), but Alexander was persistent. He constantly maneuvered for a role in one of Bette's pictures, and told anyone who would listen that if he could only do a love scene with her she would respond to him "like a wildcat."

Word spread around the lot about Alexander's interest and Bette's lack of it, and he never was given a role in a Davis movie. Instead, he left a florid love note pinned to her dressing room door. As Alexander's luck would have it, Ham made a rare visit to the studio that day and found the letter inside an envelope marked, "To my beloved one, Bette." Alexander, in his ardor, had written the note in a way that implied that Bette returned his passion and that their love had been consummated. Nelson hit the roof. He confronted Bette on the set and waved the note in her face. "I want you to explain this!" he shouted.

As the cast and crew first grew quiet, then pretended not to pay attention, Bette pulled Ham off to the side behind some scenery and read the letter. As she crumpled it in her hand she told Ham, "That queer is having *pipedreams*. He's trying to prove his *manhood*—or something—and he knows I see right through him."

"I'll kill him for this," Ham sputtered.

"Deal with him as you like," Bette haughtily replied as she whirled around and started back to the set. "Just get him off my fucking *back*!"

When Nelson found Ross—in a men's washroom—he picked him up by the lapels and slammed him into a wall. "It's my *wife* you're writing mush notes to," Ham shouted, "and she wants no part of it. Leave her alone!" Alexander tried to punch his way out of the clinch, but Ham was bigger and Ross wound up on the floor, his eye so blackened he couldn't start his next picture for weeks. When Alexander didn't let up in his pursuit, Bette started to taunt him about his insecure manhood.

Crushed, he complained to Jerry Asher that Bette was "a merciless bitch."

"No, Ross," Asher replied. "She just wants you to get off it."

Jack Warner, as was the custom in such cases, was the first person notified of Alexander's suicide. Around Christmas, the actor had picked up a male hitchhiker for sex, and the man had threatened him with exposure unless he was paid handsomely for his silence. Frantic, Alexander unburdened himself to his studio publicist, who along with the Warner lawyers "took care" of the matter. But Alexander was mortified by the disclosure of his indiscretion; and the humiliation he felt at Bette's treatment of him, added to his shame over his homosexual cravings, proved too much to bear. In January, he fired a bullet into his brain.

Alexander's death left Bette stunned and guilt-ridden over the way she had treated him. She asked Jack Warner if there was anything she could do, but he advised her only to keep quiet. Even before the police were called, Warner had ordered that Alexander's house be ransacked and any letters from him to Bette Davis destroyed. The scandal would be bad enough without dragging the Davis girl into it.

While Bette grappled with her romantic problems, her twenty-five-year-old sister finally found some happiness. Bobby fell in love with the fair-haired, boyishly handsome twenty-year-old socialite Robert Pelgram, whom the Davises had known back in Ogunquit as "Little Bobby Pelgram." He wore navy blazers and white flannel pants, flew his own airplane, and had a charming devil-may-care insouciance that Bobby loved.

Pelgram was Bobby's first serious suitor; his love for her made her feel for the first time that she, not her sister, was the center of the universe. When Pelgram asked her to marry him, her emotional problems and institutionalization seemed a million years away. Accompanied by Bette and Ham, the couple was married in Tijuana on August 18, 1935—the Nelsons' third anniversary.

When Jack Warner told Bette that he had cast her opposite Leslie Howard and Humphrey Bogart in his version of the prestigious stage success *The Petrified Forest,* she was so thrilled she absolutely gushed her thanks. Warner was embarrassed by her effusiveness, especially since he knew it wasn't any more demanding a role than the ones she had complained about in the recent past. "I think I like Bette better when she's fightin' and fussin'," he told Hal Wallis.

He didn't have to wait long to get his wish. Bette had been so eager to appear in a quality production that she failed at first to see her role's shortcomings, but they became clear to her as filming progressed. Again she was little more than a female addendum to a man's picture, and her character, an idealistic young truck-stop waitress, offered her thin challenge except the chance to prove, as one critic pointed out, that she did not "have to be hysterical to give a grand portrayal."

Bette approached the end of her tether with Warner Brothers when her next two films, *The Golden Arrow* and *Satan Met a Lady,* returned her to dismal second-rate fare. The final indignity was *God's Country and the Woman,* in which Jack Warner expected her to play a female lumberjack. This one forced a noisy confrontation in Warner's office. Crimson with fury, Bette screamed at him, "I won't do it! *Satan Met a Lady* was bad enough, but this is absolute *tripe!*"

Warner tried to calm her. "Bette, c'mon. You'll have George Brent as your costar. And it will be in *Technicolor!*"

"I won't do it."

"Listen," Warner cajoled. "If you'll be reasonable and do this picture, I promise you a great role when you finish. I've just optioned a wonderful novel that isn't out yet. It's called *Gone With the Wind.* You were *born* to play the heroine."

"Yeah," Bette snapped acidly as she spun away from him and headed for the door. "I'll bet it's a *pip!*"

Preproduction began on *God's Country and the Woman* in the late spring of 1936, and Jack Warner fully expected Bette to show up for work. Instead, she fled to the house in Laguna Beach she'd purchased as a getaway, and Warner put her on a three-month suspension. It was a blow, because Bette's expenses were high. She had renegotiated her contract early in 1935, and she was now making $1,600 a week, but somehow it never seemed to be enough. A great deal of the money went to taxes, or to Ruthie to keep up the Hollywood house Bette had bought for her ("More elegant than mine"), or to helping Bobby and her husband out occasionally, or to the ever-growing expenses of keeping up appearances of being a star and paying for two houses of her own. Bette wouldn't be able to live without her salary for very long.

She had been suspended briefly several times before, but this was the longest layoff yet, and she was worried about the standard clause in her contract that allowed the studio to add the months of suspension to her total term of service. At this rate she could remain a slave to Warner Brothers for the rest of her life.

Still, she wouldn't relent. If she didn't insist on better treatment, she felt, she would be "in bondage for years, with no choice but to work in bad pictures and with bad directors—so that soon I would have no career at all." On June 6, Bette met with Warner in his office and told him that she wanted a new contract that would grant her a salary increase, the right to do radio work and make outside pictures, and approval of her scripts and cameramen.

Warner told her that he couldn't grant any of her creative requests but he assured her, once again, that he was always on the lookout for "good stories" for her. He would agree, he said, to give her a new seven-year contract that would raise her pay immediately to $2,000 per week and increase it every year until she was making $3,500 a week—but only if she would agree to do *God's Country and the Woman.*

Bette said she'd think about it. When Warner called her ten days later, she told him that he would have to talk to her attorney, Dudley Furse. At two-thirty on the excessively hot Thursday afternoon of June 18, Warner met with Furse and Bette's business manager, Vernon Wood. The two men sat in front of Warner's massive oak desk along with Warner's outside lawyer, Ralph Lewis, and in-house counsel, R. J. Obringer. After the five men commiserated for a while about the heat, Furse said that Bette was happy with the financial offer Warner had made to her, but that she still insisted on the creative concessions she had asked for.

"I cannot do that, gentlemen," Warner replied. As Wood began to speak up in argument, Warner interrupted him with a loud slap of his hand on his desktop. "It is amazing to me," Warner boomed while beads of sweat popped out of Furse's forehead, "that we can take a totally unknown individual like Bette Davis, spend money and time to groom her into a star, and pay her extremely high salaries, only to have her walk out on her contract and make outrageous demands. What are we supposed to do, give in to her whims whenever she has them?! This kind of nonsense is going to destroy this industry. Every actor in Hollywood will 'walk out' of their contracts if we give in to Bette Davis and there won't be any motion picture industry left! I will increase her salary, gentlemen—her pictures have made a lot of money for us—but I will not give an inch on any of her other demands!"

The quintessential Bette Davis character—Margo Channing in *All About Eve*, 1950.

One-year-old Ruth Elizabeth Davis on an outing with her mother Ruthie, *left,* and her nurse, Mrs. Hall, spring 1909.

(Culver Pictures)

(Photofest)

A revealing Davis family portrait, 1910—outgoing "Betty" plays to the camera while her shy baby sister "Bobby" looks sad and stern father Harlow scowls.

(Culver)

By the age of nine, Betty was already head and shoulders above her eight-year-old sister, literally and figuratively.

A rare 1917 photo of Betty with her father, who was thirty-one. Shortly afterward, he was out of her life for good.

(Lester Glassner Collection / Neal Peters)

Recovering from the burns she suffered when a candle set her Santa Claus costume on fire, 1919.

Her first stage triumph, as The Moth, 1925. Afterward, her mother and sister looked at her "as if they'd never seen me before."

Bette's acting school roommate, Virginia Conroy, shocked her when she lit up a cigarette.

Bette's first screen test, made while she was at acting school, with classmates Ted Scharf and Ginny Conroy in 1928. Nothing came of it for any of the participants.

On Cape Cod in the summer of 1928, Bette and her puppy Boojum pose with, *left to right,* Ginny Conroy, Ruthie, and Bobby.

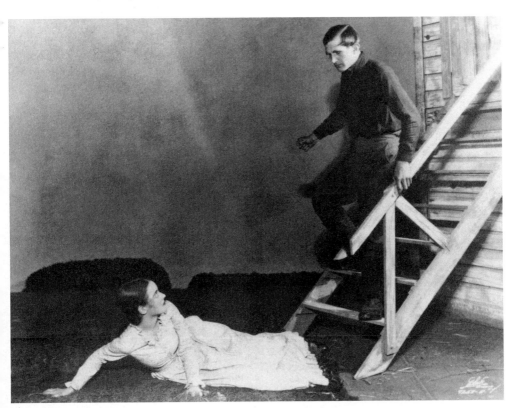

A dramatic moment with Grover Burgess in *The Earth Between,* Bette's off-Broadway New York debut, spring 1929.

A striking portrait of Bette that she sent to Broadway casting agents throughout 1929 and 1930.

Bette arrives in Hollywood with Boojum and Ruthie on December 13, 1930. A Universal representative left the train station without her because he hadn't seen anyone who looked "remotely like an actress."

A scene from Bette's first film, *Bad Sister,* 1931. Universal chief Carl Laemmle said she had "about as much sex appeal as Slim Summerville." Summerville is at the far right in this picture.

A breakthrough after six dreadful films: *The Man Who Played God* with George Arliss for Warner Brothers, 1932. The studio soon put her under contract.

(Nickens)

In August 1932, Bette married her boarding-school sweetheart, Harmon O. ("Ham") Nelson. When she first met him, Bette recalled, she found herself "wading in those velvety brown eyes."

One of Bette's earliest Hollywood portraits, 1931.

With Leslie Howard in the film that gave Bette her first great dramatic opportunity, *Of Human Bondage*, 1934.

Five indifferent films later, Bette finally had another juicy role as the alcoholic actress in *Dangerous* with Franchot Tone, 1935.

The highest accolade: Bette wins an Academy Award for *Dangerous* in 1936, along with Best Actor Victor McLaglen. She nicknamed the statuette "Oscar," Ham's middle name, because its backside reminded her of Ham's.

After too many dreary roles, Bette walked out on her Warner contract in the fall of 1936 and fled to England, where the studio sued her for breach of contract. She lost the case.

The movie—and the man—that changed Bette's professional life: on the set of *Jezebel* with director William Wyler, 1937. During filming, she and Wyler began a tempestuous extramarital affair.

The Oscar Bette thought she deserved—Best Actress of 1938 for *Jezebel*. Spencer Tracy was chosen Best Actor for *Boys' Town*.

As Julie Marsden in *Jezebel,* Bette was more controlled—and more beautiful—than ever before on screen.

September 1938: Bette meets millionaire Howard Hughes at a Hollywood fund-raiser. Their indiscreet affair brought Bette and Ham's marriage to a bitter end.

With Errol Flynn in *The Private Lives of Elizabeth and Essex*. Although she was sexually attracted to Flynn, she resisted becoming "another notch on his belt."

With George Brent in the popular 1939 tearjerker *Dark Victory*. Bette had been attracted to Brent for years, and they began an affair.

Divorced from Ham, Bette dines out with her mother in Hollywood, circa 1940. Ruthie's extravagance with Bette's money caused heated arguments between the two.

Bette and her second husband, Arthur Farnsworth, make the Hollywood scene in 1941. The marriage was marred by Farnsworth's furtive drinking.

(Nickens)

The venomous Regina Giddens of *The Little Foxes* gave Bette a meaty role, but the contentious filming marked the end of her professional relationship with William Wyler.

According to notes made by Obringer, Warner calmed down when conversation turned to the fine points of his financial offer to Bette, and the meeting ended on an amiable note as Furse and Wood assured Warner that he was being tremendously fair and that they would do their best to persuade Bette to accept his offer and return to make *God's Country and the Woman.*

She refused, and with that she made it clear that her main concerns were creative, not monetary. Convinced that he would not be able to sway Bette any other way, Warner began a press campaign designed to pressure her through public disapproval. The studio quietly leaked the word to columnists that Bette was making $5,000 per week and expressed outrage at her dissatisfaction with this salary at the height of the Depression. The gossipist Louella Parsons, always the ally of the studios in conflicts of this kind, wrote dismissively on June 20 that Bette was just "pouting about money and other things."

Bette was, of course, making less than one-third what the studio claimed, but still she wasn't likely to garner much sympathy among the masses: the average *annual* salary in America was only slightly more than Bette made in a single week. Her contention that her problems with the studio had nothing to do with money, on the other hand, was no less deceptive than Warner's exaggeration of her salary. In fact she had been badgering Warner for a raise for months; she argued that her Academy Award had brought prestige to the studio, and her name was now, as she put it, "directing people into the theaters." Her recent films had grossed between $400,000 and $800,000 at the box office, princely sums in those days, and Bette felt she deserved a heftier share of the profits.

She later explained why. "Your professional life is short and if you do not make enough to protect yourself after the public is tired of you, you will be broke and jobless when your career is ended. . . . Your pay must equal that of other performers whose popularity and drawing power are comparable to your own. . . . I make these observations gratuitously because money was not a point at issue."

Of course it was, but when Bette refused to accept the raise Warner offered her without other concessions, she made it clear that the quality of her films was the main issue for her. If Jack Warner wasn't willing to grant her more control over that quality, she would just have to sit out this suspension.

Bette's layoff might have gone the way of the others—with her return to work amid glowing promises of better scripts—had it not been for the appearance of Ludovico Toeplitz, an Italian producer working in

England. Toeplitz convinced Bette that Jack Warner did *not* have the right to keep her from working, and that furthermore she should be working for *him*—for $60,000 a film.

She decided to do so, and thereby set in motion a series of events that led her to flee the United States under cover of night and face a groundbreaking—and personally devastating—lawsuit in Britain.

NINE

B ette heard a sharp rap on the ship cabin's door. She jumped out of bed and scurried into the bathroom to hide as Ham got up and opened the door to a young porter who announced, "There's a cable for Mrs. Nelson!" Ham signed for the wire, and once the messenger was safely gone, Bette came out and read some words of encouragement from Ruthie. For the entire trip, Bette said, "I spent all my time hiding in the johnnie so that Warner Brothers couldn't serve me with papers."

Bette had signed a contract with Ludovico Toeplitz to star in two of his productions, including one with Maurice Chevalier as her costar. She liked the projects and she had admired Toeplitz's work, which included Elisabeth Bergner's *Catherine the Great* and *The Private Life of Henry VIII*, which won a Best Actor Oscar for Charles Laughton in 1933. Toeplitz, a dapper man with a beard that made him resemble England's King George V, produced quality films, and he promised Bette everything Warner wouldn't: top-notch production values, first-rate directors, script approval.

He also came through with his promise of $60,000 per film, nearly a year's salary for Bette under her Warner contract. When the studio threatened to seek a court order against her deal with Toeplitz, the producer assured her that they wouldn't be able to win one because he planned to make the pictures in England. As long as she could get out of the United States without being served legal papers, Bette was assured, she'd be home free.

She went to great lengths to avoid process servers. She and Ham flew from Los Angeles to Vancouver at midnight one Saturday, since legal service couldn't be made on Sunday, with Bette wearing a Garboesque hat pulled down to cover half her face. "Every time the plane stopped in the U.S.," she recalled, "I felt like a convict." The Nelsons then took a train across Canada—where they felt safe from American authorities—and sailed from Montreal to Britain aboard the

Duchess of Bedford, where Bette cowered in the bathroom whenever there was an unexpected knock on the door. She needn't have—Warner Brothers didn't know she had left the country until she surfaced in Scotland.

The ship docked at Greenock on August 18—Bette and Ham's fourth anniversary—and Bette was in a carefree mood. She was convinced that nothing would stand in the way of her films with Toeplitz; even if the case went to court, she was advised, she would win it. She was excited to visit a foreign country for the first time, and she looked upon this sojourn as a second honeymoon, one that might salvage her deteriorating marriage. Six thousand miles away from Hollywood, she reasoned, "we might find ourselves again."

The visit began well. She and Ham rented a car and toured Scotland; they gaped at centuries-old castles, bicycled over heather-dotted hills, and played darts in village pubs. Bette made an emotional pilgrimage to Wales, her Davis ancestral home, but couldn't find any relatives. Then she and Ham trekked south to England, where they stayed at the beach resort of Brighton "to watch the people" on their way to London. There, they stayed at the Savoy Hotel and Bette met with Toeplitz and the director Monty Banks to discuss *I'll Take the Low Road,* her first project. By now the English press had latched onto the story of Bette's flight from Hollywood, and she was startled by the enormous play it received on Fleet Street's front pages: "I had not realized how well known I was abroad."

Early in September, Toeplitz sent Bette to Paris for costume fittings, and she felt a connection to France as strong as she had to Wales; she had gone from the homeland of the Davises to that of the LeFievres in a matter of weeks. "I had the most incredible feeling of at-homeness there." She loved the French food, so much lighter than the British, which had put weight on her with its heavy, meaty breakfasts, shepherd's pies, and Devonshire creams. When she left Paris she found she had lost the ten pounds she'd gained.

By the time she left England again, she would wish she had the weight back.

❧

Bette got the bad news the moment she got back to London. While she had been in Paris, Jack Warner had sailed to England and met with Toeplitz in an attempt to convince him that his contract with Bette was illegal. The producer was adamant that he had every right to use her in pictures made outside the United States. Warner wasted no time; he retained one of Britain's most celebrated barristers, Sir Patrick Hastings, and obtained a preliminary injunction that restrained Bette from working for Toeplitz until the case could be heard in the English courts.

Bette had been sure the matter would never come to this, and she was both frightened and infuriated. As she usually did when challenged, she dug in her heels. She was Davis against Goliath, and this was no time to back down: her career as an actress, she was sure, rested on her determination to stay the course.

Her first setback came when the barrister she had hired to represent her, Sir William Jowitt, asked for a $10,000 retainer in advance, as was the British custom. Bette was at a loss: she hadn't been paid for months by the studio, she wouldn't be paid anything by Toeplitz until she began work for him, and she didn't have the money. Ham decided to return to the States since there had been some talk of a musical gig for him in New York before he left, and he told Bette he couldn't let the opportunity pass. If things turned out badly, he reminded her, they might well have nothing to live on except his income.

Bette understood his position intellectually, but emotionally she was crushed. The second honeymoon she had hoped for hadn't materialized; it was clear that her problems with Ham couldn't be solved by a change of scenery. And, rationally or not, she felt deserted by her husband at the moment she needed him most. She had supported him all the way, and now he was leaving her to "face the fight of my life alone." Any income he might make in New York, she felt, would be "negligible in comparison to the moral support I craved at that moment." As she stood and watched his steamer leave the dock at Southampton, she felt dazed and more alone than she ever had before. Fear, loneliness, emotional pain gripped her—then, contempt for what she saw as Ham's bailout. "It was the most tragic day of my life."

Bette returned to London and took a tiny inside-court room at the Park Lane Hotel—because she needed quiet, she told the manager, but in fact it was to save money. She stayed in bed most of the time, surrounded by her unopened steamer trunks, crying. What was she to do? Ham had urged her to give up the fight and return home, and so had everyone else whose advice she sought. But she couldn't bring herself to do it. She felt she was *right*, and to give up just because the odds were long went against every ounce of Yankee in her.

∾

Immensely relieved when Sir William agreed to forgo the advance payment, Bette girded herself for the trial, which began on Wednesday,
October 14, in the King's Bench Divisional Court. She recalled feeling
tremendous awe as she sat in the huge courtroom, intimidated by its
imposing aura, its heavy oak benches redolent with history, and its black-
robed, white-bewigged barristers presided over by the redoubtable Mr.
Justice Branson. She soaked in the atmosphere, excited in spite of everything, and told herself this was the greatest drama of her life.

While Bette drank in the details around her, everyone else's eyes
were glued to her. The British press had worked itself into a lather over
the case, and Bette's every move and comment had been reported
breathlessly for weeks. Reporters noted she looked wan and thin as the
trial opened, easily fifteen pounds lighter than she'd been when she arrived. And despite all the stuffy British tradition of the proceedings, the
press gave the trial something of a carnival atmosphere with its daily
reports of Bette's attire: much was made of the fact that she wore the
same blue-and-red checked tweed coat and matching beret three days in
a row. Fashion sticklers noted, however, that she did change her shoes.

As Sir Patrick Hastings began his opening arguments for Warner
Brothers, Bette caught his eye and felt a shiver. She faced a formidable
opponent, and she quickly realized that not just her studio but the entire
motion picture industry was aligned against her. Hastings's characterization of Bette's complaints against Warner, delivered in a booming baritone that filled the enormous chamber from corner to corner, made her
want "to kill him":

> "This really is a case of great importance to this industry, because
> [Bette's] contract . . . is the common form . . . on which
> most big film companies in America engage most big film
> stars. . . . What this young lady is seeking to do, in effect, is to
> tear up the contract. . . .
>
> "A series of defenses have been put forward of this nature: It
> is said, 'You (the plaintiffs) broke your contract; you wanted me
> to play more than six hours a day; you either give me too many
> films or too few.'
>
> "Regarding these, I venture to suggest that your lordship
> will doubtless come to the conclusion that this really is rather a
> naughty young lady and that what she wants is more money."

Bette fairly jumped out of her seat at that last remark, but her lawyer grabbed her arm and pulled her back. "That's just what he wants," Sir William whispered to her. "He wants you to blow up so he can point out to the judge that you're an unstable, irresponsible woman."

She had to bite her lip again and again to keep from screaming as Sir Patrick mocked her. "Miss Davis has characterized her employment at Warner Brothers as 'slavery.' The 'slavery' had a silver-lining because the 'slave' was, to say the least, well-remunerated." He cited her salary, incorrectly, as $1,350 a week and added with a smile, "If anybody wants to put me into perpetual servitude on that basis of remuneration I shall be prepared to consider it."

When Sir Patrick concluded his harangue, Bette ran the gauntlet of press and fans outside the courtroom and returned to her hotel. She was shaken. She had expected, no matter what the outcome of the trial, to be treated with respect as a serious artist concerned over the direction of her career. To be belittled as "a naughty young lady" left her uncomprehending. Her only comfort came from the knowledge that the next morning, Sir William Jowitt would present her side of the story.

Sir William's opening sentence sent a shock wave through the courtroom: "Your lordship, I will call no witnesses." The press and observers gasped and then groaned, eager as they were to see Bette's "performance" on the witness stand. Clearly, Sir William felt it ill-advised to serve up his emotional client to the opposition. Sir Patrick was so angry not to have the chance to grill Bette that he tore off his white wig and threw it across the room—a *very* dramatic gesture in a British courtroom.

Bette felt vindication near as Sir William addressed piece by piece the unfair aspects of her contract. He pointed out that Bette was required to do anything the studio requested of her, including making political appearances, but that she couldn't appear publicly without their permission. She was not allowed to work for another company, but Warner Brothers could lend her out to anyone without consulting her. She was required to work as many hours a day as her director thought necessary, six days a week. She had no say in the roles she played, nor in any aspect of any production. If she refused to play a role, she could be suspended, and the length of the suspension would be added to the term of the agreement. This, Sir William argued forcefully, could amount to "a lifetime of servitude."

Now they can see what I'm up against, Bette thought as Sir William ticked off clause after restrictive clause. *Surely Mr. Justice Branson will see that it's wrong.*

After Sir William concluded his opening remarks, Jack Warner took the stand. Under examination by barristers for both sides, Warner told the court that Bette's refusal to work for him had already cost his company huge sums of money. "We generally have many films of the artist already produced but not yet exhibited," he explained. "If the artist 'walks out' the value of the films depreciates greatly." Warner claimed that theater owners would be less inclined to exhibit a Bette Davis picture after her walkout, but presented no evidence to back up this dubious assertion.

Warner wasn't entirely honest on the stand. Asked whether Bette had ever complained to him about the quality of her film roles, he replied, "No one ever complained to me that her parts were unsuitable." Under cross-examination by Sir William, he "admitted" that "on one or two occasions, she did. Sometime in 1935 she said words to the effect that her part was not so big."

To prove that Bette's main concern was more money, Sir Patrick put into evidence a letter Bette had written Warner earlier in the year. "In reference to our talk today," she wrote, "it seemed to me our main problem is getting together on the money. You, as head of your firm, naturally know what your concern can afford. I have no desire to be off your list and I feel sure you do not wish it either. I also know that you have the right to keep me from working—a great unhappiness to me because I enjoy working. . . . I am the kind of person who thrives under change . . . mentally a change does me good, makes me do better work. I also am ambitious to become known as a great actress—I might, who can tell?

"As a happy person I can work like hell," she went on, "as an unhappy one I make myself and everybody around me unhappy. Also, I know, and you do too, in a business where you have a fickle public to depend on, the money should be made when you mean something, not when the public has had time to tell you to go to hell."

Sir William got Warner to concede that Bette was "seriously and deeply interested in her acting," and that any actress might be "heartbroken" if made to play parts that were unsuited to her. But he denied that she had ever been forced to appear in a substandard picture, and pointed to the fact that he had paid $110,000 for the film rights to *The Petrified Forest,* the highest purchase price for a play to that date.

Bette's barrister then turned to her work schedule, and Warner denied that she had to work late into the night very often. "Few people work more than eight hours a day," he said. "I think Miss Davis's record-sheets will show that she averaged five or six hours a day over twenty-five weeks." But he added that Bette's request for a 6 P.M. quitting time could make it "impossible" to complete a film on schedule.

Bette squirmed restlessly in her seat, frustrated by all this discussion of what she saw as peripheral issues. But Sir William was attempting to prove, point by point, that Bette's contract made her "a piece of chattel," that it was unfair, and thus the contract should be declared invalid.

As he closed his questioning of Warner, Sir William showed him a drawing of a scantily clad Bette in a poster for one of her movies. "Would you like to see a woman you were fond of portrayed to the public like that?"

"If she is a professional artist," Warner replied, "it is part of her duty."

"If she undertakes to act for you, it is for you to select what sort of films she should act in, and I suppose it is for you to select what sort of posters are prepared to portray the part she plays?"

"No, not exactly. There is a committee in New York to pass all posters and there is nothing lewd, licentious or vulgar allowed to be posted."

"Whatever part you choose to call upon her to play, if she thinks she can play it, whether it is distasteful and cheap, she has to play it?"

"Yes. She must play it."

Sir William's closing argument on Friday afternoon, October 16, left Bette certain she would win her case. "I do not suppose," he said, "that any artist can turn on his inspiration as one turns on a tap. His mood and inspiration have to suit. It is a contract which can be rendered tolerable and bearable by a human being only if the persons for whom the artist is working show tact, good temper and consideration." Implicit, of course, was that Jack Warner had shown none of those qualities in his dealings with Bette. Mr. Justice Branson promised to announce his decision the following Monday, and as Bette left the courtroom she shot Jack Warner an unsubtle "So there!" expression.

She left London for the weekend, staying at an inexpensive cottage in Brighton (where she had to put a shilling in a meter to turn on the heat). The wait threatened to unravel her. She paced up and down the seashore, smoking furiously, the icy late-fall winds off the Atlantic Ocean biting at her face. She ran the testimony over and over again through her mind. She was, she has said, "a wreck," deeply melancholy about being alone, fearful that she might lose the case, furious with Jack Warner for his smooth lies and Warner's barrister for his blustery derision. The hours seemed like years to Bette before Monday dawned, and she remained at the beach rather than appear in court to hear the decision.

Sir William knew the case was lost when Mr. Justice Branson, in a preface to his decision, described the circumstances that had led to the lawsuit: "In June of this year Miss Davis, for no discoverable reason except that she wanted more money, declined to be further bound by the contract, left the U.S.A., and in September entered into an agreement in this country with a third person."

Bette was appalled by the fact that her artistic frustrations had been completely dismissed by the judge, but she would have lost the case no matter how sympathetic the court had been to her reasons for breaking the contract. For Justice Branson based his decision on a bedrock legal tenet: a contract is a contract. Warner Brothers had asked for a very narrow decision—whether Bette could legally work for someone else in spite of the clauses in her contract that forbade it. The court said no. She had signed the document, Branson noted, "with her eyes open," and contracts would be worthless if their provisions could be violated at will and without penalty.

Branson did agree with precedents that contractees could not be *forced* to perform under a contract, and said that while Bette would not be "compelled" to go back to work for Warner Brothers, she "might be tempted to" considering her salary. In either event he stressed that her contract's "negative covenants"—such as those that forbade her to work for a competitor—were fair and reasonable, and he agreed with Jack Warner's assertion that Bette's walkout could adversely affect the profitability of her already finished product.

The court granted Warner an injunction against Bette's working for anyone else in England, but for just three years. Bette could return to Britain in 1939 and work, for Toeplitz or anyone else, but that was a moot point; she could not afford to remain idle and unpaid for thirty-six months.

What was left of Bette's spirit crumpled when she got all this news. She told the press the decision was "a real sock in the teeth. I'm a bit bewildered. . . . I thought at least that it would have been a partial victory for me and for everybody else with one of these body-and-soul contracts. . . . I suppose I have been made an example of as a warning to anybody else."

Over the next few days, bundled up in sweaters, Bette could be seen trudging desolately along the beach at Brighton. Sir William told the court that Bette would appeal, and Branson stayed the execution of the injunction. By now Bette had lost nearly twenty-five pounds, felt weak and sickly, and couldn't face another day alone. She cabled her mother in California and asked her to come and lend her moral support. Ruthie packed her bags.

Just before she left, Ruthie got a call from Ham, and to her shock, he asked to speak to Bette. "She's not here," Ruthie replied, her voice dripping with anger and sarcasm, "she's in *England*!" She was appalled that Ham could be so oblivious of Bette's plight not to know that she was still out of the country. She wanted, she later said, to kill him.

Ham agreed to meet Ruthie in New York, and she was somewhat placated by his obvious despair as they waited on a windswept dock for Ruthie to board the ship. "Bette promised me she'd come home," he complained. "What can you expect?" Ruthie told him. "There's a lot at stake." Just as she stepped on the gangplank, she was handed a cable. It was from Bette: "Don't sail. Coming home. Meet me in New York." Ruthie gave the paper to Ham and when he read it he threw it in the air, grabbed Ruthie, and spun her around. "I knew she couldn't do that!" he exulted. "I knew it!"

Bette had decided to drop her appeal and accept the court's verdict for a number of reasons. First among them were her rapidly mounting legal costs. The court had ordered her to pay the studio's expenses as well as her own, and she already owed $15,000. An appeal would bring the total close to $25,000, and Bette didn't have it. She was losing $1,600 a week by not working, and if the case dragged along through appeals her losses could spiral to $50,000. On top of that, Sir William was less than confident that an appeal would be successful.

She finally made up her mind to accept defeat graciously after George Arliss—at Jack Warner's behest—paid her a visit in Brighton. "Go back," he advised her. "You haven't lost as much as you think. Go back and gracefully accept the decision. See what happens. I think good things. If in time you feel you're being treated unjustly, put up another fight. I admire your courage in this affair, but now—go back and face them proudly."

Bette knew Arliss was right, and she sailed to New York in November. She had a brief reunion with Ham, but he decided to stay in Manhattan, where he had cut a record with Tommy Dorsey and was exploring a career change into artists' management.

Bette and Ruthie arrived back in Los Angeles aboard the *Santa Fe Chief* on November 18, and a chastened Bette told the press, "I'm just a working girl—not a crusader. 'Work, work, and more work' is my motto from now on. . . . Whatever I am asked to do I shall willingly do." Two days later she had a letter hand-delivered to Jack Warner, informing him that she was "ready, willing and able" to resume work at his studio. It was her understanding, she added hopefully, that her salary would be resumed as soon as Warner received the letter. Warner told her to be back at the studio on Monday morning at eleven-thirty.

To her great joy, Bette discovered upon her return to the lot that her battle of Britain had brought her at least one victory: increased respect from her studio. The fray had proven to them that Bette had the courage of her convictions, and it was equally clear that without her services, they would be poorer at the box office. To her surprise, Jack Warner "bent over backwards to be nice" once she reported back to work. He agreed to guarantee personally a $14,000 loan so that Bette could pay her legal expenses, and after she had paid half of the $10,000 she owed Warner Brothers for *their* court fees he told his legal department in a memo that it was not his wish to "try and collect the 5,000-odd dollars involved from Miss Davis," but that he would like to retain the right to collect in the future. He never did.

Warner also increased Bette's salary to $2,000 a week, as he had promised to do back in June, never again insisted that she bleach her hair, and—best of all to Bette—he sent her a script she loved, *Marked Woman,* in which she was to play a call girl who works for a gangster (modeled after Lucky Luciano) who has her viciously beaten when she informs on him. Bette has called the film "excellent" and "satisfactory in every respect." It is neither, but in comparison to *God's Country and the Woman* it's a masterpiece. Bette must have been blinded to the film's shortcomings by her sheer relief that she had a solid, fairly well-written script to play.

The film was well reviewed and successful at the box office (it took in $1.15 million), and with her next few films there was no question that Bette's product had improved immeasurably. She may have disliked working with Edward G. Robinson on *Kid Galahad* ("All of us girls at

Warners hated kissing his ugly purple lips"), but the film was called "easily the best fight picture ever screened" by *Film Daily,* and it grossed $1.5 million. *That Certain Woman,* in which she costarred with her erstwhile love object Henry Fonda, struck many reviewers as so much soap opera, but audiences liked it and *Variety* thought that Davis's performance "displays screen acting of the highest order." *It's Love I'm After* reteamed her with Leslie Howard in a madcap comedy that *The New York Times* called "a rippling farce, brightly written and deftly directed . . . an agreeable change for Mr. Howard and Miss Davis and it fares well at their hands."

These last two films grossed nearly $1 million apiece, and Bette's skein of box-office winners at Warner Brothers reached twenty-seven. Still, she had yet to appear in an A movie with a big budget, a world-class director, and high-level production values throughout. With her next picture, all that would change—and so would Bette Davis's life. She was about to enter the rarefied stratum of superstardom—by playing a beautiful, self-centered, willful socialite in the antebellum South. It wasn't *Gone With the Wind;* Bette had lost the opportunity to play Scarlett O'Hara when Jack Warner sold the rights to the project to David O. Selznick. But for Bette it was the next best thing: *Jezebel.*

From the first day of shooting in the fall of 1937, Bette knew that this film—and this director—would be different. William Wyler watched her closely as she strode through her first appearance in the picture, a scene in which Julie arrives late for her own formal-dress engagement party and sweeps in still wearing her riding clothes. At Wyler's suggestion Bette had practiced lifting her long skirt insouciantly with her crop as she entered the house in order to establish immediately her imperious, rebellious nature. She mimed the gesture on the first take exactly as she had practiced it, and she was pleased. But Wyler asked her to do it again. And again. And again.

Twelve takes later, Bette took Wyler aside. "What do you want me to do differently?" she pleaded. "I'm doing it exactly the same way every time!"

"I'll know it when I see it," Wyler replied, and put Bette through her paces *thirty-three* more times. By then she was exhausted, irritable, and certain Wyler was a madman. "Okay, that's fine," he announced, and the day's shooting wrapped.

What was fine? Bette still didn't think she'd changed her performance an iota, and she demanded to see a selection of takes. That night, as she sat in a small projection room with Wyler and watched herself on screen, she realized she was in the best directorial hands of her career: to her amazement, she could see vast improvement in the later takes, improvements she didn't even realize she was making.

"How is this possible?" she marveled. "You didn't even tell me what you wanted."

"I am not a dramatic coach, Bette," Wyler responded. "I can only direct actors, I can't teach them how to act. I knew you could give me what was right for the character, even if it took a while. I trust your instincts."

That night Bette went home in a happy daze. Here was a brilliant director who believed in her talent and was willing to spend whatever time was necessary to get the best possible performance out of her. She thought she must be dreaming: this was the filmmaking experience she had so desperately longed for.

Based on an unsuccessful stage play that had starred Bette's stock company nemesis Miriam Hopkins, *Jezebel* told the story of Julie Marsden, a spoiled New Orleans heiress whose fiancé, the handsome but stuffy young banker Preston Dillard (Henry Fonda), breaks off their engagement after Julie spitefully attends the 1850 Olympus Ball wearing red instead of the white required of single women—a shocking breach of etiquette that brings shame and humiliation on herself and Pres. He leaves for New York, and she pines away for him until she hears that he has returned. She throws a huge party, humbles herself before him, and asks forgiveness. Then he tells her he is married.

Her machinations to win Pres away from his wife result in the murder of a family friend—who loves Julie—in a duel with Pres's brother. Julie is able to redeem herself only when Pres is stricken by yellow fever during a raging epidemic, and she accompanies him to a quarantined island after she tells his wife that she knows "he loves you, not me" but that she, being a native of Louisiana and accustomed to its people's habits and idioms, can best nurse him back to health. She promises that when Pres gets well she will see that he is reunited with his wife, and she means it.

What Bette considered the "triteness" of *Jezebel*'s plot is not evident in the finished picture, thanks to both her richly modulated performance and the inspired direction of William Wyler. When the director began to shoot the Olympus Ball scene, a dramatic centerpiece of the picture, it had been sketched out by the screenwriters in just one line. Wyler turned it into a three-act mini-play fraught with tension, as Julie arrives delightedly expecting to cause a sensation and instead is greeted by shocked silence and ostracism by her friends and neighbors. Pres, determined to teach her a lesson, marches with her onto the dance floor, shooting daggers with his eyes at anyone who would dare say a word. As they dance, the other revelers shrink away from them until they are alone in the middle of the vast hall.

"Take me home, Pres," Julie pleads, realizing she has made a terrible mistake. Grim-faced, Pres holds her ever more tightly and they twirl across the floor like solitary figures on a music box. When the band leader interrupts the music, Pres insists he start up again. Finally the song is over and Julie rushes from the ball, thoroughly disgraced.

The assistant director had allotted half a day's filming for the five-minute scene; Wyler took five days before he was satisfied with it. Bette was tired but delighted; Henry Fonda was tired and irritated. He kept reminding Wyler that he had a clause in his contract that allowed him to leave the set by the second week of December to be with his wife in New York when she gave birth. "I don't see how this thing is going to be finished by then at this rate," he kept sputtering.

Bette not only didn't complain about the retakes, she seemed to thrive on abuse from Wyler that would have sent her stalking off the set if it had come from another director. "Don't wiggle your ass so much!" he commanded one afternoon. Another time he barked, "Do you want me to put a chain around your neck? Stop moving your head!"

Bette wasn't offended. "Willie corrected a lot of my bad habits. . . . When he picked away at me, I knew he was right. I'd been with too many directors who didn't give a damn about performances, just so they finished on time." She gladly worked as hard as Wyler demanded, but she still longed for some indication that he was pleased with what she was giving him. She told him that she was an actress who "desperately needs the approval of my director" and would he please let her know when she'd given him a good take? The next day, after each shot he bellowed, "That was marvelous, Miss Davis, just *marvel-*

ous!" Bette laughed and told him to "go back to being noncommittal!"

Bette let Wyler run roughshod over her because she knew he was as much a perfectionist as she, was as dedicated to his craft as she was to hers. For the first time, she had a director who was strong enough to match her in every way. He wasn't the namby-pamby sort she'd worked with so often in the past; and he was the antithesis of Ham Nelson, who in contrast seemed to her weak-willed, vacillating, and given to whining. Professionally, she admired and respected Wyler. Personally, she was falling in love with him.

The film's assistant editor, Rudy Fehr, knew that something was up between Bette and Wyler the night he and Warren Low, the editor, waited for the two of them to come to the projection room and review the day's rushes. Just as the impatient Low was about to leave, Fehr recalled, Bette and Wyler came in "with lipstick smeared all over their mouths. They looked ridiculous. They should have looked in the mirror before they came in. This happened practically every night after that. They obviously were doing some heavy petting in somebody's dressing room before they came to review the rushes."

"I *adored* Willie," Bette admitted. "He was the only male strong enough to control me." That was enough for her. Like many another woman before her, Bette was attracted to Wyler in spite of his looks. His short stature and blunt features had earned him the sobriquet "The Golem," after the ugly clay monster in the German horror film of the same name. But Wyler, thirty-six, Jewish, born in Alsace-Lorraine, was one of those men who drew women to him through the sheer force of his personality and rock-solid masculinity. The latter was a stimulating quality for many women who lived and worked in a community teeming with milquetoasts and pretty boys unsure of their sexuality. "Willie was *enormously* attractive," Bette said. "The sexual sparks were there from the beginning."

Wyler had first been given the chance to direct by the nepotistic Universal chief Carl Laemmle, a distant cousin. Derided at first as little more than one of "Laemmle's parasites," Wyler proved himself a talented director in the early '30s, and quickly established himself as a nononsense sort prone to bluntness. While she was at Universal, Bette had had one encounter with Wyler she never forgot.

Sent to audition for him in 1931 for a role in *A House Divided,* she had nothing to wear, and one of the wardrobe mistresses threw her into a tight-fitting, low-cut cocktail dress—the only outfit she had in size eight. "I was embarrassed," Bette recalled. "Girls in New England didn't dress that way, even for fun." Wyler took one look at her and said loudly enough so that everyone on the soundstage could hear him, "What do you think of these dames who show their tits and think they can get jobs?" Bette had felt like crawling home.

When she found out that Jack Warner wanted to borrow Wyler from Sam Goldwyn to direct *Jezebel,* she smelled revenge. She would meet with him, remind him of what he had said to her years earlier, and refuse to work with him. He didn't remember any of it, but he apologized profusely, told Bette they were both more mature now, and assured her that he was eager to work with an actress of her accomplishments. She was totally disarmed.

Both their working relationship on *Jezebel* and their romance were volatile. Again and again, just as she had with her mother, Bette tested Wyler's mettle with temper tantrums, arguments, fits of exasperation. Unlike Ruthie, Wyler matched her strength for strength, never gave an inch, and eventually forced her to his will. By turns he would be sarcastic and aloof, charming and treacherous, and she delighted in the fact that Wyler was able to exert control over her in spite of her every wile, something no one before him had ever been able to do. She adored him for it. Eventually, she and Wyler developed a kind of shorthand so that she often knew what he wanted from her without his uttering a word. At other times, he'd drive her to exhaustion as she tried to decipher what he wanted; then he would give a small suggestion that "turned the whole scene around and made it live," Bette said. "When I wasn't hating him, I was loving him."

With Ham now in New York most of the time, where he worked as an artist's representative at the Rockwell-O'Keefe talent agency, Bette and Wyler spent their evenings together, usually at his place, where she would cook a simple dinner and they would go over her scenes for the following day. She listened raptly as Wyler explained to her why, in his opinion, none of her previous movies had come close to tapping her talent. "Those were *performances,* Bette," he told her. "You were acting, and acting very well. But I never got the sense that you *were* those people. A great actress *becomes* the part she is playing, and that's achieved not by overwrought mannerisms but by an understanding of the subtleties of the character."

"I think I truly understand Julie," Bette whispered.

"I think you do too, Bette."

She was now deeply in love with Wyler, and terrified that Ham would hear about their affair. When she recalled her husband's reaction to an imagined liaison with Ross Alexander, she shuddered to think what he might do if he found out about her and Wyler. It was a blessing Ham was in New York so much; as long as he stayed back East she wouldn't have to deal with him—or with the increasingly tenuous state of their marriage.

❧

If Bette was thrilled by Wyler's demands for retake after retake, the Warners front office was not. Hal Wallis, now the Warner production chief, sent a memo to *Jezebel*'s associate producer, Henry Blanke, complaining about Wyler's excesses on one scene: "Wyler is still up to his old tricks. . . . With all of the care he used in making closeups, certainly he must expect that we would use the greater portion of the scene in closeup. Yet, he takes the time to make sixteen takes of a long shot. What the hell is the matter with him anyway—is he daffy?"

Jack Warner thought so, and when Wyler fell nearly a month behind schedule and several hundred thousand dollars over budget, he threatened to bring in William Dieterle to replace him. Beside herself when she heard this, Bette went to Warner and pleaded with him to let Wyler finish the job: "He's making a great movie, Jack. I promise you it will make a lot of money. And it will establish me as a box-office draw, I'm sure of it."

"That's all well and good, Bette," Warner replied, "but what good will it do if the thing costs so much we wind up losing money no matter how well it does?"

Finally, Bette said, "If you don't fire Mr. Wyler, I will work every night until nine or ten o'clock, and be ready to shoot the next morning at nine—whatever it takes to finish."

Warner agreed, but Bette's willingness to work late solved only a few of the picture's problems. Chief among them was Henry Fonda's looming December 17 deadline, which forced Wyler to shoot the actor's scenes in bunches, out of continuity. When Fonda left the set to join his wife Frances back East (where she gave birth to daughter Jane on December 21), Bette had to perform her closeups without her costar to react to, a difficult task for any actor.

The workload took its toll on Bette's health. A scene where Julie defies a quarantine and tramps through a swamp to get to Pres in New Orleans was filmed at midnight; when it was completed, Bette was drenched, shivering, and exhausted; she caught a "miserable cold" that put her in bed for two days. Wyler was under so much pressure to finish the picture that he asked Bette to work on New Year's Day, 1938.

During the filming of another difficult scene that day, Bette received a telegram: her father had suffered a massive heart attack in Boston. He was dead.

TEN

Bette lay alone in her bedroom in the sprawling new house she and Ham had recently moved into at 1700 Coldwater Canyon and thought of her father. As she listened to the sound of rain beating against the roof and windows, she told friends, she felt strangely detached, as though the memories drifting through her mind were scenes from someone else's life. She would think of the rare happy times, those Christmases when Harlow would put on his Santa suit and shout "Ho! Ho! Ho!" as he handed her and Bobby their gaily wrapped presents. Then her mind would sharpen and flash on one of his cruelties and she would shiver with the memory of his steely glare. Then anger would course through her as she thought of his cavalier treatment of Ruthie, and the financial hardship he had allowed his ex-wife and daughters to suffer.

Mostly, she cried. Each new memory—of Ruthie's gaunt face as she hunched over her negatives, of Harlow's awkward backstage attempts to reach out to her, of Bobby's silent year in a mental hospital—would wash a new wave of sorrow over her. How could her father have been so unfeeling? Why had he kept Bobby waiting for hours the one time she visited his Boston office, and then granted her an audience of only ten minutes? Why had he come to visit her and Ham in Hollywood only once, and then refused to give her any compliments on her achievements?

She had heard that he had tossed a copy of *Photoplay* with her picture on the cover into a trash can and grumbled to a coworker that "a stage career would have been more dignified." In spite of herself, she laughed, recalling how little he had encouraged her stage acting in the first place. Maybe if her father had lived to see *Jezebel* he would have finally given her some credit. . . .

She longed for the father he might have been. She knew that with *Jezebel* so far behind schedule it would be very difficult for her to attend his funeral in Boston, and she felt oddly relieved. She was exhausted, fighting a bout of bronchitis and a still-lingering cold, and she knew she would never be up to the rigors of a funeral three thousand miles away. When angry memories flooded back, she was glad she was bound to finish *Jezebel*—"I wouldn't go if I could!" Then she would sob at the thought that she held such ambivalent feelings about her own father's funeral. In the end, she didn't go.

Bette's return to work on *Jezebel* diverted her emotions somewhat, but she was close to collapse. Filming dragged on through January, and her physician wrote to Jack Warner that Bette would have to be given at least two months off once shooting was completed. "She is going on grit alone," he warned. "She is not actually medically ill, but her general physical and emotional makeup is such that if we rush her into another picture she will be in danger of collapse."

Jezebel finally wrapped on the 17th of January, a month behind schedule and hundreds of thousands of dollars over budget.* Depleted, Bette fairly crawled down to Laguna Beach, where she holed up, exhausted and depressed, and deftly avoided Warner messengers bearing new scripts. Adding to her state of near collapse was the volatility of her relationship with Wyler. She had been testy and irritable the last month or so of filming, and the two had frequently descended into arguments on the set. While Bette admired Wyler's strength, he could only dominate her so far—then the masculine side of her personality would rear back, unwilling to be completely tamed by any man. "We fought and made up and fought and made up and fought and made up," Bette said. "We were both miserable."

Her reflections on her father's death had made Bette sense how much like Harlow William Wyler was. The director's stern, uncompromising ways, his talent and intelligence, his taciturnity, his reluctance to praise her—all of it reminded Bette of Harlow. As contemptuous of psychoanalysis as she was, she was intelligent enough to figure out that in her relationship with Wyler she was seeking a loving version of Harlow Davis. The realization served only to make her more ambivalent about Wyler.

---

* In order to have the film finished by then, Henry Blanke had asked John Huston, who had worked on the script, to direct the scene in which Julie's admirer and Pres's brother duel, thereby freeing Wyler to complete his scenes with Bette. It was Huston's first stab at directing.

The release of *Jezebel* on March 10 offered Bette and Wyler a happy respite from their troubled relationship; the film was a major success (it took in $1.46 million at the box office, for a profit of nearly $400,000) and Bette's performance in it was lavishly praised by the critics. Wyler's attempts to tone down his star's more overwrought mannerisms led her to the most controlled, sustained characterization of her career, so that the few instances in the film when Bette is allowed free rein have far greater impact. One such moment stands out: when Julie learns that Pres has been stricken with yellow fever, she pleads to be allowed into New Orleans to see him. Outwardly she seems under control, but Bette expresses all of her character's terror and frustration by frantically opening and closing her left hand. It's a riveting and highly effective moment.

James Hamilton of the National Board of Review praised *Jezebel*'s writing, direction, and photography and added, "At the center of it is Bette Davis, growing into an artistic maturity that is one of the wonders of Hollywood. . . . Her Julie is the peak of her accomplishments so far, and what is ahead is unpredictable, depending on her luck and on the wisdom of her producers."

Her producers, to Bette's great chagrin, still sorely lacked wisdom when it came to her career. As he had with *Of Human Bondage* and *Dangerous,* Jack Warner failed to follow up Bette's triumph in *Jezebel* with scripts that would build on her accomplishments. The first movie he offered her was *Comet Over Broadway,* a soapy backstage drama she refused to do; she was put on suspension. The second, *Garden of the Moon,* had a plot that was described thus: "Nightclub owner Pat O'Brien and bandleader John Payne have a running feud. There is time out for numerous Busby Berkeley numbers." Bette remained on suspension rather than play O'Brien's girlfriend.

Warner's relentless myopia toward her career didn't improve Bette's precarious state of mind. Her fights with Wyler escalated, and their periods apart grew longer. When Ham Nelson was in town, Bette felt herself on tenterhooks, trying to hide her relationship with Wyler, loath to end her marriage, yet aware that she and Ham were drifting inexorably apart. Her New England sense of propriety, flexible though it had become in matters sexual, dreaded the specter of a public divorce. But living with Ham was becoming more and more difficult.

Nelson's insecurities about the marriage led him to bouts of anger, self-pity, and frustration. He knew Bette was unhappy, knew that her romantic longings were far afield. Although he imagined dalliances around every corner, he didn't suspect Wyler. He did worry about Henry Fonda after seeing *Jezebel,* especially since he knew about Bette's girlhood infatuation. (He wasn't the only one who suspected Bette was still smitten with Fonda. Hedda Hopper approached Bette after the premiere and whispered salaciously, "Bette, I know one thing for sure—you had to be in love with Henry Fonda. Oh, the way you looked at him!" Bette laughed and waved away the suggestion so convincingly that Hopper never mentioned her hunch in her column. "I couldn't tell her," Bette said, "that all those closeups of me showing love for Hank had been shot after he had finished all of his scenes for the picture and had left the lot. It was Willie—off camera—I was looking at!")

Ham's jealousy boiled up again when Bette began work on *The Sisters,* a melodrama set in 1906 San Francisco. Bette's costar was Errol Flynn, one of the handsomest actors of his time and a legendary ladies' man. Flynn played a charming, feckless newspaper reporter who deserts his pregnant wife (Davis) soon after their elopement. She survives the city's great earthquake and continues to search for him until they are reunited and he begs her to take him back. She does.

Flynn used his most seductive wiles to get his leading lady into bed, but Bette was wary of him on a number of levels, and she resisted. His reputation as a heartbreaker preceded him, and rumors were rife in Hollywood that it was not only women who shared Flynn's sexual favors. Several young men in his thrall were said to have committed suicide after he broke off the relationships.

Like most people during this unenlightened period, Bette felt a deep discomfort with homosexuality, and Flynn reminded her uneasily of Ross Alexander. She needed to respect a man's masculinity in order to feel truly attracted to him, and in her mind bisexuality was a major point against a suitor's manhood. She also needed to respect a man professionally; Flynn's careless work habits and cavalier attitude toward his craft left her puzzled. Flynn was a huge box-office star, paid twice as much as she, and yet he seemed to walk through his roles, while Bette felt she worked "like ten men" on her films. Two or three times a week, the assistant director would have to scour the local bars to get Flynn back to the set after lunch. This infuriated Bette. She later said that Flynn "was certainly one of the great male beauties of his time, but a terrible actor—not because he didn't have the basic talent, but because he was lazy, self-indulgent, refused to take his work seriously, and tended to throw away his lines and scenes."

Jack Warner didn't help Bette's feelings toward Flynn when he told her that their billing would read "Errol Flynn in *The Sisters,* with Bette Davis." Aghast that her Oscar and her performance in *Jezebel* didn't seem to matter a whit to Warner, Bette lobbied to have the billing changed. After months of haggling it was—to "Errol Flynn and Bette Davis in *The Sisters.*" Hal Wallis said in 1964 that the initial slight was purposeful; Warner had told him, "That dame needs to be brought up short now and then; she's an egomaniac and I like to get her sweating at times."

Flynn was never able to get Bette into bed, although his finely honed sexual instincts told him that she was ripe for the picking. He was right. Her fragile emotional state made her susceptible to any male attention, and she found herself responding to him during some of their love scenes. Every time Flynn felt her weaken, he would make yet another pass at her. Tempted she was—she later called Flynn "utterly enchanting"—but her pride won out: she wasn't going to let herself become just one more of Errol Flynn's sexual trophies.

Jack Warner, for one, felt that Bette's resistance was a real battle for her. "She always acts better when she's in love," he said, "and though she'd have killed me for saying so, I felt she was in love with Flynn all through the shooting. But she'd be damned if she'd let him or anyone else know." Ham, of course, sensed it, and his imagination tortured him as he conjured up all kinds of sexual shenanigans between Bette and Flynn. The tensions between them grew; they fought over the telephone when she was working, they fought when she got home. Ham started to spend his nights at friends' homes or in hotels.

Bette continued to see Wyler, but their relationship had become "tempestuous to the point of madness," as she put it. As much as she was drawn to "his strength, his brilliance," she was also terrified that he would "run my life from sunrise to sunset. . . . I resisted the loss of my sovereignty to the end." But she couldn't walk away from him.

With two tenuous, bombastic relationships tearing her apart emotionally, Bette longed for a solid, quiet romance. In September she thought she'd found it. Instead she became embroiled in a "catastrophic" love affair that would finally give Ham Nelson cold, hard proof that he was being cuckolded.

It was at a party in September 1938 that she first saw him, a benefit at the Beverly Hills Hotel for the Tailwaggers, an organization Bette headed up that cared for lost and abandoned dogs. She looked lovely at the gathering, her hair falling softly around her bare shoulders and her low-cut, tight-fitting pink lace dress revealing more than a touch of cleavage. She carried a wicker basket over her arm, filled with raffle tickets, and when the tall, handsome man approached her, she felt first a thrill, then a certain amount of relief when he stared into her eyes, not her bosom. She recognized him immediately as Howard Hughes.

People and activities and talk and laughter swirled around her as she stood next to Hughes in the ballroom, but it all seemed to fade out as she looked up into the face of the rangy, gawky, shy man who reminded her so pleasurably of the young Ham Nelson. Hughes, thirty-three, was world famous as the filmmaker who had launched Jean Harlow to stardom in 1930 with *Hell's Angels,* and as an aviator who had recently won the Congressional Medal of Honor after navigating the world in just over ninety hours. Bette had heard he was a cocky, arrogant sort, but when she met him she was taken aback by his sweetness. There were no fireworks between them, she professed, but rather an instantaneous warmth: "He bought scads of raffle tickets from me and asked for a date. He was so debonair and handsome that I was flattered." She also found it titillating that Hughes was enmeshed in a very publicized relationship with Katharine Hepburn, a woman Bette had always envied for her striking beauty—and now Hepburn's beau wanted *her.* Ham was in New York again, Wyler was out of town, and Bette was lonely.

The date turned into an affair. Their rendezvous were discreet and held at odd hours when Bette wasn't working. Hughes was a night owl, and they would sit up until the small hours of the morning in front of the fireplace in Hughes's rented house just feet from the gently lapping surf of the Pacific Ocean in Malibu, talking quietly while Hughes stroked her hair. To Bette's surprise, this apparently experienced man of the world was shy and fumbling in bed, much as Ham had been at first, and she was stunned when Hughes, so insecure about his attractiveness that he was often petrified by a first encounter with a woman, struggled with impotence. Hughes saw himself, his associate Mickey Neilan recalled, as "a great gangling buffoon of a guy."

Bette was patient with him, never made him feel that she was disappointed or thought less of his manhood because of his problem, and she helped Hughes come around until the potency problems evaporated. Hughes's gratitude knew no bounds. One warm sultry night, an evening Bette would never forget, Hughes covered his bed with gardenias and made love to her amid the intoxicatingly rich aroma of the exotic flower.

With Ham still away, Bette became more brazen. She and Hughes began to meet at the Coldwater Canyon house, making love in the bed she shared with Ham. By now, the affair was a poorly kept secret in Hollywood, but nothing so much as a blind item appeared in the newspapers—because, as Bette put it, "since I had always cooperated with them and treated them fair and square, they stood behind me. . . . Brother, was I lucky!" Her luck ran out when Ham, visiting with friends in New York, heard the rumors about his wife and the eccentric millionaire. Now, he had had enough. He would return to Hollywood immediately, but he wouldn't confront Bette. Nor, he resolved, would he punch Hughes in the mouth. Instead, he would get *proof* that his wife was an adulteress—and he would use it against her in divorce court.

Ham and his brother-in-law, Bobby's husband Robert Pelgram, worked feverishly in the basement of the Coldwater Canyon house on the afternoon of September 22 while Bette was at the studio. Ham drilled a hole in the bedroom floorboards, then Pelgram carefully ran the recording wire up a basement wall, along the ceiling, and through the hole. Ham pulled the wire up into the bedroom, attached a small microphone to it, and nailed the microphone to the baseboard under the bed. Then he tested it, while Pelgram listened below. It recorded Ham's voice perfectly. There was nothing to do now but wait.

That night, Ham lay sleepless in a motel room, his imagination conjuring up images of what was occurring in his bedroom, images that ripped at his heart. When he and Pelgram returned to the house late the next morning, the sounds on the small disc confirmed his worst fears. Ham's face contorted in agony as he listened to his wife, his childhood sweetheart, making love to another man. Pelgram tried to soothe Ham's tears of pain, calm his fits of rage against Bette, against Hughes, against the Fates. Finally they left the dank basement, taking the recorder and the disc with them, and Ham returned to his motel room.

Around midnight, Ham went back to the house, barged into the bedroom, and caught Bette and Hughes in the act. Hughes jumped up and threw a punch at him, which missed, and a fierce struggle ensued that left Bette screaming in her bed. Finally, with both men exhausted but unhurt, Ham started to back out of the room. "You'll regret this, you bitch!" he hissed at Bette. "I've got tapes of the two of you, and don't think I won't release them! Then your lousy career will be over! You'll be finished! *Finished!*" On the verge of tears again, he bolted out of the room.

Hysterical by now, Bette threw Hughes out of the house and frantically called Bobby, who was over in a flash. The sisters searched the house in a frenzy looking for the eavesdropping equipment. *Ham is bluffing,* Bette kept telling herself. *Surely he's bluffing.*

Bobby later told Ruth Bailey, her daughter with Robert Pelgram, what happened next. "My mother found all this wire down in the basement," Ruth recalls, "and then she and Bette started following the wires and they wound up in the bedroom." When she saw that Ham had indeed taped her, Bette was beside herself. A disclosure like this *could* ruin her career, destroy everything she had worked so hard for. Frantic, she knew she *must* talk to Ham. He wouldn't do that to her—he *couldn't.* . . . If only she could talk this over with him, everything would be okay. But then she realized that she had no idea where he was, and her stomach sank. She fell on her bed and sobbed so fiercely she could barely breathe.

Hughes heard from Ham Nelson the next morning. He would destroy the disc, Ham said, in exchange for $70,000 in cash. As Ruth Bailey puts it, Ham and her father "figured they could use the money. There was a purpose in doing what they did—to get some money out of her." Hughes paid the blackmail, and Ham broke the disc apart in front of him. Then Ham moved out of the Coldwater Canyon house and in with a fellow agent from the Hollywood branch of Rockwell-O'Keefe. Bette was shattered. "It broke my heart. Ham was my first love."

Ruthie wasn't nearly as upset. She urged Bette to marry Howard Hughes immediately. Bette's secretary, Bridget Price, wrote Ginny Conroy to say how shocked she was when she heard about Ruthie's hopes for a Hughes-Davis wedding. It was a terrible idea, Bridget had told Ruthie, because "no one can live with Howard Hughes."

"That's all right," Ruthie replied. "She can always get a divorce."

Bridget's mouth dropped open. "Do you mean to say that you'd encourage your daughter into a marriage that you knew couldn't work? Think of all that emotional wear and tear. Think of all that bad publicity."

"Think of all that money," Ruthie sighed.

Bette's wiser head prevailed. She felt so conflicted about the loss of Ham that she couldn't concentrate on another man, and she broke off the relationship with Hughes. She borrowed $70,000 from the studio against her future earnings, to pay him back the money he had given Ham. Bette kept a soft spot in her heart for Hughes, and he remained fond of her. For years afterward he sent Bette a single red rose on the anniversary of the repayment.

When reporters got wind of the fact that Ham no longer lived with Bette, they started asking questions. Bette denied everything, but Ham was more equivocal. "I can't say anything about a separation, except that there is none contemplated at this time and we'll just have to wait a while for developments. Bette will probably have a statement to make about the situation." She did. On October 1, she sent a terse telegram to key members of the Hollywood press corps: "Ham and I definitely have decided to take a vacation from each other."

Besieged by phone calls begging for more information, Bette told the columnist Mayme Ober Peak that "we have a problem to work out, and we feel we can do it better away from each other. Then, after a little vacation, we'll see how we feel. This isn't something we can decide in a minute or two. It's too important to both of us." The vacation, she stressed, was meant to save the marriage.

She said no more. Even after Walter Winchell announced on his radio broadcast that Bette planned to "marry a millionaire," she remained closemouthed. "I will not talk," she told Peak. "Even if I should go into court, I shall not tell under any circumstances what has happened between Ham and me. It is our own personal affair."

Ham felt the same way. When he filed for divorce on November 22—an extremely rare case of the husband as plaintiff—he didn't mention Howard Hughes's name, but he did make it as clear as possible in legalese that his problems with Bette were largely sexual. She had treated him, he charged, in a "cruel and inhuman manner" by becoming "so engrossed in her profession that she has neglected and failed to perform her duties as a wife and has been inattentive, casual and distant to plaintiff, to the point of rudeness and embarrassment."

She also "insisted on occupying herself with reading to a totally unnecessary degree, and upon solicitation by plaintiff to exhibit some evidence of conjugal friendliness and affection, defendant would become enraged and indulge in a blatant array of epithets and derision, wholly unjustified, and would upset the entire household and unnerve and humiliate plaintiff."

Ham also complained that Bette ignored his friends when they visited, refused to eat meals with him, and preferred to vacation with her mother and sister rather than travel with him. All of this, the lawsuit concluded, had "caused and does now cause plaintiff great and grievous mental suffering and humiliation."

Bette didn't answer the petition, and the divorce was rushed through with the help of Warner Brothers's influence. Nelson didn't demand alimony from Bette, despite the fact that she had just signed a new contract for $3,000 a week; rather, he entered into a property settlement with Bette that split the couple's money down the middle. After a brief court appearance by Ham on December 6, in which he alleged that Bette had *told* him that her career was more important to her than her marriage, the divorce was granted. Nelson left town almost immediately and went to New York, where he took a job with the advertising firm of Young and Rubicam.

For most of the second half of the 1930s, Bette Davis had engaged in a sexual lifestyle that would certainly have horrified her straitlaced New England forebears and deeply shocked her fans, who thought of her as a bedrock of Christian values. Abortions, adultery, sexual blackmail—none of it would have passed the all-powerful Hays film censorship office if it had been part of a Davis script.

She was not without shame, and she told a friend late in 1938 that she had been wrong about much in her life, and could no longer look herself in the eye. She must regain that ability, she said—"It's doing awful things to me." She had tried to bury her troubles in the work of filming *Dark Victory* shortly after the separation from Ham, but she told the same friend that while she "adored" the script, she felt badly that she didn't "feel up to" making the movie. She had been so convinced that she couldn't do the film justice in the state she was in that she had gone to see Hal Wallis and offered to give up the part of Judith Traherne, a flighty heiress stricken with an inoperable brain tumor. But Bette had always been able to translate her personal troubles into acting brilliance, and when Wallis looked at the first week's rushes, he told her, "Stay upset."

At home, there was nothing to take her mind off the disintegration of her marriage. She told a reporter at the time, "That whole episode of my life just makes my heart ache and you can see why I can't talk about it. . . . When I split up with Ham, one of the worst things I had to contend with was living with things we had acquired together. Everything in the house reminded me of Ham. I was all set to forget about him, and up would bob an old chair, and I could see him sitting in it. My God, it was ghastly!"

Bette moved from the Coldwater Canyon house shortly after the divorce to another large home at 301 North Rockingham Road; a few months later, she moved again, this time to Beverly Grove. The nomadic existence she had spent with Ruthie for so many years left Bette with a restless spirit; after she had succeeded in Hollywood and could afford to live just about anywhere she wanted to, she continued to move frequently, sometimes twice a year.

And the closeness she had always shared with Ruthie made her very uneasy about being alone. After Ham left, Bette begged her mother to come and stay with her. Ruthie obliged, but their relationship was more fractious than ever. They fought about matters large and small: Ruthie was spending too much money, Bette was being surly and unpleasant, Ruthie was trying to control Bette's life, Bette didn't appreciate her mother's wisdom and concern for her.

Quickly enough, Bette realized that she could no longer live with her mother. Ruthie went back to her own home, hurt and angry, and a new friend of Bette's, Ruth Garland, moved in to take her place as Bette's companion.

Bette had lost both her husband and Howard Hughes, but she still, after a fashion, had William Wyler. They had drifted apart, he'd spent time in Europe, but it was clear that his love for Bette had not waned. One would have thought he'd have been wary of her. He had already been through a short, volcanic marriage to the neurotic, temperamental actress Margaret Sullavan, who had been married to Henry Fonda. Wyler was obviously attracted to vibrant, mercurial women, and even while Bette was buffeted by the Hughes debacle and Ham's divorce action, he continued to see her, making love to her one day and battling viciously with her the next. The fights with Bette didn't destroy his ardor—he wanted to marry her.

For months, Bette told him that she couldn't give him an answer yet —she was too upset, too confused. That was true, as far as it went, but that was only part of it. As much as Bette loved Wyler, admired him, and enjoyed being subjugated to him, she also feared him. She worried that the strength of his personality would overwhelm hers, that she would be consumed by him and lose the independence she so loved. Moreover, her intelligence told her it would be a mistake to marry a man so much like her father.

In October, Bette and Wyler fought badly and didn't speak to each other for weeks. Finally, she received a note from him. Still in a snit, she tossed it aside: *I'll show him!* Several days passed before she opened it, and what she read shocked her. Wyler had asked her one more time to marry him, and had given her this ultimatum: if she didn't respond within two days, he would marry another woman. Bette was beside herself. Could Willie really mean it? She had lost Ham and Howard Hughes. She couldn't lose Willie. Fear him she might, but somewhere deep in her heart she felt that he was the only man she had ever truly loved. She *couldn't* lose him!

Bette spoke to friends about how desperate she felt at that moment. Frantic, she telephoned Wyler at his home, at the studio, at his club. No one would tell her where he was. She left urgent messages. She called *his* friends, and they seemed oddly reluctant to talk to her. After half a dozen calls, Bette grew frenetic, pacing back and forth across her living room, puffing violently on her cigarette, the knot in her stomach tightening with the fear that something was terribly wrong. Nervously, looking for some distraction, she turned on the radio. She didn't like the music, and was about to turn the set off when the news began. The announcer read the report that the well-known director William Wyler had married the beautiful starlet Margaret Tallichet, who had been tested as Scarlett O'Hara for *Gone With the Wind*.

Bette stood by the radio, staring blankly ahead, and mechanically turned the knob to shut it off. She closed her eyes for a few minutes, then sank onto the sofa. She felt too numb to cry.

PART THREE

~

"The Fourth Warner Brother"

ELEVEN

Bette glided into the grand ballroom of the Biltmore Hotel in downtown Los Angeles for the eleventh annual Academy Awards presentations on February 23, 1939, and soaked in the applause that erupted around her. She was surrounded by what can only be called an entourage—ten people, including her mother, her cousin John Favour,* her Aunt Mildred, Ruth Garland, and Robert Pelgram. (Bobby, newly pregnant, felt under the weather and stayed home.)

Bette's attire this evening was the antithesis of her controversial look of three years earlier. This time, she was every inch the movie star in a stylish brown net gown with a tight bodice and full skirt, topped off with ostrich feathers that billowed up around her shoulders and a bird of paradise sewn across the front.

Bette was applauded so lustily because there was little doubt that she would again win as Best Actress. *Jezebel* had received four other nominations, including Best Picture (a first for a Davis film), but William Wyler had been overlooked for a Best Director nomination. Four hours into the ceremony, after Fay Bainter had been chosen as Best Supporting Actress for *Jezebel*, Bette accepted her second Oscar in three years. "This is the happiest night of my life," she told the crowd and an international radio audience. "I am especially proud because I loved Julie so, but in accepting the award let me ask the man who made Julie what she was to stand up and take a bow." She gestured to Wyler, who responded to the spotlight and applause and kissed Bette as she returned to her crowded table. She later said that to win this Oscar was far sweeter because, unlike her first, she felt that she had really earned it.

As tumultuous and distressing as her personal life had been over the past year, Bette's career had had the forward momentum of a tidal wave. *Jezebel* had been a huge commercial and critical success; so too had *The Sisters* when it was released in October 1938. The enormous success of

---

* This branch of the family reverted to the English spelling of "Favor."

153

Dark Victory the following April would cement Bette's position in the front rank of movie stars—and convince Jack Warner once and for all of what he had in Bette Davis.

The ad copy for *Dark Victory,* although pretentious as only Hollywood self-congratulation can be, was a clear sign that at long last her studio appreciated Bette: "Out of the blazing fires of her genius, the screen's most gifted actress has created a gallery of unforgettable women. Now Bette Davis, the winner of two Academy Awards, comes to you in the climax of all her dramatic triumphs. In the role she waited eight years to play. In the greatest picture of a woman's love that the world has yet seen."

The "eight years" was a stretch, since *Dark Victory* had played on Broadway with Tallulah Bankhead only five years earlier. And unmentioned in the ad, of course, was the fact that it had taken Bette two years of battle with Jack Warner before he agreed to let her do the picture. Warner felt that the story of Judith Traherne, an insouciant society girl who bravely battles an inoperable brain tumor, was "too downbeat" to appeal to the masses. He told Bette, "When you're just getting into high gear, why go morbid on your audience? All those women out there want to see you making love, fulfilling their dreams vicariously. Then you conk out on them!" But Bette pestered Warner more than she had since *Of Human Bondage,* and when Casey Robinson brought in a strong script and Edmund Goulding, one of Warner's top directors, expressed interest, Warner gave in—but not before he told Bette, as he had when he lent her to RKO for *Of Human Bondage:* "Go ahead and hang yourself if you want to!"

Dark Victory turned out to be the archetypal tearjerker and the quintessence not only of a "woman's picture" but a "Bette Davis picture" as well. Judith Traherne's carefree high spirits give way to bitterness and cynicism when she realizes her condition is terminal, but she soon faces reality, marries the doctor who has tried to help her, and faces death with quiet valor.

Keeping Judith free of self-pity was a struggle for Bette, she later said, because she was feeling so much of it herself: "Judith did not know what self-pity was. It was Ruth Elizabeth, damn her. She was calling the shots." But the strength and courage of the character helped keep Bette's own emotions on a more even keel, and the depletion she felt after all that had happened to her left her "docile," on and off the set.

Ruthie found this new Bette "refreshing," and so did the film crew. By this juncture in her career Bette was convinced that if her films and her performances were to be top-notch, she would have to fight—and fight and fight and fight—for every creative idea she had. Even when she respected her director, there still might be differences in their approaches to her characterization, her playing of a scene, even just a line of dialogue. She rarely backed down. If she thought her director weak or lacking in creativity, her fear that the film would be a disaster could turn her into a harridan—demanding, intractable, temperamental, sometimes even irrational.

A cinematographer who had worked with Bette several times told the journalist Adela Rogers St. Johns that when Bette felt threatened, the tension on her sets was unbearable: "She is the most exacting star, the most ruthless I have ever known. She sees everything, watches everything, will never put up with mistakes, says what comes into her head, never pulls a punch, screams and weeps and drives everybody to distraction. She can be fury or angel or clown, which doesn't make her popular —but does make her the finest dramatic actress I ever photographed."

Because of her "weakened condition" while she was filming *Dark Victory*—and because she felt confident in the hands of director Edmund Goulding, whom she called "a true genius of film-making"—Bette was a self-described "doll" on the set. The twenty-seven-year-old acting neophyte Ronald Reagan certainly thought so. In Hollywood just eighteen months after a career as a sportscaster in Des Moines, he was a Warner contract player and had been cast as one of Judith's feckless society "boyfriends," Alec; his main scene with Bette was in a nightclub, where Judith purposefully gets drunk after learning of her malignancy. Although Bette told David Hartman in 1981 that Reagan at the time seemed to her a "silly young kid," he remembers her with fondness. "She was not only a great star and probably our greatest actress, but also a professional of the highest order."

Reagan recalls that Bette took his side in a dispute with Edmund Goulding over the nightclub scene. "Mr. Goulding wanted me to play my character as if he were the kind of guy . . ." He paused to consider the most delicate way to put it. "The kind of guy who wouldn't care if a young lady were undressing in front of him. And he wanted me to encourage Bette to get even drunker. I felt that this man had real affection for Bette and would have done just the opposite. He would have wanted to help her, not encourage her to feel even worse. Goulding definitely disagreed, so when we took a break I went to Bette and told her how I felt. And she was wonderful. She agreed with me completely. In fact she said, 'That would be better for me, too.' So she went to talk to Goulding, and he didn't know that I was listening, but he told her to do it the way I wanted. Then he came to me and [instead of admitting that Reagan had been right] told me that *Bette* wanted me to play it that way."

Reagan never told Bette of his distress at the overall interpretation of Alec's character that Goulding wanted from him. "I wondered why he didn't come to me," she said. "Alec as written was a wimp. I should have insisted on a rewrite. Dammit! But I was a mess emotionally at that time. . . . I had my hands full."

Especially so because Bette was now embroiled in yet another affair. George Brent played the doctor who loves and marries Judith despite her terminal condition, and Bette was still smitten with the reliable leading man who had attracted her on the set of *So Big* six years earlier. Brent finally reciprocated her feelings after his divorce from Ruth Chatterton. At that point Brent's affection for Bette and his sympathy for her personal problems turned to sexual attraction, and they began an affair about a month before Bette's divorce was final. The studio prevailed on Hedda Hopper and Louella Parsons not to reveal the relationship (mainly because Bette was afraid Ham might use it against her in court), and the couple were able to carry out their trysts without too much fear of public discovery.

She was deeply fond of Brent. "He was a charming, caring, and affectionate man, with a wonderful sense of humor. When he became infatuated with me, I was delirious. After Ham, I needed a strong man like George." But she was amused to find that Brent, only thirty-five, had prematurely gray hair that he had darkened for years. "He used to stain my pillowcases with hair dye!"

Once Bette's divorce was final, she was immensely relieved that she could at last be public with her affection for a man other than Ham Nelson. "We went to a lot of Hollywood places together," she said, "even the racetrack, which, in those days, was about the most public place you could go." The studio, she recalled, was "delighted" with the romance; Hal Wallis felt it was making Bette's performance all the better, and the publicity would surely help the box office.

Dark Victory opened in New York on April 20, and the next day Bette had the best reviews of her career. Frank Nugent in *The New York Times* called Judith Traherne "a great role—rangy, full-bodied, designed for a virtuosa, almost sure to invite the faint damning of 'tour de force.'" And Davis in the role, he added, "is enchanted and enchanting," playing Judith with "eloquence, tenderness and heart-breaking sincerity." *The New Yorker* observed that "the bravados of her agonies will touch the nation's heart," and *Time* magazine's critic wrote that

"*Dark Victory,* if it were an automobile, would be a Rolls Royce with a Brewster body and the very best trimmings. . . . It puts [Bette Davis] well up in line for her third Academy Award."

Bette's head was swimming with all this praise as she ate lunch in the Warner commissary the day after *Dark Victory* opened, to strong box office. She was aware that all eyes were on her, some filled with admiration, some with envy. One contract player after another came to her table to congratulate her. Bette later said that she felt like running to the middle of the room and shouting, "By damn, I was right! Everyone in America wants to see a story where the heroine dies in the end! I've won my battle, and I just may win my third Oscar!"

Dark Victory was only the first of four superlative Bette Davis films released in 1939. Each of them brought in over $1.6 million in ticket receipts, and in each Bette provided a vivid and distinct characterization. The sweeping historical drama *Juarez,* released five days after *Dark Victory,* cast Bette as Carlotta, the wife of Austria's Archduke Maximilian, who is installed by Napoleon III through a rigged election as the emperor of Mexico. Benito Juarez, the rightfully elected president, wages a rebellion that ends in Maximilian's death and Carlotta's descent into madness.

Edwin Schallert, in the *Los Angeles Times,* called *Juarez* "magnificent," and James Hamilton in the *National Review* said of Bette, "[She] subdues her strikingly individual characteristics to a portrayal of the Empress Carlotta that is not only touching but overtoned with premonitions of her eventual tragedy, and her final flitting away into the darkness of madness is the most unforgettable moment in the picture."

Bette offered a starkly different portrayal in her next film, *The Old Maid,* costarring Miriam Hopkins. As a Philadelphia society girl with a terrible secret—she has a love child by a man recently killed in the Civil War—Bette was given the opportunity to play a woman who ages twenty years and displays a wide range of emotions.

To say that relations between Bette and Miriam Hopkins were strained during the filming of *The Old Maid* would be an understatement. They remembered each other vividly from the Cukor/Kondolf stock company, and each was wary. Miriam resented Bette, galled by the fact that a woman who had been an ingenue when she was a leading lady was now the biggest star in Hollywood.

Miriam was bitter too about losing the Julie Marsden role in *Jezebel*

to Bette—she had created the character on stage. At first she had held
the screen rights to the play along with its producer, Guthrie McClintic,
and he was ready to sell them to Warner Brothers. When Hopkins heard
that they wanted the vehicle for Bette, she balked, insisting that she
would not sell the rights to anyone unless she played Julie. Finally, assured by Warners that she would be given first consideration, she sold
her share for $12,000. But the agreement didn't *guarantee* Hopkins the
film, and when Bette was cast she flew into a rage. Her mood soured
further when the film was such a big hit, and it positively curdled when
Bette won the Oscar for it.

On *The Sisters,* her next picture after *Jezebel,* Bette had added insult
to injury in Miriam's view when she had a brief affair with her director,
the Russian-born Anatole Litvak—who was Miriam's husband. His marriage, like Ham and Bette's, was crumbling, but that did little to assuage
Miriam's anger. She still had a sexual hankering for Davis, and for Bette
to dally with her *husband*—well, that was too much. Bitterly, she characterized Bette as "a greedy little girl at a party-table who just had to
sample other women's cupcakes. First she wanted my husband and then
she wanted Hepburn's boyfriend [Howard Hughes], and her own husband was all but forgotten!"

Hopkins threatened to name Bette as corespondent in her divorce
action against Litvak, but Jack Warner talked her out of that potential
disaster. When his divorce was final, Litvak shook his head thinking back
on events. "Marriage with Miriam—an affair with Bette—I've had
enough of crazy, temperamental women to last me for years. Now I need
a rest, no?"

Around this time Warner Brothers signed Hopkins to a picture-to-
picture contract, promising her high-quality vehicles and hinting at a
possible costarring stint with Davis. "If I get into a picture with that
husband-stealer," Hopkins sputtered, "I'll show her what acting is *really*
about!"

That set the stage for the first working relationship between the two
women in ten years, *The Old Maid.* Bette knew she was in for trouble on
the first day of shooting, when Hopkins swept onto the set wearing one
of Bette's costumes from *Jezebel.* Bette refused to give Miriam the satisfaction of a blowup and simply ignored this flagrant provocation. Her
sanguinity, however, didn't rub off on Miriam. "Ensuing events," Bette
said, "prove[d] she wanted even more to be in my shoes than in my
dress."

Bette marveled anew at Miriam's cache of tricks and stratagems designed to upstage her. As they exchanged dialogue, Miriam never looked

directly at Bette; her eyes would wander as though she were impatient for her costar to stop speaking so that she could say her next line. During a scene on a couch, Hopkins continually slid farther and farther back on the seat cushion until Bette had to face away from the camera in order to look at her. It took twenty takes before she would stop it. Often when Bette had a highly emotional scene with Hopkins and gave a wonderful take, Miriam would spoil it by announcing that one of her buttons had popped or one of her hairpins had fallen out. The ruses changed, but the goal was always the same—to keep Bette off balance, to make sure she didn't give *too* good a performance.

Within a week Bette was so enraged that she would go home at night and "scream at everybody"—but she never blew up at Miriam. Bette knew that in her attempts to sabotage her, Hopkins was actually sabotaging herself. Cast as a hard, vengeful woman, Miriam chose to play her with sweetness and Southern charm in the hope of gaining audience sympathy. But Bette could see that Miriam was turning her character into a mushy nonentity, and in the process handing the picture to her. Although she worried that the film as a whole might be hurt by the weakness of Hopkins's characterization, by now Bette disliked Miriam so much she had adopted one of Jack Warner's favorite attitudes: *Go hang yourself!*

Despite all this strife, *The Old Maid* was the third of Bette's string of 1939 successes—and her biggest moneymaker to that date. The critics cheered the film and her performance, her third indelible characterization in three and a half months. Frank Nugent wrote in *The New York Times,* "Miss Davis has given a poignant and wise performance, hard and austere on the surface, yet communicating through it the deep tenderness, the hidden anguish of the heartbroken mother."

Although she badly needed a rest after making three films in a row, just one week after *The Old Maid* wrapped Bette reported for work on a grueling costume drama: the film version of *Elizabeth the Queen,* Maxwell Anderson's blank-verse play about the relationship between Elizabeth I of England and Lord Essex. Her costar was Errol Flynn. She had fought with Jack Warner for months over the project, her first and only color film at Warner Brothers. She had been unhappy with her second billing under Paul Muni in *Juarez,* but capitulated because Muni was, after all, the title character. She wouldn't make the same mistake again. When Flynn balked at Anderson's original title (which excluded Essex),

Warner suggested *The Knight and the Lady* or *Essex and Elizabeth*. Bette rejected both because Flynn's role was given precedence. Warner finally came up with a title Bette liked: *The Private Lives of Elizabeth and Essex*. At this point she demanded top billing, and Flynn let her have it: his main concern was money, and he was getting twice as much of it as she was for the picture.

Bette was unhappy about Flynn's casting as Essex; she knew he wouldn't do the role justice and lobbied for Laurence Olivier. "Mr. Flynn had no right to play Essex whatsoever," she felt. "He wasn't that kind of actor. He just wasn't up to the gorgeous blank verse of this play." But Warner was unsure about the commercial potential of the film and wanted Flynn's proven box office strength to complement Bette's. They stood fast on Flynn.

Worried about her costar and the exigencies of so big a picture and so demanding a role, Bette was overwrought as production loomed. Concerned, the film's associate producer, Robert Lord, sent a memo to Jack Warner on April 30. "How about health insurance on Davis?" he wrote. "Once she starts shooting we have no work without her. If she folds up, we stop shooting. I have been studying the lady and in my opinion she is in a rather serious condition of nerves. At most she is frail and she is going into a very tough picture when she is a long way from her best."

As a precaution, Warner tested the actress Geraldine Fitzgerald as Elizabeth, but Hal Wallis refused to consider anyone but Bette. Production began on May 24, and there was immediate friction between Bette and the front office when she insisted that her makeup man, the redoubtable Perc Westmore, shave her head, since Elizabeth was bald. There was no way the studio would allow her to appear in any scene without hair, but Bette convinced them that if Westmore shaved a few inches off her hairline and she wore a wig, it would be clear that she was bald without putting the audience off. Bette had studied the Holbein portraits of Elizabeth, and when she posed for her first makeup and hair tests, she was amazed at how much she resembled the monarch.

Michael Curtiz, Bette's old nemesis, was assigned to direct the picture. (It was Curtiz who had muttered in 1932 that Bette was a "goddamned-nothing-no-good-sexless-son-of-a-bitch.") She savored the chance to work with him again from her new position of power, and in short order the two had their first clash—over her costumes. Curtiz thought they were too big and bulky; Bette and the designer, Orry-Kelly, knew they were historically accurate. When Hal Wallis sided with Curtiz, Orry-Kelly made a new, scaled-down wardrobe for the tests.

Once filming began, Bette switched back to the original, larger outfits. No one noticed, and she had little further trouble with Curtiz. Whenever he forgot just whom he was dealing with, Bette would remind him with a sharp "Shut up, Mike! Shut up and let's get on with it!"

She had much more trouble with Flynn. Feckless as usual, hurt by her ill-concealed dissatisfaction with him as a costar, and stung once again by her resistance to his advances, Flynn childishly bedeviled Bette at every turn. He pinched her behind, yawned broadly or made rude gestures off camera while she emoted, aped the heavy walk she was forced into by her cumbersome costumes. Bette usually ignored him, but she lost her composure one afternoon and threw a candelabrum at him when he said she walked "like she had shit in her panties" and asked, "Shall I help you to the porcelain throne awaiting you in your dressing room, Your Majesty?"

By now, Bette strongly disliked Flynn. "He was just not my kind of actor." To get herself through the experience, she imagined Laurence Olivier emoting with her in scene after scene.

Despite her trials, Bette took the time to help a frightened newcomer in the cast. Nanette Fabray, an eighteen-year-old appearing in her first movie, admitted she "knew nothing about markings or positionings or what one is supposed to do when the camera is on."

Fabray remembers that the set was so hot during shooting that Curtiz would call breaks every few hours to keep the soundstage's fire sprinklers from going off. The cast and crew would disperse to their air-conditioned dressing rooms or the commissary to cool down. Bette remained on the stifling set and gave the lovely ingenue playing her lady-in-waiting some pointers. "Bette was wearing these enormously heavy costumes," Fabray recalled. "The heat must have been unbearable for her. And yet in her very first scene with me, when I kept missing my marks and didn't know where to look, she very patiently sat in her chair after the others had left for a break and gave me some very quick acting lessons. I didn't realize until later how unusual it was for someone in her position, under such terrible conditions, to take the time to stay on a set and work with me. She was just wonderful."

Fabray was struck by the fact that Bette had a retinue of people around her at all times to do her bidding—even someone whose only job was to light her cigarettes. Years later, she asked Bette why she had needed all these attendants. "I think I was being a little sarcastic, you know, maybe a little jealous," Fabray recalled. "But her answer stunned me. She said, 'All the people around me wouldn't have had jobs if I didn't have them do all those unnecessary things.' "

The Private Lives of Elizabeth and Essex was released on December 1, and proved to be Bette's fourth smash hit of the year. The critics, as usual, raved. As Frank Nugent put it in *The New York Times,* "Bette Davis's Elizabeth is a strong, resolute, glamour-skimping characterization against which Mr. Flynn's Essex has about as much chance as a beanshooter against a tank."

By now, the same could be said of Jack Warner. Bette Davis in 1939 had the kind of year actresses dream about: an Oscar, four diverse and juicy leading roles, four movies that among them won nine Oscar nominations and brought in over $3 million in profits for the studio. There was no doubt now that Bette was a bona fide superstar, and the results of a national poll had proclaimed her, at thirty-one, "The Queen of Hollywood." Best of all to Bette, the critics were close to unanimous in the opinion that she was now America's finest actress. It was almost as though these brilliant twelve-plus months had erased all the struggles and indignities Bette had suffered in Hollywood for the prior nine years. So great was her power now that she was dubbed "the fourth Warner Brother," and that brought her no end of delight.

Still, she remained wary. She knew how much she had had to fight her studio for every tiny concession; she knew that they thought of her as "uppity" and wanted to "keep her in her place." She was convinced that she would *always* have to fight, that she couldn't let her guard down for a minute or the studio might still force her to play a female lumberjack. By now that was very unlikely, but Bette was never convinced it was impossible. Since her arrival in Hollywood she had honed to rapier sharpness her "me against them" attitude, and no matter how wonderful her roles, no matter how much success she achieved, it was so deeply ingrained in her that she never was able to relinquish it.

What she had learned, more than anything else, was that if she were to get anywhere in her battles with the members of Hollywood's exclusive, all-male circle of moguls, she would have to prove herself equal to the fight. She refused to charm them, win them over with her feminine wiles, make them feel sorry for her, or sleep with them. She preferred to win their *respect,* the same regard they automatically gave any man. The only way to do that, she knew, was to be tougher than the women of her day were supposed to be—to stand her ground, to go up against them without flinching. In short, to fight like a man.

Bette had been tickled when she heard the old stage adage "An actor is something less than a man; an actress is more than a woman"—so much so that she had it inscribed on her silver cigarette case. What it had originally meant is unclear. Perhaps it referred to the fact that all actors have to be in touch with both their masculine and feminine natures in order to give their best performance; perhaps it mocked those whose sexual preferences leaned toward their own gender.

To Bette, it meant just one thing: to succeed in her profession, an actress must be stronger, more ambitious, pushier, more belligerent than society expected—or most men wanted—her to be. Katharine Hepburn, looking back over her career, said, "I have lived my life as a man." Bette took that old adage on her cigarette case to heart. To stay on top, she was convinced, she would have to remain "more than a woman."

TWELVE

R uthie knocked softly on the door to the guest room of the Laguna Beach house Bette had recently bought for her. She hadn't heard a sound from Bette all day, and she was worried. When her raps went unanswered, Ruthie gently turned the knob and entered. The room was dark, the curtains drawn against the afternoon sun. Ruthie walked over to the four-poster bed and looked down at her daughter. Bette was awake, but she lay stock-still, her eyes fixed straight above her as though she were in a hypnotic trance. Ruthie sat down on the edge of the bed and took Bette's hand. "Sweetheart," she murmured, "you should get up now. Dell's made some wonderful sandwiches. Why don't you come down and eat?" Bette just shook her head. "I'm tired, Mother. I want to rest." Her daughter had been like this for over a month, and Ruthie was getting scared.

Ever since she had completed the grueling filming of *The Private Lives of Elizabeth and Essex* in the summer of 1939, Bette Davis might as well have been a zombie. She had done six pictures in a row with very little rest in between, and she was close to a physical breakdown. "I just went to bed," she recalled, "and slept fourteen hours a day. My friends and family thought there was something seriously wrong with me. I began to worry myself."

Jack Warner, with his usual insensitivity, hadn't helped much when he told Bette her next film would be *'Til We Meet Again,* and that he wanted her to begin work on it immediately. She had refused. The film wasn't in the same league as her last six triumphs, and she would once again be cast as a dying heroine. (*How quickly these moguls change their minds about what the public wants to see,* Bette thought bitterly.) She had also told Warner she must have four to six months off, and hadn't waited for J.L. to stop sputtering before she set off for Laguna Beach, where she ignored the increasingly frantic phone calls from Warner and his minions.

What worried Ruthie now was that Bette seemed to have fallen into a clinical depression. None of the tried-and-true methods that had perked Bette up in the past did any good now. She had little appetite; by September she had lost nearly twenty pounds. She seemed unable to summon up the strength to do much of anything except agonize over the failure of her marriage. "I was wearing myself out, thinking of Ham and the breakup, which never should have happened, because I wasn't the type."

Most alarmingly, she seemed to lose interest even in her profession, which had been the center of her life for over a decade. "I was overfull of acting," she said. "I was gorged with it, surfeited with it, exhausted with it." Her avoidance of the studio's calls and refusal to open the door to messengers with scripts put her on suspension for the umpteenth time. Finally, her lawyer informed the studio that she would not return to work unless her contract was amended: she wanted to make no more than two films a year, or three if one was a light comedy. Warner refused, and Bette fell ever deeper into melancholia, weary to the bone of her constant struggle with her employer.

As Ruthie sat on the edge of Bette's bed and held her hand, she knew that something would have to be done to snap Bette out of this. If not, she feared, Bette might wind up in an institution as Bobby had, miserable and mute, her career at an end.

"Bette, darling," Ruthie began as gently as possible, "you can't go on like this. You simply must get away, do something fun, get your mind off things. This isn't you. Where's that spunk of yours that always drives everybody crazy?"

"Oh, Mother," Bette whispered, squeezing her hand. "I'm just so *tired*. Tired of everything. I hate all this Hollywood crap. I wish I could go back to Newton and have no responsibilities and never have to take another phone call from Jack Warner."

"So why *don't* you?" Ruthie chirped. "You're on suspension anyway. Go back to Newton. Don't think of anything except having fun. Fall is just around the corner—think of how beautiful the leaves will be. Think of the crisp apples and the fat pumpkins and the children trick-or-treating. Think of how wonderful the cold night air will feel against your cheeks."

Bette looked at her mother, and for the first time in weeks, she smiled.

❧

Two weeks later, Bette put her dependable old station wagon on a train and headed East. She went first to New York, where she stayed several days to see some Broadway shows and visit friends. Then she drove up to Massachusetts, to begin a sentimental tour of all her old haunts. She went to Newton, to Lowell, to Cape Cod, to Boston, to Ocean Park. She visited Newton High, Mariarden, Cushing Academy, the Cape Playhouse.

But her memories proved to be only that. "There were gas stations in back yards where I used to play. Strange faces looked out of windows where familiar, friendly faces used to welcome [me]. All the pictures of my childhood I had expected to see again were gone."

After two weeks of this, Bette sagged again, more tired and depressed than ever. Her reunions with old girlfriends and schoolteachers upset her; they treated her as though she were an irreplaceable Dresden doll. "I was wondering whether I was still a human being, or whether I was a kind of painted shadow, Hollywood model. . . . I realized that we can't go back. There isn't any 'back.' "

She ended up in Maine, sitting atop the huge boulders along the seacoast and staring out at the ocean, overcome with sadness. She watched the waves crash against the rocks, methodically pulverizing them into tiny grains of sand, and wondered whether that was what was happening to her. She thought again of Ham, and an empty ache returned to her stomach. *Why can't I have what every one of these fishermen's wives has?* she thought. *I don't want to end up alone at fifty— unsafe, desperate, pitiable—without someone who needs me.*

She called Ruthie, who knew the moment she heard her daughter's voice that Bette's emotional state hadn't improved. "If you find yourself falling to pieces, Bette," Ruthie advised her, "go to Peckett's. You'll find rest there."

Ruthie was right. Bette loved Peckett's Inn, a rustic retreat at Sugar Hill, New Hampshire, where she took long walks among the ever-deepening reds and golds of the oak and maple and butternut trees, picked berries, sipped clam chowder, gained weight, and started to recover her emotional equilibrium. Her state of mind was helped along nicely by the attention paid her by the thirty-four-year-old night manager and host of the inn, Arthur Farnsworth, Jr.

She saw him for the first time during the evening meal her first day there. Across the homey dining room with its red linen tablecloths and rough-hewn wooden walls, she glimpsed an imposing figure of a man as he spoke animatedly with some of the other guests. He was six feet tall, light-haired, robust and handsome in an Arrow-shirt-ad sort of way. His eye caught hers and she was brought up short when he moved quickly over to her table.

"Good evening, Miss Davis," he greeted her in a strong, masculine voice, extending his hand. As Bette took it she noticed how blue his eyes were, how straight and white his teeth. "I'm Arthur Farnsworth, and I must say it's both an honor and a pleasure to have you with us."

"Thank you very much, Mr. Farnsworth," Bette replied, a little more formally than she meant to.

"I didn't mean to interrupt your meal," Farnsworth apologized, picking up on her coolness. "I'll be playing the piano in the music room after dinner. I do hope you'll join us."

Bette said she would and returned to her meal, lifting her eyes furtively to watch Farnsworth walk away. He had stirred her emotions pleasurably, and she found herself impatient to be finished with dinner. When she was, she and a few other women gathered in the music room, and she requested her favorite song, "Stardust." When Farnsworth switched from piano to violin, he played it again for her. Then the group gathered in the lodge's station wagon and drove to Franconia Notch, where they sat under a bright autumn moon and harmonized together, eventually letting Farnsworth's pleasing baritone carry on alone.

The next day, Bette made discreet inquiries about Farnsworth to Robert Peckett, the owner of the inn. She discovered that he was the son of a well-regarded Rutland, Vermont, dentist and his wife Lucile, and that his family came from rock-solid Vermont stock. Bette liked that.

Something of a Renaissance man, Farnsworth had been a pioneering aviator as well as a musician. As a student pilot in 1931, he had won praise and made headlines when he successfully landed his plane in the waters of Boston harbor after he ran out of gas. He had toured the country in a musical act with his sister Barbara and brother Dan, and had worked at Peckett's in various capacities since 1934. For the previous two years his job as "host" had primarily meant entertaining the single ladies registered at the hotel, and E. J. Tangerman, a local resident, recalled that Farnsworth's duties earned him a reputation as a gigolo. If Bette became aware of this she didn't let it stand in the way of her new romance.

Farnsworth and his wife, Betty Jane Aydelotte, were divorcing after a four-year marriage, but the decree wouldn't be final for another fourteen months. He and Bette began their affair almost immediately, and it did wonders for her state of mind. Much to her delight, Farnsworth was no fumbling Ham Nelson or impotent Howard Hughes in bed. Best of all, he wasn't the least bit intimidated by her star stature. Farnsworth seemed to all the world like a man's man, a tower of strength—just the kind of man Bette felt she needed "to control me."

Bette had planned to stay at Peckett's for a few weeks at most, but she couldn't bear the thought of leaving, and she extended her sojourn to nearly two months. The man she nicknamed "Farney" proved a healing tonic for her, and the couple made no secret of their attraction to each other. They swam, hiked, boated, played tennis together day after day. At night, they were discreet about their rendezvous. Each would retire to a separate bedroom, then one or the other would stealthily switch rooms. But their affection for each other was so obvious that soon everyone within a fifty-mile radius of Sugar Hill knew that Arthur Farnsworth, local, and Bette Davis, movie star, were (as they say in Hollywood) "an item."

The news got back to George Brent, and he wasn't happy. He and Bette had never broken up; their romance had simply wound down. The director Irving Rapper, a friend of Brent's, recalled that he had gone up to Brent's house one afternoon and found him standing by the fireplace, sadly holding a single rose. When Rapper asked what was wrong, Brent replied that Bette had made an appointment to accept his marriage proposal but had instead sent a note to tell him she had changed her mind because "it wouldn't work out." After that, the romance foundered; according to Bette, the bulk of the communication between the couple went through their secretaries, who "were so busy courting each other for us that it was inevitable they would take over our romance."

Now that Bette seemed to be involved in an important new relationship, Brent was worried that he would lose her forever, and he wanted to know where he stood. He telephoned her several times from Hollywood, but she was maddeningly noncommittal. Finally he boarded a plane, flew into Boston, and called Bette from his hotel in Copley Square: he wanted to come to Sugar Hill and see her.

"No," she told him, "you just sit tight. I'll come down to Boston and see *you*." No one but Brent and Bette knew what transpired between them in his hotel room, but once Bette left Boston, her romance with George Brent was over—and she knew she'd done the right thing when all she could think of during the drive back was Farney.

Jack Warner called. Hal Wallis called. Anatole Litvak called. Bette took none of the calls, and returned none. Then Jack Warner telephoned again to say that he was willing to discuss her contract demands. During that conversation on October 26, Warner agreed that Bette would not be required to do more than three movies a year and could have one twelve-week vacation without pay and one four-week vacation with pay a year. Warner also agreed to raise her salary $500 a week to $4,500, but he refused to allow her to choose her own scripts or do outside radio work, and he wouldn't guarantee her the services of cinematographer Ernest Haller. Bette accepted the compromise.

Warner told Wallis he was pleased to have the matter resolved, but the Warner Brothers lawyer R. J. Obringer was skeptical. In a memo to the New York office, he commented that Bette hadn't lasted a year under her August 1939 contract and added that it was "unpredictable" how long these new concessions would keep her happy.

She was certainly happy at first. Warner informed her shortly after their peace-making conversation that he wanted her to star opposite Charles Boyer in a lush costume drama, *All This and Heaven Too*. He sent Bette the script, she liked it, and she promised to return to Hollywood by the end of the year.

First, however, she wanted to put down roots. A few days after she had arrived at the inn, the Pecketts had shown her a ninety-acre, heavily wooded piece of property "up the road a spell" with a one-hundred-fifty-year-old house and barn surrounded by butternut trees. It was for sale, and Bette fell in love with it on sight. Before she had gone to Peckett's, she had stayed with a friend who owned hundreds of acres, and she sat with him and his wife on their front porch during a sultry Indian-summer evening. "You know, Bette," the man said, "I've worked hard all my life. We've owned this place for fifteen years and yet I never sit down and look out over my land that I don't get a lump in my throat and say to myself, 'This is *my* land.'"

Now that Bette had the contract she wanted—which would allow her four months off every year, three of them consecutive—she knew that she would be able to enjoy her beloved New England as she hadn't for nearly a decade. She bought the property, christened it "Butternut," and the day after the sale was final, walked up to the property alone and remembered what her friend had said a few months earlier. "I looked at my acres," she recalled. "I felt them under my feet. You have never seen such trees in your life. It was too exciting. I knew what my friend meant. And I knew that I would know it more and more as the years went by. It was the best thing that ever happened to me. Davis went home!"

But not before she had to return to Hollywood and make another movie. She left New England early in December in a three-car caravan led by Farney and Bette in his car, a friend in her station wagon, and several other friends in a third car. Farney remained with her as far as Ohio, then had to return to New Hampshire and his job. Bette switched to her own car, kissed Farney good-bye, and promised she'd be back within a few months.

"You look *wonderful!*" Bette heard again and again when she started to make the rounds back in the film capital. When she began work on *All This and Heaven Too* at the beginning of February, United Press reporter Frederick Othman devoted an entire dispatch to Bette's new glow. Under the headline "Bette Davis Looks Fine After Rest," he wrote that she looked "only vaguely like the tired woman who appeared in *Dark Victory,*" and was "a walking example of the theory that maybe an actress deserves an occasional rest. Her eyes were bright and her cheeks were round. . . . She gained thirty-five pounds and immediately had to lose fifteen of them because she couldn't zip her skirts on."

A weight of 116 pounds, Bette told Othman, was perfect for her, and she didn't cotton to the vogue for rail-thin actresses. "They can't be healthy when they're underweight," she opined, "and to make it worse they seem to have set the fashion for women all over the country to be too thin. I'm glad to see curves becoming fashionable again and I know that when I retire from pictures, I'm going to be a nice, plump, comfortable-looking middle-aged lady. There'll be no streamlined figure for me."

Still, it was a struggle for Bette to keep weight on in Hollywood. Almost the minute she got back, she faced myriad problems that turned her once again into a jumpy, short-tempered, chain-smoking bundle of nerves, the antithesis of her contented, carefree, placid personality in New Hampshire. Not only were there the preparations for her new films —always guaranteed to cause her stress—but there were also the family problems that never seemed to go away.

If Bette was the Queen of Hollywood, Ruthie was the Queen Mother, and she expected, as always, to be able to project the appropriate image. Despite the fact that Bette had been on suspension for months and wasn't receiving a paycheck, Ruthie's spending on gowns, furs, and jewels was so profligate that Bette was shocked to find when she returned that the Davis coffers were nearly depleted. Bobby and her husband (with Ruthie's encouragement) had also spent too much, mostly on preparations for the new baby, using the store charge accounts Bette had established in both her name and theirs. (It was around this time that Bobby nicknamed Bette "The Golden Goose.")

When Bette confronted Ruthie for the umpteenth time about her spendthrift ways, waving her bank statement in her face and railing against her, Ruthie came up with one of her usual blithe responses: "But Bette, you're going back to work soon—there'll be more money than we know what to do with!" Exasperated, Bette canceled all the store accounts.

And soon there was the baby to add to Bette's nervous condition. Bobby had given birth to her daughter, Ruth, at Hollywood Hospital on October 1, and soon the chemical imbalances caused by childbirth and the rigors of new motherhood had sent her reeling into postpartum depression. Her behavior deteriorated so badly—to the point of screaming fits and paranoia—that Ruthie called an ambulance and Bobby was hospitalized once again. When Bette returned to Hollywood she took baby Ruth into her home and told the press that she would keep her "until Bobby is stronger. She's been so ill since the baby's birth."

Bette felt guilty about having been away when her sister's latest breakdown occurred—"I felt I had let her down." Typically, she attempted to make up for it by plunging headlong into surrogate motherhood. She remodeled one of her bedrooms into a nursery, complete with every known piece of baby furniture, colorful wallpaper, and shelf after shelf of toys, and lavished the child with attention and love. She even pretended, in her actressy way, that the little girl was hers. "It's the first time I've ever had a baby in my house and I love it," she told a reporter. "Yes, she does look like me—even I can see it."

But Bette was driven to distraction by the infant's constant demands and nightly crying fits, and she hired a full-time nurse to care for her. Still, the minute the child would begin to cry Bette would sit bolt upright in bed, and with her new film requiring a 6 A.M. wake-up, she was soon exhausted again—a condition that caused some controversy the night of the Academy Awards banquet on February 29.

Bette had been nominated for Best Actress for *Dark Victory,* along with Irene Dunne for *Love Affair,* Greta Garbo for *Ninotchka,* Greer Garson for *Goodbye, Mr. Chips,* and Vivien Leigh for *Gone With the Wind.* Bette had been considered a shoo-in to win until *Gone With the Wind* was released on December 20. Bette was so certain Leigh would be the victor—and so tired during the pre-award dinner at the Ambassador Hotel—that she told Ruthie she wanted to leave before the award presentations began.

"Are you mad?" Ruthie gasped. "Everyone will think you're a bad loser. You'll stay right where you are!"

She did—until two in the morning, when, as expected, *Gone With the Wind* took the vast majority of the Oscars, including Best Actress. Bette joined in the applause for Vivien Leigh—she has always maintained that Leigh deserved the award—then turned to Ruthie and announced, "We're going home now."

Although she slept for only three hours that night, Bette soon learned that her "sacrifice" for the sake of appearances went for naught when catty comments began to circulate around Hollywood the next day: "Did you see Davis leave in a huff when she lost? She walked out in a rage!"

"There is nothing anyone can do," Bette sighed, "to avoid the preconceived and desired reactions of Hollywood."

Bette had felt so much pleasure at the purchase of Butternut that in February—armed with her new weekly salary of $4,500—she bought a home very much like it in Glendale, quite close to the studio, for $60,000. (She put $22,000 down and had a monthly mortgage payment of $1,000.) She christened the rustic, thatch-roofed cottage "Riverbottom," and she and Ruthie furnished it with overstuffed chairs and sofas covered in plaids and ginghams, knickknacks from local thrift stores, and hurricane lamps that gave the place the homey New England look that Bette loved so much. It was the closest thing she had had to a "real home" in California, and she vowed to put down roots at Riverbottom.

All This and Heaven Too turned out to be Bette's biggest hit to date, amassing a $1.24 million profit, and she won high critical praise for her controlled and understated performance as a governess accused of murder in nineteenth-century France. The film garnered three Oscar nominations, including Best Picture, but it was Bette's other 1940 performance, in *The Letter,* that won her a third consecutive Best Actress nomination. The film reunited her with both William Wyler and Somerset Maugham, who wrote the original story, a lurid melodrama of a

Malaysian plantation owner's wife who kills her lover as the film opens and remains unrepentant throughout her trial, at which she is acquitted when her lawyer suppresses an incriminating letter. Finally she tells her husband, "With all my heart I still love the man I killed!" Then—since no one could get away with murder in the movies of the period—she allows herself to be stabbed to death by her slain lover's wife.

With Arthur Farnsworth three thousand miles away, Bette was lonely and sexually frustrated during the filming, and her feeling that she was single and could sow some wild oats resurfaced. Her daily proximity to Wyler stirred up her dormant romantic feelings toward him, and he too felt there was unfinished business between them. They began another affair, but it was short-lived; after a few months Wyler deferred cordially to a young man the restless Bette also had her eye on, an actor in the production ten years her junior named Bruce Lester.

Bette found Lester winsomely sweet, like the young Ham Nelson, and he stirred her newfound maternal instincts pleasurably. They made no secret of their mutual attraction; they ate lunch together every day and left the studio in a single car each night. "This is the first time in my life that I've been free and able to have fun, have dates, have romances," Bette explained to a reporter. "Now I can play the flirt and be the young-woman-about-town. . . ."

Characteristically, Bette quickly tired of Lester's genial passivity. "She found Bruce attractive and sweet," her friend Jerry Asher recalled, "but he was a bit tame for her speed." She got herself out of the entanglement by telling Lester the truth: that Arthur Farnsworth was on his way to Los Angeles. He had read Bette's "young-woman-about-town" comment and didn't much like it; he left for Los Angeles by train a few days later.

Farney stayed with Bette at Riverbottom for two weeks, and the romantic fire between them flared. During a motor trip to Death Valley with some friends, as reporter Sally Jefferson put it in a dispatch, "Arthur's devotion to Bette was observed by all. It was plain that he worshipped her." Farnsworth wasn't happy that his romance with Bette Davis had hit the newspapers; his divorce still wasn't final, and he didn't want to jeopardize it. He and Bette agreed that it would be best for him to return to New Hampshire before any more press stories about them appeared.

"I was pregnant during *The Letter*," Bette confessed years later to her friend Whitney Stine. "Tony Gaudio, the cameraman, kept looking at me sideways. Obviously, I couldn't have the baby and I was upset as hell. I had already had two abortions. I was only thirty-two and thought to myself that if I married again and wanted to have a baby, my insides might be such a mess that I couldn't. I cried and cried, but I knew what I had to do. I went to the doctor on a Saturday and showed up for scenes on Monday wearing a form-fitting white eyelet evening dress for a scene, and that damn Tony said, 'Jesus, Bette, it looks like you've lost five pounds over the weekend!' "

Bette never told Stine who the father was, but the list of candidates is clear. Arthur Farnsworth, William Wyler, and Bruce Lester are all possibilities, but so too is Bob Taplinger, the head of publicity at Warner Brothers, with whom Bette had had a clandestine rendezvous during a Hawaiian vacation just before she began *The Letter*. In typical Hollywood fashion, when reporters noticed both Bette and Bob disembark from the ocean liner upon their return the two of them said it was merely coincidence and that neither had even been aware of the other's presence on the ship. It took only a few transpacific inquiries for the newsmen to learn that the couple had danced in close clinches every night at the Royal Hawaiian Hotel, and that Bob had sent flowers to Bette's room every day.

Rumors of the romance popped up in the press when Bob and Bette continued their romantic dancing in a series of New York nightclubs— Arthur Farnsworth's proximity notwithstanding. According to two people very close to Taplinger, the romance was a serious one. Taplinger's sister Doris recalled, "Bette told me that she very much wanted to marry Bob, but he told her that marriage wasn't right for her, that she couldn't be a wife—her career should be the most important thing to her. She told him she would give up her career for him, but he said no, she would be depriving the world of her talent."

Public relations man that he was, Taplinger knew that this rationale would both flatter Bette and let her down easily. Executives at Warners were contractually forbidden to "date" the studio's stars; Bob could deny anything more than a friendship with Bette as long as matters didn't progress too far. But there was another reason that Taplinger didn't want to marry Bette. According to Bertha Kelley, his longtime assistant, "Bob was a confirmed bachelor. As much as he loved Bette, he was just too devoted to his family. His mother, his father—all came first. He just liked to keep single."

According to Bob's sister, "It's a foregone conclusion that they were intimate," but she doesn't think Bette's pregnancy was Bob's doing. "He was a little bit too careful for that to have happened, especially because of that Warner Brothers policy. . . . I don't even know how their romance managed to take off, because he was very cautious about that."

We will never know whose baby Bette was carrying in 1940, but she offered what may be an oblique clue to Whitney Stine. After telling him of the pregnancy and abortion, she fell sadly quiet. Then she said softly, "I should have married Willie."

Instead, she married Arthur Farnsworth. He began to press her to marry him when his divorce was final early in December, but Bette vacillated. For her, there were pros and cons to consider. On the one hand, she found Farney very attractive; he was forceful and manly in some ways, gentle and pliable in others. He seemed to respect her career, and was willing for their marriage to be bicoastal (he would live in New Hampshire a good deal of the time); that appealed to the freedom-loving side of Bette. On the other hand, as she put it in her memoirs, "I was not violently in love with Farney. I loved his loving me, and our mutual love of the New England way of life was the tie that finally bound."

If it wasn't exactly grand passion, it was enough for a somewhat older, wiser Bette Davis who still felt twinges of New England guilt about her voluptuous love life. "Ruthie had raised Bobby and me in such a straitlaced way," she recalled, "that we had to get her okay to go to the bathroom. And we were lectured that a girl never, ever lost her virginity before marriage." Bette hadn't, but she had more than made up for lost time before and after her divorce from Ham Nelson. Now it was time, she felt, to make an honest woman of herself.

Despite Ruthie's strain of lingering Victorianism, she wasn't thrilled by the idea of Bette marrying again. Even with their continual bickering, Ruthie had felt closer to Bette after the divorce from Ham than she had in years, and she feared that her daughter's remarriage would drive a wedge between them again. "She had me back again and I'm afraid didn't want to let me go," Bette said. But the materfamilias didn't put up much of a fight. Farney was handsome, charming, and exceptionally well mannered, and he came from a good family. "I really think Ruthie found it hard not to like him," Bette conjectured.

The wedding took place on the eve of the new year 1941 in Rim-rock, Arizona, at the ranch of Bette's friend, the former actress Jane Bryan, now Mrs. Justin Dart. Bette wore a white dress dotted with lilies of the valley; Bobby, fresh out of the hospital, tentative and wan, was the matron of honor. Bette had chosen the holiday for her wedding so that newspapers would have no more than skeleton staffs, and the gambit worked—many reporters had no inkling of the marriage until January 2, when several of them were greeted by a telegram from Bette that tersely announced the nuptials.

"Bette's Marriage Jolts Experts," one headline read, but most of Bette's friends, especially in New England, had long been aware of the possibility. As another dispatch pointed out, "In Boston, in Littleton, in Franconia, friends of Farnsworth and of Miss Davis talked the kind of talk that will remain forever mystifying to Hollywood folk in general and to Warner Brothers in particular. For what none of the press departments of the film colony, none of the columnists, none of the top-flight executives knew about the impending nuptials was all 'old stuff' to Bette's and Arthur's friends here in New England. From a distance of some 3,000 miles, any of the friends of the pair could have tipped Hollywood off . . . none did."

Several people who knew Bette, however, had tried to tip Farnsworth off to the fact that it might be a mistake for him to marry Bette. One of these was her cousin, Elizabeth Carmichael. When Farnsworth showed Carmichael the wedding ring he had purchased, she said to him, "Are you sure you want to do this? It isn't going to be easy, you know."

"I know," Farnsworth replied, "but I want to do it."

"Are you *sure?*" Carmichael pressed him. She wasn't talking about Hollywood and the exotic lifestyle he was about to enter, she says, but rather "I was thinking about Bette. Because she wasn't easy—especially when she was working." But Farnsworth assured Carmichael that he was going into this marriage with his eyes open.

Mr. and Mrs. Farnsworth had scant time for a honeymoon. Married on a Tuesday, Bette had to be back at the studio the following Monday to begin work on a slight comedy with Jimmy Cagney, *The Bride Came C.O.D.*, which proved unworthy of both their talents. Bette had worked on *The Great Lie*, a soapy melodrama with George Brent, up until a few days before the wedding, but she was too happy to be angry about Warner's sweatshop schedule. She and Farney drove around the desert

Southwest, awed by the sprawling mesas, enormous rock formations, and exotic plant life. They stayed each night in Spanish adobes or rambling ranch-house inns.

By Sunday, Bette was back at Riverbottom and her husband was on a train to New Hampshire. The Farnsworth marriage—in its modern, unconventional way—had begun.

THIRTEEN

Bette marched into the imposing, high-ceilinged meeting room of the Academy of Motion Picture Arts and Sciences in her patented no-nonsense way, wearing a tailored black suit and carrying a portfolio of papers. She sat down at the head of a sprawling oak table and faced a dozen starchy, middle-aged men. "Good *evening*, gentlemen," she said as she opened her portfolio, her speech just a tad more clipped than usual. "Shall we *begin*?"

Nothing could have been more symbolic of Bette's lofty new status in Hollywood than her election in January 1941 as the first woman president of the motion picture academy. Not her four nominations and two awards in the prior five years, not her selection as "The Queen of Hollywood," not her sobriquet as "the fourth Warner Brother," not even the fact that her last three films—*All This and Heaven Too; The Letter;* and *The Great Lie*—had each brought in over $1.2 million in profits to her studio. To be chosen as the academy president, in Bette's mind, was the highest honor she had yet received—and a responsibility she was determined to live up to.

"My dear Miss Davis," one of the elderly chaps interrupted as Bette shuffled through her papers. "There's plenty of time for the business at hand. First, we of the board all want to welcome you as our newly elected president!"

The men applauded and Bette stood to accept their welcome. But she sat down again quickly, eager to get down to work. She knew from the academy by-laws that her position gave her a good deal of power, and she came to this first meeting intending to use it. Once the minutes of the previous gathering were read, and the board's greeting was entered into the record, Bette laid out her agenda.

"Gentlemen," she began, "there are a number of important issues I think we should address. First, as you know, there has been some talk in the community that holding our usual banquet at the Biltmore might seem frivolous in the light of the terrible struggle that our British and European friends are engaged in against the Nazis. Some have suggested we cancel it. I think a better solution would be to hold the award ceremony in a theatre, charge a minimum of $25 a seat, and donate the proceeds to British War Relief."

The board members sat in stunned silence. "*Charge* to attend the Academy Awards?" one finally stammered. "But—but—that would be so *undignified.*"

Bette forged ahead. "Another matter of great importance is the issue of extras. Many of these individuals don't even speak English, and few are capable of judging technical excellence in motion pictures. I move that we no longer allow them to cast votes in the Oscar competition." Again no one said a word until Walter Wanger, Bette's predecessor as president, balefully asked, "Miss Davis, you have won two of our awards. What do you have against the Academy?"

As the meeting progressed along similar lines, as each new suggestion triggered shock and disapproval, Bette began to feel that she had been chosen only to be a glamorous figurehead and had no real power to effect change. Two days later, she resigned the position, despite a warning from the 20th Century–Fox production chief Darryl Zanuck (who had sponsored her for the presidency) that if she quit the job "you'll never work in Hollywood again."

In her memoirs, Bette points out that her positions were soon vindicated when Jean Hersholt, elected to replace her, denied extras the right to vote, and again when the awards ceremony was switched, in 1943, to theaters rather than banquet halls. Her implication was that her gender and her position as a movie star had caused the board to ignore her suggestions.

It was just as likely that Bette's brash way of offering her ideas did them in. Blunt, impatient, never a politician, Bette was no more capable of gently lobbying people to her way of thinking in a boardroom than she was on a soundstage. When she made up her mind that a change was necessary, she wanted it made, and fast. Through patience, Jean Hersholt managed to succeed when Bette saw no recourse but to quit.

It might have taught her a lesson, but it didn't. She still looked upon the Warner lot as a war zone. "I spent my days in battle," she said, never imagining that her own fighting style always made the skirmishes worse. Never was the atmosphere more belligerent than on her next picture, *The Little Foxes.* "We fought bitterly," Bette said of the experience. Her opponent? William Wyler.

When Sam Goldwyn, one of Hollywood's premiere independent producers and widely famous for his malapropisms, was told by an aide that *The Little Foxes,* the Lillian Hellman play he wanted to option for the screen, was "very caustic," he replied, "I don't give a damn how much it costs. Buy it!" The 1939 Broadway success had starred Tallulah Bankhead, who triumphed as the steely, rapacious, down-at-the-heels daughter of the South, Regina Giddens, who connives with her brothers to build a cotton gin that will exploit cheap labor. When her banker husband refuses to put up her share of the money for the scheme, she withholds his heart medicine and does nothing as he struggles and dies. Their daughter, appalled when she learns all, renounces Regina and leaves her a lonely, miserable wretch, a victim of her own greed.

When Goldwyn asked Wyler, who was under contract to him, to direct *The Little Foxes,* Wyler told the mogul that the only woman in Hollywood who could do Regina Giddens justice was Bette Davis. Goldwyn blanched. He knew that Jack Warner was unlikely to lend out the services of his top box-office attraction; he hadn't done so since *Of Human Bondage.* The request, as Goldwyn expected, was turned down. But he was able to change J.L.'s mind by refusing to lend him Gary Cooper for *Sergeant York* unless he got Bette—and by agreeing to reduce a $425,000 gambling debt Warner owed him to $250,000. Goldwyn agreed to pay Warner $150,000 for Bette's services, while Bette continued to receive her $5,000 weekly salary during the twelve-week production. Bette wasn't happy about Warner's $90,000 profit on the deal, but she was eager to play Regina and remained quiet.

Once all the peripheral issues were settled, the real trouble began. Bette hadn't wanted to see Tallulah Bankhead's performance because she was afraid that it would influence her too much. Wyler insisted that she go to the National Theatre, where Bankhead had brought the show back to New York after a road tour. The depth of misunderstanding between Bette and Wyler over her interpretation of Regina can be gauged by their remarks over the years. Bette insisted that Bankhead had played Regina as written—brittle, cold, unrelenting in her manipulation and greed— and that there was no other way to play the role. Wyler has said that he sent Bette to see Bankhead because the actress had given the role more shading than Hellman had written into it. "[Regina] was a woman who was greedy and high-handed," he felt, "but a woman of great poise, great charm, great wit. And that's the way Tallulah had played it on the stage. But Bette [wanted to play] it all as a villain because she had been playing bitches—this is what made her at Warner Brothers. She thought when I tried to correct her that I was trying to make her imitate Tallulah Bankhead, which I was not."

It was clear on the first day of filming in May 1941 that problems loomed. When Bette appeared wearing calcimine on her face—to make her appear older and to give her the pale, white-powdered look many Southern women affected during the play's early 1900s time frame—Wyler scowled at her. "What's *that* for?"

"It's to make me look older," she replied.

"What you look like is a clown," Wyler snapped. "Take it off!" She didn't, but she did have Perc Westmore tone it down a little.

As she looked around at the opulent set that Stephen Goosson had designed for the Giddens home, Bette felt it wasn't true to the play; rather she felt it should have a "decaying grandeur" to underscore Regina's need for money. She lost that fight, and the next several as well, and within a few days of the start of filming she was a mass of raw nerves, a stick of dynamite about to explode.

Wyler, by all appearances, was eager to set off the charge. He challenged Bette at every turn, demanding retake after retake to get from her the more finely shaded interpretation he wanted. Bette had loved the chance to refine her performance in *Jezebel* this way, but now she resisted. More confident of her abilities, more convinced of the validity of her characterization, she bristled now under Wyler's direction, bucking against his strength like a bronco, determined not to give in to him. With every retake he demanded, with his every plea to soften Regina, Bette's performance grew only more brittle.

Wyler was shocked by how differently Bette behaved toward him now. No longer was she pliable, open to suggestion. Raucous screaming matches erupted between star and director, rocking the soundstage, her dressing room, his office. Teresa Wright, twenty-two and appearing in her first motion picture, burst into tears one day listening to the vicious, scatological insults Bette and Wyler hurled at each other. Neither would give an inch, and the usually courtly Wyler's nastiness toward her shocked Bette. One stiflingly hot afternoon—the temperature was over one hundred degrees—Wyler was rehearsing an elaborate dinner scene at which he wanted Bette to convey the height of Southern charm and hospitality. She played it instead with a razor-sharp edge, and at its conclusion Wyler announced loudly, "That's the lousiest goddamn dinner scene I ever saw. Maybe we'd better get Bankhead!"

Bette lost all her reserves of composure. She burst into tears, pushed herself away from the table, and ran to her dressing room, slamming the door with a resounding crack. Then she walked off the set, for only the second time in her life, and fled to her mother's house, where she took to her bed, Ruthie in hand-wringing attendance.

Farney was in Minneapolis, where he had taken a job with the Honeywell corporation, and could offer little consolation. While Goldwyn and Wyler considered replacements for Bette (including Bankhead and Miriam Hopkins, who had lobbied for the role before Bette was cast), her doctor informed them that she was on the verge of a nervous breakdown and could not return to the set for several weeks. The studio sent an examining physician from Lloyd's of London to see Bette, and he concurred that she needed several weeks of rest.

After Goldwyn decided that in spite of everything, there could be no *Little Foxes* without Bette, Wyler shot around her for three weeks until she returned on June 7, scarcely better able to cope with the heat and the stress, but determined to get the ordeal over with. Wyler, too, was in a more conciliatory mood. Resigned to the fact that he couldn't alter Bette's interpretation, he let her play Regina her way and concentrated instead on turning what had been a talky, static stage play into vivid cinema. With the help of photographer Gregg Toland, he succeeded. The film's centerpiece—and one of Bette's most famous film moments— is the scene in which Regina allows her husband (played by Herbert Marshall) to die by denying him his heart medicine.

They could have shown Regina's reactions as the sounds of her husband's struggle up the stairs to get his medicine are heard off screen; they might have cut back and forth between the two actors; they considered shooting both Bette and Marshall in hard focus, a technique Toland had pioneered with great success in *Citizen Kane* a few months earlier. Instead, he and Wyler decided to keep the camera trained on Bette's hard, unfeeling face while showing her husband in the background, in soft focus. It created a memorable cinematic image.

When filming wrapped in early July, Bette felt a palpable relief, and a deep sadness. "To be happy to have a film with Wyler as the director finished was indeed a heartbreak for me," she said. But Bette long maintained that she could tell whether a movie would turn out well by the amount of strife on the set—the more, the better—and *The Little Foxes* proved her point. Released on August 21, 1941, the film was a box-office success and won high critical acclaim. In February it received nine Oscar nominations, including Bette's fourth consecutive nod as Best Actress.

Bette had proven that her interpretation was a valid one, but at a high price. She maintained as late as 1974 that one of her few remaining ambitions was to do "one more film with Willie before I end my career." But Wyler—who went on to win three Oscars as Best Director—never again offered her a role in one of his pictures.

The minute she was finished with *The Little Foxes,* Bette went back East to rejoin Farney in New Hampshire. (His job with Minneapolis Honeywell didn't require him to relocate to Minnesota; his base remained in the Northeast and he commuted several times a month.) As before, the sojourn to Sugar Hill rejuvenated Bette physically and mentally. She had the rugged, down-to-earth Farney as her reality anchor; she looked forward to the fall foliage and the freshly shucked clams and the crisp fall air to renew her and remind her of her roots. And she had Butternut.

While Bette was in Hollywood, Farney and a team of construction workers had followed her and Ruthie's sketches and rebuilt the main house. "The only thing we could salvage from the original building was the fireplace," Bette recalled. The new house was built around it, so that it rose from the middle of the living room, two sides open. The small, barnlike structure—with its white pine walls, its comfortable overstuffed chairs and antiques that Bette and Ruthie had gathered from throughout New England—felt more like home to Bette than any other place she had ever lived.

More than ever now, Bette possessed two distinct personalities. In Hollywood, she was Bette Davis, movie star. In New Hampshire, she was Ruth Elizabeth, New England girl. She and Farney puttered around Butternut in plaid flannel shirts and work pants, cleaned house ("Too small for a maid," Bette explained), burned leaves, planted bulbs for next spring's tulips, drove their six-wheel truck to market for freshly picked produce. What social life they enjoyed centered around skiing, ski dances, "sugaring-off parties," and sitting around the kitchen table making small talk with their neighbors.

One reporter who observed Bette at Butternut described her as "divinely happy." She was probably incapable of ever achieving such a blissful state, but the love she and Farney felt for each other, she said, was "a low but steady light." Amid some rocks on the Butternut property, she installed a plaque in tribute to her husband: "In Memoriam to Arthur Farnsworth, 'The Keeper of Stray Ladies,' Presented by a Grateful One." Later she admitted that what she liked best about the marriage was that it was "classically European" and allowed her a good deal of freedom.

"He didn't have an ounce of jealousy. He never questioned me about anything I did. He let me run my own life."

Which meant, of course, that he allowed her full rein to pursue her career, and unlike Ham, made little issue of the financial disparity between them. *He's got a good, important job,* Bette told herself, *and he's secure enough that he can enjoy the life my money brings us without feeling his masculinity is being threatened.* She liked that. She liked him. She felt content. And in New Hampshire, surrounded by families with small children, she yearned to have a child at last.

Bobby was able to care for her baby Ruth now, and Bette missed her. Georgie Farwell, a neighbor, recalled how Bette reacted to Georgie's son the first time the Farnsworths visited her home. "My baby was on the living room floor, playing on a quilt. Bette made a beeline for him, and got right down on the floor and started playing with him and you could tell that she was captivated." Farnsworth wanted a baby too, but Bette's career was still more important to her than motherhood. She continued to feel—irrationally at this point—that a pregnancy would be disastrous to her career, and she had at least two more abortions during her marriage to Farney. There could be no better indication of Bette's priorities. Even as she tried to create a normal life for herself at Butternut, nothing could be allowed to impede her career.

After nearly two months in New England, Bette was back in Hollywood to shoot the three movies she was contractually required to make every year. The first of these was a quick shoot, *The Man Who Came to Dinner,* a light comedy and box-office success with Monty Woolley in which Bette accepted a secondary role as a secretary and won plaudits for her restrained playing.

By October 9, she was already in costume fittings for the second film, *In This Our Life,* when she got word that Farney had taken seriously ill with pneumonia in Minneapolis. The news turned her frantic. She refused to wait for a commercial flight, which would require several delaying stopovers, and instead called an aviator friend of Farney's, who told her he had only a single-engine plane. "We'd have to stop every hundred miles. And the weather's bad."

Jack Warner and Hal Wallis told her not to take the risk, and more frenzied than ever, she spoke to Howard Hughes for the first time since the Ham Nelson debacle. He warned her that the weather was "thick," but when she insisted he agreed to put a TWA plane at her disposal. After a sleepless night and a conversation with Farney during which he sounded alarmingly weak, Bette left the following morning on a harrowing, wind-buffeted, fog-enshrouded flight that seemed to take forever (the weather forced an unscheduled stop in Des Moines) and left her a sheet-white, trembling mass of nerves.

In Des Moines, a studio representative called her with the news that Farney had rallied, his temperature was normal, and that she should return to Los Angeles. Instinctively, she knew this was a ruse. When she arrived in Minneapolis, she found her husband in intensive care, and to her horror he was too ill to recognize her. Her emotions wavered between terror at losing Farney and fury at Jack Warner for lying to her.

Farney's physician, Jay Davis, found Bette so overwrought when she arrived that he was almost as concerned about her as he was about her husband. He insisted there was nothing she could do at the hospital and ordered her to get a hotel room and rest. She did, but the next morning she demanded the room next to Farney's. It was against hospital policy, Dr. Davis told her. She moved into the room that afternoon.

While she sat by Farney's side, holding his hand and praying for his recovery, Bette was handed a telegram. Hal Wallis expressed his sorrow about Farney but asked when she would be back at the studio. Furious, Bette had Dr. Davis wire back that she was in no condition to return, that the traveling had exhausted her, and she was near collapse over Farney's condition.

When Farney rallied toward the end of the week, he insisted that Bette return to L.A. and promised her that he would come out to the Coast to recuperate. She agreed, but Dr. Davis wired Hal Wallis that he had ordered her to travel by train in order to get some rest. Just before she left, another cable came from Jack Warner: he insisted she report to the studio directly from L.A.'s Union Station to finish her costume fittings for *In This Our Life*.

It could only have been Bette's frazzled state over her husband's health that led her to play the film's classic bad girl, Stanley Timberlake, in such a fevered manner that one critic wrote, "Such optimistic souls as believed that Bette Davis's success with a relatively normal role in *The Man Who Came to Dinner* presaged a permanent filmic discharge from the neurological lists are doomed to disappointment. The actress converts *In This*

Our Life into an excuse to have a complete relapse [and] bug her eyes, twitch her hands and maneuver her lower extremities as though in performance of some esoteric Charleston."

John Huston, directing only his second film, made a conscious decision not to rein in Bette's raw emotionalism. In his autobiography he wrote that she "fascinated" him: "There is something elemental about Bette—a demon within her that threatens to break out and eat everybody, beginning with their ears. The studio was afraid of her; afraid of her demon. They confused it with overacting. Over their objections, I let the demon go; some critics thought Bette's performance was one of her finest."

The plot of *In This Our Life* was absurdly melodramatic—the spoiled, willful, bored Stanley runs off with her sister Roy's husband, causes his suicide, then returns home and tries to win back the husband she deserted, who is now in love with Roy. When she fails, she becomes infuriated and in her anger accidentally kills a baby with her car. She flees the scene and blames the family cook's son, a "colored boy," who is jailed. She is found out and runs to her lecherous old Uncle William for help. When he tells her he has only six months to live, she screams hysterically, "You don't care a thing about *me!*" and flees. She is killed in an automobile accident as she tries to elude a pursuing patrol car.

Few actresses, least of all Bette, could have remained restrained in their performance of such bathos, and the ad campaign cried, "Nobody's as good as Bette when she's bad!" The critics may have sniffed, but the fans loved it: the film became her biggest hit to that date, netting $1.7 million in profits.

At the end of filming, the studio gave Bette notice that she was to begin her annual three-month layoff immediately. Since she had promised the publicity department that she would pose for photographs and give some interviews about the film, she arrived at the studio a few days later and was in makeup when Bernie Williams, a publicity man, charged into the room and insisted that she leave the lot immediately. When she asked why, Williams replied, "You're on layoff! If you stay we'll have to pay you a day's salary!"

The fury rose in Bette like volcanic lava. She was so angry she didn't remember getting to Jack Warner's office. She tore past his startled secretary and barreled into the inner sanctum, where she found Warner staring out the window. *"How dare you!"* she hissed as Warner spun around. "How *dare* you treat me like a chorus girl! How *dare* you order me off the lot! You should have known I had made dates to do publicity work for the film. You should have known I would keep those dates—

pay or no pay! Now I *am* getting off the lot and it is just possible I may *never* come back!"

She stalked out and refused all communication from the studio for weeks. She had never been angrier with Jack Warner—this time, he had made her feel *cheap*. Finally, a desperate Warner pleaded with Bette's business manager, Vernon Wood, "What does this woman want?" *Revenge*, Wood thought to himself. Instead he replied, "She wants a new contract."

"A new contract?" Warner parroted as his throat tightened.

"Yes. She wants her salary increased, and she wants to do no more than two pictures a year, of any kind."

What was J.L. to do? Bette Davis was his biggest star, his most prestigious actress, and his strongest box-office draw. *Each* of the thirty-eight films she had made for the studio had made money, for a grand total of $21.4 million in profits. Warner relented. He raised her salary to $5,500 per week and agreed that she wouldn't have to make more than two movies a year.

They always hang themselves, Bette thought when Wood told her that Warner had capitulated to her every demand. *They're penny wise and pound foolish, these moguls.*

When the Japanese staged a surprise attack on Pearl Harbor, Hawaii, on December 7, 1941, the struggle against Nazism and fascism that had begun in Europe in 1939, once remote for most Americans, hit home with a shock. President Franklin D. Roosevelt declared war against Japan the next day, after which Germany and Italy, honoring their pact with Japan, declared war on the United States.

Bette immediately wrote to Roosevelt, one of her idols, to offer whatever help she could provide. The President took her up on her offer. Rather than vacation in New Hampshire, as she had planned, she joined the government's "Stars Over America" program and traveled across the country to sell war bonds, raise money, and rally the populace. Her first stop, in Iowa, was so successful that the government asked her to make a special trip to Missouri, where she sold more bonds in one day than anyone else had in two months. Tirelessly, she crisscrossed the country visiting private homes, aircraft factories, square dances, state fairs, schools, and Rotary clubs.

Still, she created controversy. If she didn't sell enough bonds by signing autographs, selling memorabilia, and being gracious, Bette would harangue an audience until they were cowed into shelling out their money. "Do what you can do—to the level you can do!" she'd rasp, her voice about to go, "or you're not my idea of an American!"

When press reports that likened Bette to a drill sergeant filtered back to Jack Warner, he was worried. He counseled her to show a little more tact. "They want you warm, gracious, kindly," he told her. "Don't get strident. Don't disenchant them."

"I know what I'm doing, J.L.," Bette snapped. "You and your brother in New York just sit around and count the money I make for you. I'm the one who has to deal with the public. The only way to get them to contribute, to develop enthusiasm, is to let 'em have it straight, no holds barred!"

She was right, of course, and it's astonishing that even by now Jack Warner seemed not to understand Bette's appeal to the public. Moviegoers might occasionally accept her onscreen as "warm, gracious, and kindly," but it was characters like Mildred Rogers, Julie Marsden, Regina Giddons and Leslie Crosbie in *The Letter*—real *bitches*, Bette called them—that her public responded to most strongly. When Bette sold *two million dollars'* worth of bonds in two days (and a picture of herself in *Jezebel* for $250,000), criticism of her sales pitches ceased.

Bette returned to Hollywood in April, irritated that all that greeted her was an empty house. Farney had indeed come to Riverbottom to recover, but he had returned to New Hampshire before long, and Bette had seen him only sporadically for the preceding six months. As much as she could appreciate marital freedom, she hated it when she needed Farney and he wasn't there. Her spirits improved when she convinced Hal Wallis and Jack Warner to cast her in *Now, Voyager* rather than borrow Irene Dunne from Columbia for the part. "I'm under *contract* here," she pleaded, incredulity in her voice. "Why can't I play Charlotte Vale? As a New Englander, I understand her better than anyone else ever could." For once, she got her way with very little argument.

Olive Higgins Prouty's bestseller offered a juicy part for an actress: a repressed, dowdy, mother-dominated Boston spinster who, with the help of a sympathetic psychiatrist, transforms herself into an attractive, stylish woman and finds love with a married man, Jerry Durrance (to be played by Paul Henreid), during a South American cruise. Charlotte knows Jerry cannot divorce his wife, a clinging hypochondriac, and when she returns to Boston she becomes engaged to another man. When she runs into Jerry again, she realizes that she still loves him, and breaks her engagement. Her domineering mother is enraged, and during an argument with Charlotte she dies of a heart attack.

Shattered, Charlotte returns to the sanatorium where she was first helped by psychiatric counseling, and meets a young girl very much like herself before the transformation. The child, it turns out, is Jerry's daughter; Charlotte helps her to blossom and takes her into her home. Finally Jerry offers to marry Charlotte, but she tells him he must stay with his wife, while she remains a foster mother to his daughter.

The plot, which comes perilously close to bathos, was saved—as are so many of Bette's films—by a fine script, strong performances, and Bette at the center of it all. Convincing as the dumpy, heavy-browed spinster, touching as the physically altered but still painfully shy traveler, and believable as the self-sacrificing woman in love, Bette as Charlotte Vale delivers one of her half-dozen finest characterizations.

Now, Voyager was Bette's biggest hit, turning a profit of $2.38 million for Warners, and brought Bette her fifth straight Oscar nomination. It also brought her more mail from moviegoers than any other film. Charlotte's physical transformation moved many audience members who thought themselves unattractive and gave them hope that they, too, might be able to take control of their lives and find happiness. More importantly, the film's theme of sacrifice and redemption through selfless love touched a deep chord in the hundreds of thousands of women whose husbands, fathers, boyfriends, brothers, and sons were fighting a war in Europe and Asia.

The film became an enduring classic, and provided one of those indelible movie moments that have remained instantly recognizable: at the film's end, Paul Henreid lights two cigarettes and hands one to Bette. Then she tells him that their decision to part was the correct one: "Oh, Jerry, don't let's ask for the moon—we have the stars."

As she had so often before, Bette made major contributions to the excellence of *Now, Voyager*. The initial costume and makeup tests of Henreid, a thirty-four-year-old Austrian actor making just his fourth Hollywood picture, depicted him with slicked-back hair and a silk smoking jacket, and Bette was appalled. "He looked just like Valentino," she said. "He was wrong for the part in every way. I thought that was how he wanted to look, but when he told me he hated it too, I insisted on another test. Luckily, it was approved. He would have ruined the picture looking like that."

In nearly every scene, Bette restored original dialogue from the Prouty novel that had been altered in the script. She fought with the film's director, Irving Rapper, over matters large and small until, he said, he would go home evenings "angry and exhausted." Ilka Chase, who played Charlotte's sister, recalled that Bette was "a fine, hard-working woman, friendly with members of her cast, forthright and courteous to technicians on her picture, and her director's heaviest cross. She will argue every move in every scene until the poor man is reduced to quivering pulp . . . she is what atomic energy draws on when it really wants to gather its forces. To make a picture quietly, a procedure so wearing that it leads many others to the doors of a sanitarium, would exhaust Miss Davis about as much as a bout with a six-year-old contender . . . would tire Joe Louis."

To Paul Henreid, Bette's willingness to battle was a godsend. "She was the soul of kindness to me all through the shooting, as she was to all the cast," he recalled. "I have never understood these stories of how difficult she was to other cast members. On the contrary, she would fight *their* battles with the director."

FOURTEEN

Huge klieg lights sent beacons swirling into the low-hanging clouds in the sky over Hollywood. On Cahuenga Boulevard near Sunset, swing music blared from loudspeakers and filled the night as thousands of servicemen jamming the street cheered every time they caught sight of one of their favorite movie stars pushing through the throng. It was Saturday night, October 3, 1942, and the Hollywood Canteen had opened in a swirl of glamour and excitement to rival the most lavish movie premiere.

The crush became so great that when Bette arrived she feared she wouldn't be able to get in to give her welcoming speech in time. A security guard escorted her to the back of the building, where she clambered through a bathroom window. After Bette and John Garfield offered their opening remarks, Abbott and Costello did their comedy routine, "Who's on First?" Then Kay Kyser, Rudy Vallee, and Duke Ellington started to swing, and hundreds of fresh-faced, wide-eyed young men danced with movie goddesses like Rita Hayworth, Carole Landis, Joan Crawford, Betty Grable, and Marlene Dietrich. None of these men had ever seen so much beauty, glamour, and excitement in one place. It was enough to make them forget for a while that they were headed out to war.

Bette helped found the Hollywood Canteen because making films made her feel guilty. The United States was locked in a potentially apocalyptic struggle with Germany across the Atlantic and Japan across the Pacific. Hundreds of thousands of American boys were being shipped off, many to their deaths, leaving behind widows and orphans and heartsick parents. In the midst of all this, lines of dialogue, or the line of a dress, seemed absurdly unimportant.

Even before America entered the war, Bette had said, "With France, beautiful, brave France, collapsing, England with its back to the wall, and Hitler's hordes trampling down democracy everywhere in Europe, mak-

191

ing faces at motion-picture cameras seemed utterly inconsequential. My feeling about my work was, 'What does it matter?' "

Although she had already done a good deal for the war effort during her last layoff from Warners, and had joined Lena Horne and Ethel Waters in Hattie McDaniel's touring troupe to entertain all-black army divisions (she was the only white member), Bette couldn't shake the nagging feeling that she wasn't doing enough, and that spending her time making movies was frivolous. Hal Wallis reminded her that films—particularly her special brand of "women's pictures"—were a diversion and a comfort to lonely wives and grieving widows, and of course that was true. But somehow it didn't seem enough.

It was John Garfield who gave Bette the chance to make what she considered a major wartime contribution. The handsome twenty-nine-year-old cinema anti-hero had been classified 4-F, and like many men in that position, he felt frustrated and impotent at not being able to fight in a war that the vast majority of Americans believed to be morally right and necessary for the survival of the free world.

Garfield decided that the best contribution he could make would be to establish a servicemen's club in Hollywood, where embarking and returning soldiers could dance and mingle with movie stars—and not have to pay a cent for it. When he brought the idea to Bette during the late spring of 1942, she shouted *"Yes!"* the minute she heard it, and she plunged into the preparations with her indomitable energy. Between shots of *Now, Voyager,* she helped Garfield with the mountain of details that needed to be worked out—at this point they didn't even have a building to house the club.

They found a run-down former livery-stable-turned-nightclub called The Old Barn on Cahuenga Boulevard. Bette persuaded fourteen guilds and unions to donate the labor and materials to renovate the building. The carpenters' union pounded nails; the electricians' union replaced the wiring; the musicians' union supplied an orchestra. Studio artists and cartoonists decorated the walls, Cary Grant donated a piano, Jack Warner shipped in linoleum.

Bette also enlisted the help of Jules Stein, her agent and the powerful head of MCA, who was able to raise hundreds of thousands of dollars for the Canteen. Stein invested and managed the money so well that there was always a surplus of funds despite a weekly bill of $3,000 for food alone.

The Hollywood Canteen was an enormous and instantaneous success. There was music, dancing, fun, and good food, usually served by people these men never thought they would have a chance to meet, and their excitement was palpable night after night. Bette rarely danced with the men, but she scrubbed floors, served meals, and signed autographs, often after a long day's shooting. Whenever there was a shortage of celebrities, Bette could be counted on to show up. "Couldn't have a night when there was nobody," she said. And to the surprise of many, Bette usually won the lion's share of the attention, even when women of sexier reputations and more conventional beauty were present.

The actor Jack Carson, who had appeared with Bette in two films prior to the Canteen opening, recalled how surprised he was by the magnetism she seemed to hold for the servicemen. "There were some real lookers there, but Bette was the one they clustered around. . . . She would jump out of costume and race from Warners down to the canteen and when she showed up she'd look like something the cat dragged in—hair unkempt, makeup still partly smeared over her face, and with any old thing thrown on, and those guys would drop whatever cutie-pie starlet they had on hand and would make a bee-line for her. Within two minutes of showing up, she'd be mobbed by them."

Charles Morton was a young navy recruit when he visited the Canteen, and he vividly remembers his awe and excitement at "so many celebrities performing, washing dishes, mopping floors. . . . I wonder now what stars like Joan Fontaine, Bob Hope, Marlene Dietrich, and Olivia De Havilland thought when instead of asking for their autograph I would ask them, 'Where is Bette Davis?' "

She was arguably the most famous actress there, but more than that, the servicemen responded to Bette's genuine concern and feeling for them. They knew she *wanted* to be there. Others, it was clear, showed up primarily for the publicity it would bring them. More than once Bette got on the phone and harangued some star or other to show up—"'and not just when the newsreels are here!'"

The intermingling of so many people from different parts of the country occasionally caused trouble. "Oh, the black/white problem we had!" Bette recalled. "We had black hostesses, white hostesses. We had millions of southern men—you know how they deal with blacks—and if at any time there was a row, if a black man was dancing with a white girl, or whatever, we would play 'The Star-Spangled Banner' and that would stop it."

As the war dragged on, more and more wounded and disabled servicemen visited the Canteen, confined to wheelchairs or walking on crutches. Bette put together a thoughtful primer to help the volunteers deal sensitively with these men. "Forget the wounds, remember the man," she instructed. "Don't be oversolicitous, nor too controlled to the point of indifference. Learn to use the word 'prosthetics' instead of 'artificial limbs.' Never say, 'It could have been worse.' And when he talks about his war experiences, *listen,* but don't ask for more details than he wants to give."

Bette's next two films, released in 1943, kept her solidly in touch with the wartime fervor. Lillian Hellman's antifascist Broadway success, *Watch on the Rhine,* gave her a chance to underplay once again as the wife of a leader of the underground anti-Nazi movement in Germany. The film was the first time Bette had been able to "fight the war on-screen," and she was gratified by its solid box-office profits and positive reviews. Bosley Crowther in *The New York Times* called it "the first Hollywood film to go deeply into the fundamental nature of fascism. . . . It also reveals with shocking impact the unforgivable carelessness of those who are morally opposed to fascism but who do nothing positive to check it."

Thank Your Lucky Stars provided a complete change of pace. A musical pastiche, its thin plot centered around a wartime charity show and featured Bette and a pantheon of other stars in over a dozen musical numbers. Each guest star was paid $50,000, which was then promptly donated to the Canteen.

The film turned out to be a mixed bag. Talented singers like Dinah Shore, Eddie Cantor, and Dennis Morgan delivered as expected, but most of the rest—Errol Flynn, Jack Carson, Alan Hale, Olivia De Havilland, and Ida Lupino—were conspicuously ill at ease with a song. The best turn by a nonsinger was Bette's; her number actually turned up on the Lucky Strike Hit Parade after the film's release. Bemoaning the lack of available men after the draft, she torchily talk-sang that "They're Either Too Young or Too Old." Bette brought out all her most beloved (and often criticized) mannerisms in the number—popping eyes, fluttery hands, clipped inflections—and they worked brilliantly in what was meant to be caricature.

At the end of the song, Bette is approached by a young man who swings her into an athletic jitterbug that left audiences cheering. A dance contest winner, Conrad Weidel, played the young man. He was terrified. "If I hurt you or drop you, Miss D-Davis," he stammered, "the top guys will pr-probably put me in a cement mixer."

"Forget about who I am or who you think I am," Bette replied. "Just let your instincts come to the fore and do it, boy!" Weidel then handled her so expertly that Bette enthused, "He made me look like the dancer I distinctly was not."

Thank Your Lucky Stars pulled in a $1.5 million profit at the box office; added to the donations of its stars' salaries the film brought in more than $2 million for the Canteen.

Bette's long work days and her frequent harried evenings at the Canteen left her in a perpetual state of near exhaustion. Friends wondered how she managed to keep at it. "Thank God I was blessed with so much energy!" she replied. But too often now, that energy threatened to desert her. On her days off she'd sleep twelve to fourteen hours; when Farney was in Minneapolis or New Hampshire she'd feel lonely and dissatisfied, and when he was at Riverbottom with her she would be too tired and draggy most of the time to be much of a companion. What even Arthur Farnsworth didn't know at this time was that Bette kept herself in perpetual motion in part to avoid facing the fact that her marriage was crumbling.

It wasn't just because Farney was away so much and Bette was so often tired. As she had with Ham Nelson, Bette had come to resent rather than enjoy Farnsworth's frequent passivity, and she took to goading her husband to "Be more of a man!" or "Show some life, for crissakes!" Farnsworth's reactions ranged from withdrawal to secret drinking to hitting Bette. "He got violent at times to take out his frustrations," she said.

By this point Bette had realized that Farnsworth was "an alcoholic who was tied to his mother's apron strings . . . and what a mother. *Christ,* what a cold bitch!"

Bette, who could belt back a drink with the best of them, didn't realize the extent of Farnsworth's alcohol problem until she found a cache of empty bottles he had hidden. "I couldn't understand that," she told Whitney Stine. "If you drink, then drink! He didn't have to hide it from me."

Furtive drinking, Bette later learned, was a problem in Farnsworth's family. His brother, too, was found to have hidden a large number of liquor bottles under a bed. Bette sensed that his drinking wasn't the only secret Farney tried to hide. "As much as I loved my husband, I realized that he had problems he hid from me. Maybe I caused some of them, I don't know." She never did find out what most of them were.

According to her cousin Sally Favour, Bette may have been the only one who didn't realize the extent of Farnsworth's drinking from early on. "He was drinking heavily," Sally avers. "He didn't drink that much at first, but he got to drinking more and more as they were married. You know, being married to Bette would be very difficult for anybody, and it was for Farney. It's pretty hard for a guy to live as Mr. Bette Davis, and to live with a human dynamo like she was."

The marriage was heading for disaster, Bette knew, and now a new problem arose that she found unbearable: their sex life dissipated as Farney's drinking rendered him impotent more and more often. Both of them began to dally with others, and when Bette found out about one affair of Farney's, she exploded to a friend, "He can do it with *her* for crissakes!" Finally the innuendoes around Hollywood about the Farnsworths' marital problems cropped up in the gossip columns, but Bette denied them all. "Farney and I are *divinely* happy," she lied.

In November 1942, Bette fell into a troubled cauldron of a different kind when she was cast again in a picture opposite Miriam Hopkins. Her better judgment had told her not to do it, but the script was too good to turn down. *Old Acquaintance* was the story of two lifelong friends, both writers, one down-to-earth and noble, the other pretentious, bitchy, and suspicious, and their real and imagined rivalries over their careers and men. The script, written by John Van Druten and Lenore Coffee (based on Van Druten's play), featured much delicious bitchiness; when a reporter makes a gaffe in front of the Hopkins character and says, "I guess I should cut my throat," Miriam replies, "There's a knife over there on the table." It also gave Bette one of her best movie lines: "There comes a time in every woman's life when the only thing that helps is a glass of champagne."

Bette was cast as the sweet character, and Miriam Hopkins typecast as the bitch. Immediately, Hopkins caused trouble. With her picture-to-picture deal with Warner Brothers, she demanded to be paid $10,000 a week, twice as much as Bette, and to be allowed complete autonomy over her own makeup, wardrobe, and hairstyling. The film's director, Edmund Goulding, began to look for a replacement, and considered Margaret Sullavan, Janet Gaynor, and Constance Bennett, but it was clear that none of these women could play this harridan as well as Miriam. Jack Warner personally pleaded with Hopkins to reconsider and assured her that she wouldn't be paid any *less* than Bette. When Warner agreed to her personal grooming and wardrobe requirements, Hopkins signed on at $5,000 per week.

Then Goulding found himself beleaguered from the other side. When Bette said she would accept no cameraman but Sol Polito, whose work she had loved in *Now, Voyager,* Goulding fired off a telegram to Hal Wallis: "I am either working for Warner Brothers or Miss Davis and there is a difference. Urge you not to commit to any promise on cameraman until after talk with me. That would put me in a position of Davis, Hopkins, moods, fads, and nonsense."

Caught between Bette's demands and Miriam's, and besieged by late-night telephone calls from both of them to make sure he wasn't siding with one against the other, Goulding suffered a heart attack. He recovered with near-miraculous speed once he was removed from the picture.

Several other directors turned down the assignment. "I might be able to work with Hopkins," one said, "and I might be able to work with Davis. But together? Never!" Finally, the relative newcomer Vincent Sherman accepted the challenge. Bette had wanted to work with Sherman in 1940 after George Brent recommended him to her, but he didn't like the script she wanted to do with him (*Affectionately Yours,* which she never made), and wrote to tell her so. "I never heard from her," Sherman recalled, "and I didn't know whether she was angry. But whenever I passed her on the lot from then on she'd ignore me."

Bette was skeptical about Sherman as director of *Old Acquaintance;* he had made only seven B pictures before this. But Hal Wallis assured her that his most recent film, *The Hard Way,* was excellent, and that Sherman had pulled a first-rate performance out of his star, Ida Lupino. Bette acquiesced, but she was still worried. As the November production date approached and Los Angeles was battered by a series of rainstorms, she developed strep throat and took off for Palm Springs to recover. She didn't report for work the first week, and Sherman filmed around her. When she finally arrived, she did so in the company of her agent's partner, Lew Wasserman, with an obvious "show me" attitude toward Sherman.

Sherman saw her arrive on the set as he directed Miriam in a scene. After he yelled, "Cut!" he walked over to Bette and said, "Hello." He thought she would say, "Well, at last we're working together," but she was more terse than that. "How are things going?" she asked. Sherman replied that things were going very well; why didn't Bette stay and watch some rushes? "Oh, *may* I?" Bette purred.

"That was why she had come to the set in the first place," Sherman says. "She wanted to see the rushes of what I'd been doing and if she hadn't liked them you can bet she would have gone to the front office and told them she didn't want me to continue." As Bette watched four days' worth of filming, she was delighted to see that Sherman had beautifully captured Miriam's worst qualities—her harshness, her coldness, her vicious edge. She called Sherman that night. "I think it's delightful," she told him. "You're doing a *wonderful* job with Miriam! When do you want me to come to work?"

"Tomorrow morning at nine." Bette said she'd be there. "She came in and we went through the picture," Sherman recalls. "There was no problem—except the two ladies."

As before, the main problem was Miriam. Bette Davis's status as a movie star had taken a quantum leap since the filming of *The Old Maid;* she was now the undisputed queen of the American cinema. If Miriam had been insecure about working with Bette early in 1939, she was rendered frantic by it in 1943. Her antics and machinations escalated throughout the filming until they had just about careered out of control.

Two days into shooting with Bette, Miriam called Sherman and complained that he was giving Bette more close-ups. She didn't believe his protestations to the contrary, and she continued to badger him with phone calls. After a week of this he sent her a letter: "Miriam, if I had my own mother in this film I wouldn't favor her over any other actress because I do what I think is best for the film and not what I think is best for any individual."

Still unconvinced, Hopkins reverted to the tried and true tactic of scene stealing. She asked Sherman if she could use a cigarette holder in one scene, and then covered Bette's face with it during an over-the-shoulder shot. More than once she slowly blew cigarette smoke in Bette's face until her costar's eyes began to tear; whenever she was supposed to do no more than listen to a Davis monologue, she did every bit of business she could think of to distract attention away from her costar.

Bette fumed, but she'd be damned if she would give Hopkins the satisfaction of a blowup. Instead she constantly took Sherman aside to advise him on how best to "handle" Miriam, something Sherman made the mistake of complaining about to Miriam. "There's going to be a showdown," he told Hopkins. "Either she directs the picture or I do. I'm not going on in this way."

Sensing success, her Southern belle side rushing to the fore, Miriam cooed, "She's bin runnin' roughshod over me from th' beginnin', Vince. Ah'm an innocent in this matter. I never did any harm ta her. Ah don' know what she's talkin' 'bout." When Bette heard about this exchange, she felt she had been betrayed by Sherman, whom she always suspected would side with Miriam because of their mutual Southern backgrounds. She began to harangue Hopkins about her performance, but whenever she did Miriam would take a hearing aid out of her purse, put it in her ear, and pretend it wasn't working. Bette would stalk off to her dressing room, red-faced with fury, and soon a game of one-upmanship began: when Bette muttered that Miriam had just played a scene as though she were dead, Hopkins showed up the next day dressed entirely in black; every time Miriam came in with a revised script page on pink paper, Bette would quickly present Sherman with a blue page of her own changes.

For the last third of the movie, after the two characters have aged nineteen years, Bette added gray to her hair and some subtle aging makeup. Hopkins did nothing. "That *bitch*," Bette seethed to Sherman. "I'm going to be looking old and she's going to be looking younger than she looked at the beginning!"

The friction took its toll on both women. Each was out sick ten times in January; they alternated sick days during one week so that no scenes of them together could be filmed. When a columnist printed these statistics and repeated the stories of the two stars' mutual antipathy, the anticipation of many in Hollywood for the film's upcoming set piece mushroomed: the moment when Bette's character, sick to death of Miriam's selfishness and treachery, shakes her senseless and leaves her collapsed on a sofa. When *Life* magazine asked Jack Warner to allow one of their photographers on the set for the scene, he refused. "I don't think it's good for the picture, two dames hating each other," he explained to Sherman. "What they feel about each other isn't good publicity. I'd rather not have it."

On the morning the scene was to be shot, Bette noticed far more observers on the set than usual. "The rafters above the stage were full of excited spectators," she recalled. "It was rather like a prizefight ring below." Bette told Sherman that for the sake of realism, she intended to shake Miriam just as hard as she could. But, she warned him, "She's gonna try to fuck up this scene, Vince." When Miriam arrived on the set she told Sherman, "Vincent dear, ah know Bette has t' shake me, but ah slipped badly and have a crick in mah neck, an' ah just hope she won't be *too* vio-lent."

Sherman mentioned this to Bette. "Goddamn it!" she growled. "I knew she'd come up with *something!*" When the big moment arrived, hundreds of observers watched Bette grab Miriam by the shoulders and shake her as hard as she could. Sherman was prepared for anything except what happened. As he explained it, "When you shake someone, they try to resist you, and their head moves back and forth as part of the push/resistance struggle. Miriam did just the opposite. She put up no resistance, just let her head relax so it went all over the place, like a broken doll." (This despite the "crick" in her neck.)

Bette turned in fury to Sherman and screamed, "She just went *limp!*" and stormed off the set. Sherman took a deep breath and walked over to Hopkins. "Miriam, it looks phony and weird that way, with your head wobbling like that."

"Ah was only tryin' to coah-perate," Miriam sighed. "I didn't want ta fight her, ah just wanted to let her do it." When Sherman shot the scene again, Miriam stiffened up enough so that with careful editing he was able to make the confrontation look, as he later resignedly put it, "all right."

All this professional tension left Bette drained and more emotionally needy than ever. Farney provided her no solace; he still spent more time in Minneapolis or New Hampshire than he did Los Angeles, and when he was on the West Coast he and Bette fought so much about his drinking that they wound up avoiding each other at separate ends of the rambling Riverbottom.

Always in need of professional allies on a picture ("Us against Them"), Bette sought romantic and sexual soothing as well, and she found it with Gig Young, the handsome thirty-year-old newcomer playing the fiancé she loses to her rival's daughter. Appearing in only his third film, Young was immensely flattered that a star of Bette's magnitude would find him sexually attractive. In spite of his marriage of less than three years to Sheila Stapler, Gig embarked on an affair with his leading lady that found them sneaking assignations in her dressing room suite or at Riverbottom after a day's filming. According to Young biographer George Eels, Gig told Sheila his late nights were the result of the strife on the set between Davis and Hopkins. She had read and heard about it, so she had no reason to disbelieve him.

Young, five years Bette's junior, played a naval officer ten years younger than Bette's character. When it came time for Hopkins to deliver a put-down of her friend's romance ("She wants to be a sailor's bride—of forty-two!") she spoke it with just enough extra malice that Bette couldn't miss the dig. The affair with Young was cut short when he was drafted into the Coast Guard; he reported for duty as soon as *Old Acquaintance* production wrapped in February.

On the last day of filming, Bette and Vincent Sherman worked until two o'clock on a Sunday morning to finish the picture, and Bette asked him for a lift to Ruthie's house in Laurel Canyon, where she stayed frequently to allay her loneliness. On the way, Bette spotted Simon's drive-in restaurant on the corner of Ventura Boulevard and Laurel Canyon. "Can we stop for a hamburger?" she asked Sherman. "I'm starving!"

They placed their orders, then Bette turned and looked into Sherman's eyes. "Well, Mr. Sherman," she said, "I just want you to know that it's been fun working with you and despite all the trouble we had with Miriam, you handled her beautifully." Then she paused and added softly, "I want you to know that I love you."

"I love you, too, Bette," Sherman replied cheerily, assuming this was typical Hollywood hyperbole.

"No, Vince," she whispered, and took his hand. "I mean, I *really* love you."

Sherman looked at her and felt chills that he recalled vividly forty years later. "You must remember *who* Bette Davis was at this time. She was very attractive, a great actress, and a powerful star. I was a new, impressionable director." Sherman, who was two years older than Bette, admits that he was "enamored" of her during filming: "I admired her, and she appealed to me tremendously, both physically and mentally. But I never made a pass at her. I was happily married, with a wonderful wife and a three-year-old daughter. And Bette was married. I didn't know what to say to her. Finally I just said, 'Well, Bette, I can't tell you how flattered I am.' "

They left the restaurant about 3 A.M., then parked in front of Ruthie's house and continued to talk. Bette confided in Sherman that her marriage was in name only, and asked him how he felt about her. He admitted he was attracted to her, but he made no moves. "She was too far above me—in standing, in salary, everything." Sherman feared that "if I made a pass at her, it would have offended her New England sense of values. Also, it had to be *her* idea."

Of course, Bette *wanted* Sherman to "make a pass at her." She saw in him many of the same qualities that she admired in William Wyler; Sherman even reminded her physically of Wyler. Something might have transpired between the two of them in his car that night—except for Ruthie. "It was about four o'clock in the morning by now," Sherman recalls, "and Bette's mother came out on the front porch in her bathrobe and called out, 'Is that you, Bette Davis?' Bette replied, 'Yes, Mother.' And her mother said, 'Do you realize what time it is? You come into this house at once!' " Sherman burst into laughter. "What's so funny?" Bette asked. "I haven't heard that kind of talk since I was in high school," he replied.

"Here was Bette Davis," Sherman mused, "twice married, twice the winner of the Academy Award, and her mother was talking to her as if she were a sixteen-year-old out past her curfew." As she got out of the car, Bette turned back to Sherman and said, "Ruthie means well."

Sherman didn't follow up on Bette's amorous revelation to him, so she initiated a dinner date a few weeks later. It was clear that Bette wanted a sexual relationship, and he enjoyed the thought: "I would have loved to have put my arms around her and made love to her." But again, the pull of his family proved stronger, and he let the opportunity pass. Soon thereafter, Bette joined him for lunch at the studio and mentioned that she was about to take a vacation trip to Mexico—did he think he might be able to join her in Acapulco? He told her he would try, but in fact he had no intention of going. "I tried to hedge a bit by saying that Warners might want me to stay to work on the final cut of *Old Acquaintance*, but I did tell her that I would try to get away."

Bette left for Acapulco the first week of March, already in a poor frame of mind because on March 4 she had lost the Best Actress Oscar most observers had expected she would win for *Now, Voyager*. (Greer Garson won the award for *Mrs. Miniver*.) She registered at the Hotel Los Galmingos, and waited for Sherman's arrival. "I waited and waited," Bette recalled. "To my chagrin, he never came. He stood me up." According to Sherman, he did call to tell Bette that he wasn't going to join her. What he didn't tell her was what had happened to make his decision final: Arthur Farnsworth had telephoned him at the studio and said he had something important to discuss with him. Could he come and speak with him?

"Farnsworth was a very nice guy," Sherman recalled. "He came to my office and told me that he and Bette had had too many drinks the night before she left for Mexico and got into a terrible fight, during which she told him everything: that she was in love with me, that she and I were going to Mexico together, the whole thing. He begged me not to go."

Sherman wasn't sure what to do, so he told Farnsworth the truth. "Arthur," he began, "I can tell you that nothing has happened between Bette and myself. Honestly. Yes, there was some talk about Mexico, but I haven't made any plans to go." He looked Farnsworth directly in the eye and added, "I promise you, I will not go."

In Bette's view, Sherman had rejected her, and she was angry. By the time she received a telegram from Jack Warner asking her to appear at a reception with the president of Mexico to launch his country's Red Cross, she was in a very foul mood indeed. She snapped back that she was on vacation and that once again Warner expected her to "work for free." Tentatively, Warner drafted and redrafted his reply. (By now, whenever he faced the Davis dudgeon, J.L. handled her as gingerly as possible.) Despite his long, carefully worded response to her objections, and his argument that Bette's appearance was important to the United States's war effort, she did not appear at the function.

Instead, she went to stay at the Acapulco home of Dorothy, Contessa di Frasso, an American-born beauty who had married an Italian count and whom Bette knew only as a wealthy California hostess. What she didn't know was that the contessa was under FBI surveillance because of her friendships with the Los Angeles gangster Bugsy Siegel and the Italian dictator Benito Mussolini. The United States government suspected that di Frasso was a paid agent of Mussolini, but the FBI's close watch of her activities in 1943 revealed nothing, and the surveillance was called off. Bette never did know that she was being watched while staying with the contessa; had she found out, she would surely have breathed a sigh of relief at Vincent Sherman's failure to keep their illicit rendezvous.

Crushed by Sherman's rejection, Bette resolved to make one last attempt to salvage her marriage to Farney. In April, she left Mexico and went directly to Butternut. At first, the reunion went well. Bette was unusually docile and pliable, and she helped Farney around the house, socialized with the neighbors, did everything she thought one should do to be a good wife. It didn't last long. Issues that should have been laughed off gnawed at Bette; whenever some small problem resurfaced, she would snap, Farncy would withdraw, and silence would hang over Butternut like a pall. Before long the Farnsworths were drinking and battling more seriously than ever, and the husband was taking the worst of it.

Bette was always able to get the better of Farney verbally. His sister, Lucile de Besche, recalled that Bette "had the superior intellect of the two," and Bette later said that all of her husbands "loathed my brightness." When she was angry, Bette would turn into a harpy, cruelly goading Farnsworth until he couldn't take it any longer and hit her. Their marriage descended into violence more and more often now.

In June, according to Bette, she and Farnsworth were sitting in the loft when the telephone rang downstairs. He got up to answer it, and as he started down the stairs in his stocking feet, he slipped and plummeted to the bottom, cracking his head on the floor as he landed. Bette ran to him, but he protested that he was all right. Bette has never said whether Farnsworth had been drinking.

For the next few days, Bette noticed that Farney was acting oddly. He appeared woozy and forgetful; sometimes he would move sluggishly or go into a limp as he walked. But he was an uncomplaining sort, and he pooh-poohed the symptoms. Finally, he seemed to return to normal, and in early July he and Bette boarded a train back to California. She was set to begin a new film, *Mr. Skeffington,* and he had been hired by the Disney Studios to help prepare an instructional film for the Air Force on the use of the new Norden bombsight for bomber planes.

Renewed tension hung over the trip West. The couple rarely spoke to each other as they sat in their compartment and stared out the window at the passing scenery. When either did say something, it usually signaled the start of an argument. One morning, as the train passed through Nevada, Bette and Farney got into a verbal clash that grew so intense that Farnsworth rushed toward Bette as if to strike a blow. She bobbed out of his way, knocking him off balance, and he fell to the floor. Once again, he struck his head, but he seemed to be okay. That night, the last of the trip, the two slept in separate cars.

FIFTEEN

Monday, August 23, 1943, was a typically hot, dry summer day in Southern California, the sky cloudless, the sun beating stark and bright on the sidewalks of Hollywood. At about 3:30 in the afternoon, according to witnesses, Arthur Farnsworth walked past the Regent Tobacco Shop at 6249 Hollywood Boulevard, carrying a briefcase. The store's owner, Dave Friedman, later said he was standing just inside the door of his shop, and had heard a "terrifying yell that made my blood curdle. It came from a man walking just inside my view, and as I heard him yell, I saw him suddenly fall straight backward and land on his head. He made no attempt to break the fall with his arms or hands, so that's why I think something happened to him before he hit the ground. Blood rushed from his ears and nostrils."

Another witness, advertising man Gilbert Wright, said he had seen Farnsworth walk past the store entrance. "When he was almost past, he let out a throaty cry, and the next moment he came down on the back of his head, just as if he were doing a backflip and hadn't quite made it. I ran to him but it was all I could do to hold him because he was in convulsions. The blood was flowing from his nose and ears." Friedman's sales clerk, Rosalie Fox, called an ambulance and the unconscious Farnsworth was taken to Hollywood Receiving Hospital, where his physician, Dr. Paul Moore, arrived at 4:30 and found him semiconscious and unable to speak. The hospital telephoned Bette at Riverbottom to tell her that her husband seemed to have had an epileptic fit. Her reported response was odd: "There are a great many things my husband may have had, but I assure you an epileptic fit is not one of them!"

Bette asked Dr. Moore to transfer Farney to Hollywood Presbyterian Hospital, where X-rays revealed a fractured skull. Deeply distressed, Bette arrived there about 5:30, accompanied by Ruthie, and when Farney did not recognize them she seemed about to pass out. Dr. Moore helped her into a chair, and she remained at the hospital, sleeping in Farney's room along with his mother, Lucile, who had flown in from

205

New Hampshire, for the next two days. He wavered in and out of con
sciousness, sometimes seeming to recognize her and his mother, and
other times not. On Wednesday evening he took a turn for the worse,
and at 7:05 P.M. he died. Bette seemed to take the news stoically, but
when Ruthie took her back to Riverbottom she collapsed and was put
under sedation.

Arthur Farnsworth's death certificate listed the cause of death as a "basal
skull fracture right temporal and occipital." It seemed clear that the
injury was the result of his fall, and the matter was about to be closed
when Lucile Farnsworth demanded an autopsy on her son. She argued
that his war work at Honeywell, and his top-secret consultations with the
Disney Studios on the Norden bombsight, made it possible that his
death involved foul play. When she learned that Farnsworth's briefcase
was missing, her resolve hardened, and the Los Angeles County Coroner's Office scheduled an autopsy for the next day.

On Thursday afternoon, Dr. Homer Keyes, the assistant coroner's
surgeon who performed the autopsy, issued a surprising finding: Farnsworth's skull fracture was more likely the *cause* of his fall than the result
of it. "The blood in the fracture was black and coagulated, not merely
purple and partially congealed as it would have been if the injury had
been received only last Monday," Dr. Keyes told reporters. "The fracture could have been inflicted as long as two weeks ago, and, conceiv-
ably, Farnsworth had been walking around ever since with the condition
fructifying until it eventually caused his death."

The press strongly played up Keyes's finding; headlines called the
death "mysterious" and the *Los Angeles Examiner* suggested that Farnsworth's "connection with the Honeywell concern, which manufactures
precision instruments for aircraft, would furnish a powerful motive for an
attack by agents who wanted to acquire valuable secret data."

When Bette heard of Keyes's report, she asked to speak to a detective. Detective Sergeant H. R. Johnson went to Riverbottom, where
Bette was reported to be "prostrated." She described to Johnson Farney's tumble down the stairs at Butternut two months earlier, and
blamed it for her husband's death. "I realize now that little things that
happened since, which I thought nothing of at the time, were the result
of that fall, all of which have been confirmed by Dr. Moore," she was
reported to have said. "At least to find a reason for a seemingly ridiculous accident is a relief and a comfort to me."

Accounts of Bette's statement in the next day's newspapers reminded readers that Homer Keyes had found that Farnsworth's skull fracture could not have been inflicted more than "two weeks ago," spoke of "new mystery developments," and suggested that Farnsworth must have suffered another head injury more recently than the one at Butternut. Faced with growing skepticism, Los Angeles County Coroner Frank A. Nance announced that he would hold an inquest into the death on the following Tuesday, August 31.

At the funeral on Saturday, Bette wore a black suit, her hair tucked into a black snood, and sunglasses. She wept during the recitation of the 121st and 123rd psalms, "Farney's favorites." As the mourners began to file out, she pulled Jack Warner aside and spoke with him privately for nearly twenty minutes. The veteran Hollywood reporter Hector Arce recalled that "the details of their conversation were not heard by anyone . . . but he must have agreed to use his influence to get the inquest settled quickly. Certainly he had that power, because look what happened."

The following Tuesday at 10 A.M., Frank Nance began the inquest into Arthur Farnsworth's death at the Los Angeles Hall of Justice. The transcription of the testimony, never before available to a Bette Davis biographer, strongly suggests that the proceedings were designed not to ascertain the truth but rather to present the jurors with a prearranged set of facts from which they could reach only one possible verdict: that Farnsworth's fall on Hollywood Boulevard had been caused solely by his injury at Butternut in June.

Nance alone posed the questions to the ten witnesses who appeared. Again and again the transcript reveals the coroner's lack of interest in discrepancies in their testimony, and the reader is struck by his leading, biased questions and his interruptions whenever a witness begins to fill in unwanted details. Each time Nance asked the six male jurors whether they had any follow-up questions, they did not. But Nance invited queries from the jury after only four of the witnesses. In five of the six cases where he didn't, the witness had made at least one statement in direct contradiction of either himself or one of the other witnesses, a contradiction that Nance had neither pointed out nor asked to be explained. It is difficult not to suspect that Nance was very deftly trying to avoid placing any doubts in the minds of the jurors.

The first witness in the stiflingly hot courtroom was Bette's attorney,

Dudley R. Furse, who testified that he had met with Farney in his law office, near to where he fell, between 2:45 and 3:30 on Monday afternoon. Nance's initial questions to Furse established little beyond Farney's full name, birthplace, birth date, time and place of death, and the name of his wife. He then asked Furse if he had learned the cause of death—a strange question to a lawyer, especially when expert medical witnesses were waiting to testify—and Furse replied that he had "an opinion" that "it resulted from an accident" and further that "the information that has come to me" indicates that Farney's death was caused by the fall on Hollywood Boulevard "and possibly a previous injury before that."

In light of the press hints that Farnsworth's "secret war work" might have made him the victim of foul play, Nance was oddly uncurious about what business Farney was engaged in on the day he died. "Was he talking to you about personal business?" he asked Furse. "Yes," the attorney replied, and that was that—Nance posed no more probing questions. The same thing happened with the next witness, Mary Marshall, a secretary at the Walt Disney Studios, who testified that Farnsworth telephoned her around 3:30 "to make an appointment with my immediate superior for him to come in to see him before five o'clock that afternoon, inasmuch as he was working with us at the studio at the time."

Since Farnsworth's work on the Disney film involved his knowledge of the top-secret bombsights and may have endangered his life, the testimony of Mary Marshall's superior might have provided key information for the investigation. Incredibly, Nance didn't even ask the name of the man, or whether Marshall had any idea what the meeting was going to be about. Instead he asked, "That was the last you heard of him?" When Marshall replied, "Yes, sir," Nance said, "I think that is sufficient." He didn't invite the jurors to ask any questions.

Next on the witness stand was Ralph William Dorn, a young attendant at a parking lot next door to the Regent, where Farney had parked his car that day. Early in his testimony, Dorn dropped a potential bombshell when he said that Farnsworth had left his car in the lot on two separate occasions the day he fell. "He came in once towards noon," Dorn said, "and then again about 2:30 or quarter to three." Completely ignoring this intriguing new information, Nance asked Dorn nothing about Farney's demeanor or activities during the first visit, and he did not recall Dudley Furse to the stand to ask if the first visit was also to Furse's nearby office and if so what business was discussed.

When Dorn told Nance that he did not see Farney fall but did see him lying on the sidewalk, Nance asked if the young man went up to him. Dorn began to reply, "I went up there and Mr. Wright and Mr. Friedman—" but Nance interrupted him. "Was he unconscious?" Dorn replied, "No, he wasn't unconscious." After asking if Farnsworth had said anything (he hadn't), Nance then quickly wrapped up the questioning.

Nance: Was there any evidence of an obstruction or anything that would cause him to fall?

Dorn: No sir.

Nance: The sidewalk was perfectly clear?

Dorn: Yes sir.

Nance: And nothing to interfere with careful walking?

Dorn: No sir.

Nance: Do you know of anyone who contributed to his falling?

Dorn: No sir.

Nance: That is all.

Again, Nance invited no questions from the jurors. Dave Friedman, the owner of the Regent, climbed into the witness box next, and offered no major departures from what he had told the press following the accident. He did supply further details of Farnsworth's condition after the fall. "His body was quivering. He didn't say anything. The only thing, he just looked dazed and his eyes were glassy. He didn't say a word, but he was groaning or moaning. He was quivering and trying to get up. The blood was coming from above his ears, and his mouth and his nose." In response to Nance's question—"Was it your impression from the way he acted that he had a sudden seizure of some sort and fell backwards and lost control?"—Friedman replied, "That's correct. The reason I thought that something happened to him at first, he didn't throw his arms out, trying to save himself."

After Friedman's straightforward testimony, there was a brief recess, then the court reconvened and Nance began to question Gilbert E. Wright. At three separate points in the transcript one is stunned by Nance's failure to ask follow-up questions. When the coroner asked whether Wright agreed with Dave Friedman's testimony about what happened outside the tobacco shop that day, Wright replied, "Practically," but Nance never asked him to enumerate the points on which he disagreed with Friedman. Contrary to his earlier statement to the press that he had seen Farnsworth "walk past the store entrance" before hearing his cry, Wright now testified that he did not notice Farney until his scream "attracted my attention that something was happening," and Nance did not question him about the discrepancy. After Wright contradicted Ralph Dorn's statement that Farney had been conscious during the seizure with the statement that "he was unconscious all the time," Nance ended the advertising man's ninety-second testimony without asking the jury if they had any questions.

Friedman's sales clerk, Rosalie Fox, added little to what her boss and Gilbert Wright had said, and she was dismissed after about a minute. Next up was Dr. Moore, whose most interesting testimony was that he had not seen Farney since the first week of June and had no indication that he had had an injury to his head at Butternut until he saw Bette the day after Farney's death and she told him about the fall. Nance did not ask Moore whether he thought it strange that a man with a skull injury that would later cause him to go into convulsions would not have complained to his doctor of dizziness, headaches, or other symptoms of a neurological problem.

As reporters and court personnel studied her every move, the day's star witness, Bette Davis, took the stand next. Her testimony is fascinating when one interprets it as an attempt to push forward a certain scenario of Farnsworth's death. She appeared to observers "wan and nervous" and looked haggard without makeup, her eyes underscored by dark circles. Once again she wore a black snood and suit jacket, but her skirt was punctuated by a dull green-and-red flower pattern.

Nance treated Bette with a deference he accorded none of the other witnesses. "I learned from witnesses," he told her, "that your husband, Arthur Farnsworth, not only met with an accident on the 23rd day of this month while walking on the street in Hollywood, but that he had an accident sometime previous to that while he was on a visit in the East. Is that true, Miss Davis?"

Bette's reply was odd in the extreme: "That is from the autopsy, I believe." Nothing of the sort was contained in the autopsy; the information that Farnsworth had fallen at Butternut came only from Bette, and Homer Keyes had said five days earlier that the fracture that caused Farney's seizure could not have occurred more than two weeks before his fall. Clearly, Bette was attempting to lend official credence to her version of the events, and Nance let the blatantly untrue statement go unchallenged. Instead he spent several minutes prodding Bette for irrelevant details like whether the fall was "in the daytime or nighttime" and whether the staircase on which Farney fell at Butternut was "winding or straight."

Bette's replies were terse, as though she had been coached to say as little as possible. When Nance asked her whether Farney had complained after the first fall, she replied, "Never heard him mention anything." When he asked her whether Farney saw a physician, she replied, "Evidently not."

After Bette added that Farney "wasn't one to complain very much" and that he might not have told her if he didn't feel well, Nance proceeded to tell rather than ask her how she felt when she heard of his fall on Hollywood Boulevard: "So that you were not prepared for the surprise and the shock you received on the 23rd when you learned he had fallen on the street. Did you at that time think about this fall?"

"I just couldn't imagine what it was."

"You never thought about this fall?"

"I never thought of it until the autopsy and they asked me of any kind of an accident he could have had."

"Your relations were always pleasant and nothing in your home life that could in any way contribute to his condition?"

"No."

"There is nothing else you can tell us?"

"That is the only thing I know anything about. I even asked the man who takes care of our horses if he had a fall from one of the horses while I was away, but not that he knew anything about. I think he would have known of that."

"Gentlemen of the jury, have you any questions?" Nance asked. There was no response. "I think that is all, Miss Davis, thank you very much."

This blithely unprobing inquest continued with the next witness, H. R. Johnson, the Los Angeles police investigator who had interviewed Bette at Riverbottom. The detective sergeant testified that he had conducted a probe into Farnsworth's death and had been "unable to locate anyone that knew anything of any prior injury that [Farnsworth] had complained of or received." In any proceeding truly intent on unearthing the truth, that information, which seemed to contradict Bette's story of the fall at Butternut, would have created some doubt as to her veracity, and would at least have prompted further investigation. Instead, Nance immediately retreated from it and turned Johnson's testimony around to show that the detective was in full agreement with the direction that the inquest was obviously taking:

Nance: You did verify the fact of his falling there on Hollywood Boulevard?

Johnson: We did.

Nance: You talked to these witnesses who testified here, and what they have told you in your investigation is substantially the same as they have stated here?

Johnson: It is.

Nance: Have you any reason to believe there is any contributing act on anybody's part in connection with his death?

Johnson: None at all.

Nance: I think that is sufficient. Thank you.

Homer R. Keyes, the man who had performed the autopsy on Farnsworth's body the morning of August 26, was the last to step into the witness box. Court observers leaned forward in anticipation of Keyes's testimony; it was, after all, his finding that Farney's initial injury could not have been more than two weeks old that had first cast doubt about the cause of death. Since it was clear to all in the courtroom by now what direction the inquest was taking, reporters and observers wondered how Nance would deal with Keyes's contradictory finding.

Keyes first described when and where he had conducted the autopsy, and read into the record his highly technical official report that concluded that the "immediate cause of death" was a "basal skull fracture." Then Nance zeroed in on the heart of the matter: "How about this old dark clot that you found? Was that sufficient to incapacitate the man?"

Keyes: Yes, indeed. The surface of the brain is a very sensitive area. You might say it is a ticklish spot, and is capable of throwing a person into convulsions resembling epilepsy.

Nance: Could it have taken practically eight weeks to develop that?

Keyes: Yes, I think it would be very likely. It would take about that long to develop.

Keyes had completely reversed himself, but Nance didn't question him about the contradiction. Instead he proceeded, as he had with Bette, to put words into the witness's mouth:

Nance: You heard the history of a fall while at his home in New Hampshire. . . . Could the hemorrhage and the injury to the brain develop a leak of some small blood vessel, so the hemorrhage would accumulate slowly, so it would take eight weeks to reach a point where it would cause a convulsion?

Keyes: I think that is what happened. I think there was a slight leak in a capillary.

Despite his report five days earlier that "the blood in the fracture was black and coagulated, not merely purple and partially congealed as it would have been if the injury had been received only last Monday," Keyes now reversed himself and testified that "I don't think there was a previous skull fracture."

After prodding Keyes to say that he didn't find it the least bit odd that Farnsworth hadn't complained of any symptoms following the fall at Butternut, Nance turned to the jurors. "All right, gentlemen, are you satisfied? Please retire to the jury room and see if you can agree upon a verdict and the responsibility for the death, if any."

At that, Bette left on the arm of Dudley Furse. There was little reason to stick around: the verdict could be easily predicted. After a short deliberation, the six men came to the only conclusion they could have after hearing the evidence they were presented. Farnsworth's death, they ruled, was "the result of an accidental fall on the sidewalk. . . . We find this death to be accidental and no person to blame."

In the fifty years since Arthur Farnsworth's death, rumors have been rampant that Jack Warner used his considerable power in Hollywood to orchestrate and control the investigation. Former Los Angeles County Coroner Thomas Noguchi, after reviewing the transcript, agrees that "the questioning of the witnesses by the coroner's office at the inquest seemed like it was just a formality. In fact, it seemed as if it was done almost to appease those who might have questions. The questioning of Bette Davis was fairly innocuous and she was handled with kid gloves . . . she was very much allowed to say whatever she wished . . . her testimony was a cold, calculated statement."

It seems clear that this inquest was designed to protect Bette, but from what? The most benign of the cover-up theories is that Jack Warner merely wanted to spare his biggest star the agony of a protracted, genuinely probing inquest—and his studio the attendant bad publicity— and stepped in with coercion and money to make sure that the matter was kept short and sweet. Others suggest that Bette was desperate to keep her marital difficulties out of the public eye, and to avoid revealing her husband's fall after their fight on the train back to Los Angeles.

But there is evidence to suggest a third possibility, one that would have left Bette and Jack Warner with no choice but to make certain that the inquest jury would find exactly the way it did: Bette may have been with Farnsworth that fatal day, and she may have pushed him, albeit accidentally, to his death.

The writer Fredda Dudley reported only a few months after Farnsworth's death that Bette had been with her husband when he met with Dudley Furse, in order to discuss how best to deal with the tax matters arising from Bette's recent formation of her own production company, which she had incorporated in June primarily as a tax shelter.

Miss Dudley made no further implication, but the man Bette married next, William Grant Sherry, recalls a very strange moment three years later as he and Bette walked along Hollywood Boulevard. "We were crossing the street," Sherry says emphatically, "and we walked between a couple of parked cars. All of a sudden Bette started shaking and looked frightened. I said, 'What's the matter?' She pointed down to the ground and said, 'That's where I pushed Farney. I thought he was drunk and I pushed him and he fell and hit his head on the curb.'"

What are we to make of this? A number of scenarios are possible. Farnsworth could have suffered vertigo from his prior head injuries, leading Bette to think he was drunk and push him away from her in anger, causing his fall. (There were no signs of alcohol on his breath at the hospital.) It is hard to imagine that Bette meant to injure him or left him knowing that he had been injured. She could have pushed him and stalked away so quickly that she never realized he had hit his head. She could have realized he was hurt and remained, without being recognized in her sunglasses, then slipped away unnoticed to avoid a scandal once she was sure Farney was being cared for. Or she might have remained with Farney at all times and Warner Brothers was able to use its formidable power to cover up the facts, coach the witnesses with their stories, and ram through the inquest verdict.

If Bette had been responsible for her husband's fall, Warner Brothers could not have allowed a full investigation. As Hector Arce has said, "She had no intention of killing him, and if she was charged, she would [have been] acquitted. But if there was a trial the details of her shaky marriage and her infatuation with Vincent Sherman might have come out. Her reputation and her career might have been seriously affected." Clearly, Jack Warner had too great a stake in his biggest star to risk a full disclosure.

This wasn't the first time Jack Warner had exercised his power in Los Angeles. Meta Carpenter, a script supervisor on a number of Bette's films in the '40s, recalls that "Jack Warner and Walter Huston were able to get John Huston out of a very, very difficult situation when he hit a young woman with his car on Sunset Boulevard and she died. She was the bride of a man in the business, and it could have been very serious for Huston. But Warner was able to get him off."

It would have been easy enough for Warner to convince Frank Nance, Homer Keyes, and the witnesses to cooperate, and not necessarily with an offer of money. This was the height of World War II, and all that Warner would have had to tell them was that because of Farnsworth's Honeywell work the national security would be jeopardized unless the inquest jury found the death to be accidental. The government, he might have said, would make sure that justice was done. The most charitable explanation for the shoddiness of Nance's inquest is that he thought he was acting in the national interest.

Perhaps the strongest evidence that Warner Brothers participated in a cover-up of Arthur Farnsworth's death is provided by the studio's legal files on Bette, which are housed at the University of Southern California and which are available for research perusal. For the first three and a half years of the 1940s, Bette's file bulges with memos, cables, letters, contracts—so much so that nary a week goes by without some written mention of Bette among the paperwork.

There is absolutely *nothing* in the file, however, for the three months between August and November, 1943.

Still another scenario exists to explain the untimely death of Arthur Farnsworth. The press accounts after his death quoted medical experts on what might have caused the basal skull fracture that Dr. Keyes originally said could not have occurred more than two weeks earlier. The *Los Angeles Examiner* reported that "a blow with a blunt instrument such as a blackjack or the butt of a gun, medical authorities agreed, would cause a fracture precisely such as was at first believed to have resulted when Farnsworth suddenly fell."

Several months after his death, Bette learned that Farney had been having an affair with a married woman, whose husband was blindly jealous. Only a few days before Farney's death, the man had followed his wife to a Sunset Boulevard motel and caught her in bed with Farnsworth. A furious fight ensued, during which the man hit Farney on the back of the head with a lamp. This would have meant that Arthur Farnsworth had suffered at least four blows to his skull in less than two months; in retrospect, his death may have been inevitable.

Immediately after the inquest, Bette flew to New Hampshire, where Farney's body had already been taken for burial at Butternut. There was first a funeral service in Vermont, then another in New Hampshire— Farnsworth's third. Stories have cropped up over the years of great dissension between Bette and Farnsworth's mother, Lucile, over details large and small—tales of Bette forced to sit in vigil with her husband's body all night, of an aunt of Farnsworth's hysterically pulling at his body in its coffin. According to his sister Lucile de Besche, this is all nonsense. "There was only one disagreement at the wake. Both the minister and I wanted the coffin closed. Bette and my mother wanted it open, so we went along with their wishes."

It has also been written that Mrs. Farnsworth insisted that her son's body be moved to Vermont shortly after Bette had had rocks blasted away and trees leveled on her property in order to bury him at Butternut, and that this caused great conflict between the two women. This too, Mrs. de Besche said, is not entirely true. The removal did occur, but not until two years later, after Bette had remarried and Mrs. Farnsworth felt it would be less hurtful to her. Bette seems to have been equally solicitous of Mrs. Farnsworth's feelings. "For a long time after Arthur's death," Mrs. de Besche adds, "Bette was extremely thoughtful of my mother and her grief over losing Arthur." Mrs. Barbara Briggs, Farnsworth's other sister, has said that "Bette and my mother were both very strong ladies, but they had no fight over my brother's death."

Whatever the secrets of her second husband's death, Bette took them to her grave. "There were certain topics Mother would not go into," her daughter B.D. wrote. "That was one of them."

Two months later, a small urchinlike boy walked up to the Warner studio gate, incongruously carrying a briefcase. When he said he wanted to see Bette Davis, the guard started to shoo him away. Then the boy said it was a matter of life and death, and the guard remembered something about Bette's husband and a missing briefcase. When he telephoned the set and spoke in hushed tones to Bette, she asked that the young man be brought back to her dressing room.

Sitting on a small sofa across from Bette, the boy nervously confessed that he had snatched the briefcase amid the confusion after Farney fell. Guiltily, he handed it to her. Stunned, Bette took the case and laid it on her lap, fumbled in her purse for a few dollars, handed the money to the boy, and asked him to leave. He scurried away. As a wave of fresh sadness washed over her, Bette snapped the lock and opened the case. In it were half a dozen bottles of alcohol, both empty and full. She looked down at them for a few moments, then she burst into tears.

SIXTEEN

Vincent Sherman yelled, "Roll 'em!" and looked to Bette to begin a scene from *Mr. Skeffington*. She sat in a chair on the right side of the set—the opulent Skeffington living room—and picked up the telephone. Everyone waited for her first line, but she said nothing. After a few minutes, Sherman spoke up.

"We're ready to begin, Bette," he said softly.

"I can't do it," she replied, putting down the phone.

Sherman called, "Cut!" and walked over to his star. "What's wrong, Bette?"

"I don't think I should be sitting on this side of the room. It doesn't *feel* right."

Sherman wasn't sure what to say to her. "But Bette, if we do it anywhere else, I'll have to knock a wall out to accommodate the camera. We're already behind schedule. Please, couldn't you give it a try?"

She was unsympathetic. "I can't play the scene here, Vince," she insisted.

By this time, Sherman was ready to throttle Bette Davis. "I wanted to kill her at times," he says. "She challenged me on *everything*. She was a complete bitch." At first, Sherman didn't understand what was going on. "When we did *Old Acquaintance*, she welcomed all of my suggestions, we worked together beautifully. Now she was rejecting everything I said, and I realized that it was a personal thing. She was striking back at me for what she saw as my rejection of her. It got so bad, crew members were coming up to me and asking, 'What's going on?' Her costar Claude Rains told me, 'I've never seen her like this.' "

Sherman felt himself on the verge of a nervous breakdown. "I couldn't sleep at night, my hair was falling out. Finally my wife said to me, 'What the hell is going on? You're not eating, you toss and turn every night. . . .' I broke down and told her everything that had transpired between me and Bette. She said, 'Oh my God. You've got a problem. It's not going to get better, it's going to get worse. If I were you I'd get the hell off the picture.' "

Mr. Skeffington had started out amid high optimism. Bette and Sherman both loved the script that the twin brothers Philip and Julius Epstein had fashioned from the bestselling novel by the pseudonymous "Elizabeth." The story concerned Fanny Trellis, a beautiful, vain, and flighty young woman in 1914 New York who marries a much older millionaire, Job Skeffington, in order to save her brother from prosecution for embezzling from Skeffington's firm. When the brother is killed in the war, Fanny divorces Skeffington and allows him to take their daughter to Europe because the child's growth reminds her of her fading youth.

Fanny, rich and idle, pursues much younger men until she contracts diphtheria. The disease ravages her, and her well-preserved beauty vanishes until she looks closer to seventy than fifty. Devastated, she refuses to leave her home. Finally a friend tells her that Job Skeffington has been a victim of Nazi persecution and has returned to America penniless. She offers to help him financially, but refuses to see him because of her appearance. The friend convinces her to change her mind, and she is stunned to find that Job is now old, frail—and blind. She realizes how selfish she has been, and that to Job she will always be beautiful. She accompanies him upstairs after telling the household staff, "Mr. Skeffington is home," and she recalls what he told her years before: "A woman is beautiful only when she is loved."

Sherman had asked Bette to play Fanny Trellis shortly after they completed *Old Acquaintance,* and although she had turned down the project two years earlier based on a script by John Huston, she liked the refashioned story by the Epsteins, who had written *Casablanca* (with Howard Koch) and would go on to win an Oscar for it. What intrigued Bette most about Fanny was her description as one of the great beauties of New York society. "I was far from being beautiful," Bette admitted, but she knew what could be done with makeup, hairdos, and lighting. Her hairdresser, Maggie Donovan, designed a curly Gibson Girl style that "gave me the illusion of beauty"; her makeup man Perc Westmore gave her a soft look and made her eyes seem even bigger; and her cinematographer, Ernest Haller, lit her with diffuse fill light that further softened her features and made her face appear more youthful.

The rest Bette supplied herself. During her opening scene, in which

Fanny descends a staircase to greet a group of young admirers, she kept repeating a mantra to herself: *You are the creamiest thing that ever existed, Fanny. You're Venus and Mrs. Harrison Williams combined. You're just too beautiful to live.*

Bette needed all the help she could get to look her best in *Mr. Skeffington*, because emotionally she was a wreck. Still shattered and guilt-ridden by Farney's death, she was more high-strung than ever, sexually frustrated, furious with Vincent Sherman for rejecting her, and terrified that she was losing control of her life and her career. All of these factors, Sherman believes, contributed to the extraordinary difficulties she created during filming.

Jack Warner had offered to let Bette take as much time off as she needed after her husband's death, but she felt that work would be the best palliative, and she reported for costume and makeup tests only three weeks after Farney's final funeral. Filming began a month later. As soon as she turned up on the set, Sherman realized that she should have taken a longer rest. "Just about every decision she made was wrong, and she wouldn't budge on any of them. It was a combination of a personal vendetta against me and a fear on her part that she was losing control. She felt helpless about everything else in her life, so she wanted at least to exert control over the picture. But her instincts this time were terrible."

Sherman couldn't persuade Bette not to raise her voice an octave to make Fanny seem more feminine; he thought she sounded ridiculous. He wasn't able to talk her out of the heavy, grotesque mask she wanted to wear after Fanny is devastated by diphtheria. As Ernie Haller put it, "She began to go to extremes. She wanted to look ravishingly beautiful in the opening scenes, and then ugly as sin in the last shots. She had a ghastly rubber mask designed to make her look older. Instead it made her look like something out of a horror movie, but she insisted on wearing it."

When Sherman arrived on the set one morning, he saw Bette in her rubber mask, half bald, wearing a patchy red wig. "My God, Bette!" he exclaimed. "If I shoot you like that you'll look like a witch!"

"Don't you worry, Vince," she replied. "My audience will take me in this kind of thing. They don't mind if I do this to myself."

"Well, *I* mind," Sherman retorted. But once again he lost the battle.

At first, the friction between Bette and Sherman seemed little more than honest creative differences. Bette had strong opinions as always, and now she had the power to make them stick. Sherman concedes that Bette thought her characterization of Fanny "was honest and real. I suppose to some extent she was right . . . perhaps she was more right than I was, although I think I was more right in other places."

What angered Sherman far more—as well as the Epsteins, Jack Warner, and everyone in the cast and crew—was Bette's sometimes unfathomable behavior on the set. During a dinner-party sequence, she insisted on introducing all the guests to each other as the scene opened, a time-consuming process, even after Julius Epstein reasonably pointed out to her that the audience would assume the introductions had been made before the scene started. In another party sequence with dozens of guests, Bette improvised lines of dialogue with everyone. As Epstein recalls it, "She'd go up to someone and say, 'How is Aunt Tilly?' Then she'd go up to someone else and say, 'How are the children?' It was ridiculous. The first cut of the movie was three hours and twenty minutes long, and that was the main reason why." Julius and his brother argued with Bette again and again over things like this, but she stood her ground.

The day that Bette insisted on reading her lines on one side of the set instead of the other, Sherman had had it. "I looked through the finder and saw that I couldn't shoot the scene the way she wanted it unless the carpenters completely re-did the set. But Bette wouldn't budge. So I told them to do it, threw the finder down and said, 'Goddamn her!' She was standing in the wings and snarled, 'I heard you, you son of a bitch! Don't you ever do that to me!' I just kept walking to the men's room."

Later that day Sherman was in Jack Warner's office, asking to be let off the picture. Warner pleaded with him to stay. "Vince, you know she's high-strung. Her husband's just died, for crissakes, and she's very emotional. Finish the goddamn picture."

Warner persuaded Sherman to tough it out, but the Epsteins were next in line at the exit door. A series of notes that the film's unit manager, Frank Mattison, sent to Jack Warner vividly outline the producer's complaints. "It sure is tough," Mattison wrote in one memo, "to sit by with a show that goes like this where she is the whole band—the music and all the instruments, including the bazooka. I suppose she wants to have her finger even in scenes in which she does not appear." In another memo he warned about Bette's script revisions: "I am sure that when the Epsteins see [them] they will be spinning on their heads like tops."

The brothers gritted their teeth at most of Bette's rewrites, but her constant attempts to keep herself chattering away nearly drove them crazy. In one scene where Fanny goes to her husband's office, the script has the scene open with Bette in front of Job's desk. Bette insisted that her husband's secretary should announce her and waited for the woman playing the secretary to call out her name before she walked across the full width of the set to his desk. Julius Epstein told Bette that the secretary would know her well and would simply wave her into the office.

"But she's a *new* secretary!" Bette explained.

Epstein looked at her in disbelief. He had written the script, and the secretary (as much as he'd given consideration to her employment history) was not new. "How do you *know* that, Bette?" was all the man could muster in reply.

Finally, when Bette refused to do a retake the Epstein brothers wanted from her, they walked off the set and into Jack Warner's office. He sided with them. "She'll do the retake," Warner announced, and headed out for the inevitable confrontation. "When he got to the set," Julius Epstein recalls, "he took one look at Bette, who was shooting daggers from her eyes, and put his arms around her. She didn't do the retake, and my brother and I took the next flight to New York."

By this time the cast and crew of *Mr. Skeffington* had had their fill of Bette Davis. She had always been popular with her crews, who saw her as a good ol' gal, not that far removed from being one of them. But her behavior on this picture shocked and angered them, and they no longer cared that she was a recent widow or an artist fighting for her vision: they had come to think of her as nothing more than a bitch.

On Saturday, December 2, something remarkable occurred. Bette went to her dressing room and splashed some eyewash in her eye from a vial, as she had done every day for weeks, to alleviate irritation caused by her makeup. This time, when the liquid hit her eye a piercing pain shot through her head and she screamed in agony. Perc Westmore, standing outside her dressing room, bolted to her side just as she hit the floor, writhing in agony. He splashed castor oil in her eye, picked up the eyewash, and rushed Bette to the infirmary.

There, as Bette lay on the cold steel of an examining table, the doctors continued to flush out her eye while the eyewash was quickly analyzed. The results were a shock. The vial had been laced with acetone, a corrosive substance used as a solvent in paint and varnish, and Bette was in danger of permanent blindness in the affected eye. It was hours before she could see clearly again, and she was under treatment from eye specialists for a week before it was certain that the damage to her corneal tissue was not irreversible. Bette later said that she preferred to believe that the solvent had been put in her eyewash by mistake, but Julius Epstein points out that if he and his brother had still been on the set "we would have been the suspects . . . as it was they could have rounded up any number of likely perpetrators."

Bette attempted to explain her behavior on the *Mr. Skeffington* set in her autobiography. "When I was most unhappy I lashed out rather than whined. I was aggressive but curiously passive. I had to be in charge but I didn't want to be. I was hated, envied and feared, and I was more vulnerable than anyone would care to believe."

It was this vulnerability that finally led to a resolution of the "Bette Davis problem" on the set. Vincent Sherman was so frustrated and angry with his star that when Jack Warner asked him to shoot a Red Cross promotional film with her on Sunday, December 10, he considered faking a back injury so he wouldn't have to do it. He went ahead, however, and afterward, when everyone had gone home, he sat alone on the edge of the set, in darkness, trying to figure out what had gone wrong and how he was ever going to finish this picture without losing his mind.

Suddenly he heard the staccato *click-clack* of high heels on the soundstage floor, and he knew it could only be one person. *Oh my God,* he thought. *She's still here!* He hoped she wouldn't see him. "I thought, *I'm in the dark and I've got my back to her and why should she stop and talk to me anyway, we haven't been talking very openly to each other for the past five weeks.*" But as the footsteps got closer they suddenly stopped. Then he heard the booming voice and its unmistakable rhythms. "Why are you still *here*? Why are you sitting in the *dark*?" Bette demanded. *Just like a schoolmarm*, Sherman thought.

He told her he was "just thinking," and Bette said, "Would you like a drink? I've got a bottle in my dressing room." Sherman agreed, and as she poured Scotch into paper cups, she told him, "I know you wanted to get off the picture, and I just want to thank you for staying. I know I've been a perfect bitch, but I couldn't help myself."

Bette then started to cry, and Sherman recalled that what followed was "one of the greatest scenes Bette Davis ever played. She told me everything that had happened between her and Farnsworth, everything that happened since his death, everything that had been going on in her mind for the past five weeks. She said she hadn't slept for weeks, she wasn't eating properly. She said she had wanted to come to me and put her arms around me and tell me how sorry she was, but she couldn't. There were tears streaming down her face when she finished."

Sherman was touched. "I was so smitten with her in spite of everything, and I felt so sorry for what she'd been through. I put my arms around her and told her how sorry I was and asked if she'd like to have dinner with me. She said yes, and we went to dinner. Then I took her home, and I stayed with her until one in the morning. That was the first time we had ever been to bed together.''

The next morning, Sherman told his wife Hedda what had happened. "Well," she said, with remarkable understanding, "that's one way to solve the problem. But just be careful."

Sherman was unsure what effect his nascent affair with Bette Davis would have on their movie. He worried that it might make matters worse, but the next day's shooting eased his mind. "She was just delightful on the set," he says. "So much so that I was embarrassed. Ernie Haller said, 'She's like a different person today, isn't she?' I didn't know what to say, but inside I was laughing like hell. I thought maybe I should have done that earlier."

Bette and Sherman continued their affair over the next two months, and he was fascinated by her sexual psychology. Whenever they had been intimate, he says, "she would be wonderful for three or four days, then she'd begin to tighten up. Then we'd meet again for an evening, and she'd be fine for a few more days."

As much as Bette clearly needed sexual release, it didn't seem to Sherman that she genuinely enjoyed the sex act. "There wasn't a great deal of foreplay, or a great deal of afterplay. I had a feeling that after the deed was done, she didn't want to talk about it anymore. She had sort of a puritanical streak. I don't think she liked feeling vulnerable or submissive during sex. I think she resented it. And I think that after all was said and done, she deeply distrusted men.

"Sex was a biological need for her, that's all. And when it wasn't there, all the nervous energy you saw in her was because her sex drive had no outlet."

Little more than a week after their first night together, Bette asked Sherman to divorce his wife and marry her. "We had a terrible fight," Sherman recalls, "because of course I said no. She knew from the beginning that there was no way I'd leave my wife and baby. It would come up again and again, usually after we hadn't been intimate for a while and she was tightening up, and she'd be angry. Then we'd get together and everything would be fine for a few days. I tried to keep away from the subject as much as possible."

Even had Sherman not been happily married, he would not have wanted to spend his life with Bette Davis. "I knew after what I went through the first several weeks of *Skeffington* that life could be hell with her. By that time I had made up my mind that no matter what happened I could never marry a woman like this."

The filming finally wrapped on February 17, 1944, two months behind schedule, and Vincent Sherman decided at that point that he had had all he could take of Bette. "I avoided her after that. I refused to return her calls. She tried to make trouble [for me]. But Jack Warner didn't care, as long as the picture was made."

While he was editing the film, Bette accosted Sherman on the sidewalk in front of the Warner studios. "Everyone says the picture is wonderful," she chirped. "I want you to direct my next one."

"Bette, do me a favor," Sherman replied. "Get yourself another director." And he walked away from her as fast as he could.

Several years later, Sherman began a three-year affair with Joan Crawford, and he found the two women surprisingly similar. "Even though they hated each other, they were sisters under the skin. Both had been deserted by their father, which left them with an eternal distrust of men. When a father deserts a family, it leaves a wound in his daughter that's impossible to overcome. It leaves a scar the rest of her life. And even if a man treats her decently, she'll always think, *Someday he'll leave me.*"

Mr. Skeffington opened at the Strand Theatre in New York on May 25. As Julius Epstein recalled, "It didn't do too well critically." A number of critics thought Bette had once again fallen into self-parody, and the formulaic "woman's picture" she and Warners had patented came under ridicule by the esteemed critic James Agee in *The Nation:* "It is another of those pictures in which Bette Davis demonstrates the horrors of egocentricity on a marathonic scale; it takes just short of two and a half hours' playing time to learn, from her patient husband (Claude Rains), that 'a woman is beautiful only when she is loved' and to prove this to an audience which, I fear, will be made up mainly of unloved and not easily lovable women. . . . Essentially *Mr. Skeffington* is just a super soap opera, or an endless woman's-page meditation on What to Do When Beauty Fades. The implied advice is dismaying: hang on to your husband, who alone will stay by you then, and count yourself blessed if, like Mr. Rains in his old age, he is blinded."

The Epsteins cut twenty minutes from the film for its national release, and it proved popular with enough viewers other than "not easily lovable women" so that it became one of the studio's top three box-office hits of the year. Bette received her seventh Oscar nomination in nine years for the film, but lost the award to Ingrid Bergman in *Gaslight*.

With *Mr. Skeffington* out of the way and her affair with Sherman at an end, Bette's diversions were again provided largely by the Canteen. In the spring of 1944 she made a short cameo appearance in *Hollywood Canteen,* Warner Brothers' self-congratulatory all-star paean to the club, which brought in $3.3 million in profits, most of it donated to the Canteen. To assuage her loneliness, Bette sometimes showed up at Cahuenga Boulevard five or six nights a week. She still drew many of the same satisfactions from the Canteen as she had from the outset, but now there was an added element. Rejected by Sherman, pining with rose-tinted memories over her marriage to Farney, Bette was a mass of sexual frustrations. The Canteen, early in 1944, went a long way toward filling that void.

Her sexual dalliances with the servicemen at the Canteen, in fact, were so frequent and so blatant that some of the most jaded Hollywood insiders were heard to mutter, "What's *happened* to Bette Davis?" The actor Jack Carson, a friend, was puzzled less by Bette's behavior than by the number of handsome, muscular servicemen who seemed always to surround her, often to the exclusion of far more beautiful actresses. He asked one of them what the attraction was. The young man replied, "I hear she screws like a mink."

"I thought that an ungentlemanly remark considering how Bette was knocking herself out night after night for those guys," Carson told author Lawrence J. Quirk, "and I was about to call the loudmouth son of a bitch on it, and then it struck me, *Well, ain't it the truth?*"

The fan mail for Bette that arrived at the Canteen was usually opened by young female volunteers, and Carson recalled that it soon became a running joke to see how many of Bette's correspondents would rhapsodize about the glorious hours they had spent together.

These brief encounters, of course, did little to fulfill Bette's deeper emotional needs—but a big, ruggedly attractive, well-built army corporal about twelve years her junior named Lewis A. Riley soon did. Bette found his looks "smashing," but what really set him apart from so many of the other handsome, supple youngsters around her was his quick wit and the fact that his family, among the founders of Acapulco as a vacation spot, was worth millions.

A year after Farney's death, Bette shed her widow's weeds and began to date Riley publicly. She dined with him at glitzy Hollywood night spots like Chasen's and La Rue, and pictures of them together popped up in the gossip columns and fan magazines. When they began to attract a little too much public attention, they slipped up north to the Mira Mar Hotel in Santa Barbara, California, after Perc Westmore darkened Bette's skin to a deep olive and gave her a black wig. The couple registered as Mr. and Mrs. Riley, then went down to the lounge for a drink before dinner. Bette was sure she had pulled off the masquerade until the woman sitting next to her turned and said, "It's no good, Miss Davis, you aren't fooling anyone." When Bette looked flabbergasted, the woman explained, "It's your *voice*! You can't change that!"

Bette went upstairs, took off the makeup, and came back down for dinner undisguised.

After several blissful months, Bette's affair with Riley was interrupted when he was transferred to Fort Benning, Georgia, and she began work on a grueling new film.

With her corporal three thousand miles away, Bette was predictably agitated, temperamental, and exasperating on the set of *The Corn Is Green* during the summer of 1944. The story, based on Emlyn Williams's play, concerned Miss Moffat, a sixty-year-old schoolteacher in Wales who works indefatigably with a brilliant but desperately poor miner's son to prepare him for a scholarship examination at Oxford that, if he passes, will help lift him out of his life of poverty and hopelessness.

As so often before, Bette battled with her studio bosses over details large and small. Ethel Barrymore, sixty-one, had brought Miss Moffat memorably to life on stage, but the studio felt that the character could have been any age and wanted Bette to play Miss Moffat close to her own age. Bette preferred to wear a gray wig and add padding to her clothes to give herself a middle-aged frumpiness that seemed to her more suitable to the character. The studio balked, but Bette wouldn't be swayed, and she got her way.

This early skirmish put Bette on a wartime footing once again as filming began, and the set was torn with strife from the start. Bette's concern for every detail of her pictures was stronger than ever now because so much rested on her shoulders as the premiere actress in Hollywood. She had seen too many fabulous careers crumble after one or two failures, and she knew that no matter what, a bad Bette Davis picture would be blamed on Bette Davis. The pressure weighed on her heavily.

Few of the people around her, who should have been her creative partners and support system, took the time to consider all this; most of the people at Warners had grown sorely short of patience with Bette. It now seemed to most of them that she created a battlefield mentality around her either because that was the only way she could work or, less charitably, because she was simply, terribly, and irredeemably a bitch.

The film's director, Irving Rapper, who had found himself "angry and exhausted" at the end of most days during filming of *Now, Voyager*, reached the end of his tether with Bette on *The Corn Is Green*. He was infuriated by her habit of telling everyone—the grips, the sound men, the lighting men, and, most annoyingly, *him*—how to do their jobs. Struggling to keep his temper, desperate to avoid a confrontation that might threaten the picture's completion, Rapper bit his tongue, tolerated humiliation, placated Bette at every juncture. But finally, in the middle of filming, she went too far and Rapper snapped.

"*I* am the director of this picture, Bette, *not you!*" he bellowed at her.

"Well, you're doing a damned *lousy* job of it!" Bette screamed back. "Why do I have to do everybody's work for them?"

Rapper's face grew crimson. "Maybe if you'd concentrate on your part and your lines, you'd keep out of other people's hair!" He stalked away from her and yelled over his shoulder, "I've had it with you, Bette!"

As the cast and crew stood in shocked silence, Bette remained stock-still and yelled after him, "You go one step farther toward that door, you son of a bitch, and you're fired!"

Rapper wheeled around. "Only Jack Warner can fire me, Bette, you know that. But he won't have to: I quit. I've had enough of your tantrums and your sadistic bullying."

"Tantrums! *Sadistic!*" Bette seemed about to explode with fury. "Listen, you no-talent third-rater, you ought to go down on your knobby knees in *gratitude* that you're directing a *Bette Davis* picture!"

Unable to muster up any more anger, Rapper issued a cold, even reply. "I'm not directing, Bette, *you* are," he told her, and left the set.

❧

Rapper returned, and Bette's oft-tested theory that the best films are made amid creative conflict proved correct once again when *The Corn Is Green* was released in March 1945. The film posted a profit of $2.2 million, and critics praised Bette's performance in it. E. Arnot Robinson in *Picture Post* wrote, "Only Bette Davis, I think, could have combatted so successfully the obvious intention of the adaptors of the play to make frustrated sex the mainspring of the chief character's interest in the young miner. This would have pulled down the whole idea of their relationship into something much simpler and more banal—more suitable to the sillier film audiences—than the subtle interpretation she insisted on giving. Drab outwardly, the schoolmistress, in her hands, became someone consumed by inward fire, by the sheer joy of imparting knowledge."

A few days after she completed *The Corn Is Green* in the fall of 1944, Bette took a train East, with Bobby in tow, and rented a house in Phenix City, Alabama, just across from the Georgia border and Fort Benning—so that Corporal Riley would be in close proximity.

Bobby had separated from Robert Pelgram early that spring, after trying for several years to make a badly disintegrating relationship work. Shortly after Pelgram moved out of the house, she had suffered another nervous breakdown and had spent the better part of the year in a mental hospital. Now she was on the rebound emotionally, awaiting her final decree of divorce (which would come the following March), and Bette thought a change of scenery would be good for her. While Ruthie cared for young Ruth, Riley found no shortage of fellow soldiers interested in dating the pretty, pliable Bobby, and often the four of them would double-date. The Davis girls bubbled with contentment.

Except for the fact that Bette expected Riley to ask her to marry him during the visit, and so far he hadn't. Before Bette and Bobby's three-month stay in Alabama ended, Riley received his orders to report overseas, and Bette was sure he would want to get married before he left. To her intense disappointment, he again failed to pop the question. He did ask Bette to wait for him until his return. "Maybe he was scared to marry me and then go off and be killed," Bette mused.

Riley shipped out and Bette returned to Hollywood, where she spent inordinate amounts of time at the Canteen, meeting men. She and Riley corresponded for months, but then Bette decided she was tired of "living my life in a mailbox." She sent Riley a Dear John letter and broke off the relationship.

A soldier who was with Riley when the letter arrived recalled that it devastated the corporal, who went on a three-day bender and didn't get over Bette for a very long time. Told this years later, Bette exclaimed, "My God! Then Riley really *did* love me! I wish I had married him. . . ."

The Hollywood Canteen remained in operation for three years, until World War II mercifully ended with the Japanese surrender in August 1945. Its $500,000 surplus was applied to a veterans' relief fund. In its three years of operation, the Canteen had often entertained three thousand men a night, one thousand in each of three shifts. Hundreds of thousands of men passed through, and it was an experience they never forgot.

Neither did Bette. More than forty years after the Canteen's doors closed, she spoke about that period with undiluted passion. "Christmas tore your heart out," she told the reporter Gregory Poe. "The servicemen were all so lonesome and sad. One Christmas Eve Bing Crosby came through the kitchen door with his four little boys. He said, 'Thought maybe we could help out tonight,' and he got on that stage with those four little boys. Everything those men were fighting for were those four little boys! He sang carols for an hour and a half. Oh God! There were so many wonderful rewards from the Canteen. So many."

SEVENTEEN

On the cool Saturday evening of October 20, 1945, Bette and Ruthie attended a cocktail party in Laguna Beach at the ocean-front home of Russell Leidy, a ceramics artist. As soon as Bette finished her new film, *A Stolen Life,* early in August, she moved into Ruthie's guest room and spent the next two months resting, walking along the beach, shopping in the local art galleries, swimming, and sun-bathing. The extended vacation had left her relaxed and relatively mel-low, but she was still lonely and melancholy over the state of her romantic life. It had been two years since Farney's death, she had not had a serious romance since Lewis Riley, the Canteen was closed, and she was beginning to wonder if she had any appeal left to the opposite sex.

The party guests noticed that Bette was quieter than usual, more reserved. After a few minutes, she wandered out onto a balcony that overlooked the ocean and stood alone, staring out at the night-black-ened water. After a few moments she turned around, and that was when she saw him: a tall, strong-featured, wavy-haired, powerfully built man dressed in sailor whites who couldn't seem to take his eyes off her. When she smiled slightly and nodded to him, William Grant Sherry picked up another drink for her at the bar and joined her on the balcony.

"Bette and I just seemed to gravitate toward one another," Sherry recalls. "We talked and talked about all kinds of things, and it irritated everyone else at the party, because she wasn't sharing herself with them. Finally some of the guests started saying things like, 'Why don't you come in here?' But we never did. We just kept talking away."

At thirty, Sherry was seven years younger than Bette, but he liked older women because "they were more mature and I enjoyed being with them better than the young ones." Bette, he noticed, "was in pretty good condition," and he found her very attractive. As they stood and chatted, he liked her even more: she seemed so pliable and yielding that he thought of her as a girl who needed his protection.

Their conversation was largely about him; Bette learned that he was soon to be discharged from the navy, and that he had been hospitalized for many months after an explosion on his ship that burst one of his eardrums. He told her he had been a boxer, that he was an artist who had done surgery renderings for a medical journal and had ambitions to be recognized as a fine artist, and that he was a licensed physiotherapist and worked out with weights regularly.

When Sherry asked Bette, "What do *you* do?" she realized to her delight that he did not recognize her. She didn't clue him in. "I'm an actress," she replied, and Sherry says he assumed she was a member of the local Laguna Beach theatrical company. "She didn't tell me she was a movie star, and she certainly didn't seem like one." They talked about their mutual New England backgrounds—Sherry was born on Long Island but spent summers with his family in Maine and Vermont—and both grew more smitten by the minute.

"No one ever paid court with the singularity of purpose that Sherry displayed," Bette said. After their initial meeting, the couple saw each other day and night. "We spent all our evenings on the beach," Sherry recalls, "or sitting around the barbecue at her mother's place, which was a very simple house. I'd stay there until the early morning hours. And all I could think of was that I was falling in love with this girl."

Sherry's obvious adoration, Bette admitted, "excited" her, and he had no doubt that she shared his feelings. "She acted like a person in love," he says. "She melted with me, and she just seemed so *proud* to be with me. I was a good-looking person."

When Sherry returned to his naval base in San Diego a few days after meeting her, he found that he could think of nothing but her. The following weekend, when he drove back up to Laguna (where he shared a house with a friend), he and Bette were once again inseparable. On the final day of that weekend, Sherry told her that he was "crazy" about her, and that he would be getting out of the service in a week. He said he didn't have much money, but there was a gallery in New York selling his paintings and, "I'll work something out." Would she marry him?

"I really believe I couldn't have avoided becoming his wife," Bette said, and she claimed to have realized later that Sherry had made up his mind to marry her on first sight—"perhaps before."

It was the suspicion implicit in that last aside—that Sherry was a gold digger who had known precisely who she was—that led most of Bette's family to oppose the notion of their marrying. Bette's cousin Elizabeth Carmichael didn't believe Sherry really loved Bette—"it was just like getting the gold ring or something." Sally Favour, married to Bette's cousin John Favour, said, "I felt that he was an opportunist." Ruthie and Bobby both vehemently denounced him to Bette; Ruthie didn't think Sherry was of the proper social station to marry Bette Davis, and she was "aghast" to learn that Sherry's mother, the widow of a theatrical carpenter, was working as an elevator operator in San Diego. Icily, Bette told Ruthie she admired Mrs. Sherry for supporting herself—something, she reminded her mother, that Ruthie hadn't done since Bette became a star.

But Ruthie's opposition to Sherry only hardened. She and Bobby both engaged private investigators to delve into his background, and the reports, apparently, contained enough of interest that Ruthie badgered Bette to read them. She refused. "Ruthie . . . so continually criticized him," Bette recalled, "that she drove me right into his arms."

When Bette told Ruthie that she was of a mind to accept Sherry's proposal, Ruthie asked her plaintively, "Why, Bette, why?"

"He's damn good in bed, that's why!"

"You don't have to *marry* him for that!" Ruthie sputtered.

Sherry didn't like Ruthie at all. He thought she was "a very domineering woman who spent a lot of Bette's money and always wanted more things," and he suspected that she and Bobby disliked him so much only because they were "afraid I was going to take Bette away. There was no other reason they should dislike me."

Bette told Sherry that she wanted to marry him, but she asked if they could put off the wedding until after she returned from a planned trip to Mexico City—"something about a film down there," as Sherry recalls it. He told Bette, "Let's get married first and then go down together. What's the point of going down yourself?"

She agreed, and in order to placate her mother's misgivings about Sherry, she asked him to sign a prenuptial agreement assuring that he would make no claims on her property in the event the marriage ended in divorce. He did so. On November 16, Hedda Hopper broke the news that Bette Davis planned to marry William Grant Sherry on the thirtieth of November.

The date was less than a week after the sixty-year-old Ruthie planned to marry fifty-three-year-old Robert Palmer, a Belmont, Massachusetts, businessman she had known for some time. After nearly thirty years as a divorcée, Bette's mother had decided that she had had enough of living alone, that she wanted the company of a man who was friendly and accommodating and unthreatening—"a nice little fellow," as Sherry considered Palmer.

Palmer, like Ruthie, was divorced, but on the marriage license application, Ruthie described herself instead as "widowed," an indication of her continuing shame over the divorce from Harlow. When she was asked to list her occupation, she wrote "Housewife."

Sherry didn't think the marriage would be very successful. According to him, "Ruthie just ran that poor man ragged. He should never have married her. The poor guy."

William Grant Sherry contends to this day that he had no idea who Bette Davis was until after he married her, but that's hard to believe. He must have been aware of the Hopper story revealing their wedding plans, and he gave an interview to the *Los Angeles Examiner* a few days before the marriage. He was also questioned by reporters about the last-minute change in plans necessitated by the refusal of St. Mary's Episcopal Church in Laguna to marry the couple because of Bette's 1938 divorce from Ham Nelson. If Bette was only a local actress, why was there so much press interest in her marriage plans?

In any event, the ceremony was scheduled for Friday afternoon, November 30, at the chapel of the Mission Inn in Riverside. But Ruthie's constant fussing over Bette just before the ceremony caused an altercation that nearly made Bette change her mind about marrying Sherry, according to him. Bette had been a nervous wreck all morning, and Ruthie told Sherry, "You go off somewhere. You're making Bette nervous."

"*You're* the one who's making her nervous!" Sherry shot back. Ruthie immediately told Bette what Sherry had said to her, and Bette later told him she had been so furious with him "I almost didn't come down and marry you—that you would talk to my mother that way!"

Dressed in a blue wool suit and a blue Breton sailor hat trimmed with goose feathers, Bette was escorted down the aisle by her brand-new stepfather, Robert Palmer, who had walked the same path to marry Ruthie one week before. The newly divorced Bobby was the matron of honor and Sherry's Laguna Beach roommate, Seymour Fox, was best man. Once he and Bette were pronounced man and wife, Sherry kissed Bette "fervently," according to witnesses. Bette's only comment: "That was the longest aisle I ever saw!"

Afterward, sixty guests crowded into a reception at the Inn's galleria, where Bette cut a three-tiered cake and Ruthie took the wedding pictures. Then the Sherrys departed for Mexico in Bette's enormous 1944 Buick, laden with trunks and gifts, as hot dry Santa Ana winds kicked up throughout southern California, bringing the kind of burning static air that Raymond Chandler said "curls your hair and makes your nerves jump and your skin itch. On nights like that every booze party ends in a fight."

Indeed, the heat got to Bette and her bridegroom. The arid air and the merciless sun undid both their tempers, and Sherry ordered Bette out of the car at one point halfway through the trip. As they drove along endless vistas of Southwest desert, the roads were so hellish that the tires began to blow out, and no sooner would Sherry replace one than another would go. By the time they got to Guanajuato, three hundred and fifty miles from their Mexico City destination, all four of the Buick's tires were useless and there were no spares left. Finally they had no choice but to sit by the side of the road in the suffocating heat, share a bottle of Scotch they'd brought along, and await rescue. When it came, just as night began to fall, it was in the form of a fleet of official Mexican government cars carrying soldiers, policemen, politicians, and reporters.

When the first man out of the first car, a policeman, saw Bette, he called out to the others, "She's here! She's here!" All the men greeted her effusively, and Sherry recalls that he turned to his bride and commented, "Boy, they're making quite a fuss over you!" Bette dismissed it with an airy "Yeah, well . . ."

The Sherrys were driven directly to Mexico City—where, Bette finally explained to Sherry, she was scheduled to appear at a gala screening of *The Corn Is Green,* which the Mexican government had selected to kick off a campaign against illiteracy. After a quick shower and change of clothes at their hotel, they were hustled over to the theater. Sherry says he finally realized at this point that his bride was more than a Laguna Beach actress, but he was still stunned as he and Bette entered the movie theater and thousands of people rose in unison from their seats in acclamation. "Who *are* you, anyway?" he asked her.

"I'm *Bette Davis,*" she replied, acknowledging the cheers.

"The name doesn't mean anything to me."

"Well, you'll find out," Bette murmured as she took one last bow and sat down.

After the screening, the Sherrys were treated to a round of nightclub entertainment at which they were the guests of honor. Then they were taken back to their rooms, the bridal suite in a lovely hotel in San Juan

Hill, outside the city. *Isn't this wonderful?* Sherry thought, and when he saw that Bette's maid Dell Pfeiffer—whom Bette had flown down for the occasion—had placed his pajamas on the bed next to Bette's nightgown, he was overcome with emotion. "Tears came to my eyes. This was so wonderful to me. I was married, I had a wife, and I had wanted one for so long—but I had never found anyone that I wanted."

Bette saw the tears in her husband's eyes as he gazed at the bed. "Oh, Sherry, you big sap," she said.

Sherry soon learned that it was electricity in a relationship that stimulated Bette, not sentimentality. She managed during this working honeymoon to infuriate her groom so badly that he threw a steamer trunk across the hotel room at her. "I never seemed to bring out the best in men," she admitted with some understatement. According to Sherry, Bette thrived on conflict and strife in their relationship. "She was always doing something to make me lose my temper to the point where I'd throw something at her. And she loved it. She'd always have that certain look of satisfaction on her face that she had made this man lose his temper."

When they returned to California, the Sherrys set up housekeeping in Bette's rented Toluca Lake home, where she had moved after renting out Riverbottom not long after Farney's death because the memories were too sad. (She sold the property in 1946 for a $5,000 profit.) Back at the studio, Bette asked to have some of her films screened for her new husband, who didn't think he had ever seen one of her movies—a fact she found vastly amusing and repeated to anyone who would listen. After Sherry had watched a couple of pictures, he recalled that he had seen them but had found Bette less than memorable. "I never liked the person she was on screen," he says. "I always enjoyed the men in her pictures better, and her I just put out of my mind. I told her that she didn't come across on screen the way I liked her. She wasn't the type of person I'd be interested in. But at home, she was."

Sherry enjoyed treating his bride like a queen. "I took care of her, you know, did all kinds of things for her, and if I went for a walk, I'd always bring back some little flower or something. It was a lovely romance with her. I *really* loved her."

This first blush of love left Sherry nonplussed by the wiles of Joan Crawford, who had recently come to Warner Brothers from MGM. Ever since their 1935 competition for Franchot Tone, there had been bad blood between Bette and Joan, and one afternoon a few months after his wedding, as Sherry strolled through the Warner lot, Crawford hailed him from across the street. She strode up to him and extended her hand. "Mr. Sherry? I've wanted to meet Bette's new husband. How do you do?"

Sherry said it was nice to meet her, and then Crawford extended an invitation for dinner. "That would be very nice," he replied. "I'll tell Bette."

"I don't want Bette," Joan responded. "Come alone."

Taken aback, Sherry stammered, "Well, Miss Crawford, I-I-I . . . don't go anywhere without Bette. Thank you just the same." When he got to his wife's dressing room and told her what had happened, Bette laughed. "Oh, she does that with all the men. That's nothing new. Are you going?"

"Of course I'm not going!" Sherry exclaimed. Bette let loose with another of her raucous laughs and that was the end of that.

On May 1, 1946, *A Stolen Life* was released, and Bette had a special interest in its success at the box office: it was the first of a series of films she was to produce for Warners under the aegis of her new production company, B.D. Inc.

As she admitted in her memoirs, Bette didn't produce the film in any real sense. "I simply meddled as usual. If that was producing, I had been a mogul for years." The formation of the production company was in large measure a concession on Jack Warner's part to Bette's ego and her power. There were some minor tax benefits for her as well, but Bette's main interest in producing her own pictures was that she would finally get to choose the movies she wanted to do.

Warner braced himself, certain that Bette would choose some esoteric piece sure to flop at the box office. But if she had learned anything in her fourteen years at the studio it was that financial success was everything, and everything good came from it. She chose *A Stolen Life* for two reasons. First, she was convinced it would be popular with audiences. Second, it would provide her with a showcase for her acting versatility: the script called for her to play twins, one good, one evil.

If some observers expected Bette to have a scene-chewing field day with the parts, they were disappointed. Instead she gave a subdued, effective performance, subtly delineating the character differences between the two women, and touchingly portrayed the heartbreak of the good twin after her sister steals away the man she loves. But the film turned out to be talky, static, and oddly uninvolving. The director, Curtis Bernhardt, who had begun his career in Germany, gave the picture an incongruous high-contrast *film noir* look; too many scenes were so dark they were difficult to see.

The reviews of *A Stolen Life* were generally poor, but audiences flocked to it, and the picture became Bette's biggest hit, netting a $2.5 million profit at the box office. The overriding reason for its success has to be Bette. She had been off the screen for more than a year, and in *A Stolen Life* audiences could see her play both the characters she had always been best at: the long-suffering, noble martyr and the willful, selfish barracuda. Whatever the shortcomings of the picture itself, Bette's fans loved it.

Bette never did produce another film; she found that worrying about everything was far more debilitating than merely meddling when she felt so moved. She had proven that her instincts could produce a huge financial hit, and she was content to go back to fighting creative battles and leave the accounting to others.

The first time Bette brought Sherry to Butternut he fell in love with it. "It was a wonderful, beautiful, dreamland place," he recalls. "Just right for me because it was down-to-earth—a great big old barn that had been made over, with thick posts to hold up the upstairs loft. It was really New England, with boxes of nails and horseshoes lying around, things Bette's mother had picked up at auctions. Upstairs she had a delightful four-poster bed."

At Butternut, Bette was usually happy and mellow, just as she had been the day Sherry met her, and he came to covet the time they spent there. "She was just herself" in New England, Sherry says, "the person I loved." Bette's cousin Elizabeth Carmichael recalled that Bette seemed very much in love with her husband. "She used to try to bolster him by raving about his painting, and complimenting him all the time."

Things were different back in Hollywood; Sherry didn't like the Toluca Lake house. "I was uncomfortable there, because nothing is yours in a rental. And I didn't like Los Angeles. I felt like a fish out of water." To keep Sherry happy, Bette purchased a woodsy home on Diamond Street in Laguna, near Ruthie and the water, with a wall of north light for Sherry's painting. But when she was making a film, Bette stayed in Los Angeles during the week, and if Sherry wanted to see her he had to stay there too. He did at first, but soon he began to spend more and more time in Laguna—because when Bette was making a picture, she wasn't the same woman with whom he had fallen in love.

This first struck him five months after the wedding, when Bette began *Deception* on the Warner lot at the end of April 1946. As she admitted in her autobiography, she "never either saw or heard anyone" while she was working. Work came first in her life, and everything else—even her husband—was "a necessary refreshment, a comma, a dash in my life sentence of work."

The filming of *Deception* was a trial for Bette for a number of reasons, few of which had anything to do with her home life. Her marriage was barely beyond the honeymoon stage, and Sherry indeed provided her with "refreshment" from her perennial creative struggles with Jack Warner. But those struggles were worse than ever, all of them stemming from Bette's self-doubts and her increasing sense of betrayal at the hands of the studio. "She was nervous about everything to do with films," Sherry recalls. "She argued with everybody on the set all the time. She was a very insecure person."

Her nervousness wasn't assuaged by the script she was filming. *Deception,* as one critic described it, was "like grand opera—only the people are thinner." Bette wasn't thrilled by the melodramatic turns Warner was adding to the story, based on a successful stage play about the reunion of a concert pianist (Davis) and her cellist lover (Paul Henreid) following World War II. The woman attempts to conceal the fact that she has been kept in high style for a number of years by a composer (Claude Rains). Following a series of complications, Davis shoots Rains to prevent him from revealing all, then she confesses her act to Henreid after he has triumphantly presented Rains's latest opus. They agree she must go to the police, and as they leave the concert hall, an onlooker calls to Davis, "You must be the happiest woman in the world tonight!"

After barely a week of filming, Bette was about as unhappy off screen as her character was on screen. She was upset by the addition of the Rains character to what had been a two-person play, especially since Rains was quite handily stealing the movie out from under her and Henreid with an over-the-top performance. While she had rewritten *Mr. Skeffington* to her heart's content, now she was infuriated by the constant rewrites of others—so much so that after one last-minute alteration she stormed into her dressing room and slammed the door on her finger, resulting in huge swelling and an ugly, blackened fingernail.

Matters went from bad to worse. Bette's nervous condition weakened her resistance, and she caught colds and other infections repeatedly, including an outbreak of boils on her face. On Saturday evening, May 14, she was driving down to Laguna Beach for her Sunday off when another car made her veer off the road and smash into a tree. Her head shattered the windshield, and she was in a daze when someone arrived and offered to take her to the hospital. She wanted to be taken home, she insisted, and when she got there she went to bed despite the protests of Sherry that she should see a doctor.

The next day her physician, Dr. Wilson, told her he was worried she might have a hairline fracture of the skull, and that she should remain in bed, as still as possible, for several days. She felt dizzy and ill, and at one point blood began to trickle down her chin from her jaw, which she had also injured. Dr. Wilson told the studio that Bette was in "a very hazy condition" and could not report to work for some time.

Within a week she had mustered up the strength to return to the set, but she suffered from dizzy spells and went back to Laguna. On May 25 she phoned the studio to say she had the flu, a strep throat, and a fever of 101. She finally returned to the studio on June 13, with the picture now weeks behind schedule, and asked Jack Warner to push back her morning call from 9 A.M. to 10 A.M. Warner, once again eager to keep his biggest star happy at all costs, reluctantly agreed to try out the arrangement.

On June 22, just before noon, the Warner executive Steve Trilling came to the *Deception* set on Stage Seven and knocked on Bette's dressing room door. Inside, he told her that the picture was alarmingly behind schedule and over budget and she would have to return to a 9 A.M. call. Furious, Bette shot back that Jack Warner had agreed to the change in her starting time and if she had to come in earlier she was likely to get sick again and further delay things. "If Jack Warner wants me to change the arrangement agreed to," she told Trilling, "why doesn't he have the courage to tell me himself?"

Trilling tried to placate Bette, but his efforts only heightened her anger. Unconcerned now that others might hear her, she began to shout. "They keep adding dialogue! I have to stay up at night learning lines for the next day! And they're long, difficult lines! You, Steve Trilling, have a lot of nerve coming on the set during a shooting day! And when you *know* that we're working and I'm trying to concentrate and I'm about to go into a scene five pages long with difficult, complicated lines!" Then she started to cry, and Trilling left.

When Bette got home that evening, she took to her bed and remained there for three days. She soon received a telegram from Jack Warner: "Dear Bette: I am at a loss for words to express myself after having learned of the turmoil that existed last Saturday afternoon with respect to the production of your picture. You must not lose sight of the fact that you are in a profession that calls for certain fulfillment of moral obligations to say nothing of legal ones. You are taking the wrong attitude towards our company and me personally on this whole matter in that you would create conditions that are not fair to our studios. We are not responsible for the working hours under which the industry is making its pictures. We have done everything in our power for you, but now you ask us to change the working hours which I find we cannot do after having honestly tried, which was our distinct understanding when I discussed this with you in my office several weeks ago. Am sure you realize our rapport was radical departure from our normal studio operations and if we continue it will create a complete change in our production methods and prove very costly to us. I implore you as a friend and business associate to use your good reasoning. Am sure in the long run you will realize that what you are doing now is not the proper thing and am asking nothing unreasonable from you."

Bette didn't respond to the telegram, but on June 29, back at work, she halted filming and asked the crew to gather around. She complained that the studio seemed "indifferent" to her health problems and added, "I am appalled that the crew has been called in to work every day I've been off sick when Trilling *knew* you would be wasted because I couldn't come in. It shows terrible lack of consideration for you. I hate being put in a position like this—when Trilling and Warner make it seem my fault the crew is called in every day, when they know it's impossible for me to come to work."

The crew was unmoved by Bette's speech—by now her latenesses and absences had made them resent her as much as the *Skeffington* crew had, and nothing she said could convince them that she wasn't simply being her usual bitchy, temperamental self. Jack Warner was livid, and came very close to dismissing her from the picture. But every movie featuring Bette Davis had made money for his studio, so Warner bit his lip, held his tongue, and turned his back.

The troubled production of *Deception* came to a close in August 1946, and when the film was released two months later, it disproved Bette's theory that a discordant set guarantees a successful picture. The costliest of Bette's films to date, the movie lost over half a million dollars—the first time a Davis film had flopped after forty-nine straight successes.

Box-office failure was a new experience for Bette, and she didn't like it a bit. Sherry and her friends soothed her anxieties with assurances that her next film would be yet another blockbuster. But just as disturbing to her was the way she looked in the picture. Bette was approaching forty, the witching hour for most actresses of the period, and it was clear on screen that the battles and the problems and the illnesses had all taken their toll on her. For the first time, she looked every bit her age on screen. Upset, she cornered the film's cinematographer, Ernie Haller, and demanded, "Why can't you make me look like I did in *Jezebel*?"

Haller looked at her, the picture of contriteness. "Well, Bette," he explained, "I was eight years younger then!"

EIGHTEEN

"Everything was wonderful between me and Bette," recalls William Grant Sherry, "until the child was born." The nine months his wife was pregnant, Sherry thought, were the happiest period of the marriage. "She was lovely at that time. She had that expression on her face that all new mothers have, in love and having a child. She had the angelic look and I had a photograph of her that was so loving. This was the Bette that I adored. The world just couldn't have been more beautiful."

Bette wanted to have her baby in New England, and she and Sherry moved to Butternut in the fall of 1946 after Jack Warner gave her an indefinite period off, with pay. Six months before the baby's expected arrival, Bette proudly displayed a brown leather photograph album with gold lettering across the front: "Our Baby—Bette and Sherry." (Almost without exception, Bette called her husband by his last name.)

While Bette puttered around the house, Sherry would jump into his jeep every morning and drive up into the mountains to ski. "Then I'd come back down in the afternoon and we'd go for walks in the snow." Once a week they drove to New Haven to see Bette's doctor, and as the New England winter hardened she began to worry that the snow might make it difficult for her to get to the hospital in an emergency. Reluctantly, she and Sherry returned early in March to Laguna Beach, where Bette was told that her baby was in the breech position and would have to be delivered by cesarean section. She decided to have the surgery on May 1—because she hoped for a daughter, and felt that May Day would be "a fun birthday for a girl."

Sherry was convinced the child would be a boy, and Bette recalled that when her seven-pound daughter was born at 7:15 A.M. on May 1, she said to him, "Poor Sherry—you married an old woman and I gave you a daughter—not a son." Nonetheless Sherry was delighted to be a father, and he suggested that the child be named Barbara, after Bette's sister. "Bobby was a very pathetic person," he recalls. "Inside a lovely

person, but dominated by Bette, who treated her terribly. She was nothing. She depended on Bette for her income and Bette used her as a
servant. Bobby put up with it because she knew she was a little bit off
mentally and she depended on Bette."

The infant was christened Barbara Davis Sherry, but her father took
to calling the little girl BeDe because of her initials, and later he painted a
portrait of her with the nickname appearing on a book she was holding
while he painted her. Bette turned it into B.D., and that became the
girl's name for the rest of her life—which effectively obliterated the tribute to Bobby.

Bette's age prompted whispers that she had feigned her pregnancy
and had adopted B.D. ("Hollywood is a suspicious town," Bette said.)
To check out the rumors, the gossip columnist Hedda Hopper arrived,
uninvited and unannounced, at the Sherry house. "She burst through
two gates and into the secluded guest cottage where I was resting,"
Bette recalled.

"May I come in?" Hopper asked.

"It looks like you're already in," Bette murmured sweetly.

According to Bette, Hopper "scrutinized the child's features and the
condition of my anatomy, and the next day it was officially recorded for
Hollywood posterity that I had indeed given birth."

Just then Bette's husband came in, wearing only bathing trunks.
Hopper was gaga. "I'd met 'Sherry' before," she wrote, "but in a suit
you couldn't possibly guess what a handsome Greek god he is. Now he's
run up fresh from the sea with the water still glistening on his mahogany
tanned skin." When Hopper exclaimed, "Ah, the bronze giant," Sherry
laughed and said, "I'll leave you two alone."

Hopper spent the better part of an hour with Bette as she lay on a
yellow chaise longue after feeding the baby. "I've wanted Barbara for so
many years I can't tell you," Bette reflected. "I used to think it was awful
I hadn't had her when I was twenty-one. But now I realize how perfect it
is to have her at my age. When I was a youngster, I was struggling so
hard to get somewhere. Now I've got the time to enjoy her."

Prior to B.D.'s birth, Bette had hired sixty-three-year-old Bessie Downs,
the mother of her business manager, Vernon Wood, as the baby's nurse.
Eighteen months later, Bette and Bessie were trading charges in court
when Mrs. Downs brought suit against the Sherrys for breach of con-

tract when she was dismissed three days after Bette's return home from the hospital. In her deposition, Bette explained that she had let Bessie go because she wasn't following doctor's orders on feeding the baby. "The instructions were from the hospital and the doctor," she testified. "They were that she was to be fed every three hours, a very important thing to a young baby. . . . I asked that the baby be brought down to me to be fed and . . . on the second day the baby did not appear to me until every four hours. She was an hour late again, and I asked Mrs. Downs had she contacted Dr. Carroll to get permission to change the feedings and she said, 'No, I hadn't,' and she said she would now if I wanted her to. I said it was a little late. I told her, 'You just can't switch babies back and forth, one day give them three hours and one day four hours. It's very upsetting to them.' "

Downs's attorney, taking the deposition, interjected. "I will have to take your word for it—"

"It is!" Bette exploded. "I found out! I had had a cesarean and it wasn't very good for me at the time to discuss many things, but I myself was so enraged by this I brought it up with Mrs. Downs. I was being treated like an invalid! . . . She would not let me have anything to do with the baby. She explained to me that it would take four days for the nipples to be right, and in these four days she did not want me to feed the baby . . . the baby for twenty-four hours was not brought near me at her insistence. . . . Because it was a great emergency Dr. Carroll found another nurse. At the time Mr. Sherry asked Mrs. Downs to leave, she was an old friend of the family and as it had worked out so badly, for what reason we did not know, he mentioned that it was clashes of temperament. That was his way of telling her to go without insulting her."

In her testimony, Downs countered that Dr. Carroll had given her verbal permission to reduce B.D.'s feeding schedule. "It's not the time of the feeding," she said, "but the ounces."

The Friday afternoon she was let go, Bessie testified, Dr. Carroll came to see her at Bette's behest. "He seemed quite upset and he said, 'What's this all about? I can't come around here three times a day to settle family quarrels.' I said, 'Well, I am sure as far as I am concerned, everything is all right.' And then he said, 'While Bette was in the hospital she was fine and since she has been home she has deteriorated. I don't know whether it is you or her mother or her sister. But I feel that your personality clashes with Bette.' "

The jury agreed that Downs had indeed been dismissed for that reason, and not because of incompetence or failure to obey doctor's orders. They awarded her damages of $1,500 and court costs of $243.90. Bette appealed, and the damages were reduced to $680. She didn't pay Bessie Downs until November 23, 1949.

"The first months of a child are spectacularly exciting," Bette wrote in her memoirs, and she added that although she never considered giving up her career, suddenly it wasn't all that important—"my life seemed full without it." Sherry was delighted by his wife's new domesticity; he worshiped her and the baby and secretly hoped that she would remain content to be just Mrs. William Grant Sherry. But it was not to be. Although Bette claimed that she reveled in motherhood and was reluctant to return to Warners, Sherry tells a different story.

Within a few months of B.D.'s birth, he says, Bette shocked him by announcing, "I'm sick of being a cow. I've got to get back to work." She telephoned Jack Warner and asked him to prepare a new picture for her. "From that day on she changed completely," Sherry recalled. "She became manager of everything. It was almost like, 'I don't need you anymore.'" Sherry feels today that "she got from me what she wanted— a child. And then, I was of no more use to her." Friends told him that they suspected Bette married him because of his good looks and robust health in order to "have a strong baby." Sherry isn't sure they were wrong.

He couldn't persuade Bette not to return to the studio, and it soon became clear that it wasn't just because she felt like a "cow" that she wanted to get back to work. She was afraid for her career. She had had at least three movies in release every year through 1943. In 1944 she'd had two, and in 1945 just one. The poor box-office showing of *Deception* gnawed at her; she was well aware of the old Hollywood axiom, "You're only as big as your last picture." Even if she returned to work immediately, by the time her new film would be in release, she would have been off the screen for nearly two years, with *Deception* festering in the public mind. She needed to do something quickly.

Although she professed to have been completely absorbed in her baby, Bette had remained acutely in touch with what was happening in Hollywood, and she didn't like what she saw. The best women's roles were going to actresses years younger than she: Ingrid Bergman in *The Bells of St. Mary's*, Gene Tierney in *Leave Her to Heaven*, Loretta Young in *The Farmer's Daughter*, and Susan Hayward in *Smash-Up—The Story of a Woman*. Actresses her own age were copping Oscar nominations in the few roles she might have played: Greer Garson in *The Valley of Decision*, Rosalind Russell in *Mourning Becomes Electra*.

Worst of all, her old nemesis, Joan Crawford, had won the 1945 Best Actress Oscar for her first Warner Brothers film, *Mildred Pierce* (in a role Bette had turned down); she also got a nomination two years later for *Possessed*, while Bette was ignored for both *The Corn Is Green* and *Deception*.

It is fair to say that by August 1947, Bette was deeply worried that her career had flagged, and she was eager for a major film with a meaty, rangy role. She lobbied Jack Warner hard to let her do two stories: *Ethan Frome* and a biography of Mary Todd Lincoln. The former, a novel by Edith Wharton that had been a critical success in a Broadway incarnation, concerned a nineteenth-century New England farmer who is driven into the arms of a gentle young hired girl by his cold, unpleasant wife. After the pair run off together, they are maimed in a sledding accident, and the wife dedicates her life to caring for both of them.

Bette wanted to play Mattie, the hired girl, opposite either Gregory Peck or Gary Cooper as Ethan Frome. Even though she was too old for the part, Jack Warner might have been willing to let her try it even a year earlier. But Bette had aged noticeably after the birth of B.D.; she now seemed closer to fifty than forty. Although Warner told her *Ethan Frome* was out because it was too downbeat a story and he "hated costume stuff," his real reason for nixing the project was Bette's appearance.

Mary Lincoln, the emotionally unstable wife of the sixteenth president of the United States, was a far more appropriate role for Bette. Initially a source of strength for her husband, Mrs. Lincoln became undone by charges that she was a Confederate sympathizer during the Civil War, the deaths of several of her children at early ages, and the assassination of her husband as he sat next to her in Ford's Theatre. Finally, her eldest son committed her to a mental institution in Illinois.

Bette sent a barrage of letters and telegrams to Warner begging him to let her play Mary Lincoln. In one she wrote that she found Mrs. Lincoln to be a combination of Scarlett O'Hara and a *Back Street* woman and added, "To me this is the story of so many women—not just a figure out of history—it is a story of any woman who believes in her husband and pushes him ahead." She felt the theme was "apt to be box office," and noted Katharine Hepburn's success in *State of the Union*, a very different kind of film. "Anyway," she concluded, "stubborn Davis is asking you to think more about it—I am so truly sure someone in the theater will do it soon—the Theater Guild has always been interested— or could I do it as a play?"

Bette got no further with Warner on *Mrs. Lincoln* than she had with *Ethan Frome,* and this time the mogul's reluctance had little to do with Bette. Again, three years earlier, he might have okayed the project, but by 1947 the economic fortunes of his studio—and all the others—were on a distinctly downward slide.

The motion picture box-office boom of the first half of the 1940s—especially for "women's pictures" and innocent-minded musicals—had been fueled primarily by the wives, sisters, mothers, and daughters left behind by the millions of fighting men who had led the United States and Great Britain to victory in World War II. Once the war ended, complex factors combined to both lower movie attendance and change audience tastes. With their husbands home, and in many cases in need of physical or emotional nursing, many women no longer had the luxury of free time to take in two or three movies a week. Others were soon busy as well with new babies.

The men who had fought the deadliest war in world history had little taste for frivolous, naïve entertainment or soap operas that revolved around issues that paled in comparison to what they had witnessed. They were more interested in stark melodramas that dealt honestly with the dark side of human nature they had come to know, or patriotic war films that filled them with pride.

For Warner Brothers, the general downturn in box-office receipts (and the even poorer showing of the studio's recent women's pictures) was compounded by two other factors: the coming government decision that it was a violation of antitrust laws for the studios to own their own movie theaters (which was final in 1948), and the threat of television, which sent a shiver down the spine of every studio employee.

Jack Warner was no longer certain what kind of movie would attract audiences. Creatively his output foundered, and the years 1946 through 1949 were among the poorest in overall movie quality in the studio's history. Financially, Warner pulled in the reins, lowered budgets, and nixed any project that was likely to cost too much. This was his main reason for rejecting *Mrs. Lincoln:* its costumes, its Civil War battles, the kind of director he would need to keep it all together, would have meant the kind of budget Warner was no longer willing to approve.

Instead, he convinced Bette (who was now making over $6,000 a week, a budget buster unto herself) to appear in a relatively modest picture based on a little-known novel with a neophyte leading man and an untried director. Years later, Bette said of the film, "I should have stopped that picture in the middle and said, 'Boys, it's just not working,' and gone to Jack Warner and asked him to shelve it."

❧

Ethel Vance's novel *Winter Meeting* hadn't exactly set bestseller lists on fire, but it had been a *succès d'estime,* and Bette liked its story of Susan Grieve, a virginal spinster, and her unlikely love affair with a handsome young navy war hero who intends to enter the ministry. What appealed to her most was Vance's explorations of the differences between the Protestant Grieve, a minister's daughter, and the Catholic sailor, and the awkwardness and confusion Susan feels at her first sexual experience as she nears forty.

Bette felt the project might be as prestigious as *Ethan Frome* or *Mrs. Lincoln,* and she was impressed when Bretaigne Windust, a well-regarded Broadway director, signed on to helm the project, his first film. William Grant Sherry recalled a visit Windust made to the Sherrys in Laguna Beach. "He was such a gentleman, and the more I listened to him, I realized what good taste he had. He explained to me that he knew there was something about Bette that hadn't been brought out, by any director." What Windust wanted to highlight in Bette was a new "softness" and "femininity." Unfortunately, this new concept amounted to little more than lighter makeup and a pulled-back hairdo topped with Mamie Eisenhower bangs that served mostly to make Bette look spinsterish.

Bette suspected that Windust's attempts to "soften her image" had been prompted by Jack Warner and were meant to make her look younger. She realized she was right her first day on the set. "Ernie Haller had set up enormous banks of lights behind huge silk screens just outside of camera range," she recalled. "As a young actress I had seen these same screens on the sets of Ruth Chatterton and Kay Francis, when they were nearing forty, and I knew what they meant. I went back to my dressing room and cried my eyes out."

As filming progressed, Bette became just as unhappy with her leading man. Jim Davis, a handsome six-foot-three-inch thirty-three-year-old with a handful of minor films to his credit, was handed a starring role opposite Bette Davis primarily because his $500-a-week salary fit well into the *Winter Meeting* budget. He tested for the role; Bette liked what she saw and approved him—over the objections of her husband. "Davis was a nice-looking guy, and big," Sherry recalled, "but he was a little awkward. I said to Bette, 'I think you can do better,' but she said, 'Oh, I think he'll be all right.' I didn't know too much about this, so I backed off."

Sherry's instincts proved correct—Jim Davis was indeed stiff and awkward in *Winter Meeting,* and there was little chemistry between him and Bette. She blamed the "over-analytical approach" of Windust for the fact that Davis "never again during filming showed any signs of the character he portrayed in the tests that made me want him for the part. No help I tried to give him could offset the effect of the detailed direction of Windust. He was lost and openly admitted it."

The script of *Winter Meeting* was unusually talky, and Windust, from a Broadway background, saw no problem in that. Bette knew it could be fatal for the picture, and tried to overcompensate. According to William Grant Sherry, "Bette decided to show everyone that Windust wasn't the director he was ballyhooed to be. She began to do things in the film that I could see from his expressions weren't to his liking at all. She started hamming it up. It embarrassed me for her. He would take her aside and say, 'I want to explain something.' And she'd snap back, 'Well! I think I know what I should do, and when I should do it.' And you could see that he was afraid to buck her."

The film's producer, Henry Blanke, called a meeting with Bette and Windust that Sherry also attended. "The rushes are terrible," Blanke told them bluntly.

"You get a decent director and then we'll have something," Bette snapped.

"Bette was a very insecure person," Sherry recalled, "and that was why she'd try to take the upper hand with everybody and put everybody down. Had I been married to Bette longer than I was at that time, I might have gone over and talked to Bretaigne and said, 'Hey look, start smacking her around, and get what you want.' Because that's what the big directors did with her. They'd just say, 'Bette, we'll do it all day until you do what I want.' And then she'd finally have to do it their way. She liked that."

Janis Paige, the second female lead in the film, was a twenty-five-year-old newcomer "very much in awe" of Bette. "She was *the* star," Paige recalls. "She was the epitome and number one. But she seemed confused on this picture. She was battling Warner Brothers for better roles, she thought Jim Davis wasn't strong enough for her. Windust wanted to 'change' her, and I think she had an actor's paranoia about being changed. We actors fight very hard and work very hard for whatever image we have, in order to be different. I think she was scared.

"You could hear the fights on the set. She was extremely outspoken and that doesn't always sit well with people. I think she always felt alone—Bette Davis against the world. For the most part that was true.

She fought so hard for women's rights. She was a remarkable human being when you think about it, so far ahead of her time, in every possible way."

Among Bette's many frustrations with *Winter Meeting* were the censorship restrictions on the script. The very elements that had most intrigued her about the novel had to be jettisoned for the film, and that drove her to fury. "We were not allowed to be honest about the differences of opinion between a non-Catholic and a Catholic" for fear of offending either religious group, she said. And neither would the censors "allow Jim and me to be shown in the bedroom, let alone in bed. . . . With no Hays [censorship] office [the film could have shown] how difficult it was for Susan to have sex for the first time—with a man who really wanted to be a priest! Think of all those meaningful conversations in the dark over cigarettes after making love!"

All of Bette's worst fears about *Winter Meeting* proved correct when it was released two days after her fortieth birthday on April 7, 1948. The box office was disastrous (it lost nearly $1 million), the reviews scathing. Bosley Crowther wrote in *The New York Times,* "Of all the miserable dilemmas in which Miss Davis has been involved in her many years of movie suffering, this one is probably the worst. For it offers Miss Davis no salvation. As a neurotic spinster who falls in love with a young Navy hero whose passion, ultimately revealed, is to become a Catholic priest, it leaves her no recourse save to send her young man on his way. And that she does with such slow anguish as to make it seem interminable."

There was anguish for the Davis women on the marital front as well. In January 1947, Ruthie had separated from Robert Palmer, their longtime friendship undone by daily proximity and the disinclination of both of them to change well-established habits to suit the other. Still another factor, if William Grant Sherry is correct, was Ruthie's propensity to run her husband "ragged."

Two years after her divorce from Robert Pelgram, Bobby, now thirty-eight, seemed to have found happiness again when she married David Roscoe Berry, a well-built man of imprecise occupation in his early thirties. The wedding took place on June 9, 1947, in Las Vegas, and Bette told her sister, "Now we're Mrs. Sherry and Mrs. Berry!" Although Bette knew that Berry had struggled with alcoholism, she sent the newlyweds a dozen cases of liquor as a wedding present.

Bobby's daughter Ruth, eight years old, liked Berry. "He was a nice man," she recalls, "but he had a problem with alcohol." William Grant Sherry thought that the marriage was a big mistake. "I don't know who got the idea that they should get married. Bobby was a mess, he was a mess, oh gosh. He turned out to be a drunk and the worst thing that Bobby could have."

Bobby came to realize this herself when Berry began to drink heavily again and failed to keep a job for more than a few months. Eighteen months after the wedding, Bobby sued for divorce in Orange County superior court on the grounds that Berry had "failed to provide the necessities of life" for her due to his "idleness, profligacy and dissipation." In the court documents, Bobby told a harrowing tale of domestic discord.

She charged that Berry was "habitually intoxicated" during most of their marriage and that when he was drunk he would "inflict on her severe bodily injury" and cause her great anxiety about the "safety and well-being of herself and her minor daughter and other members of her family."

On November 28, 1948, Bobby threw her husband out of their Laguna Beach house, and on December 3 she filed her divorce petition. The next day, Berry returned to the house at four in the morning, drunk, and demanded to be let in. When Bobby refused, he broke a window and clambered through it, threatening to "really raise hell around here." Bobby grabbed little Ruth out of her bed and ran toward the front door, but Berry blocked her passage. Finally she was able to get out of the house and fled to the local police station, where she was told that because there was no restraining order against Berry, the police could do nothing.

On December 5, a judge issued the restraining order, which forbade Berry even to speak to Bobby. He denied all of his wife's allegations and told the court that he shouldn't have to pay Bobby's legal expenses because she "has sufficient funds and ample income, as well as separate property to pay her own legal fees." The court decided that all of Bobby's charges against Berry were true, and ordered him to pay her legal expenses. The restraining order was made permanent, and the divorce was granted on March 4, 1949. Berry was denied even California's customary community property division.

This latest personal failure sent Bobby reeling once again into a mental hospital, where she remained for nearly two years. When she was released, she seemed more disconnected from reality than ever. Within a few years she developed a great passion for a Laguna Beach man to whom she signed over her home (much to Bette's fury, since she had bought the house for her). They lived together for nearly three years, Bobby's friend Betsy Paul recalls, then he "threw her over and went to Paris to marry another woman. Bobby changed. She just fell apart."

Bobby suffered yet another breakdown, yet another hospitalization. She never married again, and during the next decade she was more dependent, emotionally and financially, on her sister than ever before.

As though to sadly complete the Davis women's catalogue of domestic failure, Bette's marriage to William Grant Sherry was coming irreparably apart throughout 1948.

NINETEEN

ette and Sherry sat across from each other at their sprawling Spanish-style dining room table, fully set with the finest china, crystal goblets filled with wine, and sparklingly polished silverware. While candles flickered around the floral centerpiece and in the wall sconces overhead, the cook brought out their salads and placed one, then the other, on the table as the Sherrys sat in stony silence. As soon as the woman had returned to the kitchen, Bette renewed the scathing attack she had launched against her husband during predinner cocktails.

"You're *nothing*," she hissed at him as she unfolded her napkin. "You don't make a living. *I* make a living. I have to worry about everything!"

"Bette," Sherry replied, trying to stay calm, "you know that I take as much as I can off your hands, as much as you'll let me do. I can make a living anytime." But Bette would have none of it. Between deep gulps of her white wine and mouthfuls of her salad, she lobbed zinger after zinger at Sherry. "You don't make any money! I have to make all the money."

Sherry clenched his teeth. "I can make money *anytime*. I've always made money in my life. But your lawyers tell me not to sell a painting because our income tax is so terrific. Give it away, they tell me, but don't sell it. If you want me to make money, I'll go out and make money."

"You live like a prince!"

"What do you want me to *do*? Live out in the garage, go begging? I don't know what you want. Do you want me to get a job?"

"No!" Bette exploded.

Finally Sherry could take this irrational harping no longer. He shot up from his chair, lifted his end of the heavy oak table, and turned it over on top of Bette. "She was under the table," he recalls, "with dishes, lettuce, crystal on top of her. I walked out of the room, and I don't know how she got out from under that mess."

Later that evening, the two were back in bed together and all was fine. "She loved it, you see. She had to dominate her men, and when they wouldn't let her, she liked it."

But Bette soon began to carp again, even less rationally. She continually harangued Sherry about not contributing to the family finances, while at the same time she thwarted at every turn his efforts to strike out on his own. He vividly recalls one morning when he and Bette were reading the newspaper in bed and Bette saw a Harrison Carroll column in which Sherry talked about attending UCLA film school in the hope of directing a nature film for children. "Bette tells me that she will be the last one to stand in my way if I really want to get into the film business," Carroll quoted Sherry.

Bette threw the newspaper across the floor and stared angrily at Sherry. "How much did you pay Carroll to write *this?*"

"I didn't pay him anything. He was just interested in what I was doing, that's all."

"Let me tell you something—there's only room for *one* star in this family!"

"You're always hollering at me to make money—I just thought I'd try my hand at making pictures."

"Well, you can *forget* it!"

Sherry learned that Bette meant what she had said when he spoke to one of the technicians with whom he had discussed the project. Sheepishly, the man said, "I've got to tell you that your wife is against you doing this. She has told every one of us that if we go with you, she'll see to it that we never work in this town again. And she's got the power to do it."

It became clear to Sherry that he couldn't win with Bette no matter what he tried. When he decided that the way to keep his wife happy was to make her as comfortable and relaxed as possible after a hard day's work, the plan backfired. "She was the breadwinner," Sherry said, "and I was the housewife. And I loved doing it. I'd always have dinner ready for her when she got home. I'd take off her shoes and bring her slippers and fix her a drink. I pressed her dresses when her maid wasn't there. I'd draw her bath and give her massages. I felt it was a privilege to do things for her. All I asked in return was love and affection. I'm a man who needs a lot of that. But when she'd come home from work she'd always say she was too tired. I wouldn't get as much as a kiss from her. She was too absorbed in her work."

Her latest absorption was in *June Bride,* a slight comedy that would add little luster to her fading career. Oddly, Bette agreed to be directed again by Bretaigne Windust, and to have her image altered one more time. For this film, she was given a smart, tailored, "modern" look as Linda Gilman, the high-powered editor of a slick woman's magazine who disrupts an Indiana family's life when she decides to feature their daughter's upcoming wedding in her magazine.

The picture turned out forced and largely unfunny, and Jerome Cowan, who played Linda's publisher, recalled being "sorry that Bette had elected to do [the film]. But she told me she was desperate at the time and felt a comedy—which was never her strong suit, in my opinion—would represent a 'change of pace.' . . . Windust had no talent for light comedy . . . and the depressing, spiritless atmosphere on the set carried over, regrettably, into the final result on screen."

Bette, upset enough to find herself mired in a potential turkey, found little comfort in her leading man. Robert Montgomery, a forty-four-year-old MGM player on loan, was an accomplished actor, adept at both drama and comedy. Always insecure (and rightly so) about her comedic talents, Bette feared Montgomery would outclass her, and she had lobbied instead for a Warner contractee as her costar, suggesting Dennis Morgan or Jack Carson. But Windust and producer Henry Blanke convinced her that Montgomery was stronger box office, and she relented. Years later Blanke admitted that there was another reason he favored Montgomery as Bette's leading man: "Since she had her baby, she looked much older. . . . Bob was in his mid-forties and we felt he might make her look younger. As it turned out, *she* made *him* look younger. I think he knew that when he saw the rushes, and it delighted him."

It hardly delighted Bette, and neither did Montgomery's frequent criticisms of her less-than-gossamer comedic touch. "Bette, my dear," he would tell her loudly, "this is not the court of Queen Elizabeth, and certainly not the castle of Lady Macbeth!" But her deepest resentment of Montgomery stemmed from his ardent support of Republican presidential candidate Thomas E. Dewey in his campaign against Harry S. Truman. Every public opinion poll suggested that Dewey would win, and Bette loathed Montgomery's smug confidence in the election outcome. "Montgomery got Bette's pressure up more than Miriam Hopkins had ever done," Jerome Cowan recalls, and when Truman pulled off the political upset of the century three days after *June Bride* opened, Bette sent Montgomery an exultant, gloating telegram.

She had got back at him during filming, too. After a hayride scene, she complained loudly to Windust, Blanke, her agent Lew Wasserman, and her husband (who happened to be visiting the set that day) that Montgomery had been copping feels under the hay. "He's trying to make everybody think he's still young by feeling my leg," Bette reasoned torturously.

"When I heard that," William Grant Sherry says, "I could feel the heat come into my face. I got up and went to his trailer and told him, 'Robert, if you do that scene again, just keep your hands off my wife's legs.' He said, 'I don't know what you're talking about.' And I said, 'Yes, I'm sure you do.' And I left. They closed the set down because he got so furious he wouldn't work. Bette loved it. She and Lew Wasserman were laughing. She said, 'That's the kind of husband I have.' "

The comedienne Mary Wickes played one of Bette's assistants in the film, and her recollection of the hayride incident suggests that what Bette thought was lust may have been nothing more than scratching. According to Wickes, "The hay had just come in and it was full of fleas. It got so bad they had to replace it with fresh hay."

June Bride got mixed reviews when it opened on October 29, 1948. Some critics felt it was "one of the merriest entertainments of the movie season" and "pure, unadulterated fun," while others were less easily amused. As for Bette, *The New Yorker* critic carped, "she conducts herself throughout the film with the grim competent air of a prison warden."

The film did respectable business, pulling in half a million dollars in profit, but that wasn't enough to offset Bette's prior two failures and justify her salary, which now had reached nearly $9,000 a week. Despite that, Jack Warner gave Bette a new, four-picture contract in January 1949 that paid her $10,285 weekly. She was now the highest-paid woman in the United States.

Amazingly, while Jack Warner seemed willing to throw money at Bette, he still would not grant her script approval. The abysmal quality of the next film he insisted she do, in fact, suggests that even as he signed Bette's new contract, Warner harbored doubts about whether Davis, draining his coffers by nearly half a million dollars a year, remained an asset to his studio.

"Jack, *please* don't make me do this picture!" Bette pleaded. "Give it to Virginia Mayo. She'll be much better in it!" She sat in Warner's office, wearing sunglasses as she always did when talking to her boss "so that he couldn't look into my eyes," and tried to get out of doing *Beyond the Forest*. She hated Lenore Coffee's script of a Stuart Engstrand novel about Rosa Moline, a small-town Wisconsin housewife who tries any-thing—including self-induced abortion and murder—to escape from her boring husband and go to Chicago to marry an industrialist with whom she has had an affair. (The ad copy for the finished film called Rosa "a twelve-o'clock girl in a nine-o'clock town.")

"I'm too old for the part, Jack," Bette argued. "I'll look ridicu-lous!"

"Now, Bette," Warner cajoled. "This is a part you could really sink your teeth into, like Mildred. You're always telling me you want gutsy roles. Well, Rosa Moline is just as strong and snakelike as Mildred. She's a man hater, she's scheming and climbing and ambitious in the same cheap, sluttish way Mildred is. Your fans will eat this up!"

When Warner went on to tell her that the respected King Vidor would direct, and that her beloved Max Steiner, who had won three Oscars, including one for *Now, Voyager,* would write the score, Bette began to feel that the project might just work. "I thought Rosa Moline would be a challenge. I hadn't played a bitch in years. . . . The book was great, and it could have made a marvelous movie."

But too many of the creative decisions of all concerned conspired to turn the film into a wretched mess. The first of these was the casting of the attractive forty-four-year-old Joseph Cotten as Rosa's husband, who in the book is far less physically appealing. According to Bette, "The husband was supposed to be a man like Eugene Pallette [who played Bette's husband in *Bordertown*]—a fat, *horrible* man. So when they told me that Joseph Cotten would be my husband, this adorable man, I said, 'What in the world would she leave *him* for?' "

Other decisions were no better, including one to deck Bette out in a jet-black wig that one critic described as "Dracula-like." With heavy lipstick and eyeliner, wearing frumpy print dresses and plaid shirts, she looked little short of ridiculous, and she knew it. She could see too that King Vidor, who had triumphed with *The Fountainhead* earlier in the year, was doing little to elevate the film from its absurdly melodramatic story line.

As filming progressed through the late spring and summer of 1949, Bette dreaded having to act the scenes where Rosa throws herself down an embankment to induce an abortion, develops peritonitis and raging fever, drags herself out of bed, smears on her makeup, and then crawls toward the train in a desperate last-ditch effort to get to Chicago, then dies with her hand outstretched toward the track.

With each day of filming Bette grew more and more terrified that she was making her worst picture, one that might well drive the final fatal stake through the heart of her cherished career. She feared she would make a fool of herself, and as so often before her insecurities resulted in temperament, tantrums, and absences from the studio. "She had so many excuses for not going to the set," William Grant Sherry recalled. "Her favorite was laryngitis. One day she sent a note to [the film's producer] Henry Blanke saying she'd lost her voice totally. A little while later Jack Warner telephoned to ask how she was. She grabbed the phone and started screaming at him."

Before long, Bette rebelled. During an argument with Vidor and Henry Blanke in her dressing room, she reiterated her reservations about playing Rosa at her age, about the casting of Cotten, about everything. Vidor explained that he thought Rosa was "a fine variation on Mildred" and that a woman of forty-one could be "desperate for new experiences."

"Don't give me that *crap*!" she bellowed. "Warner just thinks this will be less expensive than *Frome* or *Lincoln*. He wants something trashy and cheap that he thinks will sell to lowbrows. I didn't work all these years for better pictures to be relegated, at this stage, to *horseshit* like this!"

A few weeks before the film was completed in August, Vidor asked Bette to retake a scene in which he felt she hadn't flung a bottle of medicine at Cotten viciously enough. She refused to do it again, and left the studio. At home that evening, according to William Grant Sherry, "She was furious and fretting and talking about quitting Warners. She asked me what I thought and I told her, 'It seems to me, Bette, that with your fame and ability, there would be an awful lot of scripts that would come your way from other studios. It's a gamble—you'd have to give up that salary—but if you're brave enough and take a chance, it might work."

Soon thereafter Jack Warner called, and Marion Richards, a twenty-one-year-old woman who had just joined the Sherry household as B.D.'s governess, recalled that "she yelled so loud at Jack Warner that there was practically smoke coming out of the phone. Neither of them would budge an inch on anything." Finally Bette told Warner, "If you want me to finish the film, let me out of my contract."

To her shock, Warner agreed without hesitation, and even before she arrived on the set the next morning, he had released her. "It was dirty pool on my part, but I was that desperate," Bette said, suggesting that she had forced Warner to let her break her contract against his will so that he could avoid losing the $800,000 already spent on *Beyond the Forest*. But if Bette had come to the end of her rope with Warner, so had he with her. He was tired of her demands, her temperament, her tantrums, her enormous salary. The Warner legal department notified Bette to stop telling the press she had forced the studio to release her, because "it was a mutual decision."

"I was relieved to see her go," Jack Warner wrote in his memoirs.

On her last day at Warner Brothers, Bette dubbed a particularly apt line of dialogue—"I can't stand it here anymore"—and sat around all night on the back lot drinking until dawn with Henry Blanke and three of her favorite crew members. Then, "three sheets to the wind," she drove through the Warner gate for the last time in tears. She grieved for the loss of the working relationships she had loved, the loss of the "second father" she had respected as much as she hated, and, worst of all, the loss of the secure career that the studio had provided her over the last eighteen years. Sherry had predicted she'd be flooded with great scripts now that she was freelance, and part of her believed it. Another part of her chilled with the fear that her age, her spotty recent box-office record, and her reputation as a troublemaker, might cause other studios to shy away from her.

Within a few months, Bette realized that her worst nightmare had come true. "Nothing happened," Sherry recalled. "There were no good scripts, it was all just terrible stuff. It got pretty bad."

"Why are you sending me this *crap*?" Bette bellowed to her agent. His reply cut into her like an ice pick: "Because that's all I'm getting, Bette." To a woman for whom work was a lifeline, the news was shattering. She fumed and she fretted, she raged against the fates and the powers that be, she beat up on herself for giving up her contract. And she turned on her husband, the most convenient object of her wrath. According to him, "As time went on, Bette completely became another character. She was no longer the Bette that I was in love with. I began to wonder what was going on. I thought it was something with me. . . ."

Sherry tried to keep his wife happy, tried to placate her, tried to buck her up. It didn't work, and her denigration of him grew merciless. Now she not only accused him of living off her, she questioned his manhood.

Sherry was able to take less and less of it before he would lose control of his temper. "One night she needled me all through dinner and when we went into the living room to have coffee she got me so mad I threw my coffee cup at her. It hit the fireplace and splashed all over and she went racing out of the room."

In her memoirs, Bette says that "Sherry's physical violence was a thing of terror to me." She admitted that it was natural for a husband to want to be dominant in a marriage but "with me this is impossible." She accused Sherry of throwing her down a flight of stairs, hurling an ice bucket at her head, and throwing things at her while she held their baby. Sherry denies all of this. "Whatever I did throw at her never hit her. I'd throw it across the room just to scare her."

Sherry's frustration mushroomed, and so did his violent outbursts. "I fly into a temper at the slightest provocation," he admitted at the time, "sometimes without provocation. Bette told me she was afraid of what I might do to her and to the baby when I was in one of my rages."

In a feeble attempt to calm things down and take Bette's mind off her professional inertia, Sherry tried three times to paint her portrait. He wasn't able to do it. "Each time," he says, "the meanest-looking expression would come out in the painting. It would just come up. I paint what I see. I tried to change it and put a smile on her face, but those eyes . . . I'd tell her, 'I can't do it, Bette, sorry.' She'd say, 'Can I see it?' and I'd say, 'No, you can't' and I'd destroy the painting before she could sneak a look at it."

Caught in the middle of all this marital tension was Marion Richards, the twenty-one-year-old girl Bette had hired in August as a governess for B.D. after another "personality conflict," this one with the woman who had replaced Bessie Downs two years earlier. Marion had a feeling that Bette liked her because she could "take or leave" the job and she didn't "kowtow" to her. As Marion recalls it, "she was more nervous than I was during the interview."

The pretty young woman, who had appeared as a model on the covers of several magazines, was struck by the fact that whenever the Sherrys were together, they argued. "She was always on his case, calling him a prince, saying that she was making all the money. Then he'd offer to go to work, and she'd say no because then she'd have to pay more taxes. He was damned if he did and damned if he didn't."

Marion also noticed that Bette never seemed to let Bobby, recently released from a mental hospital, forget that she was financially indebted to her, either. "Bobby was like a whipped dog," Marion recalled. "She looked like she was below the servants, and she didn't dare say the wrong thing or else she'd be reprimanded. When she got depressed, she would just hang her head down. And it seemed that when she would get into that state of mind, Bette would kind of gloat over it. She loved it in a way. She never showed any empathy, she would only get angry with Bobby. That was the cruel side of Bette. She could be wonderful and darling, but then she would go into this other, almost sadistic person. She liked exercising her power over people. There were days when she thought she had the world around her little finger, and she was going to exercise it to the max."

Marion's biggest shock when she started working at the Sherry house was the condition of two-year-old B.D., who seemed deeply maladjusted. "When I first got there, this little girl would hide behind chairs, and sometimes she would defecate back there. She just looked scared. Whatever she did it was her *duty* to do. Bette hadn't been much of a mother to that child. She was too wrapped up in her career and herself. I never saw her really close to B.D. She didn't like having to deal with her."

A few weeks after Marion began to work for Bette, they had a furious row, and when it was over Bobby told Marion, "Don't worry, Bette's had a tough day. It's not you, she has other things going on. I've told her that she'll never find anyone who's as wonderful with B.D. as you are. She needs a young person, not those old fuddy-duddies she'd always had. The child's just blossomed since you've been here."

What Marion did to help B.D., she says, was to treat her like a child. "I just started tickling her and playing with her, and she started opening up. We even started drawing on the wall, which Bette allowed. She could be wonderful at times. She just didn't know how to relate to a child."

Bette came to like and respect Marion Richards, mainly because the young woman never allowed her boss to "walk all over her" the way Bette did so many others. "If I came home late, even on my day off, she'd be pacing back and forth like a wild animal: 'Why weren't you *home?*' And I didn't even discuss it with her, I just looked her right in the face, and she *knew* that if she went too far, I'd say *forget it.* Most people would say to her, 'Okay, Bette, oh yes, Miss Davis. Kick me in the you-know-where. I'll take anything you say.' But I was firm with her. I knocked the wind out of her sails. If enough people had done that, she wouldn't have acted the way she did—like a spoiled brat.

"She was careful with me because she knew I had my own independence. When I showed her that I wasn't going to let her step all over me, she started catering to *me*. It was weird. It showed her insecurity. She actually brought me coffee and toast in bed the morning after we had had a confrontation and I hadn't backed down."

As the last months of 1949 dragged on without a suitable script for Bette, she became all the more overwrought and volatile. Sherry was desperate with anxiety over the state of his marriage, and the situation disintegrated further after Bette began to humiliate him in public, carping about everything from his unemployed status to his thinning hair. At a party in Hollywood thrown by MCA, Bette's talent agency, Sherry, for the first time, wasn't allowed to sit next to his wife, who was at a table "with the big shots." Several people asked him why he wasn't with Bette, and he was at a loss to explain it. At one point he walked over to her and said, "Bette, let's dance." She looked up at him as the others at the table fell silent. "I'm not dancing with you!"

Without another word, Sherry leaned down, put his arm around her waist and lifted her out of her chair. He pulled her out onto the dance floor, and every time she struggled to get away from him he hissed, "You're not going anywhere!" Finally the music stopped and Sherry loosened his grip. Bette charged off the floor, and as Sherry started after her Joseph Cotten grabbed his arm. "When you catch up to her," Cotten advised, "punch her in the mouth." Bette never returned to the banquet, and Sherry later learned that she had climbed out of the bathroom window and taken a taxi home.

On October 21, Bette filed for divorce, claiming that Sherry had threatened her, and obtained a court order restraining him from doing her "bodily harm." She left him alone in the Laguna house and fled to what the press described as a "secret hideaway." Four days later, Sherry agreed to undergo psychiatric treatment in order to "curb his temper" and change Bette's mind about the divorce. "I've told her I'll do anything to preserve our marriage," Sherry said to reporters who had jumped on the story. "The whole trouble is due to my violent temper. It's hooked up with the war, I think. It's one of those nasty things. But I adore Bette and I'd be miserable if anything happened to this marriage."

Sherry consulted Dr. Frederick Hacker, who had a strong reputation as a "shrink to the stars." During the first session, Hacker informed Sherry that he wanted Bette to accompany him on his next visit. When Sherry told Bette this, she retorted, "No way! No psychoanalyst is getting to me. What's the matter with him? *You're* the crazy one!" Sherry explained that it wasn't a matter of who was sane or who was crazy, but only that Dr. Hacker felt it would be advantageous for both partners to see him. Bette snorted, and Sherry went back to Hacker alone.

During the sessions, Sherry confronted a number of issues in his marriage and his life, including his ambivalent feelings toward his father, who "wanted me to be a tough guy. I really wasn't. I was a tender person." After a fall from a fire escape, he had grown up thin and delicate, "not what my father wanted as a son at all, I'm sure. He wanted me to beat up the kids who took pokes at me on the street, so I started playing with the girls instead of the boys because they were gentler. My father made me feel like I was a sissy."

Hacker explained to Sherry that he had overcompensated for these feelings with bodybuilding and boxing, and that his repressed anger caused his fits of violence. Hacker suggested that Sherry see a female associate of his, and she presented him with Rorschach inkblots that she asked him to interpret.

"All I could see in those blots were drawings I had made during surgeries while I was in the service," Sherry recalled. When he told the woman that one blot looked "like something I drew up of a kidney operation," she said to him, "You mean to tell me that this doesn't remind you of a woman's vagina?"

Sherry winced. "If it did, I'd have nothing more to do with women."

The next day, Dr. Hacker told Sherry that he had upset the woman because "you didn't come up with the answers she thinks you should."

"You mean, I should answer the way *she* thinks I should answer? I don't get it."

Hacker laughed. "We're not going any further with this," he concluded. "I have surmised what's wrong. You're a red-blooded American man who's married to the wrong woman."

The same thought had occurred to Sherry a year earlier, when Bette hired Marion Richards as B.D.'s governess. To this day, Sherry remembers what Marion was wearing when she first came to the Laguna Beach house to apply for the job. "Bette and I were in the living room and Marion came in wearing this lovely navy blue suit. With white gloves. She was beautiful, with hair down to here, a lovely looking person." Sherry found himself staring at her and thinking, *I got married too soon.*

Still, Sherry tried to keep his marriage to Bette intact, and they reconciled early in 1950. The friction between the two was eased considerably when Bette finally began work on a new picture—for Howard Hughes at RKO. *The Story of a Divorce* had not only a prophetic title, but a plot line that uneasily paralleled Bette's marriage to Sherry. She played Joyce Ramsey, a driven career woman who pushes her easygoing husband David (Barry Sullivan) into business success that he neither wants nor enjoys. Cold and obsessive about her career, Joyce unwittingly drives her husband into an affair with a gentle schoolteacher who gives him the comfort and affection he craves. Finally he asks her for a divorce after twenty years of marriage. When she learns of his affair, she countersues him, demanding a large settlement in cash and property.

Later, after their daughter's wedding, Joyce and David decide to reconcile. The next morning, Joyce is as nasty and domineering as ever at the breakfast table, and David leaves her once again, this time for good. Director Curtis Bernhardt shot the film's final scene from above, as Joyce sits alone in her enormous house, having pushed away everyone who loved her.

After the shot was completed, Bette turned to Betty Lynn, the young actress who played her daughter in the film, and said, "This is the great fear of my life. That I'll end up just like this."

By all accounts, Bette was less temperamental on this film than she had been in years. Both her costar Barry Sullivan and Leonard Shannon, the film's publicist, recall dire warnings from a number of people that Bette would be impossible to work with, but both found her "a real pleasure." Shannon believes that Bette was so shaken by the six months she had spent without a good script that she was determined to prove herself "considerate" of cast and crew on this picture. "Of course," he adds, "it was also true that by that time a lot of people had figured out how to handle Bette Davis. If you wanted her to do something, you had to tell her just the opposite. If you wanted to take lunch off the lot with her, you couldn't say so, because she'd say, 'Ah, it's too much trouble, let's eat in my dressing room.' You had to say, 'Bette, it's a really crappy day. It isn't the kind of day that you'd want to go out and have lunch.' Then she would say, 'Hell, it's a *beautiful* day out there! Of course I'll go out and have lunch!' She would do what you wanted her to do without ever knowing you wanted her to do it—just as long as she could be contrary."

Bette was also made more docile by the presence of B.D. on the set. She had decided to have her nearly three-year-old daughter make her screen debut in the film, and for one scene between Bette and B.D., Curtis Bernhardt asked for six retakes. After the fifth, B.D. shot him a look of exasperation. "I've seen *that* look before," Bernhardt mumbled.

"Bette was screwing Barry Sullivan at night," Leonard Shannon recalls. "He was always hanging around her dressing room after the company broke. That wasn't a secret." Although Sullivan denies having had an affair with Bette—he was married, he says, and didn't find her attractive —the rumors got back to William Grant Sherry that his wife and the handsome thirty-seven-year-old leading man were having late-night tête-à-têtes in her dressing room. Sherry arrived on the set on April 5, the final day of filming, and angrily demanded that Bette come home with him. She refused and ordered him off the lot. When studio guards blocked him from entering the commissary to accompany Bette to a combination wrap party and birthday bash the crew was throwing for her, he put up such a fuss that Barry Sullivan intervened. He and Sherry got into a verbal clash, Sherry recalls, and "I let him have one and knocked him down. The studio cops broke it up."

The incident made front pages around the country, and Sherry told the Hollywood columnist Harrison Carroll that "my wife is a troubled, mixed-up girl. She has never been really happy. . . . I tried to help her as much as I could, but I can't go any further alone. . . . If she would join me in consulting my psychiatrist, I am positive that our marital problems could be worked out. But whether she continues with me or not she ought to have the treatment. If she does not, she will be a miserable woman all her life."

Instead, Bette reinstated her divorce action against Sherry. This time, he didn't contest it, and he remained in Laguna Beach while Bette holed herself up in a new house she had rented in Beverly Hills. Sherry was granted visitation rights with B.D. while the divorce suit was pending, and he told Bette he wanted to take her down to Laguna with him. Bette agreed, but only if Marion Richards, still the child's governess, could accompany her each time. "Well," said Sherry, "if you insist."

≈

A few days before she completed filming *The Story of a Divorce,* Bette had received a telephone call on the set. When she heard the call was from Darryl Zanuck, the head of 20th Century–Fox, she knit her brows: she hadn't spoken to Zanuck since he had told her she'd never work in Hollywood again after she resigned her Academy presidency in 1941. She took the call and was on the phone for about five minutes. When she returned to the set "her eyes were blazing," Betty Lynn recalled.

"You'll never guess who that was," she said to Lynn, and without waiting for a response, she told her. "It was Darryl Zanuck. He's sending over a script that Joe Mankiewicz wrote and will be directing for Fox."

"He just won two Oscars for writing and directing!" Lynn exclaimed.

"Yes, he did," Bette replied dreamily. "And Zanuck wants me to replace Claudette Colbert in this new picture. She's hurt her back and can't do the part."

"What's the movie about?" Lynn asked.

"Zanuck wouldn't tell me much except that it's about a theater actress."

Bette sat in her chair and stared straight ahead, her mind abuzz with limitless possibilities. "Zanuck wants me to do some tests with my leading man this weekend." Then she turned back to Lynn. "Do you know an actor named Gary Merrill?"

TWENTY

Bette couldn't believe her eyes. She sat in an overstuffed chair in the corner of her bedroom, a fire crackling across the room, a glass of Scotch beside her and a cigarette between her fingers, and read the script that Darryl Zanuck had sent over. Entitled *All About Eve,* it was based loosely on a short story by Mary Orr that had appeared in *Cosmopolitan* several years earlier. With each page she turned, Bette's excitement grew.

The plot had grabbed her instantly: What was Eve Harrington (to be played by Anne Baxter), the seemingly innocent, loyal young fan, really up to as she insinuated herself into every aspect of the life of Margo Channing, Broadway superstar? The supporting characters jumped off the page at her: Margo's lover Bill Sampson (Gary Merrill), a director, pretentiously grandiloquent about the theater but a rock of masculinity and loyalty to Margo; her best friend Karen Richards (Celeste Holm), warm and witty but not above a few Eve-like machinations of her own; Karen's husband Lloyd (Hugh Marlowe), a playwright, admiring of Margo but resentful that her star personality often overwhelmed his characters; Max Fabian (Gregory Ratoff), Margo's producer, a victim of chronic indigestion; Birdie Coonan (Thelma Ritter), Margo's personal maid, a wise and wisecracking ex-vaudevillian; and Addison DeWitt (George Sanders), the cynical, Machiavellian "critic and commentator" who is, by his own admission, as "essential to the theater as ants to a picnic."

But it was the character that Zanuck wanted Bette to play—Margo Channing—that made her actress's heart flutter more than it had since she read *Of Human Bondage.* "A Star of the Theater," Addison DeWitt describes Margo, who "made her first stage appearance at the age of four in *Midsummer Night's Dream.* She played a fairy and entered—quite unexpectedly—stark naked. She has been a Star ever since." Throughout the script, Margo is described variously as "talented, famous, wealthy," "beautiful and intelligent," "a junk yard," "childish," "ageless," "maudlin and full of self-pity," "magnificent," "a body with a voice," "paranoiac," "an hysterical, screaming harpy," "Peck's bad boy," and finally, in her own words, "a foursquare, upright, downright, forthright married lady."

Clearly, this character was a marvelously layered creation, larger than life, a mass of contradictions, the true possessor of the "fire and music" used in the script to describe Eve Harrington's surreptitious reading of Margo's role during an audition. Bette's only reservation had been that she would be playing someone other than Eve in a movie entitled *All About Eve*. As she put the script down, however, the kind of thrill only an actress can feel when offered a magnificent role coursed through her body. The movie could just as easily have been called *All About Margo*. And it was probably the best script she had ever read.

It was also the wittiest, replete as it was with ultrasophisticated aphorisms, biting theatrical in-jokes, and epigrammatic observations. Bette howled as she read some of the lines Joe Mankiewicz had written. As Birdie finishes snapping up the back of Margo's dress when she prepares for a party, she proclaims, "Voilà!" Margo turns to her and mutters, "That French ventriloquist taught you a lot, didn't he?" When Birdie tells Margo that she ordered domestic gin by mistake, she replies, "The only thing I ordered by mistake is the guests. They're domestic, too, and they don't care what they drink as long as it burns."

After Margo and Bill fight over his attentions to Eve, Lloyd Richards arrives at the party and comments, "the general atmosphere is very *Macbeth*ish." Then Karen says to Margo, "We know you, we've seen you before like this. Is it over—or just beginning?"

"Fasten your seat belts," Margo replies. "It's going to be a bumpy night."

When Margo is told that a famous movie star has arrived at her party, she says, "Shucks. And my autograph book is at the cleaner's." When Addison tells Margo that Eve's performance of her part for an audition was "made of fire and music" and that "in time she'll be what you are," Margo shoots back, "A mass of music and fire. That's me. An old kazoo with some sparklers."

It went on like that, page after page, glittering wit sparkling off a rock-solid story of backstage chicanery. The next morning, Bette called Darryl Zanuck and told him she would love to play Margo Channing. He said she would need to be in San Francisco, ready to film at the Curran Theatre, in two weeks. She still had four days' work on *The Story of a Divorce*, but she told Zanuck she would be there.

The night before Bette left for San Francisco, Sherry came up from Laguna to try to talk her out of divorcing him. Bette had banished him from the Beverly Hills house, and she wouldn't let him in after he knocked on the door. Instead, she came out on the lawn to talk to him, still in her nightgown, and within a few minutes their discussion had degenerated into a vicious fight.

Illuminated only by the lamp over the front door, Bette and her husband stood a few feet across from each other and yelled. She baited him with her usual taunts about his manhood and his lack of a job, and then she lobbed a new one at him—she told him she was having an affair with Joe Mankiewicz. "He's a *real* man," Bette hissed. "He's a genius! He makes a living *all his own*!"

"Shut up!" Sherry fairly roared as Bette broke for the house and barricaded herself behind the door. Within a few minutes, she looked down at the lawn from her bedroom window. All was quiet; Sherry was gone. But Bette wasn't able to sleep that night—she had screamed so loudly that she ruptured a blood vessel in her throat.

The next day, Saturday, April 15, Bette arrived in San Francisco with B.D., her nurse Marion Richards, and a bodyguard to protect her from Sherry, who she feared would follow them. The broken blood vessel in her throat had left her barely able to speak, and when Joe Mankiewicz heard her he nearly panicked—filming was to start in two days. He called in a doctor who advised Bette that if she used her voice as little as possible over the weekend, she would probably have no trouble with it come Monday.

When Bette showed up at the Curran Theatre, where the interior stage scenes were to be filmed, her voice had come back only enough to leave it coarse and husky. She apologized to Mankiewicz, but he loved it. "It's just the whiskey-throated voice Margo should have," he told her. "If your throat improves, make sure you keep your voice deep throughout the picture."

Hollywood can be a serendipitous place. Film lore is rife with stories of the tortuous paths traveled by screenplays and their characters before they met up with the actor or actress who would so memorably bring them to life that it would become impossible to imagine another performer in the role. Judy Garland played Dorothy in *The Wizard of Oz* only after 20th Century–Fox refused to make Shirley Temple available to MGM for the part; Vivien Leigh wasn't chosen to play Scarlett O'Hara until after filming on *Gone With the Wind* had begun; Barbra Streisand won the Broadway role of Fanny Brice in *Funny Girl* only after Mary Martin, Anne Bancroft, and Carol Burnett passed; Liza Minnelli got the chance to play Sally Bowles in *Cabaret* only because Streisand turned it down.

There are many other such happy accidents, but few more resonant than Bette and Margo, a pair destiny seemed determined at first to keep apart. Although Bette was Joe Mankiewicz's first choice, her work on *The Story of a Divorce* overlapped the late-winter 1949 start date Darryl Zanuck had set originally for *Eve*. Mankiewicz's second choice, Claudette Colbert, was under contract to Fox and available. She signed to do the picture, but she ruptured a vertebra filming a violent jungle rape scene in *Three Came Home* and was forced to bow out. "I cried and cried," Colbert recalled. "I was in agony with my back and in emotional despair at losing such a plum role."

Mankiewicz then sent the script to Gertrude Lawrence, the great theater musical comedy star (*Private Lives*), who was ten years older than Margo Channing and hadn't made a film in thirteen years. Lawrence's attorney, the redoubtable Fanny Holtzman, intercepted it and told Mankiewicz that she thought Gertrude might be interested, but he'd have to make some changes. "For one thing," Holtzman said, "the character drinks too much. I would prefer she not drink at all. And in that party scene where she's at the piano, don't you think that would be a nice time for Gertie to sing a song?"

"You mean like 'My Bill'?" Mankiewicz asked mockingly.

"Well, it *has* been done," Holtzman replied.

"I know it's been done, but it ain't gonna be done by me, Miss Holtzman," Mankiewicz said just before he hung up.

By now the start date had been put back several months, and with *The Story of a Divorce* nearing completion, Bette Davis suddenly became available. Thus was another actress melded with a role that was absolutely perfect for her.

The morning Bette's signing to play Margo was announced, Joe Mankiewicz got calls from several of her directors warning him of the most dire consequences. He recalled Edmund Goulding's the most vividly. Goulding had directed four of Bette's films, including *Dark Victory* and *The Great Lie.* "Have you gone *mad?*" Goulding asked. "This woman will destroy you, she will grind you down to a fine powder and blow you away. You are a writer, dear boy. She will come to the stage with a thick pad of long yellow paper. And pencils. She will write. And then she, not you, will direct. Mark my words."

Forewarned and wary, Mankiewicz watched Bette closely as she arrived on the set the first day. She was carrying nothing but the script; she didn't look around to check out the camera angles or the lighting setup. "Bette didn't even glance at the set," Mankiewicz recalled. "She lit a cigarette and opened the script—not, I noticed at once, to the scene [of hers] we were doing that first morning."

Mankiewicz called a rehearsal. "Bette was letter perfect. She was syllable perfect. There was no fumbling for my words; they had become hers—as Margo Channing. The director's dream: the prepared actress." Over the next few days, he saw no temperament from Bette, no attempts to change his words, no bridling at his direction. He was astonished— either Ed Goulding was crazy or this actress was an impostor.

Mankiewicz told Bette about the warnings, and added that while he had expected Lady Macbeth, she was more like the virtuous Portia of *The Merchant of Venice.* Bette just snorted, then laughed. ("Her snort and her laugh," Mankiewicz said, "both should be protected by copyright.") Then she responded. "I am neither Lady Macbeth nor Portia. . . . But yes, I suppose my reputation, based upon some experiences I've had, is pretty much as advertised. . . . [But] you're a writer, you're a director, you function behind the camera. You do not appear upon the screen, forty feet high and thirty feet wide. . . . Me, I'm an actress, and I do appear upon that screen, that big. What I say and do, and how I look, is what millions of people see and listen to. The fact that my performance is the end result of many other contributions as well, matters to them not at all. If I make a horse's ass of myself, on that screen, it is I—me—Bette Davis—who is the forty-feet-by-thirty-feet horse's ass as far as they're concerned."

Bette added that Mankiewicz's script—tight, gripping, sparkling on every page—was "heaven" because most scripts were damaged by compromise, and when she had a bad script she could turn only to the director for "salvation": "With his help, you think, it'll turn out fine. Or, at least, hold together. Then, one morning, the director drops by your dressing room . . . and in a very strange voice asks what you think of the scene you're about to do that day, and do you really like it? That *does* it for me. . . . Bells and sirens go off inside me. I know at once that *he* doesn't like the scene—that *he* doesn't know what to think about it. Invariably, rehearsal proves me right. The director can't make up his mind whether we're to stand, sit, run, enter, or exit; he hasn't the foggiest notion of what the scene is all about or whether, in fact, it's a scene at all. . . . Pretty soon there's quite a gathering [of producers and executives] on the set, throwing worn-out clichés at each other."

Bette took a deep breath and continued with her aria. "By this time, I am back in my dressing room. Fully aware that the result of it all, nine times out of ten, will be a botched-up, abortive scene which will wind up with me as a thirty-by-forty-foot horse's ass on the silver screen. So yes, I'm afraid there have been times—and probably will be again—when the responsibility for what I say and do on the screen is one I feel I must meet by myself."

It took Mankiewicz only a few days to realize that the mutual admiration society between Bette and himself had inspired her to contribute layers to Margo Channing that no other actress could have. His only direction to her had been that Margo Channing was a woman who would "treat her mink coat like a poncho." Bette's first appearance on screen indelibly establishes Margo's character—without a line of dialogue. As Addison DeWitt describes her undraped entrance into show business at the age of four, she looks up with a heavy-lidded, cynical world-weariness that lets us know immediately that this woman has seen it all. Her long hair falls sexily around her bare shoulders. She takes out a cigarette and deftly lights it herself with a lighter—Margo Channing waits for no man. She pours herself a drink, and Addison DeWitt offers her some seltzer from a bottle. As if she has done this a million times before, she pushes the bottle away to prevent the dreaded diluting liquid from sullying her liquor and gives Addison a small smile, as if to say, "You know better than that."

None of this is in the script exactly the way Bette enacts it. Mankiewicz had written that Addison offers Margo the water and she "looks at it, and at him, as if it were a tarantula and he had gone mad." Bette's weary gesture, wonderfully offhand, characterizes Margo instantly—as, in a different way, does the cigarette. Mankiewicz's screenplay doesn't mention that Margo smokes, but to have Bette Davis's first scene in a film where she plays an actress so prominently involve a cigarette, her most famous film prop over the past ten years, telegraphs to the audience that there might just be a dollop or two of Bette Davis in Margo Channing. That subtext lends immediate electricity to her characterization, the sparks from which never wane throughout the movie's two-hour-eighteen-minute running time.

It is startling to realize that Bette completed her role in *All About Eve* in three and a half weeks. The entire film had only a six-week shooting schedule; the solid script, Mankiewicz's sure-handed direction, and Bette's confidence in both helped keep things moving smoothly. What makes the brevity of Bette's contributions so breathtaking is not only the enormity of Margo Channing's impact on the Bette Davis legend (she is remembered for Margo more than for any other character), but the equal impact the film had on Bette's personal life. For it was on the set of *All About Eve*, of course, that she met Gary Merrill.

She had already been captivated by his charms on the silver screen four months earlier in the Oscar-nominated World War II drama *Twelve O'Clock High*. So much so that after she and Sherry attended an industry screening in Hollywood in December, they got into a nasty argument over Bette's effusive talk about how "attractive" Merrill was. Apparently, Merrill's name hadn't rung a bell to Bette when Darryl Zanuck originally told her over the phone that Gary would be her *Eve* leading man, but when she met him she was as impressed as ever by his rugged good looks, and pleasurably stirred by his unforced masculinity and lack of pretension. During an early scene, Bette waited for Merrill to light Margo's cigarette. He didn't. Finally she said, "Well, aren't you going to light my cigarette?"

"I don't think Bill Sampson would light Margo's cigarettes," Merrill replied, and Bette knew he was right. She also sensed that Gary Merrill wouldn't light her cigarette either, and she liked that. *This fellow Merrill,* she thought, *might have possibilities.*

He, too, was intrigued. He found Bette a "magnetic" woman with a "compelling aura of femininity. I was irresistibly drawn to her. My first feeling of compassion for this misunderstood, talented woman was quickly replaced by a robust attraction. Before long we were holding hands, going to the movies, and doing other things together. From simple compassion, my feelings shifted to an almost uncontrollable lust. I walked around with an erection for three days."

The two made little effort to hide their ripening romantic feelings. Following a scene in which Bill comforts Margo after she reads a scathing Addison DeWitt attack on her, they remained locked in an embrace for so long that Mankiewicz called out, "Cut! Cut! This is not swing and sway with Sammy Kaye!"

When William Grant Sherry heard the rumors about his estranged wife and her leading man, he sent Bette a telegram pleading with her to reconcile with him. "It was a beautiful, tender, sweet letter," Marion Richards recalls. "And what does Bette do? She reads it aloud in front of the entire cast, laughing all the time, until finally everyone was howling. The only one who didn't go along with ridiculing it was Anne Baxter. She was offended by the whole thing. As was I. I knew Grant was doing whatever he could to save his marriage. But when I saw Bette do that, I knew there wasn't the slightest chance they would ever reconcile."

According to Marion, the attraction between Bette and Gary didn't become a physical affair until *All About Eve* filming wrapped, but they seem to have made up for lost time after that. Bette's lease on the Beverly Hills house expired May 1, and she, B.D., Marion, and their "big, black bodyguard" began "running around" when they returned from San Francisco: "We stayed at Joe Mankiewicz's house, at other producers' houses," Marion says. "After the picture was finished we were living in Katharine Hepburn's house in Beverly Hills."

It was there that Marion became aware that Bette and Gary Merrill were sexually involved. "B.D.'s and my bedroom was just below Bette's. Gary would come over and I'd hear the bed going up and down all night. Then you could hear him leaving in the morning. He wouldn't stay for breakfast, he would leave."

Bette and Gary continued their indiscreet behavior despite the fact that Sherry could easily have used it against Bette in a custody battle for B.D. Marion Richards feels that Bette was so proud of her hot new romance that she couldn't help but flaunt it. Lest Marion miss the implications of Gary's visits, Bette called her to her bedroom one morning moments after Gary had left. With the musky scent of her lover's sweat still heavy in the air, Bette stood before Marion stark naked and discussed inconsequentialities. She made no move to cover herself. Marion stared at her face and prayed to be dismissed from this bizarre command appearance.

Gary's nocturnal visits to Bette's bedroom were possible only because, weeks earlier, he had loudly announced at a party—in front of his wife—

that he would marry Bette Davis if she'd have him. The next day, the woman he had married nine years earlier, the former actress Barbara Leeds, threw him out of their Malibu house. "All hell broke loose," Barbara recalls. "We had had separations and reconciliations for years. He was a real womanizer. I knew about his affair with Mercedes Mc-Cambridge. We broke up over that one—and I had my pregnancy terminated as a result—but we got back together just before he went into *Born Yesterday* on Broadway. But when he said that about Bette at that party, I'd had it. That was it."

Gary was delighted to spend his nights with Bette, but he was getting very nervous about her husband. According to Barbara Merrill, "A few days after we broke up, Gary came pounding at the door of the apartment I'd moved into. He was frantic and screamed, 'Let me in! Let me in!' I opened the door and asked him, 'Good God, what's the matter?' He said, 'Sherry's got a pistol and he's trying to get me! I'm being followed! He's a very dangerous man.'"

Barbara, inured by now to Gary's penchant for histrionics, simply sighed, "Oh, God," and let him hide out until he calmed down. Whether or not Sherry actually presented that serious a threat, Bette certainly thought he did. Marion Richards recalls Bette waking her up in the middle of the night and insisting that she come down to the kitchen, where Bette was going to cook them a meal. As she fidgeted over the stove, Bette turned around and said, "I wonder if he's going to come after us and kill me?" Marion didn't think he would, and she suspected that Bette's fears were mere hysterics. "After a few drinks the actress side of her would appear. She'd play these big dramatic scenes. I thought it was very funny."

While Bette struggled with all this domestic upheaval, her mother decided once again to give marriage a try. On April 24, 1950, the sixty-four-year-old Ruthie eloped to Las Vegas to marry a retired army captain named Otho Williams Budd, also sixty-four. An Arizona native and a pottery packer in Laguna Beach before his retirement in 1947, Budd had been a neighbor of Ruthie's for several years. When Ruthie telephoned Bette on the Fox lot from Las Vegas to give her the news, Bette was rendered speechless at first. Then she wished her mother luck and promised that she and Gary would come down to visit as soon as they could to meet Bette's new stepfather.

They drove down the following Sunday, and after meeting Otho

Budd they motored through town in Gary's yellow Oldsmobile convertible, with the top down, kissing and laughing and acting like college kids in love. It would have been enough to provoke Sherry, who lived near Ruthie, to fury, but he never saw them.

Bobby did. With her mother newly married and her sister so obviously in love, Bobby withdrew again into her shell of depression, her two marital failures gnawing freshly at her mind. It was little consolation to her eighteen months later when Ruthie divorced Otho Budd, charging that for over a year Budd had treated her with extreme cruelty and had driven her to "grievous mental anguish" that had impaired her health.

When the divorce was final on December 12, 1951, Bobby had her mother's full attention again, but this latest domestic collapse made her wonder achingly—*Will the Davis women* ever *find happiness?*

The moment she finished shooting *All About Eve,* Bette went to court to gain custody of B.D. She had never withdrawn the divorce petition she had filed against Sherry the previous October, and she asked the court to decide the question of B.D.'s custody while the divorce action was pending. Apparently beaten down by now, Sherry didn't appear before the judge or challenge Bette's request. On May 9, the couple signed an agreement that allowed Sherry only the vague right to "visit [B.D.] at a reasonable time and place."

Less than a month later, Sherry told Bette's lawyer, Jerry Geisler—and the press—that he had changed his mind and would contest the divorce because Bette had allowed him to see B.D. only for "two hours on Tuesday and two hours on Thursday. She's acting so ridiculously. The struggle I'm having to visit my own daughter is becoming so embarrassing I'll have to go to court to have it adjusted."

Sherry also said that he still hoped to reconcile with Bette. "She's acting on impulse. I really should try to hold our marriage together. Her charges are ridiculous. She has me built up in her mind as one of the greatest monsters who ever lived. [But] I went to her house Sunday and told her I came over because I was lonely. She was very pleasant and asked me to take Barbara to the zoo. When I returned two cops were outside to keep me from getting back in. She left a note that said she was afraid of me and I had no right to come in. That's really laughable. . . . I'm only concerned about the welfare of my daughter and keeping our family together."

By now, one of Bette's main concerns was that Sherry not interfere with her plans to marry Gary Merrill. She began to put pressure on him; she closed out their joint checking account and put both the Laguna Beach house and Sherry's small nearby studio up for sale. "I had to move into a smaller house down the street," Sherry recalled. "It was a shack where her sister Bobby had lived. If you drove a nail in the wall to hang a picture, it went through to the other side."

If Sherry still doubted that Bette was serious about a divorce, he soon found out that she'd stop at nothing to make sure she got one. "Weeding outside one day, I found a strange-looking wire and traced it up to the attic. Bette had the place bugged. There were microphones placed in the ceiling over the bedroom. She was doing the same thing her first husband did when he found out she was having an affair with Howard Hughes." Sherry says he later found out that Bette was prepared to have two men swear that they had had sex with him. "I couldn't believe this was the woman I had loved and married."

Aware that her refusal to give Sherry reasonable visitation rights posed a threat to a smooth divorce, Bette reversed her tactics. She agreed to allow B.D. to visit Sherry in Laguna every weekend, but she insisted once again that Marion Richards had to accompany the child. Over the next few weekends, Sherry, B.D., and Marion spent idyllic hours together in Laguna. "We'd have all kinds of fun," Sherry recalled. "We'd go up in the hills, we'd walk on the beach. When the child was sleeping at night Marion and I would sit and chat, and I'd just look at this person and think in the back of my mind . . ."

Two weeks later, during another visit, Sherry told Marion, "I feel like a washed-out dishrag. But I think you're the most wonderful person. Would you consider marrying me?"

"Oh, no," Marion replied. "I wouldn't think of it."

"I just didn't like him," she says. "I thought he was self-centered. I had *no* intention of marrying him."

The next weekend, Sherry repeated the question. Marion turned him down again, but this time he sensed a softening in her refusal. He remembers her telling him, "Since I've been coming down I've seen a different person than the one who was always fighting. It was the way you treated your daughter. You're so loving with that child that I see a different side of you."

Encouraged, Sherry bought an engagement ring. "I know you don't want to marry me," Sherry said as he gave it to her. Marion didn't know how to react. "I said, 'Thanks a lot.' I never did say yes. Before I knew it the ring was on my finger, and I'm the kind of person who hates to hurt somebody's feelings. So I thought, *Well, I'll go along with it and then I'll get out of it."*

Despite Marion's lukewarm feelings, Sherry was so overjoyed that she had accepted his ring that when he took her and B.D. home to Beverly Hills he called Harrison Carroll to give him the news. Bette's secretary overheard the call and immediately telephoned Bette. She rang back in a flash and demanded to speak to Marion. Sherry intercepted the call. "She started cursing and calling Marion names and claimed we were having an affair. I just put the receiver down and hung up on her. It wasn't true that we had had an affair, of course. Marion was a virgin. In fact, I hadn't even kissed her. I asked her if I could that day, and she said 'Yes.' I kissed her and I almost fainted. It was the loveliest experience of my life, kissing that girl. Just one kiss, and she kind of melted. It was so wonderful."

Bette's divorce from Sherry was final on July 3. "It cost me a bundle," Bette said. "Houses, cars, the usual things. And for the first time in my life, I had to pay alimony to a man." As usual, she exaggerated; Sherry received only his artist's studio in Laguna, and he vehemently denies that Bette paid him alimony. "I had my own money in our joint checking account. She closed it out and all of a sudden my checks were being returned. She owed me that money. I met with her and her lawyers and said, 'I want my money.' They said, 'Well, she doesn't have it. She can't come up with it all at once. . . . She could arrange to give you $700 a month.' And I said 'Nothing doing'—with Bette sitting right there. 'She'd call it alimony.' I got up and they all came running after me. She said, 'Grant, I will never call it alimony.' And of course, that's exactly what she did call it."

Three days after the divorce was final, Sherry told the press of his engagement to Marion. Bette was furious, particularly about the way Sherry characterized his intended. "Here is a girl who can make my life happy," he said. "She is beautiful and calm and spiritual and wants the really worthwhile things in life. She has no complexes." Just the opposite, clearly, of Bette Davis.

Sherry and Marion were married on August 6, and their financial situation was so tight by November that he was forced to advertise in the local Laguna Beach paper for work as a handyman. When the story made the papers—"Bette's Ex Doing Odd Jobs in Laguna"—Sherry was nonchalant. "I'll do any kind of work," he told a reporter, "as long as they pay me $2 an hour."

But before long Sherry's paintings began to sell, and he eventually was able to develop a self-sufficiency he had been denied as Mr. Bette Davis. He and Marion are still married today, despite some rocky stretches and a 1954 divorce action that Marion withdrew. In the 1960s, Bette and Sherry came into contact again when Sherry went to visit B.D. while he was in New York for a show of his paintings. "I have to hand it to you," Bette told him. "You've done very well by yourself—the paintings in New York, and you've got a big job in Florida."

Sherry was polite. "Well, sure I have—" he responded. "What I really wanted to say was, 'You told everybody that I'd marry some rich bitch or become a bum. Instead, I married this beautiful girl.' That was what *really* infuriated Bette. She just never got over it."

Marion believes Bette's anger pushed her into marriage with Gary Merrill. "They would never have gotten married if Grant and I hadn't," she said. "Bette pushed Gary into it. She was saving face. She didn't want it to look like her husband had thrown her away for a young girl."

Joe Mankiewicz may also have influenced Bette's decision to marry Gary. In a speech Margo makes to Karen Richards about her need for more in life than just a career, Bette could not have failed to see an astonishing similarity to her own situation, a manifesto for Bette Davis in 1950:

> Funny business, a woman's career. The things you drop on your way up the ladder, so you can move faster. You forget you'll need them again when you go back to being a woman. That's one career all females have in common—whether we like it or not— being a woman. Sooner or later we've got to work at it, no matter what other careers we've had or wanted . . . and, in the last analysis, nothing is any good unless you can look up just before dinner or turn around in bed—and there he is. You're something with a French Provincial office or a book full of clippings—but you're not a woman.

PART FOUR

"Ten Black Years"

TWENTY-ONE

Bette and Gary Merrill were married in Juárez, Mexico, on July 28, just hours after his divorce was final. Immediately they embarked on their honeymoon trip, a cross-country drive from Mexico to Massachusetts. The journey was disturbingly similar to the one Bette had taken *to* Mexico with Sherry. Nearly a dozen suitcases and other paraphernalia jammed the car, and the newlyweds hardly had room to move; the heat as they drove through the desert Southwest was suffocating; and their patience dried up quickly. "For five long days I drove that damn car," Gary recalled. "It felt more like horsing a truck around."

They bickered constantly, and several times their tempers erupted into shouting matches. Whenever they stopped at one of the few roadside inns along the way, Bette didn't like it. "Each time we checked into a place," Gary recalled, "something was wrong with it, and out we'd go. I'd be tired, saying, 'What the hell, it's a bed.' But no, it had to be better. Before the trip was over, my normally easygoing attitude was wearing thin, and I began to wonder."

Bette had sent Bobby and Bobby's daughter Ruth ahead to Massachusetts with B.D., and the Merrills met up with them in Gloucester, a small, picturesque fishing village and art colony near the border with Maine, where they had rented a house as a honeymoon cottage. Ruth, then eleven years old, found her new uncle's presence disturbing. "It seemed like Gary was always drunk," she recalls. "All I can remember about him was drinking and yelling. The screaming between them got so bad that I left the house and went down to the shore to do some crabbing. I could still hear them going at it, even from that far away."

Like Gary, Bette later professed that shortly after the marriage she felt that she had made "a terrible mistake." But she wasn't going to let go easily of Joe Mankiewicz's romantic vision of love conquering all.

283

Years later, she admitted that she had fallen in love with Bill Sampson and Gary had fallen in love with Margo Channing—"and we woke up with each other." Still, Bette had a new mission—finally to be the "four-square, upright, downright, forthright married lady" Margo Channing had wanted to be. No matter what, she was determined to make this marriage last. Even the battles with Gary, that had begun almost the minute they were married, gave her as much pleasure as they did pain. Bette thrived on confrontation and drama, and Merrill gave as good as he got.

The Merrills spent the rest of their honeymoon, alone, on Westport Island, Maine, near Squirrel Island, where Bette had been conceived forty-two years earlier. They rented a campsite, complete with oil lamps and an outhouse, and took boat trips for groceries and five-gallon jugs of fresh water. With none of the stress of the outside world to impinge on her happiness, Bette felt as though she were "blooming," that her hopes were "never higher," her "chance for a life, never surer." With this marriage, she felt, it was "do or die."

"I'm a hausfrau at heart," Bette told the press, "the little woman." Never one to do anything halfway, she threw herself into domesticity with her usual single-mindedness. When she and Gary rented their first house, a furnished cottage at Prout's Neck, Maine, Bette became so fervid about turning it into a home that she rearranged everything in it. When Gary returned from a round of golf with a friend and saw what Bette had done, he told her that the place "looks like something out of *Good Housekeeping.*" She threw a piece of chicken at him.

She had ample time for such frenetic housekeeping because once again there were no offers of work. Gary, on the other hand, was considered "hot" after *Twelve O'Clock High,* and scripts came in for him just about daily. Shortly after they moved into the Prout's Neck house, Gary left for Germany to make the World War II drama *Decision Before Dawn.* In his absence, Bette flew to Los Angeles to attend the opening of *All About Eve* and try to find a West Coast house for the family. She did—a spacious bungalow on the beach at Malibu.

Bette and Ruthie strode onto the forecourt of Grauman's Chinese Theatre as flashbulbs flared and reporters shouted questions at them. It was October 13, and the world premiere of *All About Eve.* Bette basked in the glory that reflected from the film; advance word in Hollywood was that it was little short of a masterpiece and that Bette had orchestrated the comeback of the year. She didn't stay to watch the film, however, because she had promised Gary she wouldn't until he returned.

The advance word was right on the mark—the critics were rhapsodic. Leo Mishkin's opinion in the New York *Morning Telegraph* was typical: "Let's get right down to cases on this. *All About Eve* is probably the wittiest, the most devastating, the most adult and literate motion picture ever made that had anything to do with the New York stage. It is also one of the top pictures of this or any other recent year, a crackling, sparkling, brilliantly written and magnificently acted commentary on . . . the legitimate theater. And just to show you that I haven't yet run out of superlatives, *All About Eve* is also a movie in which Bette Davis gives the finest, most compelling, and the most perceptive performance she has ever played out on screen. Including *Of Human Bondage*. . . . You have my word for it: *All About Eve* is one of the great pictures of our time."

The film brought in $3.1 million at the box office, and after the dismal failure of *Beyond the Forest* a year earlier, represented a stunning return to form for Bette. She was the talk of the country for months, and on December 24, Hedda Hopper wrote a profile of her headlined "Comeback in 'Eve' Proves Bette's Still Film Queen." Hopper wrote that "Hollywood's most thrilling comeback in 1950 was made by its finest actress. . . . Just a year ago her long and brilliant career was never in worse shape. A succession of bad pictures had proved that not even the queen was immune to the skids. Thinking that *Beyond the Forest* was the worst thing she'd ever done, I wrote in my column, 'If Bette had deliberately set out to wreck her career, she could not have picked a more appropriate vehicle.' . . . Hollywood wondered: Was Bette Davis through? The answer is that a girl like Bette is never through until the last gong has sounded. . . . For my money, her performance in *All About Eve* topped anything she ever did, including the two pictures that brought her Oscars. . . . If the job doesn't get her a third Academy Award, I'll miss my guess."

On February 12, 1951, *All About Eve* received a record fourteen Oscar nominations (one more than *Gone With the Wind*), including Best Picture, Best Director, and Best Screenplay. Bette was nominated for the eighth time as Best Actress, along with Anne Baxter; Celeste Holm, Thelma Ritter, and George Sanders were cited in supporting categories. Bette had already won the New York Film Critics Award, her first, and most observers considered her the Oscar front-runner. Still, it promised to be a tight race; also strongly contending (along with Anne Baxter) were the silent-screen great Gloria Swanson for her own extraordinary comeback in Billy Wilder's *Sunset Boulevard,* and Judy Holliday for her effervescent comic performance in the movie version of Garson Kanin's Broadway success *Born Yesterday.*

In an upset, the award went to Judy Holliday. Bette was crushed, and she wasn't very gracious about the reasons she thought Holliday had won; she complained that it wasn't fair to pit an actress who had honed her performance for two years on Broadway against someone, like her, who had created the role of Margo with ten days' notice. More to the point was the fact that Bette and Anne Baxter were the first two actresses ever nominated for starring roles in the same film. "Bette lost *because* Anne Baxter was nominated," Joe Mankiewicz says. "Annie lost *because* Bette Davis ditto. Celeste Holm lost because Thelma Ritter was nominated, and *she* lost *because* Celeste ditto."

But it has to be said as well that Bette's unpopularity hurt her just as much as did all these other factors. Too many directors, writers, producers, and technicians in Hollywood had spread stories—fair or unfair—about what a monster she could be on a set, and the movie community dislikes few more than temperamental superstars. Considering Bette's reputation in the film colony, there was little chance she'd ever win another Oscar.

Bette took some solace in the fact that *Eve* won six Oscars, including Best Picture (the first time a Davis film had been so honored), and she was thrilled that Mankiewicz, for the second year in a row, was chosen Best Director and Best Scenarist. According to George Sanders, however, Bette was bitter that he alone among the cast won an Oscar.

Sanders recalled that he and Bette hadn't gotten along too well during filming. "I matched her snarl for snarl and bite for bite. Of course it was great for the picture, as it made for some nice confrontational conflict. . . . Later, when she lost the Oscar and I won for Best Supporting Actor, I met her at a party and she turned her back on me without a word. I couldn't resist the temptation to purr over her shoulder, 'Sour grapes, Bette?' and do you know what she did? She turned around and spit at me!"

All About Eve was kept in the public mind for months by a highly publicized "feud" between Bette and Tallulah Bankhead, who claimed that Bette's performance was little more than an imitation of her. On her national radio show, Tallulah missed few opportunities to get in digs at Bette, both about *Eve* and the fact that her rival had played several roles on film that Tallulah had originated on Broadway. When she was asked if she had seen *All About Eve,* Tallulah replied, "Every morning when I brush my teeth." She called the film *All About Me.* In the middle of a recitation of her career achievements, her cohost asked, "And what happened next?"

"Bette Davis," Tallulah sighed.

There's no question that Bette looks, sounds, and acts like Tallulah Bankhead in *All About Eve.* The long hair, the cut of her cocktail gowns, the self-mocking, world-weary sophistication, even her huskier-than-usual voice, all call Bankhead to mind. And yet both Joe Mankiewicz and Bette denied that Margo Channing owes anything at all to Tallulah. Bette's hair just happened to be that length when filming began. Her taffeta gowns, designed by Edith Head and Charles LeMaire, were the height of 1950 fashion. Her husky voice was a result of her throat injury after the fight with Sherry. "There was no intentional imitation of anyone," Bette assured a reporter at the time. "I feel in this picture I played myself more than any part I ever played in the last ten years. Maybe Miss Bankhead and I are alike, you see. That could happen."

In any event, Bette as Margo never fails to summon up memories of Tallulah, and Bankhead was able to parlay the controversy into radio ratings. Finally, in a backhanded sort of way, Bette had given a boost to a career that her mere presence in Hollywood had prevented from blossoming on screen.

"I would make the most ghastly mother that ever lived," Bette told a reporter in 1937. "I am not the maternal type and I know it. . . . I'm horribly possessive. I love the feel of things being mine. I could never adopt a child because I would have to feel that the child belonged to me, was my own flesh and blood or not at all."

Marion Richards hadn't thought Bette a very good mother to B.D.; the child's bizarre behavior didn't change until the governess began to treat her like a human being worthy of attention. "Mother always said that I was the one thing in her life she loved the most," B.D. later said. "The operative word there was 'thing.' "

Gladys Young, the woman who replaced Marion Richards as B.D.'s governess, found the four-year-old "spoiled rotten." Bette, she says, "never disciplined the child. We were staying at a fancy hotel once, and I took B.D. for a walk in these beautiful, formal gardens. She rushed up to a rose bush and started to pick a flower. I said, 'No, B.D., don't pick that because that sign says, 'Do not pick the flowers.' B.D. was a lot like her mother, so she pouted. I never touched her, but I disciplined her very well."

Later that evening, when Bette, Gary, and B.D. came back from dinner, B.D. was carrying an armful of roses. "Look! Mommy let me pick the roses!" she cried. As Gladys put it, "That was how well Bette disciplined her."

After Gladys left Bette's employ, a later nurse told her that B.D. "simply runs wild and behaves like an absolute little pig at the table—so disgusting I can hardly eat. I'll be relieved when I don't have to have my meals ever again with her."

Bette often had little time or patience for B.D.; she usually relegated her care to governesses. When she was in a maternal mood, she would smother the little girl with love, treating her like the doll she had thought her sister Bobby to be when she was eighteen months old. Sometimes, when Bette wasn't available to B.D., the child would manifest symptoms of illness. Betsy Paul was a Laguna Beach neighbor of Ruthie and Bobby's, and she remembers an occasion when Bobby threw a party for about eight people. Bette was there (Gary was away on a film), and her cousin Sally Favour was baby-sitting B.D. at her nearby house. About an hour into the party, Sally called to say that B.D. was having a bad asthma attack. Bette picked up the phone and said, "Well, just put her to bed, that's all you can do."

Sally called back three times within the next hour to report that B.D. was getting worse and that Bette should come over. Bette decided not to, and Betsy Paul's husband David was concerned. "She may be having anxiety because she needs you," he told Bette. "That very often causes it."

"Well," Betsy Paul recalled, "you never saw such a fight, my God. Bette was just furious with my husband. Finally Sally called a fourth time and David said, 'Bette, I *really* think you should go and get B.D.' And Bette said, 'Well, if you feel that way, *you* go and get her!'"

David went, and brought B.D. back to Bobby's house. "We all gave her a hug," Betsy says, "and Bette tucked her in bed, and when we all went in to say goodnight, she was perfectly fine. There was no more of that gasping for breath."

Bette's hot-and-cold mothering left B.D. confused and rebellious, and often her behavior was designed to gain her mother's attention, whether positive or negative. Every six months, "as if on schedule," Bette said, she would have to spank B.D. "She would push me and push me and push me and finally *wham*! You've got to give your children a little bit of hell; if your children don't hate you from time to time when they're growing up, then you're not doing a very good job."

Shortly after their marriage, the Merrills decided that Gary should adopt B.D. Bette called William Grant Sherry to ask his permission, but he was reluctant. When she persisted, he told her that Gary could adopt B.D. if he paid him $250,000. "That was the dumbest thing I ever did," Sherry says, denying that he wanted money to give up B.D. "Bette kept asking me to do this, and I thought, *This is ridiculous,* so I threw out this absurd figure—an amount I knew she didn't have—just to let her know that there was no way I was going to let that child have *his* name."

In his memoirs, Gary Merrill claimed that Sherry "settled for $5,000" and B.D. became Barbara Davis Merrill. Now that Gary had a daughter, he wanted a son. Bette's doctors had told her after B.D.'s birth that she could have no more children, so they agreed to adopt a boy as soon as the proper arrangements could be made.

In January 1951, Gary was in the Virgin Islands making a film when Bette called him bubbling with excitement. "You're the proud father of a beautiful baby girl!" she announced.

"Wrong fucking sex!" he replied.

According to Gary, "Bette hadn't consulted me, but went ahead on her own, and her high-handed way of doing it irritated me." Still, when Gary returned and saw the newborn child, he melted. "She was a little blonde doll."

"A real live doll" was Bette's description of the girl, whom the Merrills decided to name Margot after Margo Channing. The day she brought the baby home, Bette had B.D. go into the living room, sit down, and close her eyes. When she opened them, B.D. recalled, "there was this big 'present'!" Just as young Bette had had when her sister Bobby was born, B.D. now had her own "big doll."

On February 15, 1951, *The Story of a Divorce*—retitled *Payment on Demand*—opened in New York after a long delay. Bette was unhappy about the title change (she thought it made the film sound like a cheap melodrama), and she was angry that Howard Hughes had forced her to reshoot the ending. Rather than have her character abandoned again by her husband when she reverts to her bitchy ways, the new scene leaves their reconciliation up in the air, with a happy ending a distinct possibility. Bette hated all of it, but critics and audiences didn't seem to mind. Typical were *The Hollywood Reporter* critic's comments: "If *Payment on Demand* has been withheld from release until the Bette Davis hit in *All About Eve* had been cemented, it wasn't necessary. The picture . . . stands on its own firm feet, and Miss Davis on the powerful range of her acting talent. It's a superb part and the actress plays superbly, reading nuances of the modern woman into it that her fans will recognize and understand."

Publicly, Bette's comeback had lost none of its steam, but privately she was worried that she hadn't been sent a decent script since *Eve*. To her relief she finally got a film offer she could accept—from, of all people, Douglas Fairbanks, Jr. He wanted Bette to star in *Another Man's Poison* as a murderous English mystery writer who lives in a murky mansion on the Yorkshire moors. Neither Bette nor Gary much liked the script, but the film's coproducer, Daniel Angel, offered Bette "nearly the whole world," as Gary put it, and promised to give Gary a part and transport the entire family—including Bette's long-time maid and cook Dell Pfeiffer, Margot's nurse "Coop," and B.D.'s governess Gladys Young—to England. When he also agreed to allow Irving Rapper, a favorite of Bette's, to direct, the Merrills agreed. Bette found herself excited about returning to England, which she had loved so much despite the unhappy outcome of her trial in 1936.

"We were a small troop," Gary recalled, "and took up a good deal of space—just about the entire top deck of the *Queen Elizabeth*" when it set sail from New York to Southampton on March 21. The ship arrived on March 26, and Gladys Young was amazed at the mob scenes the Merrills created when they arrived at the Savoy Hotel in London. She wrote in her diary that "crowds of fans pushed and crowded until a London Bobby had to escort us. Autograph hunters, Bette Davis Fan Club members, etc. Very exciting." At another point "the crowds of people in front of the hotel had to be dispersed by the police before the Merrills came out to their car. Most all day there are little groups of people standing around, hoping for a glimpse of them."

Bette had been warned that the English press had become increasingly hard on American stars visiting their shores, so she decided to court them and opened the hotel suite to the Fleet Street reporters. She provided hors d'oeuvres and alcohol, and patiently answered questions for several hours. The next day, Gary recalled, all the papers "sang the same song—about rich American actresses with hundreds of pieces of luggage, fur coats, and a mention or two about kids and 'Mr. Davis.'" Bette was further hurt by their characterization of her as "a middle-aged matron" and, two days later, their barbs about her Oscar loss to Judy Holliday.

After a few weeks in London, the Merrills moved into what was meant to be their permanent home while in England, the grand manor–hotel Great Fosters, a former Tudor palace built in 1550 by King Henry VIII in Egham, Surrey, about eighteen miles outside London. An imposing structure amid acres of lush, manicured topiaries and gardens, Great Fosters boasted ornate rooms with enormous stone fireplaces, decorated with priceless antiques and elaborately ornamented twenty-foot ceilings. It had been a fitting residence for a king, and it offered the same opulence to Bette (whom Gary now called "The Queen") and her entourage.

The Merrills were in Great Britain for three months, and Gladys Young recalls that it was a tempestuous and debilitating period for all concerned. "B.D. was only four, and she was forced to witness so many disgusting exhibitions of drinking and violent quarrels between Bette and Gary, all of them started maliciously by Bette."

The battles usually followed drinking bouts, Gladys says. "It was obvious to me that Bette's intent was to get her husband drunk. Her capacity was much greater than his and she'd keep pouring double martinis down his gullet as rapidly as possible. I didn't think about it at the time, but now I realize that her masochistic aim was to get him to the point where he would lose control and quarrel with her. Then she would remain in pretty good fighting trim long after he was fair to becoming hysterical.

"From that point on, the very staid English people who were also staying at the hotel would stand down in the garden among the peonies and sweet Williams, mouth agape, listening to the unspeakable language which was wafted down to them from the Merrills' suite. Eventually the booze got to her, and then she'd go on a crying jag, with throaty sobs and accusations. She'd tell him he wasn't as good in bed as her third husband, and the poor guy would tell her he never claimed to be. Millions of people considered Bette a superb actress for her realistic portrayals of the bitchiest of bitches, but—*she wasn't acting!*"

The battles grew so disruptive that the manager of Great Fosters approached Douglas Fairbanks to complain. "We hate to do this," the man said, "it's very embarrassing, and we're very honored to have these distinguished people, but they imbibe so much and then they argue so much and in such a loud voice that we've lost several customers—they've moved out on us. I'm going to have to ask you to move them to another hotel."

Chastened, the Merrills returned to the Savoy, but the situation didn't improve. They fought on and off the set, and their on-set battles—usually over Gary's laziness while Bette labored to improve the script—did little to endear them to the cast and crew. Neither did the fact that Bette, in the midst of the postwar British meat rationing, had steaks flown in every few days from New York. "She would eat them on the set, in front of everybody," Fairbanks recalls. "I advised her not to do it. I thought it was indiscreet, but she pooh-poohed the idea, and continued to do it her way—defiantly. It was not very popular."

Bette was even less popular at home. According to Gladys Young, "She was so miserable to everybody. She used to drive Margot's nurse Coop crazy. Whenever Coop was out of the house, Bette would rearrange everything in Margot's room—her diapers, her blankets, her bottles, everything. When Coop got back she could never find anything and it would take her hours to put everything back where she wanted it. That was just Bette's sadistic personality at work.

"Finally Coop became so fed up with the treatment she was getting from Bette that she and Dell Pfeiffer went out to the nearest pub and had a few beers. Coop was feeling no pain when they got back, and she said, 'I'm gonna tell that bitch what I think of her.' And I said, 'Oh please don't, go to bed, Coop.' But she wrote her a letter and went upstairs, slipped it under Bette's door, and banged on the door. She hoped to get away before Bette got to the door, but Bette never walked, so you could hear her run to the door and she opened it before Coop could get away. She read the letter, then gave Coop one hour to get ready and leave to go back to the U.S."

Gladys found it wearing on her physical and mental health to work for Bette. Despite the fact that Gladys was ill one day, Bette insisted that she take B.D. for a walk. Gladys tried to explain that she was unwell and experiencing bladder problems, but Bette would hear none of it. Finally Margot's nurse said, "For God's sake, can't you see the woman's sick? I'll take B.D. out."

Gladys longed to tell Bette off the way Coop had, but she didn't want to be shipped back to the States without a job. When the Merrills returned to California in July, however, both Gladys and Dell—who had worked for Bette for over fifteen years—took their leave. "Dell was wonderful and she adored Bette," Gladys recalled. "But Bette could be very unkind to her and one day she came into my room and she was almost crying and I said, 'Why do you work for a woman like Bette Davis? What did Lincoln do for you people?' And she straightened up and said, 'He made it possible for us to taste of the tree of life.' And I said, 'Well, you're sure as hell grovelling in the roots when you work for Bette Davis.' And I made her promise she'd quit, and she did."

Gladys wrote a letter to Bette on July 11, explaining that her doctor had advised her not to return to the Merrill house until she had "regained the weight I have lost, and the general state of health I was enjoying when I left for England."

Bette responded with a snippy letter telling Gladys she had made a wise decision because she was "physically and mentally" unsuited to be a governess. She argued that weight loss was seldom an indicator of poor health and that Gladys wanted to lose weight anyway. She concluded that she and Gladys did not get along because one "definite" person should work with another.

Gladys had to laugh. "I've never wanted to lose weight in my life. Bette was so deluded; she could never ever admit that she might have been at fault, for *anything*. But it got so bad that the Frosch Employment Agency in Beverly Hills blacklisted her. They wouldn't send any help over to her any more. She had to go out to the hinterlands to get help."

❧

Bette's unhappiness with *Another Man's Poison* had helped put her in such a foul temper in England. She had tried to improve the script during shooting, but nothing seemed to work. She had hoped that in spite of everything Irving Rapper would make a great picture. He didn't. Merrill called him "a real run-of-the-mill" director, which angered Bette, who feared it was true. Worst of all, she was afraid that after two excellent comeback films she would again be caught in a turkey.

She was right. When the picture opened on January 7, 1952, it was met by scathing reviews and lukewarm box office. As she had before when struggling with a sub-par script, Bette had attempted to make up for its deficiencies through sheer acting power. The critics, however, were less willing than ever to accept her more mannered histrionics. *The Hollywood Reporter* reviewer commented, "The melodramatic gamut seldom has experienced the workout it is given in *Another Man's Poison,* a wild and fanciful saga. . . . Bette Davis, queen of the vixens, combs her hair, lights cartons of cigarettes, snaps her fingers and bites her consonants, and it all adds up to a performance you'd expect to find from a night club impersonation of the actress."

The feeling in Hollywood that Bette's comeback had petered out was reinforced by her next effort, *Phone Call from a Stranger*. It wasn't a bad film, but Bette's role in it amounted to less than fifteen minutes. Gary was the star, and Bette asked the producer to let her play the small but flashy role of an invalid. "I have never understood why stars should object to playing smaller parts if they were good ones," she told the press. Left unsaid, of course, was that she had no other offers, and she was being paid $35,000 for a role originally budgeted at $1,500. "The producers got back more than that in publicity alone," Gary said, "the 'star playing a bit part.'" But despite all of Bette's protestations, the cameo appearance only served to reinforce the feeling in Hollywood that Bette Davis could no longer land a starring role.

Two months after *Phone Call from a Stranger* was released, with Gary swamped with film offers and Bette getting none, she decided to make her television debut on Jimmy Durante's variety show. Appearing live from Los Angeles, she first read a commercial ("It takes two cans of Pet Milk") and then did her best at farce in a fifteen-minute skit with Durante. The *Daily Variety* critic wasn't kind. "That her coming-out in the channel set was not too auspicious can be traced to an apparent nervousness . . . and a lack of sufficient elasticity to 'unbend.'"

"I was scared to death," Bette admitted. "That I got through it at all was a source of great wonderment to me!"

Bette was spared more television chores when she was finally offered a meaty part, the title role of Margaret Elliott in *The Star,* an overblown Hollywood saga about a washed-up, self-destructive Oscar winner obsessed with regaining her star stature. The script had been written by Katherine Albert, a disgruntled former employee of Joan Crawford's, and Bette was gleeful not only to have a good part but to be able to do a sendup of her least favorite actress. "Joan was famous for saying 'Bless You' to everybody in that pious way of hers," Bette laughed, "and I actually got to say that in the script!"

Bette seems not to have realized that Margaret had more in common with her than with Joan Crawford. She is unbending, hates producers, rails against the "tripe" she's been forced to do. Moreover, she is sick of supporting her parasitic sister and her husband, and Bette plays the scene in which Margaret refuses to give them their monthly stipend (because she hasn't got the money) in such an overwrought manner that one can easily imagine she wasn't acting at all, but thinking about spendthrift Ruthie and dependent Bobby.

The Star isn't a very good picture. Its script is full of implausibilities, its production values are cheapjack, and its ending, in which Margaret decides to give up a juicy role that would mean her comeback to marry the man who truly loves her, far too facile. Bette's performance is typical of the kind she had often given since the late '40s—overheated and caricatured one minute, nuanced and affecting the next. As *Time*'s critic put it, "Her performance as an ex-first lady of the screen is first-rate. . . . It is a marathon one-woman show and, all in all, proof that Bette Davis—with her strident voice, nervous stride, mobile hands and popping eyes—is still her own best imitator."

The Star provided Bette with yet another "comeback," bringing with it her ninth Oscar nomination (along with Joan Crawford, who had choreographed a small comeback of her own in *Sudden Fear*). Bette lost the award to Shirley Booth in *Come Back, Little Sheba*, a film she had turned down, and once again her career resurgence proved short-lived. She didn't make another film for more than three years.

Bette stood in front of Margot's crib and shrieked uncontrollably. "Shut up! Shut up! *Shut up!*" It was four in the morning, and she was at the end of her rope. Every night, the baby screamed and cried, rattling the bars of her crib. "Nights were something to dread," Bette said. "Five minutes after we had put her to bed she would be up shaking the crib bars and screaming. We would take turns putting her down, telling her it was time to shut her eyes and go to sleep. By two or three o'clock in the morning, exhausted from lack of sleep, she would be in a nervous rage. And sometimes, I am afraid, we were too."

It wasn't just Margot's nightly screaming fits that worried Bette. The child seemed "different" somehow; her behavior was unsettling. First she ran away from her governess, not too alarming an event. But then she tried to strangle the family kitten. Bette left her alone in the car for a few minutes, and when she returned Margot had removed all her clothes. "Children often strip, and often run away," Bette's friends would reassure her as they laughed at Margot's antics. But she wasn't convinced. "There was something about the *way* Margot did these things, and the frequency with which she did them, that worried me. She seemed driven."

Bette tried to put her mind at rest about Margot. She told herself this was a phase, that the child would come around. But at night, lying in her bed, listening to Margot's wails, fear would gnaw at her and "all the disturbing thoughts I had pushed away during the day would come floating to the surface."

The Merrills had a happy distraction from Margot's problems in January 1952 when they adopted another child, the boy Gary had always wanted. Fair-skinned and blond-haired, the infant came to them at five days of age, and they named him Michael Woodman Merrill. His ancestry, according to Gary, "was good on both sides, probably better than either Bette's or mine."

Bette doted on the placid, well-behaved Michael, whom she called "Woody" for a time; throughout his youth she treated him as a little prince, sparing him her anger and vitriol. Not so B.D., who by five had developed a willful personality uncomfortably reminiscent of her mother's. The clashes between them, even at B.D.'s young age, were vivid. B.D. was "a hardheaded, stubborn little girl," Gary recalled, "who was prone to come up with stories not based on fact." Bette didn't seem to mind that, but when B.D. would dig in her heels and defy her mother, Bette would treat her as an adult rather than a child, prompting verbal fireworks that depleted both of them but did little to set B.D. straight. "B.D. needed a great deal more disciplining than she had received," Gary thought.

All of this turned Bette into a wreck. Her career, the safety valve she had always relied upon when her home life threatened to undo her, had come to a dead halt, and she had no escape from B.D.'s temper tantrums and Margot's bizarre, frightening rages. Ruthie's and Bobby's failed marriages had left them more emotionally and financially dependent on Bette than ever. Early in 1952, Bette was close to distraction.

Then, a blessed reprieve: the young producer Mike Ellis offered her the singing and dancing lead role in a Broadway revue, *Two's Company*. "I was not a little apprehensive," she admitted. She hadn't appeared on stage in over twenty-two years. She was neither a singer nor a dancer. Still, she had no choice but to accept the offer, because her expenses, as usual, were enormous; Gary's income, although high, wasn't always enough. She needed the money. She was also eager to return to the East Coast—"I wanted the children to be brought up in my beloved East." She hoped that if the family "got out of Hollywood our personal situation might change. I would have done anything for that."

Bette picked up the family and moved to Manhattan, where she furnished a Beekman Place penthouse with enough of their belongings to make it feel a little like home. Then she embarked on what was arguably her greatest professional challenge, her spirit infused with optimism for her life and career.

TWENTY-TWO

On the stage of the Alvin Theatre in New York, the boys and girls of the chorus—Broadway's gypsies—were rehearsing a sketch for *Two's Company*. They had been told that at some point that day they would finally meet Bette Davis, the star of the revue, and their excitement was palpable. In the middle of a complicated routine, the show's producers, James Russo and Mike Ellis, walked down the middle aisle and announced, "Bette Davis is here and we'd like you to meet her."

Swathed in mink despite the mid-June heat, Bette swept in with her best Margo Channing flourish and called "Hello!" She bounded up the steps to the stage and removed her coat. Florence Brooks-Dunay, one of the dancers, recalls that as Bette greeted them and shook hands, "she dragged her mink coat across the filthy, dusty stage. It was a very Hollywood thing to do, and pretty shocking."

Then, as quickly as she had come, Bette was gone. "She said, 'Hello,' and out she flew," May Muth, her understudy, says. "We weren't sure if she was embarrassed or didn't want to be introduced to us, or what. She certainly wasn't very loving toward us."

Bette's involvement with *Two's Company* came about by accident. Late in 1951, Russo and Ellis, neophyte producers, had been approached by Charlie Sherman, a Broadway and television comedy writer, about producing a Broadway revue, and he suggested Judith Anderson as the star. After several meetings, she decided that she would not be up to the musical numbers, and passed. Aware that they needed a big star to put the show over, the pair's ears perked up when Ralph Alswang, a scenic designer who shared an office with them, put a call through to his friend Gary Merrill early in February. "Hey, Ralph," Russo called over, half in jest, "ask Gary if Bette would like to do a musical revue in New York."

Bette's reply—"Sure, if the material is right"—sent Russo and Sherman whirling across the country in a borrowed car to present the project to Bette in person. "Charlie sat in the back seat with a typewriter the whole time," Ellis recalls, "putting this thing together. When they got to California they spent three hours auditioning the material for Bette, and she was rolling on the floor with laughter. She told them she wanted to do it."

In the meantime, Vernon Duke and Ogden Nash were fashioning the music and lyrics, and when Bette heard them she told Ellis she thought they were "heaven." On March 11, Ellis wrote her to explain the format of the show. "It is our plan to have you run through a gamut of characters, from wealthy and sexy types to thoroughly slatternly housewife characters. . . . Also, since the nature of the show is intimate, with the emphasis on the sketches, there will be at least once in the show when you'll come on in the middle of someone else's sketch and say nothing more than 'Dinner is served.' We are most anxious to retain the small, intimate format, with everyone on a friendly basis helping everyone else throughout the show, except that you will be the star."

After Bette made her verbal commitment to the producers, telling them that "Gary says it's about time I got off my ass," serious negotiations began. Bette asked for approval of the choreographer and all cast members. The choreographer, in her view, was the most important person in the equation, and should the producers' first choices, Michael Kidd or Jerome Robbins, be unavailable, she felt it was "of the utmost importance to my security" to have veto power over any alternate choice. "I must get along with, be understood by, and believe in the man who has this job in the show."

As to the cast members, Bette was blunt. "If an actor were fine in every way for everyone else, and there was some reason why I did not click with him, I would want the freedom of having the right to ask you to change him." She assured Russo and Ellis that she had only used such discretion "once in twenty years" and had no intention "of being the Hitler of any production, all rumors to the contrary. Nor am I the type, in case of an argument, who argues just for the sake of winning my point."

Bette signed a standard run-of-the-play contract with Russo and Ellis on June 11 that guaranteed her $3,000 a week against 10 percent of the gross weekly box-office receipts. Riders to the agreement granted Bette all the approvals she had asked for and an additional 5 percent of the net profits. The producers also agreed to provide her with first-class transportation for herself, her three children, two nurses, and a maid.

"I just can't tell you how excited the boys are about the whole idea!" Ellis said in a letter to Bette. "We will have a long, pleasant and enthusiastic relationship with this show and possibly many others. It's marvelous!"

Bette went into rehearsals in July for the scheduled October 20 opening, working with director Jules Dassin, choreographer Jerome Robbins, and costars Hiram Sherman, Nathaniel Frey (later replaced by David Burns), and Nora Kaye. Almost at once, everyone in the cast realized that Bette, the legendary Hollywood star of whom they were in awe, was all wrong as the star of a musical comedy revue. According to Florence Brooks-Dunay, "She was unattractive and klutzy. Her line readings were impossible. *Everything-was-the-same.* I mean, the woman had no range. And really no sense of humor. Or if she had one, it didn't come out on stage. She was obviously much more comfortable in front of a camera."

Shortly into rehearsals, Bette too realized that she was ill equipped to handle the material, and Jules Dassin saw that she had become "terribly nervous and afraid." She began to tinker with the production, much to Mike Ellis's annoyance. "She used to sit there and try to rearrange the routine of the show. And we'd tell her we couldn't do that because this scene has so and so in it and he's also in the next scene and there would be no time for the costume change. She had no feeling for that sort of thing. It was very difficult."

Because Bette had no experience in musical comedy, she was easily influenced by the retinue of people she had gathered around her for advice. As Dassin remembers it, "Someone said to her, 'You mean, you're rehearsing without *props*?!' So, by God, one Sunday she came to rehearsal with a truck full of furniture and props—just because she was quite lost."

Bette had expected that to work with a director and a choreographer of the stature of Dassin and Robbins would make up for her deficiencies, and she was shocked that she drew so little support from either of them. This shook whatever confidence she had left. "I must admit," says Dassin, "that I was not much use to her during all of this. First, I hated the material. Second, I was being hounded by the House Un-American Activities Committee. They sent guys to rehearsals every two minutes telling me that I had to come to Washington."

Dassin had been blacklisted a year earlier along with many other artists for alleged leftist ties during Senator Joseph McCarthy's Communist "witch hunts," but Ellis and Russo wanted him because they thought he had the strength "to handle a star." When they told Bette that there might be problems hiring Dassin because of the blacklist, Bette replied, "Fuck 'em." He still remembers Bette fondly for that, but in the end his harassment by the HUAC process servers cost her much needed directorial support.

Why did Dassin agree to direct *Two's Company* if he "hated" the material? "I had something to prove—that the whole blacklisting thing was phony and that with my name up in lights, there would be no American Legion demonstrations outside the theater and all that." Moreover, Dassin had hoped to convince Bette to lobby for better songs and sketches and to bring in outside help. He told her, "Look, you can get the best people in the world to write for you. I've contacted Noël Coward, and he said he would be delighted." But, Bette protested, she *liked* the material. "That was the tragic mistake," Dassin says. "It was a lot of junk."

Even more devastating to Bette than Dassin's distractions was the indifference of Jerome Robbins, the brilliant, mercurial choreographer who had burst on the Broadway scene in 1944 with *On the Town* and scored triumphs with *High Button Shoes* and, most recently, *The King and I*. Bette was sure she was in the best of hands, and that if anyone could help her turn her "klutziness" into grace it was Robbins. She was sorely disappointed.

Rather than focus his attention on Bette, as she reasonably expected he would, Robbins left her to her own devices after the first few weeks of rehearsal. "Jerry may have felt that Bette was hopeless as a dancer," Mike Ellis mused, "and that he should concentrate on Nora Kaye and Maria Karnilova, the lead dancers in the show, who were no slouches. Bette was not the most graceful woman in the world, and choreographers tend to like to work with dancers."

Dassin agrees. "Jerry, in my deficiency, really should have taken over more. But he didn't. He was much more concerned with the ballet than anything else." Even when Robbins did pay attention to Bette, his approach grated on her, as it did some of the others. Buzz Miller, one of the dancers, points out that "Jerry was not very helpful to *anyone*. He's a perfectly delightful person off-stage, but when he's working, he can't help himself, he's just a monster. Everything that comes out of his mouth is a put-down."

On September 23, with the October 20 opening date already unreachable, Bette refused to work with Robbins any longer and threatened to walk out of the show. Advance ticket sales had been tremendous, primarily on Bette's name, and Ellis and Russo were desperate to keep their star happy. Ellis wrote a contrite, comforting letter to Bette for Robbins's signature. ("I was a better writer than Jerry," Ellis explains.) In it he told her, "I want you to know that the only reason I signed for this show was because of you and I have a clause in my contract to that effect. I believe, now more than ever, that you will be marvelous and I am more excited about the idea of working with you than with any other star I've worked with. If I have not seemed to demonstrate that to you, I ask you to forgive me. . . . I feel that your numbers will present no problems to you. I suppose it's because I'm so sure of that and not at all worried that I have given the impression that the numbers are being slighted." The letter went on to assure Bette that Robbins would hire an assistant to free him up "so that I can devote as much time to you as you feel you need," and that "your success in this show is so important to me that I have withdrawn from my next assignment, *Carnival in Flanders*."

The letter placated Bette, as did Ellis's hiring of Viola Rubber, a former Broadway producer whose job, in Ellis's words, was "to do nothing but try to keep things with Bette running smoothly."

Bette's new sanguinity lasted only until the beginning of out-of-town tryouts. She had been feeling tired and run-down, and moments after her entrance for the first public performance of *Two's Company* in Detroit on October 19, she collapsed to the stage floor with what one observer called "a terrific bone-jarring bang." As Gary jumped out of his seat, a stagehand dragged Bette into the wings and slapped her face hard. "Get up, Bette," he pleaded. "Get up."

She regained consciousness and within five minutes was back on stage with a comment that brought the house down: "Well, you can't say I didn't fall for you." She got through the rest of the show without incident. "If there's one word to describe Bette Davis," Jules Dassin observes, "it has to be *trouper*."

Over the next few weeks, Bette continued to feel terrible. Her lack of energy was completely alien to her; the only thing she could attribute it to was the grueling work of taking a major show to Broadway. As worried as she was about the way she felt, that wasn't her most gnawing concern—she was terrified that *Two's Company* was headed for disaster. "She realized we were in bad shape during the out-of-town tryouts," Jules Dassin recalls. "She lost faith in herself and the material. She thought people would laugh, and they weren't laughing."

Bette had asked Bobby to travel with her during the out-of-town tryouts in her customary position as personal maid and factotum, and Bobby ministered to her one night in Detroit when she felt too sick to go on. By now, the producers were wary of Bette, and they suspected her illness was feigned, merely an attempt to pressure them into something or other she wanted. Her star power was so important to the show, they knew, that if she didn't appear the revue would never work. "We had a conference," Ellis recalls. "Everybody was there—me, Jimmy Russo, Vernon Duke, Ogden Nash, Jerry Robbins. And we sat around saying, 'What should we do?' It was hard to know what to do because we didn't know what *she* was going to do. So I said, 'I'll find out.'"

Ellis called Bette's room and Bobby picked up the phone. "How is Bette feeling?" he asked.

"Oh, Miss Davis isn't feeling well at all," Bobby told him. "Miss Davis is really quite sick."

Ellis was concerned. "Has she seen a doctor?"

"Oh, Miss Davis is much too sick to see a doctor," Bobby replied.

"I didn't know what to say to somebody who made a remark like that," Ellis says. "And I'm not usually tongue-tied."

As the show plodded through Boston toward the latest Broadway opening date, December 15, the petrified Bette adopted a wartime footing and began to enlist allies, pitting one camp against the other. According to Mike Ellis, "Her allegiance would move from person to person as she felt less secure," and she was deeply suspicious now of anything Ellis tried to do to improve the show. When he asked the esteemed director Joshua Logan (*Annie Get Your Gun, South Pacific*) for a critique, she refused to complete her performance. "Bette had eight appearances in the show," Ellis recalled, "and when she found out Logan was there she only performed three and then left. Logan had one of the two or three best minds in the American theater and he came not because of Jimmy Russo or me—he came because of Bette Davis. Then she refuses to perform. And that's the way it went."

In Boston, Jules Dassin left the show, and the producers asked the elderly John Murray Anderson to step in; Bette agreed to allow this only with the proviso that any criticisms her former teacher might have of her performance be given to her in private and not in front of the cast. Anderson didn't keep the bargain. Much to Bette's chagrin, after a few days of observation he told a number of the cast members that he hadn't thought Bette had much talent when she came to his school in 1928, "and this just proves how right I was."

Distrustful of everyone by now, Bette relied only on herself and her entourage. "Whenever an artistic decision had to be made," Ellis says, "she always fell back on her own instincts and resources and they were always wrong. She wouldn't listen to me or Jerry or whomever. No, she was going to do it *her way*. Then she'd be proven wrong and she'd be very angry. It's too bad, because if she had just done what they said, it would have been tremendous."

By now, the cast of *Two's Company* had pretty well had it with Bette. "She was quite a disappointment," Florence Brooks-Dunay felt. "Really, she was a wreck." When May Muth rehearsed a new scene with her, she found that Bette didn't know her lines, so she prompted her. "Don't you *ever* throw me a line!" Bette hissed. "She almost *killed* me!" May recalled.

To May, Bette seemed jealous and possessive whenever Gary would visit. "She didn't like him being too friendly with the girls. We all got the message that if he came over to say hello, we were to fly." Bette got along much better with the men in the show, according to Buzz Miller. "She was just terrific with the dancing boys, who worshipped her. She was warm and appreciative. I guess she figured they were no threat. I mean, they weren't after Gary Merrill."

Miller feels that much of the resentment the cast felt toward Bette was generated by her entourage. "She had Viola Rubber around her, and everybody wanted to stick pins in *her*. Bette had all these henchladies and advisers who kept rushing into her dressing room and pumping her with nonsense. They just stirred the pot and made her go absolutely nutty. No one was allowed near her. If she'd had some good gypsy folk around, she could have just laughed it off and gone on."

Miller was amazed at how inconsistent Bette could be. "The cast would hang around in the wings and watch her every night, because it was unbelievable—you never knew how she'd be. She would do a scene and it would be so absolutely fabulous that we were all awestruck. Or it would be so terrible that we were awestruck. Like the last song, 'Just Like a Man.' When she did it badly, it was just so embarrassing that everyone would just sneak out of the theater. But once in a while she would do it and just annihilate you, she was so terrific."

As the New York opening night loomed, Bette's terror grew. She was drinking, Ellis noticed, and she broke into screaming matches with Gary in her dressing room night after night. She was still feeling tired unto death, and now she was frequently nauseated as well. She felt so exhausted the day before the New York opening that she went to see Dr. Max Jacobson, who was gaining a reputation as "Dr. Feelgood" because of his extraordinarily energizing vitamin injections. Within a half hour of her shot, Bette felt peppier than she had in months, and the effect didn't wear off for eight hours. Thrilled, she asked Jacobson if he could come to her Beekman Place apartment before every show and give her an injection. "Of course," he replied.

With as much optimism and energy as she could muster, Bette opened in *Two's Company* at the Alvin Theatre on December 15. The audience, packed with her most rabid fans, cheered, stomped, and applauded her every move, and when the show was over Bette was convinced that the seemingly impossible had happened: she had a hit.

The critics were more discriminating, and all but one had deep reservations about the show. The influential Walter Kerr's opinion was typical: "It's always fun to see a distinguished actress unbend, and in *Two's Company* Bette Davis unbends all over the place. She trucks right out and lets herself be tossed into the air by four or five chorus boys. She ties an old bandana around her hair, drapes herself in a moth-eaten sweater, and slouches in sneakers through a sketch about tenement passion. She blacks out her teeth, jams a corncob pipe in her mouth, and lets loose with the yowls of a hillbilly ballad. Indeed, Miss Davis unbends so much that there's some doubt in my mind whether she'll ever be able to straighten up again. The trouble with this business of encouraging a serious performer to let her hair down, climb off the Hollywood pedestal, and rough it up with the lowbrow comics is that it all adds up to a single joke. . . . Unless the performer has hitherto unsuspected and thoroughly genuine talents of the music-hall sort—which Miss Davis would not seem to possess—the descent from Parnassus thins out into a stunt. . . . It's a lot like listening to Beethoven's Fifth played on a pocket comb. You marvel that it can be done at all. And five minutes is just about enough of it."

Bette was devastated by the reviews, particularly because they affected the box office. When the initial surge of Davis fans began to wane after about six weeks, the show played to less-than-capacity audiences, and Bette was forced to agree to have her weekly guarantee reduced from $3,000 to $100 in order to help keep the show open. Her mood wasn't improved two months after *Two's Company* opened when another movie star, Rosalind Russell, won rave reviews (and, ultimately, a Tony Award) with *her* Broadway musical comedy debut in *Wonderful Town.* "When Rosalind Russell made such a hit with the critics," Buzz Miller recalled, "that was the crowning blow. And that's when she really got sick."

She had been feeling worse and worse for weeks; even Dr. Jacobson's injections did little to help her now. She missed performances, and everyone involved with the show suspected that she wasn't ill at all, but only trying to get out of her contract. Several doctors told her she had a low-grade infection and prescribed penicillin, but the drug was of little help. Finally Bette insisted that the antibiotic be stopped, and at that point her jaw began to ache and the left side of her face swelled so badly that she was barely recognizable. She missed the matinee performance on Sunday, March 8, and called in an oral surgeon that afternoon.

Dr. Stanley Behrman came to see Bette at the Beekman Place apartment and from the looks of her suspected that she had a badly infected tooth. "I told her that she had to go to the hospital immediately so that we could drain the infection and see exactly what was wrong," Behrman recalls. Bette told him that she had to do an Actors' Equity benefit performance that evening. He strongly advised her not to do it. "I have to," Bette insisted. "If I don't everyone will think I'm afraid to perform in front of my peers."

Behrman made her promise that she would meet him at New York Hospital after the benefit. In pain, her face and lymph nodes swollen, Bette went on, and after the show—at midnight—Behrman did a complete set of X-rays of her mouth. What he saw shocked him. "Instead of the infected tooth I expected to see, it looked like the moths had been at her jaw. The whole left side was just riddled with holes."

For months, Behrman realized, Bette's body had been fighting osteomyelitis of the jaw, a potentially life-threatening bacterial infection that had been eating away at the bones around her teeth. (It was the same disease that had afflicted Ruthie in 1921.) The penicillin had checked the infection only enough so that it could slowly destroy her jaw, and Dr. Jacobson's injections had allowed her to "run on empty," further endangering her health.

Behrman told Bette that he would have to perform surgery on her jaw the next day, and she remained in the hospital overnight. Blood tests while she was there showed that her body was suffused not only with the infection from her jaw but also with amphetamines, "speed" drugs that provide artificial energy, and can be addictive and debilitating to the body. Dr. Jacobson's injections, it turned out, had been more than just vitamins, and could have cost Bette her life. According to Dr. Behrman, when Bette insisted that the penicillin be stopped, she also told Dr. Jacobson that she no longer wanted his "Feelgood" injections. "But he insisted," Behrman recalls, "and she had to lock him out of her apartment to keep him away from her."*

Bette's stay in the hospital caused quite a stir. "People lined up in the halls when they heard she was there," Behrman marvels, "and her X-rays were stolen by somebody as a souvenir." A worried Gary Merrill spent the night in Bette's room, and the next morning he told Behrman, "That woman in there is my wife, the mother of my children, she's a housewife and that's how she should be treated." Meaning, Behrman felt, that he should treat her as he would any other patient. "There's a tendency sometimes to treat someone like that with kid gloves—'Well, I won't do this test because it's going to be uncomfortable' or whatever. Merrill wanted us to do whatever we had to in order to get Bette well again."

As Bette waited to be operated on Monday morning, she asked May Muth to pay her a visit. When May arrived, Bette begged her to take her side against the producers, whom she was convinced would think she was faking. "She asked me to go back and tell everybody she was really ill," Muth recalls. "But I wasn't about to get into the middle of it. She was going to win no matter what, and I wasn't going to speak against the producers, who I loved. I don't think she was faking it, I just feel that she didn't want the show to keep running without her."

Behrman was faced with a difficult problem when he operated on Bette's jaw. He had to remove large areas of diseased bone and marrow while preserving Bette's teeth and keeping her jaw intact. "Ordinarily, I would do this operation from the outside and collapse the bone. But that would have scarred her and perhaps even have caused her face to cave in. So I did it the hard way. I went in from inside her mouth. I had to remove

---

* In the 1960s, after he had treated President and Mrs. Kennedy, Peter Lawford, Sammy Davis, Jr., Judy Garland, Tennessee Williams, Marlene Dietrich, and many others with his "vitamin injections," Jacobson had his medical license revoked.

nearly half the jaw, but I left enough so that all of the bone would grow back. It's a great deal more painful that way, but it would eventually be as if nothing had happened."

After the surgery, Behrman packed the cleaned-out areas with what he describes as "a thin strip of gauze covered with Vaseline that was miles and miles long." Most of it encircled her main jaw nerve, and the first few times he changed it, Bette was under general anesthetic. Afterward, the changes were done while Bette was awake, and they put her in agony. She rarely complained. "She was an incredible lady," Behrman thought. "A gal of steel in some ways."

The day after the surgery, Behrman wrote to Ellis and Russo to say that for Bette to return to work "in the next three to four weeks" would be "hazardous" to her health. The producers considered several replacements, but on Monday, March 16, they accepted the inevitable and posted a closing notice for the cast and crew. *Two's Company* had played ninety performances, and lost money. "It took me seven years to get out of debt," Mike Ellis says. "I had bill collectors following me all over town."

The entire experience was "excruciating" for Ellis, "a nightmare." He places the blame largely with Bette. "If she had just trusted the people involved with the show and had done what they wanted her to do, she would have made it." Bette, of course, felt differently. When Ellis ran into her and Gary at the Coconut Grove Playhouse in Miami in 1956, "Bette took one look at me and *ran* out of the theater."

For her part, Bette never entertained the idea that she was responsible for the failure of *Two's Company,* or that she was in any way deficient as a singer, dancer, or farceur. In January 1953 she took part in the recording of the original-cast album of the show, which contained only the songs, not the sketches, so that she appeared on only two or three cuts. Years later she was asked to explain the commercial failure of the album. "They made the biggest mistake *in the world* on that album!" she cried. *"I'm not on it!"*

TWENTY-THREE

Bette lay in her hospital bed, restless, uncomfortable, her jaw aching miserably. She thought the radio might take her mind off the pain, and she switched it on. Within a few minutes, Walter Winchell began his nationally syndicated gossip report, "Coast to Coast," with words that sent an icy finger of fear down Bette's spine: "Bette Davis has been operated on for cancer of the jaw."

Nearly hysterical, she called Dr. Behrman at home. "Do I have cancer, Doctor?" she asked, her voice shaking with fear. "You must tell me if I do."

"No, Bette, you don't have cancer," Behrman replied. "What you had was an infection, not a tumor."

Bette's relief soon turned to fury at Winchell. She told Gary to demand a retraction in Winchell's daily newspaper column, but he cautioned that more people would read the retraction than heard the original item and think Bette really did have cancer. The story, however, refused to die, and other columnists, including Dorothy Kilgallen, picked it up. "One young doctor in town who wanted publicity told the press that I had missed the diagnosis and that Bette had cancer," Behrman recalled. "My mother pulled me aside and said, 'You can tell *me* the truth. Walter Winchell wouldn't say it unless it was true.' It got so crazy that we took out the slides and studied them again, just to make sure."

Finally Gary persuaded Dorothy Schiff, the publisher of the *New York Post*, to print a prominent article that accurately described Bette's illness. Winchell then admitted in print that he had been misinformed. "It certainly helped," Bette recalled, "although no retraction ever completely does it. The rumors persisted."

She languished in the hospital for six more weeks, a long and difficult period that gave her an opportunity to reflect on her past, and her future. "My head was bursting with pain. I wondered if my life was over. Two things sustained me as I lay in the hospital trying to keep control of my life: I thought of my husband and my three children . . . and I mentally reviewed the long years of my career. Thinking of my family gave me courage; reviewing my career became a fascination. It was almost a form of psychoanalysis. . . . Each picture brought back a memory—of my continuing fight for independence in Hollywood, of the unhappiness that dogged my personal life, of the good wholesome existence that finally came to me."

With Gary constantly concerned and attentive, with Bobby reliably supervising the household ("Without her . . . I don't know what I would have done," Bette said), with the children visiting her for an hour every day and B.D. often spending the night in a cot at her side, Bette was able to reflect pleasurably again on marriage and family and forget for a while the drinking and the battles with Gary, the willfulness of B.D., her nagging doubts about Margot. *Maybe,* she thought, *Margo Channing and Bill Sampson might just have a chance.*

It took more than a year for Bette's jaw to heal completely, and longer for the numbness that replaced the pain to disappear. She didn't even think about working; Gary had enough film offers to keep him busy for the next eighteen months, and this gave Bette her first real chance to see whether she could be truly happy simply as a wife and mother. The Merrills moved from Beekman Place to an inn in Maine, where they remained for six months before moving into a sprawling white clapboard house at Zeb's Cove in Cape Elizabeth on the Maine coastline.

Bette loved the house, just as she had loved Butternut. "The porches," she wrote, "the stacked lobster pots, the open fires, the pond for skating in winter, the cove—everything made it the perfect home for a family to be happy in. Its kitchen was my new amphitheatre; and I never wanted to get off the stage!" She named the house Witch-Way because so many people asked "Which way?" when seeking directions and because, as she put it, "A witch lived there—guess who?"

Bette and Gary became a part of their community, much like any other parents. B.D. entered the first grade at Waynflete, a private school fifteen miles away in Portland, and the Merrills joined the PTA. Bette suspected the locals expected Theda Bara "in satin sheaths" when she arrived, but they found instead a surprisingly down-to-earth New Englander. When Gary joined the local ice-hockey team, which played on a nearby pond, Bette would supply the players with cocktails and cheer the team on.

The Merrills maintained a small animal farm on their property; Gary butchered their sheep and pigs for food in the fall and replaced them in the spring. He also caught lobsters from a kayak, and the children combed the beaches for mussels and steamer clams. The first summer, Bette decided that her family should reap the full harvest of the land and water around them and took a recipe from a naturalist cookbook for seaweed pudding. As a blissful Bette ate bowl after bowl of the delicacy, B.D. recalled, the rest of the family choked on every mouthful.

Bette and Gary now presented a heartwarming picture of domestic bliss to the world: the "good wholesome existence" Bette had alluded to. In a series of magazine and newspaper interviews, they spoke about their happiness in Maine. One article, entitled "The Present Is Perfect," quoted Bette as saying, "This is the only marriage I've ever had." Gary added, "She's sweet and wifely and I'm sweet and husbandly." The reporter, Ida Zeitlin, closed the piece with the observation, "Now there's a house whose warmth is like a welcome. If Bette's been tops with you for more years than you care to remember, you go away feeling good."

The reporter had spent a day, seen the performances, and left with a warmed heart. But Bette and Gary's neighbors and friends knew that things at Witch-Way weren't as the Merrills would have them seem. Dark rumors swirled around Cape Elizabeth about very odd goings-on in that house. There was the procession of hired help that came and went, each with a new story of violent battles between the couple, of Gary's drinking and peculiar behavior, of his physical abuse of Bette. One live-in young couple had left the morning that Gary wandered into the kitchen at dawn, said "Good morning" to them, and started to fix himself a martini—stark naked. As the woman ran upstairs in shocked tears, her husband screamed and shook his fist at Gary. Then Bette barreled in, spouting venom at her husband that added considerably to the decibel level. Unbothered, Gary finished his martini and wandered off.

There were whispers that Margot was insane, that she had been placed in a straitjacket and confined to a third-floor bedroom where she screamed and howled all night. The rumors gave Witch-Way the gothic aura of a mad doctor's isolated mansion. Unfortunately, the gossip wasn't that far afield of the truth.

For Margot's behavior *had* become increasingly erratic and disturbing. The two-and-a-half-year-old's nightly disturbances had grown longer and louder. She spoke only rarely, and when she did she would repeat a word—"Hi! Hi! Hi! Hi! Hi!"—until she drove Bette to distraction. Worst of all, she frequently grew violent now. She pushed over

*A*n evocative study of Bette as the transformed spinster Charlotte Vale in one of her most popular films, *Now, Voyager*, 1942.

A lovely Davis portrait of the period.

(David Polanco Collection)

In 1942, Bette helped found the Hollywood Canteen for America's World War II soldiers. Here she helps serve cake to a serviceman at its New York counterpart, the Stage Door Canteen

Director Vincent Sherman shows Bette how he wants her to resist a man's advances in *Old Acquaintance*. In real life, the situation was quite the reverse as Sherman tried to keep an amorous Bette at bay.

An hysterical Miriam Hopkins lights into Bette, who remains maddeningly calm in *Old Acquaintance*, 1943. The on-set dynamics between the two stars were similar.

Haggard, Bette testifies at the Los Angeles inquest into the mysterious death of her husband in August 1943.

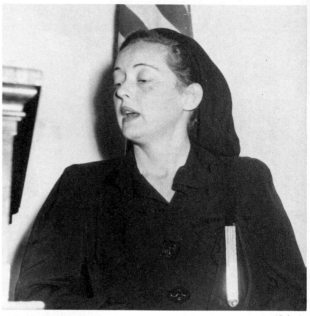

Bette plunged immediately back into work on *Mr. Skeffington* in September. During filming, Vincent Sherman finally agreed to have an affair with Bette.

In November 1945, a lonely Bette takes her third husband, William Grant Sherry, an artist seven years her junior. Flanking the newlyweds are Sherry's mother, Marion, *left,* and Ruthie.

Eighteen months later, the Sherrys' daughter Barbara Davis is christened in Hollywood. Bette's sister Bobby wears Bette's old wedding outfit.

A ridiculous publicity still from a ridiculous movie, *Beyond the Forest,* Bette's final Warner Brothers picture. She dubbed her last line on her last day at the studio: "I've got to get out of here!"

B. D. Sherry makes her film debut with her mother in *Payment on Demand,* filmed in 1949. By this time Bette's marriage was disintegrating.

Bette on the set of her comeback film, *All About Eve,* with director/writer Joe Mankiewicz and costars Anne Baxter and Celeste Holm, 1950.

Bette as the irrepressible, volcanic Margo Channing, one of her most indelible screen creations.

(Nickens)

Inset: Bette leaves her hand- and footprints in the forecourt of Grauman's Chinese Theatre, November, 1950.

(Nickens)

(Photofest)

March 1951: Bette leaves for England with her new husband Gary Merrill, B.D., and newly adopted baby Margot. Also along were, *clockwise from upper left,* Margot's nurse "Coop," B.D.'s governess Gladys Young and Bette's maid Dell Pfeiffer.

Unable to find work in Hollywood, Bette returns to Broadway in the musical review *Two's Company,* 1952. The show was a disaster.

The Merrills with Margot and B.D. on the beach near their home in Malibu in 1952. Not much later, Margot was institutionalized after she was diagnosed as mentally retarded.

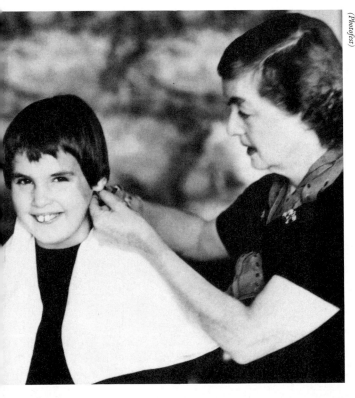

In the mid-fifties, Bette cuts Margot's hair during one of the girl's visits home.

Gary and Bette whoop it up at a party, circa 1955. By now their marriage was crumbling amid drinking bouts and outbursts of violence.

Bette as the dumpy housewife Agnes Hurley in *The Catered Affair*, 1956. "She looks old enough to be my mother," Joan Crawford sniffed.

Fourteen-year-old B. D. poses with her newly divorced mother in 1961. Two years later, B.D. would marry a man nearly twice her age.

In *The Night of the Iguana* on Broadway, 1962. The backstage strife made the plot of *All About Eve* seem like *Little Women*.

(Nickens)

Joan Crawford and Bette as the Hudson sisters in *Whatever Happened to Baby Jane?*, 1962. The filming was rife with feud-fueled problems.

Bette poses with her adopted son, Michael Merrill, and his bride, Chou Chou Raum, at their wedding in May 1973. With them is the bride's mother, Alix Snow.

Yet another try at the stage for Bette, in *Miss Moffat*, 1974. The show never made it to Broadway.

With Gena Rowlands in the critically acclaimed TV drama *Strangers*, 1979. Bette won an Emmy for her performance.

Bette and her grandson, J. Ashley Hyman, in *Family Reunion*, 1981. The experience, his mother said, was a nightmare for him, but others tell a different story.

Jimmy Stewart with Bette in their TV film, *Right of Way,* 1982. The two studio-era veterans adored each other.

Bette in a scene from her first TV series, *Hotel,* 1983. She filmed only a few episodes before she was stricken with breast cancer and a series of strokes.

Three years later, Bette makes a miraculous comeback in *Murder with Mirrors,* a TV movie costarring Helen Hayes—whom she totally intimidated.

With Vincent Price, Lillian Gish, and Ann Sothern in *The Whales of August,* 1986. Whenever she autographed this picture, Bette scrawled her name over Lillian's face.

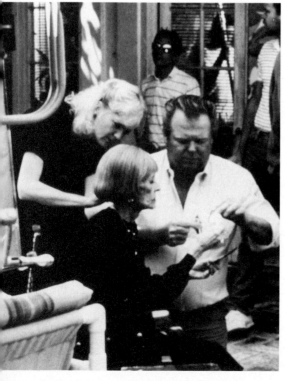

Bette is attended to during filming of her last picture, *The Wicked Stepmother,* in 1988. She walked off the set after two weeks.

One of Bette's last public appearances, at the American Cinema Awards, January 1989. She collapsed at her table that night, and nine months later, ravaged anew by cancer, she died in Paris.

Michael Merrill with his wife Chou Chou, their sons Matthew and Cameron, and their dog Tam in October, 1991.

furniture, lashed out in anger at her nannies, her parents, her siblings. She viciously hit Michael and pulled his hair out in chunks. She indeed had to be restrained with a straitjacket while she slept, for her own protection. What finally convinced Bette and Gary to seek professional help for Margot was the terrible day Bette heard the crash of breaking glass and raced into the den. There, in front of the bar, stood Margot. Next to her, on the floor, sat Michael—bleeding amid shards of shattered cocktail glasses.

In despair, Bette and Gary took their little girl to New York's Presbyterian Hospital for examination, and after a week of tests they heard the devastating news—Margot was retarded, a result of brain damage she had sustained either at birth or afterward. She would never achieve an IQ above 60. There was little that could be done for her, the doctors said, and they recommended that she be sent to the Lochland School, an institution for the retarded in Geneva, New York.

Frantic, Bette called Laguna Beach and spoke to Ruthie, who suggested that Margot be returned to the adoption agency as "damaged goods." Bette couldn't bring herself to do that, and when she told Gary she thought the doctors were right about the institutionalization, he snarled, "You do what you please with *your* daughter, but not with *mine*! Margot will not be shut away in a mental home!" He brought her home from New York determined to give her a chance at a normal family life.

B.D., in her memoir *My Mother's Keeper,* wrote that Bette and Gary now began to have "vicious" fights about who was "to blame" for Margot's condition. B.D. recalled that Bette maintained that the doctor who delivered Margot must have misused his forceps; Gary argued that a nurse Bette had "then fired for drunkenness" had dropped Margot on her head and caused the injury. (Since Coop was the only nurse Bette fired for "drunkenness," Gary must have meant her.)

This placing of blame may have been Bette and Gary's way of diverting suspicion from themselves. Gladys Young, who was with the Merrills in England when Coop supposedly dropped Margot, is adamant that nothing of the sort ever happened. She denies as well that Coop was a drinker, except for the night she returned home from a pub not drunk but "fortified," and was fired after telling Bette off in a letter.

Gladys Young's suspicion is that either Gary or Bette dropped Margot—or, more disturbingly, that one or the other of them struck her in frustration with her nightly crying spells. Although Gladys never saw either of them hit Margot, she says that "we all did feel that with Bette's short fuse, she was capable of striking Margot and causing a problem." Nancy Smith, who replaced Coop, wrote to Gladys when she heard the news. "She said to me, 'Poor little Margot. That's what we thought might happen,' " Gladys recalled. "And eight years later, Nancy mentioned Margot again in a letter to me, reminding me that Margot was so normal and responsive as a baby, and so joyous."

Whoever or whatever caused Margot's injury and retardation, it soon became clear that she could not remain at Witch-Way. She continued to endanger Michael, and it was impossible for the Merrills to keep a governess for more than two weeks. Finally Gary agreed to enroll Margot in the Lochland School, after being assured that it was a small, loving environment in a Victorian mansion. He was impressed that the school's proprietor, Miss Florence Stewart, would not agree to take Margot until she had come to Witch-Way to meet the Merrill family.

Lochland would remain Margot's home for the rest of her life. At the school, Bette felt, "Margot could be brought along slowly with children of her own capacities. In that way she wouldn't have the pain of competing throughout her formative years with normal children who would be too advanced for her and therefore add to her frustrations. It was heartrending to part with her, but we felt that not only for her own future, but for the future of our other two children, we must."

Bette couldn't bring herself to accompany Gary and Margot to Lochland; instead she carefully dressed the little girl in a sailor suit and kissed her good-bye at the Portland airport. When he arrived at Lochland, Gary was relieved to see that the school was indeed more like a home, a tree-shaded, three-story clapboard structure reminiscent, in fact, of Witch-Way. But he was disturbed to see the obviously retarded Down's Syndrome children at the school who would become Margot's new family; Margot's condition *couldn't* be the same as theirs. "As I looked at her after saying good-bye," he reminisced, "she looked so pretty, so normal—but, of course, she was not."

At Lochland, however, Margot quickly calmed down and came to seem more normal, and it became clear that her violent outbursts had been a reaction to the tumult that had surrounded her at Witch-Way, the angry words and the nasty fights between Bette and Gary that she was subjected to so often. Al and Mary Beardsley worked at the school when Margot arrived, she as a housemother and he as a speech therapist. Neither could recall a single incident of violence involving Margot. "She was outgoing and wanted attention," Al says, "but that was all. Her speech wasn't perfect, so I worked with her on that." According to Mary, Margot responded very well to the patient, caring instruction and attention she received at Lochland. "She fit into the school very well. I don't remember any conflict with the other children."

❦

In stark contrast to Margot's placid new life at Lochland, the atmosphere at Witch-Way grew ever more violent, ever more bizarre. Although Bette liked to call herself "a hausfrau" and "the little woman," she had lost none of her obstinate willfulness. As she had with Sherry, Bette loved to goad and belittle Gary. His brother Jerry recalls sitting with Bette at his place and listening to her "taking off on my brother" for the better part of an hour. "Finally I flipped and told her off, and she walked out the door. It was very difficult to stay with Bette for more than an hour, because she'd make some comment that made absolutely no sense, and if you didn't agree with it, you were done with. If something was undeniably white, she'd say, 'No, it's black.' So you couldn't deal with her. I'm an easygoing sort of guy, but after an hour with Bette I'd have to leave the room."

Bette, with her obsessive-compulsive attitude about order and cleanliness, ran roughshod over everyone on the domestic front as much as she had on a film set. One New Year's Eve, Bobby had carefully prepared table settings for a party, strung banners, hung balloons. Bette arrived after most of the guests, took one look at the room, and announced, "You've done it all wrong, Bobby! Jesus! Do I have to do *everything* around here!" The guests waited a half hour while Bette rearranged everything—which, in their view, had been perfectly okay the way Bobby had it.

When Bette purchased a new house for her mother in Laguna Beach, Ruthie's friends and neighbors helped her move in. The house was smaller than the one Ruthie had left, and she had some big wood pieces. Everyone struggled to find just the right place for everything, and finally, about eleven at night, all were convinced the arrangement was perfect. Exhausted, they started in on pizza and beer. At that point, Ruthie's friend Betsy Paul recalled, Bette swept in wearing a mink coat. "She took one look at the place and announced, 'It's all *wrong*! We'll have to do it again!' Whereupon we spent two more hours moving things around to Bette's satisfaction. And you know what? When we were done everything was exactly where it had been before Bette barrelled in."

Gary mocked Bette's housekeeping fervor—"How clean can a place be? You're not Mrs. Craig; you're Bette Davis!" He made fun of her in other ways too, taunting her about her spreading waistline, comparing her unfavorably to younger actresses. He even belittled her Oscars and continually tried to remove them from the mantel; once he gave one of them to a puzzled cab driver, who returned it the next morning. Bette retaliated by humiliating Gary outside the home; his friend Bob Jurgenson recalls that Bette told him Gary was "sexually lazy" and that the only time she "got any" was at Christmas and her birthday, "if I'm lucky."

According to Jerry Merrill, Bette and Gary's drinking "exacerbated" their frequent quarrels. B.D. has offered a harrowing recollection of a drunken brawl between the two when she was eight. It followed a party at which one of Gary's friends accused him of sleeping with the friend's wife. As B.D. listened to the argument from her bedroom she thought of the times she had come down into the living room while Bette was away to find Gary "sprawled" on the couch with a woman.

B.D. listened to the argument, and soon heard the door slam as Gary's friend left. Then, as they had so many times before, her parents started to fight. "You make me sick!" Bette screeched. "You think you're such a hotshot with the broads? *Ha!* You haven't laid *me* in years. The only time you touch me is when you beat me up. *Bastard!* That's all you're good at!"

"What are you bitching about?" Gary sneered. "Getting slapped around is the only thing you enjoy, you stupid cunt. If it doesn't do anything for you, why do you beg for it all the time?"

"Oh, my God! That's what you always say and you know it isn't true. You know that violence terrifies me. All I want is to be loved like a woman."

"*Bullshit!* You're no woman—you're a friggin' ice queen. Without an audience you're not worth a shit! Maybe if I knocked you on your friggin' ass on the stage of the London Palladium and then jumped you, you'd perform. Outside of that, a knothole in a tree is more exciting than you!"

B.D. buried her head under her pillow, but she couldn't drown out the terrible words. *"Jesus!"* Bette exploded. "You really are something! I suppose all the other men in my life didn't know what they were talking about? One of them even—"

"*Jesus Christ!* Are you going to hand me that crap about Howard Hughes screwing you on a bed of gardenias again? He fucked every two-bit twat in Hollywood and you're proud of holding out for ten bucks worth of gardenias! . . . The only people who can be around you for long without wanting to kill you are faggots, so don't waste your time telling me about all the men—"

"So my other three husbands were fags, were they? Well let me tell *you* something . . . at least *they* were men! They—"

"*They* nothing! They all kicked the shit out of you. You've told everybody who would listen to you about it."

"Stop it! Stop it! I can't take any more!" Bette screamed, and ran up the stairs to the second-floor landing. When Gary followed, showering her with curses and threats, she frantically whispered for him not to disturb the children. By now B.D. was looking through the crack in her door, and Gary turned toward her bedroom. "Maybe the little slut should come out and see what you get for starting a fight!"

"Gary, get out of my house!" Bette shrieked. "Leave this instant! Leave B.D. out of this for God's sake!" B.D. scurried back to her bed, but within seconds Gary stumbled into her room. "You want to listen? You might as well have a clear view as well!" He started to laugh as Bette lunged at him and pounced on his back. He knocked her to the floor, and she ran for the stairs—an attempt, B.D. thought, to get Gary out of her bedroom. He grabbed Bette at the top of the stairs and began to strangle her. Frantic, B.D. watched as Gary lifted Bette off her feet. "Mother was making gurgling, choking noises and I couldn't stand it anymore," B.D. recalled. She charged at Gary and pounded his back with her fists. "You're killing her, you're killing her!" she howled. Gary kicked B.D. away while still strangling Bette, then let her go, whirled around, and knocked B.D. against the wall. Bette fell down the stairs, and B.D., as far as she could remember, passed out.

The next thing B.D. recalled is hearing Bette and Gary talking to the police in the living room. Bette was hysterical. She told the officers that Gary had attacked her, and showed them her neck bruises. Gary, according to B.D., twirled a drink, winked at the two men, and told them, "A domestic quarrel. You know how that is." The police told Bette that they could do nothing unless she filed formal charges. She didn't want to do that, she said—there would be bad publicity. Couldn't they do something informally? No, they told her. Bette never pressed charges.

These terrible rows frightened and deeply disturbed B.D. Michael, however, seemed to take them with an almost preternatural calm. It helped that Gary, while he had come to despise B.D., doted on Michael, considering him "his" son while B.D. was "her" daughter, and always shielded him from the violence. Jerry Merrill recalled the day that his daughter visited Witch-Way to play with Michael, and Bette and Gary got into a fight. "My daughter started to cry, and Mike just said, 'Don't cry. You come with me. We'll go to my room and hide. Don't worry about a thing.' Mike knew exactly what to do."

Shaken by the violence of her relationship with Gary, emotionally barren and sexually frustrated, Bette became desperate for the love and attention of her children. When she didn't think she had gotten enough of that, B.D. recalled, she would cry and wail. "Neither of you care a damn about me! Well, we'll just see how you feel after I'm gone."

To prove her point, according to B.D., Bette staged several mock suicide attempts when she and the children were alone in the house. The first time, B.D. was frantic and Michael in tears after Bette threw an empty bottle of Nembutal sleeping pills on the hallway floor, announced that she had swallowed them all, and locked her bedroom door. B.D. became hysterical. She pounded on the door and screamed, "Mommy, Mommy, please open the door! I *do* love you . . . of course I love you . . . you know that. Let me in . . . don't die . . . oh, please don't die!"

There was no response, and finally, exhausted, B.D. fell asleep in front of the door. The next morning Bette emerged. "I hope that taught you a good lesson," she announced. "I deserve better from you. I love you more than anything and I expect you to love me in return."

Never again would she believe such a scene, B.D. vowed.

By the end of 1954, Bette hadn't worked for two years, and she itched to get back before a camera. "She was the type of person who, unless she was working, was not really happy," Jerry Merrill believed. But it was more than that. Gary's contract had been dropped by 20th Century–Fox earlier that year, and he had done only some sporadic television work over the prior six months. With Margot at Lochland and B.D. in private school, with Ruthie and Bobby still dependent on her, and with the expenses of running the sprawling property that comprised Witch-Way, Bette needed to go back to work to keep the bills paid.

Happily, she had an offer she loved: to reprise her role as Queen Elizabeth I in 20th Century–Fox's CinemaScope and Technicolor production *The Virgin Queen*. Early in 1955 she took B.D. with her to California (leaving Michael in Maine with Gary), rented a house in Los Angeles, and returned to the Fox lot, where she had last worked on *The Star*. She felt she could now do even further justice to Elizabeth—in 1939 she had been thirty-one playing sixty; in this screenplay she would, at forty-seven, be playing Elizabeth at fifty.

If anyone had expected that Bette would be chastened by Hollywood's lack of interest in her and would soften her film-making temperament, they were wrong. Instead, her terror at facing the cameras again, and her determination to make this film the hit that would put her back on top, prompted her to argue with director Henry Koster over everything from blocking to interpretation. She railed against cinematographer Charles G. Clarke for not taking the care with her that Ernie Haller had, and she froze out her beautiful young costar (and rival for Sir Walter Raleigh's affections) Joan Collins.

"I tried to be understanding and flexible," Collins said, "and keep out of the way of her icy glares and sharp tongue as much as possible—offscreen that is. She would finish a scene in which she was telling me off, and I always felt she wanted to keep right on going after Mr. Koster yelled 'Cut!' So I would turn and walk away quickly as soon as my stint was completed."

In the middle of filming, Gary and Michael flew to California and visited Bette on the set. It was Michael's first experience on a soundstage, and Bette called it "a wonderment" that he recognized her with her shaved head and eyebrows and bejeweled scullcap. While Mike stood and watched Bette, as Elizabeth, verbally lash Richard Todd as Raleigh, he turned to Gary and asked, "Why is Mommy mad at that man instead of you?"

❧

When Bette returned to Maine in May 1955, the violence in the Merrill home resumed. B.D. recalled that Gary not only beat her and Bette, but that on one terrible, drunken night she found him terrorizing her quarterhorse mare, Sally, with a length of barbed wire, forcing the animal to smash into the walls of her stable until she had injured her knees. Frantically trying to stop the attack, B.D. opened the stable door, allowing the horse to escape, and Gary went back to the house. B.D. then saw that Sally had lacerations on her neck, shoulders, and face from the barbed wire. When she told her mother about the incident the next morning, Bette dismissed it, saying, "Gary's an idiot. He was roaring drunk and probably decided to go for a ride in the middle of the night."

"If that were the case, Mother, why was he in her stall slashing at her with barbed wire?"

Bette started to walk back to the house. "He probably mistook it for a lead rope," she replied.

While Bette was able to shrug off Gary's more bizarre behavior, the neighbors weren't. Most of them had liked him at first, had appreciated his down-to-earth friendliness and humor. But before long they turned against him. A neighbor, Jenny Sprague, tells of the day that she and her husband, Shaw, were horseback riding along a one-lane dirt road through the woods near their home. Suddenly Gary came roaring down the road in a convertible. He stood up on the seat and waved his arms, leaving the steering wheel unattended. It was all that Jenny and Shaw could do to keep their horses from rearing. "Shaw was furious," Jenny recalled. "In fact, he told Gary never to come near our house again, and he didn't."

Stories about Gary's eccentricities proliferated in Cape Elizabeth. He would show up at the country club wearing no shoes and cloves of garlic around his neck. He wore kilts while playing hockey, and at certain moments observers noticed that he wasn't wearing any underwear. When Bette and Gary attended a college football game between Colby and Bowdoin, Gary's alma mater, Gary arrived wrapped in a raccoon coat and carrying a large suitcase. Another Bowdoin alumnus, Frederick Goddard, watched Gary take a portable bar out of the suitcase, unfold it, and set up a row of liquor and glasses. Then, Goddard recalls, "He filled a baby's nipple bottle with booze and sucked on it for most of the game. Miss Davis did not appear amused."

Gary would make no movies between 1954 and 1960, and he appeared on just one television show between 1956 and 1957. "I didn't mind," he said. "I was living where I wanted to and loving every minute of it." The family's bills were still prodigious, however, and the Merrills needed money. (Gary had to borrow $50,000 from a wealthy neighbor to pay back taxes.) Once again, rather than "the little woman," Bette became the breadwinner, and she belittled Gary as "lazy," "a worthless husband," "a terrible provider." In 1956 she made two movies, *The Catered Affair,* in which she played the dumpy wife of a Bronx cab driver, and *Storm Center,* in which she played a dumpy librarian fighting censorship. Like *The Virgin Queen,* neither of these films made much of an impact at the box office, and Bette's stature as a movie star dropped to an all-time low. She did not play a lead role in a motion picture for another five years.

In 1940, Bette had predicted that "when I retire from pictures, I'm going to be a nice, plump, comfortable-looking middle-aged lady." By 1956 her prophecy had come true, but the problem was that she had not retired from pictures, and her appearance hurt her career. She looked frumpy now, every bit her forty-eight years, and she was no longer considered for the kinds of romantic leads that her contemporaries Joan Crawford, Loretta Young, and Barbara Stanwyck were still able to play because they had kept themselves in shape.

Television, however, proved a godsend for her. The relatively new medium was eager for big Hollywood names to attract viewers, even if they were over the hill, and shows like *Schlitz Playhouse, G.E. Theater,* and *U.S. Steel Hour* gave Bette the chance to play some interesting roles and make between $5,000 and $10,000 for a week or two of work. Television helped keep Bette creatively fulfilled, paid the bills, and gave her an occasional respite from her increasingly troubled marriage.

Early in 1957, the Merrills' financial situation had turned so dire that Bette insisted that Gary go back to work. They closed up Witch-Way and rented a house in Malibu in order to be closer to the center of television production, and Gary did eighteen guest shots over the next two years, while Bette did seven. Together they earned over $100,000 in each of those years, money they used to pay for B.D.'s and Michael's enrollment in the Chadwick School in Rolling Hills, as well as Bobby's move from Laguna Beach to a house nearby so that she could be at Bette's beck and call on a moment's notice.

On the surface, ten-year-old B.D.'s life seemed to be a charmed one—private schools, a pet horse, riding lessons, the finest clothes. But she was constantly buffeted by the battles of her parents, and she had become extremely wary of Gary. B.D. was very much like Bette—intelligent, willful, short-fused, sharp-tongued—and Gary by now directed as much of his anger at her as he did his wife. Aware that Gary might turn on her violently at any time, B.D. tried to avoid him, and she never had friends over to the house when he was home. Once, when she did invite a girlfriend to stay over for a weekend, she waited until Gary was out of town and not expected to return for a week, just to be sure. To her horror, on Saturday night she heard a drunken Gary stagger unexpectedly into the house. He began a nasty quarrel with Bette, then headed upstairs. When the violence in B.D.'s bedroom was over, her friend was bruised and hysterical. Bette drove her home to her parents and pleaded with them not to press charges against Gary. Furious, they insisted they would. Bette offered them a large sum of money for their silence. They agreed—but only after their daughter was examined by a doctor to make sure she hadn't been sexually abused.

This was the last straw for Bette. On June 6, she filed a divorce action in Santa Monica Superior Court, charging that Gary had treated her with "extreme cruelty" and "wrongfully inflicted upon [her] grievous mental suffering." She asked that Gary be ordered to pay her child support and alimony.

When the story made the papers, Ray Stricklyn, a young actor Bette had befriended when he played a small role with her in *The Catered Affair,* went to see her at Columbia Studios, where she was playing (for the second time on television) Mary Todd Lincoln. Stricklyn wasn't surprised that the Merrills were divorcing—he had spent a boozy weekend with them a year earlier in which they reminded him most of Edward Albee's slashingly vitriolic couple George and Martha in *Who's Afraid of Virginia Woolf?* But he was fond of Bette, and he wanted to offer her some condolence.

"The moment she saw me," Stricklyn recalled, "she rushed into her dressing room and began to sob, almost uncontrollably. No longer was she the tough, brittle dame. . . . She reached for a Kleenex and began wiping away the smeared mascara." Bette apologized to Stricklyn for losing control, then sank into the chair in front of her makeup mirror. "She stared at her own reflection for a long time. Then, shakily, began to apply fresh eye makeup. Suddenly, she stopped, and moaned. 'Ooooooh, Ray, at my age, having to start all over again. Four husbands! I'll never marry again.' Then, quick as a flash, she was back on the set—too professional to ever hold up shooting—heaping venom on Abraham Lincoln."

Bette dropped the divorce action a few weeks later. When B.D. asked her mother why she didn't leave Gary, Bette cried, "I can't! I won't face being alone again. I've been alone since my father walked out on me when I was a little girl like you. Nothing I did pleased *him* either. . . . What goes on with Daddy and me . . . doesn't make any difference. All men are the same in the long run . . . the bastards can't stand a bright, strong woman."

The reconciliation proved rocky; B.D. recalled that Gary "came close to killing [Bette] a couple of times." Bette felt it best for her to spend more time apart from Gary; he remained at Witch-Way while she lived as much as possible in California. Bette was thrilled in late 1957 when she received an offer to star in a Broadway version of Thomas Wolfe's novel *Look Homeward, Angel,* and she rented another house, this one on Bundy Drive in Brentwood, to prepare for the Los Angeles rehearsals of the show.

Strolling through the new house one day, Bette opened the door to what she thought was a walk-in closet. She reached for the light switch, stepped inside, and fell ten feet to a concrete basement floor. She suffered a concussion and serious spinal cord bruises, and had to withdraw from the play. Miserable with disappointment and pain, she filed a lawsuit against the owners of the house (which she won) and took to bed at Ruthie's house in Laguna. There, as she had so often in the past, she turned herself over to Bobby's ministrations and Ruthie's pep talks. They did little good. Bette was totally dispirited; she wondered that, with everything she'd been through for the past eight years, she hadn't lost her mind.

The close proximity to Bobby and Ruthie, at first a blessed relief, soon threatened to unravel her. Bobby's mood swings infuriated her, as did Ruthie's incessant chattering, and she found herself screaming at them both within days, heaping upon them the kind of vitriol they were now used to and took in their usual stoic, resigned way.

Mother and sister nursed their unhappy patient back to health and even temper well enough so that in May 1958 she, B.D., and Bobby left the United States aboard the ocean liner *Independence* in order for Bette to make two motion pictures in Europe. *John Paul Jones* cast her in a small cameo as Catherine the Great; *The Scapegoat* gave her a showier, but not much larger, role as a bedridden dowager addicted to cigars and morphine. Neither film was truly worth Bette's time, either in terms of remuneration or role. But she was eager to get away from Gary for a while, she had had no other offers, and she looked forward to seeing Europe once again. "The three Bs," as Bette called them, motored through most of Spain, visiting cathedrals and monuments at each stop. "Mother was riveted by every detail," B.D. recalled, "and in the same way that she attacked acting or gardening in Maine, she applied her energy and enthusiasm to being a tourist. No stone was left unturned, her feet were never tired, and she missed nothing."

The filming of *John Paul Jones* in Spain left Bette less satisfied. She thought the film's star, Robert Stack, was "the dullest actor who ever *lived.*" Bette was sure the film would be a dud, and she wasn't surprised when it enjoyed only scant distribution in the United States. In England, she was disappointed to find that *The Scapegoat* was little more than a showcase for the distinguished actor Alec Guinness in a dual role. There was scant rapport between the two stars, according to Guinness, who recalls that "All invitations I sent to her for lunch or dinner were declined. I think she was suspicious of me in some way, but I can't imagine why." B.D.'s recollection of her mother's opinion of Guinness offers a clue: "He's overbearing, egotistical, haughty, snotty, insensitive to play opposite and a dreadful actor."

Both *John Paul Jones* and *The Scapegoat* were greeted by mixed reviews, as were Bette's performances. The films made little money, and Bette's film career had again ebbed to a new low. When she returned to the United States, no movie offers awaited her, and she made the difficult decision to try her hand at series television. She filmed a pilot, "The

Elizabeth McQueeny Story," that was aired as an episode of *Wagon Train* on October 28, 1959. To Bette's chagrin, after she had deigned to offer herself for a series, the pilot was not picked up.

She had no choice but to look again to the stage. The writer/producer Norman Corwin approached both the Merrills to tour the country in a reading of works by Carl Sandburg. Bette was unfamiliar with most of Sandburg's writing, but her ignorance turned to enthusiasm after she immersed herself in his poetry and prose. Gary was enthusiastic, too, and Bette wanted to prove that she could succeed on the stage. They agreed to do the show, which would begin in Maine, and Bette moved back into Witch-Way as rehearsals began. In the back of her mind she hoped that working together this way would bring her and Gary closer and revive their marriage.

The experience had exactly the opposite effect. The couple began to fight almost immediately, and by the time rehearsals had begun in earnest, she had moved out of the house. "It didn't make the tour an easier one," she admitted, "but a contract is a contract and there was no out." Norman Corwin recalls no strife between Bette and Gary during the tour (which took them from Maine to the West Coast), possibly because by then both had accepted the fact that their marriage was over and there was little reason to continue battling.

The World of Carl Sandburg was a hit, especially in Hollywood, where Bette's old friends came out in force—not, as she had feared, to gloat over the fact that she was "through in pictures," but to cheer her. Her mother, now seventy-four, was in the front row as she had been so often before, and she looked surprisingly frail and elderly to Bette that night. Staring into Ruthie's eyes as she took her curtain call, Bette reveled in the thunderous applause. "It was also Ruthie's night," she wrote. "Her little girl was back in the chips."

When *The World of Carl Sandburg* got to San Francisco, Bette and Gary stayed in separate rooms at the same hotel they had occupied during the making of *All About Eve*. Margo Channing and Bill Sampson had had a "bumpy night" that lasted ten years. Bette had recently told Joe Mankiewicz, "You never warned me about the sequel," but maybe he had. At one point in the script, Margo says, "Bill's in love with Margo Channing. He's fought with her, worked with her, loved her . . . but ten years from now—Margo Channing will have ceased to exist. And what's left will be . . . what?"

Perhaps it was the memory of their unlimited dreams of happiness in 1950 that led Bette and Gary to shed the civilities they had carried with them from town to town and unleash, as Bette put it, an "explosion [that] could be heard around the world."

Gary left the show in San Francisco, and went to Hollywood to make a movie, his first in six years. He was replaced by Barry Sullivan, and later Leif Erickson stepped in. Bette didn't have the same chemistry with either man that she had had with Gary, and the box office suffered. The show drew only mixed reviews in New York and closed after several months.

At that point, Bette filed for divorce from Gary. "There was no longer any point in even trying," she wrote in her memoirs. "I am sure I have been uncompromising, peppery, untractable, monomaniacal, tactless, volatile and ofttimes disagreeable. I stand accused of it all. But at forty I allowed the female to take over. It was too late. I admit that Gary broke my heart. He killed the dream forever. The little lady no longer exists."

TWENTY-FOUR

O
n July 6, 1960, Bette stood before a judge in the Portland, Maine, superior court, her stance weary, her eyes downcast, and heard that she had been granted a divorce from Gary on the grounds of "cruel and abusive treatment." Her complaint had accused him of "excessive drinking, physical cruelty and irresponsibility." The judge granted Bette custody of B.D., Margot, and Michael, but allowed Gary visitation rights at "reasonable times and places." He was ordered to pay Bette $1 a year in alimony, $250 a month in child support for B.D. and Michael, and $200 a month for Margot.

This set the stage for nearly four years of ugly court battles between Bette and Gary, which began on July 31, 1961, after she petitioned the superior court of Santa Monica to strike all of Gary's visitation rights.

The court documents in the case reveal a furious struggle between Bette and Gary, carried out on both coasts, over his visitation rights to Michael, now nine, who became an unwilling pawn in his parents' attempts to wreak revenge on each other. In the 1961 filing, Bette charged that Michael and B.D.'s scheduled five weeks of vacation with their father would "disrupt the acclimation of the children in their schools and social life in the East . . . disturb them and make them recalcitrant and difficult to manage and supervise." For these reasons, she said, she was seeking to have the vacation rescinded. The court denied her request.

Undeterred, Bette was relentless a year later in her efforts to prevent Gary from seeing Michael, who was scheduled to spend one half of the 1962 Christmas holiday with his father. (B.D. had told the court that she didn't want to spend time with Gary, and she wasn't made to.) On November 26, Bette's attorney informed the court that "Michael [does] not wish to spend any of the Christmas vacation with the defendant [Merrill] nor alternate weekends with him. . . . He prefers to be at home with his mother and sister and it is more pleasant for him and he particularly wants to spend the entire Christmas vacation at home. Barbara and Bette Davis Merrill told me that he [Gary] has been intoxicated at many occasions and has committed acts of physical violence on these occasions."

The judge delayed a decision, and in December Bette's tactics hardened. She filed a court brief to say that "Gary is not a fit and proper person to have visitation rights with any of the children away from the home. He drinks to excess and becomes violently drunk on many occasions. He has been notoriously associating with at least one woman [Rita Hayworth] to whom he is not married and has travelled with her extensively, which has been highly publicized and proved to be a source of great embarrassment and humiliation to the children." Gary offered only this lame response: "It is untrue that I was intoxicated in the summer of 1962."

In a later statement, Bette attempted to show that Gary's house was "an unsuitable abode" for a child. "[It] is in an area which is cold, damp and foggy, which would be injurious to Michael's health. [Gary] does not have anyone to care for Michael's cooking, laundry or transportation. The beach building is not in an area which is for the best interest of a minor child. He is not a fit person to care for Michael."

Gary defended his residence: "This house is right on the beach front [in Malibu] and consists of three bedrooms completely furnished with all the necessary facilities. I am renting it for $4,000 a month. It is well heated and insulated." Gary then produced a loving note Michael had written him to prove that his son did want to be with him.

When the judge refused to curtail Gary's Christmas visitation rights, Bette asked that she be allowed to take Michael on a Christmas vacation to La Quinta, a resort near Palm Springs, during a period that would have sharply cut into his time with Gary. On December 21, she requested a hearing on the issue, and appeared with Michael in tow. Before making a decision, the judge took Michael into his chambers and spoke to him privately. When he again took his seat at the bench, the judge sternly instructed both Bette and Gary not to ask Michael what had occurred. The gist of the conversation could easily be guessed at, however, after the judge ruled that Michael must stay with Gary from December 26 to January 1, and that Bette would not be allowed to take him to La Quinta.

The ruling, the judge stated, was contingent on Gary's "not [being] under the influence of intoxicating liquor during that period and the defendant shall not subject himself to unpleasant notoriety or publicity."

Again, Bette was undeterred. On Christmas Eve, she demanded an emergency hearing and told the court that Michael was very upset at the prospect of spending Christmas vacation with Gary and had wanted to tell the judge why at the last hearing, but was not permitted to do so. She then produced a map that Michael had drawn that she claimed was an escape route to a hideout on Gary's Malibu property that he planned to use if he was forced to spend the holidays there!

Unconvinced, the judge declared that the visitation plan would remain in effect, and Michael spent the week with his father, apparently without incident. In January, another court hearing was held at Bette's insistence, at which Gary's weekly and Easter visitation rights were not only upheld but extended.

Over the next two years, Bette and Gary filed court briefs eight times. Bette continued to attempt to deny Gary visitation rights; Gary charged that Bette had violated the court order by refusing to allow him to see Michael; both filed "nuisance" charges against the other on several occasions.

Finally, Bette brought out the big guns: she hired Fred Otash, the private detective to whom Peter Lawford had gone for help the night Marilyn Monroe died, to follow Gary while Michael was in his custody and gather hard evidence of his irresponsibility. One of the items Otash gave to Bette was a photograph of Gary that showed him passed out, fully clothed, on his hotel bed, a half-empty bottle of liquor on a chest at the foot of the bed.

According to Otash, one of his men discovered Merrill in a sexual tryst with a male politician from Maine. This information did not turn up in court documents, but other observations by one of Otash's men, Michael Parlow, did. In a March 1964 petition by Bette to once again strip Gary of his visitation rights, Parlow contended that he had observed that "on January 24, Merrill left Michael in [their] room [at the Newporter Inn in Newport Beach, California] at 10:07 p.m. and returned the following morning at 7:18 a.m., and Gary was partying and drinking at various public places in the Newport Beach area but away from the Newporter Inn. On Saturday, February 1, 1964 from 9:45 p.m. to 7:20 a.m. he did the same thing. . . . On January 25 in the early morning, about 3 a.m., he had been drinking alcoholic beverages on and off the entire day and he entered a public highway and failed to observe two stop signs and one red light."

Parlow also reported that on February 1, Gary "engaged in a vulgar conduct in the presence of a minor child while pretending to sell a coat to a female from Chicago," and that on February 3, he was seen "associating with a young female in a room near where Michael had been left alone."

Despite all this sordid evidence, Bette was never able to curtail

Gary's visitation rights, in part because of his impassioned rejoinders. "Unfortunately," he said in one, "these repeated court appearances can have only the effect of causing great unhappiness to my son Michael who like any other boy loves both his mother and his father and can only be upset by the constant and recurring court appearances which are neither of his choosing or within his control. For visitations I have flown in from San Francisco, New York and even from San Juan, Puerto Rico to be with my son. I know my son enjoys these visitation periods and only the gravest emergencies would prevent my being with him on these occasions."

Gary claimed that the "incidents" in Newport Beach were "grossly untrue, exaggerated and misinterpreted. A warm close relationship has developed between Michael and myself over the past year and I know that the court will recognize that this relationship is in the best interest of Michael."

Bette tried to secure a restraining order against Gary twice more, and each time it was denied. The last court record of these battles is March 9, 1964, at which time Bette apparently gave up and allowed Gary to see Michael at the times originally set by the court.

In his autobiography, Gary says that Bette "shattered all my dreams, with her disdain for everyone's feelings but her own, her insensitivity, and her often humiliating insistence on having her own way. She did not care who was cut down with the sharp scythe of her tongue, she was self-righteous in her desire to be the queen, and she demeaned everyone who opposed her will. She had totally cut herself off from others. I finally understood why she had chosen *The Lonely Life* as the title of her [autobiography]—and she was welcome to it. I began to laugh at the marvelous joke. I felt a sense of liberation when I realized that Bette had been as big a fool as I."

Bette's decision to write her memoirs was prompted more by financial necessity than by a desire to share her most intimate memories with the public. With a contract already signed, she and Sandford Dody, a well-regarded ghost writer, began a lengthy collaboration late in 1960 that exhausted and perplexed the writer. After a promising beginning, as he and Bette sat in the den of her Manhattan townhouse, a fire popping in the fireplace, Bette inexplicably began to goad Dody, and she drew him into a heated disagreement over, of all things, the television commentator David Susskind. When Bette couldn't get Dody to agree that Susskind was brilliant, she exploded. "Bette was being Bette in one of her own films," Dody recalled. "She was having one of her famous 'let him have it' outbursts. She was seething, contemptuous, lethal."

When Dody continued to buck her, she "pulled out all the stops. Smoke and flame were escaping from her every orifice. Eyes were rolling, hands were flying, cigarettes waving. . . . Expletive followed expletive. Her range of invective was endless. . . . I was frightened. . . . This was a sorceress, and if at the end of her maledictions I was not dead or turned to stone, I was surely going to be out of a job. This was not a scene one survived, much less forgot."

But Dody never backed down, and finally Bette stopped screaming and sat silently for half an hour. Dody moistened his dry lips and ventured a question. She answered it. After an interruption by a phone call she returned to the den, stoked the fire, and turned to him. "You're not in awe of me, are you, Sandy?" she said.

"As an actress, as an artist, yes. Perhaps I am," he replied. "As a woman and a subject, *no*. If I were we would have a lousy book."

Bette walked over to him and extended her hand. "We will never have another argument, my dear," she said.

They never did, but Dody soon found himself frustrated by Bette's unwillingness to be completely frank about her life in Hollywood. Loquacious about her early years in New England and New York, she turned tight-lipped about her glory days; after more than half the book, she has only just won her first Oscar, and the rest of the memoir glosses over the very material her fans most wanted to know about. She is frank about two of her abortions, but mentions nothing about her affairs with Hughes, Wyler, Brent, or anyone else.

She *was* honest with Dody about her ambivalent feelings toward her mother, and in June he sent her half the manuscript. When Bette called him on July 1 (even though he was on vacation), he was sure it was because she'd loved what she read so much she just couldn't wait to tell him.

"Bette! How are you, darling? How did you ever find me—"

"Sandy," she sobbed. "Ruthie—Ruthie just died. That marvelous woman whom we've destroyed! Ruthie—gone! We can't, just can't go on with the book. Ohhhhhhhh!" Then she hung up.

Ruthie had died of coronary thrombosis at 8 A.M. in her home at 655 Ramona Street in Laguna Beach, with Bette and Bobby at her side. She was seventy-five years old. Bette was devastated; although her relationship with her mother had been mercurial and strained, she was convinced she wouldn't be able to function without her. Just as she had when her father died, Bette tortured herself with her conflicting memories of Ruthie's honesty and deceit, her sacrifices and extravagances, her strength and her childishness. Scenes of life with Ruthie rushed past her mind's eye: watching her make pies that filled the Winchester house with marvelous aromas; the exhausted Ruthie sitting in the audience at her graduation from Cushing; Ruthie hunched over her negatives in Norwalk; Ruthie coaching her night and day for her role in *The Wild Duck;* Ruthie dragging her out of the shower to take George Arliss's phone call.

Now that her mother was gone, Bette was racked with guilt. How could she have resented Ruthie's well-intentioned meddling in her life, or the indulgences she allowed herself when Bette was the highest-paid woman in the United States? "How dared I not understand that this cultivated, talented woman had given up everything for me; and then— only after my success was assured—exacted a price that could never nearly approximate her value?"

Bette always knew that she could count on Ruthie, no matter what, and that knowledge had provided her with a psychological crutch for fifty years. Now she was gone, and Bette knew that she would miss her desperately.

The orderly, organized Ruthie who had given Bette a detailed letter of instructions when she departed for the Cukor stock company in Rochester also left instructions to be followed after her death. "I intend to die as extravagantly as I have lived," she wrote. "I want my casket to be one of those silver things." Bette smiled when she read this, and later said that Ruthie could have had gold if she wanted it, but she was in no position financially to grant this last wish. Instead, she buried her mother in an oak casket at the Fairhaven Memorial Park in Orange, California. Later she decided she would rather have Ruthie moved to an elaborate crypt she had purchased for the family in Forest Lawn—overlooking Warner Brothers Studios. She would, she vowed, be buried right alongside her mother.

Bette's niece Ruth Bailey feels that "Ruthie would have had a screaming fit if she'd known that they had dug her up and took her way up there. But I always laughed, because there's no way I want to be buried there—with Bette and Ruthie arguing like crazy!"

At first shattered by Bette's apparent decision to shelve her autobiography, Sandford Dody was persuaded to go ahead with his work, and by the time he was finished Bette was in a more sanguine mood about publishing it. Still, Dody was not prepared for what happened when he submitted the final manuscript to her. She began to edit the book "with a butcher knife," he recalled. "Stories that she had told me with great feeling either disappeared or were changed radically. . . . Chunks—pages long—were removed, only a line or two replacing them with a rickety bridge between the remaining thoughts."

Most of Bette's cuts concerned Ruthie. When Dody protested, Bette snapped, "Just don't ever confuse my darling Ruthie with Gypsy Rose Lee's mother! Ruthie might have pushed but she was nothing like Rose, and never interfered with my work. Mother was a lady!"

Ruthie's death did little to change the curious relationship between Bette and Bobby. In 1959, while Bobby was hospitalized with appendicitis, tests revealed that her emotional disturbances, always vaguely called "nervous breakdowns," were actually a manifestation of manic-depressive syndrome. Her condition finally understood, Bobby was prescribed the relatively new drug Lithium to control her mood swings. According to her daughter Ruth, Bobby was "fine after that."

But still she was meek, withdrawn, and completely subservient to her sister, and their relationship continued to puzzle and concern Bette's friends. Their most frequent description of the sisters' interaction was that Bette treated Bobby "like a servant." (According to B.D., Bette once snapped at her for doing some work Bette wanted Bobby to do: "I *pay* her to do a job!") One anecdote is particularly revealing—and disturbing. Don Ovens, a longtime friend of Bette's, recalled a memorable dinner party at Bette's in the early '60s. Present were Bette, Bobby, B.D., Michael, Ovens, the lyricist Fred Ebb, and the actress Kaye Ballard. During lively cocktail conversation, Bette frequently, almost compulsively, applied fresh lipstick without looking into a mirror, and as her cocktail count mounted she unknowingly painted the tip of her nose bright red. Without a word, Bobby walked over to her and wiped off the misdirected lipstick. Bette didn't stop talking for a second.

When dinner was over, Bobby got up from the table, walked into the kitchen, and reappeared carrying small square slips of paper in her hand. She circled the table and put one square next to each guest's plate. On each she had written a dollar amount. *"Bobby!"* Bette thundered. "I told you we are *not* giving out dinner checks tonight!" Bette barreled around the table retrieving the squares and explained that her sister had recently been hospitalized. Bobby fled back into the kitchen, then reappeared shortly later to announce that the dishes were ready to be washed. Again, Bette responded harshly and Bobby retreated once more, never to be seen again that evening.

Bette's melancholy over the deaths of her marriage and her mother weren't alleviated by her return to work in a major Hollywood film, Frank Capra's *Pocketful of Miracles.* Based on a Damon Runyon short story, the film cast Bette as Apple Annie, a drunken Depression-era street peddler whose daughter Louise (Ann-Margret), whom she hasn't seen since infancy, is returning to New York to introduce her fiancé to Annie. For years, Annie has been writing to Louise, sending her money and leading her to believe that she is a wealthy socialite. Frantic, Annie enlists the help of mobster Dave the Dude (Glenn Ford), who believes that the apple he has bought from Annie each day has brought him good luck and protected him from his enemies.

Dave rents a Park Avenue suite, hires a staff of servants, has Annie made over by fashion experts, convinces an alcoholic judge to pose as her husband, and rounds up a coterie of hoods to pose as Annie's guests at a swell party. The elaborate charade succeeds; Louise is promised a dowry by her fiancé's wealthy father; Dave the Dude and his moll Queenie (Hope Lange) begin to think of marriage; and the alcoholic judge promises Annie he'll go on the wagon if she'll marry him.

Capra had filmed the same story in 1933, when its sentimentality and rags-to-riches theme affected audiences and made it a great hit. In 1961, the story was less likely to appeal to the day's more sophisticated audiences. Although it was her first major film offer from Hollywood in years, Bette accepted the assignment "not too enthusiastically" and primarily for the money. She had her doubts about her character. "Apple Annie lacked reality to me," she said. "I had to find a way to make it real and yet fit myself in the fairy-tale spirit of the picture. It was like walking a tightrope."

The production of *Pocketful of Miracles,* according to Frank Capra, was "shaped in the fires of discord and filmed in an atmosphere of pain, strain and loathing." Things got off on the wrong foot almost immediately, when Glenn Ford asked that Bette be moved from the star's dressing room next to his so that Hope Lange, his girlfriend, could have it.

Bette professed not to care—"You can put my dressing room at the end of the row if you like"—but studio executives were too smart for that, and Bette stayed right where she was. "It should have been this way," she conceded. "I was his costar. The request for my removal from the 'second' dressing room only showed Mr. Ford's bad manners and lack of professionalism."

The bad blood between Bette and both Glenn Ford and Hope Lange (neither of whom spoke to her except in their scenes together) worsened when Ford suggested in an interview that he had been responsible for Bette's "comeback." When she heard about his comment, she exploded. "Who is that son of a bitch that he should say he helped me have a comeback! That shitheel wouldn't have helped me out of a sewer!"

The atmosphere on the set continued to be, in Joseph Mankiewicz's wonderful phrase, "very *Macbeth*ish." Feeling embattled and outnumbered, Bette allowed her temperament to rush anew to the fore, and Capra developed crippling migraine headaches every day around noon. Asked about his star, he said he felt her behavior was prompted by "insecurity and delicate-spirited fears, especially after having been off the screen for so long." Hope Lange, for one, wasn't buying it. "Bette Davis," she retorted, "is about as delicate-spirited as a tank!"

As Bette had feared, *Pocketful of Miracles* was not a hit. Audiences failed to respond to its old-fashioned sentiment, and most reviewers found Bette's performance either one-dimensional or hammy. She preferred to forget the entire experience, she said, and she never did see the finished picture.

Bette had received no new film offers after she completed *Pocketful of Miracles* early in the summer, and her finances were at a low ebb. She had sold Witch-Way after the divorce and leased a townhouse on East Seventy-eighth Street for the New York run of *The World of Carl Sandburg* (which she kept while she also rented in California). Both Michael and B.D. were in private schools; Bette was still supporting Bobby; and she had paid for all the expenses of Ruthie's burial and reburial. The unexpectedly short run of *Sandburg* had left her strapped, and the money from *Pocketful of Miracles* and the advance on her autobiography hadn't gone very far. (*The Lonely Life* was a bestseller when it was released in the fall of 1961, but Bette wouldn't see any additional royalties from it for about eighteen months.)

Once again, however, Broadway beckoned to rescue Bette's career. She was rightly wary about the stage after the fiasco of *Two's Company* and the disappointment of *The World of Carl Sandburg*, but this time the project seemed tailor-made to Bette's talents, and a surefire candidate for success. *The Night of the Iguana* was a new drama by Tennessee Williams, one of America's greatest living playwrights, who had written some of the most unforgettable female characters in the history of Broadway. Bette accepted the offer, and she wasn't coy about her reasons: "Actors always say, 'I am returning to the stage to refine my craft,'" she told a reporter. "But that's a bunch of BS. No one leaves movies for the stage unless they can't get work. And I'm no exception."

The Night of the Iguana was far more than a poor substitute for a movie role. Her character, the vulgar, predatory, over-the-hill seductress Maxine Faulk, was one of the more vivid creations of the playwright's imagination. And not only would Bette create this typically strong, colorful Williams character on stage, but there was a good probability the show might lead to a major movie comeback for her as well. Since 1950, eight Williams plays had been turned into movies and had earned their female stars ten Academy Award nominations and three Oscars. Bette knew there was already interest in the play from Hollywood studios, and she found the prospect very exciting.

She began rehearsals in New York in the fall of 1961, more excited about a project than she had been for years. Over the next eight months, the backstage vitriol, chicanery, and fireworks of *Night of the Iguana* would make the plot of *All About Eve* seem like *Little Women*.

TWENTY-FIVE

I n the late summer of 1961, Frank Corsaro, the director of *The Night of the Iguana,* sat in a New York nightclub with Tennessee Williams and the show's producer, Chuck Bowden, and talked about how much difficulty they were having booking a theater for the show.

"They all tell me that we have to have a blockbuster name to star," Bowden said, "or we've got no theater."

Corsaro was astonished. "No theater for a *Tennessee Williams* play?!"

Williams looked up from the drink he was stirring and drawled, "Ya only ah-uz good as ya last show in this town." The playwright's last two plays had been flops, and now the theater owners wanted more of a guarantee than just his name.

"We've approached Bette Davis," Bowden announced, perking up. "She's interested in playing Maxine. It would be fantastic to have her— just incredible!"

Corsaro was skeptical. "Has she read the play?"

"Well, no," Bowden replied cautiously. "But I have sent her some material."

"What do you mean, *some material?*" Corsaro asked. "Didn't you send her the script?"

"No. I just sent her . . . because Tennessee's rewriting it, you know . . . so I thought I better just send her . . . material."

"In other words, you just sent her *her* sides?"

"Well, something like that. I don't want her to get the wrong idea."

"What wrong idea?" Corsaro shot back. "You're sending this lady material that is going to be the third lead. You're using this woman's name to get a theater and you're giving her a tertiary role? Do you think she's going to buy this?"

"Well, Frank," Tennessee piped up. "Ah think ah can work with the part, yuh know, give her some mo-ah things ta do—"

"I don't care what you do, Tenn, it's always going to be a tertiary role. Or else you're gonna have to write a whole different play."

"No, no, no," Bowden protested. "Trust us on this, Frank, it'll work out."

"I'm warning you," Corsaro said, "you're gonna have enormous trouble. I hear she's difficult under the best of circumstances. If you mislead her on this, just to get a theater on her name, you're going to have pandemonium."

The Night of the Iguana had its genesis in the late '50s when Corsaro, who had scored a success on Broadway with *A Hatful of Rain,* was asked to direct several one-act plays in Spoleto, Italy. Corsaro was a friend of Tennessee's, and he asked him if he had a one-act to contribute. Williams sent him twenty-one pages, and the minute Corsaro read them, he says, "I realized that this was a full-length play in the making. Once I got to Italy, I asked Tennessee if he could send me more, and he did. He kept sending page after page until I had a ninety-one-page script, which is a very long one-act." Still, Corsaro staged the drama in Spoleto.

The story Williams had crafted took place at a seedy Mexican resort run by Maxine Faulk, a blowsy, pot-smoking earth mother past her prime but desperately clinging to her sexual seductiveness. The drama grew out of a love triangle between Maxine and two of her guests: Shannon, a defrocked, alcoholic cleric now working as a tour guide—a man, in Corsaro's words, "who's suffering fever, an overdose of everything in his life"—and Hannah, a prim, penniless spinster who has come to Mexico with her dying grandfather.

Corsaro brought with him to Italy a troupe of Actors Studio members that included Patrick O'Neal, a handsome thirty-four-year-old journeyman actor who created the role of Shannon. Corsaro was very impressed with O'Neal's work. "What Patrick was doing was really quite spectacular," he felt. "He was just marvelous."

Once Corsaro and his company returned to the United States, they continued to refine *Iguana,* which by now had taken the standard three-act shape. They performed it at Lee Strasberg's Actors Studio in New York and at the Coconut Grove in Miami, and while there were several Maxines and Hannahs along the way, Patrick O'Neal continued to perfect his portrayal of Shannon. As plans coalesced to bring the play to Broadway, Corsaro went to bat for O'Neal to keep the part, despite the fact that he wasn't a box-office attraction. "He was giving the kind of performance that would have *made* him a very big star," Corsaro felt.

The producers agreed, but with an unknown playing the male lead, it became even more important that a strong box-office name play one of the two women. Enter Bette Davis. She loved Maxine Faulk, a character, she felt, who was "basically an animal, a good, healthy animal. She wants one thing—guys, and this one guy in particular. She's fairly direct, down-to-earth, uncomplicated. She has enormous laughter." Much of Williams's dialogue for Maxine was punctuated by a raucous "Ha!" It was very Bette, and she loved it.

After his nightclub meeting with Tennessee Williams and Chuck Bowden, Corsaro met with Bette in her East Seventy-eighth Street townhouse to discuss the role. He realized early in the conversation that she "was under the impression that her part was going to be developed. Bowden had managed to get her to sign a contract, which I wouldn't have done if I were she based on the script at that point."

The meeting was a tense one, and Corsaro got the impression that Bette was "terrified," not at all certain she could play a Tennessee Williams heroine on stage. "She had never done a dramatic role [on Broadway]. She had done that terrible musical in which she flopped so badly. She had a lot of promises from Bowden and Tennessee, but she hadn't seen anything yet. She was just a mass of fears and uncertainties. By the time we got to rehearsals, she was in a very belligerent mood."

When Patrick O'Neal heard that Bette Davis had been signed to appear opposite him, he jumped with joy. "The first time I talked to her, it was on the phone, and I didn't quite believe it. That Bette Davis voice came over the line and I thought somebody was putting me on." O'Neal's wife was as excited as he about the prospect. "Well," she said, "if you're ever going to have an affair, that's the woman I wouldn't mind you having it with."

O'Neal recalls that he felt "the highest possible anticipation," and he was flattered when Bette told him, "I would like to be in *your* play," an apparent concession that his part was the pivotal one. But he soon realized that Bette expected that to change, and he was no more optimistic about that possibility than Frank Corsaro had been. "Tennessee may have had the best intentions in the world, but there was no way that third part was ever going to lift up, because then it would be a whole other story. He could have given her all the pieces of business, all the best positions on stage and all the rest of it, and still that part is a third part. There's no way to beat that."

When she began rehearsals at the Schubert Theatre on West Forty-fourth Street in October 1961, Bette saw that so far Tennessee's rewrites hadn't enlarged her role very much. Assurances continued to fly her way, but she remained skeptical. Sensing that her back was being edged toward the wall, she attempted to exert more control over the production—both by acting every bit the temperamental star and by enlisting allies within the company. She insisted that Viola Rubber, who had been one of her "henchladies" during *Two's Company,* be named one of the producers of *Iguana,* and Chuck Bowden agreed.

The moment Bette met Patrick O'Neal, according to Corsaro, it was obvious that "she had the hots for him. She was much taken with Patrick, and she was trying to get at him to develop a romance." Despite the good-natured green light O'Neal's wife had apparently given him, he was having none of it. "It all had to do with control," O'Neal says. "That was a pattern in her life—you go for the leading man, whoever he happened to be. She resented that I didn't respond. I've often said, if I'd been Richard Burton, I'd have just done it and gotten on with it. But I was very young and terrified of being put under her control."

Bette took the opposite tack with Margaret Leighton, the lovely, sylphlike, ethereal thirty-nine-year-old British actress who had signed to play Hannah. Leighton had been delayed and arrived three days late for rehearsals. Tardiness was one of Bette's pet peeves, and the first words she said to Leighton when they were introduced were tart: "I guess we don't have to be friends in order to work with one another, do we?"

There was immediate strain between Bette and the rest of the company too, but some of it may not have been her fault. Bruce Glover, hired for a small part in his first Broadway show, was flabbergasted when Chuck Bowden took the cast aside and showed them a corner of the stage where he had placed a desk. "He told us that this was Miss Davis's area," Glover recalls, "and we weren't supposed to impose on her, weren't supposed to come within five feet of that little area. It was like he was setting up a barrier that made us all pull away. I doubt that she asked him to do that."

A few days into rehearsals, Corsaro saw that his predictions of disaster were likely to come true. Bette had long been a critic of the Method approach to acting developed by Stanislavski and taught by Lee Strasberg at the Actors Studio, and she now found herself surrounded by Method devotees. "One of the actors had to take his shoe off," she recalled, "and he spent the whole day working out the motivation for *why* he had to take it off. Finally I got so exasperated that I yelled, 'For God's sake, just take the damn thing *off!*'"

The problem, of course, went much deeper. "After about the third or fourth rehearsal," Corsaro saw, "she began to be aware of the kind of work that was taking place, which she didn't know how to do. She was afraid of the ease with which these actors worked. They didn't bang out results, they took their time and developed their characters."

It quickly became clear to Corsaro that Bette was jealous of Leighton—not just because her role was larger, but because she was a much more accomplished stage actress. "Margaret Leighton could literally transform herself into another character," Corsaro says, "but Bette was always Bette. She watched Leighton create this sensitive, many-profiled hysteria in Hannah. The coolness of the woman, her enormous stage technique, intimidated Bette."

Patrick O'Neal recalls rehearsing one long scene between himself and Margaret Leighton. "Bette couldn't wait for this 'boring' scene to be over with, and of course it was the best scene in the play! My wife and I shared a maid with Bette, and she reported to us that Bette hated to wait for that 'vampire' [Leighton] to finish so she could come back on."

As O'Neal and Leighton rehearsed this scene one day, Bette sat in the bleachers that had been set up for the cast on either side of the stage, dressed in slacks and ballet slippers, her glasses balanced on the end of her nose, her script in her lap. Suddenly she got up and began to pace back and forth in front of the bleachers, just feet away from the actors. She puffed on her cigarette, threw her head back and sighed, whirled around each time she came to the edge of the stage and started back across to the other side.

"She was doing her Bette Davis routine," Corsaro says, but the actors ignored her billowing smoke and the pounding of her footsteps and went on with their lines. Corsaro couldn't believe what he was seeing. "Bette started doing this whenever she wasn't part of a scene. It got to the point where I had to rehearse that scene at night, in secret, when Bette wasn't around. It was the only way I could get through it without disruption."

With O'Neal and Leighton creating their characters in a subtle, inward, Method way far beyond her experience, Bette apparently decided, according to Corsaro, "to come on really socko, whammo. And she got really gross. I would try to describe some bit of physical business to her, and she would grab me from behind and rub her tits against my back and say, 'Honey, you really mean like *this,* don't you?' "

A few weeks into rehearsals, sensing that her part would never be expanded and that O'Neal and Leighton were stealing the show, Bette exploded. She forgot her lines in the middle of a difficult scene, O'Neal muttered something, and that was it. "She went crazy and paranoid,"

O'Neal recalled, "and accused Frank and me of hurting her, sabotaging her performance."

"I'm sick of this Actors Studio *shit!*" she screamed. O'Neal, slack-jawed, just watched her as she ranted and raved. By now, he was a nervous wreck, drinking too much, wondering whether he would ever survive this experience. He bolted out of the theater in the middle of Bette's harangue and went straight to Max Jacobson, the same "Dr. Feelgood" Bette had relied on during *Two's Company*. "In order not to kill her," O'Neal told his wife, "I got the shot."

When O'Neal left the theater, Bette stormed off to her dressing room. Corsaro took a deep breath and followed her a few minutes later. He found Chuck Bowden on his knees in front of her, begging her to return. "It was a tableau," Corsaro says, "a scene right out of a movie."

Bette came back after Tennessee gave her further assurances of a meatier role. Corsaro saw that the playwright "was rather frightened of her, and he knew the dilemma he was in. He had gotten the theater on the strength of her name. He had to keep her happy, and he yessed her to death. But it was clear to everyone except her that any rewriting Tennessee was going to do would be of a very minor kind."

Bette quit twice more before out-of-town tryouts began (once she fled to a friend's house in Connecticut), but she was wooed back both times with flowers and telegrams and assurances that the play needed her desperately. Finally, with "fear and trepidation," as Corsaro put it, the company traveled to Rochester, New York, for their first performance before an audience on November 3. Bette had asked to open in Rochester, where she had appeared on stage professionally for the first time thirty-five years earlier. It was the start of one of the longest out-of-town tryout tours Corsaro had ever been involved in—four days in Rochester, four weeks in Detroit, five weeks in Chicago. The tour was so long, Corsaro explains, because of Bette's insecurity about her role, and the producers hoped the extra time would allow her to grow completely comfortable in the part before she brought it to Broadway.

During the train ride from Manhattan to Rochester, Bette asked Patrick O'Neal to come to her compartment for a chat. He dreaded the encounter, but instead of the harridan he expected, he found a charming, flirtatious Bette, apparently eager to make amends. "You know, Patrick," she cooed, "in Rochester your dressing room and mine are on one side of the stage, and Margaret's is on the other."

"Yes?" O'Neal didn't get the point.

"Just don't forget what side of the theater you're dressing on."

As he recalled it, "It was like a scene out of *All About Eve*. She wanted me to be her ally against Margaret. I was terrified at the thought and immediately had my dressing room moved to the other side. Very adult behavior."

The first performance of *The Night of the Iguana* in Rochester was a disaster; the audience laughed at just about every line in a play that wasn't a comedy. Some of the laughter was warranted, Bruce Glover felt —especially during one mishap that remains vividly in his memory, both as a comic moment and as an example of Bette's discomfort on stage. "The gal who played my wife came out for one scene bouncing a beach ball, and it got away from her. It bounced up in the air and came down smack on Bette's head. It bounced back off her head and went up another eight feet, so it must have made quite an impact on her. It came down and bounced again before the girl retrieved it. It was a rather amazing moment. The girl was terrified that Bette Davis would have her fired."

What astonished Glover and everyone else in the company was that Bette didn't react one bit when the ball hit her. She didn't laugh, didn't go with the moment and grab for the ball, didn't try to make it appear as though the accident was a part of the script. "She just stood there like the icon she was, without moving a muscle or expressing any awareness of the ball," Glover marveled.

"If that had happened to Geraldine Page," Patrick O'Neal says, "she'd *still* be bouncing that ball."

The first night in Rochester convinced Corsaro that the play needed a lot of fine-tuning, but the next day Bette wasn't available to rehearse. She had, she claimed, fallen and sprained her ankle backstage the previous night, and she was confined to a wheelchair. Her understudy was forced to go on in her place the second night—with script in hand.

Corsaro found the whole episode suspect, especially since Bette had appeared at a party after the performance in apparently perfect health. "Someone found out that it was only a minor sprain—she didn't need to be in a wheelchair. It was her way of getting sympathy, because the first reviews had come in that morning, and Margaret Leighton got the best notices. Bette was worried that her involvement in the show had been a big mistake."

By now, others in the company felt the same way. Corsaro hastily called a meeting of everyone except Bette, and Margaret Leighton broached the question of whether Bette should be replaced. "She really was very disruptive at this point," Corsaro felt. "She never allowed the play to take on any momentum. She insisted on revisions, revisions. We all thought the problems she was causing for the company would only get worse. By this time, she had created great dissatisfaction between her and Patrick, and there was a wall of politeness between her and Margaret. We all wondered, *What are we gonna do?*" The producers refused to fire Bette because without her they would have no theater. And so the *Night of the Iguana* company plodded on to Detroit, all the time hoping against the odds that matters would improve.

Not surprisingly, they didn't. Bette began to drink, and her behavior grew erratic, irrational. Suddenly Corsaro realized that there was a subterranean reason for this that had nothing to do with the size of her role or her distrust of the Method; it was the character Bette was playing. Maxine was a woman who was over the hill, losing her looks and sex appeal, desperate for a man, and all of this hit a little too close to home for Bette. "It was the role of a woman who was being rejected, constantly rejected," Corsaro explains, "and Bette was over fifty, she had just divorced Gary Merrill, she wasn't getting film offers. And here she was making plays for Patrick O'Neal that he wasn't responding to. I'm sure the part had an insidiously negative effect on her, and she got more and more frightened as she realized that her role wasn't going to be padded, and that Margaret Leighton was getting the best reviews. She was afraid that she was going to make a fool of herself."

In order to stand out more vividly on stage—and perhaps to prove that she still had sex appeal as well—Bette began to play Maxine far more sexily than Williams had written her. She dyed her hair flame red and wore a denim shirt open to the waist—a decision Corsaro thought was all wrong, especially when reviewers made cruel comments about her exposed flesh. Bruce Glover agreed with Corsaro. "Bette already had this little-old-lady body. She had a pot belly, boobs that were out of shape and had to be pushed up. If she'd used it to delineate the character, okay, but that wasn't why she did it. It was really Bette Davis trying to be beautiful." Despite the negative reaction, Bette did not change her wardrobe.

With O'Neal out as a conquest possibility, according to Bruce Glover, Bette made some overtures to his young understudy, Mike Basilione. "I can't say whether it was a sexual thing," Glover says, "but I know that she at least was lonely and wanted attention, and she wanted Mike as her escort. He was very unhappy because he felt he was being manipulated; he was made to feel that one way of holding his job was to be friendly to Bette."

By this time the company had divided into enemy camps, with Bette, Chuck Bowden, and Viola Rubber on one side, and everyone else on the other. Bette tried to get Corsaro in her camp, but he felt he had to retain some objectivity. "By this time I realized that Bette's participation in this show could destroy it. It was like being trapped in a nightmare. Everything was going wrong. One of the reasons Tennessee wasn't giving her the rewrites she wanted was because he was having vicious fights with his lover, Frank Merlo. He kept announcing 'It's over between us!' Then he got bit by his dog, Satan, and he was hobbling around on crutches. . . ."

Despite everything, Corsaro thought Bette gave a good performance on opening night in Detroit. "She was nervous, she was edgy, but that made her actually quite alive, and she was good. When she started to settle into the role, she became more of a caricature of Bette Davis. I could never make her understand the distinction."

Corsaro had come to realize that "there were twenty-five minutes of utter lard in the show that would have to be cut in order for this delicate play to emerge properly." He dreaded the thought, because in order to make the cuts he would have to truncate Bette's part. He was certain that would create fireworks, and so were the producers. "They told me I couldn't do that, that Bette was in a good mood, we can't upset her." Corsaro talked to his agent, Audrey Wood, and told her that unless he was allowed to make the cuts, the success of the play was in jeopardy. "I told her we had to go directly to Tennessee and get his okay. If we got that, the producers would have to shut up."

When Bette got wind of Corsaro's plans, he recalled, "She started to feel that we were all in conspiracy against her. And then, I swear to God, she started to go to the newspapers and spread stories about the play and the cast. Slanderous statements—she was convinced by this time that O'Neal and Leighton were having an affair, so most of her barbs were aimed at them."

O'Neal knew that "she had kind of a press game going on. *We* didn't have access to the press, but she did. It was just another way for her to exert control." Corsaro asked Margaret Leighton what she was going to do about Bette's behavior, and she replied, "I will not do anything about it. I will play my role, and I will not interfere in any way. You made an attempt to change this person, but you couldn't, and therefore we must take the consequences." Corsaro felt Leighton was so sanguine because "by this time she knew she pretty much had the play wrapped up herself."

Tensions heightened as the Detroit tryout continued. According to

Corsaro, "There were terrible problems, always a blow-up for whatever reason. The theater became like a battlefield. I went to talk with her, to try to ameliorate things, and I realized that this woman was like a ticking bomb. And then a very strange moment happened."

It was two or three weeks into the Detroit run. Corsaro, Tennessee Williams, and Chuck Bowden were in the empty theater one afternoon, discussing the show's many problems, when they noticed a cleaning lady carrying a bucket of water walk out on the stage and begin to mop the set. *This is odd,* Corsaro thought, and he looked at the woman more closely. It was Bette. "There she was, looking like a charwoman, with a pail of water and a mop, swabbing the floor. The three of us looked at each other and said, 'What the *hell* is going on here?'" Corsaro took a deep breath and told the others, "Let me talk to her."

He walked up on the stage and waited a few minutes for Bette to finish swabbing the floorboards. Then the two of them went backstage, behind the set. "She became the most pathetic child I've ever seen. She broke down in tears and cried out, 'Nobody likes me. Nobody likes me!' She was just self-lacerating. And I saw that I was really dealing with an eight-year-old girl. I thought, *Is this the impenetrable secret one has to find to deal with this woman? That under all that defensiveness was this rather pathetic child?*"

The Night of the Iguana limped into Chicago, and the reviews were scathing. As Corsaro recalled it, "The critic Claudia Cassidy, long a champion of Tennessee's, said that the acting was terrible, the directing was awful, *everything* was awful. Everyone knew that something had to be done, and I finally got Tennessee to agree to cut twenty-five minutes. Then came the dreadful day when I had to take the cuts to Bette." To his utter amazement, she accepted them without complaint. "There was not a peep out of her."

Bette didn't fight the changes because by now she wasn't just worried that the play might not showcase her properly, she was terrified that it could turn into an ignominious Broadway flop. After she reviewed the cuts, she called a meeting at the theater in Chicago that included Corsaro, Bowden, Viola Rubber, and Tennessee Williams. To everyone's shock, she demanded that Patrick O'Neal be replaced. His habit of improvising and experimenting with reactions and phrasing, she argued, was throwing off her concentration.

Corsaro was speechless. "This was maybe three weeks before we were supposed to open on Broadway. It was insane. Patrick O'Neal had been with this show from the very beginning, and he had been just brilliant. But his performance was suffering because of her. He couldn't stand everything that was going on around him, and he started to act like Shannon offstage, drinking and holing himself up in his hotel room. He didn't tell anyone his phone number, you couldn't reach him. He was completely incommunicado, hiding out from Bette Davis."

O'Neal wasn't so isolated that word of this meeting didn't reach him in a flash, and he turned up at the theater within minutes. Corsaro had never witnessed a scene quite like it. "Patrick went after her and almost killed her. He had to literally, physically be held back from strangling her. He called her everything in the book—'You filthy *cunt!*' He was wild, and she just stood there with a smile on her face. She seemed to be pleased that she had finally gotten a rise out of him. She was getting her vengeance."

O'Neal threw a table across the stage and stormed out of the theater. Then Bette demanded to know, once and for all, whether the substantive revisions she had been waiting for were going to be written. There was silence from everyone. *"Well?!"* Bette shouted. Corsaro turned to Williams. "Tenn," he said softly, "would you please level with Miss Davis, once and for all?"

Williams swallowed hard and drawled, "Bette, ah cahn't make any mo-ah changes. Ah think the play is just fahn the way it is." Bette's eyes popped. She glared at Williams, glared at Corsaro. Then she stomped out.

The changes weren't made, O'Neal wasn't fired, and from that point on, according to Corsaro, "it was mayhem. We were talking through lawyers most of the time." Bette started to miss performances, and Paula Laurence, who was Chuck Bowden's wife, went on in her stead. Corsaro thought she was "dreadful." And Bette repeatedly pointed out to Corsaro that without her the play's audiences dwindled. "She had this young lawyer who looked like her nephew or something," Corsaro says, "and he started to stand in the lobby holding this little mechanism that he would use to click off the number of people who asked for their money back when they heard that Bette wasn't performing that night. She'd hold that over our heads and say: 'I'm the star of this show.' Oh, it was like a nightmare."

The day after the scene with O'Neal, Bette had Corsaro barred from the theater. "She had decided that I was the enemy because I wasn't willing to do what she wanted. I had tried to talk to her quietly, but she thought I was conning her. All I was trying to do was hold the goddamn show together. But I was to leave the theater and never return. Chuck Bowden supported Bette in this. He took over and it was 'Yes, Bette, anything for you, Bette.' He kept giving her these little bits of business for her to do on stage to make her feel better."

Corsaro was still the director of record—he hadn't been fired—and whenever he could, he sneaked into the theater and scribbled notes about the performances that he slipped to the stage manager. "But Bette's young lawyer saw me and reported me." Corsaro felt as though he were "caught in the middle of a holocaust," but his frame of mind improved somewhat when Jerome Robbins sent a note to Audrey Wood. In it he reminded the agent that he had choreographed Bette in *Two's Company* and it had been a traumatic experience. "Jerry kept writing notes to Audrey telling her that if Bette had done this, this was the next thing she would do. And by God, it did seem to follow a pattern."

The producers asked the respected director Elia Kazan, in Chicago for a show of his own, to evaluate the play for them. Word got back to Corsaro that in Kazan's opinion the show was "beautifully directed, and it's now beginning to take its place, once you keep her quiet. She's not going to get any better, she's not going to get any worse. She doesn't hurt the play. Leave it alone. Leave her alone." In Corsaro's opinion, that advice from Kazan prevented things from going haywire once Chuck Bowden took over the directorial reins.

With tremendous anticipation—and four months of theater-party bookings presold—*The Night of the Iguana* opened on December 28, 1961, at the Royale Theatre on West Forty-fifth Street. Bette was a mass of raw nerves, totally unsure of what the public's reaction to her and the play would be. She could not have been less prepared for what happened when she made her entrance: a theaterful of rabid Bette Davis fans rose in unison to give her a thunderous ovation before she had uttered a word. The applause and cheers went on for five minutes ("an eternity," Bruce Glover felt), and every time Bette tried to say her first line, the cheers would increase rather than die down. Finally, she was forced to break character, walk down to the footlights, and acknowledge the hosannas—which she did by raising her arms over her head in the classic prizefighter gesture. Only then could the show continue. "My entrance followed all of that," Patrick O'Neal sighed. "And I was greeted by a flat, dead house. It was difficult."

The performance went well, but at the end of the show Bette was greeted by another, less pleasant, surprise. Now, it was Margaret Leighton who got the thunderous ovation, and it was clear that the audience felt she had given the better performance. Bette was devastated. Patrick O'Neal noticed that on subsequent nights, Bette actually prompted the tumult that greeted her entrance. "Some part of her brain knew that if she's gonna get an ovation tonight, she better get it right away. So she encouraged that and got it—and it was so transparent as to be rather touching."

The reviews didn't help Bette's self-confidence. Although the New York *Journal American* critic found her "brash and beguiling," the majority of the reviewers considered Margaret Leighton's acting far more impressive. The most influential of the critics, Walter Kerr of *The New York Times,* could muster only the faintest praise: ". . . in the coarse and blowsy effrontery of her flat-footed walk . . . there is some tattered and forlorn splendor." And Howard Taubman of the *Herald Tribune* was cruel. Bette, he wrote, "made much of her shocking flame-colored hair and her unbuttoned shirt that shows the flaccid flesh down to her waist."

Now, every performance was torture for Bette, and in another odd parallel with *Two's Company,* she began to have dental problems. "I had to reposition her teeth," Dr. Ivin Prince recalls, "because they were moving inside her mouth. They were spread out all over. She had to wear an orthodontic appliance, and for most people it would have taken at least a week to get used to it. But Bette had tremendous agility with her lips and tongue, and she went back on stage with it just like it wasn't there."

Prince recalls that during her visits Bette would wail to him about how "terrified" she was of the play. "She would tell me that she felt nauseous and ready to throw up, that's how scared she was."

While she was seeing Dr. Prince, Bette announced that she would be leaving *The Night of the Iguana* as soon as the four months of theater-party bookings were fulfilled. Tennessee Williams, afraid that the show would close without Bette as its star, frantically tried to call her at her hotel to talk her out of leaving. She deftly avoided him, but the next day Williams tracked her down at Prince's office. "Tennessee Williams came barrelling in," Prince recalls, "and started screaming at Bette that she would never work on Broadway again if she left the show so soon. Then she screamed back at him, and all the time I'm trying to work on her mouth. It was very emotional. By then I had had enough of *Night of the Iguana,* and I guess she had, too."

Bette did leave *Iguana* in April 1962, after four months and 128 performances. By this time, according to Corsaro, the cast members "had really grown to hate her. They had to keep their mouths shut to such an extent. She had made them feel like shit."

Word had spread around New York of the tension between Bette and Margaret Leighton; Bette reportedly called Leighton "a bitch" and added, "She's soooo congenial, she makes me sick." On Bette's last night in the production, she received three telegrams from Leighton telling her what a pleasure it had been to work with her. Bette was smug until she found out that Leighton had received similar telegrams signed "Bette Davis." They had all been sent by Noël Coward—because, he said, "They are two such silly bitches."

By her final performance, Bette was sick to death of *The Night of the Iguana*. She had been devastated to discover that she was not being considered for the film version, and she believed that most of the cast and crew had been in concert against her all along. According to B.D., Bette told the assembled company as they bade her farewell, "I'm soooo happy that everyone thinks Maggie is so *charming* and Patrick so *brilliant*! I'm sorry I had to irritate you for so long with my professionalism. You obviously like doing it your way much better. *Well!* Now you *can*, my dears!"

The Night of the Iguana was named the best American play of 1961–1962 by the Critics' Circle, and Margaret Leighton won the Tony Award as Best Actress. (Bette wasn't nominated.) The show ran another five months on Broadway after Shelley Winters took over the role of Maxine Faulk.

Over the past thirty years, Frank Corsaro, now the artistic director of the Actors Studio, has tried to fathom what he calls "the nightmare" of directing this show. Corsaro places the bulk of the blame with Bette, who he believes had a subconscious wish to fail. "In a terrible way, this woman was not supposed to succeed. All her life, she had had that demon. She was angry, angry to such a great degree, and at whom—her father? Who knows?

"I think she represented something of the motion picture horror.

The movies have created terrifying children who have become stars. Bette Davis's vanity was profound, and it had to be, because it masked a vulnerability that was just as profound. There is something terrifying about an industry that can create a false image of personal success and leave people clawing for the rest of their lives to live up to it."

A few months after Bette left the show, Frank Corsaro rented a summer house on Fire Island to recuperate. Sitting in a local bar one night, he noticed a man in a corner staring at him. He couldn't see who he was through the dark, and couldn't imagine why anyone would be watching him so fixedly. Then the shadowy figure got up and started toward him, and he saw that it was Gary Merrill. Corsaro thought, *Am I gonna have a fight with this guy?* He steeled himself as Merrill approached.

"You're Frank Corsaro, aren't you?" Merrill demanded.

"Yes," Corsaro replied warily.

"Why didn't you just *belt* her?" Merrill thundered. "I knocked her on her ass. That's what you shoulda done!"

PART FIVE

"Survivor"

TWENTY-SIX

Walter Blake, the personal assistant to the Hollywood director Robert Aldrich, slid out of his cab in front of the Plaza Hotel in New York. It was early summer, 1962, and he was a man with a mission: to persuade Bette Davis to star in Aldrich's film version of Henry Farrell's novel *What Ever Happened to Baby Jane?*, a thriller about a mentally unbalanced former child star living in mutual fear and loathing with her crippled sister in a decaying Hollywood mansion. In his briefcase, Blake carried a check for $25,000 made out to Bette.

"Bob Aldrich already had Joan Crawford signed to play the sister in the wheelchair," Blake recalls, "and he really wanted Bette to play Baby Jane. Bette was broke after she left *Night of the Iguana,* and she was staying at the Plaza on good will and credit. We heard she was in hock to them for $30,000."

The check Blake carried with him amounted to just about all the money Aldrich had, but he figured hard cash would be the best incentive he could offer Bette to make the movie. She knew about and liked the property, but she didn't want to work with Crawford, who had come backstage with Chuck Bowden and Paula Laurence after a performance of *Iguana* to try to talk her into making the film with her. Bette was unreceptive. "Let's make this quick, Joan," she snapped. "I'm leaving for the country in five minutes."

Crawford told her about the project and purred, "I've *always* wanted to work with you." Bette looked at her and thought, *This woman is full of shit.*

Paula Laurence recalled that after Crawford left, Bette ranted and raved that she had wanted to buy the property, that she couldn't stand the idea of working with Crawford, that she was suspicious of the whole enterprise. "If she thinks I'm going to play that stupid bitch in the wheelchair," she bellowed just before she left the theater, "she's got another think *coming!*"

And so Walter Blake's job now was to get Bette's commitment to make *Baby Jane*—by whatever means possible. "We knew she needed money, so we figured that if we got her to sign the back of the check, legally she'd have to do it." Blake first telephoned Bette at the Plaza, and the reception he got wasn't warm.

"Walter *who*?" Bette barked. "Never heard of you."

"I knew you at Warner Brothers, Miss Davis."

"Oh yeah. Waddya want?"

"I've got something that you're going to like."

"Oh yeah? Like what?"

Blake persuaded Bette to let him come up to her posh suite, where he found her in slacks and a middy shirt, her hair in a sloppy topknot, a cigarette in one hand and a drink in the other. When he showed her the *Baby Jane* script, she only glanced at the title. "I know about this. Who's gonna direct?"

"Robert Aldrich."

"Who the hell is he?"

"He's directed nine films, Miss Davis—*Apache, Autumn Leaves, The Angry Hills*—"

"I never heard of him! I bet he stinks. Who's producing?"

"I will be."

"I bet you stink, *too*!"

By now Blake feared he had made a huge blunder. "Miss Davis," he concluded as soothingly as possible, "perhaps we should meet again after you've read the script. Call me when you're finished with it and we'll talk—I'll take you to dinner."

"Can you afford it?" Bette asked as she showed Blake the door.

Bette found that she loved the way Luke Heller's script beautifully fleshed out the novel's dark, unsettling tale: as a vaudeville headliner circa 1917, precocious child star Baby Jane Hudson had played to packed houses. Resplendent in blond ringlets and flouncy crinolines, she belted out maudlin ditties like "I've Written a Letter to Daddy" (whose address was "Heaven above") to rapturous audiences. As obnoxious and spoiled offstage as she is cloying on, she completely overshadows her dark-haired, brooding sister Blanche.

By 1935, the sisters' roles have reversed; Blanche has become a top movie star, while Jane, her childhood charms vanished, gets film jobs only because of her sister's power. Jane is consumed with jealousy, then devastated by guilt when she blames herself for a car wreck that leaves Blanche permanently crippled.

The story then jumps to 1962. The aging Hudson sisters are mutually dependent. They live on income from Blanche's investments, but Blanche, confined to a wheelchair in an upstairs bedroom, must rely on Jane for her food and her contact with the outside world. Still racked with remorse about the accident, Jane has become mentally unstable and a heavy drinker. She often retreats into a fantasy world fueled by her memories of her youthful stardom. Dressed in outlandish outfits copied from her days as a vaudeville moppet, her makeup troweled on, her blond wig in ringlets, she drunkenly performs "I've Written a Letter to Daddy" in the mirrored music room as though she were fifty years younger.

Jane's descent into madness is hastened when she finds out that Blanche has secretly sold the house, and they must be out in six weeks. She cuts Blanche off from the outside world, stops bringing her food (except for her dead parakeet, and later a rat), and physically brutalizes her. At the same time she pathetically plans to stage a comeback.

When the cleaning lady discovers Blanche starved, gagged, and trussed up, Jane bashes the woman's head in with a hammer. Frantic that she'll be found out, Jane lugs her sister, now nearly comatose, into the car and drives her to the Santa Monica beach. As Blanche nears death, she confesses that it was she who caused the car crash when she tried to run Jane down. Completely gone now, Jane responds dreamily, "You mean all this time we could have been friends?"

Leaving Blanche to die on the sand, Jane joyfully performs her old dance routine on the sand as a crowd gathers and the police descend.

Bette was a bit put off by the script's Grand Guignol excesses, but she knew that Baby Jane Hudson was a great part, and that the movie could be a big hit, especially with younger audiences of the kind that had flocked to Alfred Hitchcock's *Psycho*. More importantly, Bette had no other offers—and she needed the money. She called Blake. "I read the thing," she said curtly. "I'll be playing Jane, right?"

Blake said yes, of course, then Bette barked, "So who's the *other* broad?"

"We don't know yet," Blake lied. He recalled, "I couldn't tell her it was Crawford because they were enemies. I had to get her signature on that check and then tell her, when she couldn't back out."

"I have a check with me for $25,000, Miss Davis," Blake said, "and I can give it to you if you'll sign on the back that you'll do the movie."

"Twenty-five thousand dollars for a *movie!*" Bette exploded. "Are you *crazy?!*"

"It's just a down payment, a binder to say that you'll do the movie. We can negotiate your salary, what you'll get up front, all of that."

"Oh," Bette replied, and Blake saw that he had been right: Bette did need the money. She took the check, and agreed to fly to Hollywood with him the next day to meet with Aldrich. Two days later, Bette walked into the production meeting with Aldrich, saw Joan Crawford sitting next to the director, turned on her heel, and walked out. "You've got to be kidding," she hissed at Blake. "I won't work with *her.*"

"Well, Bette, you've got to," Blake replied. "We just paid you $25,000." When she realized Blake was right, Bette went back into the meeting, seething over Joan's pious attitudes and ladylike airs. "There was no hello or good-bye," Blake recalls. "The two of them together were like a Nazi and a Jew."

Bette agreed to a salary advance of $60,000 (including the $25,000 she had already received), 10 percent of the worldwide gross profits, and $600 per week in living expenses. Crawford, in a shrewd gamble that later rankled Bette, took only $30,000 up front but 15 percent of the profits and weekly living expenses of $1,500.

Once Bette's participation was set, she made it clear to Aldrich what was paramount on her mind. During an early meeting, she turned to the rotund, forty-four-year-old director and asked, "Have you slept with Joan?"

"No," he replied. "But not for any lack of trying on her part." Bette liked Aldrich's honesty, and she felt confident that Crawford's penchant for seducing her directors in order to get preferential treatment from them would go unsatisfied this time around.

Unlike Bette, the fifty-eight-year-old Crawford was a striking beauty who had kept herself in good enough physical condition to play romantic leads through the 1950s. But she hadn't made a film since 1959, the year her husband, Pepsi-Cola mogul Alfred Steele, died. Steele had left her with little except a mountain of debt and a position on the board of his company. "I was lonely," Joan said to explain why she jumped at the chance to do *Baby Jane.* "I was worse than lonely, I was bored out of my skull. And I needed the money." Like Bette, Joan had a deep-seated need to work. "Inactivity is one of the great indignities of life," she said. "The need to work is always there, bugging me."

⁓

With his stars uneasily in place, Aldrich set out to raise money for the picture and was shocked by the chilly reception he encountered. "Four major companies refused even to read the script or scan the budget. Three distributors read the script, looked at the budget, and turned the project down. Two of those said they might be interested if I would agree to cast younger players."

Finally Aldrich convinced Eliot Hyman, the head of the small British independent company Seven Arts, to finance the picture with Davis and Crawford with a budget under $1 million and a shooting schedule no longer than thirty days. Jack Warner (of all people) agreed to distribute the film.

With Aldrich's assurances that this picture would be a blockbuster ringing in her ears, Bette decided to make a permanent move back to Los Angeles. With B.D. and Michael, she moved into a low-slung, contemporary, "flashy Beverly Hills house" that B.D. had found for them, complete with a projection room, a volleyball court, pool, and pool house. Bette had wanted a New England–style place, and when she saw this modern structure she said, "Oh, B.D., not another one."

"You told me to please *myself*," B.D. huffed in reply.

Bette's fifteen-year-old daughter was more a pampered princess than ever. She had brought her horse Stoneybrook to live with her at Grier, a private girls' school in Pennsylvania, and then sold the animal when she followed Bette to Hollywood, where her mother made sure she was cast for a part in *Baby Jane,* as a nosy neighbor's daughter. Bette let her keep the money she would be paid. B.D. told the press that she had acting ambitions, and although she would be billed in the film as Barbara Merrill, she later petitioned a court to have her name changed back to Barbara Sherry. She told the judge that she intended "to pursue a career in dramatic arts and intends to seek motion picture, television and stage engagements as a singer and actress."

On July 19, four days prior to the start of filming, Jack Warner hosted a press luncheon for Bette, Joan, and Robert Aldrich in the trophy room at Warner Brothers. The press coverage was tremendous, and there was much anticipation of a pyrotechnic feud between these two "former movie greats." Warner and Aldrich loved it, aware as they were that any publicity was good publicity. Photos of the two stars ran in newspapers around the world, and Bette pasted one in her scrapbook. Under the photo she scrawled, "W.B. gave a luncheon for the two former queens (only one in my opinion) at the beginning of *Baby Jane*. The horror is we look alike!''

They didn't really, of course, and from the outset of filming at the Producer's Studio on Melrose Avenue, it was clear to cast and crew that Bette Davis and Joan Crawford had very distinct personalities as well. Anna Lee, cast as the Hudsons' nosy neighbor, vividly recalls the two of them. "Joan would arrive at the studio sharp at one minute to nine. Immaculately groomed, she'd come in with her entourage: a makeup man, a hairdresser, a secretary—there were always seven or eight people trailing after her. She would waft very regally into her dressing room and gently close the door.

"A moment or so later, you'd hear Bette clomping down the corridor, all by herself, usually swearing like a sailor about something, using quite obscene language. She'd go thundering into her dressing room and slam the door. I really think her behavior was just to shock Joan. She was definitely needling her. She put a little card up on her dressing room door that said, 'Of all my relations, I like sex the best.' She knew it would horrify Joan, who was very straitlaced and didn't have much of a sense of humor about herself."

The film critic Judith Crist, who befriended Bette in the mid-1970s, feels that the differences between Bette and Joan ran deep. "They came from totally different classes, and your roots come out. Bette had a stage background, Joan had maybe a burlesque show or two. When you got right down to it, Bette was a lady, and Joan Crawford was not. It was ironic, because Bette would swear and lumber around, and Joan of course was all piety and refinement, but class will show. Joan would pretend to be drinking water when it was really vodka, and she'd drink herself stupid in public. Bette would never do that. And whenever Joan would call me all she'd talk about were the intimate details of her medical problems. She just didn't have any class."

Crawford was well known for showering people with little daily gifts as a way to win their affection, and Bette was no exception. The second day of filming, she found flowers in her room from Joan. The next day, a bottle of perfume. Joan had tried the same tactic when she had first come to Warner Brothers from MGM in 1944. Bette had been amused by the gesture and a little puzzled, until someone told her that Joan was sexually interested in her. She sent the gifts back unceremoniously, and never was sure what Crawford's motives had been. "How the hell do I know if Joan was a dyke?" Bette said. "I never let her get that close to me."

This time, Bette ignored the gifts at first, but when they continued coming she wrote Joan a terse note thanking her but asking that she stop. "I won't be able to reciprocate," she wrote, "because I do not have time to shop."

The note seems to have soured any possibility of a friendship between the two women. According to B.D., when Bette introduced her to Joan on the set, she extended her hand and Crawford "pulled back from me, putting her hand behind her back as if I were diseased."

"Hello, dear," Joan purred to B.D. "One thing . . . my daughters, Cindy and Cathy, are going to be on the set with me a great deal. . . . I would appreciate it if you would not try to talk to them. They have been very carefully brought up and shielded from the wicked side of the world. You, obviously, have not. I don't want your influence to corrupt them. They are so sweet and innocent, you see. . . . Thank you. Bless you, dear."

When Bette discovered that Joan had vodka in the Pepsi bottle she always kept at her side, she exploded. "That bitch is loaded half the time! How dare she pull this crap on a picture with me? I'll kill her!"

In her infamous account of her childhood, *Mommie Dearest,* Joan's eldest daughter Christina wrote, "Bette Davis was the consummate match for my mother's storehouse of intimidation tricks. She was a shrewd professional and every bit as indomitable as her costar. Years later, Mother would only have to hear her name mentioned to start a tirade."

There were no tirades as *Baby Jane* filming progressed at its breakneck pace through the summer of 1962. Bette and Joan, for all their animosities, were too professional, and too hungry for a hit movie, to slow production down with outbursts of stereotypical star temperament. Still, the atmosphere was often as frosty as the fifty-eight-degree temperature Crawford demanded on the soundstage. Joan needed the set so cold, Bette told friends, because she was always overheated from the vodka she nipped between takes.

And both actresses were frantic with insecurity. Joan fretted that Bette's much flashier role would completely eclipse her performance; Bette, always jealous of Crawford's glamour, ridiculed her comely appearance in the film. Soon they got caught in a game of one-upmanship: Bette "shoveled" on heavier and ghastlier makeup while Joan fought all efforts to make her look anything worse than a slightly faded beauty.

"Miss Crawford was a *fool,*" Bette felt. "A good actress looks the part. Why she insisted on making Blanche look glamorous, I just don't know."

"My reasons," Joan countered, "were just as valid as hers, with all those layers of rice powder she wore and that ghastly lipstick. But Miss Davis was always partial to covering up her face in motion pictures. She called it 'Art.' Others might call it camouflage—a cover-up for the absence of beauty. My character in *Jane* was a bigger star, and more beautiful than her sister. Once you've been as famous as Blanche Hudson was, you don't slip back and become a freak like Miss Davis preferred to see her character. Blanche also had class. Blanche had glamour. Blanche was a *legend*."

"Blanche was a *cripple*!" Bette snorted when told of Joan's remarks. "She was a recluse. She never left the house or saw anybody, yet Miss Crawford made her appear as if she lived in Elizabeth Arden's beauty salon."

As this struggle to establish dominance escalated, Joan and Bette both began to call Aldrich every night at home. "Did you see what that bitch did to me today?" Joan would wail. As soon as Aldrich finished with Joan, Bette would call. "What did that bitch call you about?" she would demand. According to Aldrich's son Bill, "My dad had to spend an awful lot of time trying to keep them happy."

"Mother was on the phone to Aldrich for at least an hour every night," B.D. recalled. "She would come home, take off her makeup, then, with hair flying all over the place, she would sit in her giant bed, in her master bedroom, with her papers all around her, and the phone. We would have to bring her dinner to her on a tray; then she would call Aldrich. She'd rehash everything that happened on the set that day, that Aldrich had to apologize for—all the slights she suffered that were unfair —and the terrible things Joan had done to her, which he would have to prevent her from doing the following day."

"First one, then the other," Aldrich said. "I could rely on it every night. They were like two Sherman tanks, openly despising each other."

If there wasn't a loud, raucous, public feud between these two *grandes dames,* there was a subtle and insidious one. Each woman tried to vex the other, put her off her stride, adversely affect her performance. As Joan acted a solo scene, Bette turned to Walter Blake and said, loudly enough so that Joan could hear, "She can't act, she stinks!" Afraid that Joan would storm off the set, Aldrich piped up, "I've got a terrible headache. We've got to get through this scene." When she finished, Joan pulled Aldrich aside. "Did you hear what she said about me?"

Another scene, one of the script's most harrowing, called for Jane to kick Blanche senseless on their mansion's tiled floor. To obtain the proper sound effects, Bette first viciously kicked a dummy out of camera range. Then she repeated the shot with Joan, feigning the blows. She performed the stunt flawlessly—except for one kick that grazed Joan's head.

"I barely touched her," Bette insisted, but Hedda Hopper reported that she had "raised a fair lump on Joan's head." Crawford got her revenge a few days later as Jane hauls the half-dead Blanche off her bed and drags her into the hallway. It was a difficult scene, and according to Aldrich, "Crawford wanted Bette to suffer, every inch of the way."

Just prior to action, Joan strapped a lead-lined weight lifter's belt around her waist, adding considerably to her heft. "It was one continuous take," the screenwriter Lukas Heller recalled. "Bette carried her from the bed across the room and out the door. Then, as soon as she got in the hallway, out of the camera's range, she dropped Joan and let out this bloodcurdling scream."

"My back! Oh, God, my back!" Bette shrieked. Seemingly oblivious of Bette's agonies, Joan stood up, and as a small smile of satisfaction spread across her face, walked elegantly off the set.

Joan had one last laugh on Bette. As Blanche nears death from starvation, there was no way Joan could look anything but awful, and her makeup reflected that. But Bette noticed that Joan's bosom grew fuller each day. *"Christ!"* she bellowed to B.D. "You never know *what* size boobs that broad has strapped on! She must have a different set for each day of the week! . . . She's supposed to be shriveling away while Baby Jane starves her to death, but her tits keep *growing*! I keep running into them like the Hollywood *Hills*!"

During the last week of filming, Bette pulled Walter Blake aside and asked him, "When is this goddamn picture gonna end?"

"It's supposed to wrap this Friday night," Blake assured her. "Why?"

"I want to go to bed with Bob Aldrich."

"But he's married!" Blake sputtered.

"You old-fashioned sonofabitch," Bette laughed. "What's the matter with you? What the hell do I care if he's married?"

Bette had convinced herself, B.D. recalled, that Aldrich "was madly in love with her and couldn't stand Joan." Apparently Bette felt it more honorable to sleep with the director at the end of filming, rather than at the beginning, as Joan had preferred.

"I'm going to throw a big party the last day of filming," Bette told

Blake. "I want everybody who worked on the picture to be there. And I want you to be *certain* that Bob shows up." The clear implication, the producer knew, was that Bette planned to seduce Aldrich that night.

Aldrich wanted nothing to do with Bette's romantic fantasy, and he used the heavy rain the evening of the party as an excuse not to go. Bette, however, wasn't about to let her prey off the hook that easily. Amid more than a hundred guests (they did not include Joan Crawford, who, Walter Blake says, had "high-tailed it back to New York"), Bette kept asking Blake, "Where's Bob?"

"I don't know, Bette."

"Well, *call him,* for crissakes!"

Blake did as he was told. "Do I *have* to go through with this?" Aldrich pleaded.

"We've got to keep her happy, Bob. You don't want her getting her nose out of joint and refusing to do publicity or something. Come to the party. You can finesse things."

Aldrich relented, but when he got to Bette's house his car became mired in mud. He honked his horn and Blake ran out to his boss's little sports car. "I'm going back!" Aldrich called out through the driving rain. "This is ridiculous! Find somebody to take me home."

Frantic, Blake looked back toward the house. "But what about *her?*"

"*You* take care of her," Aldrich responded, and rolled up the window.

If Bette was disappointed by Aldrich's lack of sexual interest in her, she was greatly encouraged by the word-of-mouth on *Baby Jane.* Even in rough cut, it was clear that the picture was good, the performances were vivid, and that the picture had a strong chance to be a blockbuster. Confident that she was on the cusp of a major comeback, Bette approached Jack Warner for a $75,000 loan against her share of the film's profits so that she could buy a New England–style cottage at 1100 Stone Canyon in the exclusive enclave of Bel Air. When Warner saw the picture, he wrote out a check. Bette christened her new home Honeysuckle Hill.

Back in Hollywood permanently, and certain that her star was again on the ascent, Bette was emboldened to announce to the motion picture industry—in a unique, provocative way—that she was ready for more work. On the morning of September 21, readers of the motion picture bibles *Daily Variety* and *The Hollywood Reporter* raised their eyebrows when they saw a help-wanted ad accompanied by a photo of Bette Davis:

> Situation Wanted, Women: Mother of Three—10, 11 & 15—divorcee. American. Thirty years experience as an actress in motion pictures. Mobile still and more affable than rumor would have it. Wants steady employment in Hollywood. (Has had Broadway.) Bette Davis c/o Martin Baum, G.A.C. References upon request.

For an investment of $500, Bette's ads brought her enormous publicity, but not all of it was positive. Her associates knew of her sometimes sardonic sense of humor, and saw the ad as vintage Davis cheek. But others were stunned by what they perceived as a washed-up former great begging for work. The truth lay somewhere in between, and Bette's comments at the time reflected both sides. "The ad was tongue-in-cheek," she told the press, "but it was a deep dig as well. My career was not in jeopardy; if I was truly unemployed, I could never have taken the advertisement."

Four days later, Bette spoke to the Hollywood Women's Press Club, and admitted that she had placed a lot of stock in the advertisement: "I have flung down the gauntlet. . . . I am back with a vengeance. . . . I may fail in my attempts to regain my place in the sun, but I do ask for the chance to prove whether I can or can't."

Less than a month later, her prospects looked good. *Baby Jane* was previewed at the Pantages Theatre in Hollywood, and *Boxoffice Magazine* sensed a phenomenon in the making. The picture, their critic thought, was "a memorable movie-going event . . . the applause was so tremendous at times it was difficult to hear the dialogue. Both actresses give nothing less than Oscar-winning performances." Word spread that *Baby Jane* was a stunning comeback for both these movie legends, and when a second screening was held in New York, the crush of fans was so thick that it took Joan Crawford thirty minutes to get from the theater lobby to her car.

What Ever Happened to Baby Jane? opened on November 6 in a national saturation booking. Overnight, the picture became a sensation, the movie everyone *had* to see. The film earned back its production cost in just eleven days, catapulting Joan and Bette back to the top of the heap—and back in the money as well.

While audiences—especially young viewers—loved the movie, it sparked fierce controversy among some critics whose memories of Bette and Joan were locked into *Dark Victory* and *Mildred Pierce*. The reviews ran the gamut from raves to harsh put-downs.

"*Baby Jane* is one of the best shockers since *Psycho*," Harrison Carroll wrote in the *Los Angeles Herald-Examiner*. "Robert Aldrich has extracted the utmost in shudders from this tense thriller. It makes the flesh crawl." For *Saturday Review*, Arthur Knight raved that "*Baby Jane* achieves its goal with something breathlessly close to perfection. It is a shocker, and at the same time a superb showcase for two of Hollywood's most accomplished actresses. Scenes that in lesser hands would verge on the ludicrous simply crackle with tension—or, as in the shots of Miss Davis dancing raptly on a crowded beach, they are filled with unbearable pathos."

Most of the naysayers were concentrated in New York. The *Daily News* gave it just two and a half stars out of a possible four and questioned the taste and judgment of Davis and Crawford for accepting such an "unworthy" vehicle. Bosley Crowther in *The New York Times* labeled Bette and Joan "a couple of formidable freaks" and added that the picture ". . . does not afford either the opportunity to do more than wear grotesque costumes, make up to look like witches and chew the scenery to shreds."

When B.D. saw the picture, she turned to Bette and said, "This time you've gone too far, Mother." But at least one of Bette's associates thought she wasn't acting at all. Her former secretary, Bridget Price, told Virginia Conroy after she saw the film that this was "the true Bette—screaming, laughing hysterically and generally being as bawdy as possible."

The most perceptive of the critics was Andrew Sarris in *Movie* magazine, who predicted, "Like *Psycho*, *Baby Jane* seems destined to be seen and not honored." The comparison was apt. While *Baby Jane* wasn't in the same league as the Hitchcock classic of two years earlier, both films had been crafted on a limited budget by a sure-handed director who wasn't afraid to limn some delicious moments of black humor out of a gothic horror story. Both films broke box-office records even as they polarized the critics.

Where *Baby Jane* differed most from the story-driven, delicately acted *Psycho* was in the staggeringly over-the-top performance of Bette

Davis. With her face caked with chalky-white makeup, her eyes ringed in heavy black mascara, her wig a frowsy mass of ringlets, Bette attacked the role of Jane Hudson with all the strength, courage, vigor, and abandon that only a cinematic artist of her genius could muster. Sloppy, bellicose, and bitchy, she slouches defiantly through the first few scenes in a flat-footed walk she told a friend she modeled on her sister Bobby's. In many ways her Jane is not unlike what the Mildred Rogers of *Of Human Bondage* might have turned into had she lived long enough.

Bette delineates Jane's mercurial emotional shifts with acuity. She is a vile harridan one moment, a simpering, terrified child the next. Hateful, she nonetheless evokes real sympathy when she sees her haggard, grotesque face come into sharp focus in the mirror—perhaps for the first time—in the midst of one of her pathetic vaudeville flashbacks.

Crawford's performance, far subtler, is outstanding as well, especially considering what a passive victim Blanche must have seemed on paper. Her almost masculine face and keenly expressive eyes give Blanche an inner strength that would have been missing with most other actresses and that makes her growing dependence on Jane all the more pathetic. As one critic observed, Joan's performance provided "the eye of the hurricane" around which Bette stormed. One actress was fire and wind and fury, the other granite. Together they created an unforgettable team.

Flush with the movie's success (she called it "a miracle" and "one of the greatest hits that ever *lived*!"), Bette threw herself with tremendous gusto into *Baby Jane* promotion. After the film's publicist suggested that some of the public might think she really looked like Jane, she decided to embark on a grueling three-day personal appearance tour that took her by bus to seventeen neighborhood theaters in the New York City suburbs. She appeared on stage with B.D., raffled off Baby Jane dolls, and accepted a frenzy of public adulation she hadn't experienced since the 1940s. (B.D.'s brief performance in the film, stiff and awkward, proved that acting talent isn't always hereditary.)

Reveling in the role of underdog, Bette loved to tell the story of how difficult it had been for Bob Aldrich to raise money to make *Baby Jane*. "Everybody in Hollywood told him not to make a picture with two old broads!" she cackled on national television. The next day she received a telegram from Joan Crawford: "Please do not refer to me in that manner in the future." Crawford, who professed to "hate this fucking picture," stayed home, but her lack of support for the film hardly mattered: when all was said and done, Joan made over $1 million in *Jane* profits and Bette nearly $600,000. (The discrepancy kept Bette in a stew for years.)

On February 25, 1963, *What Ever Happened to Baby Jane?* received five Academy Award nominations: Best Supporting Actor for Victor Buono as the fat, pasty mama's-boy piano player Jane ropes into helping her with her comeback; Best Black and White Cinematography (Ernest Haller); Best Costumes (Norma Koch); Best Sound—and Best Actress for Bette, her first nomination in ten years.

Observers were surprised that Crawford had been overlooked, but 1962 had been a strong year for female performances. Bette's competitors were Anne Bancroft in *The Miracle Worker,* Katharine Hepburn in *Long Day's Journey into Night,* Geraldine Page in *Sweet Bird of Youth,* and Lee Remick for *Days of Wine and Roses.*

Of all the *Baby Jane* legends, the most apocryphal is one perpetuated by Bette, who claimed that Joan, devastated at having been overlooked, actively campaigned to deny her costar the Oscar. "She told people not to vote for me," Bette huffed to friends.

Walter Blake never heard anything like that, and he doubts it happened. "For one thing, Joan Crawford didn't have that kind of influence in this town at that time. There were just as many Academy voters who disliked her as disliked Bette. And besides, both of them were hungry for money. Joan was smart enough to know that if Bette won the award it would boost the picture's box-office take—from which Joan was making more than Bette."

If Joan didn't lobby against Bette, she did make sure that she'd have the last laugh on her. She telephoned all the nominees and offered to accept the award for them if they weren't able to attend the ceremonies. As luck would have it, three of the actresses were absent that night. Joan's chances looked good.

Bette, decked out in a flattering Edith Head gown, her face temporarily lifted with tapes under her wig, left Honeysuckle Hill late in the afternoon of April 8 convinced she would win her third Oscar. She later said that before she left she had placed a rose between her first two Oscars—"those two tarnished boys"—and said, "Tonight, you're going to have a young brother."

When Anne Bancroft's name was announced as the winner, Bette said, she "nearly dropped dead. I sat there backstage and I heard her name and I thought, 'It isn't mine.' I was paralyzed with shock." Bette's disappointment turned to anger when, seconds later, Joan Crawford glided past her with a murmured "Excuse me," strode on stage to one of the night's most enthusiastic ovations, and accepted Bancroft's Oscar.

Although Bette had every right to expect that she might win, she should have realized that *Baby Jane* was not the kind of serious, uplifting, noble cinematic effort the Academy traditionally prefers to honor. (Bancroft had, after all, played Helen Keller's teacher Annie Sullivan.) Never a good loser, Bette carped (just as she had in 1951) that someone who perfects a performance on Broadway and then transfers it to film (as Bancroft had) has an unfair advantage over another actor who creates a character in a matter of weeks. And she continually blamed Crawford's meddling for her loss of the last Oscar for which she would be nominated.

At home after the ceremonies, her misery "had loads of company," Bette said. "It was an amazing experience. We all came back, Robert Aldrich and about ten of us and you should have seen us standing around like numbskulls. My children were there and they said, 'Oh, Mother, this is ridiculous'—and they *never* get involved in my career. It was a sad experience, it really was.

"That was the last amount of emotion I will give to the Academy Awards. I really don't care anymore. Quite honestly, I hope I'm never nominated again."

TWENTY-SEVEN

B.D. was miserable. She and Bette were in Cannes for the presentation of *What Ever Happened to Baby Jane?* at the city's annual film festival, and their traveling companion Viola Rubber had arranged for an escort to take B.D. to the screening. When Viola told her that her date, Jeremy Hyman, was an executive of Seven Arts, she envisaged a squat, bald, cigar-chomping mogul who would only bore her and keep her from enjoying the company of "all those lecherous Frenchmen." B.D. was sure she'd get a great deal of attention from the Gallic charmers after several of her mother's press profiles called her "a statuesque, green-eyed blond beauty." She dreaded spending the evening with someone who could only be a middle-aged toad.

Jeremy Hyman wasn't very excited either about the prospect of escorting Bette Davis's sixteen-year-old daughter that evening. *He* couldn't help but imagine he'd have an obnoxious child with braces and pigtails on his arm all night. When he knocked on the door of Bette's suite and B.D. opened it, he looked over her shoulder to find the gawky adolescent he expected. When B.D. introduced herself, Jeremy couldn't believe his eyes. His date could have been at least twenty-one—and a pretty, blond, bosomy twenty-one-year-old at that.

She was equally astonished. Jeremy, twenty-nine, was tall and handsome, and had a charming English accent. As he offered B.D. his arm and began to escort her out the door, both of them overheard Bette mutter to Viola, "My God, Viola, what have you done?! The son of a bitch looks like Leslie Howard! I thought you said he was a producer."

B.D. saw Jeremy smile slightly, and the two of them told each other how much they had dreaded the date and how pleasantly surprised they now were. As the evening progressed, Bette couldn't miss the look in B.D.'s eyes, and B.D. thought her mother seemed "in distress." For months, Bette had talked about how much she enjoyed traveling with her daughter, and B.D. suspected she would be delighted if they remained exclusive companions for the rest of their lives. Clearly, B.D. decided, Jeremy represented a threat to Bette's plans.

The couple had the good luck to be seated at a separate table from Bette's at the after-screening dinner, and in the course of the evening they found themselves alone on a balcony overlooking a glorious view of a valley. Years later, B.D. rapturously recalled their first kiss. "I saw shooting stars, heard bells and, when we finally stepped apart, I felt dizzy." She and Jeremy didn't realize it at the time, B.D. said, but they had already fallen in love.

Bette's agitation grew the next morning when B.D. left the suite at 8 A.M., wearing a revealing bikini, to meet Jeremy for a swim. She sensed a real potential for trouble here. She had treated B.D. as an adult practically since her infancy, and the girl's intelligence and strength of character had made her just about Bette's equal since she was twelve. Many of Bette's friends thought that not only had she spoiled B.D. dreadfully, but she had allowed the child far too much latitude. Bridget Price told Virginia Conroy in 1962 that B.D. "is too old for her years—only fourteen and Bette allows her to drink whiskey and soda and smoke, go on dates, etc. Do you wonder there are juvenile delinquents?"

B.D. had begun to date at twelve, and among her escorts was the handsome actor George Hamilton, eight years her senior. According to B.D., after each date Bette would accost her at the front door and demand to know if she was still a virgin. B.D. interpreted this either as Bette's attempt at a vicarious thrill or a way actually to push B.D. into her first sexual encounter. She doesn't seem to have considered that Bette might have had a motherly concern that B.D., sexually provocative beyond her years, could be taken advantage of. (B.D. has never said whether she lost her virginity during this period, but she did write obliquely that she had "been a woman since I was twelve when I had, at her instigation, begun dating.")

Bette seemed mostly concerned that her daughter not be hurt as B.D. spent more and more time with Jeremy Hyman in Cannes. At one point she warned her daughter, "You're going to get kicked in the teeth just like I always did. You're much too young for a man like that to take seriously. He's either playing you along and you'll be dumped, or he wants you because you're my daughter. Take my word for it . . . I know about these things."

When B.D. dismissed her mother's concerns and continued to see Jeremy, according to her, Bette changed her tactics. Aware that B.D. and Jeremy had a date one afternoon, Bette stalled, lingered, and changed plans during a morning in Nice with B.D. until she missed her rendez-vous in Cannes with Jeremy. When the two finally did meet up, the atmosphere was tense until B.D. proved that she had telephoned Jeremy with word that she would be late—a message he had not received.

B.D. was appalled at Bette's attempts to keep her away from Jeremy, but others were equally amazed that Bette allowed the two to spend any time alone together at all. As Bette's friend Judith Crist put it, "She was just *a little girl.*"

That was of no concern to Jeremy. After he took B.D. to a romantic dinner in St. Paul de Vence, they strolled the grounds of the Colombe d'Or, a medieval citadel-turned-hotel. On a stone bench in the midst of glorious gardens, Jeremy told B.D. that he loved her. He asked her not to respond, but to think about what he had said. On the drive back to Cannes, B.D. was afraid that at any moment she would awaken from this dream.

⁊◠◡

Back at Honeysuckle Hill, B.D. moped and pined for Jeremy. After Cannes they had spent a marvelous four days in London (where Bette had met with Carlo Ponti to discuss his new film), and B.D. had told Jeremy she loved him. When Bette agreed to make *The Empty Canvas* for Ponti, B.D. was ecstatic: it meant she would be returning to London, and Jeremy, in a few months.

Now, that seemed an eternity away, and Bette apparently felt sympathy for B.D.'s romantic anguish. When Jeremy called three days after they had left London and proposed marriage, Bette got on the phone and—to her daughter's great surprise—told him, "It's about time! B.D.'s miserable without you!" Joyful and overwhelmed, B.D. made plans for an engagement party in six weeks, when Jeremy would be able to fly to California.

Bette's friends were stunned by the news. How could she allow her teenage daughter to marry a man almost twice her age? Over the years, Bette gave a variety of reasons for her decision. She told Judith Crist that B.D. was "the kind of girl who *better* be married at sixteen"—meaning, Crist thought, that she feared that the amply developed, sophisticated B.D. was likely to "get in trouble" unless she had a marriage certificate.

Bette told several friends that she was well aware that Jeremy was a father figure to B.D., and that this had in fact helped to sway her in favor of the marriage. "She never even *knew* Sherry, for crissakes," Bette said.

"And Merrill was no father. She *hated* him. Maybe she could use a daddy in her life. Christ knows I could have!"

She didn't say quite the same thing to reporter Godfrey Winn, but she did stress that she considered Jeremy's age a plus: "I [would not] have approved," she said, "if the boy she wanted to marry had been almost as young as herself. I would have fought it tooth and nail. I consider this modern craze for marrying almost in the teens is asking for trouble. Barbara fell in love with somebody much older than herself . . . not only mature, but suitable in every way."

According to B.D., Bette's private opinion of Jeremy Hyman was quite different. During a vicious, totally unexpected fight while the engagement party preparations were underway, Bette railed against Hyman for not trying to "woo me over" and accused B.D. of caring for nothing but her "precious little love affair."

"You don't give a *damn* about me," she spat. "Well, let me tell *you* something, young lady . . . if I wanted to I could take him away from you right now!"

B.D. recalled that she turned red with fury. "Good God, Mother, are you out of your mind? One minute you can't stand Jeremy . . . the next minute you're going to take him away from me! Well, if you want to show your future son-in-law what a weirdo you are, go ahead and try it! But if you think he's one of those sycophants I used to get stuck with who went out with me in order to be able to fawn all over you, you're in for a hell of a shock! . . . Go ahead and try it! I dare you!"

With that, Bette began to sob and pleaded, "Don't do this to me, B.D. . . . not today. You know that all I want is the best for you. I know all about men . . . they're shits, every one of them. I just don't want you to get kicked in the teeth like I always was. Have it your way, but you just wait and see . . . he'll dump you. Then you'll realize that the only person who really loves you is me. You wait and see."

To this day, B.D. believes that the only reason Bette agreed to her marriage was that she was certain it was doomed and fully expected B.D. to come "crawling home" to her in six months. Equally convinced that the union would last forever, B.D. happily looked forward to her engagement party at the Bel-Air Hotel, and her wedding day, which she and Jeremy agreed would be January 4, 1964.

In the meantime, Bette went back to work. The picture, to be called *Dead Pigeon*, brought her back to the Warner Brothers lot for the first time in fourteen years. Very much a throwback to the melodramas she had done at the studio in the '40s, the story concerned a pair of murderous twins, one a wealthy socialite, the other the bankrupt owner of a bar who kills her sister and assumes her identity. The story resembled *A Stolen Life* in many ways, and just to complete the connection to Bette's past, her two-time costar Paul Henreid signed on to direct, and both Jack Warner and Steve Trilling were involved in the production.

Warner didn't like the film's title, and he asked his story department to come up with some alternates. Among those proffered were *Scream!*, *The Golden Girls, Duel Me Deadly, The Fake and the Phony, Hate the Sin*, and *The Murder of Myself*. Happily, all these were forsaken for the film's final title, *Dead Ringer*.

By all accounts, Bette was an angel on this production; her affection and regard for Paul Henreid seemed to make the difference. "I understood her temperament and her peculiar gifts," Henreid recalled. "I knew what she thought was effective for her." The film's assistant director, Phil Ball, was amazed at Bette's patience every morning during the nearly three hours it took to prepare her to face the cameras. "Bette had to go through extensive makeup. There was a lot of face lifting and that sort of thing. But she was a pro. She was always ready. Of all the actresses I've ever worked with, Bette was the most professional. I'm talking about acting ability, being on time, cooperating, her attitude, the whole nine yards. Totally professional."

Bette even showed patience with Peter Lawford, who had been cast as the gigolo lover of the rich sister. Depressed over his involvement in the death of Marilyn Monroe, ostracized from the Sinatra Rat Pack, mired in an unhappy marriage to President John F. Kennedy's sister Pat, Lawford drank heavily during production, showed up late, didn't remember his lines. When Bette finally confronted him about all this, she did so in an unusually gentle way. Peter remembered her as "understanding, kindly, patient—even maternal, if that's the word. I suspect she felt sorry for me." He was right. As Bette later said, "I could see that he was having some kind of trouble. . . . He's unfortunate, and it's too bad."

All of Bette's patience evaporated, however, whenever Jack Warner showed up. Flush with the success of *Baby Jane*, still bitter about her long years of battle with the mogul, Bette treated him as haughtily as she had at the height of her career, the $75,000 loan notwithstanding. As Phil Ball remembers it, "Warner would come down to the set, and Bette would run him off! She used four-letter words on him!" Warner just laughed it off and told Trilling, "She'll never change!"

To some, *Dead Ringer* turned out a taut little thriller, to others it was "melodramatic hokum." But it offered Bette another strong acting opportunity, and she made the most of it even as she sometimes veered into self-caricature. *Time* magazine's critic had some fun with Davis in his review: "Exuberantly uncorseted, her torso looks like a gunnysack full of galoshes. Coarsely cosmeticked, her face looks like a U-2 photograph of Utah. And her acting, as always, isn't really acting, it's shameless showing off. But just try to look away."

Immediately after she completed *Dead Ringer* in the early fall of 1963, Bette flew to Rome to appear in Carlo Ponti's production *The Empty Canvas,* directed by Damiano Damiani, in which she played the American mother of Horst Buchholz, whose father was an Italian nobleman. What little plot there was revolved around the doomed love of Buchholz, an artist of meager talents, for an amoral model (Catherine Spaak) and his mother's constant meddling in the affair. Wearyingly existentialist, the film lived up to the title of the Italian novel on which it was based: *Boredom.*

As with *The Night of the Iguana,* Bette had been promised that her part would be beefed up, and when she got to Rome she saw that it hadn't been. Desperate to give her "extremely dull" character "some flavor," she unilaterally chose to wear a shockingly blond pageboy wig and speak in a syrupy Southern accent. Barely able to understand Damiani's English, she directed herself—and everybody else—throughout the filming. Spaak, she sputtered, "thinks that trading on her looks is acting —well, it ain't." The handsome Buchholz, she complained, "went out of his way to thwart me at every turn. He's the male equivalent of a prima donna." As far as he was concerned, Bette was "a meddling bitch."

The Empty Canvas, according to the film critic for *The New Yorker,* was "one of the worst pictures of this or any other year." Bette agreed. "What that damned picture needed was a clear, linear, progressive beginning-middle-end plot and a part that I could make credible to audiences. It had neither—and I refuse to accept any of the blame." Luckily, the film was scantily distributed and did little to tarnish the glow of Bette's renewed stardom.

Back from Rome, Bette flung herself into the preparations for B.D.'s wedding and vowed that nothing but the best was good enough for her daughter. Her dress would be made to her own design by I. Magnin. The reception would lavishly entertain hundreds of guests at the Beverly Wilshire Hotel. Their wedding night would be spent at the Beverly Hills Hotel. Bette happily buried herself amid all the details, large and small, of the elaborate wedding she had planned.

Then Jeremy threw her a curve. He had consulted with his tax adviser and been told that if he married before the end of the year, he would save a considerable sum in taxes. He and B.D., he told Bette, would have to be married in a civil ceremony on December 31, then go ahead with the religious ceremony as planned at All Saints' Episcopal Church on January 4.

Over the next three days, B.D. recalled, "the shit hit the fan." Bette got hysterical, called her daughter a "barter bride" and "stormed out of the room." Jeremy suggested they consult with a minister, who told them that as long as the marriage wasn't consummated before the religious ceremony, he saw no problem. Then Rupert Allan, Bette's press agent, weighed in with his opinion that he should make an announcement to the press or else some might take the secrecy as an indication that B.D. was pregnant.

Even Bette thought this argument absurd—the difference was four days—but when Jeremy accused Allan of trying only to court the press with an exclusive, Bette turned on him furiously: "He has only my best interests in mind!" she bellowed. It was an argument that did little to comfort B.D. or Jeremy. When Allan made the announcement it served mostly to confuse the wedding guests, who wondered whether the January 4 ceremony was still on.

Despite all this, Barbara Davis Sherry's wedding to Jeremy A. Hyman went off without a hitch. B.D. wore a dress made with velvet from Lyons and rose-point lace from Venice; the ballroom of the Beverly Wilshire Hotel was lavishly festooned with pine branches and pink carnations.

Bobby's daughter Ruth, now twenty-four, was a bridesmaid, and she remembered the wedding as "gorgeous, just gorgeous. It was *huge*—my aunt spent a fortune! B.D.'s veil was specially made in France. There were ice sculptures everywhere. I was so impressed to meet Rock Hudson, and Rosalind Russell and Henry Fonda were there, too. It was a big, beautiful wedding. And all my aunt could talk about was these fabulous sheets she'd bought for B.D. as a surprise for her wedding night."

When the Hymans got to the Beverly Hills Hotel, they found that

Bette had meticulously prepared their honeymoon suite. Flowers filled every corner, the bar was stocked with champagne, canapés had been set out. The "fabulous sheets" were black silk, trimmed and monogrammed in white. On the bride's side of the bed Bette had carefully laid out a white satin peignoir trimmed with marabou feathers, and matching slippers. For Jeremy, she offered white silk pajamas trimmed in black. And in a witty nod to the practical considerations of married life, Bette placed a hammer on one pillow and a screwdriver on the other. Both were tied with white satin bows. "All of mother's forethought was greatly appreciated," B.D. later wrote. "It was a wonderful end to a most memorable occasion in our lives." The next day, the Hymans left for their honeymoon aboard a fishing boat in the Florida Keys.

With love so much in the air around her, Bette showed a renewed interest herself in romance during 1964. After her divorce from Gary, she had not only renounced marriage, but had called sex "God's joke on humanity. It is man's last desperate stand at superintendency. The whole ritual is a grotesque anachronism, an outdated testament to man's waning power."

Thus B.D. was taken aback when Bette called her at the New York apartment she and Jeremy had leased to say that she was serious about a new man. "I've found true love again at last, B.D.! Isn't that wonderful?" she gushed. "And he's *twenty-seven*. Three years younger than *Jeremy*. Can you imagine?"

B.D. kept her own counsel about the wisdom of this relationship, but she began to worry when a friend of Bette's called her to say that the young man in question was homosexual and urged B.D. to "do something before your mother makes a complete fool of herself." The next call was from Bette, who announced that she was moving into the man's Malibu beach house. That was followed by another call from a different friend of Bette's to let B.D. know that the man's beach house was a shack overrun by transients and drug addicts. Back and forth via long-distance calls, B.D. learned that Bette was cavorting on the beach in a bikini, attending "hippie parties," and otherwise behaving in a ridiculous manner.

When Bette called to say that she intended to marry this gentleman, B.D. snapped that if she wanted "to marry a homosexual, it's entirely up to you."

"Brother!" Bette boomed. "You really want to spoil things for me,

don't you? Well, maybe he was once, but he isn't now. All he needed was a real woman.''

Within a few days, Bette called back in tears to say that she had quarreled violently with the man and they had broken up. "Don't worry about me," she said, blowing her nose, "I'll get over it. It's not the first time I've been kicked in the teeth and it probably won't be the last. Men are *shits* . . . you'll see.''

Bette's longtime assistant Vik Greenfield recalled that despite this unsavory episode, her romantic ardor didn't cool throughout the next decade. Nearing sixty, terribly lonely, Bette too often deluded herself that clearly homosexual men were her "suitors." Whenever anyone pointed out that the men were unlikely to be interested in her sexually, she would announce, "I'm going to be the one to change him." Some of the men, according to Greenfield, were "obviously looking for a meal ticket," and led Bette on while cruelly mocking and imitating her in front of their friends. Others were simply delighted to meet and go to dinner with a woman they had long idolized, and were shocked when Bette would suddenly propose marriage after a few platonic "dates."

The actor Richard Tate was an exception. In his late twenties, handsome, he gravitated toward Bette at a noisy Hollywood party in the mid-'60s. After a few minutes of conversation, they moved to a quieter corner of the room and Tate told Bette that he had just come out of a five-year relationship with the actress Merle Oberon, just three years younger than Bette. Shortly after, Tate found himself "totally shocked" to realize that Bette was sexually interested in him. "She started telling me how empty her love life was because her career overpowered her intimate world so much. She said how much she adored her fans, but what vacant lovers they were. And before long it occurred to me that she was saying, 'Let's do it, baby!' ''

Tate offered to take Bette home to Honeysuckle Hill, and when they got there she nervously invited him in. She fixed him a drink and sat next to him on the couch. After some coy conversation and a few more drinks, Tate ran his fingers through her hair and kissed her. She stood up, tugged his hand, and said, "Let's go into the bedroom." When they got there, Tate recalls, "she started to direct me—'This is acceptable, and that's not, we can't do this, but we can do that.' I was being choreographed. Which I didn't adjust well to at all."

After what Tate describes as "our first burst of energy," during which he felt manipulated, he told Bette that she was too "rigid" in matters of sexuality. "I told her she had to break down those walls. I wanted her to be feminine, and not manipulate sex, just let it happen, and trust that it will happen without her controlling it. She was driving me to distraction and I went outside to smoke a joint. Then I told her she should 'grass out' with me."

Tate shared the marijuana with Bette. "After that," Tate says, "she was less rigid—and I was more rigid! I was the first one to turn her on to grass—which broke down many of her inhibitions." The couple spent the next three days together, during which Tate "functioned as a sex therapist," teaching Bette to enjoy many of the preliminaries she had avoided before; goading her on to "Enjoy it!"

Richard Tate's rendezvous with Bette Davis, in his words, was no more than "a four-night stand." They drifted apart after that, but whenever they would run into each other at some Hollywood function or another, Tate could always count on a smile and a wink from Bette.

She accepted her next film project primarily to pay the enormous bills for B.D.'s wedding. *Where Love Has Gone* was the highly publicized producer Joseph E. Levine's big-budget film version of Harold Robbins's bestseller, loosely based on the Lana Turner/Johnny Stompanato/Cheryl Crane murder scandal of seven years earlier. Bette didn't much like John Michael Hayes's script, but her relatively small part as a manipulative dowager would require just a few weeks' work, and Levine was paying her $125,000.

When Susan Hayward signed to costar as Bette's daughter, she became only the fourth actress of equal stature to play opposite Bette in her long career. Among her precursors—Miriam Hopkins, Anne Baxter, and Joan Crawford—only Baxter hadn't wound up in a feud with Bette. Hollywood observers held their breath and waited for the fireworks to start.

They weren't disappointed. B.D. recalled that from the outset her mother had been "loudly vocal about her dissatisfaction with the whole project," and this put Susan Hayward on tenterhooks from the first day of filming. The film's director, Edward Dmytryk, recalled that "Susan was scared to death of Bette. Susan was a very difficult person to know. She was very reserved, nervous and withdrawn. Bette mistook that, apparently, for rudeness. They were exact opposites."

Bette's vociferous demands for script revisions further alienated Hayward, who was certain that her costar's main goal was to enlarge her own part and truncate hers. Threatened, insecure, Hayward insisted on a private meeting in Levine's office and presented him with an ultimatum: "If the script is changed, I walk." Levine then issued a dictum of his own: not one word of the script will be altered. At this, the bad blood between Bette and Hayward completely curdled.

The next day, as they rehearsed a scene, Hayward suggested a change in Bette's blocking. To everyone's astonishment, Bette reacted by tearing off her gray wig and throwing it in Hayward's face. "Why don't you just play *both* roles?" Bette hissed. Susan whirled around and started off toward her dressing room, muttering, "Bitch! Bitch! *Bitch!*"

Bette folded her arms and planted her feet apart. "*What* did you say, Miss Hayward?"

Susan wheeled around. "Bitch!" she shouted at the top of her lungs. "That's what you are! An old bitch!"

Bette remained speechless as Hayward left the soundstage, and the next day, apparently chastened, she sent Hayward a note asking for her help to improve their "stinking, lousy script." Hayward ignored the overture, and she and Bette never spoke to each other again except while acting.

Mike Connors, cast as Hayward's husband, recalled that "they were both on the defensive. Bette felt insecure up against a ten-years-younger woman, Susan, who was better looking and, moreover, the star of the film. . . . And Susan, who was sullen and defensive anyway, found that hers and Davis's temperaments were too much alike. . . . I remember it, and so did Eddie Dmytryk, as an atmosphere of armed truce—and a mean, icy truce it was, too."

Bette happily left the Paramount lot when she completed her work in *Where Love Has Gone,* but a few months later Levine ordered her back for an additional scene: he wanted her to lose her mind and slash her daughter's portrait at the end of the film. Bette was appalled; such an action would be grossly out of character for the woman she had played, who had been in total control all her life. When she refused to film the scene, Paramount took her to court. "I am completely unable and incapable of performing the additional scene as it is presently written," Bette told the court. The judge decided in her favor, and as B.D. recalled it, "she thumbed her nose at all of them with great satisfaction." Levine convinced Susan Hayward to slash Bette's portrait instead, which she did with something close to glee.

Bette was proven right about *Where Love Has Gone.* Like so much of Joseph E. Levine's output, it proved crass, vulgar, and sensationalistic. But Levine's great genius was hype and promotion, and both helped make the film a box-office winner. The reviews, though, were disdainful. "The story," *Newsweek*'s critic wrote, "is a typical Harold Robbins pastiche of newspaper clippings liberally shellacked with sentiment and glued with sex. . . . Still, Bette Davis is splendid, with her eyes rolling and her mouth working and her incredible lines to say. Sitting in the ugliest chair in Hollywood, she lowers her teacup and pronounces, 'Somewhere along the line the world has lost all its standards and all its taste.' . . . The gang at Embassy and Paramount are probably congratulating themselves on their monumental restraint and good taste—simply because they didn't try to cast Lana Turner in the leading role."

Just weeks after she completed her scenes in *Where Love Has Gone,* Bette steeled herself for a new movie. It was an assignment once again abrim with temperamental minefields: a reunion with Joan Crawford.

TWENTY-EIGHT

ette sat on the chartered flight that was taking her and other cast and crew members to Baton Rouge, Louisiana, to film *Hush . . . Hush, Sweet Charlotte,* the "blood cousin" to *Baby Jane* that Robert Aldrich had concocted with Henry Farrell and screenwriter Lukas Heller. Directly behind her, the young actor William Campbell, cast as an aggressive tabloid reporter in the film, excitedly tried to watch every move of the woman he had unabashedly idolized for years.

"The stewardess came around with drinks," Campbell recalls, "and of course, on a chartered flight they weren't those little ponies they give you on commercial flights. I had a glass of wine, and then I heard Bette tell the girl, 'I want a double Scotch. And not much water. As a matter of fact, *forget* the water. There's water in the *ice!*' "

When the stewardess returned with an old-fashioned glass full of Scotch, Campbell peered through the space between the seats in front of him to see Bette reach into her purse and pull out a small case covered in paisley material. "I thought the case contained her reading glasses," Campbell says. "But it was a flask! She opened it up and laid in another shot!"

Bette may have felt she needed the fortification to face another picture with Joan Crawford, who had decided to take the train from Los Angeles to Baton Rouge rather than spend any more time than necessary in close proximity to Bette. Neither actress relished the idea of working again with the other, but both realized there was potentially a great deal of money to be made. Still, Robert Aldrich faced headaches from the minute he began negotiations with the two wary superstars.

Aldrich had approached Bette first with the script for *What Ever Happened to Cousin Charlotte?* Like Jane Hudson, Charlotte was a reclusive, unstable middle-aged woman haunted by a violent past. In this instance, she lives in an antebellum mansion outside Baton Rouge, tormented by memories of the ghastly decapitation of her young married

378

lover thirty years earlier. The murder was never solved, and the locals consider Charlotte the killer. She harbors fear that her possessive father committed the crime.

As Charlotte faces eviction from the family home to make way for a highway, her kind and elegant cousin Miriam arrives and offers solace. But in fact, Miriam has hatched an elaborate plot with Charlotte's doctor to drive her insane and gain access to her fortune. After she sees "hallucinations" of severed heads and walking zombies provided by her tormentors, Charlotte realizes what they've done and kills them. As she is led away by authorities she learns that it was her lover's wife who killed him all those years ago. Now, at last, she can be at peace.

The script was shamelessly melodramatic, the shocks blatantly heavy-handed. But once again Bette would have the chance to play a multi-layered character who, while far more sympathetic than Jane Hudson, still had the chance to chew the scenery to shreds every so often. She told Aldrich she'd do the film if he would change the title and find someone other than Joan Crawford to play Miriam.

Aldrich blanched. "Bette, every studio in town wants to do this picture—with you *and* Joan. If we get anybody else, they'll lower the budget, I'll have less money to pay you, and quite honestly, it won't do as well at the box office."

Bette came around when Aldrich upped her salary from $120,000 to $160,000 (plus 15 percent of the net) and agreed to change the title to *Hush . . . Hush, Sweet Charlotte,* lyrics from a theme song Frank DeVol and Mack Davis had already written for the picture.

Now that he had Bette signed, Aldrich went to work on Joan. Aware of how she felt about Bette, he was sure she would decline the film, and he flew to New York to persuade her to change her mind. He needn't have bothered; since *Baby Jane,* Joan had made only the box-office dud *The Caretakers* and William Castle's B-movie thriller *Strait Jacket,* and she was eager for another big hit. She agreed to take a salary of $50,000 and 25 percent of the net profits, then added, "But there is one small request I have to make. In the billing for this picture my name comes first, *before* Miss Davis."

Later that night, all trepidation, Aldrich broached the idea to Bette. "In a pig's eye!" she exploded. "I will not have my name come second to Joan Crawford, not now, not *ever*!" Before he returned to Los Angeles the next day, Aldrich assured Crawford he would work on Bette. When he met with her again, he offered to raise her pay to $200,000 if she'd take second billing. Aldrich could afford it. As Walter Blake recalls,

"It was the exact opposite of the first picture. After the success of *Baby Jane,* the studios were throwing money at Bob. He was the new Messiah."

When Bette still wouldn't budge, Aldrich told her, "This is the same amount I'm getting for directing and producing, Bette. So that makes us partners for this picture."

Bette's eyes brightened. "Okay, Bob," she replied. "I'll do the picture. And we'll be *partners,* like you said. All the way down the line. I'll *hold* you to that!"

Within weeks, Aldrich wished he had kept his mouth shut. When he decided to replace screenwriter Henry Farrell, and did not consult Bette, she fired off a blistering tirade. "You are stubborn and have to be totally in charge," she wrote. "You do not function well with someone of my type. That was obvious throughout the filming of *Baby Jane*—and the suicidal desire this put me into many times, was almost more than I was able to bear.

"The machinations of the new film from the very beginning have been tricky. . . . I do not wear well with tricks designed to make me do what someone else decides I will do. We have not been partners—and you do not intend that we will be." She went on to say that Aldrich wanted no more than to remake *Baby Jane,* and accused him of plotting to sabotage her appearance on film. "No matter what I look like on the set—you can order the cameraman to 'Fix me up.'

"I could never trust you again. . . . I truly do not feel I can work with you again. If you are wise for the good of the film you will re-cast and pay me off. It will be cheaper in the long run."

After flowers, an apology, an increase in her profit participation, and a promise from Aldrich that her billing would be the same size and on the same line as Crawford's (and accompanied by an asterisk to indicate "Alphabetical Order"), Bette calmed down. Finally, on May 31, after a month's delay so that Crawford could attend a Pepsi-Cola sales convention in Hawaii, the cast and crew headed off to the Baton Rouge location. "I hope we live through it," Aldrich muttered.

Bette made no attempt to show the slightest civility toward Joan Crawford. If she had to work with the woman, she had apparently decided, she could at least make her life miserable. "After the business with the Oscar," Bette's assistant Vik Greenfield recalled, "this was war." It was a war of attrition and a war of words. The film's publicist, Charles Moses, recalls that "Joan would take an awfully long time making up in the morning. Bette was there *before* she was needed, and I was with her when she'd make stinging comments about how long Joan took in makeup." Bette was just as likely to remind anyone within earshot that, despite the fact that Joan claimed to be the same age as Bette, "She's five years older than me if she's a day!"

And while Bette looked forward to her Scotch every afternoon, she couldn't abide Joan's secret gulps during working hours. "Crawford was a boozer!" she told friends. "Vodka was her life support system."

Bette, popular with the cast and crew, lost no opportunity to put Crawford down or alienate her from the rest of the company. The reporter Len Baxter observed the filming, and he recalled an instance when Bette apparently pulled "partner" rank with Aldrich and sat in front of the camera while Joan was playing a scene that did not involve her. As Baxter observed, "A director doesn't permit an actor to sit in front of the camera, directly in another actor's line of vision, unless the actor is part of the scene."

Bette's intentions soon became clear. She watched Joan go through the scene, then turned to Aldrich and said loudly, "You're not going to let her play it like *that,* are you?" Trembling, Joan rushed off the set and back to her trailer.

After hours, Bette hosted parties for the company and pointedly excluded Joan. During one such gathering, held in Bette's bungalow directly across from Joan's, Crawford drove off to dine at a local restaurant with her personal maid.

Joan, drinking heavily and growing more paranoid by the day, became convinced that everyone was in league against her. When Bette struck up a friendship with the character actress Agnes Moorehead, a kindred spirit flamboyantly enacting Charlotte's hillybilly housekeeper Velma, Joan imagined that their every giggly conversation was at her expense. She wasn't entirely wrong. Moorehead later confided to friends that she and Bette had "ganged up on Crawford psychologically."

Miserable, afraid once again that Bette would steal the picture, Crawford called Aldrich at his hotel room past midnight one evening and told him that she wanted to do retakes on some of her scenes. "He said I was overreacting," Joan recalled, "that my work was fine. But then I heard a second voice, talking loudly beside him. I knew immediately who it was. It was Miss Davis. She was there, in Mr. Aldrich's bed."

It's far more likely that Bette was there just to fill Aldrich's ears with her own problems, as Joan had wanted to do, but now Crawford was close to hysteria. She demanded that Aldrich beef up her part, and when he refused, she called her attorney and asked whether she had a legal way out of her contract. He told her she didn't, but Joan had a few tricks left. When she flew back to Los Angeles on June 13 (alone; the rest of the company had left while she was sleeping in her bungalow), she went straight from the airport to Cedars of Lebanon Hospital. As Bette had done so often in the past, Joan now claimed that stress and exhaustion had left her ill.

Bette and many others were certain Joan was faking, especially when her doctors couldn't seem to tell just what was wrong with her—the diagnoses ranged from dysentery to "an intermittent cough" to pneumonia. Charles Moses, however, believes she was genuinely ill. "The thing that did her in was that she drank heavily, which made her perspire profusely, then she'd go from her frigid trailer into the muggy Louisiana heat, then onto the soundstage that she kept so refrigerated, and she'd stand in front of these fans that were as big as a house. I stood next to her, freezing, and I figured *I'd* get sick. She'd just stand there and stand there. I thought, *She's gonna get pneumonia*. And, of course, she did."

Crawford wasn't too sick to talk to reporters. She told Sidney Skolsky that all the cast and crew members had sent her flowers, cards, and get-well wishes—except Bette. She confided to Hedda Hopper that she was reworking the script. "It will be a much better movie when I've recovered."

All of Joan's script changes gave her more to do and made her look and act more glamorous, and Aldrich rejected them. Still, when Joan returned to work on July 20, she stepped onto the 20th Century–Fox lot confident that her role would be augmented. Instead, in the middle of a scene between Joan and Joseph Cotten (who was playing Charlotte's doctor), Bette announced that she was "cutting some dialogue"—all of it Joan's—because "these lines hold me up."

Joan whirled around and stalked off the set. She returned, but over the next few days she complained that she was "weakened" and left the studio every day at noon. Close to the end of his patience, Aldrich hired a private detective to follow Crawford and see whether she remained at home over the weekend. The investigator reported that she left her apartment in a two-tone brown Rolls-Royce on Saturday at 5 P.M., but that he lost her at the intersection of Wilshire and Santa Monica boulevards. When Aldrich showed the detective's report to Bette, she snorted, "She gave the fool the *slip*!"

Joan continued to limp through her work, constantly pleading for time off and complaining of illness, until she was rushed back to the hospital with a relapse of whatever it was that ailed her. Finally, on August 4, Aldrich suspended *Charlotte* production and started to look for a replacement. "I kept up with her condition," Bette said, "by reading [the gossip columnist] Hedda Hopper, who received frequent bulletins from Joan from under her oxygen tent."

Aldrich approached Loretta Young and Barbara Stanwyck to play Miriam but, Crawford told another gossip maven, Louella Parsons, "both are friends of mine and wouldn't dream of taking a job away from me." Vivien Leigh was far less gracious when she was asked by the press if she'd be interested in the role. "I could just about look at Joan Crawford's face at seven o'clock in the morning," she reportedly said, "but I couldn't possibly look at Bette Davis's." Bette snapped back, "I will never make this with Miss Leigh. She would be more difficult than Miss Crawford. And wrong for [the Southern] Miriam—her British accent is *absurd*!" (Bette seemed to have forgotten that Leigh won two Academy Awards playing American Southerners.)

Walter Blake says that none of these women was ever offered the role. "Olivia De Havilland was the only actress we approached. Bob Aldrich flew to Europe to meet with her personally and show her the script. The other names were just bandied about for publicity."

In mid-August, still hospitalized, Joan Crawford heard on the radio that she had been officially replaced by Olivia De Havilland. "I wept for thirty-nine hours," she told friends. Publicly she meowed, "I'm glad for Olivia. She needs a good picture." As if to rub it in, Bette made a great show of greeting Olivia at the airport and throwing her arms joyously around her new costar as she disembarked from the airplane.

"I looked forward to working with Bette again," Joan Crawford said several years later. "I had no idea of the extent of her hate, and that she planned to destroy me. . . . I still get chills when I think of the treachery that Miss Davis indulged in on that movie."

Bette was far more congenial with Olivia, who had worked with Bette at Warners and had had a good relationship with her. She never let Bette's domineering personality get under her skin. "I am not a competitive person," she said. "If I am attacked, I simply refuse to fight back. I never said a word to her. I just did my scene, with a look that said, 'I will not fight you; I will not accept your challenge.' Bette understood."

Hush . . . Hush, Sweet Charlotte was completed in October 1964 and released in New York in March 1965. Less original and gorier than *Baby Jane,* the film served mainly as a showcase for some of the hammiest acting ever captured on film. Agnes Moorehead flies way over the top as Velma, but her histrionics are at least entertaining, while Joseph Cotten's are barely sufferable. De Havilland acquits herself well as the duplicitous Miriam, but the subtlest and most affecting performance is delivered by Mary Astor in a small role as Charlotte's lover's widow—and, it turns out, his murderer.

Which leaves Bette. Surrounded by excess, she wavers between admirable restraint and shameless scenery-chewing and manages to make Cousin Charlotte a sympathetic and three-dimensional creation. Like *Baby Jane,* the picture divided the critics, many of whom lamented the falling standards of American cinema while others championed the film, often because of Bette's contributions. Kenneth Tynan thought *Charlotte* had been "yanked to the level of art by Miss Davis's performance as the raging, aging Southern belle; this wasted Bernhardt, with her screen-filling eyes and electrifying vocal attack, squeezes genuine pathos from a role conceived in cardboard."

The film was another big hit, and although Bette bridled when one critic labeled her "Hollywood's *grande-dame* ghoul," she reveled in her fourth box-office success in three years. The film enjoyed some surprising respect, too; it captured a remarkable seven Oscar nominations. (Agnes Moorehead was cited as Best Supporting Actress, but Bette was overlooked.) Another of the nominations was for the title tune as Best Song, and Bette was hurt when the Academy turned down her offer to sing it at the awards ceremony.

She had already been disappointed when the studio chose Al Martino to sing the song over the film's end credits, and further annoyed when Patti Page's version became a top-ten hit. "They should have let *me* record that song with a group like the Brothers Four," Bette said. "They haven't had a hit in a long time, and if they could have done 'Charlotte' with me, it would have been the biggest hit *in the world!*"

Bette wouldn't give up. Before she embarked on another publicity tour of East Coast theaters to promote the film, she told Aldrich she wanted to sing the song on stage after the film. According to Charles Moses, Aldrich shouted at Bette, "You can't do it! You'll ruin the picture. What will the critics say?!"

"He had all kinds of reasons," Moses recalls, "and they had a big fight over it. I was just standing there, and I sensed that Bette was about to say, 'Okay, Bob, fine.' But he wouldn't stop. He kept berating her: 'You're *not* going to sing it. If you do I'm going to cut the trip short and send you home—blah, blah, blah.' He didn't have to do that. I wanted the floor to give way. That was the big break between them. She hated him after that."

A few days before Christmas 1964, Bette entertained two teenage fans at Honeysuckle Hill, where she held forth in her grandest *grande dame* manner on everything from her career to the future of cable television. The names of the two young ladies have not come down to us, but a tape recording of the encounter survives, and it reveals Bette in an expansive mood, her highly *definite* opinions growing more and more hyperbolic with each freshened glass of Scotch.

The conversation began with Bette discussing, with typical enthusiasm, her latest project—a television series pilot she had just finished for Aaron Spelling, *The Decorator,* in which she played an interior designer who insists on living with her clients before she will agree to redo their homes. "She really is basically a character like Margo Channing," Bette announced to the delighted fans. "She has never married, and she's bright enough to know she's too bright to marry. . . . It really is a show of enormous scope. I think television is where people see you as you are. . . . I'm really enthused about this whole thing." (*The Decorator* wasn't picked up as a series. Its pilot, which costarred Mary Wickes, is mildly amusing, but it is a long stretch to call it "a show of enormous scope.")

Bette revealed that she had "a habit" of never missing *Bonanza* or *The Dick Van Dyke Show,* which she called "the most tasteful, beautiful show that will ever be! I wouldn't miss it for *a million dollars!*" Cable television, she emphasized, "*truly* will be the death of the theaters. There isn't any question about it. When you think about it, three quarters of the theaters in the nation have gone anyway. It's an antediluvian thing. . . . There will be some theaters left in cities for kids. They'll show Westerns for the kids, because they enjoy going. But that will be all!"

Her next prediction came closer to the mark: "I think there will be a resurgence of better movies if we have [cable], because they will dare to gamble again."

When one of the fans mentioned the recently released *My Fair Lady* while Bette poured herself another drink, she let loose with a diatribe against Jack Warner's decision to cast Audrey Hepburn in the role Julie Andrews had created on stage. Then she added, "If you take *Gypsy,* and not let Miss Merman play it, that's a sin. Because it's a wonderful record of a performance that movies give us that the theater never has."

The other fan piped up, "They always think they know what the public wants. I wonder if they really do."

"Well, it's no use asking what the public wants," Bette replied, "because I don't think the public *knows* what it wants until it sees it. And I think to always encourage the public to have opinions is ridiculous. The public doesn't know *one thing* about making movies!"

"It's the same thing with children," Bette railed on, building a head of steam. "Do you say to a child every meal, 'What do you want for dinner?' If they say it to *us,* we don't know! What do we do when we go to restaurants? We look at the menu for *hours*! Somebody should just bring the dinner on!"

After freshening her drink again, Bette talked about the tour she had done to promote *Baby Jane.* "People just couldn't *believe* that I was *walking*—that I wasn't *ninety* years old. I've run into people myself who've been in the business thirty, thirty-five years, and I think, 'I can't *believe* they're still *alive*!' And then I say to myself, 'Well, *you're* still alive, so I guess *they* are!' "

When the conversation turned to Bette's singing, she called the studio executives who hired Al Martino to sing "Hush . . . Hush, Sweet Charlotte" "absolute fools" for not giving it to her. "And they made a mistake on the *Baby Jane* soundtrack too! They should *never* have let that girl sing 'I've Written a Letter to Daddy.' They should have let *me* sing it the way I sang it in the movie. It was the biggest mistake in *history*!"

Changing the subject, one of the fans complained about the cuts made in the TV version of *Mr. Skeffington.* "It is sinful!" Bette cried. "*Sinful!* It would be an interesting lawsuit, wouldn't it? For me to say, 'You're ruining my career with these cuts—you're wrecking the memory of these films.' I wonder what would happen. I bet I'd win it."

After Bette returned from the bar with yet another drink, one of the girls asked her if she had caught Joan Crawford's recent appearance on *What's My Line?* and added, "She did the whole thing in a Southern accent."

"Well, my deah," Bette drawled in response. "She did the *whole* Suth-in bit with us, you know. She was *all* Suth-in. Was her hair white?

Or did she have a turban? Did she say 'Bless you'? Did she say, 'Bless you, John,' 'Bless you, Arlene'? I'm sure she did. She says 'Bless you' to *everybody*! She's such a *doll*! She's just as sweet as . . ." Bette caught herself at this point and left the sentence unfinished. Later, she deigned to give Joan a little credit. "Whatever I say about Miss Crawford, she's a star. And whenever she appears, it's an occasion. And a star *must* make it an occasion when she appears. The *easiest* part of our job is the acting. That's the gravy, all alone on that soundstage. The greatest job is learning how to behave publicly. Now, Miss Crawford knows she's a star, in big quotes. And she's one of the few left. No question about it."

Asked "Would you ever go back to Broadway?" Bette replied, "I *hate* theater. But you know, I may. I'd love to do a musical version of *All About Eve*. There's been a lot of talk, but Fox won't release the rights. It would be one of the great musicals *of all time*! 'Cause I *adore* musicals!"

She also professed to "adore" the pop music of the day. "I think the Beatles are great. I have nothing against this kind of music." But, she added, "The dancing is revolting. The Watusi and the whole thing. It's all gotten down to a thing that's psychotic. I went to Pussycat Au Go Go. I've never seen anything like what I saw there. Half the kids are hopped-up. I know that they had dope. They had all the gestures of beating each other up. It wasn't dancing at all. And the music was revolting!"

As the interview wound down, the girls mentioned a twenty-five-year-old male fan of Bette's who had spent hours showing them his photo collection. "Is he a normal boy?" she asked. "Because, you know, at my age pansies are the ones who are the fans . . . it's unbelievable."

"Why do you think that's so?" one of the girls asked.

"Oh, my dear, because I'm a strong woman."

"Isn't it disgusting?"

"No, it isn't disgusting. You just have to get used to it. I tell you, outside the theater in New York—*nothing* but pansies. Unbelievable. There was this little boy—twelve years old. This is what he is. His mother warped him somewhere down the line. He's a *pansy* at twelve! Of course he is or he would not be obsessed with this kind of thing at twelve years old! If I had a son that did this at twelve years old, I'd *kill* myself!"

After her recent spate of box-office successes, Bette reasonably expected that her career would continue to flourish. As so often in the past, she was badly disappointed. She had no offers after *Charlotte* in the fall of 1964, and she was forced to sell Honeysuckle Hill with its huge mortgage payments and move into a much smaller apartment in Beverly Hills.

Finally, Britain's horror factory Hammer Films came to the rescue with *The Nanny*, about an emotionally disturbed woman responsible for the accidental death of one of her charges and now quite dangerous to the little girl's brother as well. Bette traveled to England in the spring of 1965 to make the film with the forty-two-year-old director Seth Holt, a high-strung bundle of neuroses who died of alcoholism six years later. Bette, he claimed, almost finished him off much earlier.

"She got the flu during shooting," he told Lawrence Quirk, "and sometimes she'd stay away altogether, holding up shooting while she sent in day-to-day reports on her condition—'It's worse!'—'It's better!' —'Oh God, I've relapsed!'—and so forth, and when she was on the set, still sniffling and coughing, she was drinking out of everyone's glasses and wheezing in her co-actors' faces. . . . Oh, it was hell! Then she was always telling me how to direct. When I did it her way, she was scornful; when I stood up to her, she was hysterical. I managed some kind of middle course and got through the film and stayed calm."

Whenever Holt felt Bette was overacting, he told her so. "I act larger than life," she retorted, "that's what my audiences paid me for all these years. If they wanted ordinary reality they'd go out and talk with their *grocer*!" According to Holt, Bette refused to watch the day's rushes because "she hated to look at herself. I'd ask her what did it matter since she was made up and dressed to be a frumpish, unattractive, middle-aged nanny anyway—and she was fifty-seven or so . . . but I couldn't get her to look at those rushes. If I had, I might have made her realize that she was pouring it on too much."

Ironically, when *The Nanny* was released in November, most critics praised Bette for her restraint. Judith Crist's comment in the New York *Herald Tribune* was typical: "In this, her fourth venture into the Hitchcock-cum-horror milieu, Miss Davis is out for character rather than hoax and comes up with a beautifully controlled performance as a jealous and voracious nursemaid . . . it is her performance and four complementary ones that give this film its distinction."

Bette told a BBC interviewer that she was proud of *The Nanny* because it was "a complete departure from anything I've ever played. It is very easy to say, 'Well, you know, she's always the same.' This is not true. This I will never accept from any critic. . . . One of the things over the years that critics have repeatedly referred to have been my 'mannerisms.' Well, that depends on what part I'm playing. I can show you just as many parts where I don't flutter one eyelid, ever!"

The Nanny was a moderate success, but Bette did not receive another film offer for two and a half years. In 1965, the producers of the ABC-TV series *The FBI* considered her for a role, but first they wanted the Federal Bureau of Investigation itself to ascertain her "suitability" to appear on the program. The Bureau's report, dated November 29, concluded that "it will not be possible to utilize Bette Davis in connection with our series"—which effectively blacklisted her. The reason, the report states, was that the FBI's files on Bette "reflect that during the 1940's she participated in the activities of the Hollywood Independent Citizens Committee on the Arts, Sciences, and Professions, the Hollywood Writers Mobilization and the United Negro and Allied Veterans of America, all of which have been cited as communist fronts. . . . In the past, she has been personally acquainted with numerous communist sympathizers and Party members and over the years has been a close associate and personal friend of [name deleted] who was a Communist Party member from 1939 to 1945. . . . In 1962, Bette Davis participated in a banquet sponsored by the American Civil Liberties Union which was given for the purpose of encouraging support for a drive to abolish the House Committee on Un-American Activities."

Bette's FBI dossier also lists as worthy of security consideration the fact that she took part in the Negro Victory Committee's War Bond Drive in Los Angeles's Pershing Square on December 31, 1942, along with Ethel Waters, Hattie McDaniel, and others, and the fact that "*The Daily People's World,* a West Coast Communist newspaper, in its issue of 3/27/43, has a photograph of Bette Davis, Robert Rossen, and Arch Oboler, who were stated to be discussing the 'Free World Theater' radio program under Oboler's direction, which was being heard every Sunday on the Blue Network."

It is unlikely that Bette ever knew of the FBI's skewed view of her undoubtedly innocent activities, or of her blackballing from the *FBI* series. Had she known, one can well imagine her reaction.

During this deadly lull in her career after *The Nanny,* Bette decided to move to Westport, Connecticut, near Weston, where B.D. and Jeremy had recently purchased a house. She was very excited about the prospect. At last, she could be close once again to her beloved daughter.

TWENTY-NINE

ette found a house just two miles from the Hymans, on Crooked Mile Road in Westport, which she christened Twin Bridges. A charming cottage that reminded her pleasantly of Witch-Way, it was also close to Loomis, the boarding school in which Michael had enrolled. Bette was thrilled to be so close to B.D.; she bubbled over with plans for shopping trips and pajama parties. Maybe she didn't have to lose her daughter after all. . . .

B.D. was having none of it, and neither was Jeremy. In her 1985 memoir, *My Mother's Keeper*, B.D. presents a litany of scenes of Bette's "interference" in her marriage. Viewed objectively, Bette's actions could just as easily be interpreted as genuine concern and generosity. When Bette sent steady gifts of clothes from Bergdorf Goodman, B.D. told her to stop because her closets were full. When Bette expressed concern about a cold B.D. had and insisted on sending over a doctor, B.D. and Jeremy saw it as unconscionable meddling.

B.D. had completely submerged herself in her marriage, and Bette didn't like it. She resented Jeremy's dominance over his wife, and she hated B.D.'s total deference to him. For a daughter of hers to behave that way in a marriage was unfathomable to Bette. "I was upset for her and by her," she wrote in her 1987 memoir *This 'n That*. "From the beginning, she did whatever Jeremy told her to do. B.D. was a daughter who knew her mother well. She was discerning enough to know how sad and hurt I would be by these decisions."

According to B.D., Bette made little attempt to hide her dislike for her son-in-law, even in public. Privately, she tried to convince B.D. that Jeremy was cheating on her, something that B.D. never believed. As B.D. attempted to distance herself from her mother, Bette grew terrified of losing her, and clung to her all the more fiercely.

Inexorably, the relationship between Bette and B.D. deteriorated. Jeremy considered his mother-in-law "the rudest, most importune person I've ever encountered, or ever hope to." She didn't really love B.D., he insisted. "The only emotions she truly understands are hate and jealousy." As the Hymans pushed Bette away, she tried more and more fiercely to convince B.D. that her marriage had been a mistake. The situation grew so volatile that B.D. couldn't spend more than a few hours with Bette before the conversation collapsed into vitriol and accusations.

In 1969, as B.D. prepared to give birth to her first child, Bette excitedly talked about "taking care of everything" in the delivery room. The thought made B.D. shudder, and she told Jeremy not to inform Bette when she went into labor. It was only after the birth of Jeremy Ashley Hyman on June 19 that Bette knew she had a grandson. She later wrote that her joy was dampened because B.D. had shunned her at so important a moment, and she blamed Jeremy. "While I did not ever ask for the same consideration she gave her husband, I did hope that every now and then she would say, 'I can't do this to Mother.' "

From B.D.'s perspective, Bette was envious of her marital happiness and jealous that she no longer had B.D. at her beck and call. Others who knew Bette and the Hymans, however, tell a different story. Alix Snow, the mother of the woman Bette's son Michael later married, lived down the street from Bette. "Any wrong that came between Bette and B.D.," she says, "was B.D.'s fault. Bette tried very hard to be friends with her daughter and her son-in-law, and B.D. half the time rejected her. . . . But Bette was always helping B.D. out financially, and B.D. didn't reject *that*. She had no pride whatsoever. Jeremy started this home-maintenance business, and as far as I could see, their only customer was Bette Davis! She had a perfectly fine kitchen, and all of a sudden Jeremy's men were redoing it. Oh, Bette paid and paid and paid. . . ."

Alix Snow considers Bette "one of the most generous women I've ever met. Whenever she was here, she would give so much of her time to the local charities. We have a museum of nature, and every year they have a fundraiser. Bette would spend two or three hours there in the evening, being helpful, being seen, talking to people. She was a tremendous draw, and she helped raise *thousands* of dollars."

Michael, as he had for years, remained unscathed by the battles between his mother and his sister. If there is one unassailable observation to be made about Bette and B.D., it is that their temperaments were too alike for emotional explosions *not* to have taken place. The opposite was true of Michael. Sixteen in 1968, he almost never saw his mother's wrath because he was a born conciliator and exerted a calming influence on her—unlike his sister, who seemed almost to enjoy putting a torch to Bette's dynamite.

When Michael came home from boarding school on weekends and holidays, there were no scenes, no arguments, no counterparts to Bette's oft-repeated accusation that B.D. was "a cold bitch." Michael was quiet, courteous, respectful of his mother, deferential to others. As Alix Snow says, "Michael is the most polite young man. He will kiss you when he arrives, he will pull a chair out for you and hold the door. He is so proper. He's so honest. It amazes me because it's so constant. So either it was the schools he went to or Bette did something right . . ."

On a snowy day in 1968, Michael, home from school for Christmas vacation, met Alix's daughter Chou Chou Raum, a lovely sixteen-year-old brunette who would later do some modeling. As her mother recalls it, "Chou had just gotten her driver's license, and it was so snowy I didn't want her to take the car. But finally I relented, and she got about five hundred feet from the house and the car skidded into a ditch. She was afraid to come home, so she sat on the sidewalk crying, not knowing what to do. All of a sudden Michael stopped his car and said, 'May I help you?' And there was Chou looking at this beautiful blond Adonis."

Chou Chou already had a date for a school dance, but she asked Michael to come with her as part of a foursome. "Chou Chou and Michael were forever talking and dancing," Alix recalled, "and soon they were together and their dates were with each other." Bette invited Chou to Twin Bridges for a day-after-Christmas breakfast, and Chou met the famous movie star who lived down the road for the first time. A few days later, Bette asked Alix and her husband Donald Snow to visit, and they found her completely charming. "She was so hospitable to us," Alix recalled. "She loved to cook, and she always wore an apron and some-times even a hat. It's funny when someone is so famous and you see them in such a casual way."

Michael and Chou Chou courted steadily for the next two years, and Bette heard some murmurs of marriage plans. She liked Chou, she told Michael, and she had no objections to the marriage, but couldn't they wait until they were twenty-one? Reluctantly, Michael agreed. Then he got Bette's permission to accompany Chou and a group of their friends on a six-week road trip throughout Europe.

Just before they left, Michael and Chou Chou made a trip to Maine with her parents to visit Gary Merrill. "He lived at Falmouth Foreside," Alix recalls, "right on a beautiful little pond. It was a lovely house, looked like something out of *Wuthering Heights*." When Michael took

Chou outside to show her around, Alix mentioned to Gary that she was a little nervous about her daughter's getting so serious, even about as fine a boy as Michael. "Don't worry," Gary replied. "They won't get married. They'll go on that trip to Europe, they don't have much money, it'll be one car full of boys and one car full of girls, and when they get through that ordeal, that will be the end of that."

Of course, it wasn't. At the end of that summer of 1968, Michael went away to college in Chapel Hill, North Carolina, and Alix vividly remembers Michael and Chou standing in her driveway, tearfully saying good-bye to each other. "Michael drove away, and it's an eleven-and-a-half-hour trip to Chapel Hill. Eleven and a half hours later, he's on the phone with Chou and they have an hour-and-a-half conversation. So I said to my husband, 'That European trip didn't help one bit!' It was obviously stronger than that, and at that point I was all for the marriage."

After Michael's graduation in 1973, he told Bette that he and Chou Chou were ready to be married. When she asked him to wait until he finished law school, he calmly reminded her that she had originally told him he could marry when he reached twenty-one. (B.D., one suspects, would have flown into a rage and created another battle royal.) True to her word, Bette offered her blessings, and she sent Chou a handwritten note signed "with love." Later, she gave the couple an engagement present—two diamonds that Michael then had fashioned into an engagement ring.

The wedding was set for Chou Chou's birthday, May 20, and Alix asked Bette if she would like to be involved with the preparations. She said no, that was up to the mother of the bride. "I did it for B.D.," Bette told her, "now you can do it for Chou."

"Bette did offer to do one thing," Alix recalls. "She said she'd arrange to have a fabulous photographer there to record everything. Well, apparently she forgot, because there was no photographer—all we have are the snapshots that the guests took."

According to Alix, Bette caused not a whit of discord during the engagement and wedding—but B.D. did. Chou Chou had decided that she first wanted an intimate, family-only engagement party, to be followed by a larger celebration. Alix sent B.D. an invitation, and B.D. told her that she had a previous commitment and couldn't come. Alix was not pleased. "Now, this isn't something you invite someone to overnight. There was plenty of time for her to get out of whatever other commitment she had. This was her brother, her one and only brother's engagement. And she didn't come."

Angry at what she considered an unpardonable snub, Alix didn't invite B.D. to the larger second party, and she was prepared to exclude her from the wedding as well. "But I decided that maybe I was wrong—this was Bette Davis's daughter and who was I? So I did send her an invitation to the wedding. She never even replied to it. I heard from someone else that she had no intention of coming."

Loath to upset Bette, Alix telephoned B.D., apologized for everything, and asked her to attend. "She did not come," Alix says. "After the ceremony, Bette drove up to Westport and pleaded with B.D. to come to the reception, if only for Michael's sake. She refused. And then she told everybody that I never even invited her. *She* chose not to come. I begged her on the phone, Bette went to see her, and she made the decision to stay home."

B.D. did, however, send Michael and his bride a wedding present. "She sent them a hammock," Alix recalls. "It was a *good* hammock, but we were all kind of confused because they were planning to move into an apartment in Boston. Where could they have used a hammock?"

B.D.'s failure to attend was the only sour note in an otherwise lovely wedding. Bette and Gary Merrill sat next to each other in the front pew, and Alix recalled that Bette was "completely charming" the entire day. "She wore a beautiful blue embroidered full-length gown, simple lines, and she looked stunning. I was very pleased to have her there."

Bette reacted to Michael's marriage so differently from the way she had reacted to B.D.'s that she could have been another woman altogether. According to Alix Snow, "She didn't interfere. She just wanted to have a pleasant relationship with him and Chou. She didn't assert herself at all. And she was so generous to them. For their honeymoon, she sent them to a Caribbean island for as long as they wanted to stay, the finest hotel, everything paid. And she spent $5,000 once to help them put in a natural border of already-grown evergreens to create a little park on their property for their kids.

"They never asked Bette for help, she always offered it. And after Michael established himself as a successful lawyer, he would only accept small gifts, tokens of love from Bette, that she was thrilled to give him and his family."

B.D. and Jeremy, on the other hand, frequently needed financial help from Bette, and this added to the friction and discord in their relationship. In light of her largesse, Bette reasonably expected to be treated well, to be welcomed into their home. But the Hymans seemed to detest needing Bette's help, and looked on a good deal of it as an attempt to buy their love. Bette grew more and more resentful of their lack of appreciation, and angrier and angrier at Jeremy for what she saw as his shortcomings as a provider for her daughter. As B.D.'s close friend Josie Hamm puts it, "I'm sure Bette, like any mother, would have preferred to have a son-in-law she didn't have to help." And Bette's anger at Jeremy deepened as she watched his control over B.D. grow, saw the way she waited on him, subjugated her personality to his, obeyed his every command.

"The funny thing about Bette," Alix Snow says with a chuckle, "was that she adored Chou for taking such good care of Michael. All the things she didn't like B.D. doing for Jeremy she loved for *my* daughter to do for Michael."

Bette's third child was rarely a part of her life now. Still at the Lochland School, Margot turned twenty in 1971, and she had learned some self-sufficiency. Like other residents of the school, she was able to take the bus back and forth to a simple job every day, keep up her room, cook for herself and others. "Margot is what would be called mildly retarded," says Barbara Huebner, who took over the directorship of the school from Florence Stewart. "She reads, she writes, but she has a very, very short attention span—she could never read a book, or even a short story. She dreams a lot, fantasizes about having a husband and a home."

In his memoirs, Gary Merrill recalled Miss Stewart's observation that Margot was "the most pathetic child at the school because she was just bright enough to know what she was missing. She wanted to have babies, hold a job, get married—all the things normal people do—and she knows she can't."

Margot's fascination with the opposite sex, Barbara Huebner says, borders on the "unhealthy," and it has gotten her into some trouble. By the time she was sixteen, she had developed into a lovely young woman with, as Gary's friend Bob Jurgenson observed, "the body of a twenty-year-old but the mind of a child of eight. Gary was very concerned that she might be badly taken advantage of, and he tried to keep a tight rein on her. But she became harder and harder to control. Once while she was visiting Gary, she climbed out of her bedroom window in the middle of the night and was found hitchhiking along the side of the road."

In 1967, when Margot was sixteen, Gary took her with him on a vacation trip to Florida. When she returned to Lochland, she told anyone who would listen that she had wandered away from Gary, met a man, and had her first sexual experience in a secluded spot on the beach. "That's all Margot talked about," the Lochland housemother, Mary Beardsley, recalls. "But nobody believed her because she said that the young man was Joe Namath. We all knew that her hero was Joe Namath, so everybody scoffed." Mary and her husband Al, however, don't doubt that the incident occurred. According to Al, "She was very explicit about what happened. She couldn't have told me what she told me unless she had really had that experience. The only part that she made up was about Joe Namath."

A few years later, Margot ran away from the school and was gone overnight. "She got picked up by some truck drivers," Mary remembers, "and she wound up over in Canandaigua [a neighboring town]. Gary Merrill and Miss Stewart were beside themselves. Thank God, the men who picked her up didn't seem to have hurt her in any way."

Margot's habit of saying whatever came to mind often proved embarrassing, particularly since what was usually on her mind was sex. Josie Hamm recalled Margot approaching her handsome young gardener and saying, "I'm Juliet. Are you my Romeo?" According to Barbara Huebner, "People come here [to Lochland] and the first thing Margot will ask the men is, 'Are you married?' If they say no, she'll ask, 'Do you have a girlfriend?' If they say they're married, she'll ask if they have any sons, and are *they* married. And she has been known to ask an attractive man sitting next to her on an airplane—right out of the blue—whether she could have his baby."

Bette found it very difficult to spend any prolonged periods of time with Margot. With her own wit so lightning fast, she had no patience for Margot's meandering mind, slow responses, and silly fantasies. She would treat Margot as though she were an intellectual equal, and when Margot didn't measure up Bette would lash out at her. Bette's friend Roy Moseley recalled that Bette, angry at Margot for not combing her hair, brushed it for her so violently "I thought she was going to break her neck." On another occasion, Bette ordered Margot to do something and the girl snapped, "You're not my mother! You can't say this to me!"

"Of *course* I'm your mother!" Bette bellowed. "What do you think I've been *doing* all these years? Where would you be without me? Who do you think *paid* for you? Who do you think paid for all your *clothes*?" Then, Moseley recalled, Bette hit her. Judging from entries about Margot in Bette's diary, she seemed, amazingly, not to comprehend her adopted daughter's mental limitations. Rather, she took Margot's behavior as a personal affront and she wrote of Margot's "perverseness" and "deviousness," concluding that "rough physical discipline is the only thing the lying black Irish girl understands."

Till the end of her life, Bette claimed that she paid all of Margot's expenses at Lochland, that she brought her home to the family as often as possible, and that she visited the school regularly. None of this is true. From 1965 until his death in 1991, Gary paid the bills, and the staff members at the school remember only Gary visiting Margot after the 1960s.

Frequently, Bette failed to send for Margot when the girl was scheduled to make a visit to Connecticut. Margot, excited, would wait for someone to come for her, but the Lochland staff would hear nothing from Bette for so long that one of them would finally have to call her to make arrangements for the visit. Almost invariably, according to Mary Beardsley, Margot would return early. "She was always hustled back ahead of time from visits with her mother. If two weeks were planned, she'd be sent back at the end of the first week. And she'd be very upset by things that had happened while she was there. Margot always felt very tense when she went to visit her mother; she wanted to do the right thing. And if she didn't do what Bette expected her to do, Bette would get frustrated and shout at Margot or cuss her. Whenever Margot got back from Bette's, she always had a new vocabulary of curse words. And she'd be crushed that her mother treated her that way."

And then there was Bobby, still in Bette's shadow, still in Bette's employ, still the butt of Bette's cavalier mistreatment. "My mother was just totally devoted to her," Bobby's daughter Ruth Bailey recalls. "She was a very passive type of person. My aunt was very dynamic. My mother worked for her and she tried to make everything peaceful in the house." She was rarely successful. "My aunt was abusive to everybody. It wasn't just my mother. That's just the way Bette was."

If Bobby didn't do something to Bette's satisfaction, Ruth says, Bette would "go into screaming fits. If she didn't like a meal my mother had prepared, she would turn on her viciously and say something like, 'Gee, this is a real good dinner you cooked! What kind of a can did you get it out of?'"

Bette's assistant Vik Greenfield liked Bobby. "She was everything

Bette wasn't, and nothing Bette was," he says. "You would never dream that they were sisters. Bette was very quick witted, and Bobby was slow, and that irritated Bette. Bette would make pronouncements like, 'Of course, you know, she was in and out of mental institutions. And *I* paid for it all!' But it never dawned on her *why* Bobby was like that. Not for a moment. Bobby being ill was an affront to Bette, rather than something that had happened to Bobby that Bette should feel sympathy for."

Ruth Bailey saw that her mother would become angry whenever Bette told an interviewer that she "supported" Bobby. "My mother worked for every dime. She had taken care of B.D. and Michael, she had full charge of them sometimes. She worked like a dog for Bette. And when Bette said these things, it was very upsetting to her, but she never said anything to Bette about it. What can you say? You can't fight City Hall."

Late in 1968, Bobby decided that she had had enough of Bette, and she moved to Phoenix to live with Ruth and her family, which by then included two sons—one of whom was a Bette Davis fan and collector. Bette sent Bobby $400 a month, which Ruth considers "a retirement fund. My mother more than earned it through the years." And Bette would call her every other day when she wasn't working; they would talk about the latest intrigues on the soap operas, the latest events in their lives. "They talked like anybody else would talk," Ruth recalled. "Sister talk."

Bette had hired Vik Greenfield as her live-in assistant in 1968. He continued to work for her off and on for six years, and they remained in touch for the rest of her life. At their first meeting, she told the young Englishman she appreciated the fact that he didn't seem to be afraid of her, and had not brought up her career: "You know when to keep your mouth shut."

Greenfield moved into Twin Bridges and began a daily routine that included bringing coffee and a newspaper to Bette's bedroom every morning. "She'd get herself ready and come down and putter around in the kitchen and make lunch for the both of us," he recalls. "I was usually working around the grounds, or going out on errands, or going back and forth to B.D.'s."

Bette loved her home, Greenfield realized, and "she was a great homemaker. She knew how to do everything properly. Beds were properly made and properly turned down, ironing was done to a tee. Her tables were beautifully laid. Bette was the best hostess in the world—until the guests arrived."

It was then that Greenfield saw another side of her. "She was very unsure and nervous and would be drinking, and if someone said the wrong thing Bette's behavior could be disgraceful. She just drank too much. She drank just about all day, and sometimes she would be so embarrassing at parties. The next morning she might say, 'I was a good girl last night, wasn't I?' and I'd look at her in total disbelief. Or she'd say, 'I was a bad girl. I've got to send them flowers.'

"You just rolled with the punches with Bette. It wasn't like that every day. There were some very pleasant periods, some good laughs. She had absolutely no sense of humor about herself, but you could make her laugh, and she had a rather harsh, raucous laugh. She was very child-like—not childish, but childlike. She *loved* parties, she loved wrapping presents, she loved surprises. She loved all of that and when it was happening she *really* enjoyed herself."

Greenfield was surprised to see another side of Bette as well. As meticulous as she could be about her home, she oftentimes seemed unconcerned about her personal hygiene. "Bette never looked after herself properly," he said. "In her house she would hardly take a bath a week, let alone wash her hair." When a friend with whom she was once staying seemed disturbed by the fact that she hadn't used her bath towels, she said to him, "I don't bathe very often, but I'm not dirty. I don't smell, do I?"

His most lasting impression of Bette, Greenfield says, was that she was a sad, lonely woman. He was astonished one day when she proposed marriage to him. "She wasn't serious, really, there was no romance between us. She just said, 'Oh, well, we might as well get married.' It was the statement of the day. Bette proposed to everybody so you took it for what it was worth.

"The tragedy of Bette was that she never found a man to sort of sit on her. She never found happiness, she never found fulfillment. She was, in my opinion, the unhappiest person I ever met. And your heart goes out to people like that in many ways. I think she was borderline manic-depressive—there were highs and there were lows. She could be impossible, but she just didn't know how to stop herself. She had *no* self-control whatsoever. It was as if the train started and just couldn't stop. And once you understood that about her, whatever she did—however tiresome it could be—you could always end up liking her. Not because she was famous, but because you realized that at the bottom of it all there was a very lonely, very frightened little girl."

As early as the late 1940s, Bette had told her friend Betty Lynn that her greatest fear was that she would "wind up as a lonely old lady, in a house up on a hill." By the early 1970s, with Ruthie dead, B.D. and Michael married, Bobby living in Phoenix, her career at a virtual standstill, Vik Greenfield no longer in her employ, and no romantic involvements to divert her energies, Bette's worst fear had become reality. B.D. recalled that Bette was fond of telling the press, "In the final analysis, work is all there is. Family doesn't last . . . they all go off. Human relationships . . . ha! . . . they're a joke. All there is is work, and I'm damn lucky to have it."

No trace can be found of any interview in which Bette said anything quite that intemperate, only that she found work the most fulfilling thing in her life now. And that was the problem. Bette had made just three films in the eight years since *The Nanny,* two of them obscure European dramas barely released in the United States. The third, *Bunny O'Hare,* in which she and Ernest Borgnine played geriatric bank robbers disguised as hippies, was arguably the artistic nadir of her career.

Financially strapped again, Bette made three more attempts at the security of a television series between 1972 and 1974. In *Madame Sin,* a two-hour movie of the week produced by and costarring Robert Wagner (who became a lifelong friend), she played a power-hungry, half-Chinese woman living in a Scottish castle filled with spy gadgetry. In *The Judge and Jake Wyler* she was cast as a retired jurist who fights crime with the help of a young parolee, and in *Hello Mother, Goodbye!* she was the domineering parent of an aerospace engineer who moves back in with Mom after quitting his job. None of these pilots was picked up for a series, and Bette did only one other TV movie, *Scream, Pretty Peggy,* a cheapjack throwback to *Baby Jane* and *Hush . . . Hush, Sweet Charlotte,* aired in 1973.

Bette made some money during this period with a personal-appearance tour of college campuses; she showed clips from her movies and answered questions from the audience, but the net effect of the experience was to depress her with the thought that she was a has-been who could merely reminisce about her long-ago glory days. She was surprised by a "This Is Your Life" tribute to her on the set of *Madame Sin,* at which Bobby (looking much like Edith Head in heavy-rimmed glasses and square pageboy-and-bangs hairdo), William Wyler, Olivia De Havilland, and Victor Buono sang her praises, but the exercise left Bette unsettled. "I felt like I had just attended my own funeral," she said later.

By the end of 1973 Bette's money was so low that her attorney Harold Schiff told her she would have to sell Twin Bridges. She had made only $26,000 in 1972, and when she turned sixty-five in April 1973 she applied for her Social Security benefits. She moved into a smaller house even closer to B.D., in Weston, and dubbed it My Bailiwick. To save face, she said that she had moved because, with Michael married, Twin Bridges was just too big. But privately she grieved at the loss of the house she had loved so much, and at her reduced circumstances.

All of this combined to push Bette into a crushing depression. She drank heavily; according to B.D. she was often insensible by ten in the morning. Her obsession with cleanliness and neatness deteriorated until her home had become a "pigsty," with dirty dishes piled high in the sink, plates of uneaten food on her bedstands, clothes strewn everywhere. "The bed was an indescribable mess," B.D. recalled, "with cigarette burns and overflowing ashtrays, dropped bits of food and spilled whiskey all around it."

B.D. cleaned the mess and tried to shake Bette out of her stupor, but nothing seemed to work. B.D. was convinced that all of this was an act for her benefit, to push her into leaving her family and becoming Bette's full-time companion. Suffering from colitis, she tried to keep a distance from Bette, but her mother's behavior, she said, worried her to the point of serious illness. Finally, as she had done when B.D. was a child, Bette announced that she was going to end it all. "Tomorrow I'll be gone," she told B.D. over the phone. "Just remember me with love."

B.D. had vowed never again to "fall for" such histrionics as she had the first time, and she ended up ignoring Bette's threat. Within a few days, Bette called and invited her to lunch. She was sober, the house was immaculately clean, and Bette chattered and gossiped as though nothing had happened.

When B.D. brought up Bette's behavior, she didn't want to hear about it. B.D. pressed the issue. "I will not go through anything like this again," she said. "If you pull another of your phony suicides, I'll walk away. To use your own words, you'll no longer have a daughter."

"I always knew you were a cold bitch!" Bette sputtered. "Jesus! There was nothing phony about it. I wanted to die!"

"Bullshit!" B.D. bellowed. "All you wanted was for me to feel totally responsible for you . . . to leave my family, like Aunt Bobby left hers,

and come home to keep poor Mommy company. I know it and you know it and I won't allow myself to be put in this position again."

The luncheon ended with neither woman conceding a point; when Bette apologized, B.D. thought, it was "without a trace of sincerity." When B.D. left, she gave her mother a peck on the cheek, and Bette said, "I'm glad to know you were so worried about me. It helps to know that you love me so much."

The entire tawdry episode left Bette convinced that she would have to return to work again as soon as possible or lose her mind. But there were no film or television offers. The depth of her desolation can be gauged by the fact that she accepted the next offer that came her way: the starring role in a Broadway musical.

THIRTY

ette sat on the floor of Joshua Logan's penthouse apartment overlooking Manhattan's East River, surrounded by the cast members of *Miss Moffat*, the big-budget Broadway musical version of her 1945 film *The Corn Is Green*. Logan, the brilliant director of such classic shows as *Annie Get Your Gun* and *South Pacific* (as well as the films *Picnic, Bus Stop,* and *Camelot*), wanted the company, many of them young Broadway neophytes, to meet Bette, who was set to reprise her role as the schoolteacher who helps an impoverished but talented student. On the strength of her name, advance ticket sales had been tremendous, and everyone was in an upbeat mood. Bette laughed and joked with her young costar, Dorian Harewood, and the other performers, among them Nell Carter and Dody Goodman.

Rudy Lowe, an eighteen-year-old newcomer at the time, remembers the evening vividly. "It changed my conception of Bette Davis. She sat on the floor with everybody else, she played around, she was very, very nice—like someone's grandmother. She wasn't like the Bette Davis you know from the movies. I guess she wanted us to be free with her. We talked about life, general things, and a few people asked her questions about her film career, but she didn't talk much about that. She was just trying to get to know everybody and be nice and be part of the group."

How could the show fail? With Bette reprising one of her most beloved film roles, with Joshua Logan directing, with Emlyn Williams, the author of the original play, writing the book and lyrics, and Albert Hague, the Tony Award–winning composer of *Redhead,* supplying the music, the show seemed like such a sure bet that Logan, who was also coproducing, had very little trouble raising the $500,000 capitalization he needed. Among the show's investors—"angels" in Broadway parlance—were RCA Records (which expected to produce the original-cast album),

Bette's attorney Harold Schiff, Mrs. Oscar Hammerstein, the Holly-wood producer Robert Evans, and Arlene Francis.

Bette had not been Josh Logan's first choice to play Lily Moffat; he turned to her only after Mary Martin bowed out because of her husband's death and Katharine Hepburn turned the part down. Bette had had some doubts about this offer—after *The Night of the Iguana*, she had vowed never to work on stage again—but she always thought she had been too young to play Miss Moffat in 1945, and she was enchanted by the new show's unusual concept: Emlyn had switched the locale from a Welsh mining village to the American South, and the student Miss Moffat helps is black. What finally convinced her, she told Logan, was the quality of Emlyn Williams's book. "This is a part with good words," she said. "The theater is so dependent on good scripts. And even at my age, I have a deep, deep desire always to play the lead. In the last script I was asked to read I ended up being hung in an attic. *Hung in an attic!* I want to tell you, I've played a lot of funny parts in my career, but I said, 'Bette, you're *never* going to be seen hanging in an attic!' "

She expressed some doubts to Logan that she would be able to do justice to the songs, but he assured her that they were easily within her range and ability as a vocalist. She asked him to come to Westport with the score, just to be sure. Bette tried out the songs for the first time at a high school near her home that had a suitable piano. Logan later recalled his amazement that Bette seemed far more interested in her chauffeur's reaction to her performance than Logan's: "She kept looking over at him rather than at me."

Comfortable with the music, Bette signed on, and tryouts began for the key costarring roles. Most important was the casting of the student, Morgan Evans. During Dorian Harewood's audition, Logan felt the handsome actor had a strong singing voice but had interpreted the char-acter in the wrong way. He was about to discuss this with Harewood when the show's coproducer, Eugene Wolsk, approached and whispered, "Tell him to go. She doesn't like him."

Instead, the director asked Harewood to meet him at eleven the following morning for further discussions. At five minutes to eleven the next day, Bette telephoned Logan. "I've been thinking," she said. "That boy in the pink shirt, I think you should work with him. Anybody who sings with that much drama must have some actor in him."

Harewood got the part, and showed so much talent in rehearsals that the entire company was sure the play would make him a superstar. Optimism infused everyone, and none more than Bette, who bubbled over with enthusiasm. "I want to do a year on the road with the show," she burbled to Eugene Wolsk. "A year in New York, then a year in London. Then the movie. And then, that's it. I'll be seventy and ready to retire." On this schedule, Bette's salary-and-profit-participation income of between $15,000 and $25,000 per week would accumulate into a sizable nest egg.

Abrim with energy and excitement, Bette plunged into rehearsals in August 1974. "At the beginning, she was fine," Rudy Lowe recalls. "But then something happened. I don't know what it was—nobody knows what happened—but I remember something seemed to click in her head, and like night and day, she switched."

"I don't understand what this woman wants!" Josh Logan cried to Rudy Lowe as they walked down Forty-sixth Street together. "What did I do? What have I done to this woman? What do you think is going on?"

Lowe didn't know how to respond. "Here I was an eighteen-year-old kid and Josh Logan is asking me for advice on how to handle Bette Davis! We were having problems with Bette, and Josh was a very nervous man—he was manic depressive—and he had a pocketful of change that he always played with when he was nervous. So he's walking down Forty-sixth Street jingling his change and wondering what to do about Bette."

As so often before in her stage endeavors, Bette's enthusiasm had quickly turned to fear that she was out of her league in a Broadway show and headed for embarrassment. Her understudy, Anne Francine, feels flatly that "she was scared. In the movies she was queen, and on stage she wasn't. She couldn't sing at all. It was embarrassing. And she had no stage technique, so she was frightened. *Nothing* could be more contrary to her emotional makeup than to be frightened. She was used to doing the frightening!"

Not all of Bette's songs were easily sung, Francine recalls. "One song would have been difficult for *anybody*. I don't know what Hague was thinking when he wrote it. Maybe he wrote it for Mary Martin. But you couldn't even suggest to Bette that she wasn't a great singer. She did the song in rehearsal, and Josh always told us to give her every encouragement, keep her spirits up. So I told her that I liked what she'd done with the song, that she sang it rather like Rex Harrison did his songs in *My Fair Lady*—meaning that she had wisely talked the song instead of sung it. She looked at me and said, 'Don't be *silly*. Rex Harrison couldn't *sing*!'

"Well, you didn't contradict Bette Davis. The worst part of it all was that it was a great role and she had done it so well in the movie, but she simply couldn't do it on stage. She had to have that camera, that small space. She couldn't fill a huge theater. It was not her milieu."

As Emlyn Williams constantly handed her rewritten sides, Bette's fear increased, and her behavior turned dreadful. "She *hated* rehearsing," Anne Francine saw, "because she hated to learn. She couldn't learn new lines very well. She would throw a *tantrum* when she was given new material."

Rudy Lowe recalls that Bette was "very jealous of Anne Francine, because Anne was prepared to go on at the drop of a hat and do a great job. She had the fire, and it was as if Bette's credo was 'Come hell or high water, you, woman, are not going to set foot on that stage.' "

"Bette was very suspicious of me," Francine concurs. "Josh Logan said to me, 'She needs someone to be friendly with her.' But a star doesn't want her stand-in at her shoulder every minute, because it's like you're waiting for her to slip on a banana peel." Bette didn't make it easy for her understudy to learn the part; she practiced her numbers privately, forcing Francine to hide under a piano one day while Bette rehearsed in order to learn a new song. "I'd sort of sneak around. . . . I'd stand outside doors listening to what was happening."

If Bette seemed tired, or couldn't remember her lines, or complained of a backache, Josh Logan would suggest that she take a break, and one of his assistants would call out, "Francine as Moffat!" signaling that the rehearsal would go ahead without Bette. Whenever Bette heard "Francine as Moffat!" Anne recalls, "this strange look would come over her face. So I asked them not to do that—just let me know I was needed somehow. We tried to spare her anything that would smack of undermining her. She had to be the queen—and as far as I was concerned, she was. I was ready to let her walk on my head if she had wanted to, if it would have helped her."

Rudy Lowe soon noticed that Bette was drinking during rehearsals, which didn't help matters. "She had this silver flask with her all the time, and I guess we all figured it was water. But one day she knocked it over, and you could smell the booze. She'd do strange things. The one time I thought she was really drunk she took off her wig during a rehearsal and handed it to one of the dancers. Now, this wasn't her Miss Moffat wig but her *own* wig—that's why we were all so shocked."

In the middle of another rehearsal, according to Lowe, Bette locked herself in her dressing room and wouldn't come out. "She and Logan were fighting constantly at this point. He said that she was making incredible demands and he thought she was crazy. She was threatening not to go on with the show. Then she started saying *he* was crazy. I overheard them both screaming 'You're *crazy!*' at each other."

Miss Moffat was scheduled to begin its out-of-town tryouts at the Mechanic Theatre in Baltimore on September 9. On August 28, Bette checked herself into the Harkness Pavilion at the Columbia-Presbyterian Medical Center in New York, complaining of pains in her lower back and legs.

"That was just Bette's usual sick act," says Vik Greenfield, who came back to work for Bette for the *Miss Moffat* tour. "Take my word for it, it was all mental and all an act."

Many of the *Moffat* company agreed, but Rudy Lowe felt Bette's woes were genuine. "She had to ride around on a big bike—not the Schwinns we have now, but an authentic, period bike that was heavy even for us. And she had costumes with all this heavy bracing in them. So she was dragging along a lot there. I remember one day in rehearsal someone said, 'Oh, she just doesn't want to go on,' and I said, 'No, I think she's got a problem.' I didn't know if it was brought on through her psychosis or whatever, but I knew there was a problem that was genuine. I think she brought the problem on, but I don't think she was faking."

The doctors couldn't say definitively what was wrong with Bette; her X-rays were negative, and they thought she might have a slipped disk. In any event, they told Logan, her hospitalization would continue for at least three weeks, maybe eight. "This would be enough to destroy us financially," Logan recalled.

With the members of the *Miss Moffat* company, faced with unemployment, moving through their days "like robots," and the producers facing financial ruin, Bette called Logan and Wolsk and asked them to come to her hospital room. When they arrived they found her sitting up in bed, with her leg in traction, wearing a nightgown, a shawl, and Miss Moffat's straw boater on her head. "It gave her a cocky and humorous look," Logan recalled, "and pumped up more hope than almost anything else she said or did."

Eugene Wolsk got down to cases immediately. "Bette, please be frank," he pleaded. "Do you want to continue with this or not?"

"Of course!" Bette sang out. "I love it! I'm passionately in love with it. I *must* do it! If you can wait for me, fine. If you can't, then I'll understand."

"If you want to do it," Wolsk assured her, "we'll wait as long as is humanly possible, so don't worry about it. Just try to get well."

Bette remained in the hospital for nearly a month, while the Baltimore segment of the road tour was put back to December and the Philadelphia run (already scheduled to begin on September 23) became the show's new opening date. That date had to be put back to October 4, but to the immense relief of everyone, Bette announced herself ready and able to return to work in time for it.

A few days before she was due to resume rehearsals, Bette's attorney Harold Schiff told Logan that she had injured her back again. Logan asked how, and Schiff said the injury happened after she drove up to Connecticut to visit B.D. "We were astounded," Logan recalled, "that sick as her doctors had said she was, she would take the chance of that long automobile ride. Again we realized she was shooting with our dice."

Finally, with the opening put back yet again to October 7, Bette told Logan she was well enough to return to rehearsals in Philadelphia. When Anne Francine returned to the theater for the first run-through with the recovered Bette, she arrived early and walked onto a darkened stage. Out of the corner of her eye she noticed someone sitting on the other side of the stage, silent, enveloped in darkness. Then she saw the flash of a cigarette lighter and she knew it was Bette Davis. "Oh, Miss Davis, it's Anne," she called into the shadows.

"I know," Bette said.

"It's wonderful that you're back. How are you?"

"I feel terrible," Bette replied, then fell silent again.

Francine's heart sank. "I thought, *Dear God, it's going to go on.*"

At a preview on October 4, Bette Davis performed *Miss Moffat* for the first time in front of a paying audience. To Joshua Logan's surprise, she was terrific and he felt newly confident he had a hit and that Bette would be wonderful in it. "She seemed more sure of herself, her performance was more clear-cut . . . and her music was handled in a much better way: she spoke a bit, sang a bit, spoke a bit, sang a bit, close to the way we had agreed . . . she seemed to be a happy, stimulated woman. Oh God, if we could only have frozen that evening."

No one was more relieved by Bette's new professionalism than Dorian Harewood, who had found it impossible to develop a rapport with her during rehearsals because of her maddening habit of stopping dead in the middle of a scene if she forgot her lines, or repeating a line she had just said, or criticizing the dialogue even as she spoke it. Now that they were in front of audiences, Harewood was certain, Bette would never do that again, and as they moved the show toward Broadway they would be able to create a stronger reality in their exchanges, build genuine emotion in their relationship.

Opening night in Philadelphia proved him wrong. To his and everyone else's mortification, Bette behaved as though this performance (the first to be attended by influential critics as well as the public) was just another dress rehearsal. As Josh Logan recalled, "[Bette] was quite often difficult to hear. She repeated lines in lyrics or left them out entirely. She forgot dialogue she had never forgotten before. . . . At one point she turned to the audience and said, to our horror, 'How can I play this scene? Morgan Evans is supposed to be onstage. Morgan Evans, get out here!' Poor Dorian Harewood, who still had minutes to wait before entering, nevertheless ran on and looked at her for a cue. . . . Almost at once she realized she had made a mistake. She turned to the audience at once and said, 'I was wrong. I want you to know that. It wasn't his fault.'

"The audience, under her spell, cheered and applauded, and laughed all through it, forgiving, even enjoying, any mistake. Bette went on. 'It was my own stupid fault, and Dorian had nothing to do with it. Go back, Morgan, and we'll start over.' He did, to more laughter and prolonged applause. The scene finally got going, but by that time the audience had lost its way. The evening was growing longer and longer. And the mistakes less amusing."

At another point, a seven-year-old cast member, aware that Bette had forgotten her lines, whispered them to her. "I was just stepping onstage when the boy told Bette her lines," Rudy Lowe recalled, "and she stopped the show cold and said, 'I remember my lines, *dear*!' And I went, 'Oooooh.' Things like that happened all the time. Once she was singing a song, forgot the lyrics, and started all over from the beginning. The cast didn't know what to do when she did things like that. We didn't know how to play it. Because if you covered for her—which everybody does for everybody sometime or other—she might embarrass you. So you were on pins and needles. You didn't know what you should do."

Josh Logan knew what *he* should do when he read the scathing reviews the next morning—he set about to rewrite and rework the show. He called the cast together that afternoon and announced cheerily, "Well, we've done it! We've opened, and now we can really get down to work!"

Anne Francine marvels at what happened next. "Bette looked at him and said, 'What do you mean?' And he said, 'Well, now we know where the weaknesses are, and we can change things and really start building—' And before he finished she just said quietly, 'I'm not going to learn one new line. I'm not changing one damn thing.' And all of us were in total shock! There must have been fifty people in the theater, and you could feel the silence and shock from everybody."

That night, Harold Schiff informed Logan that not only were there to be no rewrites for at least a week, but there were also to be no rehearsals for *anyone*. This, to Logan, "was unique in my experience of ultimatums."

After a few performances at which there were no changes, Bette seemed happier and more at ease in the role. The Philadelphia audiences seemed to like the show, even with its faults, and they clearly loved Bette as Miss Moffat. Logan was certain that if he could work out the kinks, the play would be a tremendous success. "She seemed to be getting better and better as the week went on. She seemed to be in a state of euphoria. The audience could always get her in that mood." On Thursday night Logan went to her dressing room, where she ecstatically reiterated her commitment to see the show through to New York, London, and beyond. "*Miss Moffat* has saved me," she exclaimed. "*Saved* me!"

"I felt closer and warmer to her than ever before," Logan recalled. Then he mentioned that of course there would still have to be *some* adjustments in the show, just to fine-tune it.

The next day, Bette summoned the director to her hotel suite. He found her lying on her bed, fully clothed, her eyes unfocused and wandering as though she were in a daze—looking, he said, "like an alabaster queen on an alabaster coffin." She asked him if the doctor had phoned him. "Doctor?" Logan warily replied. "No, Bette—what doctor?"

"The doctor in New York. Hasn't he told you that I can't play it anymore?"

"Play what? You mean *Miss Moffat?*"

"That's right."

"But who told him to call me?"

"I did. I can't play it anymore. There's no use talking."

Logan was dumbstruck for a moment, then found his voice again. "You mean you've decided without actually going to see another doctor here that you're not going to play it anymore? That means tonight or the next night?"

"Or any night."

Logan felt as though he were "walking naked through hell." Finally he said, "Bette, I know this sounds silly to you, but for your own sake you can't commit this kind of professional suicide. You've become sick and made two important productions suffer before. There were hundreds of thousands of dollars of other people's money lost because of it and dozens of actors put out of work. You mustn't be blamed for that again, Bette. This might be the end of your stage career."

"I can't help it. I'm in pain. What can I do?"

"You can't do anything, I suppose, except perhaps wait a few days and maybe come back for—"

"I'm not coming back—*ever*. I *can't*. The doctor will *tell* you I can't. So let everyone know, will you?"

Dazed, Logan left the suite and called Bette's doctor, who admitted that he had not examined her. "All I know is that when patients say they can't play a show, I'm powerless as a doctor to tell them to go up on the stage and play it."

Logan knew that he couldn't replace Bette without the play suffering badly at the box office. Angry and desolate, he announced to the company that he was closing *Miss Moffat*. "The blackest juices began to flow through my head and heart. On that gloomy afternoon I couldn't for one second weep for poor Bette Davis on her bed of pain. I didn't have time because I was feeling too sorry for myself . . . Emlyn . . . Albert Hague . . . and that great, blameless cast. What of them and their jobs gone askew?"

Bette was able to convince the show's insurance doctors that her legs were actually paralyzed, and the financial backers recouped some of their investment. But the cast was devastated, especially the hopeful young performers whose big break this show would have been. "We all cried," Rudy Lowe remembered. "What hurt us the most was that Bette didn't care enough to say good-bye to us. It was like a parent was leaving, and she didn't say good-bye. But we loved Bette in spite of everything. We really did."

Vik Greenfield feels that the poor chemistry between Bette and Logan sabotaged the show. "When I saw Bette in rehearsals, I thought to myself, *My God, she can't really do it—she can't cut the mustard*. I felt sorry for Joshua Logan, but he and Emlyn Williams both hid behind anybody's apron strings they could find. If only they had come forward and reasoned with her and explained things to her, maybe the show would have made it. She got the script, she learned the script, then the next night they were giving her new lines to learn for the next performance. You can't do that to a movie actress, who's used to being able to retake a scene if she messes up. Logan and Williams finally toppled the pedestal from under the statue and in many ways it was their fault."

Mike Ellis, the producer of *Two's Company,* had followed the ups and downs of *Miss Moffat* with more than passing interest. "You know," he says, "in 1961, when Chuck Bowden wanted Bette Davis to do *Iguana,* he called and said to me, 'Tell me about Bette.' So I told him everything, and later I heard he had told someone that we just hadn't known how to handle her. Then the phone rang again in the early seventies, and this time it was Josh Logan, and he said, 'Refresh my memory about Bette Davis.' So I refreshed him, and the next thing I knew he announced that he would be directing her in *Miss Moffat.* So there is a record there that indicates it is possible to have troubles with Bette Davis."

"My great energy had deserted me," Bette said to explain the *Moffat* fiasco. "I was exhausted. For the first time I realized that I was an old woman." She returned to My Bailiwick—"fully recovered" from her back problem, according to B.D.—and remained out of the public eye until March 1975. Then she took her show of reminiscences, *An Informal Evening with Bette Davis,* to Australia, returning with suitcases full of sheepskins and kangaroo coats for family and friends, and a stuffed toy lamb for her grandson Ashley.

"I am up to my ears in debt and taxes," she said, "and that's why I come out of my house in Connecticut every few years and work. I can hole up just so long, then I gotta get out and stir things up again. It's half for income, and half for me." Her one-woman show was a perfect showcase for her: no lines to learn, no meddling directors, no grueling rehearsals. Just *La Davis,* soaking up the adoration of the audience and answering questions, some posed with such reverence that she might have been the Delphic Oracle. Her answers, however, were never ambiguous, and the audiences loved it. Who, one woman asked her, was her favorite husband? "Obviously I had no favorite since I *dumped them all!*" she cackled. When another wondered whether she had ever had a face-lift, Bette asked her to come to the lip of the stage. Then she put her face inches from the woman's and asked, "If I had ever had a face-lift, would I look like *this*?!"

"When I started, I was scared," Bette said as she prepared to take the show to England, Scotland, and Wales late in 1975, "but now I love it. Nobody will ever know what love and applause means to me. Move on, never get repetitious, learn how to handle the audience—those are the things I believe in. I always walk out and say, 'What a dump!' and that brings down the house. Then they know it's not going to be a pompous evening; it's going to be a ball!"

Before Bette took the show to Great Britain, she completed her first American theatrical film in five years, a supernatural thriller that gave her top billing over Oliver Reed and Karen Black. Her agent, Robert Lantz, recalled that while Bette "had to work," she also had "an absolute rule that she would not go under the title. No cameos for Bette Davis. There were plenty of producers in Hollywood who were willing to pay her $100,000 to appear for a few minutes in their film, just to use this name celebrated the world over. Unh-unh. Not for Bette. She wasn't in a position *not* to work, but she wouldn't sell out. And it wasn't an ego trip. She really felt she had a deal with the public that when a marquee said, 'Bette Davis,' they really would see Bette Davis."

Burnt Offerings provided her with the billing and a substantial role, but as a vehicle it was barely above the movie she had turned down in which she would have been "hanging in an *attic*!" The story of an evil house that destroys its occupants was murky and riddled with horror-genre clichés, but in it Bette offers a fascinating microcosm of the Davis talent and persona. At the outset of the film, playing Oliver Reed's aunt, she is very much the public Bette Davis, spouting pronouncements in her clipped speech as though she were broadly imitating herself. Later, however, when she is defeated by the house and nearing death, she is astonishingly touching and real in her vulnerability, providing a reminder of the tremendous stores of acting talent she could still call on whenever she decided to jettison all the patented Bette Davis trappings.

The filming of *Burnt Offerings,* Bette claimed, nearly did her in. The child actor Lee Montgomery, who played Oliver Reed and Karen Black's son in the picture, recalls that the daughter of the film's director, Dan

Curtis, committed suicide shortly after production began by flinging herself out of a window. "We had that in our picture, too—at the end, Oliver Reed gets thrown out of an attic window. So we had to shut down for quite a while, and when we started up again it was very weird. People were kind of superstitious. It definitely tainted things."

Bette offered a long list of her problems with *Burnt Offerings* to Rex Reed in an interview published before the film's release. "This film has been amateur night in Dixie," she railed. "I said I'd never do another horror film after *Baby Jane,* and here I am in the biggest horror of them *all*!

"The director's daughter on this film committed suicide and we had to shut down for a week. Then the cameraman was fired because we couldn't see one thing on the screen, the rushes were so dark. That cost us two weeks of retakes. Karen Black showed up six months' pregnant, so they had to remake her clothes because they didn't fit. She changes her makeup in the middle of a scene, so nothing matches on the screen, she sleeps all day, never goes to rushes to see what she looks like, and you can't hear one bloody thing she says on the set. . . . Oliver Reed comes piling into the hotel at 5 A.M., and he's on the set at 6 with the hangover of the world. He fell down a *mountainside* the other night playing *bagpipes!*"

Bette hated what she called the "TV mentality" of the "New Hollywood." She was "appalled by the lack of discipline in current film making. There's practically no rehearsal, and the sloppy attitude on the set is unbelievable. These people who have been bred on television production have no sense of pacing or style. . . . It's all just get it in the can."

The interview angered Curtis, who accused Bette of sabotaging the film. She battled furiously with him from then on, upsetting him so badly after one confrontation that he walked off the set for two days. When Bette later heard he had gone to the men's room and vomited, she purportedly said, "Good—it got the damned puke out of him. Let's hope he took a *crap,* too—he was *full of it* when I talked to him!"

Bette didn't do much talking to anyone after that, and all the principals vowed never to work with her again. Lee Montgomery, who was twelve when he appeared in *Burnt Offerings,* remembers that whenever there was a problem, "Bette would say something, and if it wasn't changed, she'd just leave. She didn't have the patience to debate a subject. She demanded such an excellence, and it wasn't always there."

But Montgomery's strongest memory of Bette was that she treated him with kindness. "She would bring me to her room and we would play chess. She would chain-smoke and drink. She took a real liking to me. I spent a lot of time with her, and she told me stories." Montgomery remembers most vividly the day he was punch-drunk from working too many hours. "There was a lot of pressure to finish the picture because of budget problems, and they kept getting permits from my tutor to go beyond the eight-hour limit with me. This one night I was just drunk from lack of sleep, and I kept falling and screwing up, and everybody was laughing hysterically every time. Bette came on to the set, saw what was happening, and said, 'This is enough! Enough! He's been working too *long,* this kid. I'm taking him *home.*' And she grabbed me and took me home. She really stood up for me. She was a real sweetheart."

The critics weren't kind to *Burnt Offerings,* or to Bette, when the film was released in August 1976. The *Variety* reviewer felt that Davis "doesn't have much to do. Her role is that of a weak and pathetic old woman, hardly the kind of thing she does best. Unkind lighting and costuming make her resemble Baby Jane Hudson." Russell Davies in the London *Observer* wrote, "Bette Davis . . . keeps squawking around the place, doing her game old aunt act in the lay-or-get-off-the-nest tones of a veteran hen."

The results of Bette's next picture were far more satisfying. *The Disappearance of Aimee,* a made-for-television movie directed by the estimable British director Anthony Harvey (*The Lion in Winter*), concerned the charismatic Los Angeles evangelist Aimee Semple McPherson's mysterious one-month vanishing act in 1926. Bette had wanted to play McPherson in the 1940s, but the production code made it impossible to deal honestly with the likelihood that Aimee's month had been spent not as a kidnap victim (as she claimed), but rather in a love nest with a married man (as several witnesses attested).

Now, Bette was cast as Aimee's mother, and while she loved the script, she clearly resented Faye Dunaway, who was playing the fiery, much larger role of Aimee that Bette had always coveted, and who a few months later would win the Best Actress Oscar of 1976 for *Network.* "*Whoever* played Aimee wouldn't have seemed right to Bette," Anthony Harvey says. "She just had a gut feeling that she'd always wanted to play that part."

Bette began "testing" Harvey from the outset of the three-week shoot in Denver. "She appeared on the first day with a sort of *All About Eve* wig and tremendous makeup," Harvey recalls, "and I said, 'Look, you have the most wonderful hair, Miss Davis, and you have marvelous skin. You don't need all this makeup.' She said, 'Well, I've always done it and this is how I'm *going* to do it.' So I sat outside her caravan for an hour until she finally called me back. She had taken it all off and she looked marvelous. She didn't need all that stuff.''

After a morning of filming, Bette went to Harvey and demanded he replace the cameraman, Jim Crabbe. He realized he was being tested, and he felt it was imperative that he show some strength. "If Jim goes, Bette, I go," he told her. "He's a brilliant cameraman." Bette backed off, saying, "Well, I don't know if he can light me, but he sure is a looker."

"About two days later," Harvey recalls, "she saw the rushes and realized that Crabbe was bloody good . . . but she found it hard to look at herself after that. When you've reached a certain age, it must be tough. She just came in to check the first few dailies and she felt happy enough to not come again."

Bette's relationship with Faye Dunaway strained intensely under the weight of their differing working styles, and what Davis saw as Dunaway's lack of professionalism. "They worked in totally different ways," Harvey recalls. "Faye liked to build up her character [as filming progressed] and perhaps do more takes. Bette had a totally different way of working. She was there early, knew every line, was tremendously professional."

Dunaway, Bette later complained to friends, "drives around in her limousine all night drinking champagne, and she's a mess in the morning." Bette grew furious when her costar would arrive on the set late and unsure of her lines. According to Judith Crist, "Bette didn't give a damn if someone who was working with her was drunk, disorderly, high on drugs or anything else. But by God, you show up on time, and you do what you have to do, and *then* you go out and get drunk and disorderly. It was a dark period for Faye Dunaway, but Bette had no tolerance for anything that interfered with the work."

When Anthony Harvey set up a two-shot of Bette and Faye in a courtroom, by the time he looked through the view finder Bette was no longer in the frame. "She had quite subconsciously moved away [from Dunaway]. But she never said anything unkind or made any sort of scene in front of anyone." One afternoon, while a huge audience of local extras waited for over an hour in sweltering heat for Dunaway to arrive for a revival meeting scene, Bette sang "I've Written a Letter to Daddy" for them in what Harvey considered "a wonderful and scratchy voice. She sort of entertained the troops. It was great."

Harvey completed *The Disappearance of Aimee* in just under a month. It turned out to be a fascinating film, with brilliant performances by both Davis and Dunaway, and won high ratings and critical praise when it was aired over NBC as a twenty-fifth anniversary presentation of the "Hallmark Hall of Fame."

Not long afterward, Judith Crist invited Bette and Anthony Harvey to take part in a symposium at Tarrytown, New York, to discuss the film. "Is *she* coming?" Bette asked. Crist replied that she had no commitment from Dunaway, and that she suspected Faye would attend only if Bette couldn't.

To Crist's delight, both actresses showed up. She remembers the evening as a vivid example of "the old star power and the new star power." Bette, looking grand and elegant, wore a black evening gown and white gloves, and a tasteful minimum of jewelry. Faye wore chiffon lounging pajamas in what Crist calls "an exotic print," and when Crist helped her up on the stage she realized "she had absolutely nothing on underneath."

During the question-and-answer session, an audience member asked both actresses, "What kind of relationship *was* there between mother and daughter?" Bette stared the questioner down before she bellowed, "Didn't you see the *film*? It's right there in the *movie*!" Faye responded dreamily with a question of her own: "What was *your* impression?"

"Faye had this ditzy seventies approach of 'What do *you* think?'—as if it mattered," Crist recalls. "And I was just ebullient about the whole evening because I thought, *There's no way you could have a sharper contrast between two generations of actresses.* It was just a *fabulous* evening."

PART SIX

"The Lonely Lady"

THIRTY-ONE

T he neighbors were being too nice to Bette, and B.D. didn't like it. In June 1976 the Hymans had moved to a mid-nineteenth-century farmhouse in Stevens Township in northeastern Pennsylvania, about thirty miles south of the New York state line. They named the property Ashdown Farm, and according to B.D., Bette immediately began to visit every three weeks or so, "not only uninvited but unwanted."

During her visits, Bette stayed at the nearby Edgeville Court Motel, owned by Stan Frystak and his wife Fran. The Frystaks were shocked one day when B.D. called them to complain, as Fran recalls it, that "her mother liked Stanley and me too much, and that we shouldn't make a fuss over her. I said we treat her like any customer that comes in—we treat all our customers well. She was nice to us, so we were nice to her. B.D. said we were being *too* nice to her. How can you be too nice to someone? If it was my mother and she was staying at a motel and I knew the people were being nice to her, I'd call and thank them."

The Frystaks liked Bette, and they resented the way B.D. and Jeremy treated her. "Every time she came to visit," Fran recalls, "her car would be loaded down with things for B.D. But she stayed here rather than up there, because they fought all the time. It was bad. I think it was a case of, if Bette didn't do what her daughter wanted, she would just start abusing her."

One day after Bette had gone to visit B.D., Fran answered the phone to find the actress in tears. Between sobs, she asked to speak to her chauffeur, Bob Bernstein, who was staying in the room adjacent to hers. "She was crying very hard, and when I told her Bob was in the shower and didn't answer my knocks, she said, 'Please go back and keep pounding. Tell him to come up here and get me!' "

According to Bernstein, "There were many times when I would pick up Bette from B.D.'s and she would be very upset and agitated. But she kept a stiff upper lip, and she attempted to preserve the stability of the family. It's not as if she went up there just to feud. She was always helping them. She helped them expand the house, she put in a pool for them. Jeremy accepted her financial help, but then he begrudged her for it. He had no choice but to accept it, because he was strapped."

Doris Pitcher and her husband Jim went into the hay hauling business with the Hymans in 1978, and she recalls that "One summer Bette gave them a present of a pond that cost ten or twelve thousand dollars. The year before that it had been the swimming pool, and then there was the kitchen. It was beautiful, with a cathedral ceiling. Above it there were two bedrooms and a bath where Bette was supposed to stay when she visited them. The Hymans always seemed to want something from Bette. Jeremy wasn't the kind of man to be ashamed that his mother-in-law helped him. He expected it. It was like B.D. felt, 'I'm her kid, she should.' If B.D. wanted a new winter coat, her mother got it. If B.D. wanted certain things for the kids, they got it. Her mother paid for Ashley's boarding school and that was $10,000 a year. And I don't think B.D. was ever appreciative. Even though Jeremy couldn't stand Bette, he expected her to help out his family."

Much of the friction between Bette and B.D., as before, centered around Jeremy. In *My Mother's Keeper,* B.D. wrote that Bette constantly belittled Jeremy as lazy, a poor provider, a "slave driver" who took advantage of his wife. These accusations, B.D. insisted, were entirely untrue and motivated only by Bette's jealousy over her daughter's happy marriage, something that had always eluded her.

A number of the Hymans' Pennsylvania neighbors, however, feel that Bette's opinion of Jeremy was close to the mark. George Ryan occasionally hauled hay for Pitcher and Hyman Hay Dealers, Inc., which Jeremy had bought into for a down payment of $275. Ryan first met Bette when he went over to the Hymans' to get his paycheck. "Jeremy said he didn't have enough money to give me my check," Ryan says. "It was only ten or fifteen dollars, but he didn't have it. Bette Davis was there, and she gave me some money. Whenever B.D. wanted anything, all she had to do was ask Mommy. Every time they cried, she handed them money."

David Keeler became friendly with the Hymans early in 1978, and saw them close-up for a number of years. In David's opinion, "Jeremy's a little boy. He's never really grown up. He would never do much of anything. He'd waste *days,* really. He was out and about a lot, he was like the gentleman gadfly. He'd hang out at the restaurants and the shoe store—he was always hanging around the stores."

Leslie Santos, who worked at her parents' Creekside Market, tells of an occasion when a neighbor brought the Hymans a load of wood as a gift. "When they delivered it, Jeremy didn't even lift a finger to help unload the wood." The neighbors, Leslie stressed, considered this "a slap in the face of generosity."

David Keeler was disturbed as well by what he saw of Jeremy's treatment of his son. "He would lose his temper with Ashley easily," Keeler recalls. "He could be real verbally abusive. He put the kid down a lot, really did a number on his self-esteem. I took them out fishing one time, and every time the kid would do something, Jeremy would criticize it. It was embarrassing."

"No one liked Jeremy," Fran Frystak avers. "One man said to me, 'If they hadn't moved when they did, we would have had to burn them out.' I said, 'Are you kidding?' And he said, 'No.' They couldn't stand him—they thought he was very arrogant."

According to Doris Pitcher, "Jeremy was always griping about Bette. He griped if they were watching television and she called—no matter what it was, he griped. And B.D. seemed to resent her mother so much. She resented being sent to a girls' boarding school—she wanted to be raised at home by her parents. She resented her stepfather. She resented her mother's lifestyle. Everything was Bette's fault. *Everything*. She seemed so bitter. I remember her saying that one year when she was a kid they spent the whole summer eating things made out of seaweed because Bette was on a seaweed kick. But she didn't say it in a laughing, funny way. She was very bitter about it."

B.D. resented just as deeply Bette's continual, vociferous denigration of Jeremy to anyone who would listen. George Ryan recalled that Bette would say of her son-in-law, "He's cheap, lazy, he won't work, he won't do anything. He's a no-good lazy sonofabitch." B.D. hated this kind of talk from Bette, and she despised what she saw as her mother's meddling in her family's affairs. Bette's visits became more and more strained; according to B.D. her mother spent one stay "constantly drunk, dropped lighted cigarettes all over everything . . . was rude to everyone and then, and *then,* having tormented me for the entire four days and made it a period of abject misery"—Bette said that she had had a wonderful time and would stay a few days longer.

B.D. recounts that at this point she had a startling thought: perhaps what to her was "intolerable nastiness" was to Bette merely her way of conducting her life. If this really was a revelation, B.D. may have been the last person who knew Bette to have it. Any new awareness she gained, however, didn't change her attitude toward her mother. She continued to harangue Bette bitterly about her visits, telling her that she had not been invited, wasn't welcome, and only got in everyone's way. Is it any wonder Bette telephoned her chauffeur in tears so often?

In *My Mother's Keeper,* B.D. writes that Bette returned to the Frystaks' motel after one of their arguments, drank herself "blotto" in the restaurant, and regaled the other guests with a bitter denunciation of Jeremy. "That never happened!" Fran says emphatically. "*Never!* I went to our attorney about it, but he said there was nothing we could do."

On March 1, 1977, Bette received one of the highest honors of her career, the prestigious Life Achievement Award from the American Film Institute. She was the first woman recipient, and the televised event was a lovefest. William Wyler joked that if Bette had the chance she would drop everything at that very moment to redo a scene in *The Letter* that she and Wyler had disagreed about (she nodded in agreement); Jane Fonda reminded Bette that it was her birth that made it necessary for Bette to recite her lines to a stand-in rather than to Henry Fonda in *Jezebel;* Olivia De Havilland good-naturedly complained that Bette "got the roles I always wanted."

It was a thrilling evening for Bette, but her joy must have been leavened considerably by B.D.'s refusal to attend the event. Bette was the first recipient not surrounded by loved ones at the ceremony, and as Fran Frystak watched the special on television she felt saddened that there were no family members with Bette at her table. (Michael had wanted to attend but couldn't.) When she next spoke to B.D., Fran asked her, "Why didn't I see you at the awards show with your mother?"

"I wouldn't go out there for *that,*" B.D. replied.

For Bette, the best thing about the AFI tribute was that it seemed to spur a thrilling resurgence in her career, one that more than filled the void in her life left by her daughter's disdain. Soon after the telecast she began to receive regular offers of work; the requests to Robert Lantz for her services were so frequent that she was sometimes faced with a happy choice among three or more attractive alternatives. Late in 1977 Bette had agreed to travel to London and Egypt to appear as a dowager in the film version of Agatha Christie's *Death on the Nile* when she was offered the starring role in Universal's TV miniseries of Tom Tryon's thriller novel *Harvest Home.*

She wanted to do both films, but because *Death on the Nile* had a firm location start date, Lantz knew that Bette could accept the TV assignment only if the production were completed before she was scheduled to leave for London. He also knew that such assurances were virtually impossible for a studio to give because of the myriad delays that can stall a production. When Lantz told Bette about this, she suggested that he call Lew Wasserman, who had been her agent before Lantz and was now the head of Universal, and ask him to make an exception.

Lantz blanched. "You want me to call Lew Wasserman about a thing like that?"

"Yes," Bette replied. "I've always had huge respect for him, and I think he has respect for me. Just tell him, 'This is the dilemma.' They want me, I would like to do it, but I have to have a stop date."

Nervously, Lantz called Wasserman, and he was astonished by the reply. "Robbie, I'll tell you something," Wasserman declared. "We've *never* given it, we *will* never give it, it's out of the question." Then he paused and concluded, "But we will give it to Bette Davis."

According to Lantz, "Wasserman knew that Bette would work through the night, would do whatever it took, to make sure that she made that stop date. And sure enough, five days into preproduction, she called to say that I had to tell Lew that the way things were going, she didn't think the production would be finished on time." Lantz phoned Wasserman about Bette's concerns, and got a call back two days later.

"I made an inquiry," Wasserman told Lantz, "and she's right. Everything will be changed. I'm very grateful to her, she's terrific."

Bette worked through most of the night on her last day of shooting on *The Dark Secret of Harvest Home,* then boarded a special plane that took her to Westport to pack for the trip to London for her *Death on the Nile* costume fittings. The next morning she left for London. "All this at her age," Lantz marvels. "She met the designers at the hotel in London that night. She fitted all day Saturday and Sunday. And she arrived on the set in Egypt exactly as promised. She didn't have to do this, nor did she charge anybody an extra penny."

On August 7, 1977, B.D. gave birth, three weeks prematurely, to another son, whom the Hymans named Justin. Once again B.D. didn't inform Bette that the delivery was imminent. "Mother was convinced that we had done it on purpose," B.D. wrote, implying that they would have told her had there been time. But the man who delivered the baby, "Doc" Petersen, recalls otherwise. "Jeremy didn't want to tell her until after the fact. She always had to be there when B.D. had a problem, and Jeremy didn't think it was necessary to have her." Dr. Petersen recalled Jeremy asking him, "Do you want to see a scene from *Dark Victory* out in the lobby?" Petersen assumed this meant Jeremy thought Bette would only be melodramatic and disruptive.

Bette finally got the message from B.D. and Jeremy. She would not stay where she wasn't wanted. In December 1978 she left Connecticut and moved to West Hollywood, California, where she bought an apartment at Colonial House, a lovely brick high-rise on Havenhurst Drive just below Sunset Boulevard, for $195,000. Bette's move back to Hollywood was a "fantastic relief" to B.D., an assurance that her nearly seventy-year-old mother wouldn't "darken our doorway" as frequently as she had when she lived on the East Coast.

B.D.'s "relief" was Bette's heartbreak. Ruthie was dead, Bobby was ill with cancer, her daughter had rejected her. She felt like the lonely old lady she had feared for so long that she would become. She was terrified of being alone; when she first moved into Colonial House she asked her friend and former hairdresser Peggy Shannon to stay with her, and Shannon lived with Bette for three months. After Peggy left, if she wasn't working, Bette did little but sit around the apartment, suffused with loneliness, her losses and rejections hurting so acutely that she would often burst into tears.

She drank to great excess, and her behavior echoed that terrible period in Westport when she lost all motivation, drank herself numb, and threatened to commit suicide. The screenwriter Ginny Cerilla was a resident of Colonial House, and one day she found Bette passed out in front of her door, surrounded by empty liquor bottles she was apparently taking to the trash disposal, a spilled Scotch on the rocks near her hand. Ginny took the bottles to the disposal, then helped Bette, conscious again and spewing invective at her, back into her apartment.

In June 1979, however, redemption came to Bette's door in the person of Kathryn Sermak. The pretty twenty-two-year-old brunette had been sent by an employment agency to interview for the job of accompanying Bette to England as her assistant while she made a film. A graduate of the University of Southern California, she had wanted to be a clinical psychologist. But now she just needed a job, and since she had been an au pair for a year while she studied in Paris, she figured she could handle this assignment.

When Bette greeted her, Kath was impressed that she had "such a strong handshake for a woman." The interview lasted less than ten minutes; Bette asked her what her birth sign was, and whether she could boil an egg. She seemed satisfied by the responses ("Libra and yes") and hired Kathryn on the spot. Bette later told her that the quick decision was based on "a hunch."

When they returned from England, where Bette filmed the Disney feature *Watcher in the Woods,* Bette asked Kath to continue on and move into her apartment. Bette liked the young woman's efficiency and her pliable personality, and she became her mentor. Bette, Kath later wrote, "is, was and always will be a teacher. This I know: I learned from her every day."

Whenever she made a mistake, according to Kath, Bette would correct her. "Just don't make the same mistake again," she learned. When Bette once overheard Kath's side of a telephone conversation, she pointed out to her that she had said "Okay" fifteen times. "Every time you say 'Okay' from now on," Bette declared, "you'll have to give me a quarter." Within two weeks Kath had broken the habit.

Bette's friends soon came to realize that for Bette, Kath Sermak was taking the place of B.D. Many of them didn't like it; some felt that Kath had insinuated herself into a superstar's life, others felt that Bette was taking unconscionable advantage of Kath. They cringed when she would verbally abuse the girl, or force her into total subservience; they were shocked to see Kath dressed in a black velvet chauffeur's outfit, complete with cap, waiting to take Bette home from a restaurant.

Whatever outsiders thought of the relationship between Bette and Kath, it was clearly tremendously important and advantageous to both of them. And over the next ten years, as Bette's relationship with her daughter disintegrated even further, Kath Sermak would become the most important person in her life.

Bette was visiting the Hymans on her way back from England in July 1979 when she received word that her sister Bobby had died of a heart attack after a long bout with recurring cancer that had begun with a mastectomy fifteen years before. B.D. recalled that Bette fell into a chair, stricken by the news, and rocked back and forth in agony as she cried, "What am I going to do? Oh no! Bobby's dead! I can't go on. I want to die, too."

When Bette learned that Bobby's wish had been to be cremated, she insisted instead that she be buried next to Ruthie in the Forest Lawn family plot, and Bobby's daughter Ruth agreed. Bette paid for the funeral, something for which Ruth was tremendously grateful because "I wouldn't have been able to." But she didn't attend the funeral, ostensibly because she had to begin a new film the next day. But Ruth feels the real reason was that Bette didn't want to attract attention away from Bobby at her memorial. At Bobby's wedding to David Berry, Bette had stood outside the chapel while the vows were exchanged so that her sister wouldn't have to share any of the spotlight during a moment that should be uniquely one's own. "My aunt knew that anybody who came to my mother's funeral would spend the whole time staring at her. I would have been uncomfortable about that. I'm glad she didn't come—it was a very smart thing that she didn't."

Again work took Bette's mind off her sorrow. In the three years between 1978 and 1980, she starred in two feature films (*Watcher in the Woods* and another Disney production, *Return from Witch Mountain*) and three made-for-television movies (*Strangers, White Mama,* and *Skyward.*)

Strangers, aired in May 1979, costarred her with Gena Rowlands as an estranged mother and daughter who painfully come to love each other again when the daughter returns home with a terminal illness. The performance won Bette an Emmy Award as Best Supporting Actress. She and Rowlands, one of her generation's great actresses, struck up a friendship. Rowlands sensed that life had left Bette "worn and tired, and that her work, while it was the most important thing in her life, was not yielding the consolations that she had hoped for. We had many talks, and I found her more objective about herself than her publicity would lead one to believe."

That objectivity forced Bette into the realization, as the 1970s came to a close, that she would have to undergo a face-lift—despite all her protestations that she would never do so. "Professionally I had to do it," she admitted to Mike Wallace off the air during a *Sixty Minutes* profile of her in January 1980, "although personally it went against my grain. The way they shoot today, they don't take the time to light older people properly. I'm at the point where I can't wear [face lift] straps for fifteen hours at a time, and my skin can't tolerate makeup an inch thick. It's difficult enough to get parts at my age. Without lifts I looked a hundred and ten on camera."

The lifts had been torture for Bette. Sometimes it was rubber bands pulling hair tufts back across her head to pull up the skin, sometimes it was clear tape attached to her skin just under her wig line and stretched back across her scalp. Either way it was uncomfortable, itchy, painful—and when the tape was ripped off at the end of a day Bette thought she'd scream in agony.

Bette considered the surgery worth it, even with its recuperative period of pain and swelling and discoloration, because it promised to end all that and improve her looks permanently. But once she had healed, she was disappointed that the difference in her appearance wasn't nearly as dramatic as she had hoped it would be. According to her doctor, she'd waited ten years too long for the procedure to do much good. Still, she did look better, and the psychological lift proved more potent than the physical as she looked forward to the 1980s with renewed enthusiasm.

Bette was sure she had the perfect young actor with whom to costar in her latest project. Early in 1980 she had been offered the lead role in another TV miniseries, *Family Reunion,* about a retired schoolteacher from the town of Winfield, which her family had founded, who travels around the country with one of her former students, a thirteen-year-old boy, to visit her widely scattered relatives. When she returns, she finds that a powerful conglomerate—headed up secretly by her nephew, a senator—is trying to build a shopping mall on the extensive Winfield land. She gathers the family together at a reunion and is ultimately successful in stopping the mall.

In preliminary meetings with the show's producer, Lucy Jarvis, Bette piped up that she had a boy in mind to play Miss Winfield's young traveling companion. "Wonderful," Jarvis enthused. "Is it someone you've worked with?"

"Well, no, not exactly," Bette replied.

"Is it someone whose work you know?"

"It's somebody I know *very* well."

By now Jarvis was suspicious. "Bette, who *is* this boy?"

"Well," Bette said, "you don't have to accept him. You and the director can audition him. It's my grandson Ashley."

Jarvis liked the idea. "I'd love to audition him," she said. "There would be the automatic rapport you're supposed to have with this boy's character . . . and besides, the publicity would be great!"

Ashley had done some acting at school, and had expressed an interest in pursuing the craft professionally. "He was thrilled with the idea," Jarvis recalls. "He thought it would be a lark, and being away from home and school would be an even greater lark." Bette told John Shea, the actor cast as her former-student-turned-lawyer who helps her fight the mall, that she wanted Ashley to have the role because his earnings would help his parents send him to college, something she didn't feel they could afford to do on their own.

Ashley, eleven, was a big enough boy to play thirteen, and Lucy Jarvis was impressed by his audition. "He was awkward, but it was just the kind of awkwardness that you would find in a young boy that lived in a rural area." But he was clearly an amateur, and Jarvis felt he would need very close supervision and rehearsals before filming began. Bette assured her that "I will certainly be there to do what has to be done, and I'll go over the lines with him every night."

Filming began on Long Island in the late fall of 1980. In *My Mother's Keeper*, B.D. paints an unremittingly grim picture of the three months Ashley spent at work with his grandmother: she made his life miserable, she bossed him unmercifully, she criticized him and shouted at him at every turn. According to B.D., Bette wouldn't allow Ashley to call home unless she was present because he was "a liar and a sneak and he's telling you I'm a monster," and the boy was terrified and demoralized by the entire experience.

Those involved with the production, however, tell quite a different story. John Shea was impressed by the patience and understanding Bette showed with Ashley. "I spent many many hours sitting in her trailer with them. She coached him line by line, scene by scene all the way through the film. She never raised her voice to him, never criticized him, never abused him in any way. She got him the job, over much more experienced Hollywood kids, as a favor to him and his mother, and when they started to work she realized he really wasn't equipped for the job. So she started to practice his line readings with him, word for word. She tried to protect him from failure, to make sure he wasn't fired, which could have happened. She was very proud of him, and would reward him when he did well. Honestly, I thought she was great with him."

Lucy Jarvis agrees. "There was no question that Bette and Ashley had a warm, loving relationship. When I read that part of B.D.'s book I was in a state of shock! I was thinking very seriously about calling up the publisher and raving that it was just a crock—and how could they allow her to say things that were lies just to make the book interesting? Bette tutored him night and day so that he'd be as good as possible. She was strict, of course, but so would any coach have been. He had to learn his lines and how to toe his marks and all the professional gimmicks that help an actor give a good performance. He knew nothing of that, and Bette taught it all to him. And she was delighted that when he wasn't filming he would have access to tennis courts and an indoor pool.

"When the show was over we gave him the bicycle he rode in the story, and he was very excited about that. And he knew that all this wonderful stuff was happening to him because of his grandmother. He *loved* her for it."

While Lucy Jarvis saw no problems between Ashley and his grandmother, she did have some of her own with Bette. During the preproduction period, producer and star got along famously. "Bette and I were very good friends during the whole preparation phase. I spent a lot of time with her, and we saw eye to eye politically, so we were very friendly. I gave her a pillow inscribed 'No guts, no glory,' and she just loved it."

About a week before filming began, however, there was a distinct change in Bette's attitude toward her producer. "She announced to me," Jarvis recalls, "that the day we start shooting I would become her enemy. 'It's the director and the star against the producer,' she said, and that was that. When I came on the set the first day, I said, 'Good morning, Miss Davis.' She looked at me and scowled and said, 'Good morning,' then she walked right by me as though I really was the enemy. It was not easy for me."

John Shea watched "big fights" on the set between Bette and Jarvis "until Bette just had her banished. She flung her arm somewhere in the direction of New York City and bellowed, 'Be *gone* with you!' " Shea, however, had a very different experience with Bette. When the handsome young actor met the star in her dressing room, the first thing she said to him after "How do you do?" was "Do you smoke?" Shea didn't and never had, but he sensed that he had better say yes. "Good," Bette chirped. "Because I can't stand men who don't smoke!" When she handed him a pack of unfiltered Pall Malls, he took two out of the pack and lighted them both at the same time. "She laughed and immediately we were friends."

Shea found himself studying Bette, and he thought she was a fascinating woman. "She would sit up straight with her legs crossed just so and look up at me with these startling blue eyes and she'd blink them and look to the side. Over the course of time I realized that she was being unquenchably flirtatious. It was almost an unconscious thing, something she simply embodied. It was part of her vitality, and it's a force few people have. Bette Davis had this fire that I think was sexual and that I saw even when she was an old woman in her seventies. At times it made her seem like a seventeen-year-old girl—the years would just wash away and you'd see that spirit still alive in her. This was very powerful to me."

Family Reunion was aired over two nights in April 1981. Most critics noted that the story could have been told just as well in half the time, and that Ashley's performance was wooden and more awkward than the script called for. (He did, however, acquit himself far better than his mother had in *What Ever Happened to Baby Jane?*) But Bette gave one of her most subdued and touching performances as Elizabeth Winfield, and the film was a ratings success. "Bette was very believable as a prim New England schoolteacher," John Shea thought. "I had seen her work and I knew that she could fall back on mannerisms, begin to parody herself. So what I would do was simply get down and stare at her while we were rehearsing in her trailer and force her—us—to transcend the preconceptions and just *talk* as teacher and student who were now friends. Because what I found was that if you didn't *engage* her, if you weren't bold enough to penetrate her persona, then she would fall back on mannerisms.

"She was just like a Maine lobster," Shea concluded. "Really formidable and crusty on the surface, but once you broke through, she was as sweet and tender as she could be."

"Remember the most steadfast friend is your work," Bette told Gene Shalit in 1980. "My work has been the big romance in my life. No question about it. It really stands by you. You have disappointments in your work, and your ups and downs, but it is *there* when all else fails."

To Bette's great joy, the spate of offers that had come her way in the late '70s continued through the early '80s; while they were all for television movies, the projects were prestigious. In 1982 she played the matriarch Alice Gwynne Vanderbilt in the film version of Barbara Goldsmith's biography of Gloria Vanderbilt, *Little Gloria . . . Happy at Last,* and gave one of her finest performances as a woman struggling with senility in *A Piano for Mrs. Cimino.*

In 1983 Bette costarred with another legend from the Golden Age of Hollywood, Jimmy Stewart, in *Right of Way,* a touching drama about an elderly couple who decide to commit suicide together when the wife develops a terminal illness. Bette and the laconic Stewart, also seventy-five, were delighted to be working with each other, and the production was a charmed one. For Stewart it was "just a wonderful experience. . . . It's something I'll never forget. I can't say enough about Bette. Her charm and her wonderful ability and her wonderful attitude toward the acting profession—it all made something that was very worthwhile. It was one of the finest experiences I've had in my whole career as an actor."

Bette told the press that she "would have given anything to have met him when we were younger," but Stewart had been under contract to MGM and their paths never crossed. "He didn't marry until late, forty-one I think; if we had worked together before that, I would have *leapt* at him."

At the start of filming, Davis and Stewart seemed a little in awe of each other, and observers noticed that while Bette was being unusually low-key in her readings, Stewart was delivering his lines with an unaccustomed clip. "By God," a visitor to the set murmured, "they're *imitating* each other!"

"I never felt out of sync with Jimmy," Bette said. "People think that he is slow and I am fast, but the important thing is, he's a consummate actor who is always honest." Stewart concurred: "I never thought there was a contrast."

The assistant director of *Right of Way,* Steve Tramz, was impressed by the patience and caring that Bette showed toward Stewart during the production. "There were moments when Jimmy would lose his concentration, or he might muff a line and he'd look at her as if to say, 'I'm up,' and she'd pat him on the head and smile and say 'Okay, let's go again.' There was no temperament at all. These were professionals who had been at it for years, and they nurtured each other to make a good show."

When Bette felt secure on a film set, she could be an angel. Not only did she like and admire Stewart, but she had worked with the film's director, George Schaefer, on *A Piano for Mrs. Cimino,* and felt totally safe in his capable hands. Thus happy and content, Bette extended her magnanimity on this film to everyone. Schaefer recalls that Bette treated the young actress Melinda Dillon, playing her daughter, with equal generosity. One morning Bette pulled him aside and asked, "Have you seen Melinda's hair today? It's in these little curly-curls and it looks absolutely dreadful. I'm not gonna say a word." A few minutes later Schaefer followed Bette onto the set and saw her off in a corner with Dillon. "For crissakes, Melinda!" she thundered. "You're not going to leave your hair like *that*, are you?" Dillon changed the style.

Later, during a scene, one of Melinda's face-lift straps broke during what Schaefer considered a good take. While the necessary repairs were being made, he grew visibly impatient. "Melinda didn't need those things," he says. "She used them to smooth out wrinkles that I couldn't even see. But she had a thing about it."

Once the take was reshot and the crew took a break, Bette came to see Schaefer in his dressing room. "George," she said, "I went through that same phase. I used to put those lifts on. You can't imagine what a psychological help it is. You mustn't be upset with Melinda."

"Melinda worshiped her," Schaefer recalls, "and I just fell in love with her when we did *Mrs. Cimino* and *Right of Way*. She took direction beautifully. I have very few reminiscences beyond a lovely, warm glow and a regret that we didn't get to do more together."

In 1983, B.D. and Jeremy needed Bette's help. Their hay hauling partnership with the Pitchers had evolved into an interstate trucking company the year before, and a truckers' strike earlier in the year, they told Bette, had pushed the company near to insolvency. The Hymans were perilously close to defaulting on a $100,000 mortgage they had taken out on their farm.

As she had so often in the past, Bette came through for her daughter despite everything. She brought the mortgage payments up to date and continued to pay them for several months thereafter, saving the home the Hymans had come to love so much. But according to Jeremy's partners, Jim and Doris Pitcher, the facts of the situation were not as B.D. and Jeremy had represented them to Bette. "There was no truckers' strike in 1983," Jim Pitcher says. "The last one had been in 1980, and it didn't affect us much at all."

To this day, neither of the Pitchers can understand why the company ran into such problems; both believed it was doing more business than later showed up when they reviewed the books. Jim recalls several shipments that apparently were never entered and says, "I loaded one truck myself up in Portland, Maine, with a shipment going to Portland, Oregon, and there's absolutely no record of it on the books, anywhere."

Doris recalls the day that Jeremy was in her home going through the company mail and left the room to take a phone call. Doris began to rifle through the letters, some of which contained checks in payment of loads that had been hauled. "Jeremy came back into the room and very crudely snatched the checks and envelopes out of my hand and said, 'Leave these alone, this is none of your business.' We were in my house and we were partners with Jeremy and everything Jim and I had was riding on the business, including our house. Who had a better right? But he acted like it didn't have anything to do with me."

Jim's expertise was in the trucking end of the business, and today he says that whatever happened was his fault for leaving the financial matters to Jeremy and not paying more attention to them. Everything seemed to blow up during the summer of 1983, when Pitcher and Hyman couldn't pay their bills or meet their payroll. Jeremy approached the Pitchers' son-in-law with a proposal that he lease the company's fleet of trucks, but Jim, not seeing why the young man should take on the company's debt, advised him against the move.

"Jeremy was furious about that," Jim says. "He came by our house and left a highly charged note on our door saying we had tried to stop a deal that would have saved the business. He was so overwrought about this that he went driving away like a crazy man and ran his car off the road into a ditch."

Less than two weeks later, Jeremy resigned from the corporation. "He left us with all the debt—we owed about two hundred thousand dollars," Doris says. As a result, the Pitchers lost their home within a few years. Today, however, they are remarkably free of bitterness. Jim, in fact, called his former partner several years later when a load he was hauling took him near the Hymans' new home. "I asked Jeremy if we could meet at a certain place for lunch. He said, 'But that's fifty miles away.' I said, 'So what?' Now Jeremy used to talk all the time about some Mafia guy he supposedly knew who would break people's legs with baseball bats if they didn't pay their debts. So I said to him, 'Don't worry, Jeremy, I won't take my baseball bat to you.' Well, he just said he couldn't see me and hung up."

The Hymans were effusive in their thanks to Bette for saving Ashdown Farm for them. Jeremy sent Bette a note in which he praised her "immense generosity" and told her she had "saved the day for our business and did wonders for our personal morale."

B.D. was positively rapturous in her gratitude. "I will never not be indebted to you for helping us through this frightening time and saving our home," she wrote. "I sincerely hope that our boys will look back at their childhoods in Pennsylvania as fondly as I do my childhood in Maine, and that it will stand them in good stead with a basis of good and real values as it did Mike and I. I love you very much."

THIRTY-TWO

"I 've signed to do a part in a series called *Hotel*," Bette barked into the phone at B.D. early in 1983. "I play the owner and have to appear in seven episodes a year. It's at Fox studios on a soundstage instead of location all the time and I only film for one day per show. But I hate it! I'm broke and I have to do it for the money. Shit! They're paying me a hundred thousand dollars for each show . . . but I'm doing this . . . because I need the dough. Christ! I'm sick about it."

Bette didn't think much of the show's premise. It was an Aaron Spelling series based loosely on Arthur Hailey's bestselling novel, and—judging by the few scripts she had seen—was little more than typical lowest-common-denominator Spelling fare, a landlocked version of his popular but critically maligned *Love Boat*.

Still, B.D. couldn't believe Bette was unhappy with the offer. She tried to talk her mother out of her reservations, reminding her of all the amenities Spelling had promised her and the fact that she would make $700,000 a year for a few days' work. "B.D. would get into violent arguments with Bette on the phone when Bette didn't want to work," Doris Pitcher recalls. "She'd say, 'If I don't get her to do this . . .' It was like the world was coming to an end if she couldn't get her mother to do such and such. Obviously, B.D. was so concerned because if her mother wasn't working there would be no money."

Bette finally accepted Spelling's offer, because the salary he had offered her simply couldn't be overlooked. Moreover, the working conditions *were* marvelous (the Fox lot was just a few miles from her condominium), and for the first time in years the show would allow Bette to portray a stylish, successful woman in a glamorous setting. "She said she wanted to make one more picture where they dressed her up," her friend Don Ovens recalls. "Where she didn't have to be a bag lady."

After Bette filmed the pilot and one episode of *Hotel* in May, she was no more pleased with it than she had been at the outset. She felt particularly frustrated because her part was so minimal that rewrites hardly seemed worth it. She thought the scripts were "garbage," and she wondered about Aaron Spelling's motives in paying her so well. Although it seems unlikely that a producer with Spelling's track record would need to trade on Bette Davis's fame to guarantee the success of his new series, Bette convinced herself that that was exactly what he had done. Robert Lantz had spoken of Bette's implicit pact with her fans never to be "cameo-ized." Doing *Hotel,* Bette feared that she had betrayed that conviction.

With two episodes behind her, Bette flew back to Westport early in June to visit a friend, Robin Brown. One morning, while showering, she noticed a lump in her left breast. She had always felt, with her usual bravado, that "cancer would never *dare* come near me," but ever since Bobby's mastectomy she had examined herself regularly. Deeply worried, she left Robin Brown's immediately, leaving no word, and flew back to Los Angeles.

Her doctor, Vincent Carroll, performed a biopsy, and within just a few hours the terrible word came from the lab: the tumor was malignant; Bette had breast cancer. Carroll went to Colonial House to break the news to her in person. The only way to stem the cancer, he said, was for her to undergo a radical mastectomy.

In the hope that Bette might have more privacy away from Hollywood, her attorney Harold Schiff arranged for the surgery to be performed at New York Hospital–Cornell Medical Center in Manhattan. Frightened, she flew East with Kath, the young assistant holding her hand all the time. On June 9, Bette went under the surgeon's knife, and after the operation her doctors assured her that the cancer had been successfully arrested. As she thought back on the fact that Bobby had lived productively nearly fifteen years after her mastectomy, Bette's fears of death or permanent disability eased. "Thank God I discovered the tumor when I did," she said. "Any further delay and I might have been riddled with cancer. . . . I had been lucky in my life. Now I was lucky again."

But her luck didn't hold. Nine days after the surgery, just as she was about to be released from the hospital, Bette was hit by a mild stroke. Within a week three more embolisms tore at the veins in her brain, each more serious than the one before, the last leaving her partially paralyzed, her left hand knotted, the right side of her face twisted and dragging, her speech slurred.

Physically ravaged, Bette remained as sharp mentally as ever, and as she lay in her hospital bed, a prisoner of her failing body, she was able to comprehend fully her terrible condition. "I was panicked at the thought that I might be an invalid the rest of my life," she wrote. "Over and over, lying there, I asked, will I ever be able to work again? Acting had been my life. I wouldn't want to live if I could never act again."

Kath sat by Bette's side day and night, holding her feeble, gnarled hand, whispering to her, "We'll make it. . . . We'll make it." For the first time in her life, Bette wasn't sure. Her legendary strength and iron will seemed to have been cruelly snatched away; her body would no longer do what she wanted it to do. She felt like a prisoner in a torture chamber. Always fiercely independent, now she couldn't do anything herself. Her body, it seemed, had given up the fight. Bette almost did too. "Many times I wasn't strong," she recalled. "At seventy-five I probably didn't have many more years to live anyway. What was the point of the long struggle ahead? To learn to walk again? To unknot my left hand so I could use it again? I gave up so often during those weeks."

This unfathomable new defeatism in the Iron Lady she had known frightened Kath far more than Bette's physical condition. She was sure that Bette would come around, would respond to her constant reassurances, but finally there seemed to her some hellish conspiracy at play to make everything as difficult as possible for Bette. A few days after the final stroke, she developed an intense, maddening itch all over her body. Writhing and squirming, she scratched herself raw, raising ugly welts on her skin until she was in such pain she couldn't bear to be touched.

The doctors weren't sure what had caused Bette's itching. It might have been an allergic reaction to her medication, but it could also have been a symptom of alcohol withdrawal. In any event, the result was that Bette became infuriated with the hospital staff and verbally abused anyone who dared come near her. Her behavior, which drove away nurse after nurse in exasperation, delighted Kath, who was beginning to see some of the old "Miss D." fight she admired so much coming back in Bette.

"I'm absolutely convinced," Robert Lantz says, "that what kept Bette alive from that moment on was the rage, the fury that *this* should happen to her—that she should be physically handicapped." The doctors, Bette felt, treated her like a child and lied to her; the nurses "dared" to tell her what to do and "never took their eyes off me. Every time I moved an arm, a leg, or even an eyelash, they made a note of it. I felt as if I were in prison!" She thought the nurses were having great fun telling her what to do. "One nurse told me to say 'please' when I asked her to do something! She should consider herself lucky to be in one piece today."

Kath hadn't moved from Bette's side since the surgery. She stretched out at night on the sofa next to Bette's bed, frequently sleepless from her boss's jumpy itching and screams of pain. When Bette was too weak to fight the nurses and doctors herself, Kath would do it for her. "Had the illness occurred earlier in our relationship," Kath said, "I doubt that I would have been strong enough or tough enough to fight for her, when necessary, against the wishes of her nurses and sometimes her doctors."

After a few weeks, Bette insisted that Kath take some time off and fly to Paris to visit her beau. Vik Greenfield, with whom Bette had maintained a long-distance relationship over the years, suggested that his sister, Stephanie Landsman, take Kath's place. Stephanie found the job a trial. She constantly had to pull Bette back into bed when she would try to drag herself off to harangue or fire the night nurse, whom she considered incompetent. Still, Landsman's overriding memory of the experience was how "desperately frightened" Bette was.

In *My Mother's Keeper*, B.D. described herself as "terribly shaken and very worried" about Bette during this period and says it was because of Bette's "continuing protests that she didn't want visitors" that she did not go to the hospital to visit her mother—whom she had just a few months earlier profusely thanked for saving her home and told "I love you very much"—until almost three weeks after her surgery. When she finally did make the drive from Pennsylvania to see Bette, she said, "she looked frighteningly small and sad and my heart went out to her."

The rest of B.D.'s memory of the visit centered around how posh her mother's room was ("If it hadn't been for the hospital bed and the equipment around it, I would have thought myself in a hotel suite," she wrote) and Bette's dreadful behavior. When a physical therapist came in to check on her progress, according to B.D., Bette screamed at her. "Don't touch me you bitch! . . . You fucking idiot! . . . None of you are worth a shit in this place! . . . You don't know what you're doing! . . . Keep your filthy hands to yourself! *Christ!* Jesus! *Fuck!*"

At one point, B.D. said, Bette pushed her tray of food onto the floor. When she asked her mother why she was still smoking, "she screamed at me to mind my own business and claimed that the doctors had said it was perfectly all right." The only time B.D. saw her mother behave well, she averred, was when an attractive young doctor came to look in on her. In anticipation of his visit, Bette had her hair brushed and arranged as neatly as possible, applied fresh makeup, and put on a pretty bed jacket. "Gone the vicious, crumpled, foul-mouthed invalid," B.D. wrote. "Enter the wide-eyed, gutsy star. If I hadn't seen it, I wouldn't have believed it." B.D. did not visit her mother again, although Bette remained in the hospital for nine weeks.

During this period Bette found that "just the mention of any kind of food made me sick," and she began to lose weight dangerously. The doctors decided to feed her intravenously, and hooked her up to a large machine she nicknamed Bertha. "I couldn't even lift my arm without being conscious of her. . . . She became a kind of jailer."

Fear still dominated Bette's emotions. When her doctors told her that she had improved enough so that her care could be continued on an outpatient basis, she refused to leave the hospital. "They seemed to be trying to kick me out of my room, which I did not understand," she said. Every time someone asked her when she was going, Bette would snap, "I am the only person who will know when I am ready to leave."

Her hospital room, of course, represented a safe harbor for Bette, who was terrified of the difficulties that would face her in the outside world. Would she be able to function as she had before? What if she were alone and suffered another stroke? How would people react to her twisted face and emaciated body? She had had a taste of things to come in the last regard when a friend visited her soon after her strokes and started to cry. "That wasn't Bette Davis lying there," she later heard he had said. "She was gone."

Bette was finally persuaded to vacate her room (which she insisted she was "bumped" from because the Greek shipping magnate Stavros Niarchos had demanded it for his son), and she took a suite in the Hotel Lombardy on East Fifty-sixth Street for herself and Kath Sermak for her recuperation. During B.D.'s hospital visit, and several more times over the telephone, Bette had dropped unsubtle hints that she would like to recuperate at Ashdown Farm; she had, after all, paid for an addition on the house that included a suite of rooms for herself. B.D. did not extend an invitation.

Bette, screaming and cursing all the time, made slow and agonizing progress at the Lombardy toward regaining her ability to walk and speak clearly with a daily regimen of painful physical therapy. Her appetite returned, and she was delighted when her attorney Harold Schiff told her that her pencil-thin legs had begun to flesh out and return to a semblance of their former shapely glory. Now, she was starting to believe Kath's cheerleading: "We'll make it!"

But she was devastated every time she looked in a mirror. She was still pitifully thin; her mouth twisted badly, one of her legs dragged behind her as she walked. Under no circumstances, she told Kath, was anyone to be allowed to see her in this condition, only to react with shock and pity. That was the main reason she turned down Aaron Spelling's pleas to return to *Hotel*. In spite of the money, and Spelling's offer

to accommodate her in every possible way, she simply couldn't let anyone see her until she was much further improved. Call after call came
from close friends eager to pay a visit, but Kath always had to put them
off. Bette's friends deeply resented Kath for this; they blamed her for
"isolating" Bette rather than realizing that she was only doing what
Bette had told her to do.

According to B.D., Bette still didn't want even her to visit, and she
didn't go to the Lombardy until early in September, when Bette called
and asked her to come before she returned to Los Angeles. B.D. agreed,
and there ensued a lengthy exchange of telephone calls during which
B.D. said she couldn't come except when her husband could drive her,
since she had been having trouble with her back. "I don't *want* that
bastard to bring you in," B.D. quotes Bette. "I don't want to owe him
any favors."

"I can assure you he doesn't bring me to see you as a favor to *you*,"
B.D. replied. "He does it because I ask him to, that's all."

"You mean that's the only way you can get here? If *he* doesn't bring
you, *I* can't see you?"

"That's right."

Finally Bette sent a car to pick B.D. up, and another protracted
negotiation began about the day and time. When B.D. asked that the car
be there for her at 7:30 A.M., Bette asked, "Why so early?"

"So that I can be back in time to see Justin before he goes to bed,"
B.D. replied.

"Jesus! That won't give us any time together."

"We'll have four hours. I'm confident we'll be able to say all we have
to in four hours."

"God, you're a cold bitch!" Bette exploded before she hung up the
phone.

The visit, free of the usual fireworks, was remarkably mundane considering that out of it B.D. came to a momentous decision. She wanted
to "reach out" to her mother, she has said, and on the ride back to
Pennsylvania she decided that the best way to do that would be to write a
book about her.

Despite the bailout from Bette that had saved their home in 1983, the
Hymans faced considerable financial trouble throughout 1984. No
longer in the trucking business, Jeremy had very little income; B.D. had
taken to fashioning Christmas wreaths that she sold to local shops and

businesses for $200 apiece. With Bette unable to work while she recovered from her devastating illnesses, her own finances dwindled, and she was no longer able to help her daughter and son-in-law. By the spring of 1985, although B.D. had received a $100,000 advance the prior September for the book she had written about Bette, the Hymans' monetary situation had again turned so grim they left their farm and moved to the Bahamas.

They had bought Ashdown Farm in 1976 for $38,500, with a $25,600 mortgage. By 1984, the mortgage on the property totaled approximately $100,000 and the Hymans couldn't make the payments. As Jeremy's friend David Keeler, the publisher of the nearby Wyalusing, Pennsylvania, *Rocket Courier,* recalls it, "Jeremy told me that he didn't tell the bank he was leaving and running out on his mortgage. He just left. He explained to me that the bank would get enough money by reselling the house to cover the debt. Sometime after they left, a business associate of mine who's on the board of directors of the bank asked me if I knew where Jeremy Hyman was. I told him I knew he had moved to the Bahamas, but I wasn't sure where. . . ."

Doris Pitcher recalls that late in 1984 R. G. Rohrbach, a loan officer of the United Penn Bank, told her that Jeremy had sent him a registered letter containing the key to his house and an executed deed that turned the farm back over to the bank. Rohrbach asked Doris and Jim if they would mind going over to the Hymans' place to see if they were there. "So we got in our car and took a ride over the hill," Doris says, "and we saw that everyone was gone, the animals were all gone and everything was all closed up. Everything that could be was padlocked."

George Ryan, who sometimes worked for Jeremy, adds, "They up and packed and took off in a hell of a hurry. The sheriff came here, hunting for them. They owed numerous people from the business. Jeremy left a hell of a debt behind. He shafted the bank, he shafted people in the area, and there are a lot of people pretty upset. If he hadn't shafted everybody, he'd still be here. Really, because if he would have done right by the hay hauling, he could have done well for himself."

In January 1985, a judgment was entered in the New York State Supreme Court against Pitcher and Hyman Hay Dealers in the amount of $11,622. They had been sued for nonpayment by the Tallmadge Tire Company, but the judgment, according to Jim Pitcher, was never satisfied. In April, the National Bank of Wyalusing sued Pitcher and both the Hymans for $915, the balance still owing on a $2,500 business loan the bank made to Pitcher in 1983 with the Hymans as cosigners. The monthly payments had been $231. The bank served papers on Pitcher, but it was unable to serve the Hymans. After locating them on Grand Bahama Island, the bank sent certified letters to each of them. Court records indicate that both letters were returned to the Towanda, Pennsylvania, sheriff's office marked "Unclaimed."

If many of Jeremy's acquaintances in Pennsylvania consider him less than a brilliant businessman, B.D. has a startling reputation of her own in the area. In Bette's memoir, *This 'n That,* she told the story of returning home from a shopping trip with B.D. and discovering that her young daughter had taken a miniature Teddy bear from the store. She told B.D., Bette wrote, that the next time she would "have to return to the store and admit [she] took something," and it never happened again. But according to a number of B.D.'s Pennsylvania neighbors, that childhood incident was not a one-time occurrence.

David Keeler's wife Nancy worked in her father Clyde Tibble's store, the J&N Market. While she never saw it, she says that another employee told her that B.D. had shoplifted some film and that whenever Nancy worked there she should keep an eye on her. Carol Andras, the wife of Wyalusing Police Chief George Andras, worked in Honchell's Market, and although she also never saw B.D. shoplift, she recalls that "other employees who had been working in the store longer than I had" told her that B.D. "used to steal things." The police were never called, Carol was told, because no one "wanted to make any trouble for Bette Davis."

On one occasion, B.D. walked into an area market and asked for an item the store had just one of. After she left, the employee who had been there when B.D. came in noticed that the item was gone from the shelf. Thereafter, when B.D. visited the store, they kept an eye on her. Not too long after the first incident, the owner suspected before she left the store that she had shoplifted. He followed her outside and asked to see what was in her purse. He found a bottle of salad dressing and a stick of deodorant. B.D. told him that she had taken the items by accident, and she returned to the store and paid for them.

An acquaintance of the Hymans who prefers to remain anonymous witnessed the confrontation: "I was walking to my car from the market and I saw the owner pull B.D. aside and ask what was in her purse. I heard her say it was an accident, and as they walked back inside he told B.D. never to come back to his store again." B.D. did continue to shop at the market, and there were no further incidents there.

◦◦◦

Back in Los Angeles, Bette's recovery continued, sometimes more slowly and more painfully than she could bear. It took her three months to learn to use a knife and fork again. When Kath Sermak had to help her tie her shoes or button a blouse, she "felt like a baby again. I hated it!" Her frustration left her with a shorter temper than ever; she went through a succession of cooks, several of whom skulked out of the apartment in the middle of the night rather than face her vitriol the next morning.

Sometimes she turned her anger on herself. In her bedroom one morning in February 1984, she had difficulty removing her brassiere. She called for help, but when no one came immediately she lost her patience and struggled angrily to remove the bra. When she finally did, she turned and flung it at her television set. She lost her balance, fell to the floor, and broke her hip. In the hospital, doctors inserted a pin to help the hairline fracture heal, and Bette's recovery was set back badly.

Throughout all this, Bette grew increasingly dependent on Kath, and the shy assistant of old had now, in many ways, taken over for her mistress. Bette's friend Chuck Pollack recalled his amazement at the change in the dynamics between her and Kath. "When I used to go over to visit Bette or have dinner with Bette, Kathryn would either sit in her room, sit in the kitchen, or sit somewhere else. She was not part of the party." Now, Pollack felt, "Bette was nothing, and Kathryn was Bette. Kathryn made ninety percent of the conversation. She sat there drinking and having the hors d'oeuvres . . . as B.D. said, 'She became Mother.' "

Others among Bette's friends have made the inevitable *All About Eve* comparison, but there is no question that whatever benefits Kath Sermak derived from her association with Bette Davis, she was a rock of loyalty to a woman who desperately needed help and companionship if she were ever to regain a semblance of the productive, independent life she had led for so many years. Bette knew she could count on Kath, and she treasured that security.

She certainly couldn't count on her daughter, who never visited Bette in California after her illnesses. They did speak on the telephone every Sunday, but B.D. monopolized some of the conversations by proselytizing to her mother to renounce Satan and accept the Lord Jesus Christ as her personal savior. For B.D. and Jeremy, early in 1985, had "seen the light" and become born-again Christians.

Many of their Pennsylvania neighbors were surprised by the conversion. "B.D. had a mouth on her," Carol Andras recalls. "You know how some people have mouths like truck drivers? That's the way she was." Another neighbor, Nancy Lohman, recalls a St. Valentine's Day party at which B.D., "quite overweight," wore a light pink skin-tight dress that left "everything hanging out." And according to David Keeler, Jeremy had frequently made jokes about the Born Agains in the neighborhood before his own revelation. "B.D. seemed more changed by it than he did," Keeler thought. "Jeremy continued to curse and drink, and he was always trying to quit cigarettes."

The Hyman family's newfound belief in the Almighty—and His nemesis, Satan—was total and all-encompassing. When Ashley, now a strapping teenager, stayed out all night partying at a local disco, his mother confronted him upon his return and demanded an explanation. "It was Satan, wasn't it?" the impressionable, melancholy youngster said. "Boy, did he have me fooled. God wouldn't tell me to do those things, but I didn't stop to think about it." In the winter of 1984, B.D. and Jeremy had attempted to drive to Ohio to attend a Pentecostal healing service conducted by the television evangelist Ernest Angley, known for laying his hands on his followers' foreheads, screaming "Yea-yah!," and exorcising the demons that had created their illnesses. The Hymans had traveled halfway to Akron when a sudden snowstorm forced them to return home, but a few days later they were able to make it without incident to another of Angley's services. "Satan had apparently been foiled in his attempt to keep us away," B.D. concluded.

When B.D. went to Angley to be cured of chronic back pain, she brought Ashley along so that he could be rid of his partial deafness and depression. When Ashley walked on stage, the Reverend Angley placed his hand on Ashley's left ear and shouted, "In the name of the Lord, *come out!*"

Moments before he fainted, Ashley recalled, he could see an arc of red light running from Angley's eyes to his, and he felt a burning sensation in his head. "Then the red line turned blue, and my head suddenly felt cool. Reverend Angley stepped toward me, tapped my forehead gently with the palm of his hand, and shouted, 'Yea-yah.' "

When B.D. saw Ashley fall into the arms of one of Angley's ministers, she screamed out, "That's my son!" and rushed onto the stage. While he was unconscious, Ashley claimed, he saw a glorious vision of Jesus, resplendent in a white robe, walking on a lake before He rose to Heaven.

Ashley's hearing problem *was* cured, but apparently by a much more earthbound method. While Doc Petersen was examining the boy, who complained of a runny nose, he discovered a pencil eraser lodged in his ear. When he removed it, Ashley's hearing improved markedly.

One morning while watching Pat Robertson's *700 Club,* B.D. heard a special healing prayer directed at "a woman in her thirties with a severe lower-back problem." "I cried and thanked Jesus and claimed my healing," she wrote. Then she jumped off the bar stool she was sitting on in the kitchen and felt no pain in her back. Testing it, she did some turns and saw that for the first time she had a full range of movement. What she has described as serious ligament damage in her back had been cured. "It was the first of many miracles with which we were to be blessed."

"Oh, hell's bells!" Doc Petersen exclaimed when he was asked about B.D.'s miracle cure. "She just had a backache. It wasn't serious."

To B.D.'s way of thinking, her religious conversion offered justification for her decision to write a book about her mother. After hearing Ernest Angley tell his congregation that good Christians should "cast out" any member of the family ("be it mother, father, brother, sister, son") who "brought disharmony to the family unit," she decided that that's exactly what she should do with Bette.

"My daily prayers for a sign . . . as to the right or wrong of publishing my book had been answered," she wrote. At that point, she felt, God told her to write the book. For all the divine help she received in her labors, which lasted nearly eight months, B.D. never once mentioned the endeavor to her mother.

In the spring of 1984, Kath persuaded Bette to escape from the burning smog and heat of Los Angeles by renting a beach house in Malibu for the summer. For Bette, the seashore was like a loving embrace; so many of her happiest memories centered around the ocean. The soothing sea air seemed to make her physical therapy a little easier, and she made new progress every day. "I learned to walk again by dragging myself through the sand on a beach near Malibu."

That September, Bette's most fervent hope became a reality—she got an offer of work. She was aware that most of Hollywood had written her off, and finding an insurance company willing to guarantee her services to a studio or network was very difficult. But producers Alan Shane and George Eckstein came through for her, asking that she costar with Helen Hayes in a made-for-TV movie version of Agatha Christie's *Murder with Mirrors.*

She was fraught with fear. How would the public react to her appearance? She knew that eventually she would have to let people get used to her. The best way to do that, she felt, was under the controlled conditions of a movie role. She wanted to take the part, but then she was hit by a far more elementary doubt. "By now my feelings were divided equally between the desire to work again and the fear that I would be unable to make it." When she accepted the role, she said, "I was in a state of high excitement one minute, and terror the next."

Another of her fears was that she wouldn't be able to remember her lines. Although her role as John Mills's sickly wife was a small one, she set out to memorize the entire script. When she had it down cold after two weeks, she felt for the first time that she might be able to see this through.

Murder with Mirrors was to be filmed in England, and in order to make the trip less grueling Bette first flew to New York, where she and Kath stayed in a hotel for a few days. While she was there, Harold Schiff came up to see her—and so did B.D. Schiff had heard talk that B.D. was writing some kind of book about her mother, and his suspicions about its contents were aroused when he called to confront her with the rumor and she danced around the issue. In order not to set back Bette's recovery, he had said nothing to her, and he watched through narrowed eyes as B.D. effusively greeted her mother in her hotel room. "You look *marvelous!*" she gushed at Bette. "It's wonderful to see you looking so well after all you've been through."

When Schiff left a few minutes later, B.D. gave Bette a gift—a green-leather-bound version of *The Living Bible* with "Ruth Elizabeth Davis" engraved in gold on the cover. "That's great," Bette muttered as she took the book from B.D.'s hands. "I'll have to read it sometime." Suddenly B.D. began to recite from the book; she recounted the story of the Sermon on the Mount and then "shared" Pat Robertson's teaching on the Beatitudes. When she finished, she urged her mother to embrace Jesus. Bette would have none of it. "It doesn't make sense," she said. "If God is so much love and it's automatic for Jesus to heal everyone, why do I still get pain in my hip? I prayed and prayed."

B.D. explained that Jesus's healing wasn't automatic—that one must reach out to God first. Then she added, "Can't you see that He's giving you another chance, more time, to realize your need for Him? Your cancer was localized, your stroke was mild and—"

"Mild!" Bette exploded. "You think my stroke was easy? *Jesus!* I slaved my guts out to get over that stroke. Brother! What do you mean? I went through therapists weekly. I wore them out because I worked so

hard. Why should I be thankful?" The conversation went on like this, with B.D. appalled when Bette "used Christ as a profanity" and Bette arguing that she wasn't a sinner—"I'm a good girl. I always have been."

According to B.D., she had tried to convince her mother of the error of her ways, but she had once again failed. Had Bette seen the light, B.D. professed, she would not have published her book, which she had completed and for which she had already been paid the full $100,000 advance.*

A week later, Bette and Kath were ensconced in London's Savoy Hotel, where they rested for a few days before motoring to the large estate outside London where *Murder with Mirrors* was to be filmed. "The first day back on the set was a day of pure terror for me," Bette recalled. "I wondered if I would have the strength to last the day."

Bette's fears and uncertainties, as usual, exacerbated her battle-ready mindset. Helen Hayes, considered the first lady of the American theater, was cast as the wily amateur sleuth Miss Marple, and she was excited to hear that Bette had arrived on the set. "I saw her and said, 'Hello!' and put out my hand to shake hers. Bette looked right through me, and my hand dropped. I just continued on my way. A little later, our eyes met and I raised my hand in a little wave and she said, 'What's *that* for?' I said, 'I'm saying hello.' And she said, 'You said that before!' Oh God. She was just terrifying!"

Hayes realized the strain Bette was under, and a few days later she made another effort to engage her costar in conversation. "I told her I had admired her so in *The Disappearance of Aimee*. But when I mentioned it to her, all I got was this flood of invective about Faye Dunaway. I hadn't mentioned Dunaway, but that's all that came from mentioning that picture. Well, it went on like that. I was just nervous as a kitten around her."

All the more reason for Hayes to be taken aback when, on the last day of shooting, Bette turned to her after they had completed a scene and said, "You're a beautiful person."

"Well!" Hayes recalled. "It was like I'd been made a Dame of the British Empire or something!"

---

* When she had earlier asked Jeremy what they would do if Bette found salvation after the book was sold, B.D. wrote, his solution had been that if there was still time before publication they'd wrap another book into it, that is, "tell the story of how a couple of dumb agnostics came to Jesus and brought the great lady with them." If there wasn't time, they would simply tell the story as a sequel.

Bette wasn't happy with the rushes she saw of *Murder with Mirrors*. Playing a frail, sickly woman, she was unable to present any real vitality on the screen, and her tightly marcelled period hairdo and thinly penciled eyebrows did little to soften the harsh contortions of her stroke-ravaged face. When she returned to the United States, she decided to appear with David Hartman on *Good Morning, America* dressed in a fashionable outfit and spouting her usual peppery opinions. Her fans, although delighted to have her back, were shocked by her appearance, and saddened by the knowledge that Bette Davis was now only a weak shadow of the energetic, no-nonsense, hell-raising Margo Channing persona they had loved for so many years.

THIRTY-THREE

arold Schiff and Robert Lantz sat in grim silence as their car wended its way out of Manhattan, across the Fifty-ninth Street Bridge and into Queens. It was November 1984 and they were headed to Long Island, where Bette had rented a cottage for a seashore vacation before she returned to Los Angeles. As much as the two men dreaded it, the time had come for them to tell Bette that her daughter was about to release *My Mother's Keeper,* a devastating tell-all book about her.

"When I got the confirmation that such a book was about to come out, and the kind of material that was in it," Lantz recalls, "I knew what we had to do. I talked to Harold and we both felt strongly that, simply as friends, we had to face her. This could not be sprung on her by somebody else. So we drove out to tell her—because the worst thing of all would have been if she thought that her two trusted associates had not had the guts to let her know about this."

Bette was puzzled and a little worried when she learned that both her agent and her lawyer were coming to discuss something with her in person; her instincts told her that they had more on their minds than the latest offer for a television movie. Still, she couldn't have been less prepared for what they did tell her. "I don't know how to describe it," Lantz says. "It was worse than telling her B.D. had died. This was *terrible.* It was such a deep betrayal. She didn't believe it at first. She just would not believe it."

Bette paced back and forth, puffing frantically on one cigarette after another, as she listened to Lantz and Schiff. Her disbelief turned to confusion, then sorrow, and finally profound anger. "She was in a rage. In a *rage!*" Lantz recalls. "And rage is a mild word for it. We knew the most difficult thing would be for her to keep quiet, not to comment publicly. It took hours for us to convince her."

Emotionally drained, Schiff and Lantz left Bette after they had promised her they would try to intercede and prevent publication of the book. Back in his office, Schiff called B.D. and tried to "make a deal," but she stood fast. Bette then called her niece Ruth Bailey. She asked Ruth to call B.D. and plead with her not to release the book.

Bailey, who hadn't spoken to her cousin in years, made the call. While B.D. seemed pleased to hear from her, she told her blithely that the book was "on the presses" and there was no way she could stop it. "But I'll send you an autographed copy when it comes out," B.D. chirped. "I never got a copy," Bailey says.

Finally, Bette called her daughter herself. In *Narrow Is the Way*, B.D.'s follow-up book to *My Mother's Keeper* (in which she details her religious conversion), she describes the shouted conversation that ensued. According to B.D., Bette's voice was at first frail and broken—a ploy, she felt sure, for sympathy—but it very quickly turned harsh and accusing. "Just tell me why?" Bette cried. "Was it for the money?" Not surprisingly, B.D. didn't answer this basic question. Instead she tried to convince her mother that the book was written in an attempt to reach out to her. "I suppose you wrote a book about how much you *love* your mother," Bette goaded sarcastically. "I wrote it because I *do* love you," B.D. responded.

The exchange continued in a similar vein until Bette abruptly hung up. Relieved that the inevitable confrontation was behind her, and depressed mainly because her faith had not kept her from feeling the same old anger and resentment at her mother, B.D. threw herself into finishing work on the book and then into the preparations for her national publicity tour to promote its publication—scheduled for Mother's Day, 1985.

B.D. says she was horrified and indignant when *People* magazine headlined its story about her book "Bette Dearest." If this is true, she may have been the only person in America who didn't see similarities between *My Mother's Keeper* and *Mommie Dearest*, Christina Crawford's disturbing, sordid tale of life with her mother Joan.

While the Bette who emerges in B.D.'s book isn't nearly the physical sadist Crawford apparently was, the portrait B.D. paints is hardly more flattering. She recounts with great detail the most private conversations between herself and Bette. She chronicles numerous fights between Bette and Gary Merrill. She inventories the drinks Bette took, the foul words she uttered, the many instances in which her mother's selfish irrationality clashed with B.D.'s eminent reason.

The Bette Davis described in *My Mother's Keeper* is a lying, self-deluded shrew, an alcoholic who loves to create ugly, embarrassing scenes in public, tyrannizes B.D. and her family, and lives in a reality entirely of her own design. She is a humorless obsessive/compulsive who can't abide being anything less than the center of attention and is deeply jealous of her daughter's happy marriage. Nowhere in the book does B.D. mention the enormous largesse that Bette directed at her and her family.

B.D. seems to have considered her mother a prime example of Satan's handiwork. "Mother was a destroyer," she said. "And the thing that amazes me is that *I* wasn't destroyed. It is a miracle. . . . I do truly believe that the only reason is that God protected me."

My Mother's Keeper also makes it clear that except for those times when B.D. says she was pushed beyond endurance by Bette's words or actions, she was a long-suffering paragon of patience, an understanding and loving daughter, a helpful wife and devoted parent who was often driven to distraction—and nervous illness—by the dreadful harridan of a mother whom she professed simply to want to love and who thwarted that effort at every turn.

The truth, of course, is far more complex. While B.D.'s portrait of Bette is in many ways accurate, a number of the incidents she recounts in the book are apparently badly skewed by her perceptions of her mother's motivations, her own self-image, and everything that had passed between them for the preceding forty years. Although some of B.D.'s stories in which Bette gets drunk at a party and either makes a fool of herself or strikes out rudely at B.D.'s friends have been confirmed by guests, others have been denied by those present at the gatherings.

What seems clear is that B.D.'s prior experiences with Bette colored her reaction to everything her mother did. Like many adult children of alcoholics, B.D. would cringe in embarrassment at behavior that others saw as good-natured and amusing. Her stomach would knot as she watched Bette drink and carry on, certain that the evening would ultimately end in disaster—while Bette's guests often had a fine time with a witty, effervescent hostess. What others recognized in Bette as good-natured put-downs, B.D. interpreted as mortifying insults.

Several of Bette's friends have said that they did not recognize an event they had attended from B.D.'s description of it. Doug Troland, a friend of Bette's during the last twenty years of her life, says, "So much of the book is out of context. And B.D. knows that many of those statements of Bette's were said just as a way to let off steam in an amusing way. So, it's B.D.'s way of telling the truth, but not *really*."

The actor Robert Wagner, a longtime friend of Bette's, is more blunt. "The book was just a total fabrication. It's just not true. And I'm telling you, I was there."

Why, the public wondered, did B.D. do this to her mother? Most scoffed at her protestations that she wouldn't have published the book if Bette were dead because she had written it only to forge a reconciliation with her. The overwhelmingly nasty tone of the book effectively obliterated that argument; surely B.D. couldn't have expected that to write secretly and then publish such a scathing portrait of her mother would make Bette open her arms to her.

Most observers, of course, assumed that B.D. did it just for the money; *My Mother's Keeper* was an international bestseller and probably brought B.D. over $1 million in royalties. Some felt another factor could have been her religious conversion, which had convinced her that Bette was a sinner and expendable in her life. "I think Jesus got her," Robert Wagner says. "Jesus got her and sent her the wrong way. It's hard for me to believe from the times I was around Bette and B.D.—who was totally devoted to her mother and vice versa—that she could change that quickly, in a matter of a year, without some kind of outside influence."

Bette wondered too, of course. She didn't read the book until months after its publication, but she heard about most of the worst of it, and she asked her friend Don Ovens, "Why did she do this to me? You knew her all those years when she was a kid, Don. What made her do it?"

"The money," he replied. "That hundred-thousand-dollar advance was what did it."

"But Don," Bette said softly, "I would have found a way, somehow, if she needed money, to get it for her."

Bette suspected that Jeremy had been the driving force behind the book, and she may have been right. Diana Brown, a neighbor of the Hymans', typed the final manuscript, and she recalls that she never once met B.D.—it was always Jeremy who brought her new pages and discussed the manuscript with her. "He told me not to say a word to anyone about what was in the book," Diana recalls. "He said if anything got out he'd know where it came from."

When B.D.'s close friend Josie Hamm was asked, "How involved was Jeremy in the book?" she replied unhesitatingly, "He *wrote* the book." Then she caught herself and said, "She wrote it and he sort of like *edited* it." (B.D. later wrote that Jeremy did some "editing, and rewriting where necessary," but he only shared in the copyright, not in the credit for authorship.)

Bette herself may have had the last word on why B.D. decided to write *My Mother's Keeper* the day she visited her ravaged mother at the Lombardy Hotel. "B.D. thought I was going to *die*," Bette told a friend. "*That's* why she wrote that book. But I *fooled* her!"

B.D. expected to encounter a backlash against the book during her promotional tour. "The lions were loose in the arena," she wrote in *Narrow Is the Way*. "And now the Christian had to make her entrance." Other Christians welcomed her with unquestioning acceptance (and sad cluck-clucks about her miserable life with Bette) on such shows as Pat Robertson's *700 Club*, but the "lions" were far more numerous, more skeptical, and well armed with B.D.'s own past statements about her mother. On a *Sixty Minutes* segment about the book, Mike Wallace rebroadcast an interview with B.D. that had originally run along with the show's profile of Bette in 1980. Wallace's doubts about the veracity of *My Mother's Keeper* stemmed from what B.D. had said to him five years earlier.

"Was she a tough mother?" Wallace had asked.

"In certain ways," B.D. replied.

"What ways?"

"Discipline, manners. It was worth your life to forget a 'please' or a 'thank you.' And things that I consider important in raising my own children, really. As far as fun things went, she was totally lenient."

"Like?"

"Oh, we never had curfews. I was allowed to date who I pleased. She totally trusted my judgment as to who my friends were, where I went and with whom, because she felt that at a certain age—a fact that I agree with—your children have gleaned all they can from their parents. . . ."

After B.D. explained that Bette had let her marry at sixteen because she "believed in allowing me to make my own judgments, my own mistakes," Wallace commented, "You're making this sound like a storybook—"

"No, no. We had arguments, we certainly did."

"Who doesn't?" Wallace said. "But no real disadvantages to having been the daughter of Bette Davis?"

"None. None that I found."

Later in the interview, Wallace asked, "Now, Bette Davis was a huge and busy star . . . did she have time for you?"

"Yes. She *made* time. Part of the reason was that she had me travel with her almost everywhere, all the time. And I guess part of the reason also was that when she was home, she was home. She wasn't too busy. She wanted to be with her children, to do things with us."

"Was she a star at home?"

"No, never, never. She was in blue jeans and work shirts and she was a working mother when she was at home. She was in her kitchen. She was tidying up the house. She was weeding the garden and planting bulbs. She was a mother."

One "lion" B.D. apparently hadn't expected to encounter was Gary Merrill, whose portrait in *My Mother's Keeper* was no less devastating than Bette's. Seventy years old, long retired in Maine, Merrill picketed his local bookstore in Portland, carrying a placard that read, "Please boycott *My Mother's Keeper*." He then placed an ad in *The New York Times* urging readers not to "shell out twenty bucks for this book." He did no television interviews until he agreed to respond on CNN to some of B.D.'s charges in the book. When she appeared on the network, they ran the film of Gary's comments and asked for her reaction. According to her, he continually chanted "cruelty and greed, cruelty and greed" when asked why B.D. wrote the book, and kept laughing "maniacally."

"Memories from childhood flooded in on me," she wrote. "Abuse, threats, drunkenness, beatings. I recoiled as I would from a psychopath stabbing repeatedly at his victim."

Ultimately, it mattered little how much truth *My Mother's Keeper* did or did not contain, because a consensus quickly developed among the public and those who knew both Bette and B.D. that B.D. should not have published it under any circumstances. "It was so dishonorable," Robert Lantz says. "I once said to Harold Schiff that even assuming everything in B.D.'s book is one hundred percent true, she shouldn't have published it during her mother's lifetime."

B.D.'s friend Josie Hamm, while stressing that "I'm really on the side of B.D. on this," says, "I didn't like the book. I just think it was so strong that it shouldn't have been written when it was. The book killed Bette. That was absolutely the end. She didn't understand how her daughter, who she loved more than anything, could do such a thing to her."

What was most disturbing to friend and foe alike about B.D. was that she had kicked her mother when she was down. The book may have backfired, however. Far from tarnishing Bette's public image (as *Mommie Dearest* had Joan Crawford's), the overriding effect of *My Mother's Keeper* was to generate sympathy for Bette and forever brand B.D. as "the ungrateful daughter who betrayed Bette Davis."

Before too long, B.D. stopped being hurt and let the criticism roll off her back. In *Narrow Is the Way,* she describes Jeremy reading several "truly vile" articles about the book aloud to her while imitating the homosexual author Truman Capote's high-pitched voice because he "had long held an unshakable conviction, which I wholeheartedly shared, regarding the nature of the majority of my mother's most ardent fans." Jeremy's little impression reduced his wife to "helpless laughter" and "chang[ed] forever my reaction to the utterances of the most strident among my detractors."

Bette couldn't bring herself to read B.D.'s books for months, but when she finally did she felt as though she had been kicked in the face. "Bette wasn't one to cry," Don Ovens knew. "She never wanted you to see her that way. The only time I ever saw her cry in all the years I knew her was in my living room as we talked about what B.D. had done to her. She said she could get over the stroke and over the cancer, but she could not get over what B.D. had done to her. And I really think what B.D. did played a big part in her death."

The terrible year that was 1985 closed with more bad news for Bette when Kath Sermak decided to pursue a new life in France as an assistant to the clothing designer Patrick Kelly. Aware that Kath needed to move on, Bette reacted with equanimity to the news, but now she felt abandoned as well as betrayed. More terrified than ever of being alone, Bette sought the paid assistance of strangers and the live-in companionship of friends. Both arrangements always proved short-lived; few people possessed Kath's ability to put up with Bette's demands, her harsh tongue and temper—or her crushing melancholy whenever she dwelled on what B.D. had done to her and realized she would never see her daughter or grandchildren again.

A blessed respite came with another television movie offer that took Bette to Georgia late in October. *As Summers Die* cast her as a liberal-minded Southern dowager, circa 1955, who helps a young lawyer defend an impoverished black woman unjustly accused of a crime. With no one to accompany her to the location, Bette hired a local woman to act as her maid. The film's producer, Rick Rosenberg, called the quiet, gentle woman "just someone else [for Bette] to beat on"; the cast and crew could hear Bette raging against her whenever she returned to her trailer. But the woman remained, and when the filming wrapped the day before Thanksgiving, Bette stayed on after everyone else had gone home to their families for the holiday. She had been invited to join Michael and his family, Margot, and Gary Merrill for Thanksgiving dinner at the home of Michael's mother-in-law Alix Snow, but she had declined. "She never came to holidays at my house or Michael's," Alix explains. "I'm not sure why, but I think it was because she didn't want to see Gary Merrill. They had had a falling-out over who was to pay for Margot's care, and there was bad blood between them." Rather than spend Thanksgiving—that most New England of holidays—with her son and his family in Connecticut, Bette remained on a deserted location in Georgia, munching turkey with the temporary maid she had so often reviled.

Back in West Hollywood, as the winter of 1985 evolved into the spring of 1986, Bette faced anew the harsh reality that acting offers were not coming in for her. She telephoned Robert Lantz every couple of days—"Why aren't you sending me any *scripts?!*"—and Lantz tried to explain as gently as possible that there were few parts for a woman her age; what good roles there were seemed always to go to Jessica Tandy.

What Lantz didn't say—and what Bette must have realized in her rare moments of honest introspection—was that most producers in Hollywood considered her unemployable. If there were few roles for an actress nearly eighty, there were fewer still for a frail, painfully thin, obviously disabled woman. The electrifying nervous energy that Bette was famous for, the feistiness that had kept her seemingly forever young, had deserted her, replaced by a limping feebleness that inspired either pity or admiration at her ability to carry on—but in either case made onlookers uncomfortable. If an actor's greatest asset is his physicality— the body as instrument—then most of Bette's gifts as a performer had been destroyed by the aftereffects of the illnesses she had endured.

She went a year without acting. Instead, she drew heavily on the investments Harold Schiff had made on her behalf and met every day with the writer Michael Herskowitz to prepare a second memoir that she hoped would bring in large royalties and serve as something of an answer to *My Mother's Keeper.*

In the summer, a miracle: a film role for which Bette was ideally suited. The producer Mike Kaplan asked her to reconsider a project she had turned down a few years earlier: his film version of *The Whales of August,* a character study by David Berry of two elderly widowed sisters: sweet-natured, patient Sarah, and the older, blind, embittered, and cantankerous Libby. The slim plot was motivated mainly by a dispute the sisters have about a picture window Sarah wants to install in the living room of the cottage they share for the summer on a nearly deserted island off the coast of Maine. The title referred to the migrating whales that swim past the sisters' cottage each year.

Kaplan had wanted Bette to play Libby opposite Lillian Gish, the nearly ninety-year-old silent film superstar who had worked only sporadically in talkies. Although the project was prestigious, Bette reportedly was incensed at being asked to play Lillian's older sister, and she turned it down. Kaplan wasn't able to secure financing for the film, and the movie was abandoned. Kaplan revived the project in 1986, and this time Bette accepted the offer to costar with Gish. She wasn't any happier about the role, but she knew this was the most important film she had been asked to do in years, and it would be her first theatrical release since 1980. And—no small incentive—she needed the money.

The British director Lindsay Anderson brought together his company, which included Vincent Price and Ann Sothern in supporting roles, to Maine's Cliff Island, across Casco Bay from Cape Elizabeth and Witch-Way, the house that Bette had shared with Gary Merrill thirty years earlier. Whether it was this proximity to a lost dream that affected Bette, or her anger at having to play an enfeebled blind woman, or her fear that she couldn't do it, she arrived on the set in a foul mood and immediately drew a line in the sandy loam of Cliff Island.

"She arrived on location," recalls Vincent Price, "telling everyone within earshot that she wished she was doing the film with Katharine Hepburn instead of Lillian."

"She wasn't very nice to Lillian," Ann Sothern adds. "I don't know why. I think she felt threatened because Lillian is a great lady." Lindsay Anderson felt Bette's problem with Gish was basic. "Lillian was *at least* her costar," he points out. "I don't think she wanted to share the limelight. There wasn't anything else. There was nothing precipitated by Lillian. But Bette's attitude was one of hostility."

Gish, whose legendary film career began in 1912, was hard of hearing, and sometimes she was fed her lines through a concealed headset.

Whenever this was necessary, everyone on the set was understanding and cooperative—except for Bette, who was driven to distraction. "You try working with a deaf mute!" she exclaimed to Don Ovens.

Bette would sputter and harangue against her costar, but to no avail. When someone commented that Lillian looked wonderful in a closeup, Bette snapped, "She *ought* to know about closeups. Jesus, she was around when they *invented* them!" When someone said hello to Gish, Bette grumbled, "You'll have to yell—she can't hear a damn thing!" Gish heard all of Bette's off-the-cuff cruelties, but Vincent Price noticed that "whenever Bette went into one of her sustained tirades, Lillian would just turn off her hearing aid. That way she was able to just ignore her." Gish got back a little at Bette for her rudeness by pretending not to hear her line cues, which kept Bette off balance. "This surprised Bette a little," Vincent Price says. "I don't think she thought Lillian had it in her."

Gish, in fact, felt sorry for Bette. "She must be a very unhappy woman," she told Ann Sothern, and later she was heard to say, "That face! Have you ever seen such a tragic face? Poor woman! How she must be suffering. I don't think it's right to judge a person like that. We must bear and forbear."

Lindsay Anderson was less sympathetic. To him, "directing Bette Davis was like playing with a very sharp knife. She met the world like an enemy: to collaborate was to concede. She had the charm of vitality, but there was the threat of cruelty as well. Even if she wasn't offensive, she conveyed the fact that at any moment she might be."

The harsh weather conditions of the Maine coastline in October worsened Bette's bad temper. She had undergone minor corrective surgery on her hip just prior to filming, and the cold damp sometimes made it an agony for her to walk. "We should have shot the picture at least two months earlier," Ann Sothern felt. "Oh, God, it was cold, very cold! And sometimes Bette just couldn't work."

The wind was so fierce during one scene in which Bette and Lillian stand on a hill overlooking the ocean that burly grips had to hold onto the women's waists, out of camera range, to keep them from toppling over in the gusts. Vincent Price recalled that Bette kept her makeshift dressing room so overheated with three electric space warmers that he nearly passed out after having just one cocktail Bette had prepared for him.

The first Sunday into production, Bette quit the picture. "There was a terrific hubbub," Lindsay Anderson recalls, "telephone calls between her and Robbie Lantz and her lawyer. It was total nonsense, really, it wasn't about anything. It was just Bette churning things up. She was capable of a lot of bullshit." Bette came back, but she was frantic without Kath Sermak to keep her on an even keel. According to Lindsay Anderson, "There were endless problems of Bette trying to get a companion who would look out for her and cook for her [while being] continually insulted and treated very badly by Bette."

Bette was particularly touchy about how the long white wig she wore in the film should be dressed. "She had a couple of hairdressers," recalls Ann Sothern, but neither pleased her a whit. "She hit one! She just punched her right in the chest. She was terribly upset that Kathryn wasn't with her."

Lindsay Anderson found that Bette's contrariness extended far beyond the superficial. "She wasn't very open to suggestions. She had a sense of rivalry about it. I remember her saying, 'Oh, that's *twice* I've given in to Anderson today.' Which is nonsense. It was sort of a game with her, and not a helpful game. Reason didn't really come into it. It was temperamental and emotional. I said to her, 'You mustn't waste your energy fighting unnecessary battles.' The unit was absolutely on her side, extremely respectful. We did everything we could to make it enjoyable, but she was dead set against that. She didn't *want* it to be enjoyable. It was tragic, really."

When Lillian Gish threw a dinner party for the cast and crew, Bette left after a few minutes of idle chatter. Feeling obliged, Bette hosted a gathering of her own, but spent the entire time sitting in a corner, chain smoking and ignoring her guests.

As the filming drew to a close, Anderson noticed an odd shift in Bette's attitude. "Suddenly she was being friendly to everyone. She would come to the set even after she was through shooting and just hang around and be very pleasant. I realized that she didn't want to leave the island, didn't want the job to end. Because it was work, and work was everything to her."

The Whales of August was released a year after production wrapped, in October 1987. Perceived as an art film, it had limited distribution, and its reviews were respectful. Gish garnered the best notices for her magical presence; she was able to convey more emotion in one glance than most actresses can through pages of dialogue. As one critic pointed out, Bette provided a strong counterpoint with her best performance in years: "Bette crawls across the screen like a testy old hornet on a windowpane, snarling, staggering, twitching—a symphony of misfired synapses. Lillian's performance is as clear and simple as a drop of water filled with sunlight."

Bette might have basked in this small triumph, but instead she reacted with petty jealousy to Gish's acclaim. When she learned that she and Gish would share a title card at the beginning of the film, she insisted that she have her *own* card, flashed *before* Lillian's. When she sensed that Gish's performance was being hailed as the better of the two, she refused to attend the movie's world premiere at the Cannes Film Festival along with Gish and Lindsay Anderson. When she was told that the New York premiere had been scheduled on Lillian's birthday, she stayed away from that, too, telling the press her decision was based on "self-preservation."

Finally, Ann Sothern recalls, whenever Bette was asked to autograph photos of herself and Lillian in the film, "she would sign her name in big black letters—right over Lillian's face."

Bette's lack of support for *The Whales of August* may have hurt its chances at the box office, where it did only moderate business. Lindsay Anderson, however, thinks there was a more elemental force at work against the film's popular appeal. "The public likes to see Bette Davis in *Now, Voyager* or *All About Eve*. They don't want to be reminded of what life does to us, as it did to her, the age and the suffering." In Japan, Anderson points out, the elderly are far more revered than in Western cultures, and there the film did quite well.

There was much talk early in 1988 that both Bette and Lillian would win Oscar nominations as Best Actress, and Bette was badly disappointed when only Ann Sothern was cited, in the Supporting Actress category. At home in Idaho, Sothern received a call from Bette the morning the nominations were announced. "She didn't really congratulate me," Sothern recalls. "What she did say was, 'Now, listen, if you can't get to L.A. for the ceremonies, I'll accept your award for you!' "

THIRTY-FOUR

R obert Lantz couldn't believe what he had just heard. After nearly twenty years as his client and his friend, Bette had met secretly with another agent, Michael Black of ICM, and was about to switch her representation. Lantz was stunned and hurt, not so much by the fact that Bette wanted to move on as by her lack of candor about it.

Lantz had made heroic efforts on Bette's behalf throughout 1987, but the cause was hopeless. No producer would hire her, either because of the way she looked or because they feared she would be uninsurable. Bette fervently hoped to star in the movie version of the stage success *Driving Miss Daisy*, as a cantankerous Southern dowager; the role went instead to Jessica Tandy (who was only a year younger than Bette but in far better health). She flirted with the idea of appearing in the film version of the ensemble piece *Steel Magnolias*, but the play didn't have a role for a woman Bette's age.

Offers simply didn't come in to Lantz's office, and when he repeatedly told Bette he had nothing for her she became convinced that he wasn't working hard enough. "She didn't understand that she was no longer employable," Lantz recalls sadly. "She weighed seventy-five pounds or something. It was too difficult. *She* was too difficult."

When Lantz got confirmation that Bette was shopping for a new agent, he wrote her a note. "Bette, we are such close friends," he told her. "I don't want you to be uncomfortable if you talk to any other agent. We are released from one another. I am always here for you, for anything, but let's end it."

Lantz's heart broke. "She was one of the three or four people in the world that I could have called at four in the morning if I had trouble of any kind," he felt, "and she would have been there for me. She was remarkable." Lantz was further disheartened when Bette failed to respond in any way to his note. They were never in contact with each other again.

❧

If Bette was convinced that with the proper representation she could work steadily, she had no delusions about her inability to tend to her personal needs without assistance. Kath Sermak flew back from France occasionally to visit, but Bette missed her on a daily basis for countless practical and emotional reasons. The pain in her joints, the frustration of dealing with her often recalcitrant body, the maddening idleness—all of this was bad enough. Add the crushing loneliness that sometimes threatened to overwhelm her, and Bette often felt she wouldn't be able to go on.

Holidays proved especially difficult, but she was still too bitter at Gary to join Michael and his family's celebrations. Christmas of 1987, she went instead to her friend Robin Brown's house in Westport, and her young friend Doug Troland stopped by to visit. "It was Christmas Day evening," Troland recalls, "and when Bette opened the door I could tell her hip was giving her trouble; she was limping. She escorted me down to the little room Robin had put her in and I was really shocked. It was a tiny, desolate room with an electric heater and it was so cold that Bette kept her mink coat on. We sat down to talk and we were almost knee to knee, the room was so small. Bette went on and on about how Robin wouldn't light a fire in the house. She was funny about Robin, I never knew if she really liked her or not. Anyway, we were sitting there and Bette gestured around this tiny hole-in-the-wall and said, 'Well, here we are. Who would have thought that you and I would end up like this?' I wondered what she meant by that, 'you and I.' She was clearly talking about herself."

Bette constantly searched for a permanent companion throughout the late 1980s. Her old chum Peggy Shannon stayed with her off and on until Peggy herself fell ill and had to be hospitalized. Bette then approached Betty Lynn, who had remained friendly with her after they appeared together in *June Bride* and *Payment on Demand* four decades earlier. Lynn and Bette paid Peggy Shannon a visit in the hospital, and as they left Lynn was taken aback when Bette offered her a salary to move in with her. "I realized she needed someone to be with her, and that she was probably quite lonely. But as fond as I was of Bette, I just couldn't see myself working for her in that way."

Doug Troland lived on the East Coast, and when Bette made plans to spend an extended period of time in Westchester, she offered him $300 a week to be her live-in assistant. It was then that Troland realized that over the prior several months Bette had been putting him through an elaborate series of tests to see whether he would be suitable as her consort. The first was when she invited him to her hotel suite for a dinner with several executives from the publishing house that planned to bring out her second volume of memoirs. There was no reason for Bette to invite Troland to the dinner except to gauge how he would handle himself in a business situation of that kind.

He failed the first test. "I arrived wearing a nice sweater—I had always dressed casually around Bette—and when she opened the door she said, 'Didn't anybody ever tell you that you're supposed to wear a jacket and tie in a hotel?' I had had many, many visits with her in hotels and had never dressed up. I didn't realize until later that this visit was a grand audition for me."

Troland did better with the second test. "I sensed that Bette expected me to keep my thoughts to myself during the discussions about the book, and I did." After the other guests left, Bette put the young man to the final trial. "We were sitting alone in the suite and she was across from me. I noticed this glittering diamond by her shoe that kept catching my eye. Finally I said, 'Oh, what's this, Bette?' and picked it up. It was one of her earrings. I know it sounds far-fetched to say that Bette was trying to see if I'd steal it, but she did things like that."

Just before Troland left, Bette offered him the job as her assistant. "She wanted to feel comfortable around whoever lived with her, and we had a very comfortable relationship. It might seem boring, but often it consisted of us just sitting in the kitchen watching a game show. It was totally the kind of normal interaction that goes on between people. I sensed from the beginning that that was the role she wanted of me."

Still, Troland turned Bette down. "I was terrified of the prospect," he says. "I could see myself locked up with her, and while that may sound fascinating to most people, I knew that after one week it would turn into a very different experience. And she was ill. I remember having to find her medication for her, and I didn't want that responsibility. I also thought she needed a woman who could help her get dressed and that kind of thing."

Kath Sermak came back into Bette's employ in the spring of 1987 after she ended her romance in Paris and resigned her position with the fashion designer Patrick Kelly. Bette was overjoyed, particularly because she was set to embark on a publicity tour to promote her new book, entitled *This 'n That,* which she had written with Michael Herskowitz.

Robert Lantz had shopped the book around to a number of New York publishers, and at first Bette signed a contract with E. P. Dutton. They rejected the manuscript. "Bette refused to write a 'kiss and tell' book," Lantz recalls, "which was the kind most publishers wanted. She also didn't think people would be interested in an in-depth study of her work process, her relationship with certain directors, how she made creative decisions, that kind of thing."

Such a volume could have been more compelling than *This 'n That,* an uninspired hodgepodge that was missing more than just the second apostrophe. A disjointed collection of opinions, reminiscences, and proclamations, the book jumps around from Bette's hospital stay and Kath Sermak's tireless devotion to her experiences with *What Ever Happened to Baby Jane?,* her one-woman stage appearances, and the Hollywood Canteen. There are few revelations of a controversial nature, and when Bette retraces personal material she had already covered in *The Lonely Life,* she imparts very little fresh information.

Book buyers who hoped for a blistering response to *My Mother's Keeper* were disappointed. Bette treats her daughter kindly throughout the book, but at its conclusion she does write an odd note in which she takes issue with some of B.D.'s facts—but only those that involve her career; she ignores her daughter's far more damaging revelations about her private life.

Only in a postscript to the note does Bette get in anything close to a dig: "I hope someday I will understand the title *My Mother's Keeper.* If it refers to money, if my memory serves me right, I've been your keeper all these many years. I am continuing to do so, as my name has made your book about me a success." Also included in the final pages are several negative reviews of the book and letters of support to Bette, including one from Mia Farrow.

Bette appeared on a number of national talk shows to hype *This 'n That,* and she never failed to introduce Kath from the audience. She sang her young assistant's praises as Kath, sometimes dressed elegantly in a skin-tight black satin dress and a single red satin glove, stood and accepted applause from the audience. If Kath wasn't with her for some reason, Bette would show the back of the book—a full-page picture of the two of them—and talk about her companion's loyalty and devotion. Bette clearly wanted to let Kath know how much she appreciated her so that she wouldn't leave again, and she apparently wanted the public to know that if her daughter couldn't stand her, this attractive, capable young woman could.

Despite the shortcomings of *This 'n That,* Bette's popularity propelled it to number five on *The New York Times* bestseller list. When the publisher called her with the news, she snapped, "Why isn't it number *one?*"

Absent from the bestseller lists of 1987 was *Narrow Is the Way,* B.D.'s second effort, this time with Jeremy sharing authorship (and with a back-cover endorsement from Pat Robertson). In even more sanctimonious, self-serving tones than she used in *My Mother's Keeper,* B.D. details the travails of writing that book, her mother's reaction, her confrontational publicity tour, and—in a text replete with startling statements about Jesus and Satan—the story of her conversion to born-again Christianity. One wit couldn't resist the temptation to dub the book *Narrow Is the Mind.*

"My mother could fritter away half a million dollars a year without even trying," B.D. wrote. As in *My Mother's Keeper,* she didn't mention that some of that money was spent on her and her family.

It's unlikely that Bette ever read *Narrow Is the Way,* but shortly after its publication she got word that Gary Merrill was in the midst of writing his autobiography. *"Christ!"* she boomed. "What more can they *say* about me?!"

Larry Cohen sat amid the cheering audience in the hotel ballroom and watched Bette Davis slowly climb the stairs to the stage and accept one of the many lifetime achievement awards she received in 1988. As she spoke to the audience with a touching combination of feistiness and feebleness, Cohen felt both admiration and pity for her. *All this is very nice,* he thought, *but I'll bet she'd much rather somebody gave her a job.* The writer/director/producer of such low-budget films as *Black Caesar, It's Alive!,* and *The Stuff,* Cohen decided to write a film expressly for Bette. He did so several months later—during a week-long stay within a Hawaiian nudist colony.

The result was *The Wicked Stepmother,* a black comedy with supernatural overtones. His story, Cohen says, was built on a basic premise:

"Imagine Bette Davis moving into your house, and she won't go away. . . ." Cohen submitted the script to Bette through Robert Lantz, who turned it down without showing it to her. A few months later, he resubmitted it to Bette's new agent, Michael Black. Black passed it along, but strongly suggested to Bette that she not do it. Weeks passed, and then Cohen got a telephone call from Bette, who told him that the script had given her "a lot of laughs." Delighted, Cohen suggested that they get together at Colonial House to discuss the project.

When Cohen and his associate Peter Sabiston saw Bette, he remembers, "Peter was virtually in shock because she was so tiny and thin and drawn and she limped, she dragged her foot. But the spark was there, the pep was there, the humor was there." Cohen was touched that Bette "hung on to me—if she liked you she would be affectionate and hold your hand and that sort of thing." Afterward, Sabiston advised Cohen not to hire Bette, but Cohen thought she'd be perfect for the film. She agreed to make it for a salary of $250,000, and Cohen acquiesced to her demand that Kath Sermak be brought on board as a producer: "I figured what the hell—it will make Bette happy and Kathryn was sharp and extremely capable."

MGM agreed to finance the film within a modest budget even though they doubted that Bette still had any box-office appeal; according to Cohen, the studio figured they'd make their money back with a limited theatrical release and a quick turnaround into video stores.

Although Cohen found Bette "very friendly and affectionate" during the preproduction phase, her habit of "stirring things up" was also very much in evidence. After she met with the film's cinematographer, Daniel Pearl, he was ready to quit. She refused to film her wardrobe tests in Cohen's home as planned, and told Pearl that if she didn't like the way he captured her on film, she'd have him fired. Shaken, Pearl telephoned Cohen and said, "Larry, I can't work with this woman. She hates me!"

Cohen called Bette and began warily, "I understand you had a meeting with the photographer."

"A very nice guy," she burbled. "I like him!"

When it came time to choose her wardrobe, Bette asked Cohen for his input. "We did the wardrobe down at Western Costume," he recalls, "and she had all their employees terrorized. I sat there and she came out and modeled each outfit for me. Everything was black. Finally she asked me, 'What do you think?' I said, 'Everything looks too much the same. Can't we put a little sash with some color here, or a handkerchief there?'"

Bette's head flew back in fury. "Well then, let's throw it all out and start from scratch!" she bellowed. Cohen tried to soothe her. "No, Bette, all we have to do is add a few accessories—" When she started to interrupt him, Cohen stood up. "Bette, you asked me to come down here because you wanted my opinion, right?" Bette narrowed her eyes and said, "Yes!"

"Well, I'm giving you one!" Cohen concluded firmly, and Bette acquiesced.

"Everyone was looking at me in horror but I learned that that's the only way to deal with her," Cohen explains. "She needed someone to hold their ground. She scares people too easily and then she doesn't have any respect for them. After that we got along fine."

The Wicked Stepmother began principal photography on April 25, 1988, at a large house in the manicured Hancock Park section of Los Angeles. Cohen made sure, despite his tight budget, that Bette was treated like Hollywood royalty. Her dressing trailer was furnished with a small kitchen, a VCR, and a microwave oven. Worried about her frailty, Cohen offered to have a bed installed as well. "I've *never* lain down between takes!" Bette exploded. "Who do you think I am?!"

Colleen Camp, cast as Bette's daughter-in-law, recalls a similar reaction when she asked Bette if she could get her a chair. "If I want a chair I'll get it!" she barked.

"At first I was taken aback and intimidated," Camp says. "I was just trying to be nice. But then I realized this was her way of preserving her dignity, her way of saying, 'I'm not an invalid. If I need a chair, I can get it myself.'"

This fierce need of Bette's to let everyone know she was independent had an unhappy result one afternoon. As she walked from her trailer to the house with Kath, she slipped and fell to the ground. Cohen, aware of her angry reactions to offers of help, was loath to embarrass her; he shooed people away and let Bette fend for herself. She refused help even from Kath and struggled for what Cohen remembers as twenty minutes to get up. Colleen Camp thinks it was more like five minutes, "but that's a long time in a situation like that."

Finally, several grips stacked some wooden crates next to her and Bette used them to struggle to her feet. She limped back to her dressing room, where a nasty bruise quickly colored on her hip. Cohen went to her trailer and told her she wouldn't have to work that afternoon, but she insisted she could. "She did work later that day," Cohen recalls, "and she did a fine job."

Cohen found touching Bette's desire to soak up every bit of the film-making ambience she loved. "She would come out long before she was needed to where the gaffer was hanging the lights and the grips were climbing ladders and stand in the middle of all this chaos. The men would walk around her and say, 'Excuse me, Miss Davis,' and barely miss her head with a ladder or a cable. And I'd say to her, 'Bette, what are you doing in the middle of everything?' And she'd say, 'I always like to see what's going on. I don't like being in my dressing room.'"

After little more than a week of filming, Bette decided she didn't like being in *The Wicked Stepmother* either. She was appalled at what she saw of herself in Cohen's "dailies" and walked out of the picture. Although Cohen had taken every care to make Bette look good, and had staged the action so that she needed to move from one place to another as little as possible, Bette was shocked at her wizened appearance. In *The Whales of August,* she had accepted the way she looked because she was playing a frail, embittered woman. In *The Wicked Stepmother,* she had tried to appear elegant and stylish, but her wardrobe did little to disguise her feebleness, and the most careful camera work couldn't hide the deeply etched lines in her face or her twisted mouth. "I agonized over my appearance," she admitted. "Terrible! I looked so bad that [I knew] no producer would want to hire me after the film was released."

Bette left for New York, ostensibly to seek her dentist's care for a cracked denture that had impaired her ability to speak, but within a few days she called Cohen and told him, "I've made a dreadful mistake. I'm not coming back." Soon thereafter, Harold Schiff and Michael Black called the director and placed the blame for Bette's departure squarely on him. "They said Bette had complained that when she fell down, I wasn't sympathetic enough," Cohen recalled. "And they said, 'She got hurt, you electrocuted her, you gave her shocks and she hurt her eye.'"

The accident had occurred during a scene where Bette's character, in the first indication that she's a witch, places a cigarette in her mouth and it lights with no help from her. On the first take, the special effects device that provided the flame had flared up in Bette's face, and Cohen had told her that he didn't want to risk redoing the effect; he would add it optically later on. But she insisted on doing it twice more, both times coming close again to injury. "Schiff and Black blamed me for all this," Cohen says, "even though Bette wouldn't hear of doing it any other way."

At first, according to Cohen, Schiff and Black led him to believe that despite Bette's unhappiness she would return to the picture when her dental work was completed. He shot around her for about a week, but then he was informed that she wasn't coming back. Her doctor added to her litany of complaints when he told Cohen that the stress she'd been under had brought her weight down to seventy-five pounds. Curious to see what Bette's weight had been before filming began, Cohen was amazed to learn that she had somehow evaded the full medical exam required for insurance purposes. "She had managed to bamboozle and intimidate the insurance doctor to such a degree that he hadn't even *weighed* her," Cohen marvels. "Weighing someone is the most elemental aspect of a medical exam!"

With Bette irretrievably gone, Cohen scrambled to refashion his script so that he would be able to use the fifteen minutes of footage he had of Bette and adequately explain her absence from the rest of the picture. His solution was to have her character metamorphose into a beautiful young woman played by Barbara Carrera, but the movie was never the same. "The original script was very funny," Colleen Camp thought. "It was disheartening for Larry to try to rewrite it. It didn't make the sense it made originally."

The Wicked Stepmother did prove to be a disjointed, unfunny misfire when it was released directly to video in 1989. Some of the solutions forced on Cohen by Bette's departure have an air of desperation about them: in one instance an obviously mechanical cat puffs on a cigarette to indicate that the wicked stepmother's malevolent soul has taken over the family pet. Bette, present only in the film's first half hour, clearly tried very hard to play her character with the broad strokes required of farce. But her physical limitations lend her movements and speech the eerie quality of slow motion. In spite of her comely red wig and stunning fashions, the camera is dreadfully cruel to her, revealing the sunken contours of her nearly cadaverous face; in close-up, it is sometimes painful to watch her.

Bette was furious that the footage she had shot was used at all in the film, but there was nothing she could do about it legally. Instead, she took to the airwaves—notably on *Entertainment Tonight*—to denounce the movie and Larry Cohen. "I was perfectly willing to take the blame,"

Cohen says. "I was really on her side. I tried to give her a job . . . she was basically uninsurable and couldn't work anymore. I guess I should have expected the inevitable to happen."

Aware now that she would never make another film, Bette busied herself with a round of talk-show appearances. Trading quips with Johnny Carson, Joan Rivers, Larry King, and David Letterman, she reiterated long-held opinions about predictable topics like the studio system, Joan Crawford, Jack Warner, and Faye Dunaway. The only subjects she deemed off limits were her private agonies of the past few years, including B.D.'s book.

Viewers, at first shocked by Bette's withered exterior, were astounded by the undiminished sharpness of her mind as she rattled off her lightning-fast, irascible opinions, and her appearances were great successes. But the director Lindsay Anderson, for one, found them uncomfortable to watch. "She was popular on the chat shows because she was so bitchy," he felt. "I always disliked that because she was encouraged to behave badly. And I'd always hear her described by that awful word, *feisty.*"

Prodded by Kath Sermak, Bette was now something of a fashion maverick. For her television and other public appearances, she sported daring Patrick Kelly outfits: a black suit with oversized rainbow-colored buttons, a flashy red dress with three prominent question marks splashed across the front; wide-brimmed hats atop a fluffy blond wig. Some observers found the fashions (supplied her gratis as a way to publicize Kelly's line) a tad ridiculous on a woman of eighty. Others, remembering her matronly look of recent years, applauded the colorful garb as a refreshing change of pace.

"At that point," one fashion maven opined, "she couldn't have looked natural or grandmotherly no matter what she did because of her ravaged appearance. So she went for a very theatrical, contemporary look that I'm sure helped lift her spirits and that made her look much more 'with it.' She was the walking personification of the old adage—*If you can't hide it, paint it red.*"

THIRTY-FIVE

"You *can't* listen in," Bette roared. "You'll have to wait in the *dining* room!" She was about to be interviewed by the young writer and designer Gregory Poe for *City* magazine, a slick, over-sized fashion and arts periodical published in Paris. While she had taken an instant liking to Poe, she didn't want his editor in on the conversation. "She banished the poor woman to the dining room for three and a half hours," Poe recalls. "She had to sit on a chair in the corner like Dennis the Menace."

A longtime Davis fan, Poe soaked in the ambience of Bette's Colonial House condominium and picked up quickly on the interaction between Bette and Kath Sermak. "Kath was as nasty to me as Bette was polite," he felt. "I realized she really was an 'Eve Harrington' employee, and it was frightening. They had a very difficult relationship: Kath was overprotective, and Bette would scream at her in front of other people. But you could also see that they liked each other a great deal."

As Poe strolled through the apartment, he was struck by all the cigarette burns on the dining room table and the burn holes in the living room carpet. Then he sat across from Bette while she launched into a lengthy reminiscence. "She gesticulated and the cigarette she was holding flew out of her hand and ended up in the middle of the living room floor. I didn't say a word—you can't just interrupt her and say, 'I'm sorry but your apartment is on fire!'

"She wasn't aware that anything had happened, but Kathryn just came and picked up the cigarette and gave it back to her. She said, 'Oh, *that's* where it went!' I was amazed because she came so close to so many would-be disasters in the time I was there. At this point in her life she was a bit on the addled side. But the minute I would ask her about certain technical aspects of her films she would remember them like it was yesterday. It was a little difficult looking at her because her face was twisted a bit, but she was so *there* for me. She never looked away; she always looked into my eyes. I thought she was terrific. I *really* liked her."

❧

It was harder and harder now for Bette to get around. Her bones ached, her body wouldn't always do what she wanted it to do. A new fear gnawed at her, a terror that if she didn't keep busy, if she didn't have something to do or somewhere to go, that she would simply shrivel up and die. She accepted every plausible invitation that came her way for an interview or a public appearance, and she especially jumped at the chance to accept an award for her lifetime of contributions to the cinema.

Although Kath sometimes had to browbeat her just to get her going in the morning, Bette traveled tens of thousands of miles throughout 1988 and into 1989 in order to gather honors from film and performing arts societies around the world. Within an eighteen-month period, she received the Kennedy Center Honor (presented to her by her *Dark Victory* coworker, the then U.S. President Ronald Reagan), the Legion of Honor from France, the Campione d'Italia from Italy, and the Film Society of Lincoln Center Lifetime Achievement Award.

In January 1989 Bette had to travel just fifteen minutes by car from Colonial House to attend the American Cinema Awards at the Beverly Hilton Hotel, at which she was to be feted along with Clint Eastwood and Julio Iglesias. Resplendent in a white brocade gown and a fur pillbox hat, Bette thrilled the crowd with her entrance into the hotel's Grand Ballroom.

Lynn Barrington, an aspiring actress, was seated at a table near Bette's, and she recalls the evening vividly. At first she was bedazzled by Bette—"she was so tiny and elegant looking, like a sparkly little doll." But as the dinner progressed, Barrington was appalled by Bette's table habits. "I've never seen anyone literally puff on a cigarette, take a belt of booze and eat a mouthful of food all at the same time. Puff, drink, eat. It was gross. She would take a drag on the cigarette while she was chewing!"

After about half an hour of this, Bette slumped forward onto the table and collapsed. "It's a good thing someone had removed the plate of food from in front of her," Barrington says, "or she would have fallen face-first into her dinner."

Three hotel employees picked Bette up and carried her out of the ballroom. According to Barrington, "They carried her perfectly flat, as though she were levitating or something. Just as they passed my table, her hat and wig fell off. Without missing a beat, one of the men reached down, picked them up and plopped them back on her head. Mercifully, the lights were low and there was activity on the stage, so most of the people in the audience didn't see any of this."

Shocked and saddened by this spectacle, Barrington was further amazed about forty minutes later when Bette, although clearly exhausted, returned to her table and lit up a fresh cigarette. As the long evening drew to a close, Robert Wagner helped Bette up to the stage to accept her award, and Barrington thought he looked very concerned. "He knew she had collapsed earlier and he must have been worried about her tripping or something. His concern for her was obvious to everyone."

Bette clutched her award and thanked one and all. Then she announced that because it was January, the audience should join her in a rendition of "Auld Lang Syne." Lynn Barrington's boyfriend was the conductor of the band, and she could tell from his expression that this hadn't been planned. "After a shaky start, the band started to play and everyone sang. When it was over, Bette announced that we should sing it again! At the end of the second go-round, my boyfriend made a loud fanfare to discourage another chorus."

Rather than return to her table at this point, Bette began to express her thanks again for the award. "She started to ramble," Barrington recalls, "and Robert Wagner walked over to her and called out to the audience, 'Bette Davis!' to encourage applause and move her along. But in the middle of the ovation Bette shouted that she wasn't through! She continued to ramble on for another five minutes until Clint Eastwood joined Wagner on stage and they practically dragged her off as the audience applauded."

Barrington thought Bette's fans found the whole episode amusing and were delighted just to see her. But others, she said, "felt embarrassed for her and found her both pathetic and obnoxious."

In April, although she felt weak, Bette flew to New York to receive the Film Society Award at Lincoln Center. After tributes from James Stewart, Ann-Margret, and others, the audience was treated to a lengthy screening of clips from the most memorable Davis films. *The New York Times* film critic Vincent Canby wrote of the event, "When she walked onto the stage of the Avery Fisher Hall, she no longer looked like the woman we'd seen in the clips. . . . The indestructibility of thought and talent which we had been watching on the screen, and which seemed always to be reflected in those distinctive, familiar features, was not recognizable. Instead the ravages of [her] cancer were apparent, as were the rather pathetic and grotesque attempts to ignore them. Then the stranger took the microphone and said the magic words, 'What a dump!' Buried deep inside the alien presence, the woman lived. She brought the house down."

But it was tougher and tougher now for Bette to call up these fleeting moments of magic. She often felt tired unto death; sometimes, at home, she would fall asleep in the middle of a phrase. Kath became concerned, and urged her to see her doctor. She did, in the summer of 1989, and once again there was bad news: her cancer had recurred. She began secret radiation treatments at the Cedars-Sinai Medical Center a few miles from her home, and while the news didn't get out, the national tabloids took note of her increasingly skeletal appearance and suggested she was purposefully starving herself to death.

It was true that she rarely ate, but hardly by choice. The last time Doug Troland saw her was at Colonial House with Kathryn. "She was clearly very sick at this point and incredibly thin. She mentioned that she would give anything to get her appetite back and gain some weight." Troland had gone through a minor depression for which he had been prescribed the popular antidepressant drug Prozac, which he found increased his appetite. When he told Bette, "she got all excited and looked into the drug herself. It turned out that there was some reason why she couldn't take it, but I was struck by the fact that she was convinced that all she needed to do to regain her strength was get her appetite back. I don't believe she knew she was going to die. I think she figured she'd be out there fighting a lot longer."

Bette's deterioration was evident on television and in magazine photographs, and during 1989 B.D. attempted to contact her by phone several times when the Hymans visited California. Bette wouldn't take her calls. "Mother knew I was on the phone, because I could hear her voice in the background, but I never even got past Kathryn." Kath, B.D. thought, had completely supplanted her in the role of daughter. "Kathryn became what I was supposed to be. Mother found a willing victim. . . . She became an extension of Mother. She dressed like Mother. She talked like Mother. . . . She just became totally drawn in, totally as it were possessed by the presence of my mother, and became what I was supposed to be. And Mother indeed did call Kathryn her daughter at the end."

❦

Bette was in constant pain now, frequently nauseated from the radiation, and losing her already thin hair in clumps. Despite it all, when she received an invitation to be honored at the annual film festival in San Sebastián, Spain, she astonished Kath by saying she wanted to go. Her doctors expressed strong reservations about her ability to make the eight-thousand-mile trip, but they didn't forbid her to do so.

To make the journey as easy as possible, she and Kath flew first to New York, where they stayed overnight before flying on to Paris on September 14. Bette, tranquilized by painkillers, slept through most of the eight-hour flight. When she and Kath arrived in Spain, Bette needed three days of rest before she could venture out to meet the public.

Her first appearance was at a press conference. She faced many of the usual banal questions with aplomb, but she was also forced to deny that she was terminally ill; she spoke of further European travel plans and upcoming movie projects. But she seemed to offer a veiled hint of her true condition when she said that "time is getting short and I'm glad [the festival organizers] invited me when they did, otherwise I might never have been around to come."

The rain poured down steadily all day on September 22, and Bette was concerned that the weather would keep fans away from San Sebastián's Victoria Eugenia Theatre, where she was to be presented that evening with the Donostia Award. Kath wasn't sure Bette would be able to make it to the ceremony. She was sluggish and in awful pain; her heart didn't seem to be in this. After Kath had helped her into a dark beaded gown and bejeweled black hat and assisted her into the limousine, Bette slumped deep into the back seat and closed her eyes.

As the car made its way through the streets of San Sebastián, Bette looked wearily out the window. She saw people standing along the edges of the street, peering at her through the windows and waving. The closer the car got to the theater, the thicker the crowds became. "I was in disbelief," Bette recalled. "There were hundreds of people waiting in the rain to see me. The crowds went for blocks on all sides of the street. Even the plaza square was filled with people. I was overwhelmed."

Infused with a rush of adrenaline that filled her with energy, Bette asked the chauffeur to stop the car short of the theater. She struggled out and shook hands with the people who rushed up to the car, working the crowd like a politician. "Pouring rain be damned," she felt. "If they could take it, so could I."

Kath was astounded by Bette's renewed vigor, which was buttressed by the thunderous ovation she received when she walked out on the theater stage, grandly puffed a cigarette, and called out, "Muchas gracias!'' to the ecstatic throng. Her voice cracking, her eyes moist, she drank in this wave of affection and respect as though it were lifeblood. And as Kath watched her out on that stage, more alive than she had been for months, she realized how essential this acclaim was for Bette. But when she was helped down from the stage, Bette all but collapsed and had to cancel her appearance at a lavish dinner later that evening. Over the next week, she attended a few functions for local dignitaries, but her energy level had dropped alarmingly and she soon fell ill with flulike symptoms.

The hotel rushed a doctor to Bette's side, but the man seemed muddled about how to help her. Deeply worried, Kath called New York and spoke to Harold Schiff, who advised her to fly Bette to the American Hospital in Paris, the home of some of the world's preeminent cancer specialists.

On October 3, as a Learjet ambulance plane waited to take her to France, Bette insisted to Kath that she wanted to look "impeccably dressed and groomed." When the airplane's crew saw her they were surprised; according to Kath, "they were expecting someone in far worse condition." She refused a stretcher, and was talkative and alert during the flight.

At the hospital, tests showed that Bette's recent radiation treatment had failed; her body now was riddled with cancer. The doctors told a frightened Kath that Bette was much too ill to return to the United States, and that there was little they could do for her except to give her morphine injections to dull the pain. Unsaid, but clear, was that Bette would not survive for long.

Even with her body full of morphine, Bette remained awake and alert. Michael called and told her he was coming to Paris, but she asked him not to, insisting that she was going to be fine and would see him in New York when she flew back to the States. Over the next days, she talked at length with Kath, who remained by her side day and night and held her hand. "We spoke about life," Kath recalled, "the unbelievable situation we were in, the years we had spent together, and all the great fun we've had." Bette spoke of Ruthie and Bobby, of her fondness for Harold Schiff and her love for Michael and his family. She never mentioned B.D.

On Friday, October 6, Bette felt particularly weak, and she asked the nurses to leave her and Kath alone. They spoke further, Bette's words sometimes barely audible. When a doctor came by to look in on Bette, Kath recalled, "she actually apologized for having been a burden to him, for arriving so ill and then dying in his hospital. It took all her energy to say the things she so badly wanted to say."

The Paris day had been crisp and clear, but toward evening dark clouds began to gather in the sky, threatening rain. When Kath told Bette this, she smiled and said that she and Ruthie had long felt that rain brought them luck; it had always seemed as though the big professional breaks that set Bette on the road to stardom came while it was pouring outside. By 11 P.M., a steady rain splashed against the windows of her room, and she seemed to take on a preternatural calm. Kath sat on her bed and held her wasted hand as they said a few quiet words to each other. Moments later, with the sound of the rain in her ears, Bette passed away.

EPILOGUE

T he death of Bette Davis made front-page news around the world, and millions mourned not only her passing but the close of yet another chapter of the Golden Age of Hollywood. Some of Bette's friends expressed the view that she should never have made the wearying trip to attend the San Sebastián festival. Robert Wagner disagreed. "Why shouldn't she have gone? She could have very easily stayed in her apartment and died looking out the window at Hollywood and wondering what might have been. But she was thrilled with that last hurrah. And she sure as hell deserved it."

In Paris, Kath made arrangements for the body to be flown back to Los Angeles for burial. Although shaken by the death of the woman who had come to mean so much to her, Kath was able—with counsel by phone from Michael and Harold Schiff—to deal with the hospital, the American embassy, the mortuary, the airline, and the press and to make the kinds of decisions she felt would have pleased Bette.

She arrived with the body at Los Angeles International Airport on October 11. She had chosen, she said, "the most elegant casket in Paris. Its title was appropriate, 'The Empress.' " Inside its mahogany and gold-leafed panels Bette lay dressed in "a black evening gown similar to the one she wore at the Lincoln Center gala in April," Kath recalled. "I want you to know she was beautiful, her face serene and at peace."

Bette's funeral was held in the chapel of Forest Lawn Memorial Park at 11 o'clock in the morning on October 12, 1989. The air was redolent with the scent of the white roses and gardenias that blanketed the casket; the service—as Bette had preferred—was private and brief. Among those in attendance were Kath, Michael and Chou Chou Merrill, Robin Brown, Ruth Bailey, and Harold Schiff. Notably absent were B.D. and her family.

Following the service, Bette was interred alongside Bobby and

Ruthie in the striking Davis family mausoleum atop one of Forest Lawn's most prominent hills. Visitors to Bette's grave can see the Warner Brothers studios down the hill on one side and Riverbottom, the home Bette shared with Arthur Farnsworth, on the other.

Etched across Bette's crypt was the epitaph she always said she wanted: "She did it the hard way." And seemingly standing sentry over all is a graceful six-foot statue of a young woman, placed there by Bette years before. She always fancied that the sculpture bore a resemblance to B.D.

On November 2, the Hollywood community gathered for a touchingly elaborate memorial service for Bette on soundstage eighteen of the Warner lot, where she had filmed scenes for *The Letter, Now, Voyager, A Stolen Life,* and other films. Three hundred and fifty guests paid tribute to Bette, including Clint Eastwood, Ann-Margret, Glenn Ford, Vincent Sherman, Lionel Stander, Vincent Price, Janis Paige, and Robert Wagner.

The emcee of the event, David Hartman, opened the ceremonies as though he were speaking to Bette. "We're here," he said, "to celebrate how you matter to us, and recall the work that gave you such sweet joy and such dignity, not to mention so many damn awards." After a screening of clips from Bette's movies, Angela Lansbury told the audience that they had just witnessed a sampling of "an extraordinary legacy of acting in the twentieth century by a real master of the craft" and added that Bette's film performances provided "encouragement and illustration to future generations of aspiring actors."

James Woods, who had befriended Bette when he played a supporting role in *The Disappearance of Aimee,* said, "Miss Davis wrote poetry on the screen like Yeats might write." She was one of those rare actors, he went on, "who not only approach the horizon but go beyond it. . . . What kind of courage does it take to open one's soul so deeply?" He ended his remarks on a wry note: "Up in heaven they're saying, 'Fasten your seat belts. It's going to be a bumpy eternity.' "

The service concluded, amid many moist eyes, with Bette's recorded version of "I Wish You Love" as each guest was handed a single white rose. "As the song ended," Kath Sermak recalled, "Robert Wagner got up and turned on a work light, which is how a film set is left at the end of a day's filming."

As Don Ovens was leaving the service, he asked Michael Merrill about Gary, who he had heard was ill. "He's dying, Don," Mike replied. "I'm losing my whole family to cancer. Aunt Bobby, Mom, and now Dad." Five months later, Gary Merrill died in Maine.

Six weeks after Bette's death, the provisions of her will were made public. Her estate was estimated to be worth nearly $1 million, most of it the value of her Colonial House condominium, appraised at $700,000. The rest comprised $41,000 in personal property, and nearly $250,000 in savings and investments. Bette left all her jewelry to Kath Sermak, along with "all checkbooks, recipes, my gold charm bracelet, the desk in my bedroom, two place settings of Bette Davis flatware [and] the furniture in her former room at Colonial House."

The remainder of the flatware went to Michael, and all her clothing to his wife Chou Chou. To her friend Robin Brown, Bette left two paintings (one a portrait of herself) and a "pearl and sapphire watch." Her niece Ruth Bailey was willed six silver condiment holders because "it was a gift from her mother to me." The remainder of the estate was divided evenly between Michael and Kath. No provisions were made for Margot, as Bette had turned the responsibility for her care over to Gary years earlier. He had set up a trust fund for his daughter that is now overseen by Michael.

Most of the press attention surrounding Bette's will, of course, centered on just one proviso: "I declare that I have intentionally and with full knowledge omitted to provide herein for my daughter, Barbara, and/or my grandsons, Ashley Hyman and Justin Hyman."

Anyone who expected B.D. to feel sorrow or remorse at Bette's death knew disappointment. Within a few days of her mother's passing, she gave an interview to Connie Chung. "I won't shed a single tear," she said. "Her death was only a technicality—she died for me years ago."

In the ensuing years, B.D. and her family have had their share of problems. In 1989, they returned from Grand Bahama Island and moved into a modest tract home in Charlottesville, Virginia, where B.D. began to sell homemade knickknacks at local craft fairs. Jeremy, she says, is currently writing "a nonfiction book."

According to Davis biographer Barbara Leaming, early in 1990,

B.D. told friends that she had been diagnosed with ovarian cancer and had little time to live. She refused medical treatment, preferring instead to leave her fate "in God's hands." On December 7, 1990, she now claims, Jesus answered her prayers and rid her body completely of the disease. B.D.'s religious fervor was often directed at her son Ashley. For a time, friends say, she considered the boy to be the reincarnation of Jesus Christ. When he began to rebel and misbehave as a teenager, however, B.D. decided that her son was "Satan's latest means of access into her marriage." Ashley calmed his mother's fears when he announced that he intended to become a minister, but his studies toward that end were interrupted when he suffered a serious bout of manic depression that resulted in a two-year stay in a Virginia mental hospital. Helped by Lithium treatments, Ashley began to proselytize the other patients. Proudly, B.D. reports that many of these people "found God" through her son's efforts.

Around Christmas 1991, B.D. told Vik Greenfield, with whom she had stayed in touch, that another miracle had occurred when God cured Ashley of his mental illness. Ashley is now serving as a minister and has taken a bride, a young woman whom B.D. says turned her life over to Jesus after seeing Ashley miraculously healed.

In September 1991, B.D. brought her fifteen-year-old son Justin along for an appearance on *The Joan Rivers Show,* during which she repeated her familiar litany of horror stories about Bette. This time, however, there was a twist: Bette's handsome blond grandson, who was six when he last saw her, offered support for his mother's stories and told his own harrowing tale of being chased by Bette with a fireplace poker. (An event that was not mentioned in either of B.D.'s books.)

B.D.'s apparently dogged determination to harbor hatred for Bette (and make sure her children do as well) saddens Harold Schiff. "Unfortunately their mother chose to have them follow her rather than their hearts. Twenty years from now they'll say, 'That was our grandmother; why didn't we really know her?' "

Michael Merrill hasn't spoken to B.D. since her book was published; he considers it unforgivable and thinks it was prompted mostly by B.D.'s religious fanaticism. Recently elected the youngest first selectman in Brookline, Massachusetts, history, he lives in a comfortable home in Chestnut Hill with Chou Chou and their two sons, Matthew, twelve, and Cameron, nine.

The Merrills have few but the most positive memories of Bette. Chou Chou's mother, Alix Snow, recalls visiting a video store with her daughter and her family. "They had seven shelves of Bette Davis movies, and the boys were so happy to think that this was their grandmother. I wanted to take a picture of them standing next to those shelves—they had such proud looks on their faces."

During a 1981 interview, David Hartman asked Bette, "How would you like to be remembered?" She replied, "I think I would like to be missed and respected by my children always. I think that would mean the most to me, although I'll never know. They will probably say, 'Thank God she's gone!' "

As far as B.D. was concerned, Bette was prescient. But Michael fulfilled his mother's wish. At the end of an edition of Bette's autobiography updated by Kath Sermak in 1990, Michael (just as Bette had written to Ruthie at the close of the first edition of the book in 1962) wrote his mother a letter that expressed his love and admiration for her:

> Dear Mother,
> As I write this letter it seems as if you are still here to talk to me, help me and guide me through life. But you are not, and I miss you terribly. You will always be with me. My life was shaped by you. You were tough yet fair, honest, a perfectionist. Your desire to excel in your profession was unmatched. At home we had our difficult moments—what family doesn't? But the warm and loving times are those that stand out in my memory. You always wanted me to be the best and you always wanted the best for me. Thank you for everything. My love forever.
>
> Michael

Had she read her son's note, Bette would surely have cried tears of joy as much as she cried tears of bitterness over B.D.'s treachery. And, as important as her work and her art were to her throughout her life, she would be gladdened too by the fact that, like Michael, her fans miss and respect her despite the fact that she was less than a perfect human being.

ACKNOWLEDGMENTS

I am deeply indebted to a number of people for their cheerful and dedicated help during the three years it took to research and write this book. First among these is Christopher Nickens, my friend and assistant, who worked with me as closely as anyone possibly could. Himself the author of a book about Bette Davis, Chris has an encyclopedic knowledge of Hollywood in general and Bette in particular that enriched this book immeasurably. He conducted many of the interviews in these pages, did hours of library work, and generally kept things moving toward the inevitable deadline.

I much admire the incredible knack of Cathy Griffin to find elusive people and then persuade them to open up to her. A private investigator, she traveled to Geneva, New York, Westport, Connecticut, Wyalusing, Pennsylvania, and Charlottesville, Virginia, on my behalf and unearthed a great deal of important information about Bette, Gary Merrill, Margot Merrill, B.D., Jeremy, and Ashley Hyman, and Michael and Chou Chou Merrill.

Mike Szymanski spent long hours ferreting through the Halls of Records of Los Angeles, Orange, and Riverside counties for vital statistics on Bette, her husbands, and her family. He made herculean efforts to locate witnesses to, and otherwise shed light on, Arthur Farnsworth's fall on Hollywood Boulevard, poring through the Los Angeles fictitious name filings, county property records, birth, death, and marriage records, business license filings, and tax rolls, as well as the records of the L.A. District Attorney and Coroner's offices. His perseverance was rewarded when the Coroner's Office located the Farnsworth inquest transcript, which had long been thought missing.

I am always grateful to my agent, Kathy Robbins, for her belief in me and her careful stewardship of my career. My editor, Gene Young, inherited this book, but her enthusiasm was always so high one would have thought it had been her brainchild. I deeply appreciate her good cheer and excellent advice. Thanks to Steve Rubin, who enthusiastically signed up this project at Bantam, and the estimable Charles Michener, my original editor.

Thanks as well to Elizabeth Mackey, Steve Ross, Isabel Thompson, and Lauren Marino of the Robbins Office for their many professional courtesies; Lauren Field of Bantam for her legal advice; my Dutch publisher, Jan van Willigen of DeKern, Matthew Snyder of CAA, and Edgar Scherick.

I am grateful to Michael Merrill for kindly referring me to his relatives Sally Favour and Ruth Bailey, and for allowing me to quote from unpublished manuscripts in the Bette Davis Collection at Boston University.

The following people also graciously allowed me to quote from unpublished manuscripts, letters, or diaries: Dr. Howard Gottlieb of Boston University, Virginia Conroy, Ray Stricklyn, Gladys Young, and Mike Ellis.

Many other people assisted me in a variety of ways during the writing of this book, and I am indebted to them all:

In Los Angeles—Roy Moseley, Lucille Carroll, Tom Gilbert, Betty Berzon, J. Randy Tarraborelli, Bart Andrews, Tom Boghossian, Jimmy Bangley, Rick Carl, Mike Hawks, Bill Franklin, Randall Henderson, Randall Riese, Tim Nesbitt, Jim Pinkston, Eve Sullivan, Kathryn Sermak, John Sala, Tom Watson, Donald Spoto, Fred Otash, Bill Doty, James B. Pollack of Ralph Edwards Productions, Irwin Okuns and Sally Laughton of the Disney studios, Karen Swenson, J. B. Annegan, Sabin Gray, Hal Pedersen, David Rada, Marlene Mattaschiam of the Publicist's Guild, Kari Johnson of Hollywood Heritage, Sandi Gibbons of the Los Angeles District Attorney's office, Dace Taube of the University of Southern California, Marcia Ventura of Los Angeles Voter Registration, Bob Dambacher and Scott Kerry of the Los Angeles Coroner's office, Mike Battula of the District Attorney investigator's office.

In New York and New England—John Cronin of the *Boston Herald,* Richard Branson, Peter Cosenza, Duncan Chaplin III of Snackerty Enterprises, Robert P. Peckett III, Elmer Fryckman, Franklyn Lenthall of the Theatre Museum in Boothbay, Maine, David Anderson of the Maine State Archives, Madge Ames, Ruth Mitchell of the alumni association of Cushing Academy, Amy T. Logan of Cushing Academy, Dr. Laura N. Shapiro of Newton North High School, Carol Cortese of the Westport, Connecticut, *News,* George Zeno, Lou Valentino, Allison Solow, Sam V. K. Willson, Megan E. Ferrera and Eleanor R. Clise of the Geneva,

New York, Historical Society, William Castiglione of Abbey Industries, E. J. Tangerman, Laura Magnant, Pearl Altman.

Additional thanks to Milton Green, Wendy Leigh, Ed Hobart, Lee Hanna, Richard Jordan, Maggie Maskell, Johan de Besche, Lisa Zwickey of the Wisconsin State Historical Society, Florence W. Hoffman of Denison University, Dott Burns, Tom Fontana.

The staffs of a number of libraries were enormously helpful: Dr. Howard Gottlieb and Karen Mix of the Boston University Library; Ned Comstock, Stuart Ng, and Leith Adams of the University of Southern California library; Sam Gill and the staff of the Margaret Herrick Library of the Academy of Motion Picture Arts and Sciences; the staff of the Lincoln Center Library; the staff of the Los Angeles Public Library; David J. Sleasman of the Curtis Theatre Collection, University of Pittsburgh Library; Pat Gaudilo of the Geneva Free Library; Dr. Charles Bell of the Harry Ranson Humanities Research Center, University of Texas at Austin; Mary K. Knill, Lyndon B. Johnson Library, Austin, Texas; Maura Porter, John F. Kennedy Library, Boston, Massachusetts; Martin I. Elzy, Jimmy Carter Library, Atlanta, Georgia; Geir Gunderson, Gerald R. Ford Library, Ann Arbor, Michigan; Dwight E. Strandberg, Dwight D. Eisenhower Library, Abilene, Kansas; Amanda Fish, Richard Nixon Library, Yorba Linda, California; Benedict K. Zobrist, Harry S. Truman Library, Independence, Missouri; Mark Renovitch, Franklin D. Roosevelt Library, Hyde Park, New York.

And finally, thanks again to my friends and family, who put up with the craziness every few years: my father, Joe Spada, my brothers, Richard and Robbie, and my dear friends Glen Sookiazian, Dan Conlon, Jeff Leach, Laura van Wormer, John Figg, Mark Meltzer, Michael Koegel, and Kevin Scullin.

NOTES ON SOURCES

The primary source material for this book has been the over one hundred and fifty interviews with Bette Davis's friends, family, coworkers, and acquaintances conducted between 1989 and 1992. I am deeply grateful to these fine people for spending the time to share their memories of Bette with me, and I will be forever impressed with the deep affection and regard in which they hold her—even when they had less than flattering things to say. Most of the individuals listed below are quoted in the text; those who are not nonetheless added much to my understanding of Bette, her world, and her times. Each name is followed by the date of the interview:

Ruth Allen (October 2, 1991), Lindsay Anderson (November 12, 1991), Richard Anderson (January 8, 1990), Bart Andrews (July 11, 1991), George and Carol Andros (October 6, 1991), Ruth Bailey (April 13, 1991), Phil Ball (May 16, 1990), Lynn Barrington (November 26, 1991), Al and Mary Beardsley (October 2, 1991), Dr. Stanley Behrman (July 13, 1991), Bunny Bell (October 2, 1991), Phil Berle (July 30, 1992), Robert Bernstein (November 18, 1991), Jim and Cathy Black (October 12, 1991), Walter Blake (January 16, 1992), Julian Blaustein (February 28, 1990), Florence Brooks-Dunay (April 27, 1990), Diana Brown (October 5, 1991), Douglas Brown (October 5, 1991), Perry Bruskin (December 5, 1991), Chuck Bullock (October 5, 1991), Sammy Cahn (March 9, 1990), Jorge Camara (May 2, 1991), Colleen Camp (July 1, 1991), William Campbell (May 4, 1990), Robert and Jane Carey (October 6, 1991), Elizabeth Carmichael (January 22, 1990), Connie Cezon (July 24, 1991), Larry Cohen (March 23, 1991), Gary Collins (April 24, 1990), Gary Conway (August 3, 1990), Frank

Corsaro (May 26, 1990), Norman Corwin (May 29, 1990), Judith Crist (November 27, 1990).

Jules Dassin (June 9, 1990), Bill Doty (December 17, 1990), Milton Ebbins (November 3, 1989), Mike Ellis (April 17, 1992), Julius Epstein (May 2, 1991), Nanette Fabray (January 4, 1990), Douglas Fairbanks, Jr. (May 18, 1990), Georgie Farwell (November 24, 1989), Sally Favour (May 15, 1991), Rudy Fehr (July 5, 1990), Jon Finch (May 5, 1990), Charles Forsyth (January 20, 1992), Barbara Merrill Foster (December 16, 1991), Anne Francine (January 24, 1992), Harry Friedman (June 8, 1990), Stanley and Frances Frystak (October 3, 1991), John Gay (September 10, 1990), Madeline Gaylor (April 17, 1991), Bruce Glover (May 24, 1990), Vik Greenfield (July 22, 1992), Yetta Grossman (July 28, 1992).

Josie Hamm (October 10, 1991), Anthony Harvey (August 23, 1990), Helen Hayes (March 14, 1990), Bob Hendricks (April 15, 1991), Bob Henzler (April 30, 1991), Roberta Herzogg (October 6, 1991), Gordon Hessler (August 30, 1990), John B. Holt (April 18, 1991), Barbara Huebner (October 2, 1991), Kim Hunter (January 27, 1990), Janet Hutchinson (January 29, 1990), Tom Irish (May 7, 1991), Lucy Jarvis (December 31, 1991), Lynn-Holly Johnson (May 13, 1991), Ellie Jordan (July 1, 1991), Bob Jurgenson (November 9, 1990), Tom Kane (July 18, 1990), Andrea Keeler (October 6, 1991), David and Nancy Keeler (October 3, 1991), Bertha Kelly (July 8, 1991), DeForrest Kelly (January 12, 1990).

Hope Lange (September 18, 1992), Robert Lantz (November 29, 1990), Anna Lee (May 6, 1990), Nancy Lohman (October 6, 1991), Rudy Lowe (March 9, 1992), Betty Lynn (December 5, 1991), Karl Malden (June 1, 1992), Charles Mapes (October 5, 1991), Eleanor Coffin Marks (April 17, 1991), Dick Mason (July 30, 1992), Doug McClure (July 17, 1990), Jerry Merrill (June 9, 1991), Buzz Miller (April 3, 1992), Lee Montgomery (August 19, 1990), Charles Moses (July 2, 1991), May Muth (April 2, 1992), Thomas Noguchi (September 7, 1992), Patrick O'Neal (January 25, 1991), Fred Otash (July 25, 1991), Don Ovens (May 30, 1990), Janis Paige (January 4, 1990), Betsy Paul (June 24, 1991), Dr. Karl Petersen (October 7, 1991), James and Doris Pitcher (October 9, 1991, and September 26, 1992), Gregory Poe (February 19, 1992), Paul Poehler (November 27, 1991), John Poer (July 18, 1990), Vincent Price (March 12, 1991), Dr. Ivin Prince (December 1, 1990).

Ronald Reagan (November 14, 1990), Milton Repsher (December 27, 1991), Gladys Reuben (March 9, 1990), Barbara Rhodes (May 30,

1990), Florence Melanson Rogers (April 15, 1991), R. G. Rohrbach (October 7, 1991), Reva Rose (March 26, 1990), Bill Ross (December 17, 1991), George Ryan, Jr. (October 5, 1991), Mrs. George Ryan, Sr. (October 5, 1991), Janella Ryan (October 5, 1991), Leslie Santos (October 5, 1991), George Schaefer (April 23, 1990), Natalie Schafer (January 17, 1990), Bob Schiffer (July 9, 1990), Leonard Shannon (June 25, 1991), Ron Sharon (October 6, 1991), John Shea (July 17, 1991), Vincent Sherman (April 9, 1992), Marion Sherry (February 15, 1991).

William Grant Sherry (March 19, 1990), Anne Shirley (December 12, 1989), Dawn Langley Simmons (January 11, 1990), Herb Snitzer (December 6, 1990), Alix Snow (October 11, 1991), Burt Solomon (January 9, 1990), Ann Sothern (June 20, 1990), Jenny Sprague (December 6, 1991), Robert Stack (April 1, 1991), Lionel Stander (June 3, 1991), Warren Stevens (May 18, 1990), James Stewart (April 30, 1991), Ray Stricklyn (May 24, 1990), Barry Sullivan (June 2, 1991), "Doc" Sullivan (October 5, 1991).

E. J. Tangerman (November 27, 1989), Doris Taplinger (September 20, 1991), Daniel Taradash (February 7, 1990), Richard Tate (July 24, 1991), Steve Tramz (August 3, 1990), Doug Troland (January 7, 1992), Sir Peter Ustinov (May 8, 1991), Joan Van Ark (May 24, 1990), Mary Beth Voda (October 6, 1991), Robert Wagner (January 23, 1992), Mary Wickes (February 22, 1990), Meta Carpenter Wilde (June 4, 1992), Gladys Young (October 10, 1991).

The Department of Special Collections at the Mugar Memorial Library of Boston University, under the curatorship of Dr. Howard Gottlieb and the management of archivist Karen Mix, houses the Bette Davis papers and provided a wealth of primary and secondary source material. The collection contains Bette's baby books, scrapbooks of clippings of her career, magazine articles, photo albums, letters and telegrams to and from her and her family, annotated scripts, and several unpublished biographies of Bette in manuscript form by her mother and her uncle, the Reverend Paul Favor. The collection is a treasure trove for any Bette Davis biographer, and I am grateful for the access I was granted to it.

Equally rich in information on Bette's career is the Warner Brothers Collection at the University of Southern California, under the directorship of Leith Adams. The files contain contracts, memos, letters, annotated scripts, production schedules, notes of private and telephone conversations, daily production reports, and budget and profit-and-loss statements for all of Bette's Warner Brothers films. The helpful good cheer of Ned Comstock and Stuart Ng made research in the collection easier and more pleasant than it might have been.

The Margaret Herrick Library at the Academy of Motion Picture Arts and Sciences contains voluminous files of articles and clippings about Bette's films and personal life; the theater collection of the Lincoln Center Library for the Performing Arts offers thorough collections of reviews and background articles on all of Bette's stage appearances.

The U.S. Department of Justice, Federal Bureau of Investigation, released to me the dossiers kept on Bette, Gary Merrill, and Arthur Farnsworth pursuant to the Freedom of Information Act.

PART ONE

In addition to the personal interviews quoted in this section and listed above, many of the general details of Bette Davis's childhood, school years, and early stage career were gathered from her 1962 autobiography, *The Lonely Life*. Additional information was gleaned from her mother's two unpublished memoirs of life with Bette, and her uncle Paul Favor's unpublished biographical profile.

Important details of Bette's early life are contained in Gladys Hall's extended profile, "Bette Davis Life Story," in *Modern Screen*, which was based on interviews with Bette and Ruthie. Equally helpful were Bette's lengthy autobiographical article in the July 1941 issue of *Ladies' Home Journal* entitled "Uncertain Glory"; Sonia Lee's profile "The Untold Bette" in *Screenplay*, November 1935; and another Davis memoir, "All About Me," as told to Bill Davidson, in the November 25 and December 9, 1955, issues of *Collier's*.

Details of Bette's family background came from a genealogy of the Hinckley family by Emmet Charles Hinckley and the Colonel Jabez Mathews family tree located among Bette's papers at Boston University.

The 1900 U.S. Department of Commerce Census, the Maine Historical Society, and the State of Maine Office of Death Records supplied information about Harlow Davis and his parents. The City Clerk of Lowell, Massachusetts, made available Harlow and Ruthie's marriage certificate. The quote from Harlow's Bates College classmate about his scholastic achievements at the school is contained in Paul Favor's writings. Some of Bette's quotes about her feelings toward her father were given to Christopher Nickens during a telephone interview in 1985.

The quotes and observations from Bette's acting-school roommate Virginia Conroy were taken from Conroy's lengthy unpublished memoir of her friendship with Bette, "It Was a Bumpy Life." Ruthie and

Harlow's divorce papers were obtained from the Suffolk County, Massachusetts, Superior Court. The date of Harlow's marriage to Minnie Stewart is listed among his biographical data in a Bates College alumni directory.

Bette's Cushing Academy senior yearbook provided information about her popularity at the school and her appearance in the senior play. Bette offered details of her nude posing as a teenager in her 1981 *Playboy* interview. She spoke of watching Ruthie work on her retouching in Sonia Lee's profile.

Henry Fonda recalled his date with Bette in his autobiography and in *Playboy*. Ginny Conroy supplied photographs of Bette's first screen test while at the Milton/Anderson School. Harlow Davis's letter to his daughter after he saw *The Wild Duck* is a part of the Boston University Davis collection.

PART TWO

The Warner Brothers archives at the University of Southern California provided invaluable information for this section, as did the files of the Margaret Herrick Library and the Lincoln Center Library. Some details of Bette's courtship by and marriage to Ham Nelson were found in the article "Marriage Costs Bette Plenty" by Laura Benham in the August 1933 issue of *Picture Play* and Bette's piece "I Love My Husband Because He Doesn't Treat Me Like a Star" in a 1936 issue of *Screen Book*.

Background on the nominating rules of the Academy Awards in 1935 and 1936 was obtained from the "Academy Awards of Merit Text of Rules" for those years. Details of Harlow's visit to Bette and Ham in Hollywood were gleaned from a variety of Bette's interviews over the years. Harlow Davis's death certificate was obtained from the Office of the Town Clerk of Belmont, Massachusetts.

Ross Alexander's infatuation with Bette is detailed in Lawrence Quirk's *Fasten Your Seat Belts*. Mr. Justice Branson's decision against Bette in her Warner Brothers lawsuit was published in the volume *Trial —Law Reports of the King's Bench Division, 1937*.

Ham Nelson's bugging of Bette and Howard Hughes has long been rumored, but no one with firsthand information has ever gone on the record about it until now. I thank Bette's niece Ruth Bailey for confirming the incident and adding information about her father's involvement in it.

Ham Nelson's divorce decree from Bette (Case No. D1754595) was obtained from the Los Angeles County Superior Court. The information in this section and those that follow about Bette's various real estate holdings was obtained from the Los Angeles and Orange County Grantee/Grantor records.

PART THREE

The USC Warner Brothers archives once again provided a wealth of information about Bette's films. Background on Franconia, New Hampshire, and Peckett's Inn was provided by Robert Peckett III and Duncan Chaplin III. Some details of Bette's courtship with Arthur Farnsworth were gleaned from the profile of Bette, "You Can Have Hollywood," published in the Boston *Advertiser* on June 23, 1940, and Gladys Hall's "Keeping Up with Bette" in *Modern Screen*, April 1940. Some of Lucile de Besche's quotes about her brother Arthur Farnsworth are contained in written responses to queries submitted to her by the author.

Jack Carson's observations about Bette and the men of the Hollywood Canteen are contained in *Fasten Your Seat Belts.*

My re-creation of the death of Arthur Farnsworth is based on contemporary newspaper accounts and other published sources, Bette's reminiscences over the years, an interview with William Grant Sherry, Farnsworth's death certificate, No. 12857, obtained from the State of California Department of Health, the Los Angeles County Coroner's autopsy report, and the official inquest verdict. The verbatim transcript of coroner Frank Nance's inquest, provided by the Los Angeles County Coroner's Office and long thought missing, provided the basis for my conclusion that the inquest was itself a part of a studio cover-up of the facts.

The information about Bette's marriage to and divorce from William Grant Sherry was culled from his and his wife Marion's lengthy and forthcoming observations during interviews for this book, contemporary newspaper accounts and other published sources, the marriage certificate (No. 26189) provided by the County of Riverside, California, and divorce papers obtained from the Santa Monica and Orange County Superior Courts.

Hedda Hopper wrote of her visit to Bette after B.D.'s birth in "Welcome Stranger," *Modern Screen*, August 1947. The details of Bessie Downs's lawsuit against Bette are contained in the records of the Los Angeles Superior Court.

Information about Bobby's divorce from Robert Pelgram was gleaned from their divorce papers, Case No. 627591 of the Los Angeles Superior Court. The details of her marriage to and divorce from David Berry are contained in divorce papers obtained from the Orange County Superior Court, Certificate No. 51176.

Some of Joseph Mankiewicz's observations regarding *All About Eve* are contained in a letter to the author dated December 9, 1991. Other sources were Gary Carey's "Colloquy" with the director, *More About All About Eve,* and Harry Haun's article "Hollywood's All-Time Bitch is 40," in *Hollywood* magazine, October/November, 1990.

PART FOUR

Gary Merrill's autobiography provided some details of his marriage to Bette, as did her memoirs and B.D. Hyman's *My Mother's Keeper.* Gladys Young's diaries and her memorabilia of the Merrills' trip to England offered important insights into that period. Bette imparted a good deal of information about Margot's behavioral problems in a January 17, 1960, article in *The American Weekly,* "Our Daughter."

In addition to the interviews with Mike Ellis and the cast members of *Two's Company,* the University of Pittsburgh library provided contracts, memos, and letters that shed a great deal of light on that troubled production, as well as Bette's subsequent illness. Frederick Goddard's observations of Gary Merrill's odd behavior at the football game are contained in a letter to the author dated November 8, 1991. Ray Stricklyn's reminiscences of speaking with Bette after her initial divorce action against Gary are part of his unpublished memoir, "Bette Davis: A Personal Remembrance."

The voluminous, 190-page record of Gary and Bette's protracted custody battle over Michael is contained in the archives of the Santa Monica Superior Court, Case No. WEC2895. Ruth Davis's death certificate was obtained from the California Department of Health, County of Orange, Certificate No. 3000. Sandford Dody's recollections of his stormy collaboration with Bette on her autobiography are from his memoir, *Giving Up the Ghost.*

PART FIVE

My account of B.D. and Jeremy's meeting and courtship is based largely on her own in *My Mother's Keeper.* Some of the details of Bette's disagreement over the ending of *Where Love Has Gone* were gleaned from the depositions taken for the lawsuit Paramount Pictures v. Bette Davis, Los Angeles Civil Court Case No. 838992, filed May 20, 1964. My recounting of Bette's conversation with the young fans in 1964 is based on a tape of the encounter provided to me by Randall Henderson.

Joshua Logan's comments about Bette and *Miss Moffat* are a part of his memoir *Movie Stars, Real People and Me.* Rex Reed's interview with Bette appeared in the New York *Daily News* on October 12, 1975.

PART SIX and EPILOGUE

Kath Sermak's reminiscences of Bette are contained in *This 'n That,* as are B.D. and Jeremy's notes of appreciation to Bette for saving their farm from foreclosure. Much of the information about the Hyman family's conversion to born-again Christianity was provided by B.D. and Jeremy in *Narrow Is the Way.* The lawsuits and judgments against the Hymans and the Pitchers in 1985 are a part of the public record in Bradford County, Pennsylvania, and Onandaga County, New York.

Details of Bette's collapse at the American Cinema Awards were also provided to the author by Alex Gildzen in a letter dated November 27, 1989. Bette's last days were recounted by Kathryn Sermak in her 1990 update of Bette's autobiography *The Lonely Life.* Bette's will was probated in Los Angeles, Case No. P741578.

BIBLIOGRAPHY

Affron, Charles. *Star Acting.* New York: Dutton, 1977.

Arliss, George. *George Arliss by Himself.* London: John Murray, 1940.

Astor, Mary. *My Story.* New York: Doubleday, 1959.

Berg, A. Scott. *Goldwyn.* New York: Knopf, 1989.

Blum, Daniel. *A Pictorial History of the American Theatre, 1900–1956.* New York: Greenberg, 1956.

Carey, Gary. *More About All About Eve.* New York: Random House, 1972.

Carr, Larry. *More Fabulous Faces.* New York: Doubleday, 1979.

Carrier, Jeffrey L. *Tallulah Bankhead.* New York: Greenwood Press, 1991.

Carroll, Gladys Hasty. *Only Fifty Years Ago.* Boston: Little, Brown, 1962.

Collins, Joan. *Past Imperfect.* New York: Simon & Schuster, 1984.

Considine, Shaun. *Bette and Joan: The Divine Feud.* New York: Dutton, 1989.

Davidson, Bill. *The Real and the Unreal.* New York: Harper, 1961.

Davis, Bette. *The Lonely Life.* New York: Putnam, 1962; Berkley, 1990 (updated).

———, with Michael Herskowitz. *This 'n That.* New York: Putnam, 1987.

Dody, Sandford. *Giving Up the Ghost.* New York: Evans, 1980.

Dowd, Nancy, and David Shepard. *King Vidor.* Metuchen, NJ: Scarecrow Press, 1988.

Drake, Samuel G. *Annals of Witchcraft in New England.* New York: Arno Press, 1977.

Eels, George. *Final Gig.* New York: Harcourt Brace Jovanovich, 1991.

Finler, Joel W. *The Hollywood Story.* New York: Crown, 1988.

Fonda, Henry, with Howard Teichmann. *My Life.* New York: NAL, 1981.

Fuller, Elizabeth. *Me and Jezebel.* New York: Berkley, 1992.

Gabler, Neal. *An Empire of Their Own.* New York: Crown, 1988.

Goldberg, Lee. *Unsold Television Pilots.* Jefferson, NC: McFarland, 1990.

Grobel, Lawrence. *The Hustons.* New York: Scribner's, 1989.

Halliwell, Leslie. *Halliwell's Filmgoer's Companion,* Ninth Edition. New York: Scribner's, 1988.

Hayes, Helen. *My Life in Three Acts.* New York: Touchstone, 1990.

Heimann, Jim. *Out with the Stars.* New York: Abbeville Press, 1985.

Henreid, Paul. *Ladies' Man.* New York: St. Martin's Press, 1985.

Higham, Charles. *Bette.* New York: Macmillan, 1981.

Hirschhorn, Clive. *The Warner Bros. Story.* New York: Crown, 1979.

Hyman, B. D. *My Mother's Keeper.* New York: Morrow, 1985.

———, and Jeremy Hyman. *Narrow Is the Way.* New York: Morrow, 1987.

Ibsen, Henrik. *Four Plays.* Translated by Eva Le Gallienne. Franklin Center, PA: The Franklin Library, 1979.

Israel, Lee. *Miss Tallulah Bankhead.* New York: Putnam, 1972.

Kobal, John. *People Will Talk.* New York: Alfred A. Knopf, 1985.

Lawrence, Jerome. *Actor: The Life and Times of Paul Muni.* New York: Putnam, 1974.

Leaming, Barbara. *Bette Davis.* New York: Simon and Schuster, 1991.

Leonard, William Torbert. *Broadway Bound: A Guide to Shows That Died Aborning.* Metuchen, NJ: Scarecrow Press, 1987.

Logan, Joshua. *Movie Stars, Real People and Me.* New York: Delacorte, 1978.

Madsen, Axel. *William Wyler.* New York: Crowell, 1973.

Marill, Alvin H. *Movies Made for Television.* New York: Zoetrope, 1987.

Marx, Arthur. *Goldwyn.* New York: Norton, 1976.

Maugham, W. Somerset. *Of Human Bondage.* New York: Penguin, 1989.

Merrill, Gary. *Bette, Rita and the Rest of My Life.* Augusta, ME: Tapley, 1988.

Miller, Arnold. *The Films and Career of Robert Aldrich.* Knoxville: University of Tennessee Press, 1986.

Moseley, Roy. *Bette Davis: An Intimate Memoir.* New York: Donald I. Fine, 1990.

The New York Times Company. *The New York Times Directory of the Film.* New York: Arno Press/Random House, 1970.

Nickens, Christopher. *Bette Davis: A Biography in Photographs.* New York: Doubleday, 1985.

Quirk, Lawrence. *Fasten Your Seat Belts.* New York: Morrow, 1990.

Ringgold, Gene. *The Films of Bette Davis.* Secaucus, NJ: Citadel, 1966; updated, 1985.

Robinson, Jeffrey. *Bette Davis.* New York: Proteus, 1982.

Schatz, Thomas. *The Genius of the System.* New York: Pantheon, 1988.

Shale, Richard. *Academy Awards.* New York: Frederick Ungar, 1982.

Spada, James. *Peter Lawford: The Man Who Kept the Secrets.* New York: Bantam Books, 1991.

———. *Streisand: The Woman and the Legend*. New York: Dolphin/Doubleday, 1981.

Spoto, Donald. *The Kindness of Strangers*. Boston: Little, Brown & Company, 1985.

Stine, Whitney. *"I'd Love to Kiss You . . ."* New York: Pocket Books, 1990.

———. *Mother Goddam*. New York: Hawthorne, 1974.

Suskin, Steven. *Opening Night on Broadway*. New York: Schirmer Books/Macmillan, 1990.

Thomas, Bob. *Clown Prince of Hollywood*. New York: McGraw-Hill, 1990.

Walker, Alexander. *Bette Davis*. New York: Weidenfeld & Nicolson, 1986.

Wallis, Hal, and Charles Higham. *Starmaker*. New York: Macmillan, 1980.

Warner, Jack. *My First Hundred Years in Hollywood*. New York: Random House, 1965.

Woodward, William E. *The Records of Salem Witchcraft*. New York: B. Franklin, 1972.

Yurka, Blanche. *Bohemian Girl*. Athens, OH: Ohio University Press, 1970.

Zierold, Norman. *The Moguls*. New York: Coward-McCann, 1969.

INDEX

About the Author

James Spada has written thirteen books, including the international best-sellers *Grace: The Secret Lives of a Princess; Peter Lawford: The Man Who Kept the Secrets; Streisand: The Woman and the Legend;* and *Monroe: Her Life in Pictures.* Born and raised in Staten Island, New York, he now lives in Los Angeles, where he is at work on a biography of Senator Edward M. Kennedy.